Welcome to

Web Design for Beginners™

Welcome to **Web Design for Beginners**. If you are new to the wonderful world of web design, then this is the place for you – we'll take you through everything you need to know to get started. After covering the basics of HTML and CSS, you'll be able to build your first website with our simple step-by-step tutorials. After that, you'll be able to get your website online and then create stunning web graphics in Photoshop. Covering everything you need to get up and running, **Web Design for Beginners** will help you to be a master of web design in no time at all!

Web Design for Beginners™

Imagine Publishing Ltd
Richmond House
33 Richmond Hill
Bournemouth
Dorset BH2 6EZ
☎ +44 (0) 1202 586200
Website: www.imagine-publishing.co.uk

Editor in Chief
Dave Harfield

Production Editor
Dan Collins

Senior Art Editor
Danielle Dixon

Design
Anne-Claire Pickard
Charlie Crooks

Printed by
William Gibbons, 26 Planetary Road, Willenhall, West Midlands, WV13 3XT

Distributed in the UK & Eire by
Imagine Publishing Ltd, www.imagineshop.co.uk. Tel 01202 586200

Distributed in Australia by
Gordon & Gotch, Equinox Centre, 18 Rodborough Road, Frenchs Forest, NSW 2086. Tel + 61 2 9972 8800

Distributed in the Rest of the World by
Marketforce, Blue Fin Building, 110 Southwark Street, London, SE1 0SU.

ISBN 978-1908955081

Part of the
web designer
bookazine series

IMAGINE PUBLISHING

IMAGINEER OF THE YEAR DANIELLE DIXON

TEAM OF THE YEAR BOOKAZINES

Contents

Feature
Essential guide to web design
page 8

Build a site

WordPress

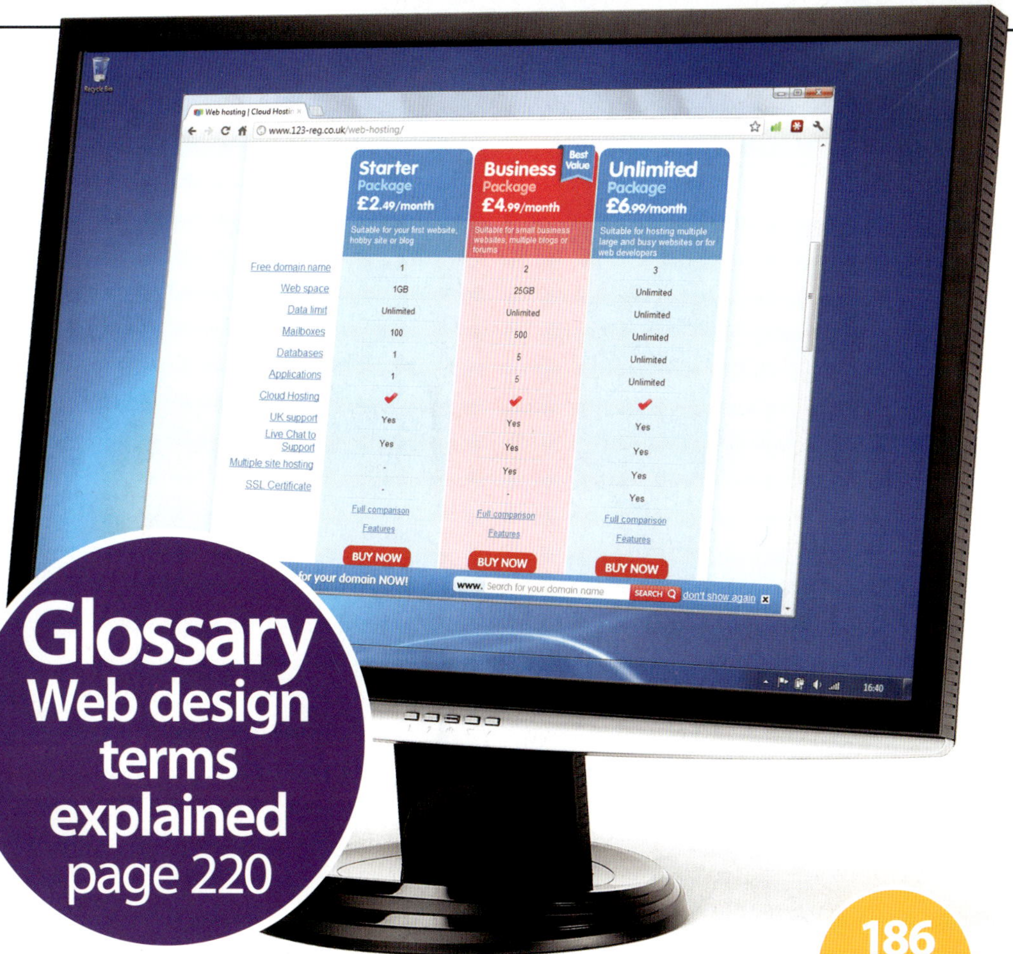

Understanding SEO

"There are plenty of ways to promote your work and share your opinions"

Glossary
Web design terms explained
page 220

Photoshop & graphics

Customise your site

186
Add a video

146
Promote on Twitter

210
Helpdesk

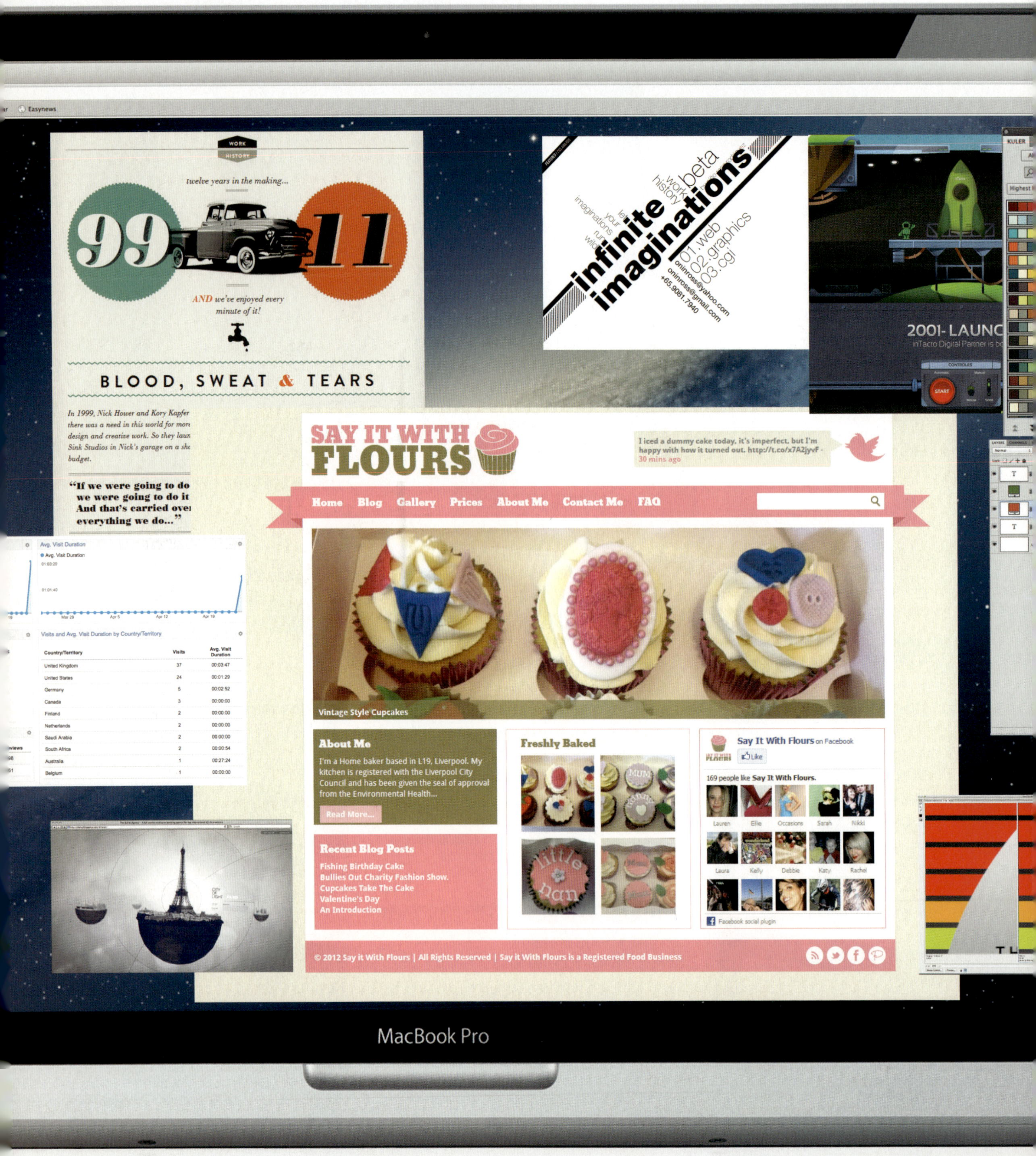
WORK HISTORY
twelve years in the making...
99
11
AND we've enjoyed every minute of it!
BLOOD, SWEAT & TEARS
infinite imaginations
beta
01.web
02.graphics
03.cgi
2001- LAUNC
START
SAY IT WITH FLOURS
I iced a dummy cake today, it's imperfect, but I'm happy with how it turned out. http://t.co/x7A2jyvF -
30 mins ago
Home
Blog
Gallery
Prices
About Me
Contact Me
FAQ
Vintage Style Cupcakes
About Me
I'm a Home baker based in L19, Liverpool. My kitchen is registered with the Liverpool City Council and has been given the seal of approval from the Environmental Health...
Read More...
Freshly Baked
Say It With Flours on Facebook
169 people like Say It With Flours.
Recent Blog Posts
Fishing Birthday Cake
Bullies Out Charity Fashion Show.
Cupcakes Take The Cake
Valentine's Day
An Introduction
Facebook social plugin
© 2012 Say it With Flours | All Rights Reserved | Say it With Flours is a Registered Food Business
Avg. Visit Duration
Visits and Avg. Visit Duration by Country/Territory
MacBook Pro

Essential guide to web design

Discover why now is the time to start building your first website

The web made its debut back in 1991, adding a graphical user interface to the internet. As such, web design was born. In its infancy web design was heavily restricted by technology and hardware, with a web presence being little more than black text on a white background. Thankfully, technology and web design have reached a far more creative and imaginative stage in their evolutions. Skipping past frames, tables and animated GIFs, web design has become far more sophisticated and will continue to grow and develop. Look back a couple of years and take note of what was 'on trend' and how the underlying infrastructure helped shape a website.

The progression of web design has always gone hand-in hand with technology and technology never takes a backward step, which in turn means that web design and the web are always going to be informative, inspirational and essential. Without it the world would be a very different place. Think about what you use the web for and how you would achieve these tasks without it. In the couple of decades that the web has been around it's gone from a plain text, email-checking entity to the key communication and information tool. And, what is it that makes the web such a crucial tool? Web pages and websites. Whatever information, service or product you need it will be wrapped up in a web page just waiting for you to say hello.

Why build a website?

It's a simple question but why build a website? There is no single answer to what is undoubtedly a >>

very broad question. However, the answer could be something as simple as 'because everyone else has got one'. And, to a certain extent, this simple answer reaches the crux of the matter very succinctly. The web is a global phenomenon and is awash with millions if not billions of websites covering every subject imaginable. There is no better place to be seen. A website can be viewed from England to Australia, while astronauts have even tweeted from the International Space Station! A 24/7 online global presence is one very powerful reason to build a website.

it also acts as a reference point or calling card where a user can promote themselves. If it's not a personal platform for opinion and promotion a site can be great a way to stay in contact and tell friends and family what you are up to. An online diary can include the latest activities and a host of photos, much like a personal Facebook. This could be another reason, for those not interested in being part of the Facebook revolution and want greater control, then a personal site is a great alternative. The web also provides the perfect platform for those looking to build a business. The outlay is minimal and the potential audience is huge. No need to rent premises, no need to keep a huge pile of stock and customers will come from miles around to pay a visit. Provide the right product and promote in the right way and the number of visits will shoot through the roof.

> "Websites cover every aspect of life, whether it's personal or business"

There is no doubt that websites cover every aspect of life, whether it's personal or business. On a personal level, everyone has an interest or hobby that they love and many simply want to tell the world what they do. A website is the perfect platform for getting across personal opinion and

What are HTML & CSS?

HTML and CSS are the key components for building web pages and sites – without them the web as we know it simply would not exist. In a nutshell, HTML provides the building blocks and structure while CSS provides the styling.

HTML is made up of a whole host of tags which all have their own identity. These consist of an opening and closing tag with all the relevant content in between. For example, '<header>web page content goes here</header>'. HTML defines a whole series of tags, ie header, nav, footer, video, etc, which all have a semantic title making them easy to identify. Custom tags, or div tags as they are known, are created when a standard HTML tag cannot be used. Again these have their own individual identities. CSS is the language applied to an HTML tag to style it. Cascading Style Sheets, CSS, will take the name of a HTML tag, ie <header> and define properties such as its height, width, colour, borders, padding and margins. Beyond the more common properties CSS3 now offers a new generation of styling options. Rounder corners, text shadows, box shadows and gradients are just a few of the properties styling today's websites.

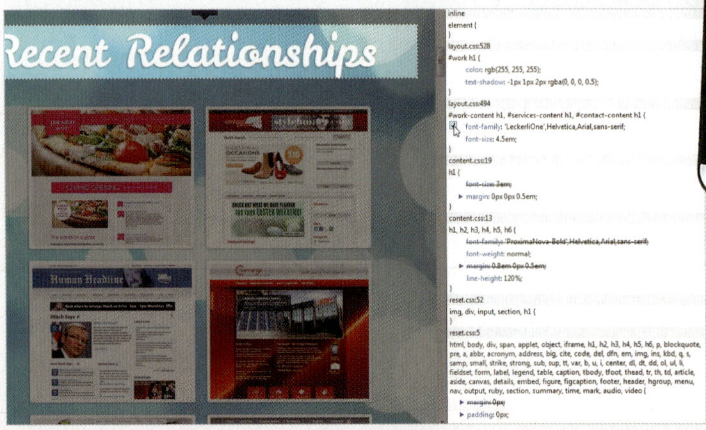

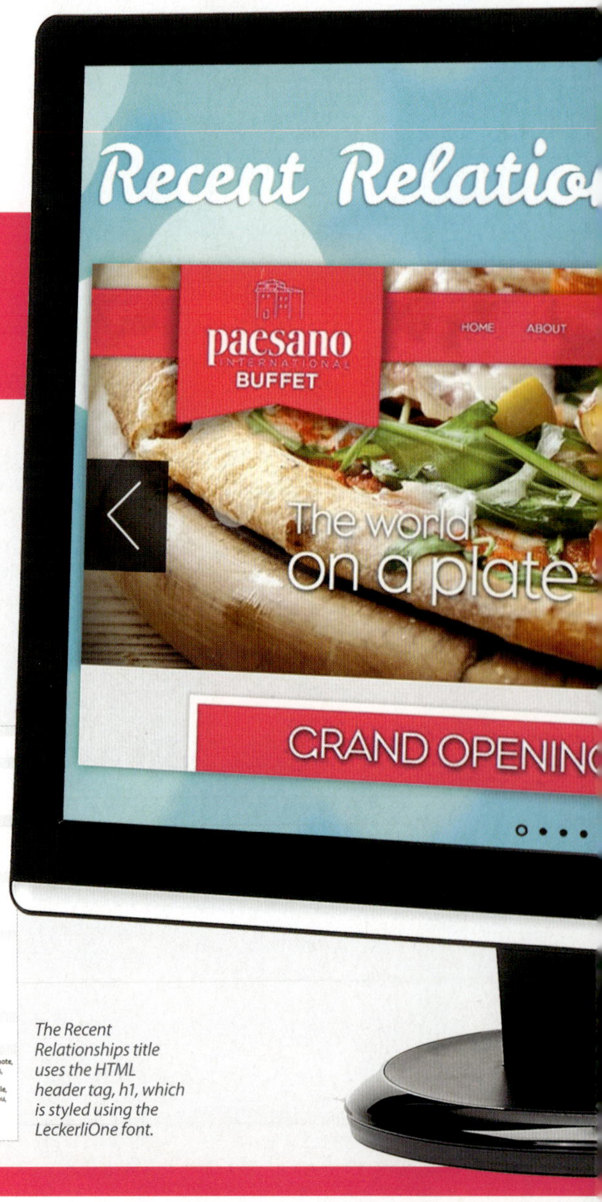

The Recent Relationships title uses the HTML header tag, h1, which is styled using the LeckerliOne font.

HTML5 is the web language you need to learn to build a site from scratch.

Combine HTML5 and CSS3 to create interactive and standout websites.

Both the title and the images use different CSS3 properties to add a shadow to both elements.

Beyond personal opinion and comment a website can have a more commercial use. Web designers instantly have the perfect platform for presenting their work. What better reason does a web designer need to build a website? A portfolio site is a great shop window for their work and a constant point of reference allowing web users to visit at any time of day or night. As already mentioned, if you're looking to build a business the web is a great starting point. A report from eMarketer.com (**www.emarketer.com**) shows that 150 million users across the United States are buying online. This is a staggering 73 per cent of all web users and demonstrates exactly how important an online business could be. Another interesting snippet of information reinforced in the report was that people like to shop online for convenience and to save money.

An online shop is the most probable and popular purpose for business, but another and less obvious reason is affiliate marketing. This is a website specifically set up to promote affiliate products, where money is made via commission.

What are websites used for?

The internet is very much influenced by what is happening outside of the web. Remember it's people that build websites and people always want information, people always need to go shopping, people will always need to go to the bank, people will always want to stay in contact – the web provides the ideal platform to replace more traditional services.

So what do people use websites for? In a nutshell: pretty much everything! But to be more concise, the purpose of a website is to relay a message or offer a service. To get a more immediate picture of what websites are used for, take a look at some of the most popular sites on the web. Facebook, YouTube, Google, Wikipedia, Twitter, Amazon, iTunes, eBay, BBC, Sky, WordPress, PayPal, Skype, Flickr, Walmart, Lastminute and Microsoft to name but a few. This brief selection of sites pretty much covers the spectrum of what websites are used for. Facebook is a huge social networking site and represents what people like to do on the web – stay in contact and tell others what they are up to. YouTube allows web users to stream and watch videos from a vast library of variety. Sitting along the same lines are services such as Netflix and LoveFilm which take the online streaming and viewing experience to a new level. Google, a service that nearly everyone in the world has heard of, presents a different tool for the web, but search engines are key to finding websites. Good luck if you're thinking of building a website to take on one of the search giants!

The online encyclopaedia Wikipedia is a fountain of knowledge. It's one of the first online locations web users will hit when looking for an >>

What makes a good site?

A well-conceived website is not only aesthetically pleasing, but also works under the hood as well. Soul Media (**www.soulmedia.com.au**) is a Melbourne-based digital agency who has put together a striking and well-constructed site that demonstrates the traits of good design. The homepage makes an immediate impact with a big, bold image and relays the company message without too many distractions. The main image is a background image that scales with the browser window ensuring that it works with all screen sizes. The site is also 'responsive', which means that it responds to the size of a screen and restyles to fit. This ensures that a site will work for smartphones, tablets and desktops.

The site itself uses the popular one-page scrolling design. This negates the need to link to other pages and wait for them to load. It is simply a matter of scrolling down the page or using the fixed position menu to jump, in an elegant manner, to the requested section. The fixed nature of the navigation system means that it is always visible and ready to use. Alongside the HTML there is good use of web fonts and CSS3 techniques – text shadows and box shadows are all here in abundance.

> "A responsive site responds to the size of a screen and restyles to fit"

Soul Media is a great example of web design working in harmony for a great visual experience.

Anatomy of a website

Websites by their very nature are made up of a few constituent parts which are arranged in a manner to suit the content. Typical websites are either two or three-column layouts with a header and footer. What sets sites apart is the imagination and variations used in the construction of the constituent parts. Characteristically, the header of a website appears at the top of the page, the footer at the bottom of a page and the main content in between.

Background images or colour will be used to create a canvas for the page. This applies to the best and worst of websites found on the web. Take a look at your favourite site and it is almost guaranteed to fit into the standard type of template. The key to a great site is bringing all the constituent parts together in a coherent and cohesive manner that suits the content.

Logo
The logo is crucial, its presents the site brand and it is a key navigation point. It should always take the user back to the home page

Content
The main area of any website is its content. This will typically appear under the header element and will be arranged in a variety of styles, ie two columns, image slider and three columns

Footer
The footer, as its name suggest, resides at the bottom of the page. This typically offers contact information, links to social media and a repeat of the navigation menu

Header
The top of the page is prime real estate on a web pages and typically includes the site logo and the navigation menu and often advertising

Image slider
A popular addition to websites is an image slider. This allows for multiple content to occupy the same space. Images, with text, slide across to reveal new content

Sidebar
Sidebars are predominately placed to the right, as this makes the content easier to access, with less mouse travel. A sidebar can contain an array of related information and interesting links

answer to a question. If Wikipedia doesn't have the answer then it will be a surprise. Again, this is a vast undertaking and the knowledge base has been built up over years by the general public, but it provides a great blueprint for anyone looking to build a creditable knowledge site.

Another big name on the web is Amazon, this is one of the pioneers of the online shopping experience and the site has developed to such a level that it is often first in the queue when a product needs to be purchased. A similar online experience sits in the hands of eBay, this is an online shopping experience, but users get to bid in an online auction rather than buy a product at a fixed price. The auction has a few imitators, but none can match its capacity and completeness. The BBC website covers a vast swathe of subjects, but it has one primary, and very popular, purpose and that is to bring the news to the masses. No matter if it's local news, international news or sports news, the BBC will have it covered.

WordPress is the most popular web publishing platform on the internet and provides the basis for over a million websites. Typically seen as a blogging platform, it has matured into something much more complete. What it also provides is a brilliant platform for people who want to produce their own website without the degree or knowledge in web design and development. Plus, it offers the user more than just one incarnation of website; almost any type of site (blog, ecommerce shop, information-based and more) can be built from the WordPress platform.

Sitting amongst the giants is Flickr, a photo storage and sharing site that provides a platform for professional photographers and amateurs alike. The Flickr platform can act as a shop window or, in the true spirit of the internet, act as a source where images are freely available for others to use. When it comes to music there are few that can match the massive entity known as iTunes. The Apple-powered store provides a shop front for a million musicians and in turn allows for an intuitive online buying experience that is hard to match.

The above does not cover every single use of a website – for example, we've not mentioned online banking – but it does offer a great representation of the scope of purpose of exactly what a website can achieve.

Where are websites stored?

The web to some degree is a mystical entity that just exists out there somewhere, but obviously this is not the case, all the information does have a home. The web is part of the internet, which is effectively a collection of connected computers that create a mass of routes around the globe. This provides the infrastructure for one computer to connect to another and view any website that exists on the web.

A web page is a file that is typically stored on a local/home computer hard drive. A collection of web pages becomes a website. However,

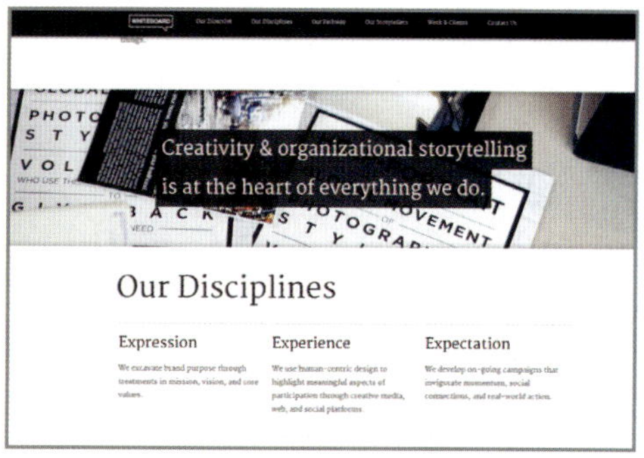

Websites tend to follow a similar layout formula.

Use exciting patterns to catch the eye.

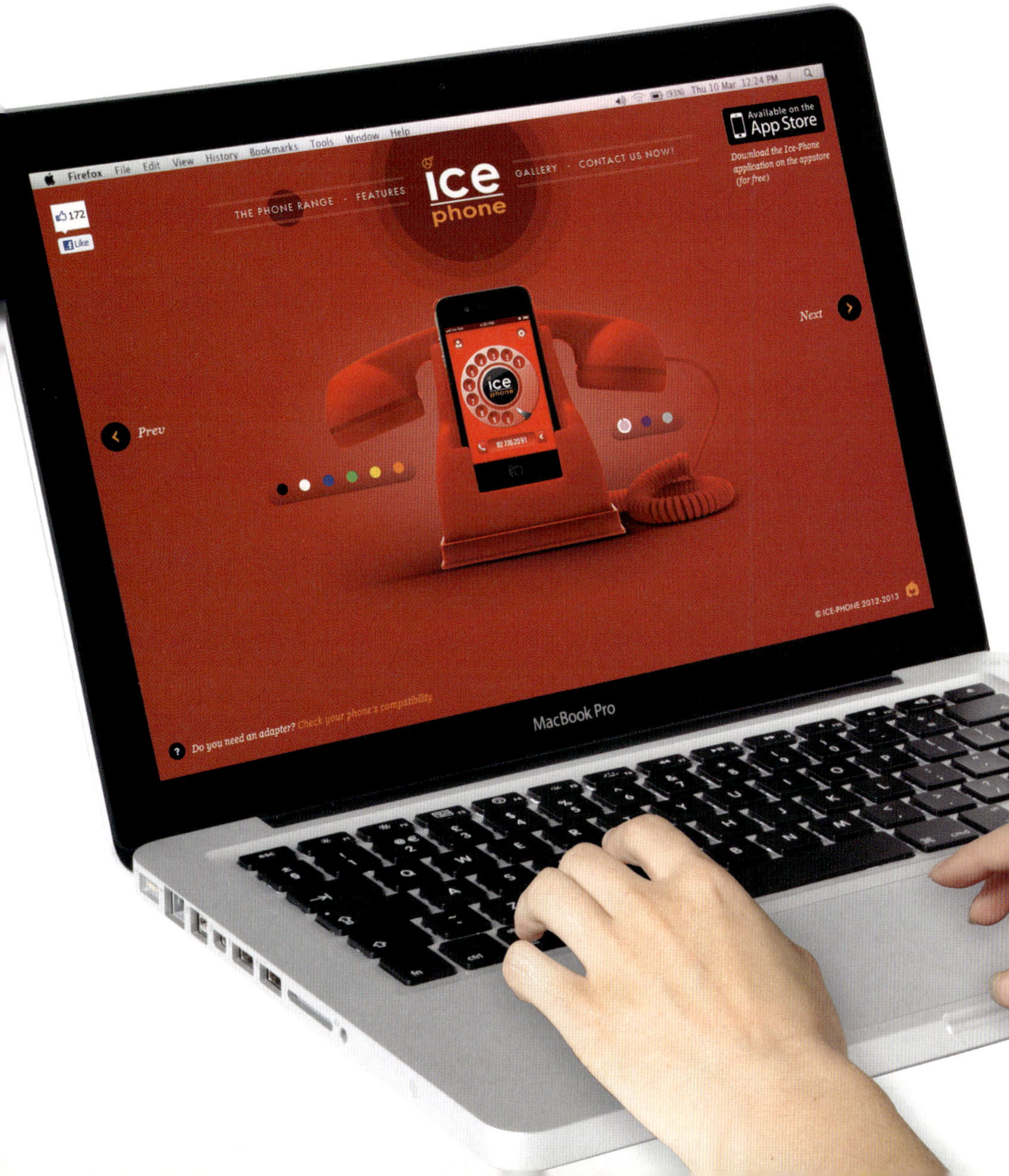

Employ clever tricks on your site to entice the reader to stay around.

What makes a good blog/ social website?

Blog sites can be bland and boring. But there are hundreds if not thousands of blogs that have stepped outside the standard template to bring a splash of creativity and originality. Ultranoir, (**www.ultranoir.com**) is an award-winning Parisian creative agency that has taken the blog format and created a striking and unique design. The Ultranoir blog, known as Blackstage, is a simple selection of posts, but the combination of fonts, typography, images, layout and effects make the blog a compelling, imaginative and engaging presence. The bespoke layout makes an immediate impression. The two-column arrangement does not simply stack post on top of post, but uses a combination of post sizes in a grid type layout to emphasise specific posts. The arrangement of individual posts does not stick to a rigid format, again offering bespoke arrangements. There are posts with images, without images, with intro text, without intro text and different size title text. The arrangement of the text and the different weights make it ultimately readable. To finish, it adds a few clever dynamic touches, with a 3D effect on post boxes, on mouse hover and moving featured images.

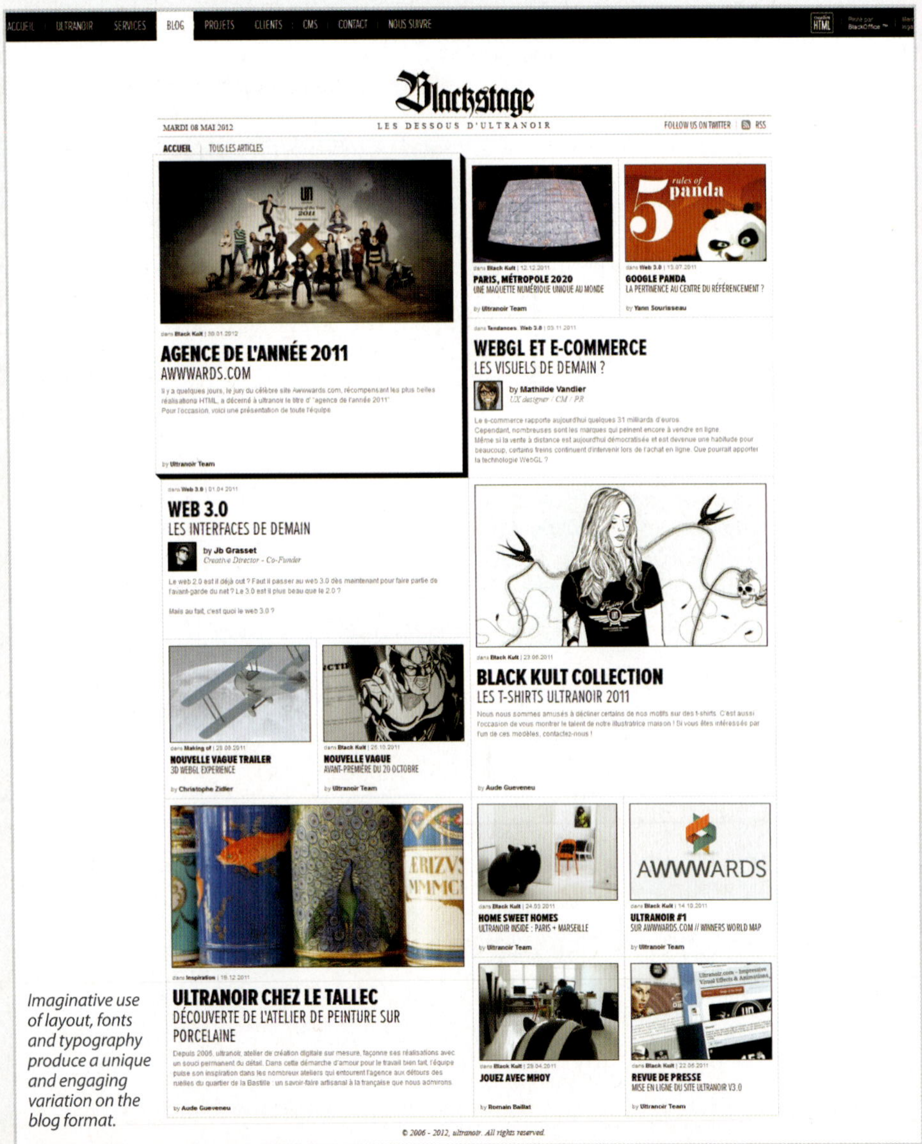

Imaginative use of layout, fonts and typography produce a unique and engaging variation on the blog format.

before any website can be seen it needs to be transferred from a local/home computer to a web server where the website is 'hosted'. A web host provides the service that gets a website out onto the internet for all to see. Web servers are like a desktop PC in the fact that they have similar hardware, but they are much more powerful and run different software.

A web host provider such as Fasthosts (**www.fasthosts.co.uk**), 1&1 (**www.1and1.co.uk**), Heart Internet (**www.heartinternet.co.uk**), Host Papa (**www.hostpapa.co.uk**) and PlusNet (**www.plus.net**) all provide a wealth of services including web space, monthly bandwidth, domain names, email accounts, databases, platforms and typically a host of web building tools. All of these services are included with a web hosting package, but each web host will have different hosting plans. The different plans provide everything from starter plans through to powerful plans for business. What type of plan is needed depends very much on what type of website is being set up. If it's a simple blog site that gets updated once a week and has an audience of around 500 visitors a month then a cheap starter plan would be ideal. If it is a company website with much more content and a lot more visitors expected then a more professional plan will be needed.

So what does all the jargon mean? The more important considerations are web space and bandwidth. Web space is storage space, the same as a hard drive. How much is needed obviously varies dependent on the content, but if it's a blog with standard text and images then it's unlikely that more than 1GB of web space will be needed. If more than text and images are going to be displayed, ie video, photos, music, then 1GB of web space can be filled very quickly. Ten gigabytes or more is a better option for such a site. It is a good idea to estimate how much web space you will need before embarking on choosing a hosting plan. Don't worry too much though, because web space can be upgraded easily and typically within 24 hours.

The other major factor is bandwidth, which is usually measured by the month. Bandwidth is the traffic, or the amount of data that is transferred to or from a website. A quick method for estimating monthly bandwidth is the sizes of the pages on a website multiplied by how many visitors are expected. For example, if a website has a total page size of 1MB and the expected visits are 500, a bandwidth of around half a gigabyte is sufficient. However, if there is a spike in visitors due to sudden interest then this could easily be doubled. Again, there is no need to worry as the bandwidth can be increased when needed.

Other considerations are databases, if setting up a WordPress blog then at least one database will be needed. If building a static brochure site that

An introduction to blogs and social media

Twitter is a good example of a micro-blogging platform that complements more traditional blogging platforms such as WordPress.

Blogs and social media websites are now an integral part of the online experience for many people. WordPress and Twitter are synonymous with web publishing and micro-blogging. WordPress has become the most popular web publishing platform due to a number of reasons. It is freely available, websites using it can be either self-hosted or hosted on **wordpress.com**, and it has a whole raft of supporting tools and themes.

WordPress is the power behind millions of websites, it is easy to install, even for newcomers, and easy to customise and navigate around. There are thousands and thousands of themes on the market, which can instantly give a website a completely new appearance with a single click. There is also a vast array of plug-ins that allow users to add special widgets that perform specific tasks, ie add polls, image sliders, tweets, featured content and so on. The beauty of blogging platforms such as WordPress is that they provide a platform for users to get their opinions, thoughts and personality online. While WordPress is the most popular web publishing platform it is by no means the only one out there. Joomla and Drupal are similar content management systems, but at the other end of the scale there are easy to set up, hosted platforms such as Tumblr and Flavors.me.

More instant web publishing is provided by the social media/micro-blogging platform Twitter. This allows users to communicate with short, concise, 140-character or less, messages (tweets). Messages are sent to all those who choose to follow you but more importantly the addition of a hashtag (#) makes a tweet subject specific. This immediately expands the reader base to include thousands more readers of a tweet. As a promotional tool Twitter is key on the web. Web sites typically include social media links encouraging visitors to follow. Conversely, it provides the perfect platform to create interest amongst followers and beyond. A well-constructed tweet will engage readers and more importantly drive traffic to a website.

The WordPress platform has become so popular that it has spawned a range of related merchandise.

Joomla is an alternative to the WordPress web publishing platform, check out all your options before choosing the one you go with.

At the time of going to press, the latest incarnation of WordPress has reached over 18 million downloads

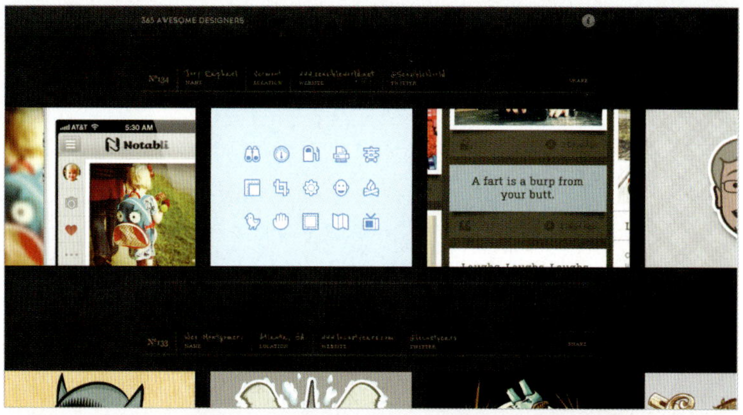

Themes not only make a WordPress site look great, but they can be tailored to your particular business or personality and can be changed in seconds.

>> just consists of text and images then a database is unlikely to be required. If setting up a site with a shop then a database is likely to be needed. As a general rule it's always worth getting a hosting plan with at least one database included. Email accounts are an obligatory addition to any hosting plan and even the most basic package will include more than are usually needed. As an example, the 1&1 Starter plan provides 1,000 email accounts. The other major web hosting consideration is the operating system (OS), typically Windows or Linux. This is not dictated by the OS your computer is running; it relates to OS that the web server is running. It only matters if you're going to build a basic HTML and CSS site. However, if a certain technology is to be used, it may only run on a certain operating system.

"Building a website is like building a house – you need a host of tools"

Tools of the trade

Building a website is much like building a house; a host of tools are needed to make sure that the job gets done. There are a few essential techniques and tools that a web designer/developer will need to know to get a website up and running. The most immediate is HTML and CSS, these are the most important elements of any website, as without them the web simply would not exist as we know it. HTML (Hypertext Markup Language) provides the base from which every website is built. Anyone looking to build a website will need to know at the very least the basics of HTML. The latest incarnation of HTML is HTML5 and newcomers to web design will need to make sure that, along with all the standard HTML tags, they also add HTML5 tags to the learning list.

Sitting alongside HTML in the web design hierarchy is Cascading Style Sheets, which is commonly known as CSS and it is just as important that website builders know at least the basics. CSS adds style to the front end of a website and defines the layout, whatever it may be, style fonts, borders, images, and create a background canvas for a webpage. In fact, any aesthetic seen on a web page has almost certainly been in contact with CSS. The latest incarnation of CSS is CSS3, which adds a host of new effects and styles that are slowly being adopted and supported by all the major browsers. Outside of the key technologies there is a trio of development platforms that are typically used in a website build. JQuery is the programming language that gives added dynamics to web pages. The jQuery language is a JavaScript library and is added to a web page to create effects that typically add movement. What can jQuery do? Typical examples include tabbed panels, image sliders, slideshows, sliding panels, expanding and collapsing accordions and tooltips to name a few.

Getting to grips with jQuery is not an essential element of design, but it is something that should be put on any web designer's to-do list when they've mastered HTML & CSS. Other backend technologies that power many websites are PHP and MySQL. PHP is a programming language that plays a big part in the makeup of the WordPress publishing platform. Typically, PHP is embedded into an HTML page and produces dynamic results. MySQL is a database application, which means it stores information entered into a site. It is often combined with PHP and a typical example of the two in action are WordPress posts where the content is stored in a MySQL database.

Getting all the essential technologies onto a page is the work of a selection of tools. An HTML editor is critical and one of the most popular software packages on the market is Dreamweaver. Part of the Adobe Creative Suite, it offers a user-friendly interface and an impressive set of tools that assist any web designer with what they need. The alternatives are explained elsewhere (see What's the best software on page 19). An HTML editor needs to be accompanied by an image-editing package to make sure that a website is beautiful while functional. The popular choice is Photoshop, favoured by the professionals, and this provides a powerful set of tools that is perfectly capable of creating any web graphic in the right format.

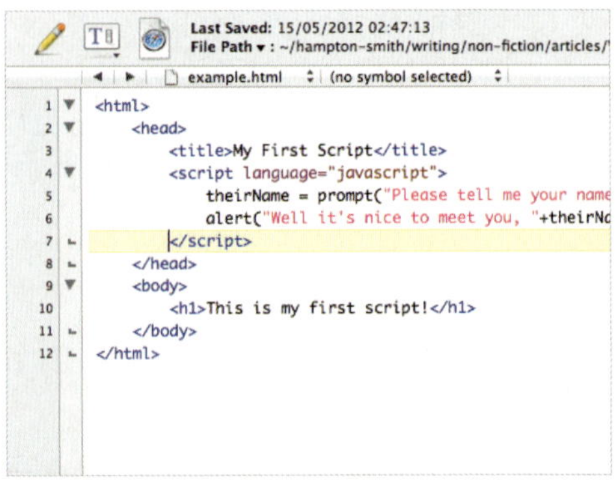

Check out our introduction to JavaScript on pages 182-185 to find out how to create your first script.

Keeping it safe

Security is an often forgotten issue when it comes to a website, and there are a few simple rules that need to be followed to ensure that a website's security is not breached. Passwords are the most popular form of securing access to a website, whether it's via an online login page, such as WordPress, or an FTP package used for transferring files from a local computer to a server where a site is hosted. One quick tip is not to use the password 'password'! As obvious as it may seem, the default password is often left and not changed. Try and choose a username that is not too obvious and ensure that a password uses upper and lower case characters and numbers. If it's hard to remember try not to write down and leave it next to your computer.

If using a web publishing platform, ie WordPress, some simple commonsense precautions are to update to the latest version. In addition, update any plugins and themes and also remove any inactive themes and plugins. Other security measures are more generic but just as important. Make sure that any OS updates are installed and make sure that any anti-virus and firewall software is kept up-to-date.

Login screens provide the typical point of access, needing a username and password to gain entry.

Beyond page building there is the web designer's favourite web publishing platform: WordPress. The beauty of the platform lies in its ability to build a complete site in minutes. The framework is provided and then it is just a matter of selecting a theme for the desired finish. The user adds content while WordPress provides the structure.

Web sites are viewed in web browsers and the four major web browsers – Internet Explorer, Firefox, Google Chrome and Safari – all offer different levels of support to HTML and CSS. And for this very reason they are an essential part of the web design process. All sites need to be tested in each browser to make sure that they work as intended, so it's always a good idea to find out a little about what browsers support when building a site. Finally, while not really tools of the trade in the traditional sense, services such as YouTube and Twitter are still key players. Both offer the opportunity to embed or integrate elements into a web page with code supplied via the mother site.

Different ways to build a website

The tools needed to build a site are all integrated into a website in different ways. A website is by its definition a web presence, and how it gets built is almost irrelevant – users want to see a functional site in action, very few care how it was built, apart from web designers of course!

The options for building a website range from the simple to the specially made. At one end of the scale there are instant, no-nonsense, no-knowledge services such as **Flavours.me**. These are services that appeal to those who want to get online quickly, or those who want an elegant, easy-to-customise web presence. Users build a page from pre-defined layout elements and styles and draw content from existing services such as WordPress, Twitter, Flickr.

Template builders sit very closely in the building process and are often found with many web hosting plans such as 1&1. These provide pre-defined elements, pages, images and so on in a logical step-by-step process and need no web design knowledge. Stepping up the ante is WordPress, which in principle is another quick and >>

1&1 Hosting (1and1.co.uk) offer several different hosting plans and packages. Pick the one that suits your needs.

Top tools of the trade

There are effectively three tools needed for the construction of a website. A knowledge of HTML and CSS, an HTML editor and a graphics editor. Sounds simple and in essence it is, but finding the right tool that suits requirements and personality is important. The first, most important tool is a HTML editor, and there are hundreds of choices available, free and paid for (see What's the best software on page 19). CSS is another text-based language and a text editor would suffice, but again a good knowledge of the language is needed. A good alternative is a CSS editor such as Rapid CSS (**www.blumentals.net/rapidcss**) or TopStyle (**svanas.dynip.com/topstyle/index.html**). A graphics editor is crucial for any web designer and the popular choice is Photoshop. This is a great package but expensive. The popular alternative is GIMP (**www.gimp.org**).

Beyond software packages there are some great in-browser tools. Firefox includes some great developer tools that help deconstruct a page. Add-ons such as Firebug (**http://getfirebug.com**) extend the browser's capabilities making the Mozilla browser the web designer's choice. There is an Aladdin's cave of online tools that will help with every aspect of the web design process. Aviary (**http://advanced.aviary.com**) is a suite of powerful creative applications, that includes an image editor, screen capture and vector editor. CSS Click Chart (**http://css3clickchart.com**) is a great tool that creates code for the latest CSS3 specification. Initializr (www.initializr.com) is a tool that helps create a basic HTML5 template which web designers can build on. For those looking for colour inspiration, Color Wizard (**colorsontheweb.com/colorwizard.asp**) offers an intuitive tool for creating complementary colour palettes.

The Aviary collection of creative online tools includes a powerful, and free, image editor.

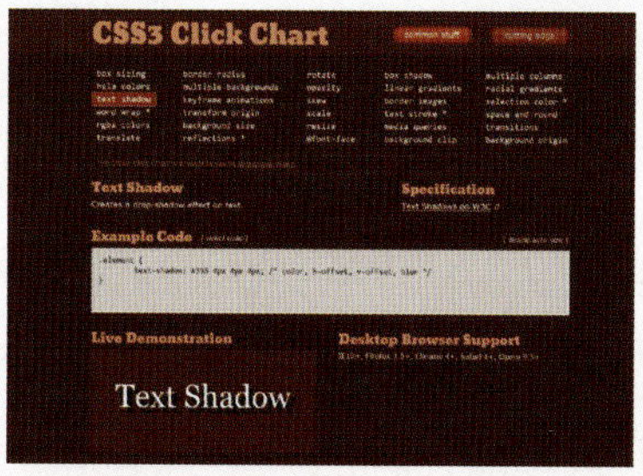

CSS3 Click Chart provides sample code for popular and cutting-edge CSS techniques.

Add a base colour and create a complementary colour palette for a website.

Essential guide

>> easy website building tool. There are two versions available; **wordpress.com**, where a site is hosted on the WordPress servers, and a self-hosted version. The .com option is created online and offers a simplified version of the platform. The self-hosted version is the full package where the user needs to provide their own web space to install the web publishing platform. Once installed users can change a theme, add plug-ins, customise the code base and completely restyle the look. Finally, at the top end of the scale is the bespoke or custom website that is built from scratch using all the latest web technologies and tools. This gives over total control of the build to the designer; the only restriction here is their imagination and knowledge.

What to do next

Once a site has been built and hosted on the web, what happens next? What more can you do with your site? Looking past the practical considerations – blogs, photographs, ecommerce and so on – a site needs to be seen. It doesn't matter how aesthetically pleasing, innovative and intuitive a site is, if no one gets to see it, it's worthless.

Any new website exists in a vast labyrinth of online experiences and promotion is the key to getting a site seen. The methodology and techniques to achieving a starring role on the web are wide and varied.

The first and maybe most important is the domain name. This is the address people will type into the browser (ie **www.iloveshopping.com**). This should reflect the name of the site. There is little point calling a site 'I Love Shopping' and using the domain name **shoppinglove.com** – the two should match for brand completeness. And, if possible, get the .com version. This is the first version of the domain name that will be searched for.

Google is the top search engine across the globe that is used by over 80 per cent of internet users, which equates to billions of people, so your site needs to be made Google-friendly. There are a host of elements that add value to a page: meta tags, sitemaps, alt tags and more. The best way to get Google-friendly is to call on Google themselves. Try out their Search Engine Optimization Starter Guide at **http://bit.ly/KGzh07**.

You shouldn't ignore social networks, either. Outside influences such as Twitter and Facebook are great communication channels with potentially huge audiences. Every time something on a site is updated, tell your followers and friends. If nothing new is happening then make it happen!

And finally, make sure your website content is consistent, error-free, current and regularly updated. Nobody wants to visit a website that has nothing new to give.

The mobile web

Smartphones and tablets are now as much part of the web browsing experience as the desktop. With the adoption of mobile devices comes a new set of resolutions and rules for web designers. Smartphones typically have a screen width of 320 pixels in portrait mode and 480 pixels in landscape mode. Tablets are a more diverse bunch, but as a typical example the iPad, the most popular tablet by far, has a width of 768 pixels in portrait and 1024 pixels in landscape. Desktops vary from 1024 pixels up to around 1900 pixels.

The variation in sizes demonstrates the issue of designing for mobile and desktop. One option is to build a mobile-specific version of a desktop website, but this not only adds to the workflow of a designer but also adds to the development cost for a company. The current solution is 'responsive design', which looks to cater for all screen resolutions and ultimately all devices and desktops, in turn future-proofing any website design. Responsive design uses CSS3 media queries, which recognise the width of a device and then switches the content to the appropriate version of the website to ensure the best on-screen display.

TheWarface (www.warface.co.uk) website is a great example of responsive design in action. Great on mobile and great on desktop.

Make a splash with your website and create something truly stunning that will have visitors returning.

What's the best software?

Writing code, typically HTML and CSS, is nothing more than a collection of alphanumeric characters, so nothing more complicated than a text editor is enough for creating code. Notepad (PC) and TextEdit (Mac) are free text editors that are perfectly capable of producing code, but they offer no assistance in the way you write it. So, a plain text editor is really for the more experienced coder.

However, while beginners and newcomers may struggle with the language to begin with, this approach will reap rich rewards down the line. Mastering HTML and CSS via hand-coding will mean that clean, semantic and lightweight code will be the eventual outcome.

Beyond the plain text editor, the next steps you'll need to conquer are the HTML editors. These are more specific text editors which incorporate related coding features. They provide an environment that offers assistance and help create a code base. These are much less expensive than high-end packages and provide enough tools to assist with the page building process.

At the top end of the scale are feature-heavy packages such as Adobe Dreamweaver, which are comparatively expensive. As you might expect, high-end packages do not simply offer a plain text interface. They offer a whole host of tools, such as pre-built templates, useful code widgets, colour-coded code, multiple views and instant code creation.

Choosing an HTML editor is very much a subjective choice and web designers will all have their favourites that they prefer to build with. The simple solution is to try a few of the free HTML editors that are available on the market and familiarise yourself with how they operate. It is almost guaranteed that one will fit your method of working.

Build a site

"HTML provides the structure, content and connection between pages"

WHAT YOU'LL LEARN

Throughout the Build a site section you'll be learning how to code your first web page using HTML & CSS, then when you're done you can get it on the internet with our hosting and uploading guides. The coding tutorials work with popular layouts like two-column and three-column, while our introductory guides to HTML and CSS teach you about some of the popular tags and properties and how they're used.

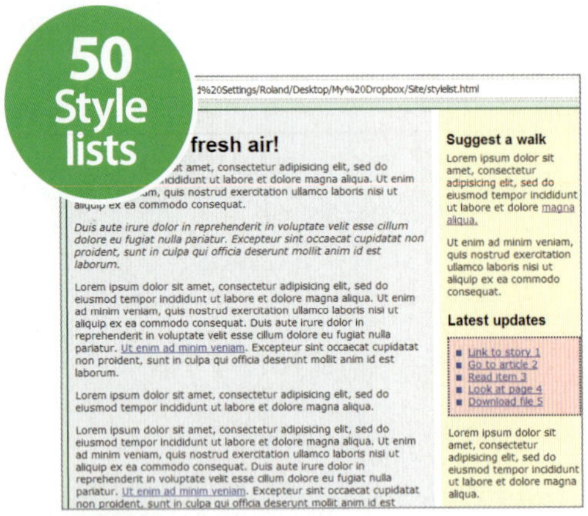

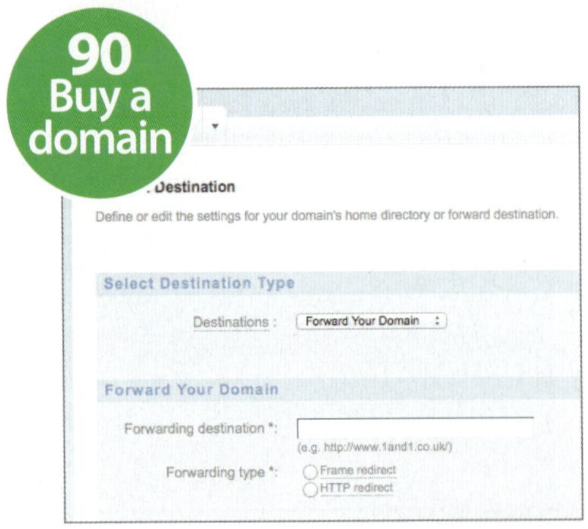

EFFECTIVE HEADER

Create a clean and clear header with our tutorial on page 70

GREAT CONTENT

Add the meat to your website with our guide on page 78

SIDEBAR

Learn how you can make and use a sidebar to its full potential on page 72

HTML

An introduction to HTML

HyperText Markup Language, more commonly know as HTML, is the basic building block of the web. It provides the structure, content and connection between pages, allowing web designers to create interactive experiences. It's easy to learn, and offers limitless possibilities…

The majority of web pages are made up of one or more files that are downloaded to a computer, which in turn are interpreted by a web browser and finally rendered out to screen. At its simplest, a web page is a plain text file that contains special instructions about what kind of content is contained within. These instructions are written in HTML – the language of the web.

HTML, or HyperText Markup Language to give it the full name, is the core building block of a web page. HTML is a markup-based, human-readable language that's designed to be simple to write, and easy to understand. A markup language is one where bits of data are literally marked as being of a particular type. So, for example, a piece of data that you want to render as a paragraph would be 'marked up' with a paragraph marker.

Marking up

Markers are referred to as tags, and they have less-than and greater-than symbols around them. This paragraph would be marked up with a <p> tag at the start to denote a paragraph, and a matching </p> tag at the end to signify the end of the paragraph. HTML offers many tags for marking up content, and browsers are programmed to interpret these tags, formatting the contents of each tag according to a set of preset rules. This allows the <strong> tag to render text in bold, and the <em> (for emphasis) tag to render in italics. One of the major benefits of this system of marking up content is that it's easy to read – you don't need any special software to either write or read HTML documents, as they're just plain text. This makes it easy to create a functioning web page using nothing more complex than a text editor.

What exactly is HyperText?

Why is the language called HyperText Markup? Because the key thing that makes the World Wide Web a web, rather than a series of disconnected pockets of content, is the ability to link one document to another – these links are HyperText because clicking on them takes you somewhere else in the vast web of pages! As well as a basic HTML (text) document, web pages can call in >>

HTML is the basic language of the web, and works no matter which browser you use, or what server provides the page

All websites are built using HTML, CSS and JavaScript

external files (or 'assets') that include stylesheets, images, audio files, video, flash and scripts. The web browser looks at the HTML document when it downloads it, and looks for any external files that are called into the page. If it finds any files called in, the browser will send a message back to the web server asking for those files. The final result you see in your web browser window may be the result of more than 20 individual files, brought together by the web browser and rendered as a single web page!

Recognising an HTML document

You'll notice as you browse around the web that different pages have different names, and more importantly they have different extensions at the end of the filename. Some end with .htm or .html, which are obviously HTML documents, but others might end with .cfm, .php, .asp or .aspx. What are these file types?

As far as the web browser is concerned, they're just normal HTML documents like every other on the web. What these different extensions signify is that some sort of processing has happened on the server before the page was sent to your browser, allowing the website to generate some unique-to-you content.

All the examples we've noted above have similar characteristics. They're scripts, or small computer programs, that run on the server and make some decisions about what content to show. This might be as simple as including your name at the top of the page when you're logged in, or as complex as a fully loaded e-commerce web store, but all these 'server-side languages' output the same final result – plain HTML. It's important that the web works this way, as every web browser only has to support one kind of page structural language, which makes it easier for both web designers and browser vendors, not to mention for users of the web who know that all they need to access any website is a web browser and an internet connection.

Who invented HTML?

In the 1980s and 90s the internet already existed, but didn't have any simple way of navigating between computers and content. Each server had different software, different protocols and methods for sharing data. Tim Berners-Lee was

What is HTML5?

HTML5 makes adding content to your web pages a much simpler process

HTML5 is the latest version of the HTML specification, which is managed by the World Wide Web Consortium (W3C). This latest iteration of the standard introduces new features and support for multimedia directly inside an HTML document. One of the key considerations for the W3C is maintaining backwards compatibility, however, and HTML5 remains backwardly compatible with all web browsers and renderers.

The most exciting aspect of the HTML5 specification is the new semantic approach to marking up content. For the first time, web designers can mark up an article as such – especially useful given the nature of blogs, news websites and the like.

> "The most exciting aspect of HTML5 is the new semantic approach to marking up content"

Over the past decade, video on the web has exploded. As bandwidth has increased, and more people have access to high-speed internet connections, the likes of YouTube and Vimeo have gripped the imagination of web users across the globe. Until HTML5, the most reliable and common method for including video on a web page was to render it using Adobe Flash. Both YouTube and Vimeo continue to use this approach by default, but both sites have started migrating over to the more accessible and standards-friendly HTML5 version as the browser vendors have updated their software to support the all-new <video> tag.

working in a computer services section at CERN – the European Laboratory for Particle Physics in Geneva, Switzerland. Tim realised that it would be useful to have a simple method for sharing information remotely, and rather than invent a completely new system from scratch, he developed a markup language based on the popular SGML format. He developed a straightforward protocol – HTTP (which stands for HyperText Transfer Protocol) – for retrieving other documents' text via hypertext links. The text format for HTTP was named HTML, for HyperText Markup Language. By keeping it simple, Tim encouraged others to build upon his ideas and to design further software for displaying HTML, and for setting up their own HTML documents ready for access. This was the birth of the web as we know it today, and led to an explosion in use of the internet. HTML itself has been further developed over time, and we're now up to version 5.

> "Every web browser only has to support one kind of page structural language, which is easier for web designers"

All new and improved: HTML5

You can't fail to have noticed the talk of HTML5 in recent years. Even non-web-savvy users have come across the term, largely thanks to Steve Jobs and the iPhone. HTML5 is the latest iteration of the HTML language, and looks very much the same as the previous versions. New tags that provide greater semantic meaning to the content being marked up have been introduced, along with native support for rich media such as audio and video. The ability to make a document self-describing offers numerous benefits, but it's worth pointing out that when the term HTML5 is used – especially in the press – it often refers to a trilogy of technologies rather than just the HTML language itself. The press interpretation of HTML5 includes both CSS3 and JavaScript in addition to the HTML5 language, and is often used to describe the experience of interactive, user-friendly web pages that incorporate all three technologies.

Apple decided to promote the use of semantic, standard HTML, CSS and JavaScript, rather than support Adobe's rich media plug-in, Flash. Adobe argued that Flash was a good solution for presenting rich content on mobile devices, while Apple insisted that open technologies with proper semantic meaning and no need for a plug-in was preferable. Time has favoured Apple's approach, in no short part due to the huge success of its iPhone and iPad products!

What are these semantics?

The HTML format is very accommodating; beyond the required elements of **<html>**, **<head>** and **<body>** you can arrange your content any way you like. This is both a benefit and a potential issue as the flexibility to present (and mark up) content in any way also means that you can quickly end up with a confusing mess! A movement to present information in a semantic fashion existed at the birth of the language, and has seen a resurgence in recent years.

The general idea is that content should be marked up according to its type and importance. **<h1>** heading tags, for example, should only be used to mark up the most important piece of info on a page, **<h2>** for the second most important and so on. If you think about the analogy of a book, the **<h1>** tag might be the book or chapter name, **<h2>** would be a section header and so on. By using this approach, the HTML describes the importance of each piece of info which helps search engines identify what your page is about, and more importantly special software, such as screen readers that translate web pages into audio for people with sight problems, can make more sense of the document.

In the past, content has been marked up using heading and paragraph tags, but content >>

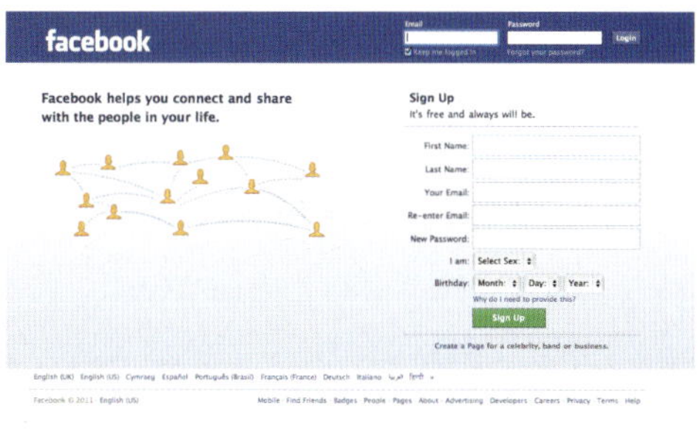

Once you know HTML you can create both websites and web apps for the likes of iPhone, Android and even Facebook!

Apple's website typifies what can be achieved with just HTML and some scripts and styles

HTML & mobile browsing

When you access the web from your mobile phone or tablet, you'll often notice special pages that have been formatted especially for these devices, rather than the full desktop version of a website. You might have wondered whether these pages use a special language especially for mobile devices? The good news is that, just like the rest of the web, they use standard HTML. The only real difference between a page optimised for a mobile device and one orientated towards a desktop computer is the CSS styles that have been applied. The content, and often the structure, of the page remains plain HTML and there's no need to learn special skills or additional languages to be able to create sites that on these devices. That's not to say that you shouldn't consider how your users are accessing the web page and what information they might need!

Typically, a mobile-optimised website will be presented in one of two ways: either it will be the full website presented to render nicely on the smaller screen size that you find on phones and tablets, or it will be a special version of the website that doesn't contain the same information as the full website. This latter approach supposes that a mobile visitor to your site is likely to be more goal-orientated than a desktop visitor, and aims to present the key information quickly, such as 'how to find us', or 'our contact details'.

Web pages for mobile devices still use HTML, it's just the CSS styles that are different.

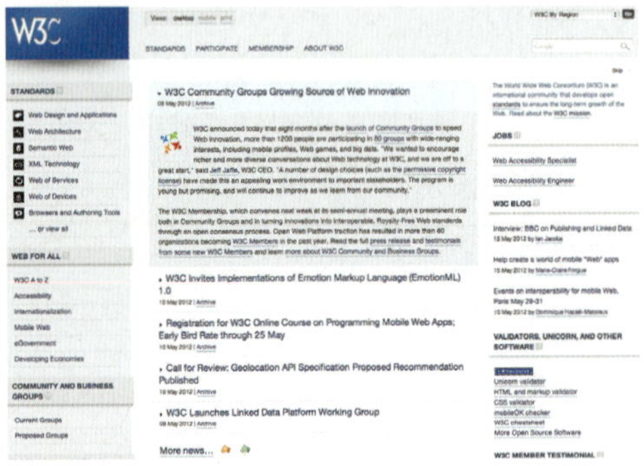

The new HTML5 specification has been drawn up by the W3C, an organisation set up to act as the gatekeeper for web standards

has been grouped using the same single nondescript tag, <div>. This tag is, by itself, nothing more than a method for delimiting different pieces of information so that it might be used around a navigation bar, or just as likely around an article on a web page. As HTML5 has been introduced, new semantically orientated tags have been introduced that allow designers to mark up navigation with a <nav> tag, headers with a <header> area and articles with <article>. There are more of these semantic tags available, but some browsers are still implementing HTML5 so we're in a period of transition where you'll still see a huge number of plain old <div> tags used.

The new features in HTML5 allow you to embed video and audio directly in your pages, and when combined with CSS can provide amazing special effects

What about Flash?

Up until the launch of the iPhone, the de facto method for presenting interactive rich content (with animated elements, video and audio) was Adobe Flash. This is a plug-in that sits inside an HTML document, but runs as a separate program within the web browser. When Apple released the iPhone it decided not to support Flash, largely because of the problems Flash had with crashing browsers, and the lack of support for touch screens. This decision helped kick-start a movement away from the plug-in towards the combination of HTML, CSS and JavaScript.

Whereas five or six years ago most interactive image galleries were created using Flash, today the majority are rendered using standard HTML and either CSS, JavaScript or most commonly both. Flash is still useful for certain types of content – it's a very popular method for showing video on the web (although this will change as HTML5 is fully implemented by browsers), and games are currently easier to code in Flash.

Flash isn't nearly as accessible as HTML, either from a developer point of view or from a user perspective, especially with regard to disability access. Adobe has worked to improve this over the years, but the technology isn't ever going to be as accessible as a plain-text-based system such as HTML.

HTML: function, not form

In the early days of the internet, HTML included a large variety of methods for changing the way content displayed. For example, an early option was the <font> tag which allowed you to specify the typeface that you'd like the content and information to be rendered in. This allowed designers to very precisely choose how their content was displayed, but when a website consisted of 50 pages and the designer wanted to change the font, it was a mammoth task to work through every page and replace every single reference to the choice of font.

As a solution, CSS was introduced. CSS, as you'll see elsewhere in this book, is a system for applying styles – defining the form and aesthetic of a page. This means that now we can treat HTML as a structural language only – we don't define the way a web page looks using HTML, just how it's structured and content arranged in a semantic hierarchy. The net result is that by separating form and function we can now change a font that's used throughout a big website with just a single change to the CSS stylesheet, saving time and ensuring design consistency throughout.

> "HTML has come a long way since its invention in a Swiss lab"

What's next for HTML?

HTML has come a long way since its invention in a computer lab in Switzerland, and it's continuing to develop. The HTML5 specification is already partially implemented in browsers, but other elements of the language are still being discussed, and there's a good probability that we'll see further enhancements in the coming years such as the ability to specify different resolution images to be downloaded to desktop computers from those sent to mobile devices.

There's been an explosion in smartphone use over the past few years which has led increasingly to the web being accessed on the move. These devices have a different screen orientation to the traditional computer, often have less bandwidth and computing power, but expect to have a fantastic browsing experience. The HTML language, through HTML5, is already adapting to meet this challenge, but as the specification matures you can expect to see further enhancements with this usage scenario in mind. It's an exciting time to be a web designer!

Common HTML tags

The <h1> tag is one of six different heading tags (ranging from <h1> to <h6>). This signifies the most important piece of information on your page, or in the section, and is akin to a chapter name or book title.

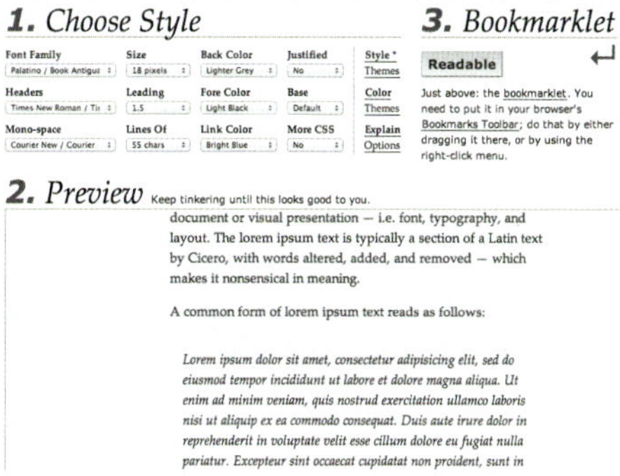

The <p> tag has to the most common in use on the web. It marks up a piece of text as being a paragraph. Individual paragraphs can also be grouped into articles with another tag as you will soon see…

The <article> tag is brand new to HTML5. This handy tag enables you to mark a set of content as being part of one story. An article can contain many heading, paragraphs, images and other assets.

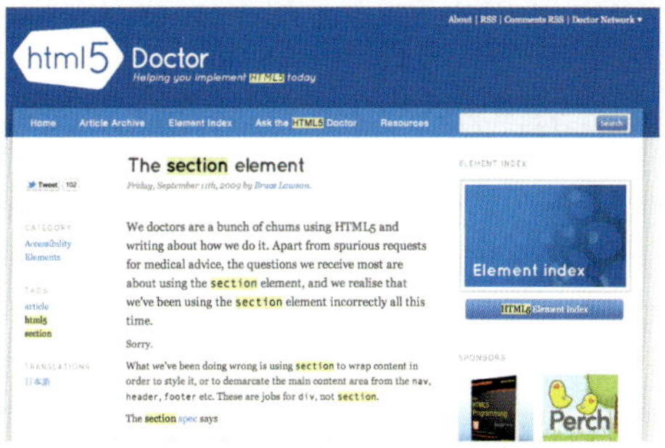

The <section> tag is also new to HTML5 and allows you to mark up content into sections. Each section can contain a single item, or a collection of related items. This tag is designed to allow you to mark up semantically, while still providing hooks for CSS.

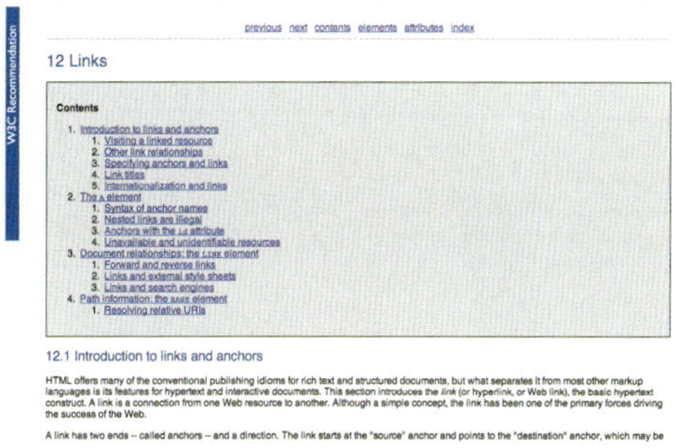

The <a> tag is perhaps the most important tag of all. This anchor tag enables you to connect different web pages together with a link. Without the <a> tag, there wouldn't be a web so much as a collection of isolated pages that you'd need to remember the addresses for.

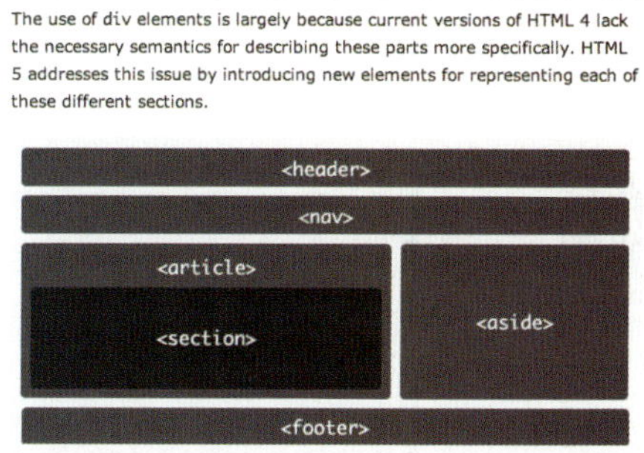

The <aside> tag is a great addition to the HTML5 specification. It allows you to mark up content as being not wholly related to the main content of your page, section or article. This is typically used for sidebars and other nonessential, but interesting, information.

The <header> tag allows you to mark up a section of your page, section or article as containing the masthead or header information for that content. For an article, this would be a heading and perhaps an image, while for a page it might be your logo and page navigation.

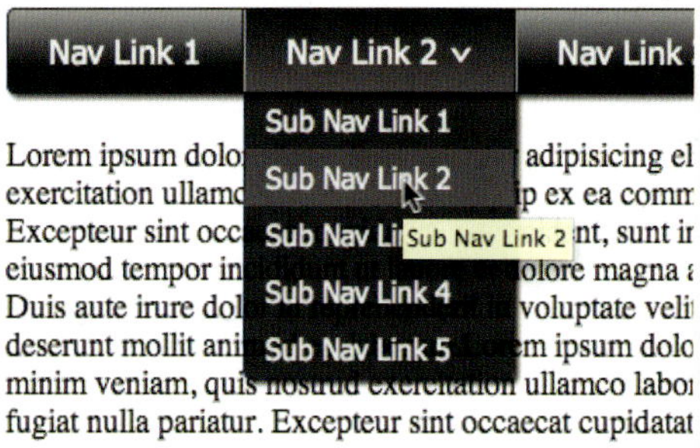

The <nav> tag simply marks up an area that's responsible for the navigation on your page. Typically it will contain many <a> tags, separated by an unordered list (using the <ul> tag) and individual list items.

The <img> tag allows you to call in images into your page. It accepts a series of attributes that specify the location of the image on the web, the width, height and some alternative text for screen readers or to be shown in the event the image can't be found.

Create a basic layout

Code up your first basic skeleton for a webpage using HTML5 – it's really quite simple to do

In this tutorial we'll make an HTML5 layout for a simple webpage. While initially HTML may look confusing, there's a relatively small amount of code that you'll need to remember. There are a few basic building blocks such as **<div>** which you will find yourself using regularly, then others such as **<caption>** which you will use much less often.

If you have made pages before in the past using HTML4 then you should feel at home, just be aware of the new tags. If you've not written any HTML before then good news, as it's now easier to understand! HTML5 has added in a lot of new elements which help the browser interpret the layout of the page easier. **<header>** and **<footer>** are two examples, and describe common top and bottom elements of a page respectively.

When starting out in web design it's important to remember to 'open' and then 'close' tags correctly. Opening a tag looks like '<example>' while closing with '</example>'. Note the '/'. Any thing within those two elements will be considered its children; they are contained within the element. This is important to remember when you later use CSS and then JavaScript. So open your text editor of choice – be it NotePad on Windows, TextEdit on Mac, or something more high-end – and let's get started!

"There's a relatively small amount of code that you'll need to remember"

A simple two-column page

The parts of the skeleton of an elementary webpage

Div tag

A div is used to group content together, in this case we use it to display our content and sidebar. Divs can be nested within each other and can have IDs and classes applied to them so they can be identified

The head tag

While usually invisible to the website visitor, the head tag contains important information for the browser, such as CSS styles as well as search engine information

Header tag

The header differs from the head, as it's contained within the body of the HTML page, meaning it gets displayed in the browser. The header usually contains company insignia, navigation and possibly an introductory image

Footer

The footer tag denotes an element that usually goes at the bottom of the content, and contains items such as author, contact info, telephone numbers etc

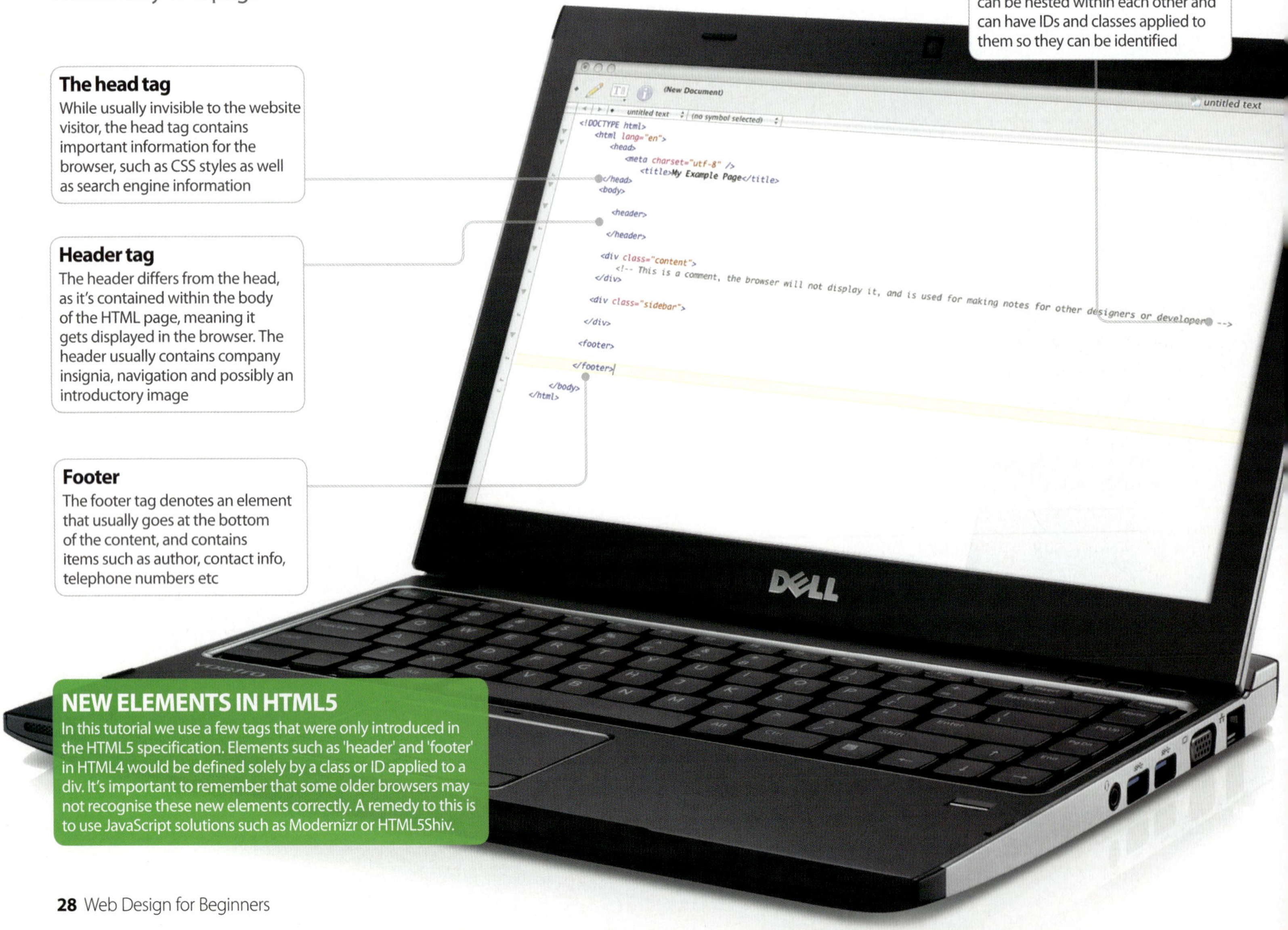

NEW ELEMENTS IN HTML5

In this tutorial we use a few tags that were only introduced in the HTML5 specification. Elements such as 'header' and 'footer' in HTML4 would be defined solely by a class or ID applied to a div. It's important to remember that some older browsers may not recognise these new elements correctly. A remedy to this is to use JavaScript solutions such as Modernizr or HTML5Shiv.

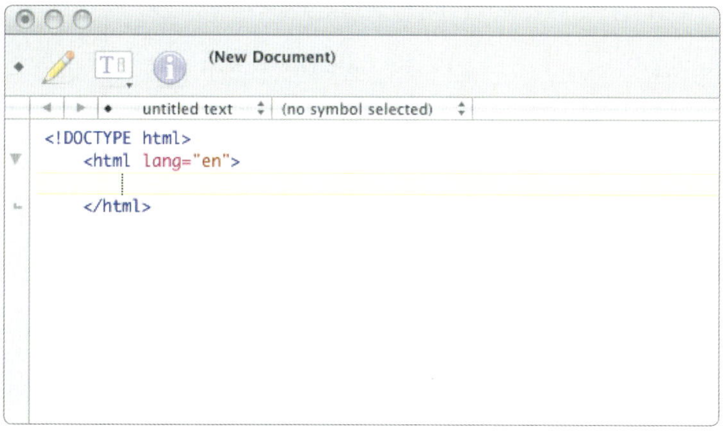

01 The HTML base

First up, the doctype tells the browser what kind of content to expect. In HTML5 it's simple: <!DOCTYPE html><html lang="en"></html>.

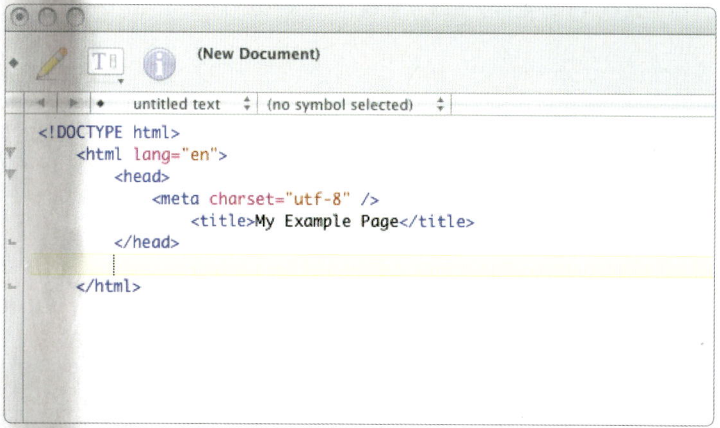

02 Create the head

Next up is the <head> element, where we place all the files we wish to include within our page, eg CSS style sheets, which we'll learn about later.

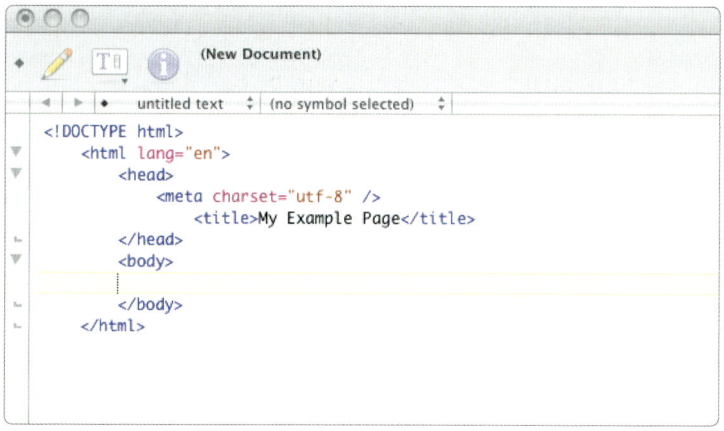

03 Add the body

The <body> is where all the viewable page content goes. In it we'll add the header, the main content area, sidebar and a footer perhaps for a sitemap.

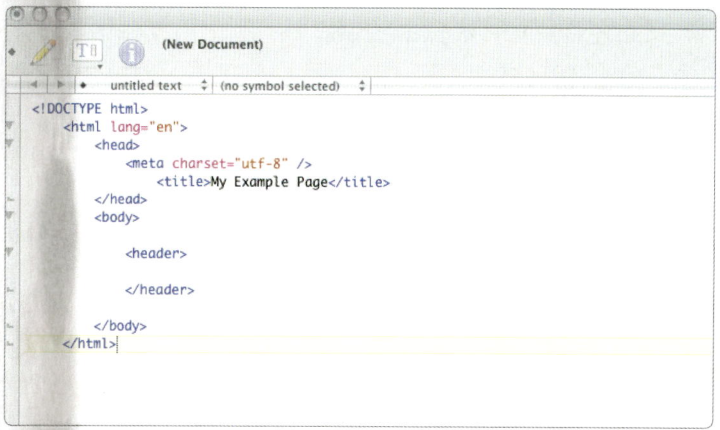

04 Add the header

The <header> is typically used to hold the main site image, with a title and possibly site navigation. You can have multiple <header> tags on a page.

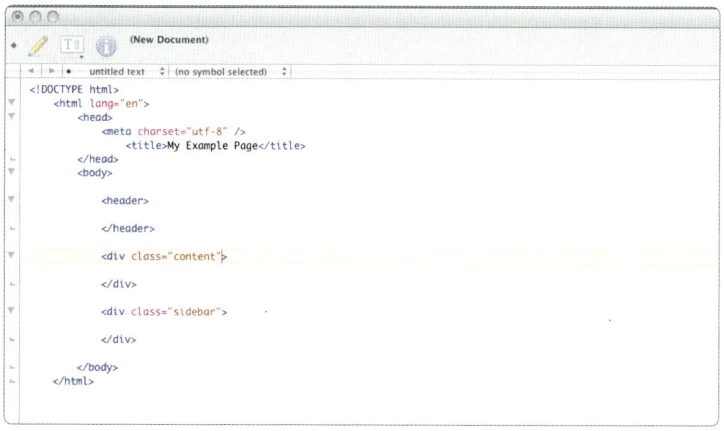

05 Sidebar and content

The main content can be placed within a 'div', then a class applied to it: <div class='content'> </div>. The sidebar can be placed after it, also with a class.

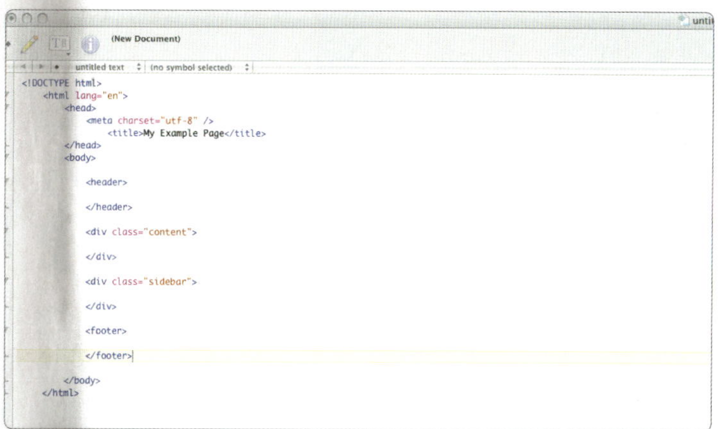

06 Add the footer

The <footer> element usually contains quick links to common areas of the site such as 'Contact us', and sometimes has copyrights or addresses.

Code a link

Adding in links to other pages in your site and external sites is a key part of web design

While links may seem like a simple element to add to a webpage, they are the key building blocks of the entire internet. Imagine having to type a different address into the browser for every single page you wanted to visit on the web! Similar to pages within a book, separate webpages within a website help to break up content by topic or purpose. Then, by adding in a navigation bar or something similar to your site, it means that visitors will be able to quickly move to the content that they are interested in.

Links are also one of the most important elements that Google and other search engines use to find and index your site. The kind of content that you link out to, and the kind of content contained within sites that link to your pages, are vital in informing the search engine on how to categorise your site for its search results.

This tutorial will take you through adding in links leading to other pages in your website, and how to link out to other people's sites. Once you have added some links, your site can start to function how it's intended to, with visitors being able to view all the content contained with ease.

"Links are the key building blocks of the entire internet"

Adding in links to pages

Adding links to other pages is straight forward

Link text

The link text is what your user will see, so make sure it's descriptive. Try to avoid using 'click here'; instead, word the surrounding text, eg view my <a href"gallery.html">gallery</a>

Default styling

Without adding in any styling of your own, links will be underlined and blue, and once visited will turn purple. Your cursor will also change appearance in most browsers

<a> tag

The <a> tag is what denotes a link, and is used on practically every webpage on the internet to link to other documents and sites

href

The 'href' part is where you enter in the destination for the link. Usually this will be somewhere else within your site, but it can also be to another page on the internet

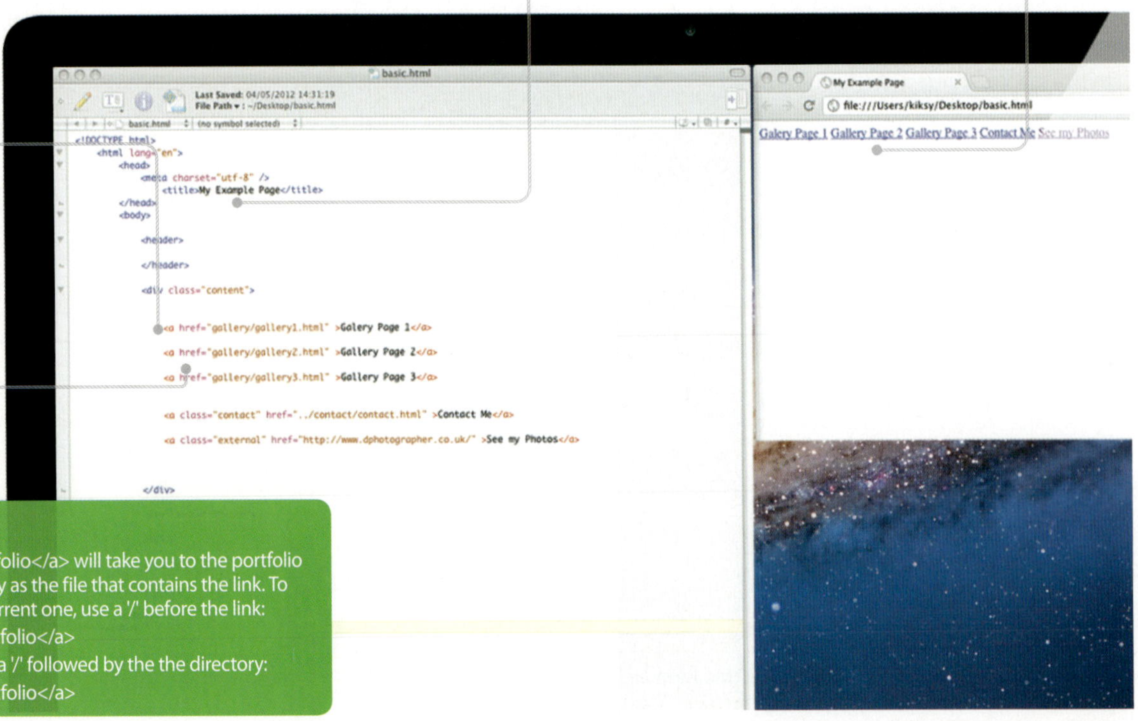

RELATIVE PATHS

Entering <a href="portfolio.html"> Portfolio</a> will take you to the portfolio page, assuming it's in the same directory as the file that contains the link. To link to a directory that is beneath the current one, use a '/' before the link:
<a href="portfolio/portfolio.html"> Portfolio</a>
To link to a file in a directory above, use a '/' followed by the the directory:
<a href="portfolio/portfolio.html"> Portfolio</a>

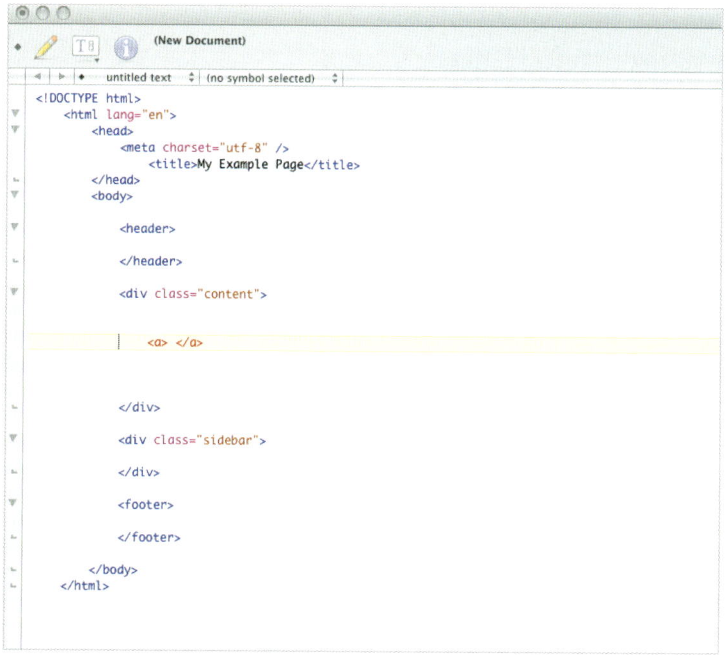

01 The basic 'a' tag

A link is denoted using the 'a' tag, short for anchor (see page 27 for more information on them). To start off your link, enter in: <a> </a>. However, unlike some other HTML tags, an anchor needs a little more information for it to work properly.

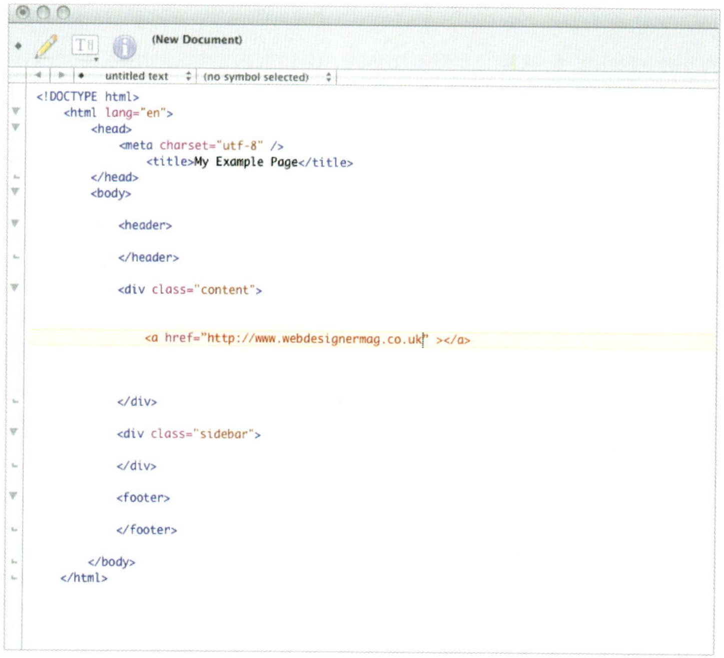

02 Href

The link needs a destination so that when it's clicked, the browser knows where to go. This is added in using 'href'. For example, <a href="http://www.webdesignermag.co.uk/" ></a> would send the browser to that external website.

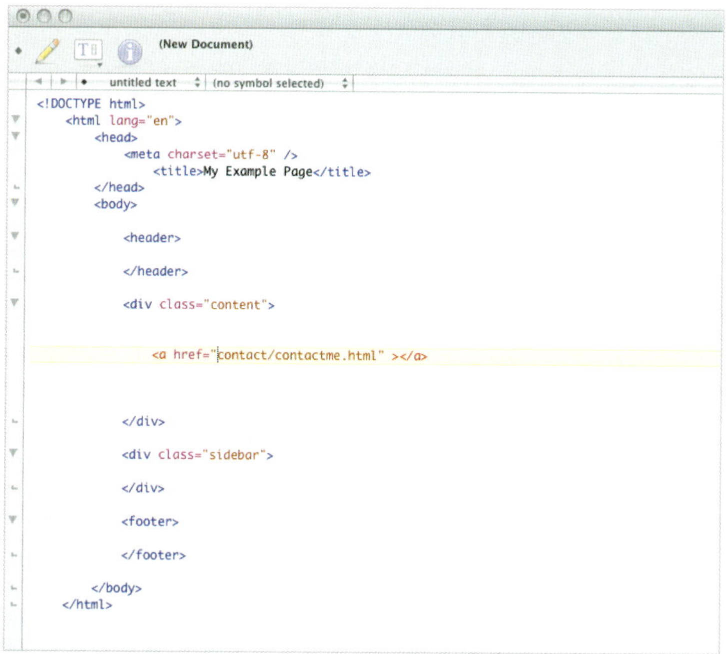

03 Internal links

To link to another page in your own site, you simply add the name of the page; eg <a href="contact.html" ></a>. This assumes that the contact.html page is within the same folder as the page we are working on. See the 'Relative paths' boxout for more information.

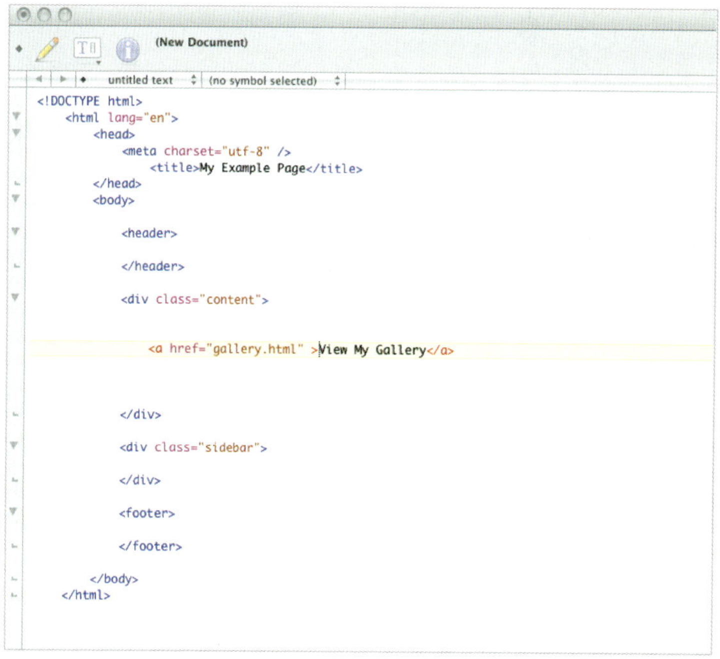

04 Add link text

To make the link visible to the user, add in some text between your opening and closing <a> tags. For example: <a href="gallery.html"> See My Gallery</a>. Open the page in your browser, and assuming the gallery.html page exits in the same directory, clicking the text will take you there.

Create lists in your website

Learn how to quickly create various lists within your webpages using HTML

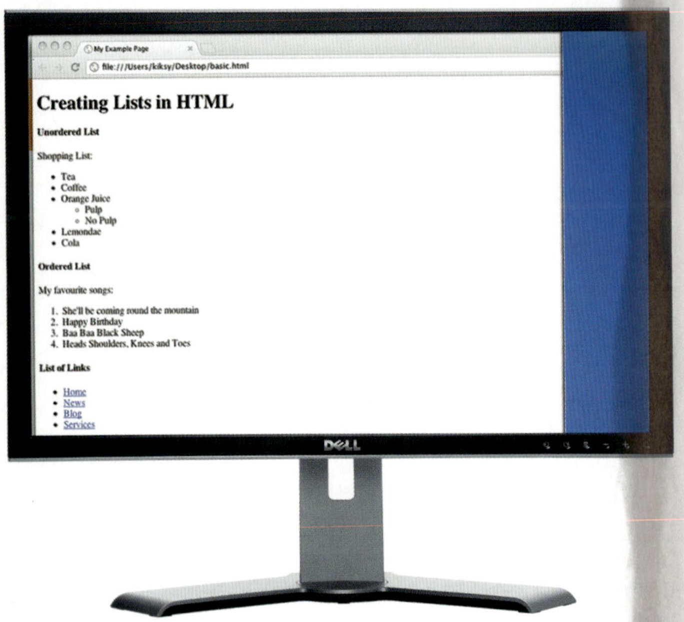

Lists are an effective way of presenting important information in a way that's quick to read and digest. They are also a good method for giving a brief description or introduction into content to follow, to help your users find what it is they are looking for.

Coding up a list in HTML is quick and very straightforward, and once you've got the hang of the basics you can start to apply your own styles using CSS to make them really stand out from the crowd, which we'll come to later

There are two main types of lists in HTML: ordered and unordered. An ordered list stars at 1 and then increases. This is useful when you need to give preference to the higher items, or you want to display a step-by-step guide.

An unordered list is simply bullet-pointed and is useful when you just need to display a list where the order is irrelevant. By default, lists will be indented from the surrounding content and have a circular bullet point. This tutorial will show you how to add lists to your pages, both ordered and unordered, and also how to create lists within lists.

> "Coding up a list in HTML is quick and very straightforward"

Types of lists in HTML

Using the list tags to create ordered and unordered lists

Unordered list

An unordered list is simply a series of items grouped together. By default they will be indented and each item will have a bullet point next to it

Nested lists

Lists can be embedded within other lists simply by opening and closing a <ul> or <ol> within another list. These are then indented further, and show a white bullet point

Ordered list

An ordered list automatically applies numbers of ascending value to each item within it. This is useful when you need to prioritise content, for example

Links within lists

Links can be put into lists simply by wrapping an <a> tag around the text. This is great for making menus and navigation items

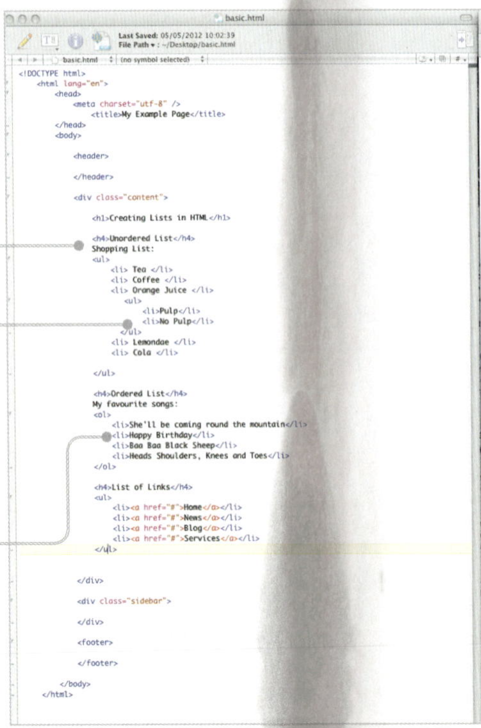

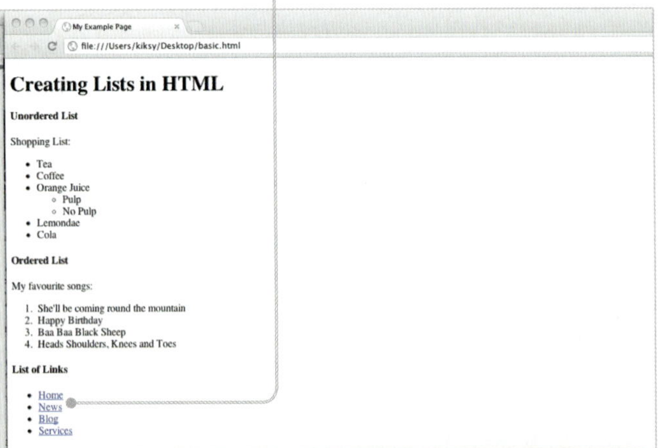

DEFINITION LISTS

There is one other type of list in HTML – the definition list. It's quite rarely used but allows an indented description to be added to each list item. An example definition list would be:

```
<dl>
        <dt>Snowboard</dt>
                <dd>- Great for freestyle tricks</dd>
        <dt>Cross Country Skis</dt>
                <dd>- Ideal for exploring on</dd>
</dl>
```

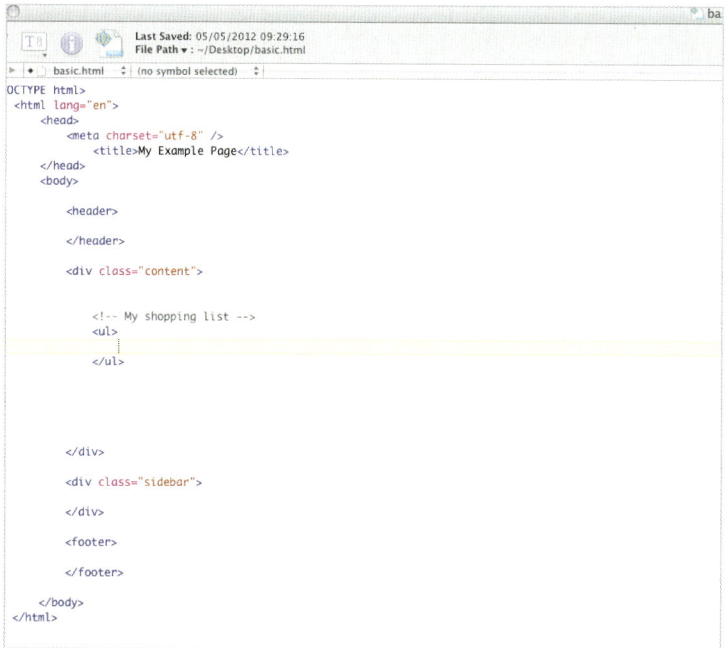

01 Unordered list

An unordered list by default is shown slightly indented with a bullet point denoting each item. To add in an unordered list you use the <ul> tag. Remember to close it with a </ul>.

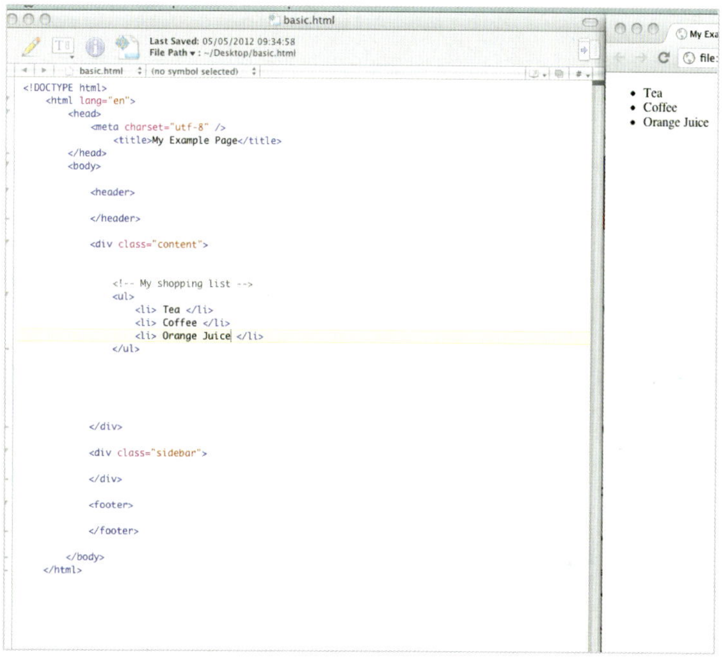

02 Add list items

Within your list, items are added using the list item tag like so: <li> </li>. Text can go between the open and close li tags; for example: <li> Tea </li>. Remember that the li tags must go within your <ul> tag.

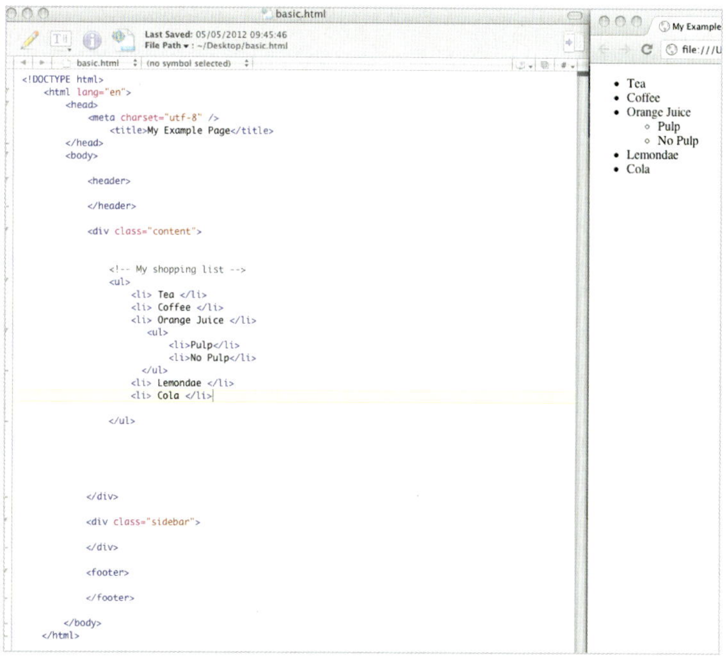

03 Nested lists

Lists can be embedded within other lists just by opening and closing a new <ul> within another <ul>, and then list items can be added to that too. They will then be indented again within that <ul>.

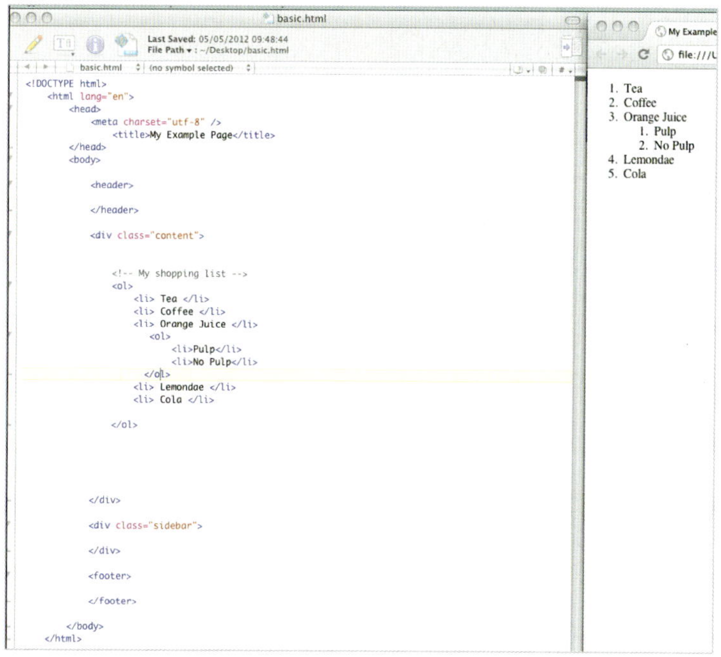

04 Ordered lists

If you wish to number your list items then you can use the <ol> tag in place of the <ul>. This will then replace the bullet points with ascending numeric values for the list items.

All about div tags

Learn about the all-important div tag in HTML and how it's used to group content

An HTML page is made up of a series of tags which tell the web browser what to display and where. The main building block of a page is a div tag, short for division. If you look at a newspaper page, you will see that text is grouped together in columns. Images with captions are also together with a margin around them. A div in HTML is similar to this, and it's usual to group together content in a similar way. While HTML5 has added a few new tags with more semantic names such as 'header' and 'footer', the main body of most pages is still constructed using divs.

There is no limit on how many divs you have within a page and most webpages you visit online will contain many, all nested within each other. Divs can contain text, images, video and audio, as well as other HTML elements such as articles and sections.

This tutorial will show you how to make your first divs and then how to apply an ID or class to them so when you're ready you can apply CSS styles, or use JavaScript on them. We'll be using plenty of them throughout the book!

Properties of the div

Divs, classes and IDs

Indenting divs
Once your pages get more complicated they can feature many divs all nested within each other. This can make it hard to track where one opens and another closes. It's standard practice to indent the content of a div using the tab button

Div classes
Classes are widely used in web development to allow CSS styles to be associated with elements within your HTML page

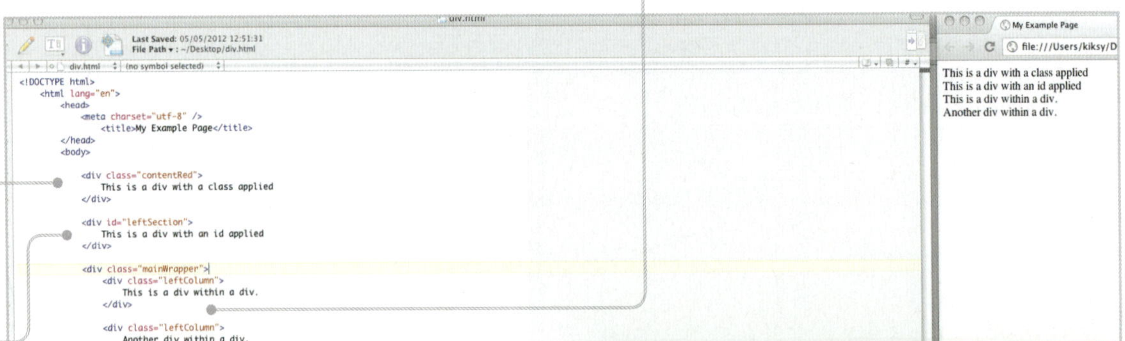

IDs
IDs are used in a similar way to classes, but there should only be one element on a page with a particular ID. IDs allow you to target specific elements using JavaScript for manipulation

Code highlighting
Most HTML editors offer code colour highlighting of some sort. This can help you when checking which divs have classes applied etc

NESTING DIVS
Many webpages are made up of a few main elements such as a header and footer, and then a main content div. Within a div it's possible to have other divs. For example:

```
<div id="content">
        <div class="leftColumn"
        </div>

        <div class="rightColumn"
        </div>
</div>
```

Doing this allows you to have a universal style to the 'content' div, and then apply different styles to the divs contained within.

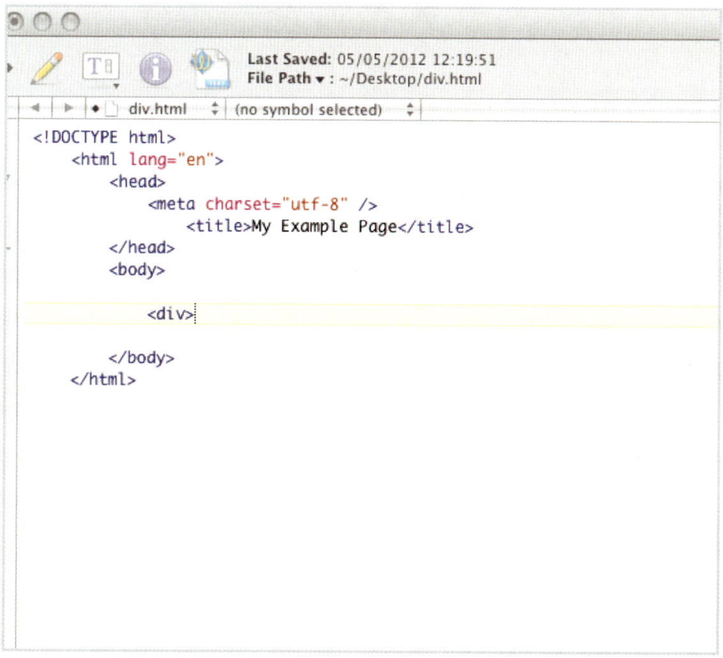

01 The basic div

A div is started by using this simple piece of code: <div>. Following on from that, you can then insert all the content you want to contain within the div.

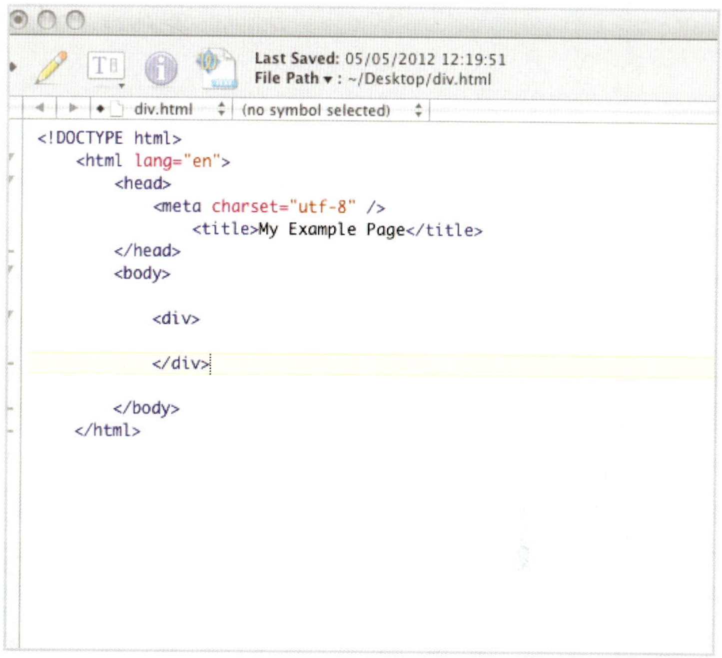

02 Closing the div

Once you have inserted all the content, you need to make sure you close off the div by using </div>. Note the forward slash denoting the ending of the current div.

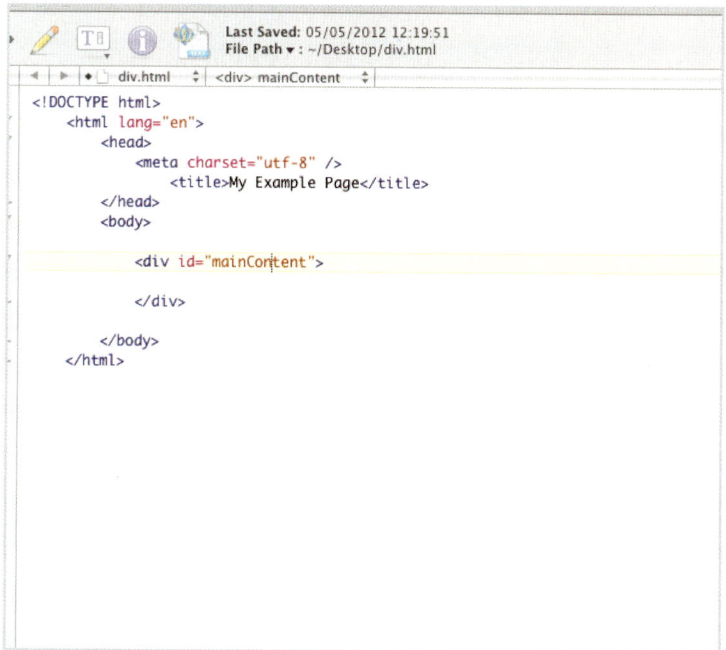

03 Adding an ID

A div can have a unique identifier so it can be recognised in a style sheet or by any JavaScript you may add. To apply an ID to a div, use: <div id="myDivId"> </div>

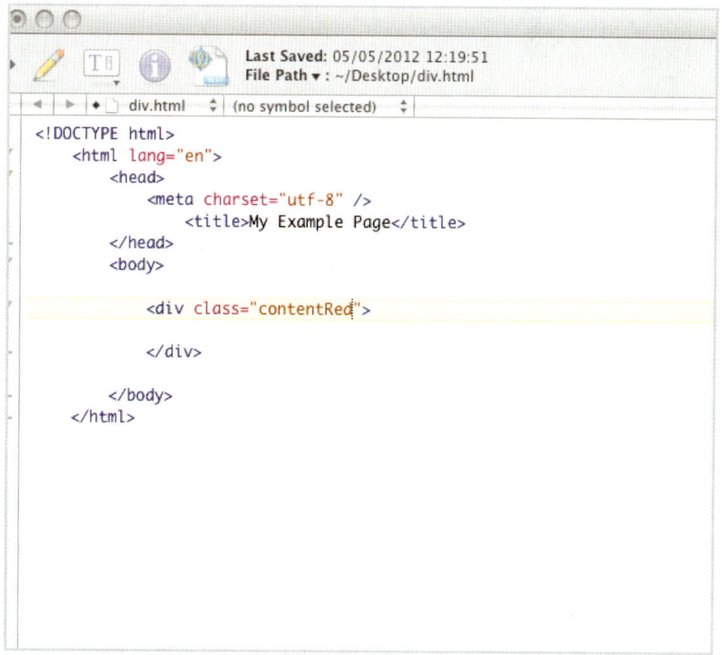

04 Adding a class

Classes are similar to IDs, but many items on a page can have the same class. To apply a class to a div, use: <div class="myDivClass"> </div>
Using classes makes styling multiple elements much easier.

Create a three-column layout

Put what you've learnt so far into practice and make the popular three-column webpage structure using HTML5

HTML and CSS essentially allow for a huge range of freedom when designing your pages, but there are a few layout principles that have developed over the years which it's a good idea to follow.

If you have a quick look at some of your favourite sites on the internet it's quite likely that they will use a column layout, akin to a newspaper. A common layout for a site is to have the site or company logo at the top of the page, then have a column down the left for navigation or links, a main content section in the centre, and then a sidebar on the right with supplementary information or Facebook and Twitter feeds. This is then commonly rounded off with a site-wide footer containing copyright information, the name of the site designer, site links and sometimes a contact address. This tutorial will show you how to code up the HTML scaffolding for a three-column layout using modern HTML5 elements. Once you have mastered this, it can then be adapted into a two- or more-than-three-column layout if you so wish.

"This tutorial will show you how to code up the HTML scaffolding for a three-column layout using modern HTML5 elements"

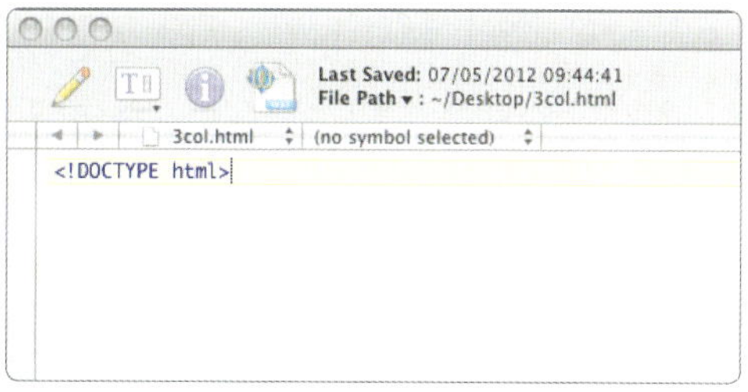

01 Set up your HTML page

To start off, open up your favourite editor and create the initial HTML elements as usual. The first thing we need to add is the HTML5 doctype declaration:

```
<!DOCTYPE html>
```

This tells our browser that we are using the HTML specification within the page, and it should be placed right at the top of your HTML file.

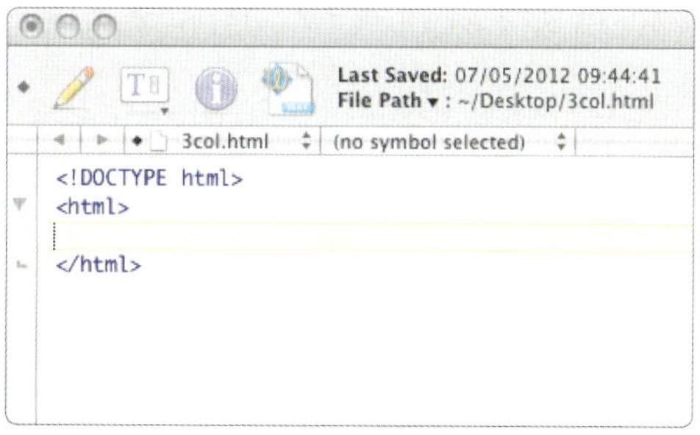

02 Open HTML tag

Next up we need to start off our HTML by entering the HTML tag – <html> – and then making sure we close this with </html>. This tag tells the browser that contained within this section is HTML code. All the page content that we will be creating will need to go within these tags.

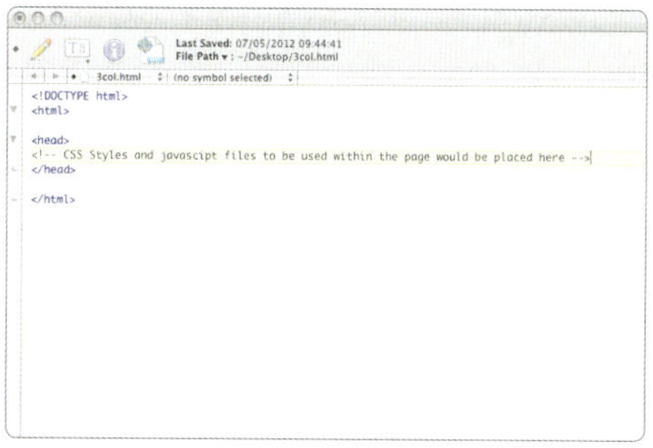

03 Insert the head

The head tag is an important one in HTML, and shouldn't be confused with the 'header' tag. Content within the head is not displayed to the user, but is used to include your CSS stylesheets, JavaScript and metadata. Within your <html> tags, place <head>, then </head> to close it off.

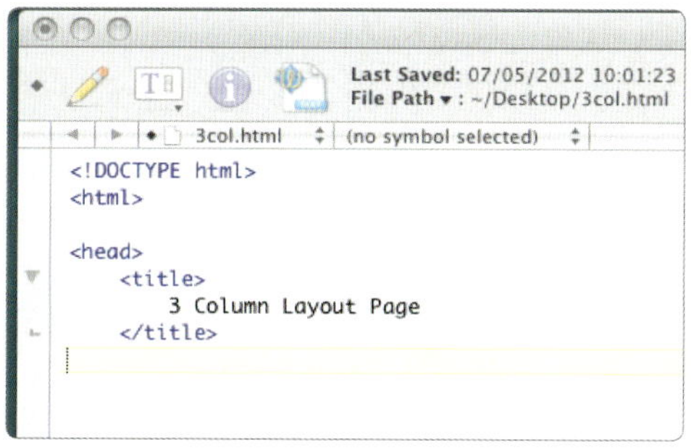

04 Add a title

The title tag is used to display text in the browser's title bar at the top (if it has one), and also used as a guide for search engines to identify what content is contained within the page. Add a <title> tag within your head. Next, add a page title to describe the content, and close the title tag with </title>.

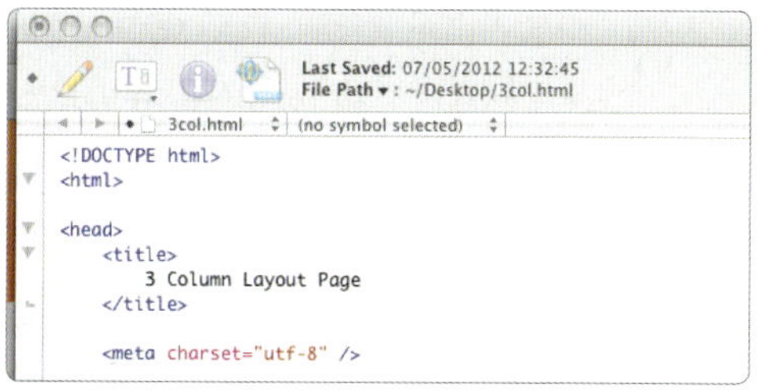

05 Define character set

There are many different ways of displaying characters in computing, and a few different standards depending on language; eg Greek or Arabic text looks very different from Chinese. Luckily for us, almost all the web uses the UTF-8 standard, which we define within our head with:

```
<meta charset="utf-8" />
```

UTF-8 does a good job of displaying most characters correctly.

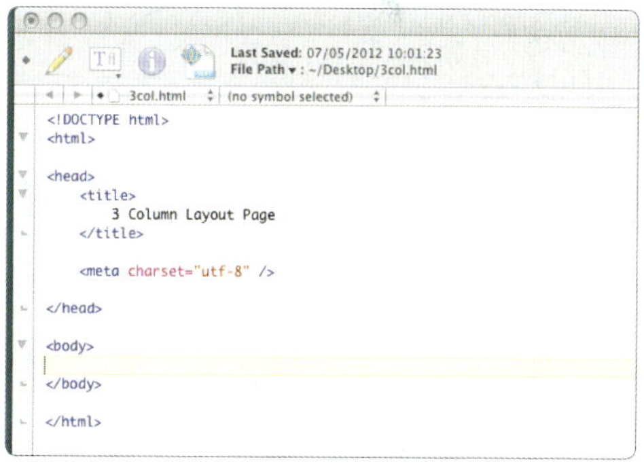

06 The body tag

All the content you wish to be displayed to the user is put within a 'body' tag. This goes after your 'head' tag has been closed, but within your <html> tag. Start it off with <body>, then close it off in the normal way: </body>. From now on we will place all code within the body tag.

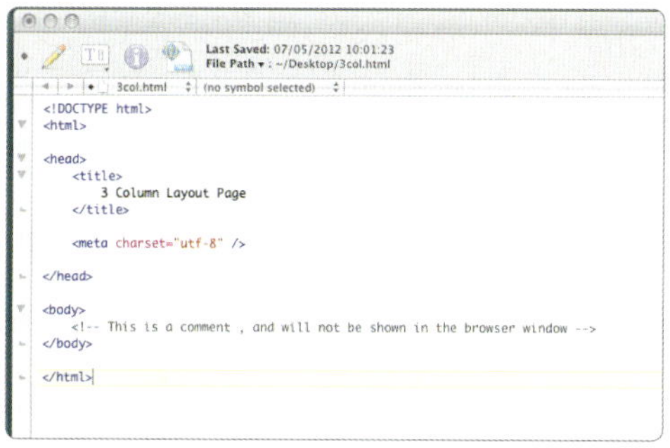

07 Adding comments

Sometimes you may wish to add a note to a location within your page, perhaps as a reminder or to make it easier to see where certain elements start or finish. Comments are started using '<!--', followed by the comment text, and then ended with '-->'. For example: <!-- Start header -->

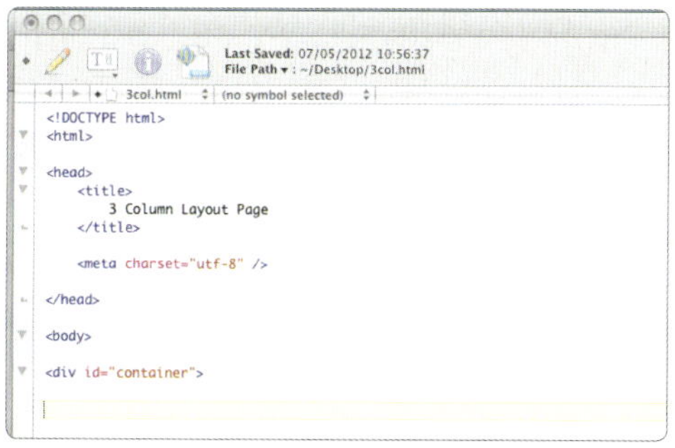

08 The container

It's quite common to wrap all the main content within the body in a 'container' div. This can make styling and centring easier when you start to write up your CSS. Add a container div within the body with <div> and </div>, then give it an ID so we can style it later: <div id="container">

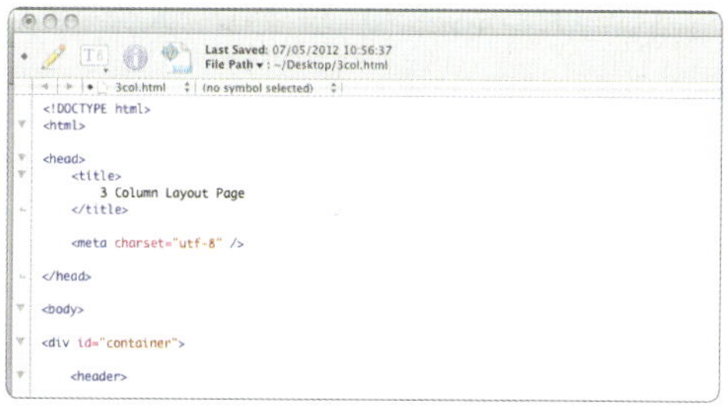

09 The header

The top element to our page is usually referred to as a 'header' and contains the site title, logo, navigation, and sometimes adverts. To create a header we use the header tag, which is new in HTML5. To open it enter <header> and then to close, </header>. A page can have multiple headers, although they cannot be contained within each other.

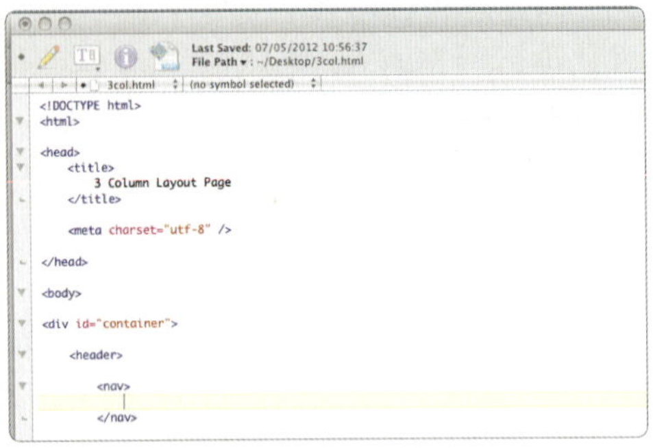

10 Nav tag

Nearly all pages contain a navigation or menu bar of some sort to allow visitors to get around the site. HTML5 now has a tag specifically for this. The 'nav' tag is where to place links to other items. Let's add one to our page – <nav> – and then close off again with </nav>.

11 Navigation items

To add links to the navigation we use the <a> or anchor tag. Eg <a href="products.html"> Products </a>. If you don't yet know your exact site layout, it's common to use a '#' in place of the link. A hash symbol can also be used to target a specific div within a page.

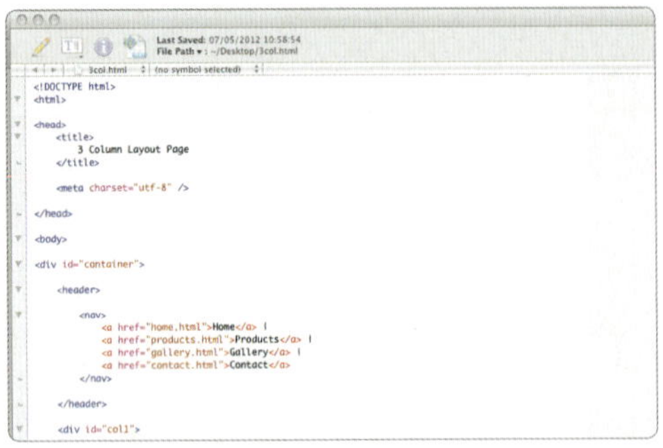

12 First column

Now we can add our first left column. This goes after the header tag, but still within our container div. Add this in with <div> and then don't forget to close: </div>. Again, you can give it an ID or class, such as <div id="col1"></div>. This column might contain a menu or adverts, for example.

13 Second column

The second column is usually the widest in the centre, and normally houses the main page content. Add it to the page the same way as before, but give it a different ID this time.

<div id="col2"> </div>

Don't be concerned if you can't see any content within your browser – as without styling, divs are essentially invisible and only the content contained is displayed.

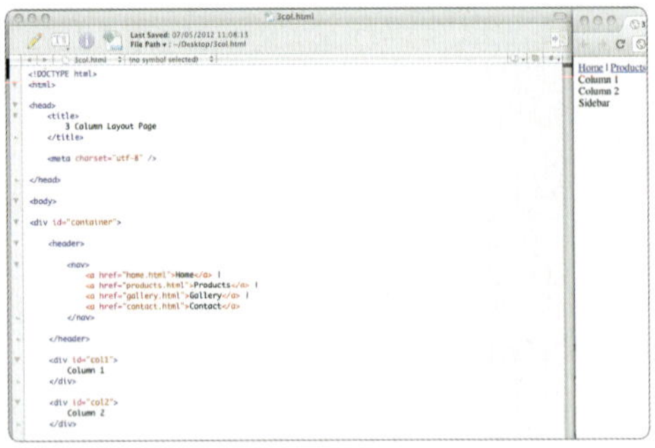

14 Third column

The third and final column is then added in exactly the same way, with a unique ID: <div id="sidebar"></div>. If you wanted to place the name within each div to see the results in the browser and help you visualise the page layout, then you can: <div id="sidebar">Sidebar</div>

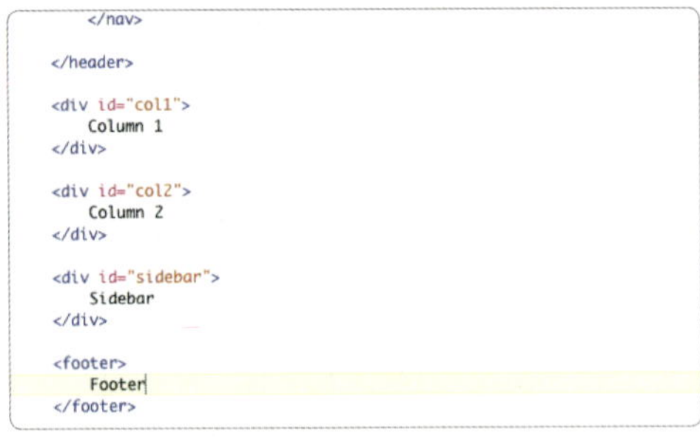

15 The footer element

The footer is used to mark the bottom of the page, and often contains a list of common links, along with copyright and/or contact information. To add a footer we simply use the HTML5 footer tag – <footer> – and as always, close it off using </footer>. Place this after your sidebar column in the code.

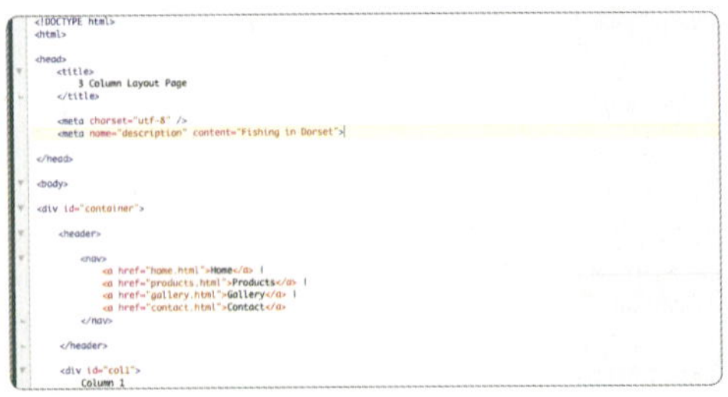

16 Metadata (optional)

If you know what content is going into the pages and wish to improve search engine optimisation, you can add meta information to the head. Meta information helps Google and other search engines to index and organise sites by content. The meta description tag is used to give a short account of the page content: <meta name="description" content="Fishing in Dorset">

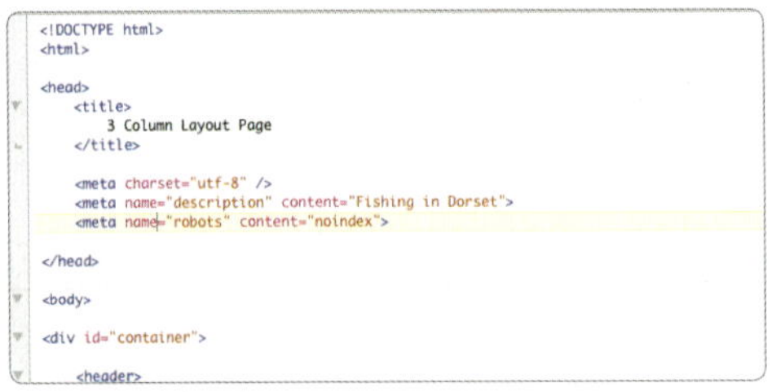

17 Stopping Google indexing (optional)

To stop Google and other search engines indexing your page, you can add the following code to your head: <meta name="robots" content="noindex">. This means the page will not be shown in Google's search results. This can be useful on client login pages, or out-of-date pages that you wish to archive.

18 The end result

Save the file now, making sure to have the .html extension at the end. Open the file within a browser to see the result. As there is no styling applied yet, it won't look particularly attractive by any means, but you've created a basic web page layout that's now ready for CSS and content to be added.

The three-column layout

The flexible three-column page structure is used by many sites

Metadata

<meta charset="utf-8" />

<meta name="description" content="Fishing in Dorset">

<meta name="robots" content="noindex">)

There are a few common meta elements which, while not displayed by the browser, help with search engine optimisation as well as how the browser renders your content

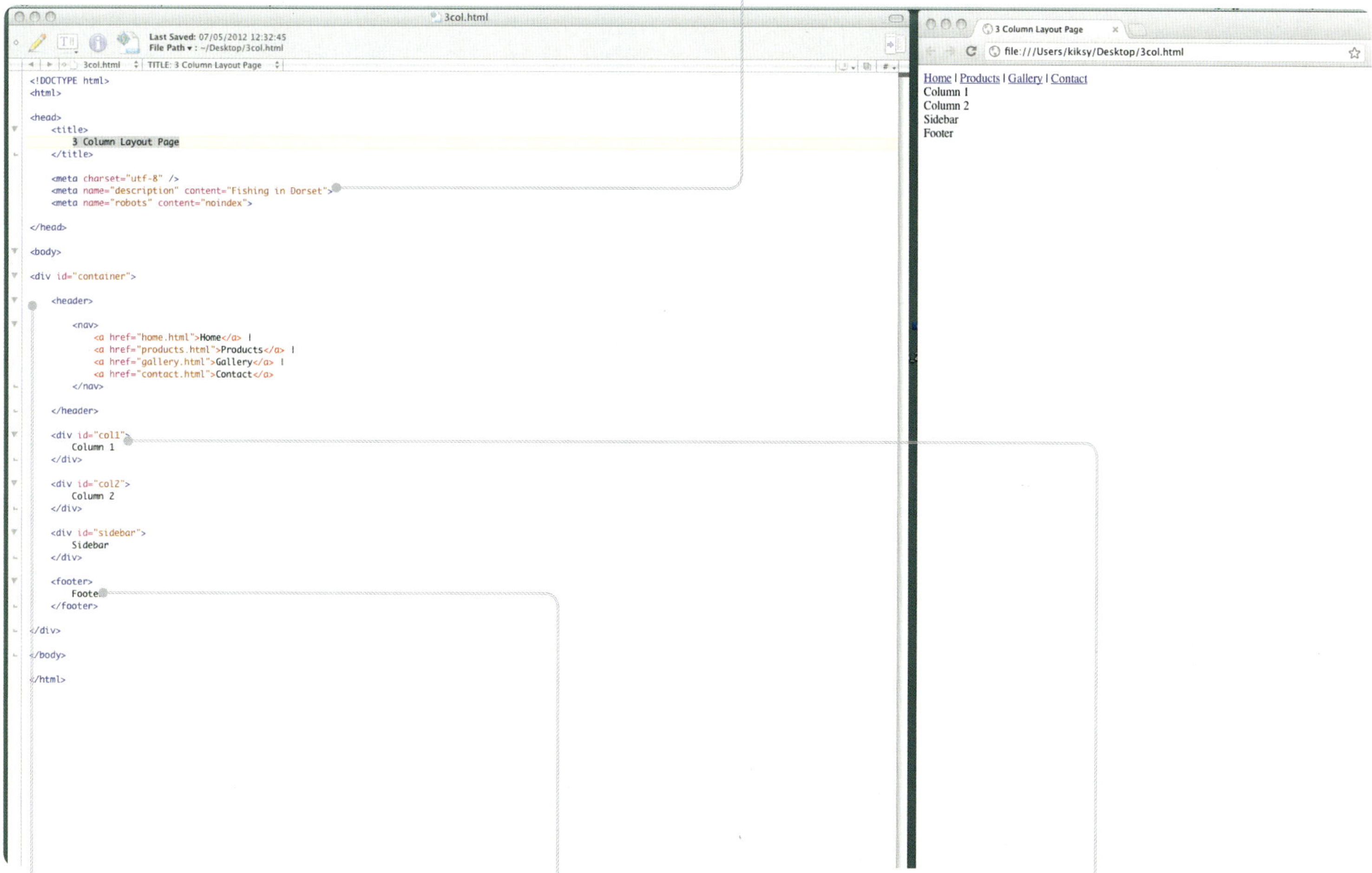

The header

In this instance the header code contains the navigation elements of the page, although it's also often used for site title and logos. Here we are using the HTML5 nav element

Footer

The footer element often remains consistent throughout a site and is usually not as tall as the header, although recently there have been some great designs featuring very prominent footer elements

Columns

The main columns are <div> elements that you can apply CSS to later, such as width, height, padding etc. It's usual to have the centre column the widest, but this isn't mandatory

Internet Explorer compatibility Ensure your HTML5 page works in IE

While most users of Chrome, Firefox and Safari run HTML5, there are still a large chunk of the internet population running older versions of Microsoft's Internet Explorer which don't support the new standard. With all the new HTML5 elements, it's required to add in a few workarounds to get everything to work satisfactorily. One of the most popular methods is to use the HTML5Shiv . This small piece of JavaScript allows us to include the new tags such as <header>, <footer> and <nav> without worry. Adding the script is simple, and as it's hosted on GoogleCode you don't even need to download any files. Simply add this to your page's head:

```
<!--[if lt IE 9]>
<script src="//html5shiv.googlecode.com/svn/trunk/html5.js"></script>
<![endif]-->
```

The <!--[if lt IE9]> part is a CSS conditional statement which says 'if the browser trying to read this page is IE and less than version 9 (which supports HTML5), then include this JavaScript file. Hopefully in the not too distant future when more people are running the latest version of Internet Explorer, hacks such as this can be avoided, but for now it's just something that we have to live with when designing pages.

Build a site

Visit www.responsinator.com to see how websites are styled on different devices

www.unitedpixelworkers.com (pictured here) is an exceptionally stylish website

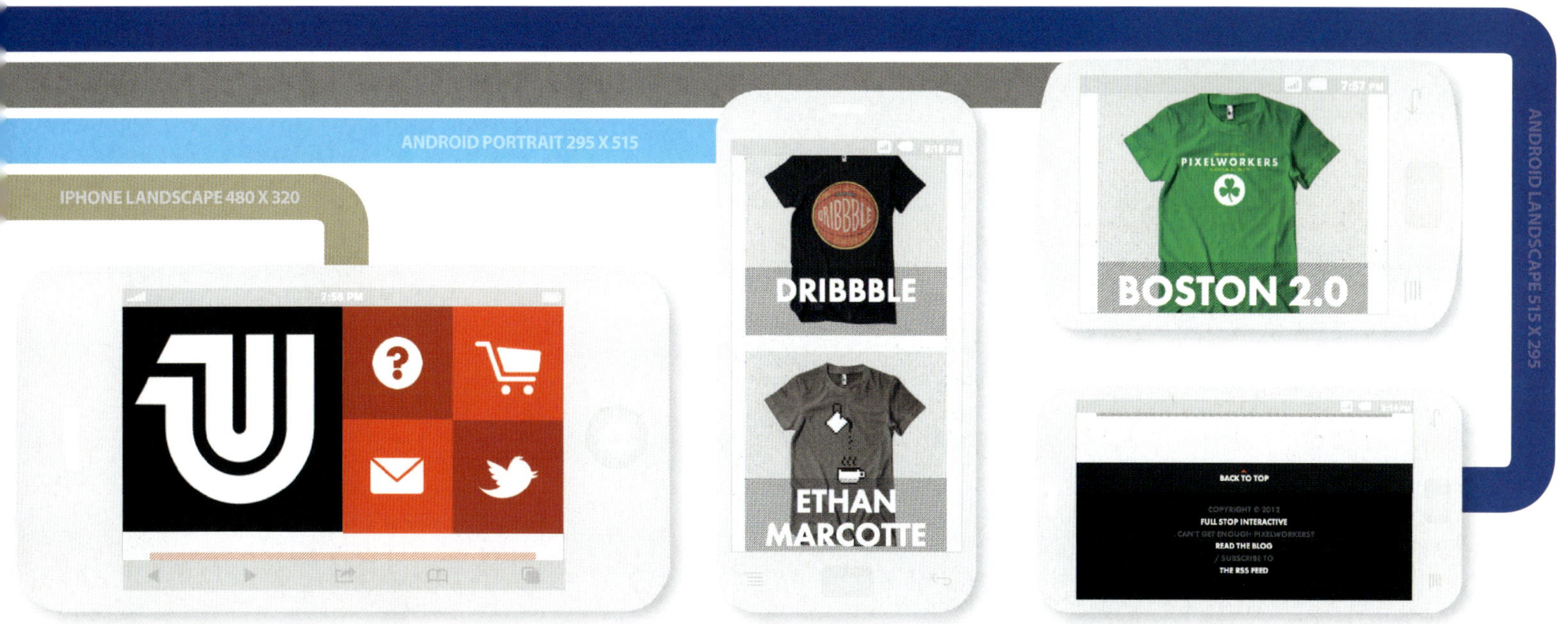

An introduction to CSS

If HTML provides the structure for a website, CSS provides the form. This is the language that will make your site stand out

Cascading Style Sheets, commonly abbreviated to CSS, is a language used for describing how HTML should be presented. CSS documents provide all the format, colour, positioning and other characteristics of a design that you will see on virtually any webpage.

Originally introduced alongside HTML4, the language was designed to separate the structure of a document from the presentation, improving the control of a design for web designers. CSS also helped to improve accessibility of web pages, reduce HTML code complexity and crucially the amount of repetition of markup that had to be created to describe how a page should look.

As well as these benefits, the separation of form and function allows different designs to be displayed to users according to their device, simply by providing a different stylesheet. This means that, for example, a mobile phone can load the same web page as a desktop browser, but present the content within the page in a different manner. Similarly, CSS can be used to present page content one way on screen and a second when printed, or to provide direction to screen reader software over areas for emphasis.

Additionally, CSS is user-configurable, so while the designer might specify that text should be shown in 18pt red Arial, the visitor to their site can load their own stylesheet to show the text in 12pt blue Times instead, should they wish to. As you can see, CSS offers a great deal of flexibility by design. To fully understand what it's capable of, we need to look a bit more at what CSS is, why and how it came about, and examine how the implementation of the language works across different web browsers.

The cascading bit

CSS is designed to use a priority scheme that determines how styles should be applied to HTML elements. The cascading bit of the language name refers to how this scheme works. Broadly, styles are applied in chronological order, but also according to specificity. If a style property is declared more than once for a particular element, the last chronological declaration will be used, unless the earlier declaration was more specific about the elements it should apply to than the latter. This sounds really confusing, but in practice it allows you to apply a set of broad styles that provide basic properties for the font that text should be rendered in, for example, and use more specific selectors to subsequently set the size, colour or font weight. To help make sense of it all, let's take a look at what CSS looks like in code.

CSS syntax

Just like HTML, CSS is designed to be human-readable in its raw form. English keywords are used with a simple syntax to describe a list of rules, style properties and style values. Each rule in a stylesheet is defined by means of a selector, which identifies the HTML elements the rule should apply to. Within the rule, a series of properties and values are defined so that the visual characteristics for an element are built up property by property. Let's take a quick look at an example:

```
h1 {
		font-family:		arial, helvetica,
sans-serif;
		font-weight:		bold;
		font-size:	18pt;
		color:			red;
		margin:	10px;
}
```

In the code above we've defined the rule using the h1 { } selector. This specifies that the style properties within should apply to all <h1> tags found on the page. Within the curly brackets we define a series of properties, such as font-family, font-size etc, and the values we'd like to set for each. As a result, every heading 1 on our page »

Recent versions of web browsers have vastly improved their implementation of CSS standards.

» would be rendered in Arial (or Helvetica if Arial wasn't available), bold 18pt red text. The entire <h1> would have a ten-pixel margin around it.

More complicated selectors

In the previous example we used a simple selector to establish which elements the rule should apply to. Selectors can be nested so that only specific elements have the rule applied. An example might look like the code that follows:

```
#content article h1 {
        color:          blue;
}
```

Here, the rule would only apply to HTML <h1> elements that are nested inside an <article> element, itself within any other element that has an ID attribute of "content". Our page would now show all <h1> tags as red, bold, 18pt Arial, with the exception of those headings inside an <article>, itself inside an element with an ID of #content where the colour would be blue instead.

This works because the CSS sheet cascades the styles and also has the priority scheme we discussed earlier. As our second rule is more specific in its selector, it takes priority over the more generic rule we created first. We could have also positioned our second rule chronologically after our first to ensure it would take priority, but sometimes the specificity rules that are a part of CSS would prioritise over chronology. By combining specific selectors with different rules, and using specificity and priority it's possible to style a document with a few SS rules.

Different ways to load a style

There are three different ways a style can be applied to an HTML element. The first is through an external file that is loaded into the HTML document in the <head> section. The second is to include a <style> declaration in the <head> section of the document, writing your rules and properties directly inside the <style> area, and the third is directly onto an element using the style attribute. The latter is referred to as an 'inline' style.

When calculating the style properties of an element, CSS is loaded first from any external files and applied, then from the <head> section of the page, and finally from any inline styles. Where the same property is set by more than one of these three methods, they apply in the order as described above.

Positioning elements

One of the most common areas of CSS that new designers struggle to grasp is how elements can be positioned on the page. CSS offers a number of different positioning systems, and these can be mixed and matched within a single page

Browser support

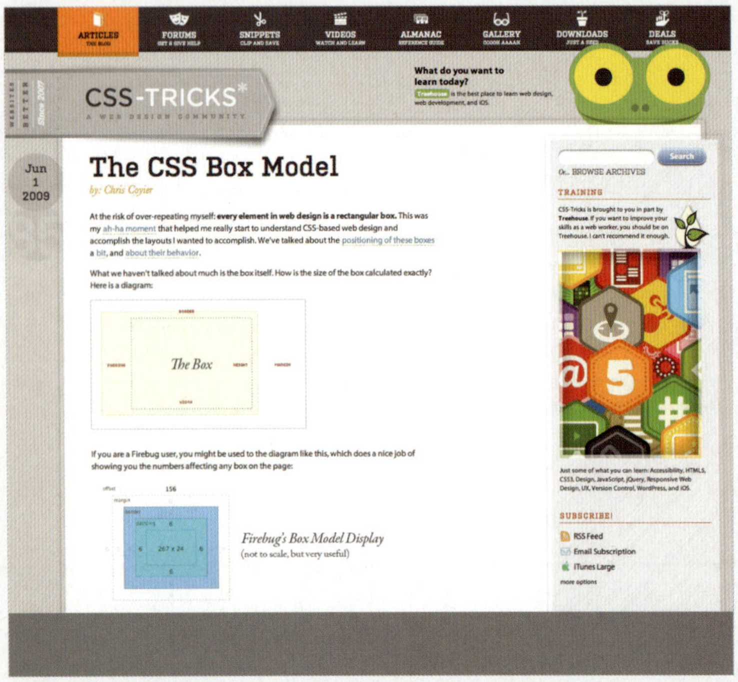

One of the biggest headaches over the past decade, at least for web designers, has been the differences in the way browsers render CSS. The original idea was that CSS would be rendered in a standard way, regardless of what software a user had. Browsers that didn't support CSS would simply ignore it, but those that understood stylesheets would display content in a predictable, consistent manner. The issues started almost as soon as CSS was introduced, however, with different browser vendors implementing their own understanding of the standards, leading to wildly different representations of a design according to which browser a visitor to a website used.

The most well-known example of this was the box-model problem where two browser vendors disagreed over whether padding should be applied to an element in addition to the specified width, or as part of the specified width. One method meant that an element set to be 200 pixels wide with 50 pixels of padding either side would render as 300px in total – 200 pixels of space for content, and 50 pixels padding each side, while the other left the element width at 200 pixels overall, leaving just 100 pixels for content. This particular disagreement lead to Internet Explorer having special stylesheets developed to work around the 'wrong' implementation for more than ten years!

Microsoft has now officially retired IE6, although IE7 and 8 both continue to support the old system, but as CSS3 properties have been introduced the W3C designers are forced to specify the same properties multiple times, targeting vendor-specific features.

design. The first, and default, positioning scheme is 'relative' positioning. This operates on the basis that an HTML document is chronological. Much like a word processor, content that appears beneath other content has its position on the page dictated by the content above which pushes it down into position.

In addition to relative positioning, CSS also offers absolute positioning where an element is positioned according to a set of co-ordinates relative to the container element. This allows elements to be very precisely positioned on the page, relative to the whole page.

Similar to absolute positioning is fixed positioning. This works, as with absolute, using a series of co-ordinates but rather than being positioned relative to the page, 'position: fixed' elements are always relative to the viewport (the visible portion of the browser screen). As you scroll, position fixed elements remain in the same place in the browser window.

The final, and often the most confusing, system is the floating element. This system allows elements to push to one side or the other of the containing element, with content and other elements automatically flowing around it. This takes some understanding and experimentation, but is fundamental to achieving some common layouts so it's worth spending a little extra time getting to know how positioning, and especially float, works.

History and potential hiccups

By now you're starting to see the value and potential of CSS, but it's not all as perfect as it might at first seem. There are a number of problems that web designers have to overcome when using CSS to style their web pages, and to fully understand those issues it's worth taking a quick trip down memory lane.

When HTML3.2 was released, a series of new tags were added that allowed web designers to specify different visual characteristics for their content. These included the likes of <font>, <b> (for bold text), <color>, <center> and many more. These tags provided the control over presentation that web designers were craving, but a problem quickly emerged: by mixing style with content the pages designers worked on quickly became unmanageable, especially when a web site had lots of pages. Something as simple as changing the font a website used might have taken days to change, working through each HTML page in the website and changing references from one font to another.

As a consequence, the W3C quickly realised that content should be separate from presentation, and developed CSS. CSS1 >>

> "CSS offers absolute positioning of an element according to set co-ordinates"

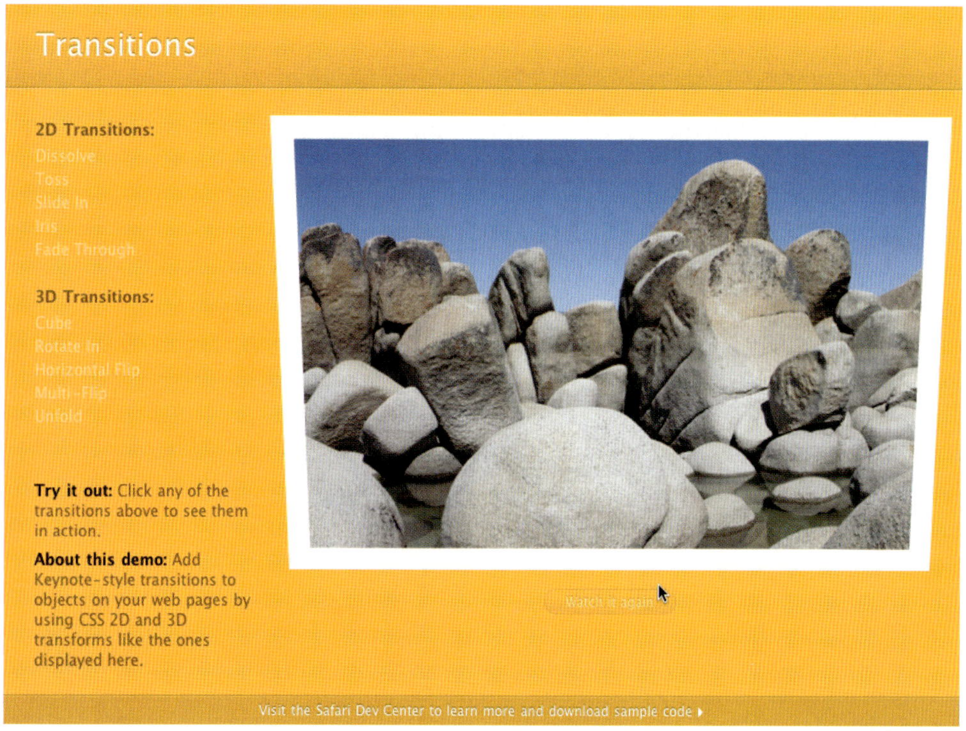

CSS3 brings animations to the mix by allowing designers to set up automatic changes in property values, altering over time.

The advantages of CSS

CSS offers many benefits over the previous idea of incorporating visual characteristics into HTML. The most obvious one is that by separating content from presentation, the aesthetic of a web page or entire website can be tailored to individual user profiles or devices with ease. A single HTML page can be rendered in many different ways, as amply demonstrated by the CSS Zen Garden experiment (**http://csszengarden.com**), and this characteristic can be used to ensure that mobile devices see a layout appropriate to their form while a desktop computer sees a different rendering more aligned to the larger screen estate. CSS supports many different usage scenarios including print and audio.

As well as the ability to tailor the presentation according to device, user characteristic or location, CSS also helps to ensure consistency across an entire website. Where multiple pages reference the same CSS sheet, a change in the CSS is instantly reflected across all those pages, saving the designer time and reducing the risk of inconsistencies. Along the same vein, CSS allows multiple elements to be selected and styled with a single selector. This reduces the amount of code required to achieve a design.

CSS makes the web more accessible; a user can choose to load their own stylesheet onto any document. Useful for visually-impaired users (who might need to see content in a larger font size) this characteristic also allows designers to separate styles into multiple stylesheets with each applying an additional layer of styling for easy organisation and adaptation of a design.

CSS3 opens the web up to more users by allowing individual stylesheets on pages.

>> debuted alongside HTML4 in 1996, but it wasn't until some years later that web browser vendors had managed to fully implement the language. In the meantime, a newer version of CSS had been created in 1998, and Netscape and Internet Explorer version 6 had both partially implemented CSS2.

As well as the slow implementation, from the start there were issues with the way the CSS specification had been written, leaving room for individual interpretation over what each part of the specification meant. This resulted in Internet Explorer rendering styles in one way, while the other popular browser of the day, Netscape, rendered differently. As well as differences in

"It's only in the last couple of years that the technology has been implemented properly"

opinion, both these popular browsers had their own bugs and quirks that resulted in strange behaviours when interpreting and rendering CSS. To further compound the issue, as the web was taking off and becoming mainstream, once the damage had been done there was no easy way to backtrack. The net consequence of these unfortunate events was that web designers had to start using workarounds to code different style rules for different browsers, taking into account the bugs, quirks and differences in rendering.

The arrival of HTML5

As the web has matured, so have the technologies used to create it and CSS is no different. HTML is now just about at version 5, and CSS3 first came into existence at the beginning of the century. It's only in the last couple of years

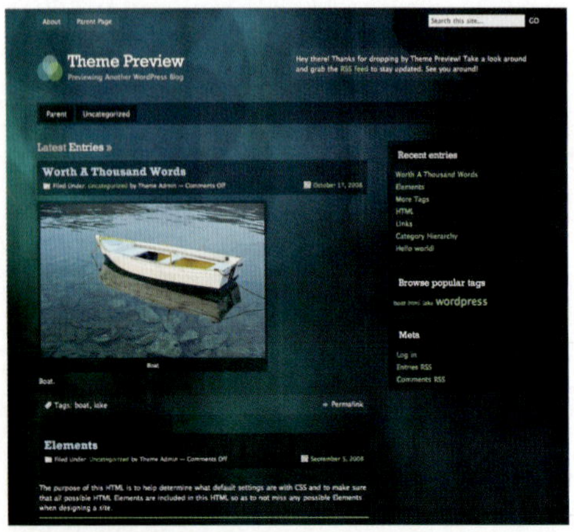

Although the technology has been around for years, it's only now we're implementing it effectively.

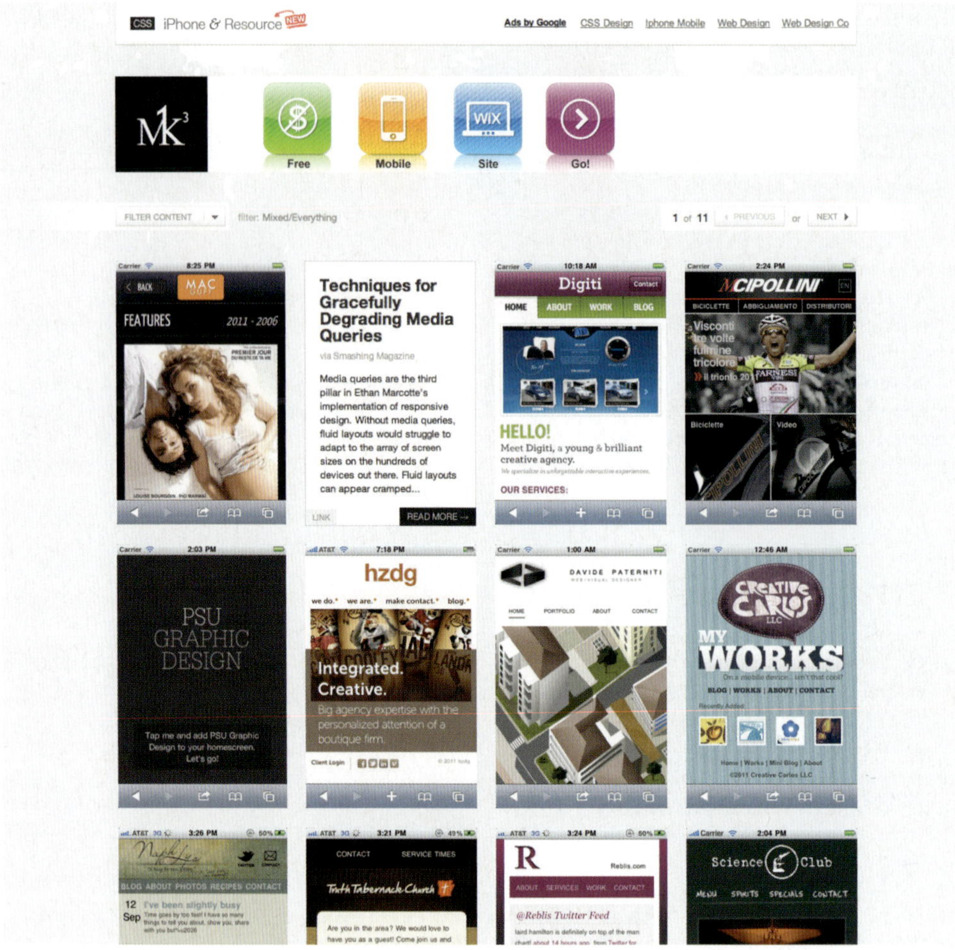

CSS allows websites to be tailored according the device upon which the website is accessed.

that either technology has started to be properly implemented by browser vendors however, and the combination of HTML version 5, CSS version 3 and JavaScript is often referred to collectively as HTML5 (erroneously it must be said!).

As mobile devices have become increasingly popular, driving the desire for access to the web on the move, and across different screen sizes, so the browser vendors have been coaxed into accelerating their implementations. This has provided quite a relief to web designers who only a year ago were still implementing workarounds for Internet Explorer version 6 – a decade-old piece of software!

Differences of opinion

Despite the recent strides towards adoption of CSS3, and the retirement of Internet Explorer 6 by Microsoft, there continues to be quite a lot of differences between the way different browsers render CSS. The most common issue today is where browsers implement CSS properties that haven't yet been fully ratified by the W3C. To ensure compliance, vendors prefix these properties with a name that represents the browser's maker. So, for example, to create a CSS drop shadow we currently have to have a rule that specifies properties for box-shadow, -webkit-box-shadow, -moz-drop-shadow, ms-drop-shadow and o-drop-shadow. The first property is the actual CSS3 specification property, while the others are the early implementations by Safari and Chrome, Firefox, Internet Explorer, and Opera respectively.

Vendor prefixes are the subject of much debate currently as they've become more prevalent in recent years as vendors rush to outdo each other in their CSS implementations. For web designers the new opportunities CSS3 presents are slightly offset by the continuing need to provide browser-specific properties for most of the modern properties.

What does the future hold?

As you've read, CSS3 is still being implemented and defined by both the W3C and browser vendors. And as for the future? Don't expect to see it any time soon, but CSS4 has been in development since 2009. It's still in early draft of course, but promises all manner of exciting new styling options and properties. If we're all still designing websites in another ten years, no doubt we'll be discussing matching selectors and reference combinators!

Glossary of common properties

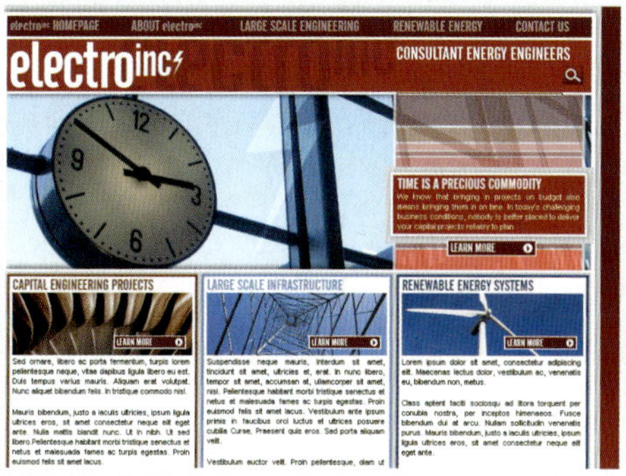

background The background property allows designers to assign a colour and background image to an element. As well as the image itself, the position of the image in the element and how the image repeats are configurable.

font-family The font-family property is the method through which all the different fonts used on a web page are designated. In the past web designers were forced to stick to a small set of 'web safe' fonts, but in recent years great advances have been made in providing web-enabled fonts on demand through a stylesheet.

color The color property sets the foreground colour of any element which has a foreground. Most commonly this is text, although certain other elements also support color. If color doesn't work, most probably you actually should be using background-color or just background for short.

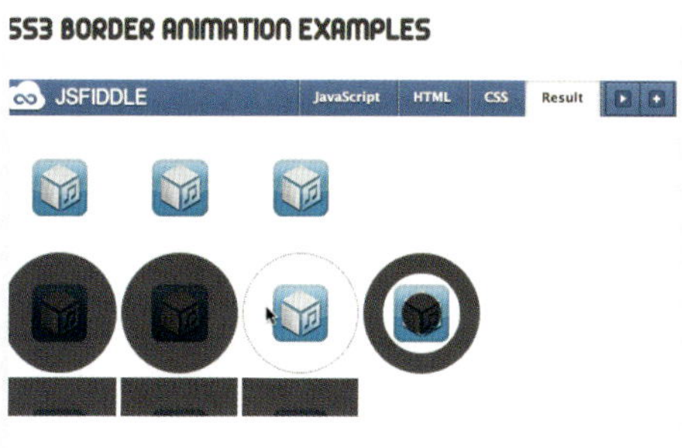

border The border property allows the designer to assign a border of varying types to any element. The options available include the weight of the border (how thick it is), colour and line style (eg solid line, dotted, dashed, etc).

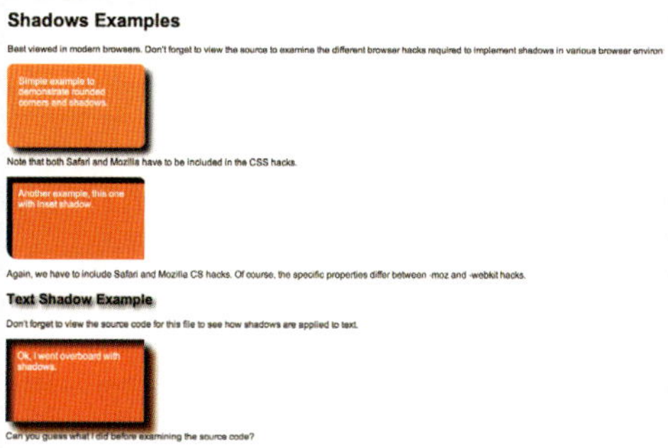

box-shadow New with CSS3 is the ability to define drop shadows on elements using the box-shadow property. An offset can be assigned independently on the X and Y axis, along with a colour and amount of blur to apply.

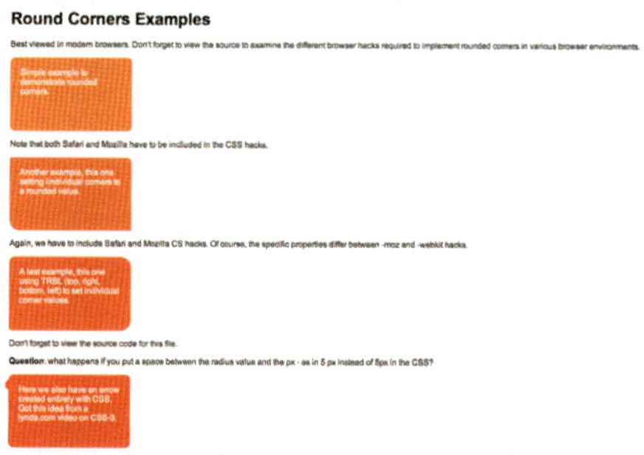

corner-radius Also new with CSS3 is the corner-radius property, which sets the roundness of a corner on any block level element. Radii can be defined independently for each corner, along with the way the curve should be applied.

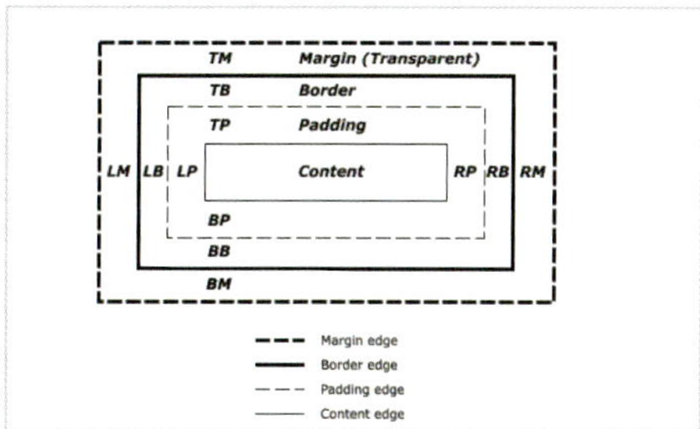

margin The margin property defines the amount of space the selected element should be away from other elements in the document. It works by pushing the other elements away from it, providing 'white space' around the element, and can be defined against each of the top, bottom, left and right sides.

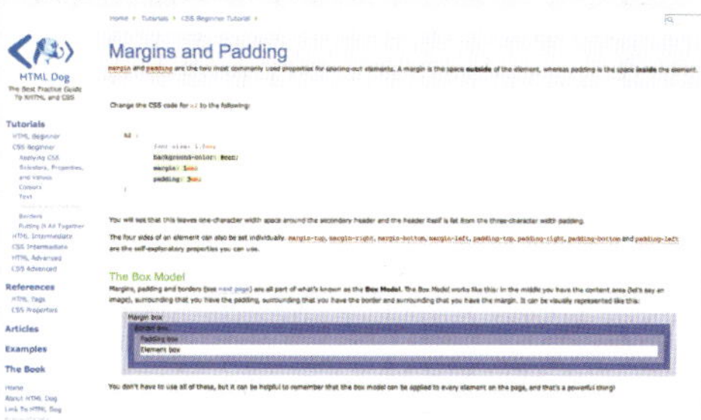

padding Similar to margin, padding also provides white space to an element, but instead of pushing other elements away, the white space exists within the selected element. If an element has a border, increasing the amount of padding will push that border away from the content within the element.

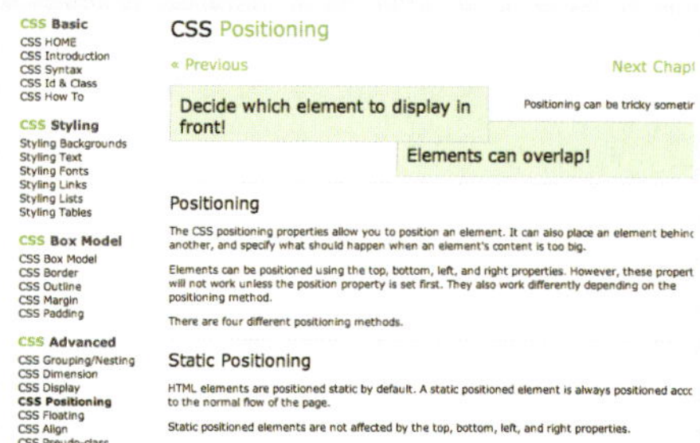

position The position property is used to define which positioning system should be used on an element in the page. Confusingly, however, should you want to use the float system you need to use the float property to define which direction the element should float to.

Centre your page

Using CSS to wrap your page's content in div tags gives you great control over the way it's displayed

When you're designing a webpage, you have to remember that a browser window can be almost any shape and size. Desktop computers have a wide range of screen sizes, and mobile phone and tablets are used to browse the web too. Your nicely designed page could be ruined if you simply allow it to flow into the browser window regardless of the latter's size or shape. By creating a wrapper you can specify the width of the webpage content and its position in the browser window. It is an essential part of the design process.

'Wrapper' is a commonly used name for a piece of CSS code that is used with a div tag to size and position the content of a webpage. A div tag is placed at the start of the page content just after the opening body tag and again just before the closing body tag, thereby enclosing or wrapping the content.

In CSS we can define how everything between the div tags – the page's content – is displayed. It can be centred on the page, positioned a certain number of pixels from the left, a border can be added, its width can be fixed or variable and so on. It is an essential component of any webpage and it's quite straightforward.

> "You can specify the width of the webpage content and its position"

A simple div wrapper

See how the CSS code relates to the content on the webpage

Set the colour
You can choose whatever colour you want for the background. If you choose a dark colour, though, you'll need to change the text to white – and that's for another tutorial!

Set the margins
Without margins the page content is displayed on the left. You can manually set them by entering the number of pixels, but a good option is to set them to auto to centre the page

Set the width
How wide do you want the page content to be? You can either set a width in pixels, as shown here, or use a percentage. 100% would be the full browser width

Borders or borderless?
This page has borders, but they are optional and leaving out these parameters will remove them. It's your choice. Padding, just above, is used for extra spacing, but it isn't needed

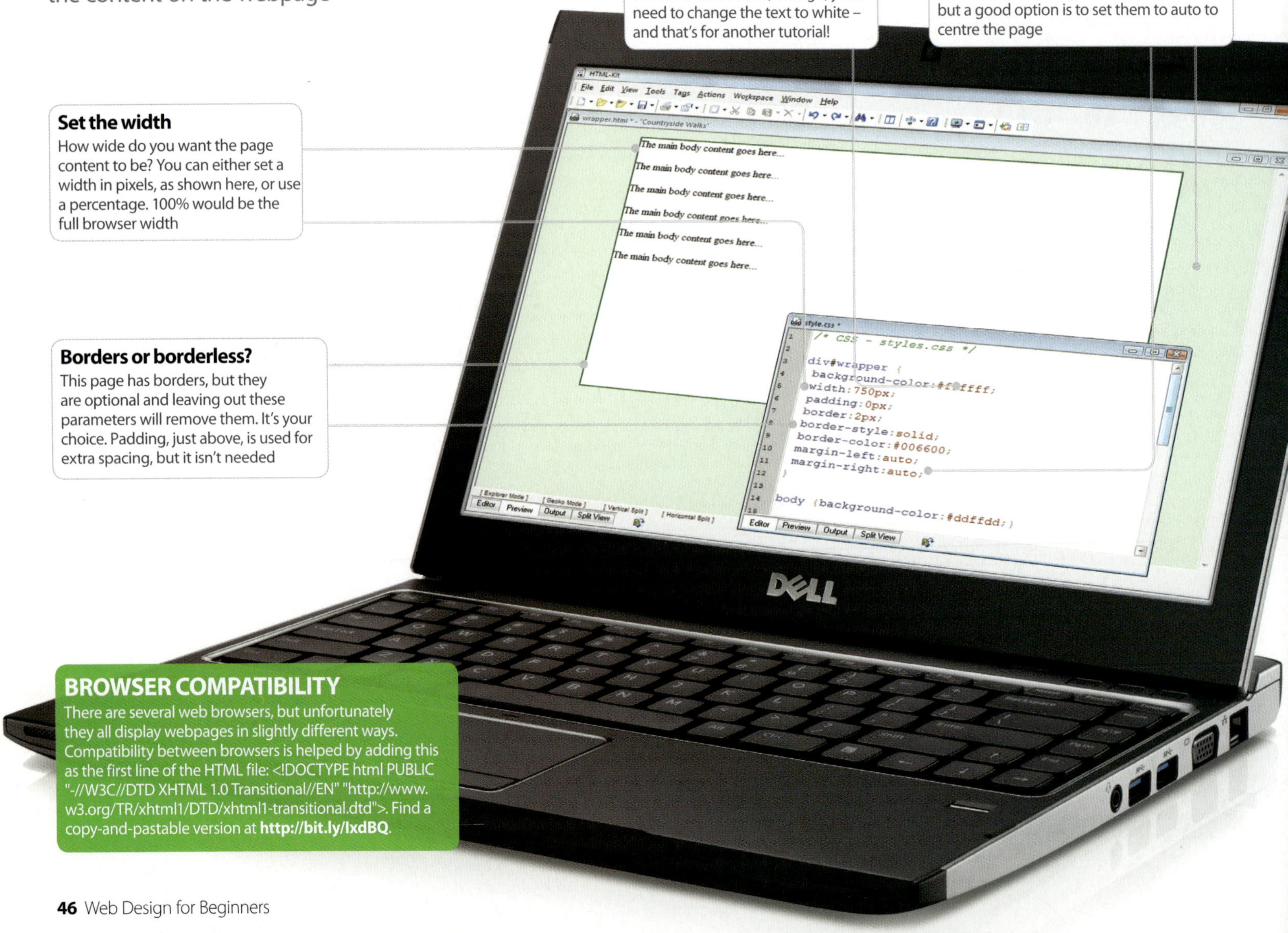

BROWSER COMPATIBILITY

There are several web browsers, but unfortunately they all display webpages in slightly different ways. Compatibility between browsers is helped by adding this as the first line of the HTML file: <!DOCTYPE html PUBLIC "-//W3C//DTD XHTML 1.0 Transitional//EN" "http://www.w3.org/TR/xhtml1/DTD/xhtml1-transitional.dtd">. Find a copy-and-pastable version at **http://bit.ly/lxdBQ**.

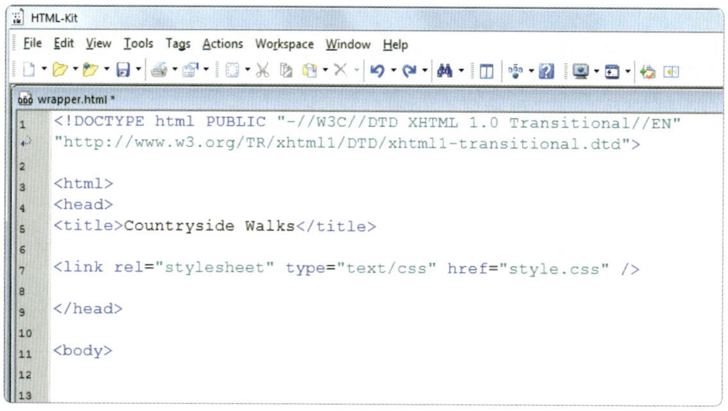

01 The CSS link

CSS definitions can be stored in a webpage or a separate file. If it is in a separate file then any webpage can access it and it saves having to add it to each new page. Add a link in the HTML header to a file called style.css.

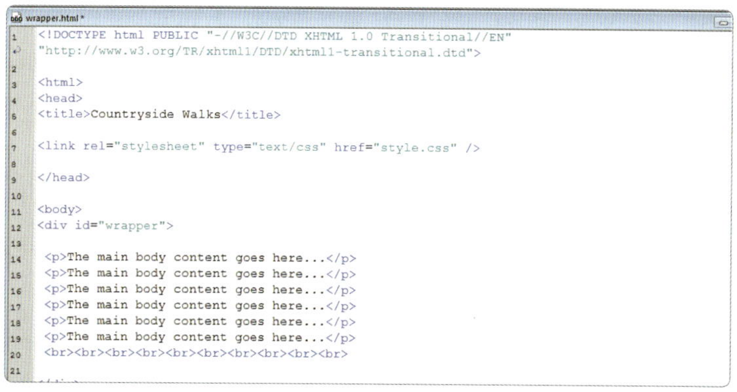

02 Add div tags

We want to specify the size and position of the webpage content, so we must place div tags at the start and end of the page, thereby enclosing all the content. The CSS definition will be called 'wrapper' and we refer to it with id="wrapper".

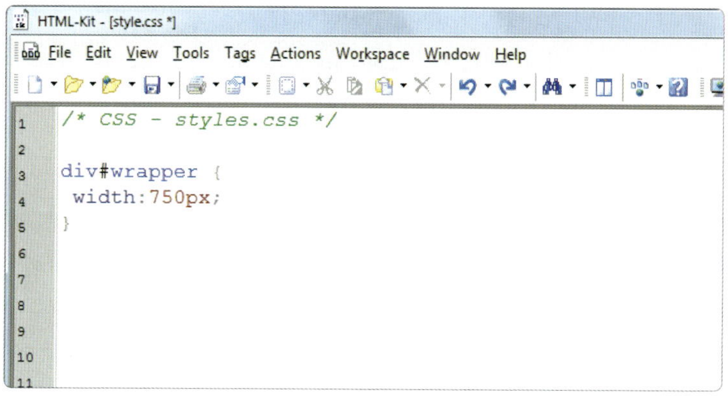

03 Create the CSS

We don't yet have any CSS, so create a new file called style.css and add a div ID called #wrapper. Set the width to 750 pixels. This value determines the width of the webpage content because everything is contained within the two div tags.

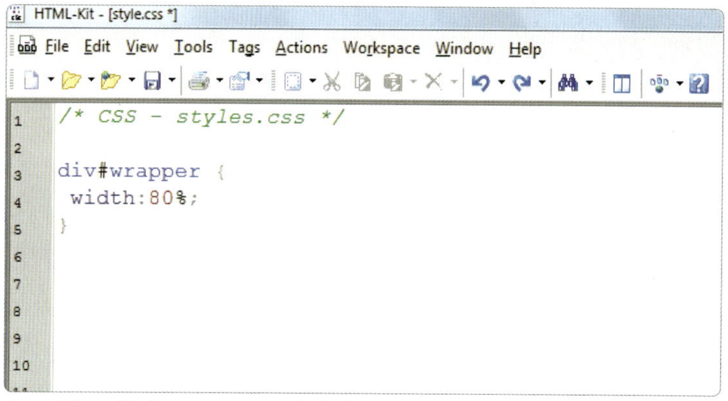

04 Flexible page width

Set the page width using absolute dimensions and it may not fit on small screens like mobile phones or tablets, or it may look tiny on computers with large monitors. An alternative is to set it to a percentage of the browser width instead.

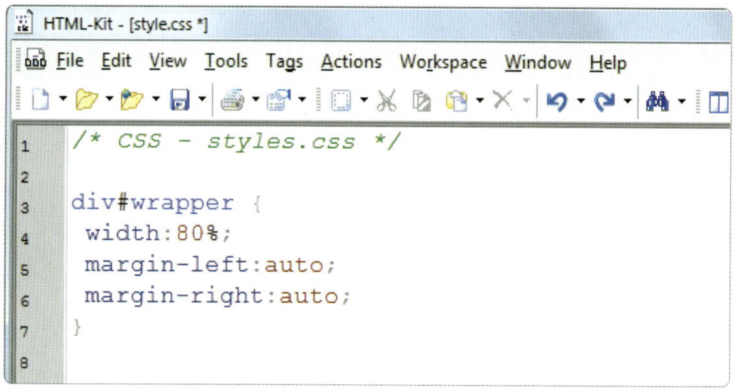

05 Set the margins

We have specified the width for the page content, but not its position. With margin-left you can specify the number of pixels from the left the content is to be displayed. An alternative is to set both margins to auto to centre it in the browser.

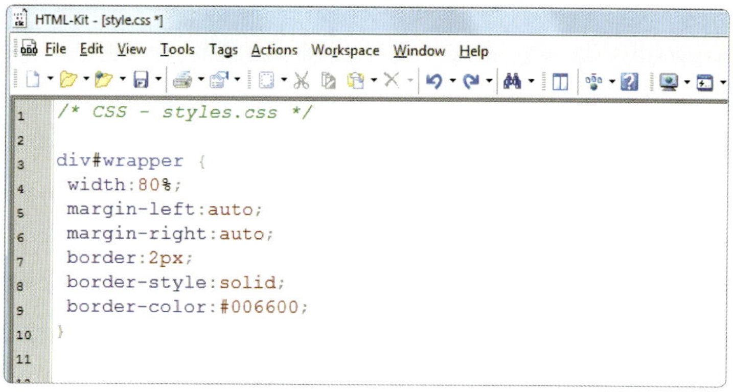

06 Add the borders

Your page design may look good if there is a border, and this specifies one that is two pixels wide. The border colour is set to dark green (006600) and the border style is set to solid. Alternatives include dotted, dashed, double and ridge.

Define body text and heading styles

Create CSS rules for displaying the text on the page

Every webpage contains text and it is frequently the main content. Therefore you should ensure that it looks good by choosing the fonts and styles to fit your design and the image you want to portray. There might only be a small amount of text if the main content focuses on images, but even so, there will be titles, links and captions. There's no getting away from text on webpages.

You can add CSS code to a webpage to define how the text is displayed, but placing it in a separate .css file and linking to it in the page's head section means that the same text styles are applied everywhere in your site. HTML font tags have been replaced by CSS font-family definitions, old-fashioned <i> and <b> tags are no longer needed, and font-style and font-weight enable you to set the styles to normal, italic, bold and so on. It might seem like extra work for one webpage, but when you are creating a site with 100 pages it is a considerable time-saver.

Writing the CSS rules for the text is simple and you can create a class that defines a text style and then use it over and over again in the page. We only look at headings and body text here, but expanding the CSS yourself should not present any problems.

"You can create a class that defines a text style and then use it over and over again"

Style the text

As you make style changes, you can see the effects on the page

Style other headings
Here you can see the style settings for the h3 tag and the heading in use on the page. The font-family, font-size, font-weight and margin-bottom have all been set

Heading style
This is an h1 heading, the largest that is available, so we have made it big and bold. The font has been set to Arial and the size is set to 30 pixels

Italic text
The p tag has already been set, so to display italic text on the page we just need to create an italictext class and set the font-style to italic. All other settings are inherited

Keep it simple
Although there are lots of CSS parameters that you can set, you don't always need to set them all. This is a minimal definition for the text that sets only what is needed

CHOOSING A FONT

When you are designing a webpage, you can choose any font on your computer, but be aware that if the visitors to your website do not have the font, another will be substituted and it may ruin your design. Safe fonts include Georgia, Arial, Helvetica, Times New Roman, Arial Black, Comic Sans MS, Tahoma, Trebuchet MS, Verdana, and Lucida Console.

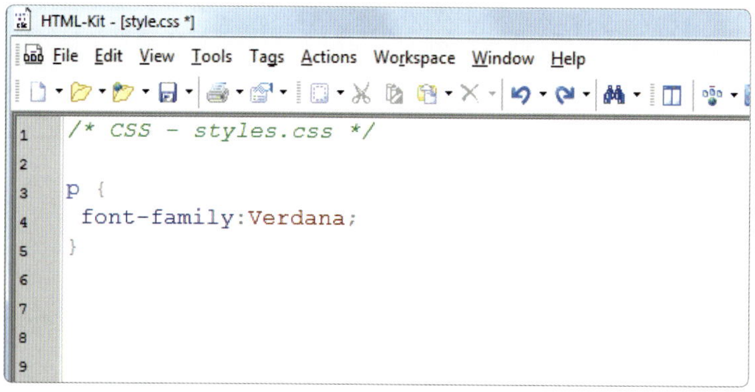

01 Pick a font

Using CSS you can set the font for all the text enclosed by <p></p> tags on all webpages with this in your style.css file. Link to it in the page header using <link rel="stylesheet" type="text/css" href="mystyle.css" />. This bit of code sets the font family to Verdana.

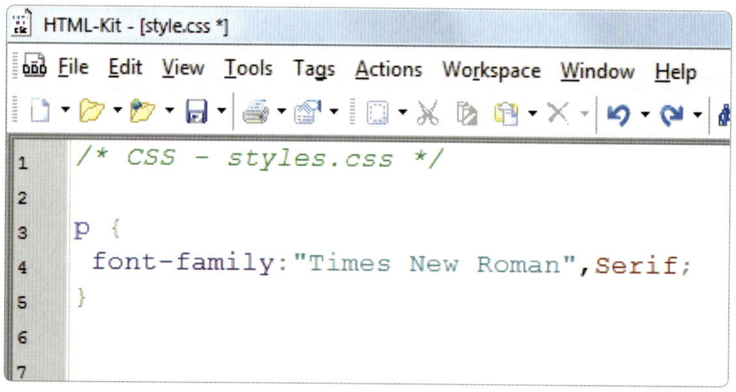

02 Select a family

When a font name contains spaces, you must put quotes around it or the CSS won't work. It is also a good idea to offer an alternative font in case the visitor to your site doesn't have the one you specified. Choose a family such as serif (fancy) or sans-serif (plain).

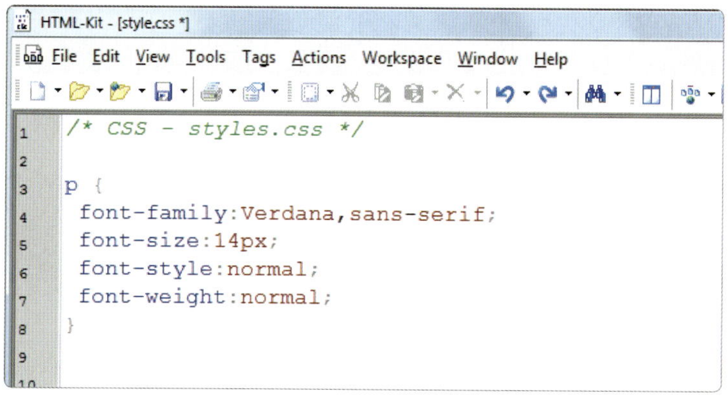

03 Size and style

The text may be fine at its default size, but if it isn't, you can set the size in pixels. The size you need depends on the font, so experiment with 10px to 16px. The font-style can be normal or italic and the font-weight can be normal, bold, bolder or lighter.

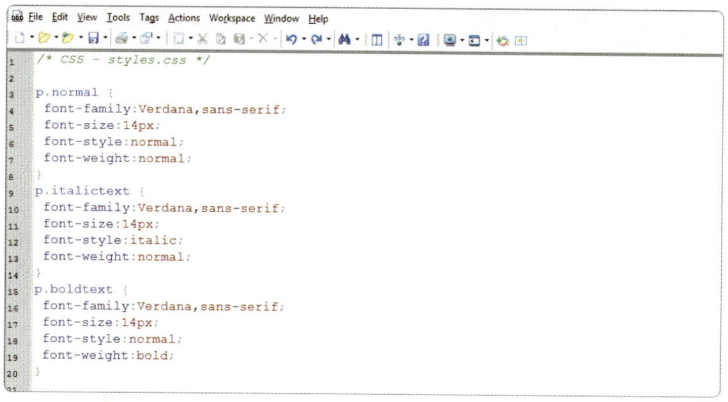

04 Define a class

There may be paragraphs that you want to make bold or italic, so here are three classes that define three styles of text. It varies the font-style and font-weight, but you could also create small text, large text, styles for panels, captions for images and so on.

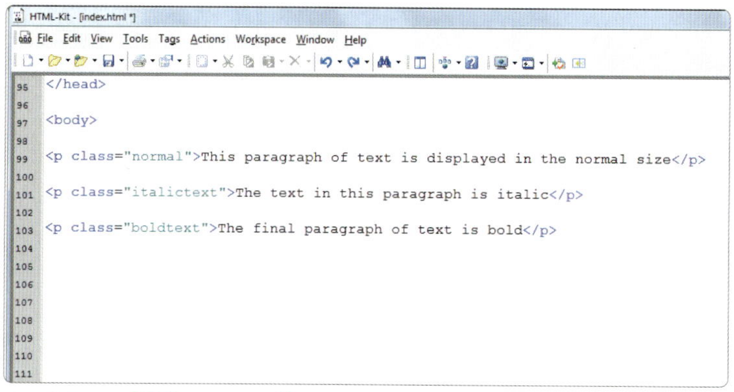

05 Use different classes

Step 4 created three CSS classes for the <p> tag. When you want text to appear in one of these styles, you add a class parameter to the <p> tag. The style is used for all the following text until you either change it with another tag or end it with </p>.

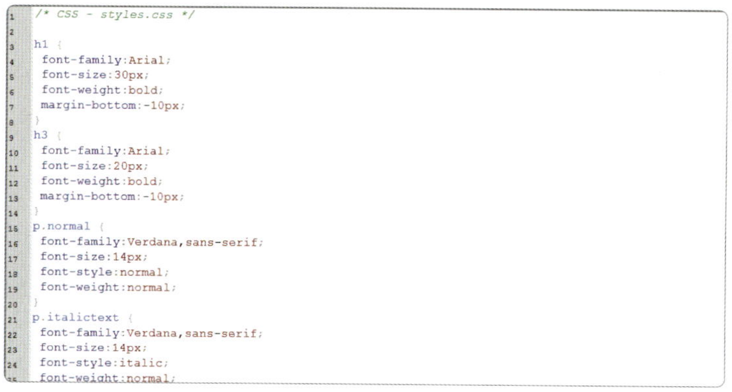

06 Define the headings

In addition to body text, there are also headings using h1 to h6 tags. You don't need to define all of them, just the ones you use. Do it exactly like the p tag and set the font, size, style and so on. We've also reduced the bottom margin below the header.

Style your lists to stand out

Standard lists tend to be a bit boring, so spice them up with some CSS styling

Although some web pages may require a lot of text, it is generally best to keep it brief and to the point. People scan a page for interesting content and then move on if they don't spot anything straight away. Lists are therefore very useful for drawing the visitor's attention to some content and for presenting it in a way that can be digested quickly.

The HTML <ol> and <ul> tags are used to create ordered (numbered) and unordered (bullet) lists, which we explored on p32-33. They are useful if unexciting, but with CSS list-style-type you can change the bullet to different shapes like a circle or square. It is even possible to replace it with an image specially created to fit in with your site's design and colour scheme using list-style-image. You can change the font used to display lists so they match the body text. If you have used HTML lists you will have noticed that they are indented, but with CSS you have fine control over the positioning using padding and margins. You can tighten up the layout or space it out – it's your choice.

> "With CSS you have fine control over the list's positioning using padding and margins"

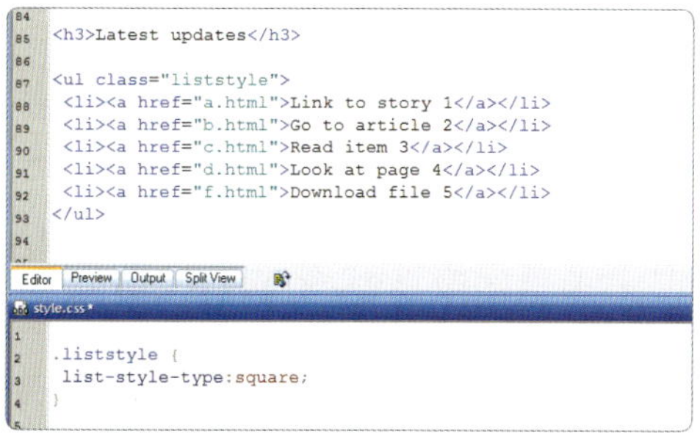

01 Create a class

You should have a separate file called style.css for CSS code, so load it and create a new class called liststyle like this. It contains just one item called list-style-type, but there are over 20 different possible values. These include circle, square, lower-roman, disc, decimal, upper-latin, and others. Try each one to see what they are like.

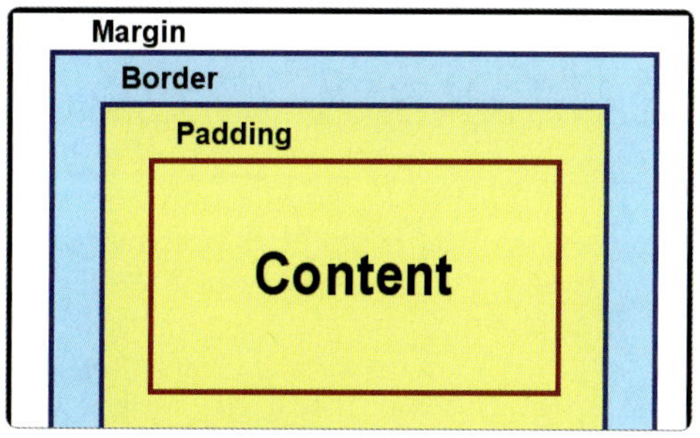

02 Boxed lists

CSS displays each element of web page content in a series of boxes. This means that a list defined by a ul or ol tag is separated from other elements on the page by a margin. Inside the margin there may be a border, but it is optional and not always used. Between the border and the content is padding or space.

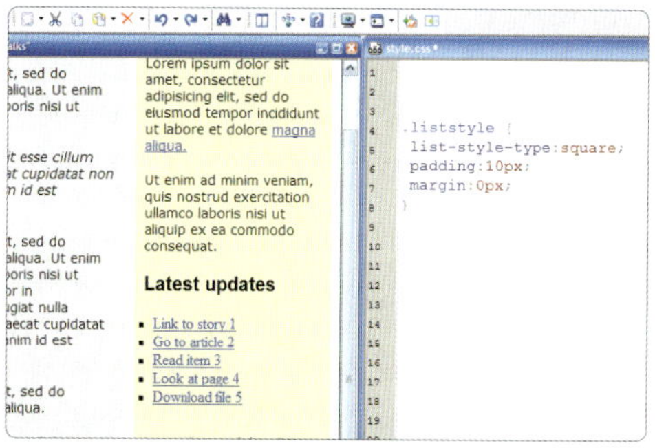

03 Position the list

With those boxes in mind, we can position the list within the space allocated to it on the page. Padding and margin have been added to the liststyle class and set to 10 and 0 pixels respectively. Experiment with different values to see how they affect the position of the list.

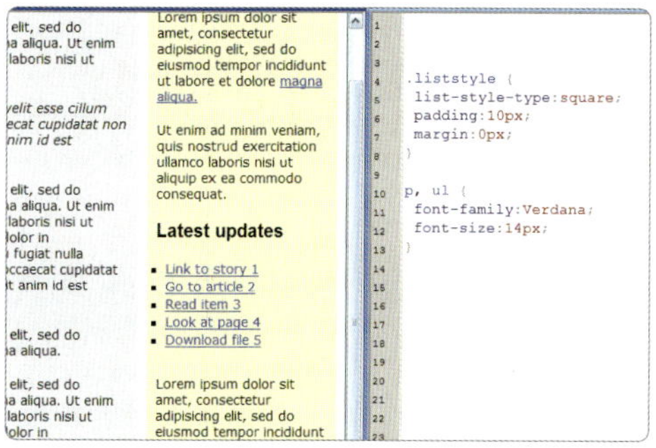

04 Style the text

Notice in the last step that the list text has a different font to the body text. That's because no style is set for lists. We defined the font and size for the body text in a previous tutorial and we can simply add ul to the p code so it uses the same font and size as the body text.

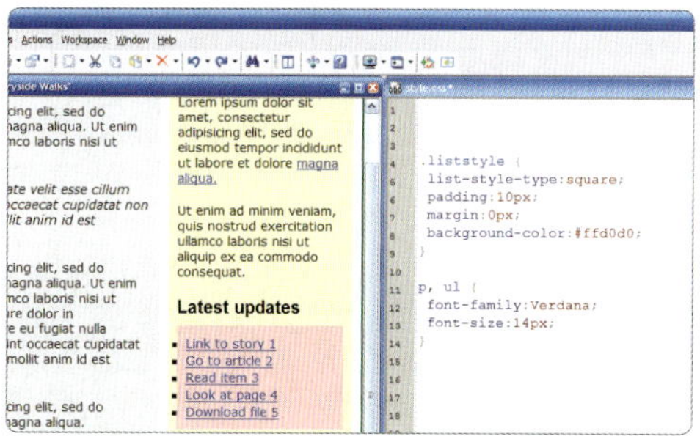

05 Choose a background

Many HTML elements can have a background colour and it is applied to both the content and padding areas, but not the border or margin. A background-color of #ffd0d0 has been set, but if you are not familiar with this notation, you can use common names like red, yellow, blue and so on. This is less flexible, though.

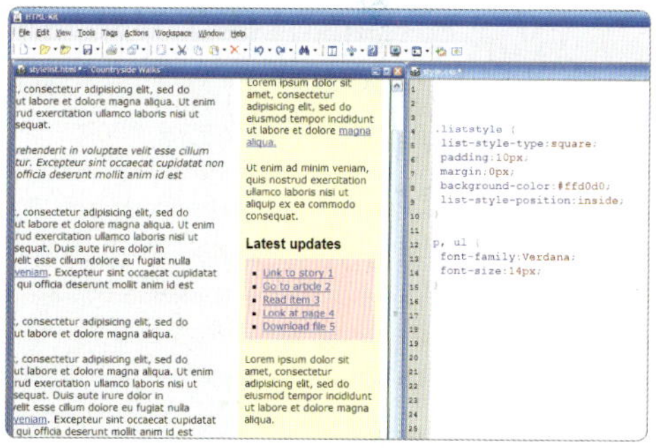

06 Inside vs outside

In the last step did you notice that the bullet blobs are outside of the background colour? This is their default position, but it's possible to change this and make them appear in the background area. In this step, list-style-position is set to inside and this makes the list look more attractive.

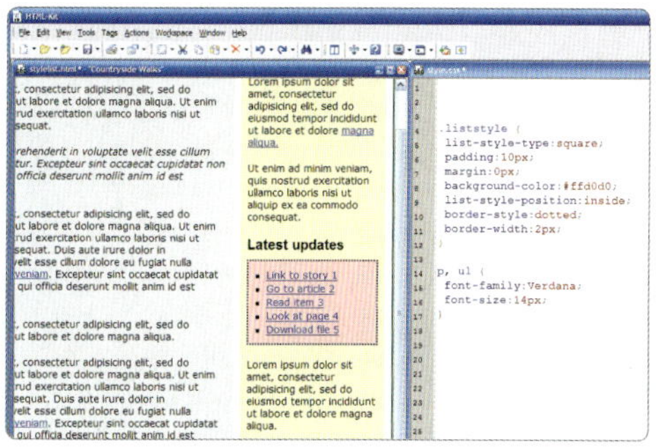

07 Add a border

As we've discussed, each HTML element can have a border. We haven't specified one so far, so one hasn't been drawn. However, we can easily define one by setting border-width to the number of pixels and border style to dotted, solid, dashed, double, groove, ridge, inset or outset.

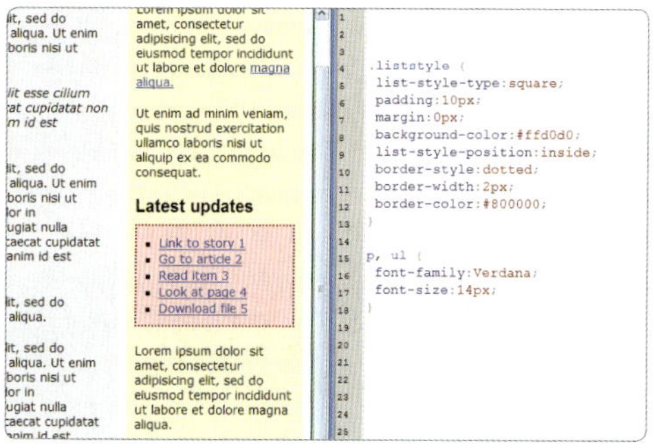

08 Colour the border

Most parts of the list can be coloured and this includes the border. The border-color has been set to #800000, which is a medium-dark red. It's a good idea to specify the colour even if it's black, because default settings for one web browser might be different to the defaults in another.

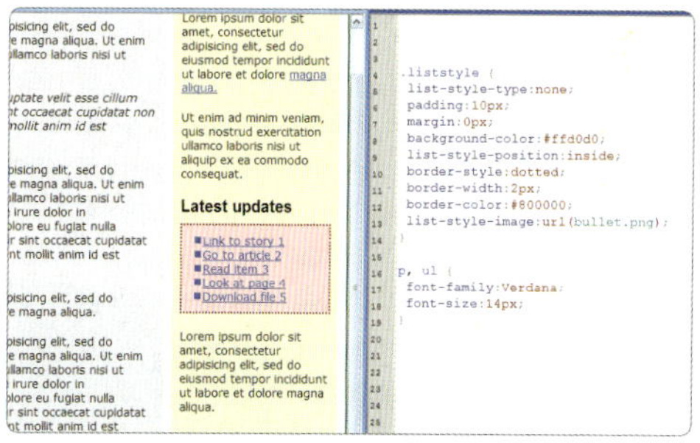

09 DIY bullets

Blue squares for bullets? Yes, we removed the standard bullets by setting list-style-type to none at the start of the CSS code. At the end we have list-style-image:url(bullet.png), which tells the browser to use an image called bullet.png that we created earlier in a paint program and saved with the web page.

Turn lists into navigation bars

Every website needs some sort of navigation, so why not use CSS for it?

Website navigation is an important topic and it is something that you need to put some thought into as you are designing your website. At one time we would have used button images created in a paint or photo program and then used JavaScript to create a rollover effect when the mouse hovered over one. But that's yesterday's technology and modern sites use CSS instead.

A CSS navigation bar looks like a regular unordered list in the HTML of the page, but using CSS we can manipulate the list elements and turn them into the website's navigation. Instead of the list running down the page, the list elements can be displayed across it instead. We can style the links just like any other text and create a custom look for the navigation bar. The result looks nothing like its original plain HTML layout and it really shows off the power of CSS.

You can copy the code into your own web pages and it will work fine. All you need to do is to change the link text to correspond to the pages or sections on your own site, and style the text to fit in with the fonts and colours that you use. It is really quite straightforward once you see how it works for yourself.

"The result looks nothing like its plain HTML layout and it shows off the power of CSS"

Build your navigation

A guide to CSS navigation menu bars

Mouse-over effects

We've sneaked in one final bit of code here. Using #navbar li a:hover, a different colour is defined for when the mouse hovers over a link in the navigation bar. It adds the finishing touch

Create an ID

The navigation menu only appears once on the page, so we use an ID instead of a class. This #navbar turns a regular list into a site navigation menu at the top of the page

Vertical to horizontal

Using float:left a vertical list of items is displayed as a horizontal list. It is the key component of this navigation menu and it would not work without it. However, display:inline is an alternative

Block links

The spacing between the items in the navigation bar is created by setting a specific width for each item. Links are turned into rectangular blocks and the width determines their size

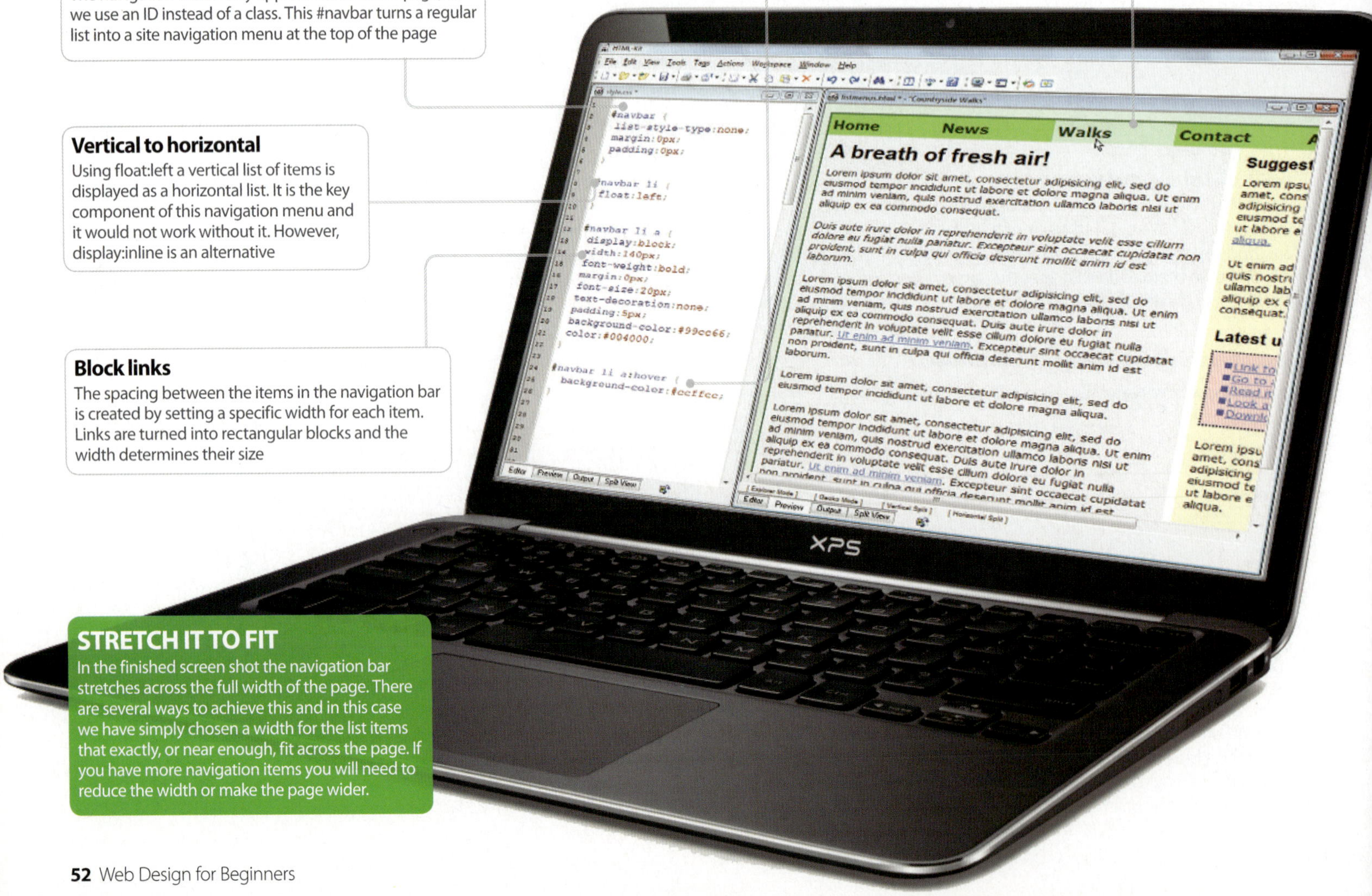

STRETCH IT TO FIT

In the finished screen shot the navigation bar stretches across the full width of the page. There are several ways to achieve this and in this case we have simply chosen a width for the list items that exactly, or near enough, fit across the page. If you have more navigation items you will need to reduce the width or make the page wider.

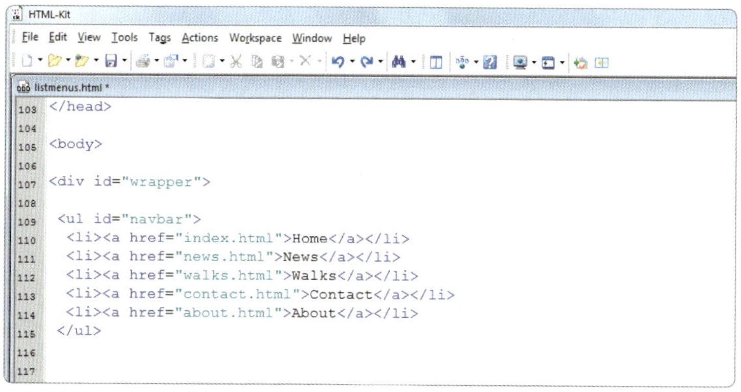

01 Create a list

An unordered list (ul) is used to provide links to other sections of the website. It's all standard HTML and it's exceedingly dull compared to CSS. Try it and see. In the ul tag though, we have added id="navbar" and we'll use it to change the way the list is displayed.

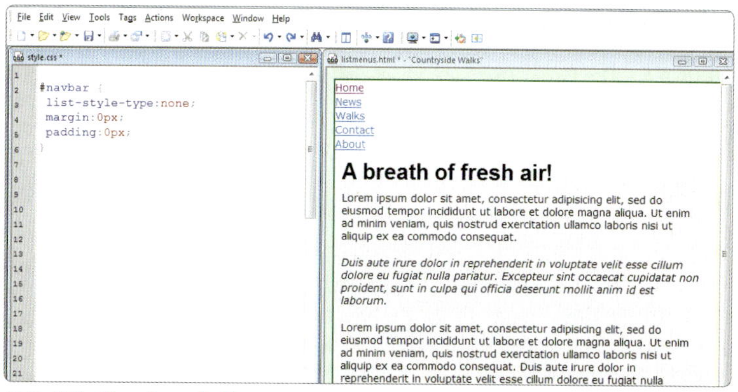

02 Make it plain

In the last tutorial we saw how to style lists and the bullets can be removed by setting list-style-type to none. The padding and margin can also be set to zero. This produces a very plain list of links at the top of the page that's not very exciting.

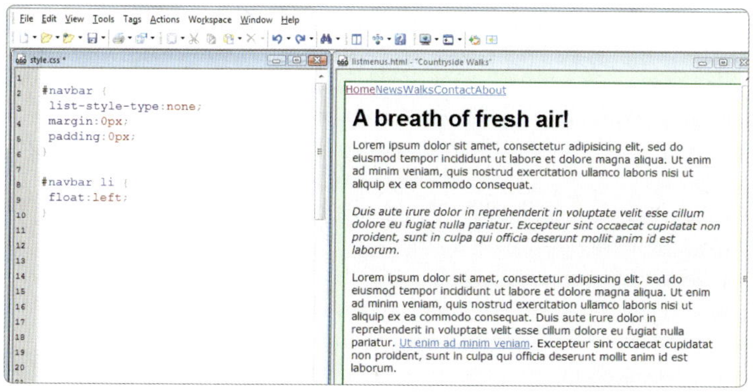

03 Floating elements

Normally each list item is displayed on a separate line, but it is possible to remove the line breaks by using float. Setting the list elements (#navbar li) to float left causes them to be displayed one after the other on the same line, like a navigation bar.

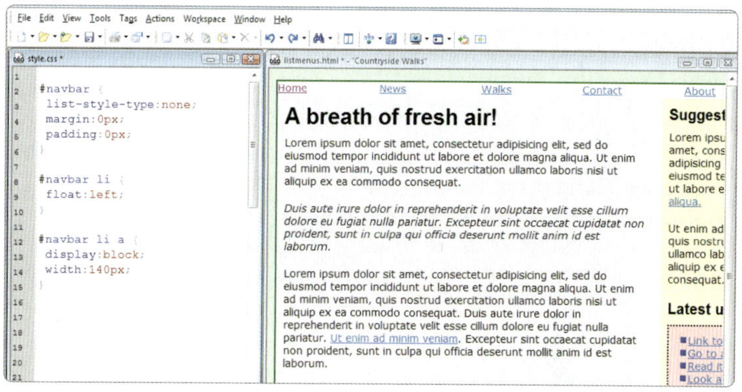

04 Spread them out

All the links are bunched up together and step 3 doesn't look much like a navigation bar. What we need to do is to make each link a fixed width. We define the a link within li of navbar (#navbar li a) as a block and set its width to 140 pixels.

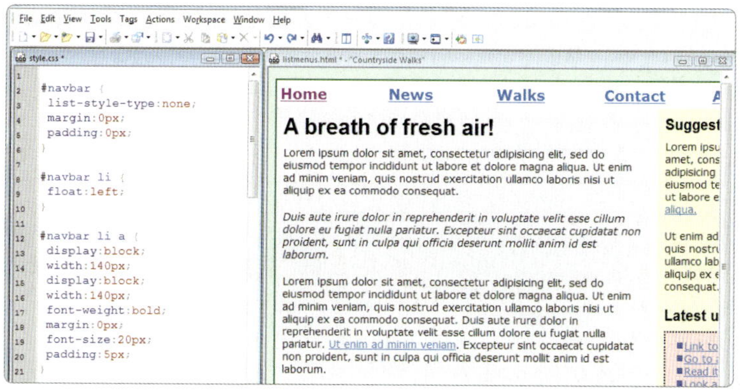

05 Style the text

Remember how we styled some text back on page 49? We can do the same here. Add the formatting information to #navbar li a to change the way that <a> links look in <li> items. Set the font size and weight, margin and padding, and so on.

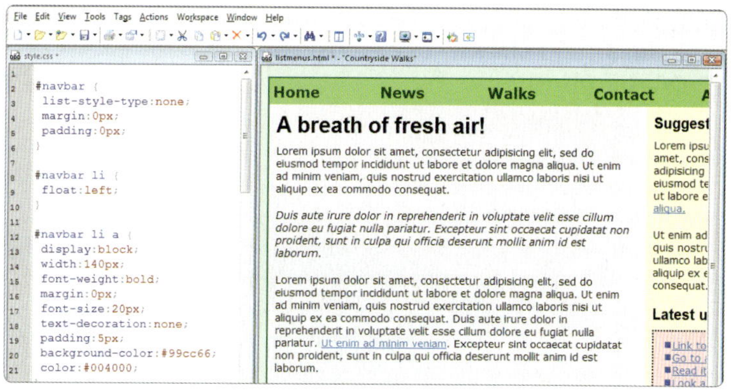

06 Colour and decoration

Three items have been added and immediately noticeable is the colour. The text colour has been set to dark green and the background has been set to light green with color and background-color. Finally, text-decoration:none removes the underline from the links.

Format images using CSS

Use CSS to gain precise control over the display of images on your website

A webpage would be pretty dull without any images on it! Some images may appear on every page, such as a graphical website logo or heading, while others may be specific to each page. You will need to create the images for your site before you start. Remember to use them sparingly and keep the file size as small as possible to ensure that webpages load quickly for visitors If you're having trouble, check out our guide on page 156.

Images are inserted into webpages using the HTML <img> tag and there are attributes to position it left and right, set the size and so on, but those are dated. If you use CSS to format images instead, there are many more options available to you. For example, you can add a border, set its thickness and its colour. The spacing around each side of the image can be individually adjusted, text can be wrapped around it on the left or the right and so on. The latest web browsers that are up to speed with CSS version 3 can display advanced image attributes like drop shadows that give the page a 3D look.

Forget the old HTML way of doing things and take advantage of CSS and its powerful features. Our tutorial will guide you through the process.

"If you use CSS to format images, there are many more options available to you"

A guide to CSS images

There are many formatting options to enhance your images

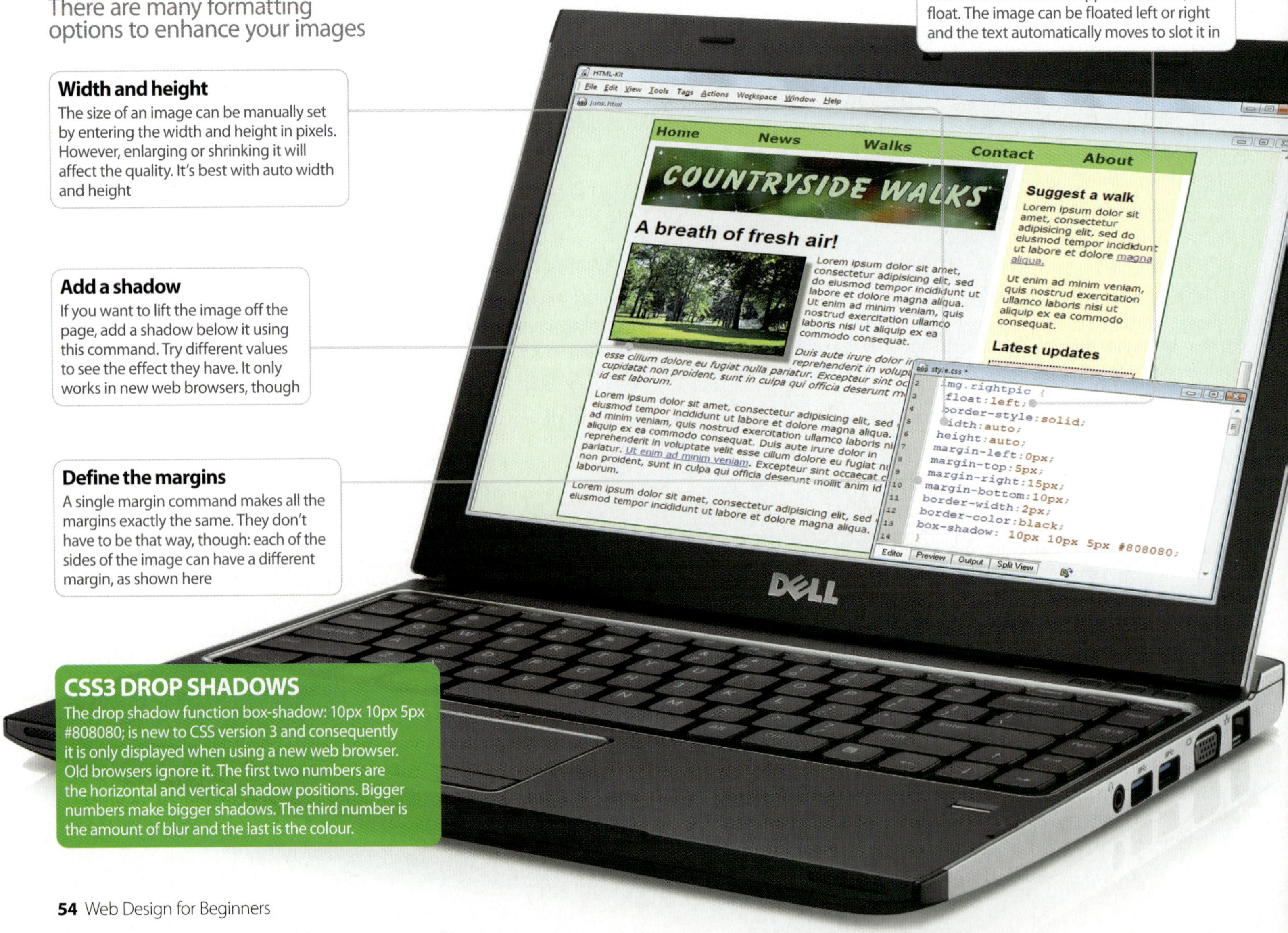

Float the image
If you want the image to appear within the text with the words wrapped around it, use float. The image can be floated left or right and the text automatically moves to slot it in

Width and height
The size of an image can be manually set by entering the width and height in pixels. However, enlarging or shrinking it will affect the quality. It's best with auto width and height

Add a shadow
If you want to lift the image off the page, add a shadow below it using this command. Try different values to see the effect they have. It only works in new web browsers, though

Define the margins
A single margin command makes all the margins exactly the same. They don't have to be that way, though: each of the sides of the image can have a different margin, as shown here

CSS3 DROP SHADOWS
The drop shadow function box-shadow: 10px 10px 5px #808080; is new to CSS version 3 and consequently it is only displayed when using a new web browser. Old browsers ignore it. The first two numbers are the horizontal and vertical shadow positions. Bigger numbers make bigger shadows. The third number is the amount of blur and the last is the colour.

01 Create the images

Load your paint program or photo editor and create the images for your webpage. There may be a graphical logo, as shown here, and one or more other images to be displayed in the page. It is usually best to save photos as JPEGs and illustrations as 256-colour PNGs.

02 Insert the images

Images are inserted into the HTML of the page using the img tag, with src pointing to the filename. Add an alt attribute as an image title: it's useful for search engines. Where the image is now, it doesn't look good. Add class="rightpic" to the img tag.

03 Build a class

Adding img.picright to the CSS file adds the class we need to format the image. The float:right; causes the image to be displayed on the right – float:left; would display it on the left. In both cases the following text will wrap around the image on the left or right.

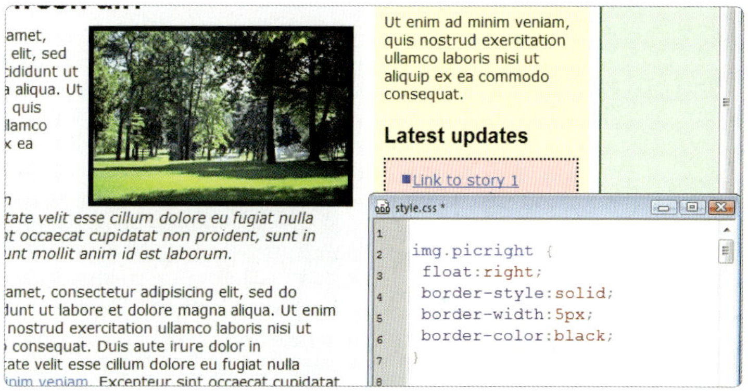

04 Add some borders

As with many other HTML elements, in CSS images can have borders. The border-style can be solid, dotted, dashed and so on, the border-width can be specified in pixels and the colour selected with border-color. Use colour names or rgb(x,y,z) values where x,y,z are numbers 0-255.

05 Define the margins

You may find that the text runs right up to the image, which might not look very attractive. It can be prevented by setting margins. We've exaggerated the effect with a 30-pixel margin; 10 is usually fine. Margin-top, left, bottom and right can be set separately if necessary.

06 Size the images

If you don't specify a size for the images, they will be displayed at whatever size they are. In some situations, though, you might want to display an image at a different size, such as when showing thumbnails. Set the width and height to the number of pixels to make the image that size.

Add a background image

A great image can really enhance your page design

The fewer images your website has, the faster it will load, but plain colours for the background and lots of text might be a turn off for your visitors. A few key images can greatly enhance the look of a website and a background image has the advantage of being used on every web page. This means that the browser only has to download it once and then it caches it ready to be used on the next page. The end result is a great page design with no time wasted downloading large images.

In this tutorial we will start with a plain coloured background and then show how to add an image. It can be a large one that fills the browser or a small one that can be stretched to fill or tiled across or down the screen. Tiled images are great for reducing the size of a page because they are so small (for more information on how to create your own, check out page 160). If you use a large image you must bear in mind the size of the file and try to minimise it without affecting the quality.

"Tiled images are great for reducing the size of a page"

CROSS-BROWSER SUPPORT

Towards the end of the tutorial there is some CSS 3 code and this is the latest CSS standard. It is new, and old versions of web browsers do not support some of the functions we have used. You need to be wary of using functions like background-position:center; and background-size:cover; because they just don't work for some people. We'd all like to create a website that works on all web browsers, but this is a difficult task. It may not always be possible and you might want to put a notice on your site asking people to ensure they have an up-to-date browser. Use Google to track down cross-browser solutions for filling the window with a background image.

Impressive backgrounds

Combine backgrounds with a wrapper to great effect

The background colour
The background colour of the page is set using CSS definitions in the body tag. It is set to the same colour as the background for the image so the two blend in like one

Background wrapper colour
If no background colour is set for the wrapper, the background colour of the page will show through. It's up to you whether you set a #wrapper background colour

Create an image
Load your photo editor or paint program. Create an image or find some clipart that you can use as is or easily modify. Save it as a compressed JPEG or 256-colour PNG

Set the repeat
In this case we want a single image that is not repeated in either the horizontal or vertical directions, so background-repeat is set to no-repeat. Tiled images repeat in both directions

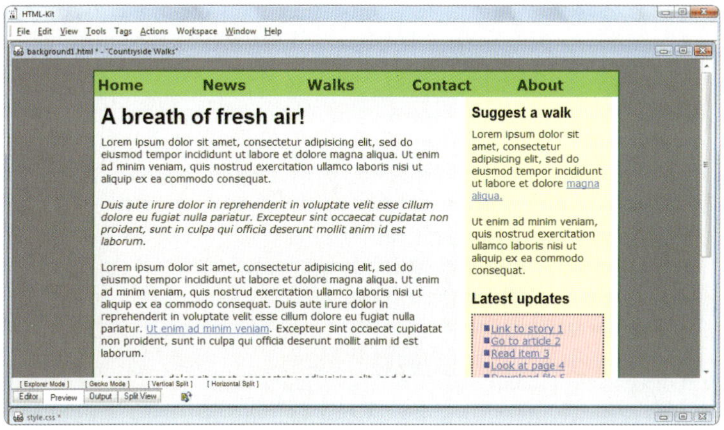

01 Pick a colour

The simplest type of background is a plain colour. This is achieved by placing a background-color style in the body tag stored in the CSS file, style.css. Use words like red, yellow, blue, green or the #RRGGBB hex value.

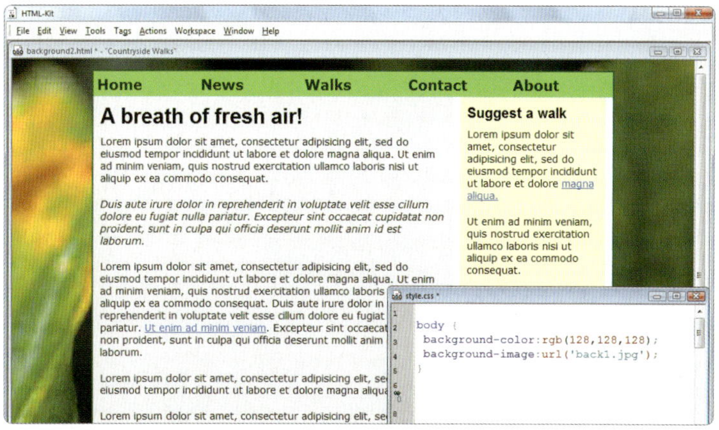

02 Use a photo

It is easy to use an image like a photo for the background and we just add a line to the body CSS that links to it. Add background-image:url('back1.jpg'), replacing the filename with whatever your file is called.

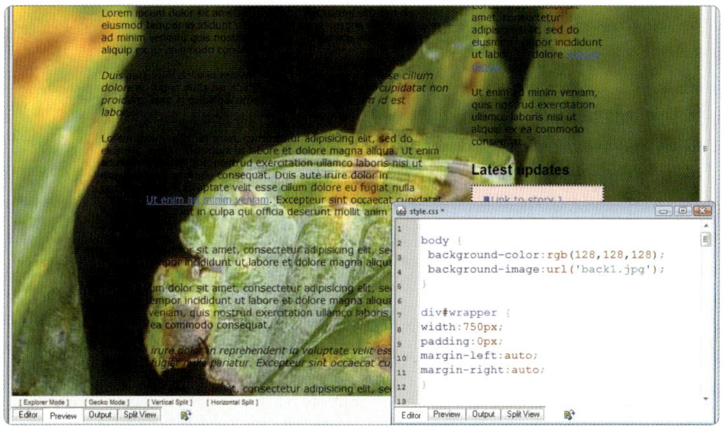

03 Modify the wrapper

The text is on a solid colour and not the background because of the wrapper we created in an earlier tutorial. Removing the background colour and border attributes results in this. You can't read the half of the text!

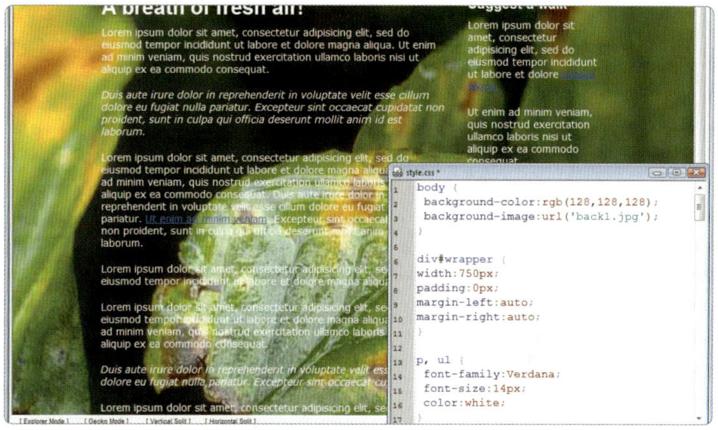

04 Change the text

We can change the text colour. We created some CSS code to set the font and size in an earlier tutorial. Now we can add color:white to the p tag definition. This image has both dark and light areas, so it's not perfect.

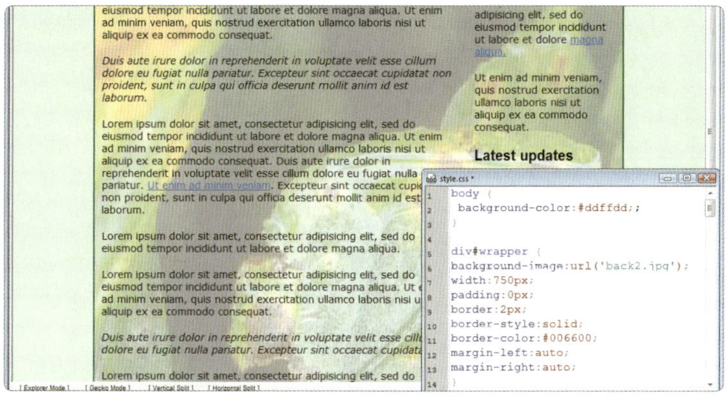

05 A background wrapper

Here, the background is solid, but the text is on an image. Anything can have a background, so we can move background-image:url('back2.jpg') from the body tag to the #wrapper definition. We chose a paler picture!

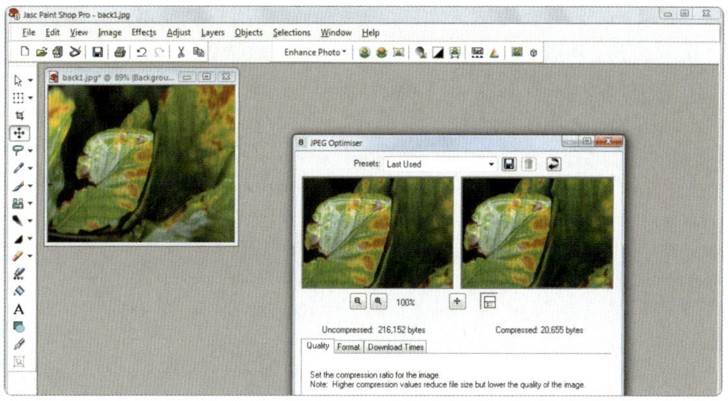

06 Resize the background

What size should the background image be? The web page should load quickly so visitors aren't waiting around, so it is best to create either a small image or use lots of JPEG compression.

07 Use smaller images

If you look down the left side it is clear that the web browser has repeated the image down the page because it didn't fill the full height. It has repeated it across the page too. It doesn't look too bad on the left, but the right edge shows all the joins. Sometimes you can get away with repeating images and sometimes not.

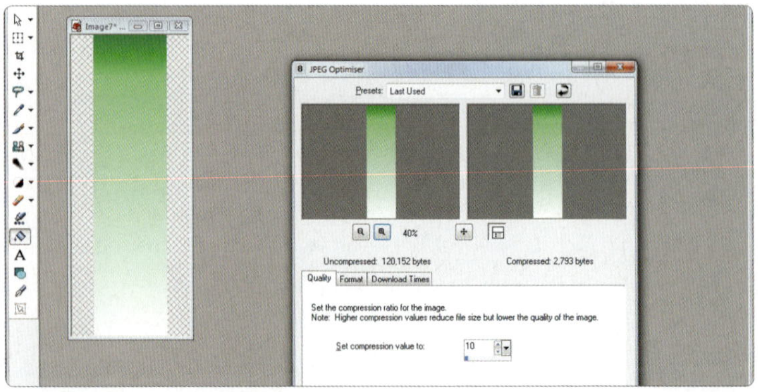

08 Create a gradient

We have created a small image that has a simple gradient that runs from dark green at the top to white at the bottom. This will be used as the background for the page and even when exported at a reasonable quality it doesn't create a very big file. Tiled backgrounds are great for creating fast-loading web pages.

09 See through wrapper

By removing the background colour in the #wrapper, the background shows through. You can see that the background image has tiled nicely across the screen and each image fits seamlessly with the next. However, it is ugly where it has been tiled vertically.

10 Tile it across

Now this is far better. What we've done here is to add background-repeat:repeat-x; to the CSS in the body definition. This instructs the browser to repeat the image across the page only (the x direction). The background colour is set to white, which is the final gradient colour so it blends in.

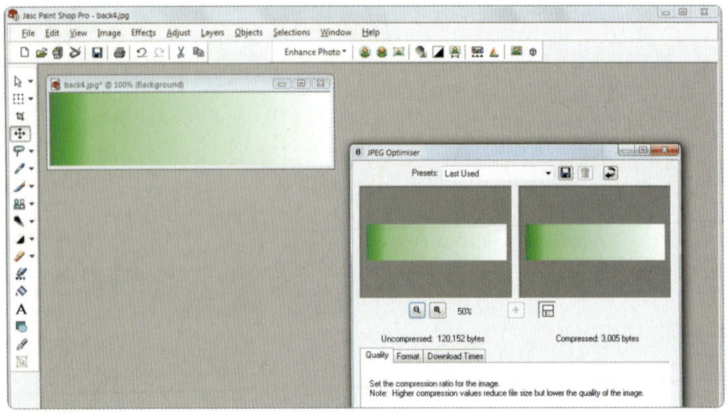

11 Horizontal gradients

The gradient background image was loaded back into the photo editor and rotated through 90 degrees to make a horizontal gradient. Notice how small it is, both in physical dimensions and in file size. The image does not need to fill the whole screen because it is going to be tiled. This reduces the file size.

12 Tile it down

The image has been tiled down the screen, but not across it. This is because of the background-repeat:repeat-y; instruction in the CSS code for the body tag. It is possible to repeat either in the x (horizontal) or y (vertical) directions. If you don't specify then it is tiled in both directions.

13 Fixed vs scrolling

The background image is tiled and the #wrapper background is white. The main difference, though, is the background-attachment in the body CSS definition. If background-attachment is set to fixed, the background stays still when the page scrolls. Set it to scroll and it scrolls with the page. You have to try it to see the difference.

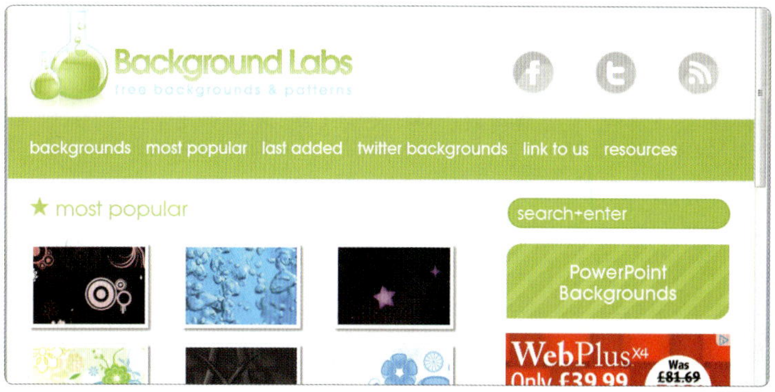

14 Grab a background

If you are not very good at creating your own backgrounds in a drawing or paint program you will find lots of sources of background images on the web. Background Labs (**www.backgroundlabs.com**) and GRSites (**www.grsites.com/archive/textures/**) have lots of images and a large number of them are textures and images for tiling on the page.

15 Resize vs stretch

This image is from Background Labs. It is a small image will not fill the browser window and it is not suitable for tiling across or down the page. You have two choices and you can either resize it in the photo editor or resize it within the page using CSS.

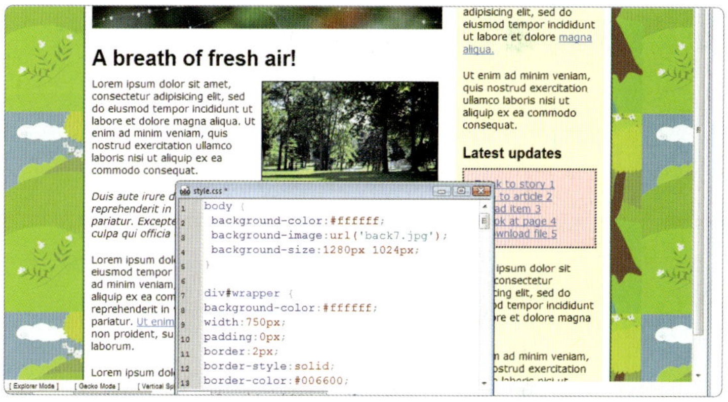

16 Resize the background

The CSS code for the body tag has been modified and background-size:1280px 1024px; has been added. This is a CSS 3 feature that is only supported by the latest versions of web browsers. This one has ignored it! In IE9, Chrome and Firefox it will stretch the image to the size specified.

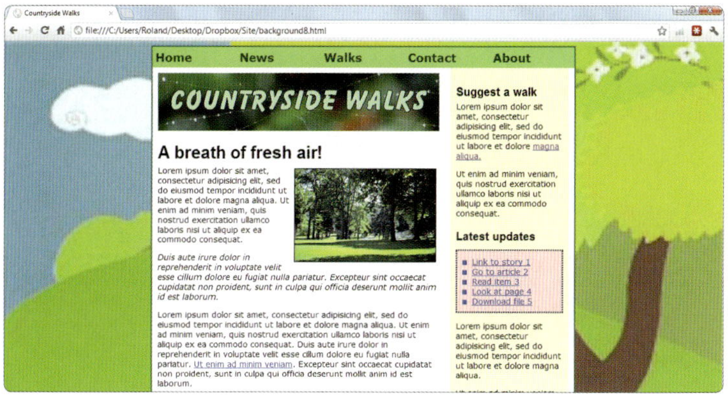

17 Cover the background

Specify a size for the background and someone with a laptop may find part of the image is hidden. Someone with a large monitor may have a browser width of 1500 pixels and then the background will be tiled. Use background-size:cover; and the image is stretched to fit.

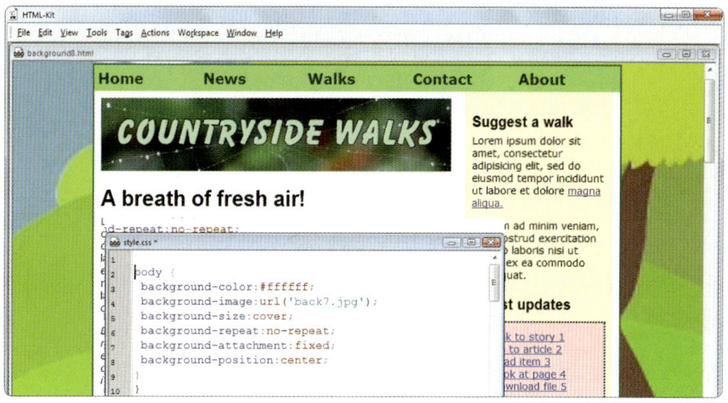

18 Background positioning

One final bit of background-related CSS is the positioning. In the body code is background-position:center; and this centres the background image in the browser window. Other values include left top, left center, right top, right center, center bottom and so on, or just use pixels like 50px.

Customise the links to fit your design

Links don't have to be blue and boring, so change the default to the style of your choice

The web is all about linking – it's what it was created for. You can link to another page on your own website or to another page on a completely different website elsewhere on the internet. Links can be made to documents like PDFs, to videos, to files and music. You will have a lot of links in your pages and they will work fine without any problems as long as you get the HTML right and the item you link to actually exists (links that don't work because a file or page was deleted or moved are the bane of every webmaster's life!).

By default, links are displayed in blue underlined text, but it is not compulsory and you can choose any colour scheme you like. However, you do need to make links obvious and it wouldn't be a good idea, for instance, to have black links in the middle of black text. If, for some reason, you wanted to have blue text then black links would be fine because they stand out. It is also possible to remove the underline on text links, and borders around image links. You can even change the background.

"It is also possible to remove the underline on text links, and borders around image links"

Luscious links in a flash

It is easy to make your links part of the site design

Highlighted links

You can do some fancy things with links, because they are simply text. However, it is best not to go overboard with the special effects or it might irritate visitors. This is a simple highlight

Linked images

This image is a link to another webpage, but it is not showing a blue border because a black border has been specified using CSS for the img tag. You can't have two borders, so black it is

The link colour

You can set the colour of a link using words like blue, red, darkgreen and so on; you can specify the hexadecimal colour value, such as #8000ff; or use rgb(x,y,z) where x,y,z are numbers 0-255

Pages you've read

Here you can see that a link that you have previously visited is displayed in a different colour to those to pages you haven't yet seen. It provides information that can be useful when browsing the web

LINKING PICTURES

If you have an image and enclose it in a link <a href="blah"> tag, Internet Explorer adds a blue border to tell people it's a clickable link. Any CSS border commands override the blue link, so set border-style:none; to remove it.

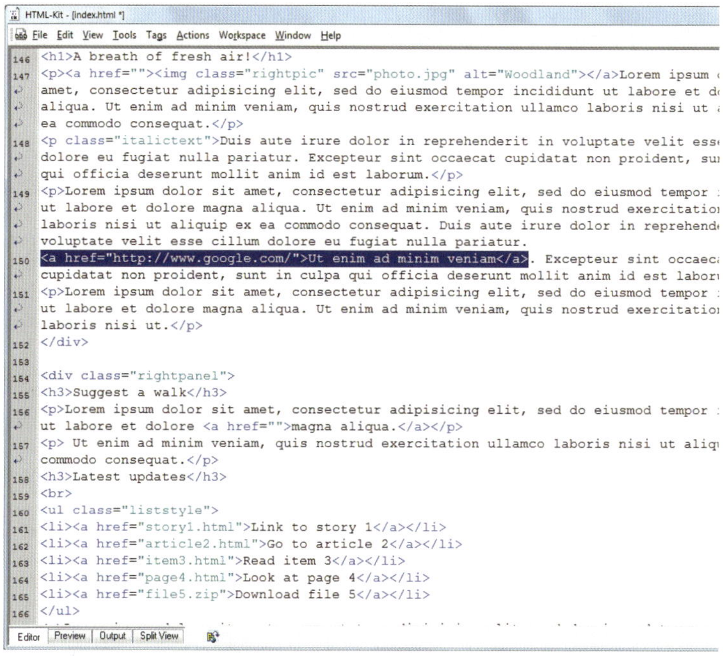

01 Add the links

There are a variety of links in this page and you just enclose whatever text or image you want to turn into a link with the <a href="blah"></a> tags. You don't need a class or an ID to use CSS.

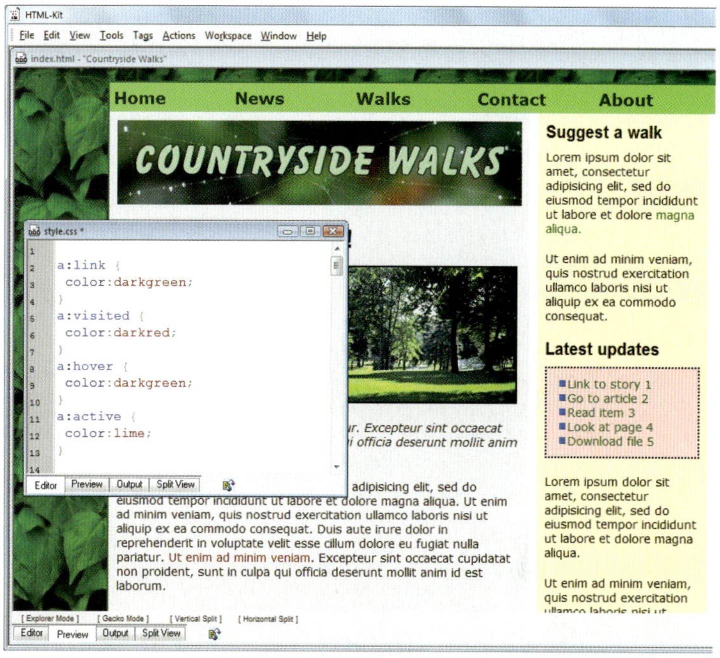

02 Choose the colours

This CSS changes the colours of text links. An a:link is a link you've never clicked, a:hover is when the mouse hovers over a link, a:active is when a link is clicked, and a:visited are links you've clicked.

03 Decorate the text

Normally the browser displays links as underlined text, but it doesn't have to be underlined. Add text-decoration to the CSS code for each link type to specify whether a link should or should not have the underline.

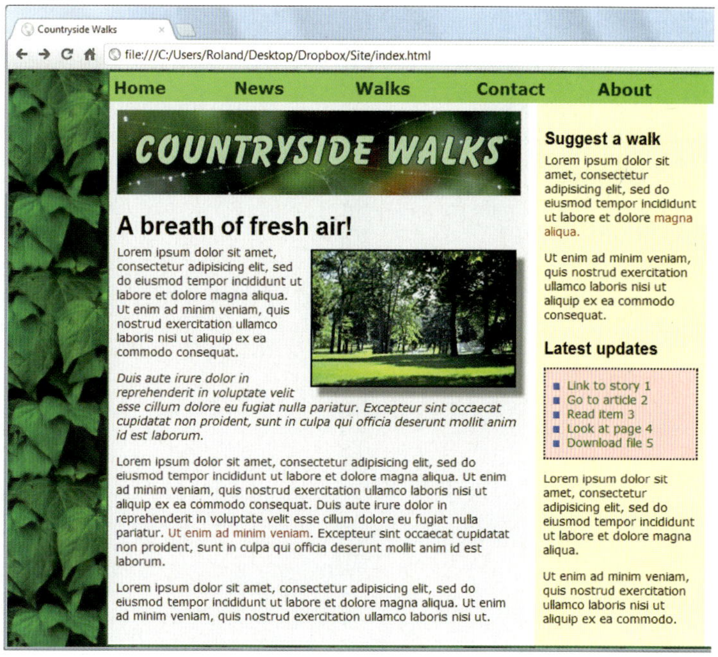

04 Set the background

Links are just text, so re-read the tutorials on styling text and navigation for ideas. For example, you can arrange for the background to change colour when the mouse hovers over a link. Here it changes to yellow.

Style a two-column layout

Use the HTML and CSS skills you've learnt so far to create and style a two-column page layout

Using HTML and CSS to create and style a two-column website layout – one of the most common layouts – is surprisingly straightforward and very flexible. Almost all websites today use some kind of column layout with at least a sidebar and main content areas. So it's one of the basic skills to have when designing websites, and once you understand these fundamentals you can move on to bigger and more elaborate designs.

In this tutorial, then, we are going to open up our favourite text editor (we will be using Adobe Dreamweaver, but the humble NotePad or TextEdit is fine) and learn how we can shorten, lengthen and swap any column we need just by using CSS. Then we will discuss CSS floats, why we use percentages and a few other tips along the way.

"Almost all websites use a column layout with at least a sidebar and main content areas"

ANATOMY OF A CSS RULE

When we write CSS, we use 'selectors'. A selector is the HTML tag is we want to style. Then within the curly braces we have the property and its value. So 'float:' is the property and 'left' is its value. Both together 'float: left;' is what is called the declaration. When we put everything together (selector and declaration) it's what we call a CSS 'rule'. Another quick thing is the fact that all tags (<p>, <div>, etc) are boxes that we call elements and are either block level or inline level. Every element follows the normal flow and stacks on top of each other vertically. When we use floats, we need to think of each element as a box that needs to be positioned outside of the normal document flow.

Taking a closer look

Let's take a closer look at what we will achieve and summarise the most important part of creating a two-column layout using HTML/CSS

The sidebar
The sidebar area is floated right and again we use margins to push it away at the top, bottom, left and right sides

The header
We'll float the header left and give it a 100% width to make sure it spans the full width of our wrapper

Main content
The main content will be floated left as we want this to be positioned far left of our page and then some margins will give us some white space

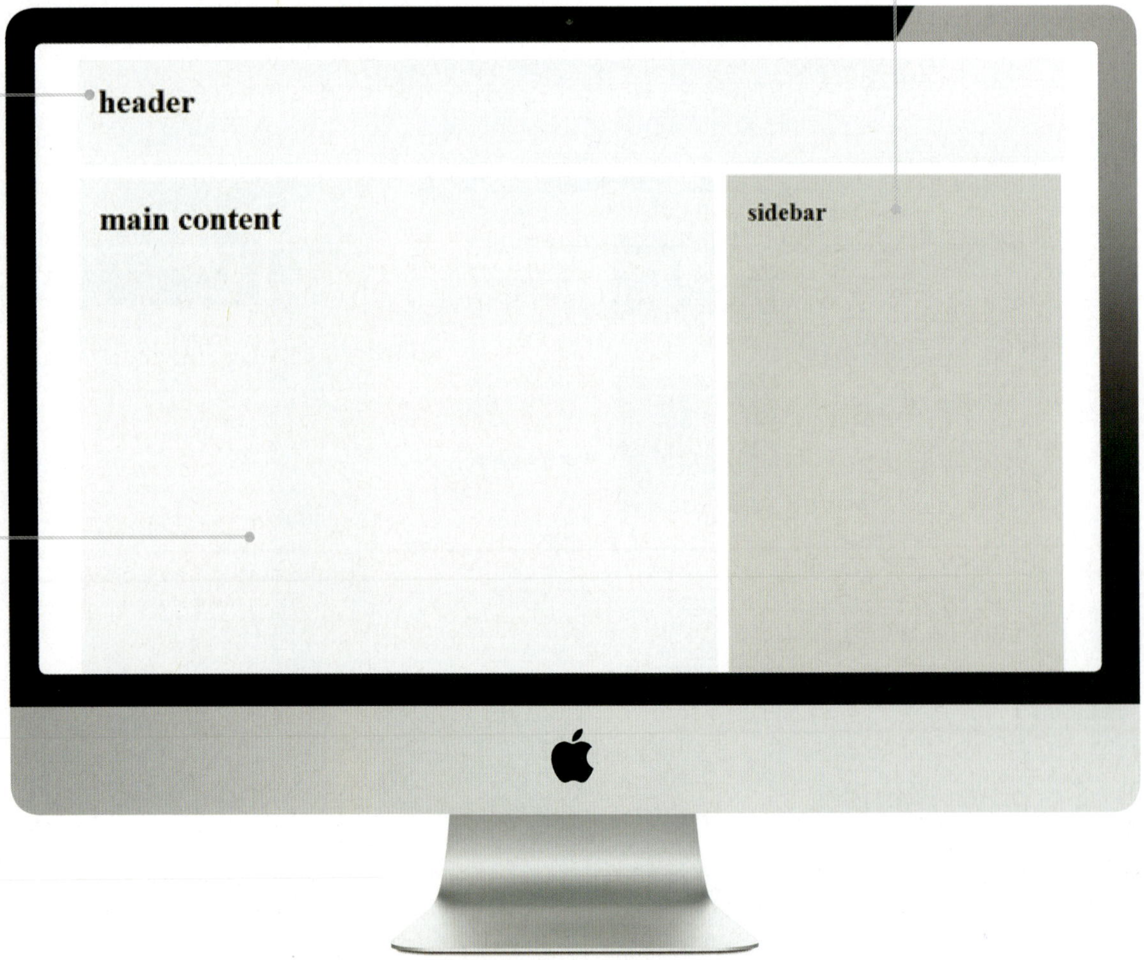

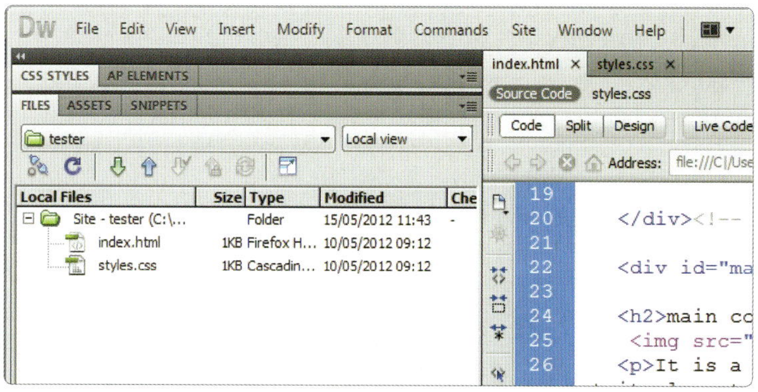

01 Getting started

First thing we need to do is create new 'index.html' and 'styles.css' files and place them in the same directory. It is considered best practice to also place all your CSS files within their own folder called 'css' as some use separate CSS files for certain things such as Internet Explorer-specific styles. However, we will keep it simple here and leave them sitting in the same location.

```
<!DOCTYPE HTML>
<html>
<head>
<meta charset="utf-8">
<title>3 column layout</title>

<link rel="stylesheet" href="styles.css">

</head>

<body>


</body>
</html>
```

02 Linking the CSS

Now that we have our new index.html and styles.css files, we will need to link them up together within the <head></head> tags of our HTML. So open up the index.html file and just underneath the closing </title> tag, type in your link to your CSS.

```
<!DOCTYPE HTML>
<html>
<head>
<meta charset="utf-8">
<title>3 column layout</title>

<link rel="stylesheet" href="styles.css">

</head>

<body>

<div id="wrapper">
```

03 The wrapper

With the 'index.html' file still open, lets add in a 'wrapper' div that will be used to centre all our content on the screen later on using CSS. What we have done here is use an ID (<div id=") instead of using a class because this is going to be a main part of our page's structure and will only be used the once throughout our code.

```
<title>2 column layout</title>

<link rel="stylesheet" href="styles.css">

</head>

<body>

<div id="wrapper">

    <div id="header">

    <h1>header</h1>

    </div><!-- END header -->

</div><!-- END wrapper -->

</body>
</html>
```

04 Header

Okay, the first real page section (element) we will add is the header. We are going to give it an ID ('<div id=' called 'header') and place this just underneath our wrapper div. Then we have added in a title of our section within an '<h1>' header tag so we can know what's what.

```
<body>

<div id="wrapper">

    <div id="header">

    <h1>header</h1>

    </div><!-- END header -->

    <div id="main_content">

     <h1>main content</h1>

    </div><!-- END main content -->

</div><!-- END wrapper -->
```

05 Main content

So next up we need to add a main content section that will be positioned on the left side. Like we did in the last step we have used an ID called 'main_ content' and added it in just underneath our 'header'. And again so we can see what section is what, we have added in a title using the '<h1>' tag.

```
     <h1>header</h1>

    </div><!-- END header -->

    <div id="main_content">

     <h1>main content</h1>

    </div><!-- END main content -->

    <div id="sidebar">

     <h2>sidebar</h2>

    </div><!-- END sidebar -->

</div><!-- END wrapper -->
```

06 Sidebar section

The sidebar is next and this is the area that will be positioned over to the right and would normally be used for extra navigation links or a search field – things like that. So again we will use an ID called 'sidebar' and add it just under the 'main_content' closing div '</div>'.

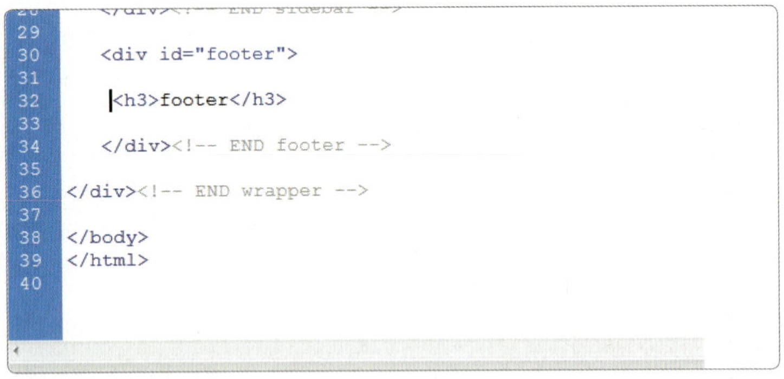

07 The footer

Now the footer speaks for itself and will be our last HTML section we will be adding. So again let's give it an ID name of 'footer' and add it in underneath the closing 'main_content' div. Then again place in a header tag using a '<h3>'. You will also notice we have added in an HTML comment to every end div tag (</div>) to give us a clear indication of where each section ends. This will help you if your HTML mark-up gets very busy.

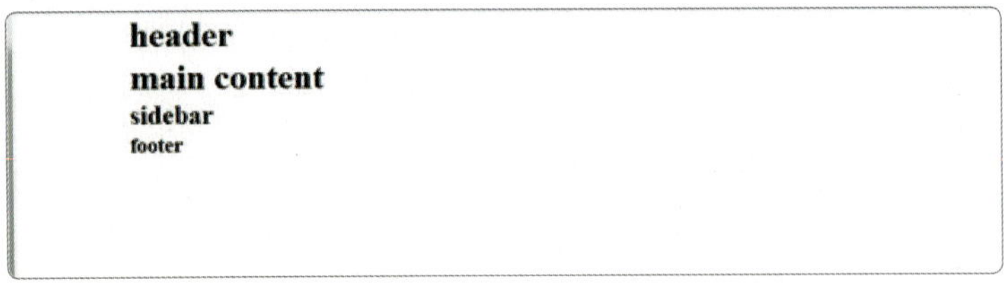

09 Wrapper styles

Now the reason for our wrapper is to 'wrap' everything within a containing section (element) so we can centre it within the viewpoint of our screen. So here we have used margin to zero out the top and bottom margins and allow CSS to automatically calculate the left and right space based on our width. Our width will be 960px because that aligns up nicely with a screen resolution of 1080 x 760px (lowest common denominator).

```
#wrapper {
 width: 960px;
 margin: 0 auto;
}
```

11 Main content styles

In this step we are going to give our 'main_content' some styles. First thing, then, is to float it left. Then give it an off-white background colour and then by using margins we can give it some breathing space – which is called 'white space'. We then specify its width and height taking into consideration the overall width of our wrapper so we have enough room for our sidebar.

```
#main_content {
	float: left;
	background: #f0f0f0;
	margin: 10px 5px 10px 0;
	width: 620px;
	height: 630px;
}
```

08 CSS reset

Now open up your 'styles.css' file and what we are going to do first is add what is called a 'reset'. The reset uses the universal selector and this just tells all browsers (including IE) to clear all default styles, such as padding, margins, line-height etc. Doing this will give you a clean slate to work from.

```
/* reset */

* {
 padding: 0;
 margin: 0;

}
```

10 The header

Now, for the header section we are going to float it left and give it a width of 100%, which will guarantee our header spans the whole width of our '#wrapper'. Then we push the header down 10px using margin. Here we have used what is called shorthand CSS, which enables us to only pick the top margin. Now give the background a colour and then 100px height.

```
#header {
	float: left;
	background: #f1f1f1;
	margin: 10px 0 0 0;
	width: 100%;
	height: 100px;
}
```

12 The sidebar styles

The sidebar will be positioned to the right-hand side and this is at most expected by the user/visitor. So it makes sense to float to right. And then use margins again to give us some white space. Our sidebar background will be a darker grey than the rest and it will be a fixed width of 324px, which should give us plenty of room for any inner content. Then we give it the same height as the main content section.

```
#sidebar {
	float: right;
	margin: 10px 5px 5px 6px;
	background: #ccc;
	width: 324px;
	height: 630px;
}
```

13 The footer styles

The footer styles should be fairly straightforward now. However, we have a new property to look at, which is the 'clear:' property. Setting this to 'both' will make all floated elements pump up over the footer allowing our footer to sit where it should be. Then we float the footer to the left and give it some dimensions.

```
#footer {
        clear: both;
        float: left;
        background: #ddd;
        width: 100%;
        height: 100px;
}
```

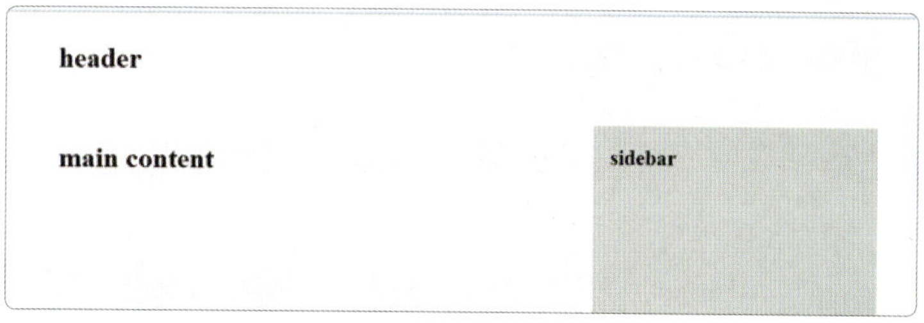

14 The headers

If you view your layout within a browser you will see we have now got a nice two-column layout with a sidebar and main content area. The only thing we need to do now is push the titles(headers) of each section away from the edges. So, we can easily achieve this by using padding on all header tags using the same CSS rule.

```
h1, h2, h3 {
        padding: 20px;
}
```

15 Moving the sidebar

Now say you wanted the sidebar over to the right, well, this is very easy to achieve and all it takes is to change the float value of the '#main_content' rule from 'left' to 'right'. But what you want to be conscious of is naming your divs. So, for instance, if we name our sidebar something like '<div id="left_side">' then this would now be a bit confusing when or if someone else looks at your code.

```
#main_content {
        float: right;
        background: #f0f0f0;
        margin: 10px 5px 10px 0;
        width: 620px;
        height: 630px;
}
```

16 Bigger two columns

As you can imagine, it's very easy to make two larger content areas and not have a sidebar at all – even though it still can be called 'sidebar'. So in your CSS, if we think about how much space we have to play with, which is 960px, and divide that into two. However, then we have to compensate for our margins, so it may take you some messing about to get the right spacing without pushing anything out.

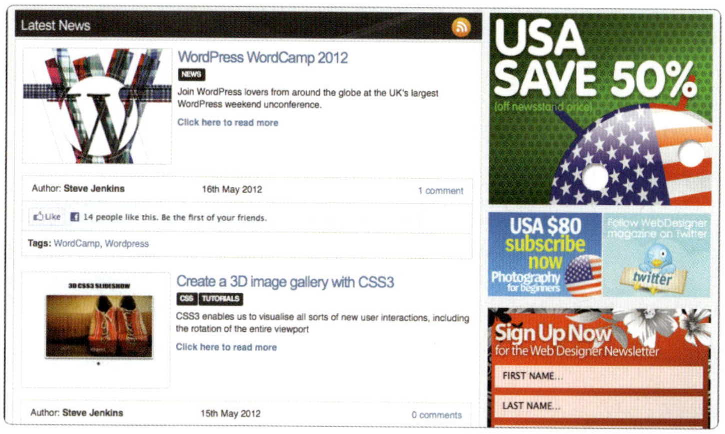

17 Be inspired

Now you've finished your basic two-column layout, take at look at some of your favourite websites and see which layout they employ. As shown above, **www.webdesignermag.co.uk** uses a two-column layout too.

18 Research alternatives

The two-column layout is in no way the be all and end all. Over the page we explore how to create and style a three-column layout, and even one-page scrolling websites (like above) are becoming more and more popular.

Style a three-column layout

Take the next step and create and style a three-column layout using HTML and CSS

Like the two-column layout, using HTML and CSS to create a three-column layout is fairly straightforward. Almost all websites today use some kind of column layout with at least a sidebar and main content areas. So it's another fundamental skill to have when building websites, and once you understand this you can move on to better and bigger things. So in this tutorial we are going to open up our favourite text editor and learn how we can shorten, widen and swap any column we need just by using CSS. As you can imagine, this will come in handy if one day you decide to try your hand at developing WordPress themes or any other blogging platform, because having a sidebar is in most cases a requirement for blogs.

> "Another fundamental skill to have when building sites"

Using floats The float property

A float is a box that is shifted to the left or right of the document flow. The most interesting characteristic of a float is that content may flow along its side (or be prohibited from doing so by the 'clear' property). Content flows down the right side of a left-floated box and down the left side of a right-floated box. The float property has four values that we can apply to it: left, right, inherit, and 'none'.

If you assign 'float: left' to an element, it will move to the left-most boundary of its parent element. The same idea applies if you were to assign 'float: right;' to an element, but to the right-most boundary of its parent element. The 'inherit' value tells an element to inherit the float value of its parent element but is rarely used if at all. The value 'none' is the default value and tells an element not to float at all, which, again, isn't really used.

Floated elements are first laid out according to the normal flow, then taken out of the normal flow and sent as far to the right or left of the parent element. In other words, they go from stacking on top of each other to sitting next to each other, given that there is enough room in the parent element for each floated element to sit. This is crucial to remember.

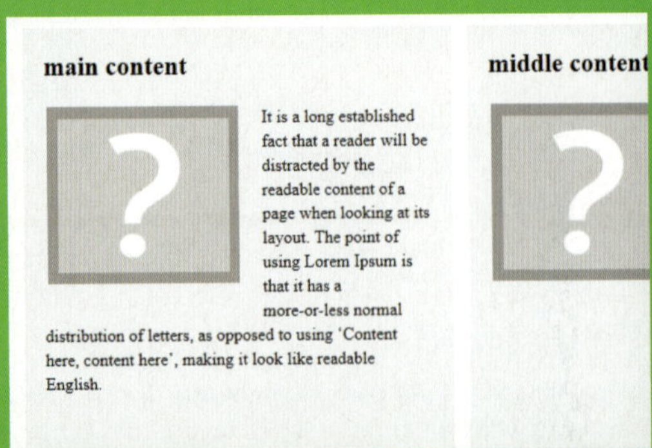

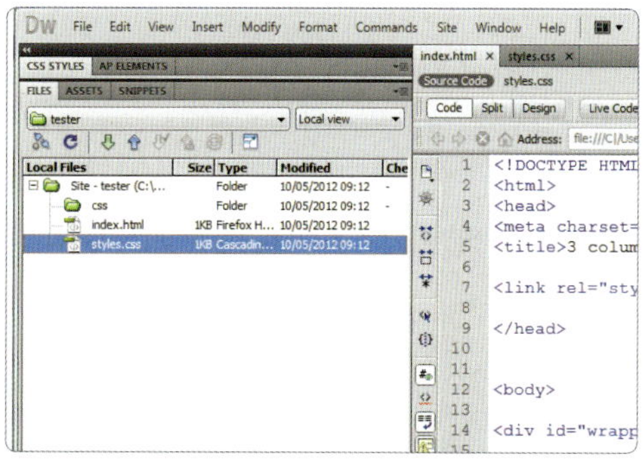

01 Getting started

First thing we need to do is create a new 'index.html' and 'styles.css' files and place them in the same location (directory). It is good practice to also place all your CSS files within their own folder, but again we'll keep it simple here and leave them sitting in the same location.

```
<head>
<meta charset="utf-8">
<title>3 column layout</title>

<link rel="stylesheet" href="styles.css">

</head>


<body>

<div id="wrapper">

    <div id="header">

    <h1>Your logo goes here</h1>
    <h5 class="tagline">Some super duper slogan!</h5>

    </div><!-- END header -->
```

04 Header

Now let's add in our header section with a text logo. So within the 'wrapper' div, create another div ID called 'header'. Then, within the header div, place in our logo using a '<h1></h1>' tag and the slogan using a smaller header tag with a class of 'slogan'. Now we can style that using CSS later on.

```
    <div id="sidebar">

    <h2>sidebar</h2>

    <ul class="list">

     <li>List 01</li>
     <li>List 02</li>
     <li>List 03</li>
     <li>List 04</li>
     <li>List 05</li>

    </ul>

    </div><!-- END sidebar -->

    <div id="footer">

  <h2>footer</h2>
```

07 Sidebar & footer

The sidebar will be positioned over to the left and include a list that can be turned into some navigation links. So we'll use an ID called 'sidebar' and include an unordered list with a class name of 'list' so we can position it later using CSS. We can now add in our footer with a header tag (h2).

```
<!DOCTYPE HTML>
<html>
<head>
<meta charset="utf-8">
<title>3 column layout</title>

<link rel="stylesheet" href="styles.css">

</head>
```

02 Linking the CSS

Now that we have our new 'index.html' and 'styles.css' files, we will need to link them up together within the '<head></head>' tags of our HTML. So open up the 'index.html' file and just underneath the '<title>' tags, place your link to your CSS.

```
</head>

<body>

<div id="wrapper">

    <div id="header">

    <h1>Your logo goes here</h1>
    <h5 class="tagline">Some super duper slogan!</h5>

    </div><!-- END header -->

    <div id="main_content">

    <h2>main content</h2>

    <p>It is a long established fact that a reader will b
        at its layout. The point of using Lorem Ipsum is
        opposed to using 'Content here, content here', ma
    </p>
```

05 Main content

So next up we need to add our first column. First let's add in the main content area that will sit over to the left. Again we are going to give it a ID name called 'main_content' and then add some content within paragraph tags '<p></p>'.

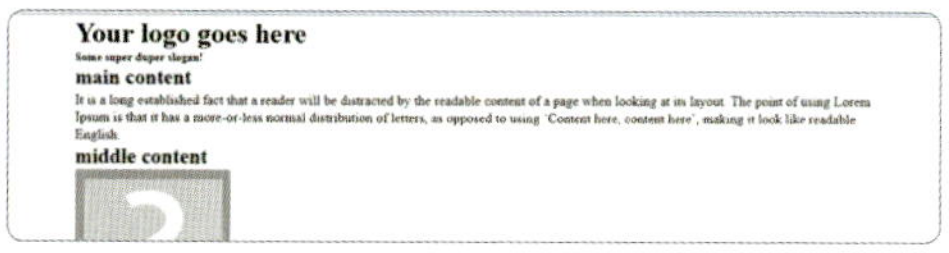

08 The CSS

Open styles.css and at the top put in our simple reset. Now we can start from a clean slate. Using the 'wrapper' div, we can give the page a fixed width and then centre it using 'margin 0 auto;'

```
* {padding: 0;
margin: 0;
          }
#wrapper {
 width: 960px;
 margin: 0 auto;
}
```

```
<link rel="stylesheet" href="styles.css">

</head>


<body>

<div id="wrapper">



</div><!-- END wrapper -->
```

03 Setting the wrapper

Now still in the 'index.html', let's add in 'wrapper' div that will be used to center all our content on the screen. What we have done is used an ID (<div id=") instead of using a class because this is going to be a main part of the page structure and will only be used the once throughout our code.

```
    <div id="main_content">

    <h2>main content</h2>

    <p>It is a long established fact that a reader will
at its layout. The point of using Lorem Ipsum is that i
opposed to using 'Content here, content here', making i

    </div><!-- END main content -->


     <div id="mid_content">

    <h2>middle content</h2>

    <img src="image.jpg" height="161" width="179"/>

    </div><!-- END main content -->
```

06 Middle content

We're going to add in the middle content, and this area will be used for adding some images. We gave it an ID name of 'mid_content' and then add in an image. We have set the dimensions of our image here and will use the '<img>' tag later on in our CSS to position it a little better.

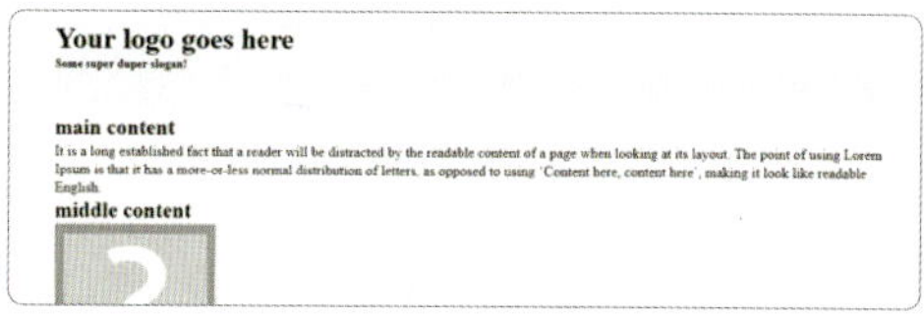

09 The header

Now we have the content centred nicely, it's time to add some styles to the header and then work our way down the page. So firstly let's float our header to the left and give it an off-white colour. Then we push it down slightly using a top margin(top, right, bottom, left) and then to make sure it spans the whole width of our wrapper, we give a '100%' width and lastly a height of '100px'.

```
#header {
        float: left;
        background: #f1f1f1;
        margin: 10px 0 0 0;
        width: 100%;
        height: 100px;
}
```

10 Main content styles

Next up is the main content section that we are going to position on the left. So first let's float it left and give it some background colour and height and width. We have then used margins to position it and create some white space (the space in between the areas). Then by using '#main_content p' we can style the text within and push it away from the edges using 'padding' and then space out each sentence by using 'line-height: 22px' to make it more readable.

```
#main_content {
        float: left;
        background: #f0f0f0;
        margin: 10px 15px 10px 0;
        width: 400px;
        height: 630px;
}

        #main_content p {
        padding: 20px;
        line-height: 22px;
        }
```

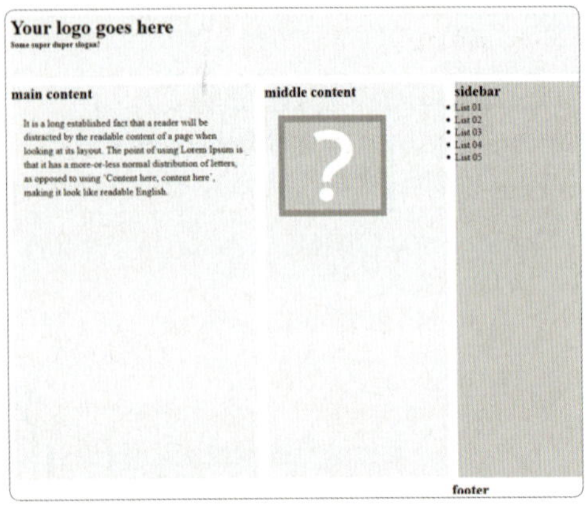

13 The sidebar styles

The sidebar is going to be the area that is positioned to the right and house our unordered list. So naturally we float this to the right; however, because of the way floats work, we can just as easily float this to the left and it will still be positioned to the right side. We then give it a darker background colour to allow us to see it more prominent. Then we set the width and height and position it better using margins as before.

```
#sidebar {
        float: right;
        margin: 10px 5px 5px 6px;
        background: #ccc;
        width: 225px;
        height: 630px;
}
```

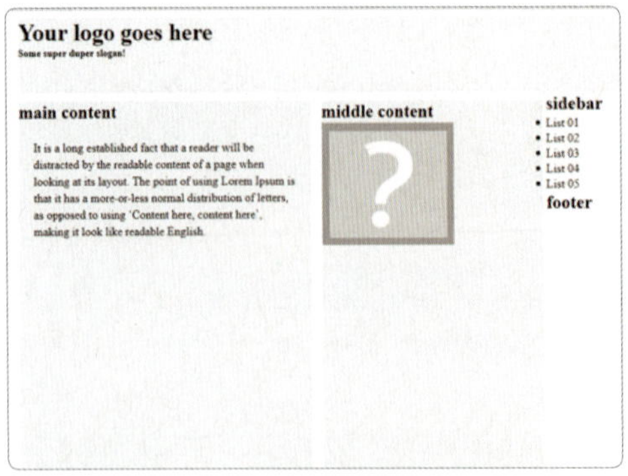

11 Middle content styles

Now we want to position our middle content area. We do this by floating it to the left which will make the element (box) move to the left-most boundary of its parent element, our parent element being our 'mid_content' div. Again we use margin to create white space and the rest is pretty straightforward by now.

```
#mid_content {
        float: left;
        background: #f0f0f0;
        margin: 10px 5px 10px 0;
        width: 300px;
        height: 630px;
}
```

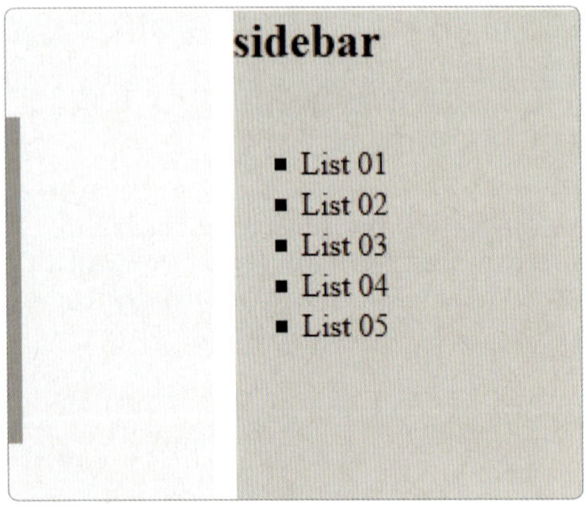

14 Sidebar list

We have plenty of options here to style our list and it's up to you to experiment with this. So for instance you can make the list items (dots) change from their default dots to squares by adding this line of code to our CSS rule 'list-style: square;'. So you have options here and in most cases designers use their own images, but let's stick to the default styles and use margin to position it better.

```
.list {
        float: left;
        margin: 35px;
}
```

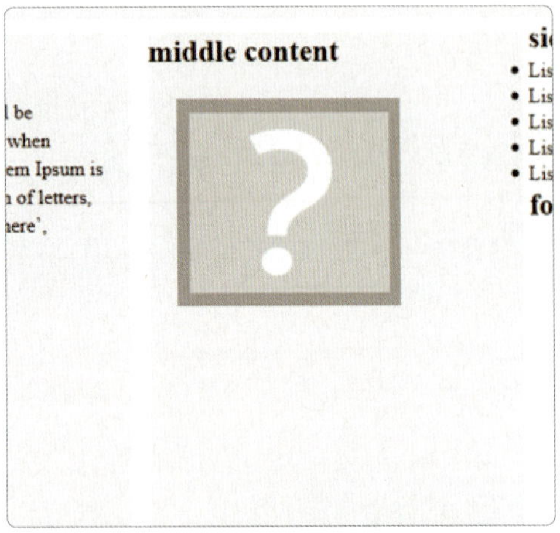

12 Middle content image

This step is going to be pretty easy and all we are going to do here is float middle content image left and by using 'margin: 22px' tells your browser to add 22 pixels all around the image giving it some breathing space.

```
#mid_content img {
        float: left;
        margin: 22px;
}
```

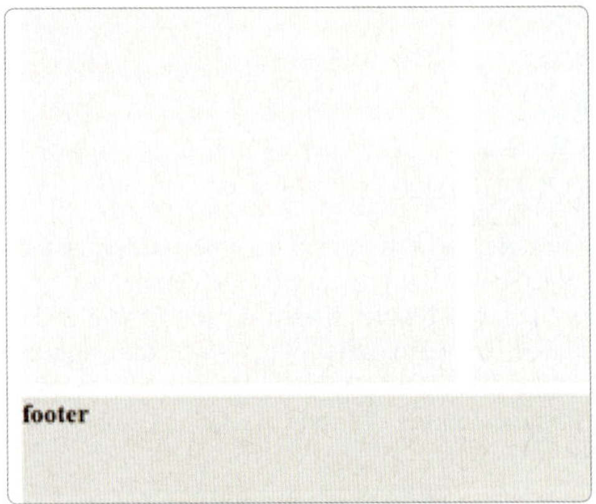

15 The footer styles

We need to float our footer left and at the same time clear both the right and left floated elements, which will allow the footer to sit underneath all other floated elements. We then give it a background colour and make sure it spans the full width of our wrapper by giving it a 100% width. And then finish off with a fixed height of 100 pixels.

```
#footer {
        clear: both;
        float: left;
        background: #ddd;
        width: 100%;
        height: 100px;
}
```

Three-column layout

Here's what we achieved as we summarise the most important part of creating a three -column layout using HTML/CSS

Main content

The main content will be floated left as we want this to be positioned far left of our page and then some margins to give us some white space

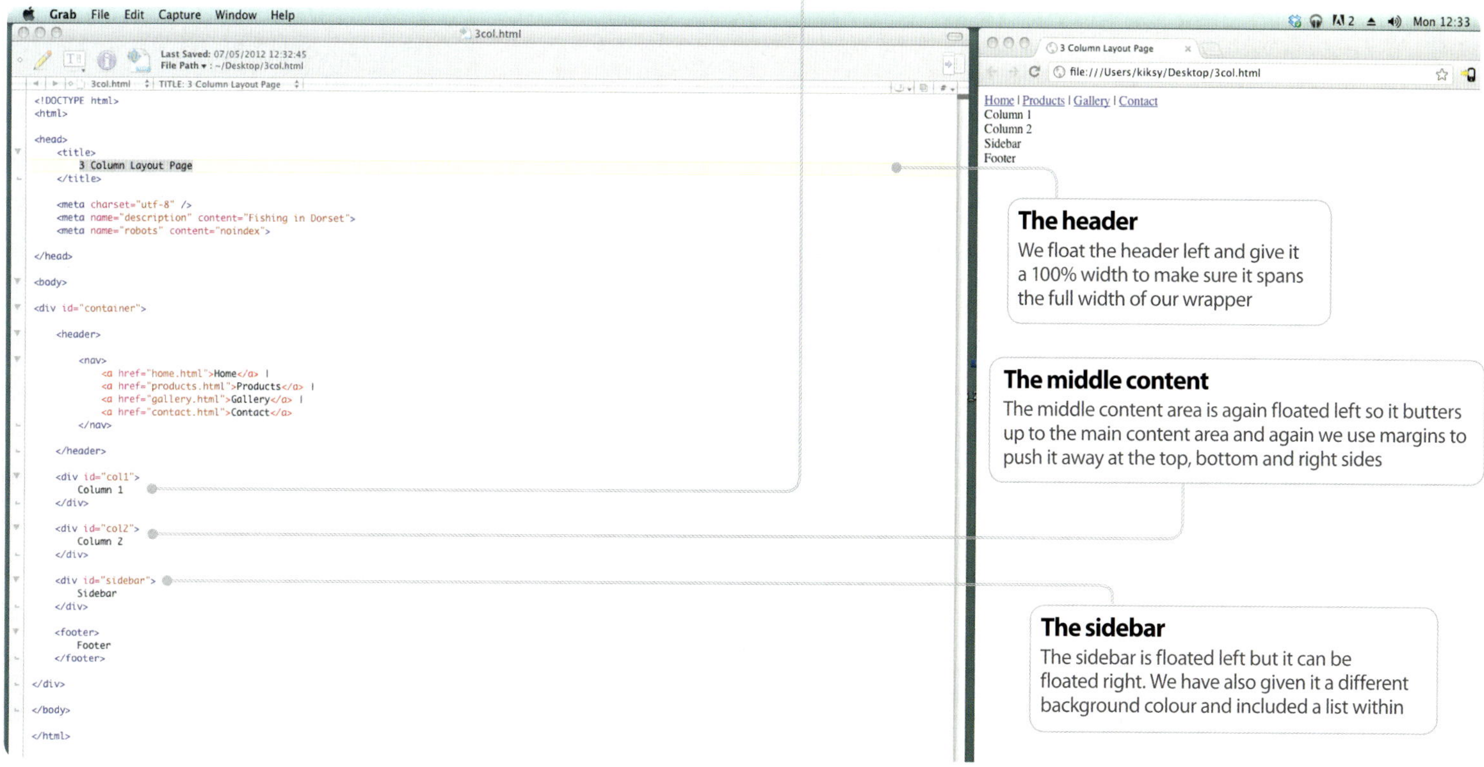

The header

We float the header left and give it a 100% width to make sure it spans the full width of our wrapper

The middle content

The middle content area is again floated left so it butters up to the main content area and again we use margins to push it away at the top, bottom and right sides

The sidebar

The sidebar is floated left but it can be floated right. We have also given it a different background colour and included a list within

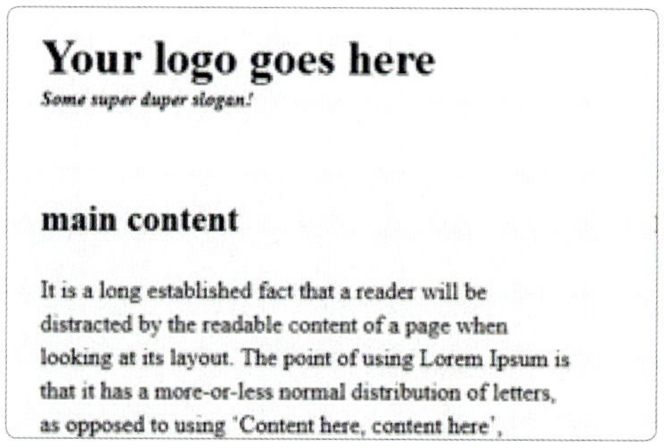

16 Styling the content

Now to finish off our page we need to style our inner content a little. So starting at the top, we are going to slightly style the slogan which is a part of our logo. Then we can style all the header tags (<h1>, <h2>, <h3>, <h4>) with some padding to push them out within its content area (parent element).

```
.slogan {
 font-style: italic;
 padding: 0 20px;
}
h1, h2, h3, h4 { padding: 20px 20px 0 20px;}
```

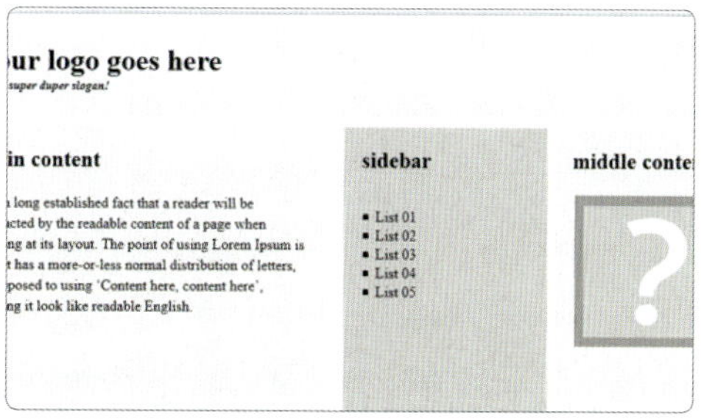

17 Moving the elements

If at a later date you decide to move your middle content to the left or move the main content to the right, this can easily be achieved by changing the float from either 'left' or 'right'. So let's replace the middle content with our sidebar by changing the float value from 'left' to 'right'.

```
#mid_content {
        float: right;
        background: #f0f0f0;
        margin: 10px 5px 10px 0;
        width: 300px;
        height: 630px;
}
```

18 Right-sided columns

Now let's say we need to columns the same size as our sidebar that sit side by side. So to achieve this we only need to change the width of the '#sidebar' and '#mid_content' and '#main_content' rules. So the '#sidebar' and '#mid_content' width can be changed to 250px and the '#main_content' to 420px.

Create a header

Learn how to create a clean, simple and effective header for your website

Having clean and clear header for your website can be the difference between a successful and user-friendly experience and a cluttered and unorganised website that no one will want to visit again! You don't want a first-time user coming to your site and not know how your navigation works, or your company branding (logo) hidden under a load of over-useless graphics or text – it doesn't even really matter how effective the rest of your layout is.

Yes, this sort of thing has been known to happen (more often that web designers would like to admit!) and this is why so many designers are turning to a relatively new role called user experience or 'UX'. So in this tutorial we will take a look at how we can create a simple, clean and useful header for your site.

"You don't want a user coming to your site not knowing how your navigation works"

LOGO POSITIONING

One of the most important things to remember is your logo. It is considered best practice to position your logo to the left and make it link to your homepage (index.html). If it's something you consider to be common practice, then not putting it there would frustrate the user. So when you design and develop your header, you first need to realise what the user would want or would expect to be there. It's also a good way of adding in more important information such as phone numbers or email addresses. The choice is yours, but be mindful of not making the header look cluttered. Check out page 168 for advice on how to create a logo in Photoshop.

How to make a header

Here are the most important things to consider when creating a header for your web page

The hover state
The hover state is nicely styled and can be easily changed whenever needed just by changing both the background colour or font colour

Separators
Adding a separator to our navigation links doesn't need to be pure CSS as we did, but it is handy using the 'border' property

The logo
The logo can be either a graphic or just text. You will also notice we have used the same font for both the logo and navigation

The background
Creating a textured background will always help stand your web page out from the crowd – gone are the days of white backgrounds with nothing but text and images

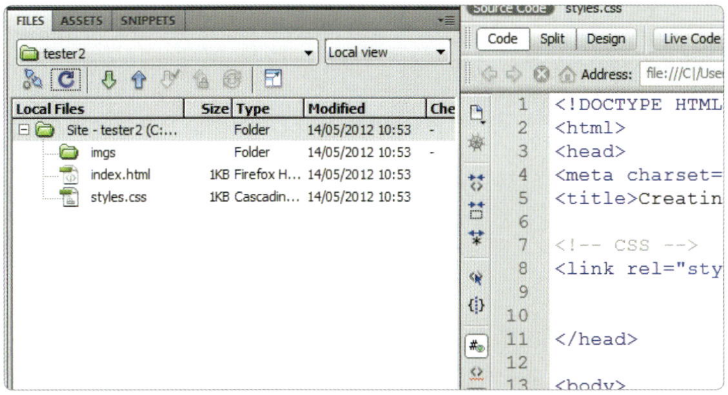

01 Getting started

First thing we need to do is create new 'index.html' and 'styles.css' files and place them in the same location. Because we will be using images for our header, let's also create an empty folder called 'imgs'. Store the logo from the disc within this 'imgs' folder and also the textured background file.

```
<!DOCTYPE HTML>
<html>
<head>
<meta charset="utf-8">
<title>Creating a header</title>

<!-- CSS -->
<link rel="stylesheet" href="styles.css">


</head>

<body>
```

02 Linking the CSS

Now we have our index.html and styles.css files, we'll need to link them up within the '<head>'</head>' tags of our HTML. Open index.html in your editor and just underneath the '<title>' tags place your link to your CSS. It's good practice to leave a HTML comment to denote where the CSS links will go.

```
<!DOCTYPE HTML>
<html>
<head>
<meta charset="utf-8">
<title>Creating a header</title>

<!-- CSS -->
<link rel="stylesheet" href="styles.css">
</head>

<body>

<div id="wrapper">


</div><!-- END wrapper -->
```

03 Setting the wrapper

Still in index.html, let's add in a 'wrapper' div to centre all our content on the screen. We've used an ID (<div id=") because this is going to be a main part of the page's structure and will only be used only once throughout. If it was going to be used multiple times, then we'd use a class (<div class").

```
<html>
<head>
<meta charset="utf-8">
<title>Creating a header</title>

<!-- CSS -->
<link rel="stylesheet" href="styles.css">
</head>

<body>

<div id="wrapper">

    <div id="header">

    </div><!-- END header -->
```

04 Header

Now let's add in our header section now. So within the 'wrapper' div, create another div ID called 'header'. You will also notice we used HTML comments to mark the 'END' of our divs. That way if our mark-up (HTML) gets too messy, we will know what end div (</div>) belongs to what.

```

<!-- CSS -->
<link rel="stylesheet" href="styles.css">

</head>

<body>

<div id="wrapper">

    <div id="header">

    <a href="index.html"><div id="logo"></div></a>


    </div><!-- END header -->
```

05 Adding the logo

Now let's place our logo within the header section; you can use your own or grab ours off the disc. We are going to use an ID again and call it 'logo'. Then we will wrap it within an anchor tag and link it to our page by adding in the index page within '<a href="index.html">'

```
<div id="wrapper">

    <div id="header">

    <a href="index.html"><div id="logo"></div></a>

        <ul class="navigation">

          <li><a href="">home</a></li>
          <li><a href="">about</a></li>
          <li><a href="">blog</a></li>
          <li><a href="">portfolio</a></li>
          <li><a href="">services</a></li>
          <li><a href="">contact</a></li>

        </ul>
```

06 Navigation list

In this step we are going to add in the navigation. What we will use here is a standard unordered list and each list item (<li>) will have a link to each page using the '<a href="' attribute. Then we will give our unordered list a class name of 'navigation'.

```
            <li><a href="">services</a></li>
            <li><a href="">contact</a></li>

          </ul>

      </div><!-- END header -->

      <div id="main_content">

       <h2>Hi, Welcome to my website</h2>

        <p>It is a long established fact that a reader wil
   at its layout. The point of using Lorem Ipsum is that
 opposed to using 'Content here, content here', making i

      </div><!-- END main content -->
```

07 Main content

We will now finish off our HTML markup with some content underneath our header. Just underneath our closing header div '</div>', let's add in a div ID of 'main_content' and add in a welcome title using header tags '<h2>' and then some dummy text using '<p>' tags.

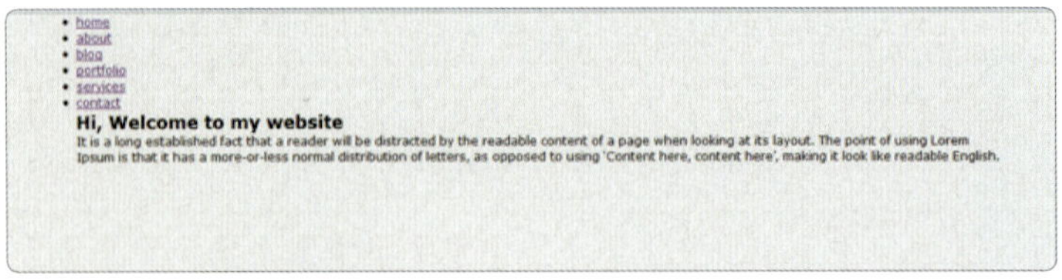

09 The wrapper

Now we are going to centre our header and content using the 'wrapper' div. What we are doing here is making sure we have no margin at the top or bottom and automatically find the difference on the left and right that is in relation to our fixed width – which we set to 960px. 960 pixels is mostly used because it fits nicely within the lowest common denominator of screen resolutions (1080 x 760)

```
#wrapper {
        margin: 0 auto;
        width: 960px;
}
```

11 The logo

Adding the logo is going to be very simple. All we are going to do is locate our logo that we have inside our 'imgs' folder and then make sure it doesn't repeat. Then position it on the left by floating it left and then specify its height and width. A thing to remember here is that if you don't specify its dimensions you will not see it on the webpage.

```
#logo {
  background: url('imgs/sc_logo.png') no-repeat;
  float: left;
  width: 200px;
  height: 200px;
}
```

08 The CSS

Now open up your 'styles.css' file and at the top put in our simple reset. The reset does exactly that – resets every element to zero, which will clear all the default styles that most browsers put on. Then, using the body tag we can give our page a textured background using an image and leaving it to repeat across the page. And then we set the 'font-family' and 'size'.

```
* {
 padding: 0;
 margin: 0;
}

body {
 background: url('imgs/bg.jpg');
 font-family: Verdana, Geneva, sans-serif;
 font-size: 12px;
}
```

10 The header

Now for our header we are going to float it left and give it a 100% width so it spans the full width of our wrapper div, then give it a height of 250px. Let's also add in a red border so we can see the header more clearly and get a better visual idea of where we need our logo and navigation, which we will add in over the next few steps – then once happy we will remove it.

```
#header {
        float: left;
        width: 100%;
        height: 250px;
    border: 1px solid #f00;
}
```

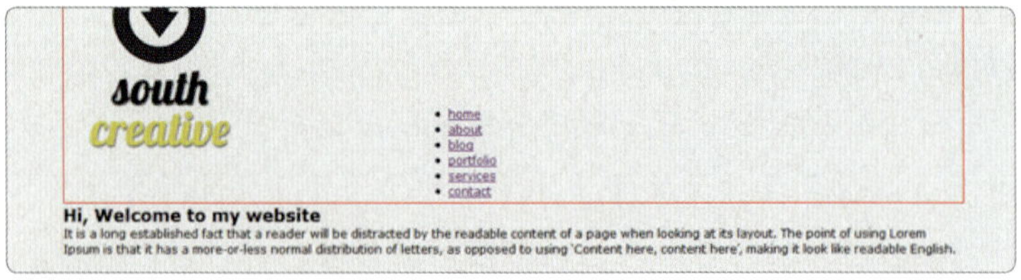

12 The navigation

Now let's style our navigation. We do this by floating the whole element right then positioning it 150px down and then pulling it over to the right using a negative margin of '-50px'. Never be worried about using negative margins as they work very well. Then we give the navigation a width of 600px.

```
.navigation {
        float: right;
        margin: 150px -50px 0 0;
        width: 600px;
}
```

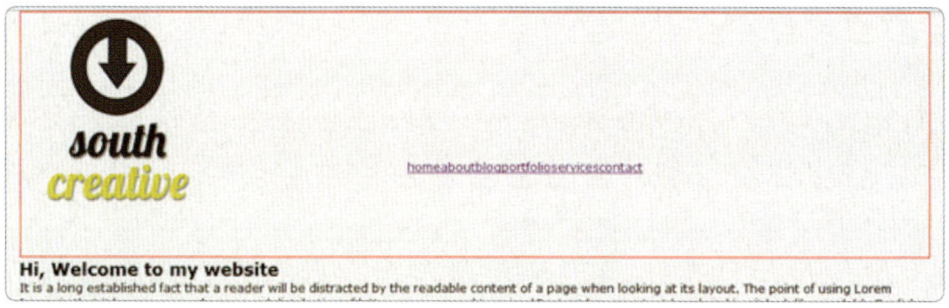

13 Navigation buttons

At the moment our navigation looks nothing like a horizontal navigation bar, more like a basic list of links. So let's make it go horizontal by floating each '<li>' item left, which will push them all horizontal. Then we can take away the default item bullets by specifying the 'list-style' being none.

```
.navigation li {
        float: left;
        list-style: none;
}
```

15 The content

Now let's style our page content, which helps to keep our page looking like a website. While we're here let's get sneaky and add some CSS3 properties to make the background have rounded corners by using 'border-radius: 6px'. We then style the paragraphs give it some padding to both the paragraph text and header tags.

```
#main_content {
        float: left;
        width: 900px;
        height: 400px;
        background: #fff;
        border-radius: 6px;
}
        #main_content p, h2 {
                line-height: 22px;
                margin-top: 10px;
                padding: 20px;
        }
```

17 Apply the Google font

Now the next step here is to click the 'use' grey button located at the very bottom right and scroll down the page slightly. What we have first is the 'link' tag line that will link straight to the Google font servers and will always be available. That way you can guarantee everyone will be able to see your chosen font. So click and drag over the link and press Ctrl/Cmd+C to copy it to your clipboard. Then paste it into your 'index.html' file just underneath our other CSS link within the '<head>' tag.

```
<!-- CSS -->
<link rel="stylesheet" href="styles.css">
<link href='http://fonts.googleapis.com/css?family=Lobster' rel='stylesheet'
type='text/css'>

</head>
```

14 Navigation anchors

Now we need to give each anchor tag some padding. Take off the underline by specifying the text-decoration as 'none' and then create a separator using 'border-right'. We can remove also the red border around the 'header'. Then we can add in a hover state that will change the background and text colour.

```
.navigation li a {
        float: left;
        color: #333;
        padding: 6px 20px;
        text-decoration: none;
        border-right: 1px solid #333;
        font-size: 16px;
}

.navigation li a:hover {

        background-color: #333;
        color: #fff;
}
```

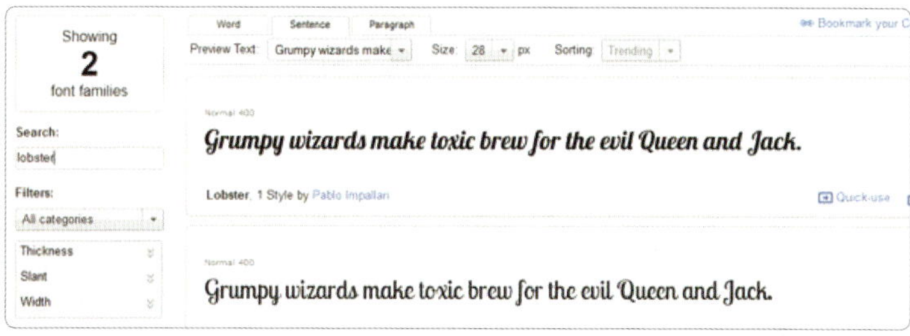

16 Find Google Fonts

Looking at our navigation, we can clearly see that it doesn't look very attractive. So let's spruce it up somewhat by heading over to Google Fonts **www.google.com/webfonts** and type in 'lobster' within the search field and you should see at least two choices of fonts. The one we want is the top style. Then click the blue 'add to collection' button to the right and now it ready to use.

18 Google font-family

Now let's Ctrl/Cmd+C to copy the 'font-family' property and then open up the 'styles.css' file and locate the '.navigation li a' rule (a CSS rule is everything within the curly brackets) and paste the new 'font-family' underneath the 'font-size' property.

```
.navigation li a {

        float: left;
        color: #333;
        padding: 6px 20px;
        text-decoration: none;
        border-right: 1px solid #333;
        font-size: 16px;
        font-family: 'Lobster', cursive;
}
```

Create a sidebar

Learn how to create a clean navigation system for your website

A sidebar is without doubt the area that is most often created by web designers, because it's the most needed. It can hold all sorts of content: things such as extra navigation links, a search field and perhaps some small thumbnail images that relate to your website – it can be anything.

So in this tutorial we're going to create a simple page layout that has a functional navigation and a nice and simple sidebar that includes some content within. We're going to include within the sidebar a list of links for that extra navigation we mentioned and a search bar above and also some thumbnail images at the bottom to act as though we have a Flickr section – very useful for any photography-based sites. So open up your favourite text editor and let's get started.

"A sidebar can hold all sorts of content: extra navigation links, a search field, even some small images"

STICK TO THE RIGHT

If you spend some time surfing the internet in some detail, the chances are that you won't see too many websites with the sidebar fixed over to the left side – it is far more likely to be over to the right. Even though it is relatively easy to swap it over, you wouldn't be doing anyone any favours if you thought you would be clever and original by plonking it on the left – internet users are now accustomed to seeing this section on the right-hand side of their screens. If you're struggling to add content in the sidebar, then you can add a short summary about you or your business or perhaps even a small YouTube video about your site.

A perfect sidebar

Your sidebar needs to be clean and crisp to keep your visitors

The width
A thin-looking sidebar wouldn't help anyone unless you have no intention of anything but small thumbnail images!

The search field
The sidebar is a great place to put your search field – and you will see this on most WordPress themes or other blogging platforms

Navigation
Having a list of links for an extra navigation will allow you to add in links that you may not have had the room to fit in the main navigation menu

The thumbnails
We added this feature because you see it all the time. People who have a blog can use a plugin that allows them to feature their Flickr photos

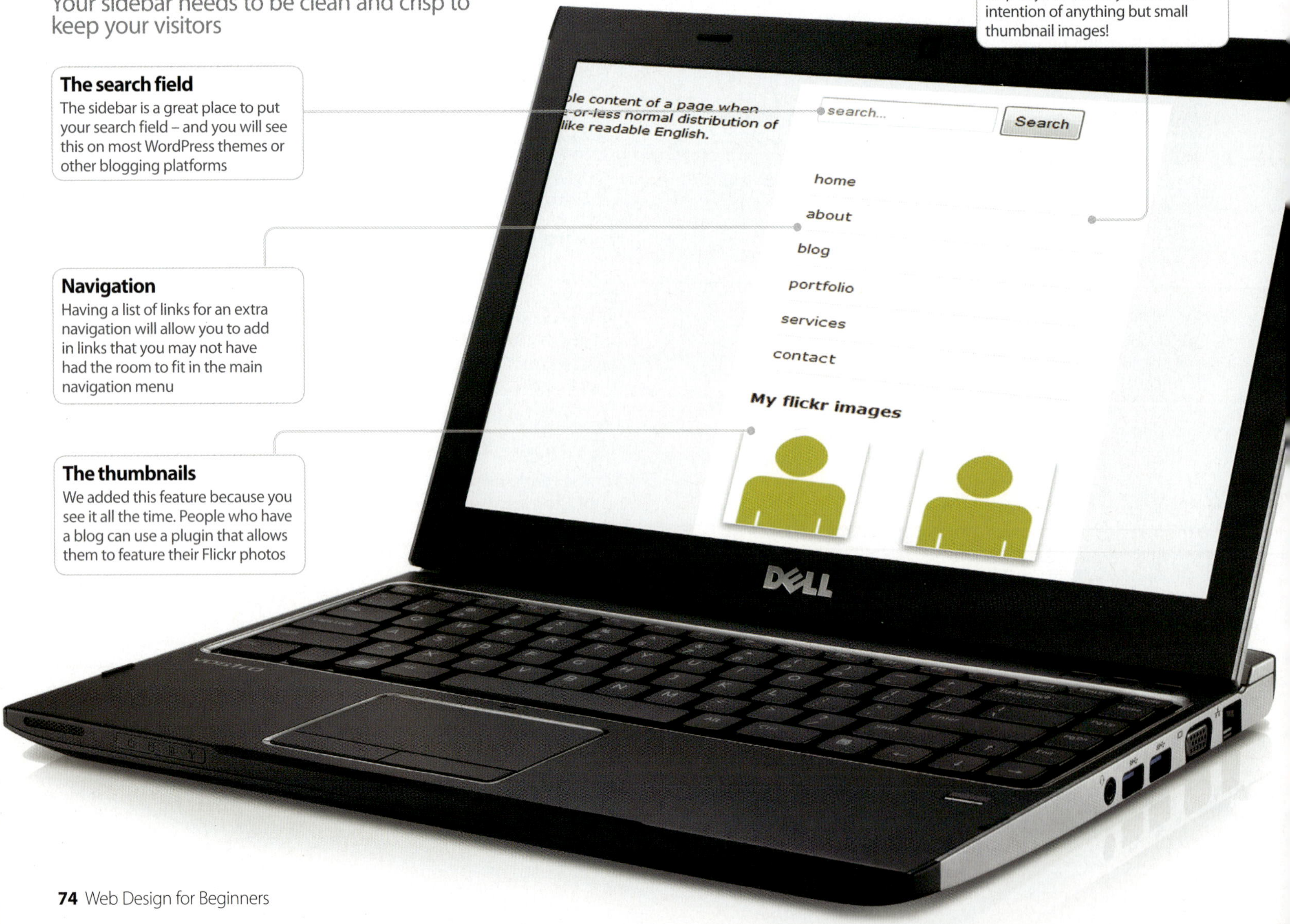

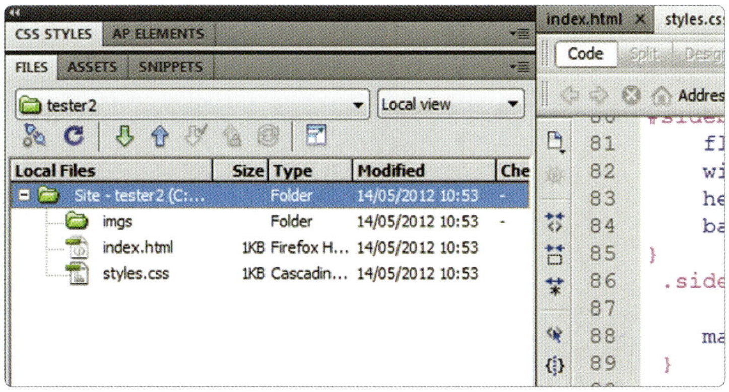

01 Getting started

First thing we need to do is create a new 'index.html' and 'styles.css' files and place them in the same location (directory). And because we will be using images for our sidebar, let's also create an empty folder called 'imgs'. Feel free to carry on with what we created last time.

02 CSS and wrapper

If you open up the index.html file and just underneath the '<title>' tags, place your link to your CSS. Then we want to add in a wrapper div that will help us contain everything on the page and allow us to centre it all using CSS.

03 The header

Next we want to add in a header for our page and we do this by adding a div with an ID of 'header'. Then within the header we are going to put our type-based logo that is wrapped within an anchor tag that links back to the home page (index.html)

04 Navigation

In this step we are going to add in the navigation. What we will use here is a standard unordered list and each list item (<li>) will have a link to each page using the '<a href="' attribute. Then we will give our unordered list a class name of 'navigation'.

05 Sidebar and search

Let's now add in our sidebar section. All we do here is create a div ID with the name of 'sidebar' just underneath the closing header div '</div>'. Then, using the code above, within our sidebar section let's add in a search field that will just sit there and look pretty.

06 Sidebar navigation

Now what we need to do is now is add in what will be our sidebar navigation. This is the exactly the same code as our top main navigation so it's just a case of copying and pasting that into the sidebar. But we will need to give it a different class name, which can be 'sidebar_list'.

```
    </form>

    <ul class="sidebar_list">
      <li><a href="">home</a></li>
      <li><a href="">about</a></li>
      <li><a href="">blog</a></li>
      <li><a href="">portfolio</a></li>
      <li><a href="">services</a></li>
      <li><a href="">contact</a></li>
    </ul>

  <h3>My flickr images</h3>

  <img src="imgs/thumbnail.jpg" height="100" width="100" class="thumb">
  <img src="imgs/thumbnail.jpg" height="100" width="100" class="thumb">

 </div><!-- END sidebar -->



</div><!-- END wrapper -->
```

07 Sidebar images

We'll now add some images to sit below our navigation list. We have the same image here for both, set to the size of 100x100px. We've given them a class name of 'thumb' so we can use CSS to position them better without relying on the 'img' tag. Also we've given this section a title with the '<h3>' tag.

```
   <img src="imgs/thumbnail.jpg" height="100" width="100" class="thumb"
   <img src="imgs/thumbnail.jpg" height="100" width="100" class="thumb"

  </div><!-- END sidebar -->

  <div id="main_content">

   <h2>Hi, Welcome to my website</h2>

    <p>It is a long established fact that a reader will be distracted b
       the readable content of a page when looking at its layout. The p
       of using Lorem Ipsum is that it has a more-or-less normal distri
       of letters, as opposed to using 'Content here, content here', ma
       look like readable English.
    </p>

  </div><!-- END main content -->

</div><!-- END wrapper -->
```

08 The main content

To finish off our HTML markup, we will add in a main content section. Again let's use an ID and name it 'main_content'. Then within the 'main_content' section we can add in a 'welcome' title accompanied by some dummy text wrapped in a paragraph tag '<p>'.

09 The CSS

Open up your 'styles.css' file and at the top add in the universal selector that will allow you to reset every element(<p>, <h1>, div, etc) to zero margin and padding. Then using the 'body' tag we can set the background colour to an off white '#f1f1f1' and set our default font style and size.

```
* {
 padding: 0;
 margin: 0;
}

body {
  background: #f1f1f1;
  font-family: Verdana, Geneva, sans-serif;
  font-size: 12px;
}
```

10 The wrapper

So with our wrapper acting as a container for all our page content, we can center everything using a fixed width and margin. We're specifying 0 pixels on top and bottom, with auto margins on the left and right. This is an easy and most often the best way of centring your page on your screen.

```
#wrapper {
        margin: 0 auto;
        width: 960px;
}
```

11 The header & logo

We're styling our header by giving it a 100% width with a height of 250px. Adding the logo is also going to be very simple as we'll only be using text for now. We've given ours a drop shadow using the 'text-shadow' property.

```
#header {
        float: left;
        width: 100%;
        height: 250px;
}
#logo h1{
        font-size: 35px;
        float: left;
        margin-top: 130px;
        color: #dac91a;
        text-shadow: 1px 1px 3px #333;
}
```

12 The navigation

Now let's style our navigation. We can do this by floating the whole element right, positioning it 150px down and then pulling it over to the right using a negative margin of '-50px'. Then we give the navigation a width of 600px. To bump everything to a horizontal position we float all the '<li>' left, then create our button separator by adding a 'border-right' to the 'navigation li a' selector.

```
.navigation {
        float: right;
        margin: 150px -50px 0 0;
        width: 600px;
}
.navigation li {
        float: left;
        list-style: none;
}
.navigation li a {
                float: left;
        color: #333;
        padding: 6px 20px;
        text-decoration: none;
        border-right: 1px solid #333;
        font-size: 16px;
}
```

13 Navigation hover state

At the moment our navigation looks nothing like a functional navigation menu and it still needs a couple of things added. The hover state will be the first thing we are going to add here, and then in the next step we will shoot over to Google fonts to download the 'lobster' font and use that.

```
.navigation li a:hover {

        background-color: #333;
        color: #fff;
}
```

15 The sidebar

Now in this step we are going to style our sidebar. So first we are going to float the sidebar over to the right and set a fixed height and width. Then we can style the '<h3>' header tag and just push that off the left side using padding. Then give the text a dark grey colour of '#333'.

```
#sidebar {
        float: right;
        width: 300px;
        height: 100%;
        background: #fff;
}

#sidebar h3 {
        padding-left: 20px;
        color: #333;
}
```

17 The search field

In this step let's style our search field. First of all we push it down slightly and then make sure anything underneath it is 50px away. Then we slightly push it away from the left edge using 20px. And lastly we give the input field some padding to make it a bit more attractive.

```
#search_form {

        margin: 10px 0 50px 20px;
}

        #search_form input{

                padding: 5px;
}
```

14 Google fonts

Now let's go to **google.com/webfonts** and search for 'lobster'. Add it to your collection and click 'use'. Then add the '<link=' code to the index.html file just underneath your main CSS link. Then locate the '.navigation li a' rule and add in the 'font-family' property. Do the same for your '#logo' rule.

```
<!-- CSS -->
<link rel="stylesheet" href="styles.css">
<link href='http://fonts.googleapis.com/css?family=Lobster' rel='stylesheet'
 type='text/css'>

.navigation li a {
        float: left;
        color: #333;
        padding: 6px 20px;
        text-decoration: none;
        border-right: 1px solid #333;
        font-size: 16px;
        font-family: 'Lobster', cursive;
}
```

16 Sidebar list

Now we are going to style the sidebar navigation list. We are going to push it away from the edges by using a 20px margin all round. Then we add in a nice subtle dotted line using the 'border-bottom' property.

```
.sidebar_list {
        margin: 20px;
}

.sidebar_list li {
        list-style: none;
        margin: 10px;
        padding-bottom: 10px;
        border-bottom: 1px dotted #ddd;
}

 .sidebar_list li a{
        text-decoration: none;
        color: #333;
        font-size: 13px;
}
```

18 Finishing off

To finish, we need to style our thumbnail images. So we float them left so they bump up to each other and then space them out by using margin.

```
.thumb {
        float: left;
        margin: 22px;
        border: 1px solid #fff;
        box-shadow: 0px 4px 6px #999;
}
```

Add content to the main area

How we can add content to the main content area of your website

Adding content to your website is either done dynamically using a content management system (CMS) or by hand. Either way, you are going to have to learn how it's styled and what options you have. For instance, will you have just text or text with images? How about a video that's either embedded using YouTube's, or your own flash or HTML5 player?

Of course your choices should be dependent on what niche your website caters for and thus knowing who will be visiting your website. So in this tutorial, we will add a few elements of content where one will include a video (which you can grab whatever video you want, you don't have to use our one) and also some text and an image. So open up the index.html and styles.css files within your text editor and let's get cracking!

> "Your content choices should be dependent on what niche your website caters for"

THE RIGHT STUFF

Adding the right amount of content to any website is vital and can mean the difference of having a successful, clean website to a cluttered and confusing one. The layout needn't be the main concern here as you can have multiple columns throughout. But it's the white space and the way that your sections are aligned that will give your web page a better and more readable layout. We also used horizontal rules to add separators to section out our content even further. But there is no real need to use a horizontal rule; we can just as easily use an image here or in some cases a bottom border. Just remember that if there's no content, you won't get many visitors.

Content is king

Let's check out the most important parts of adding content to your web page

The top section

It's a good idea to add some text about your website so users can see what you are all about before going any further

The width

You will need to think about the width of your main content area(s) and plan ahead accordingly

The middle section

We have added a video from YouTube here, but of course this could just as easily be a image of your company or yourself!

The bottom section

The bottom section is again used as a text-based section that describes the middle section video

01 Getting started

Open the Sidebar index.html file on the CD or carry on from last time and you will see we have most of the template done. We have a logo, a navigation and the sidebar to the right. On the left we have our content area.

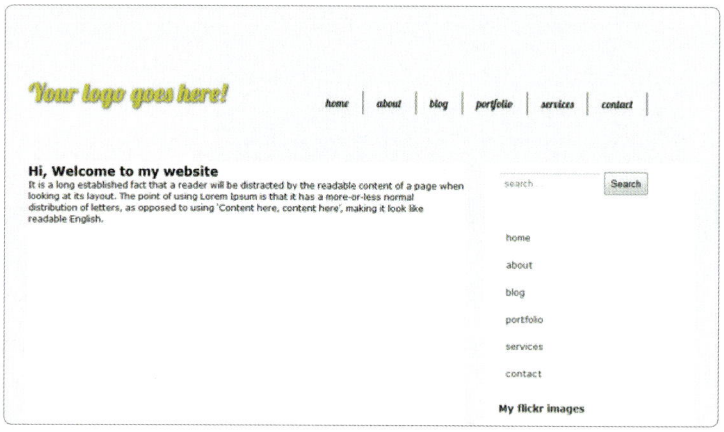

03 Welcome text

Now we need to add some 'welcome' text. This is normally a good way of letting the user know what your website is all about from the off. Here we will just wrap about three or four sentences within some '<p>' tags.

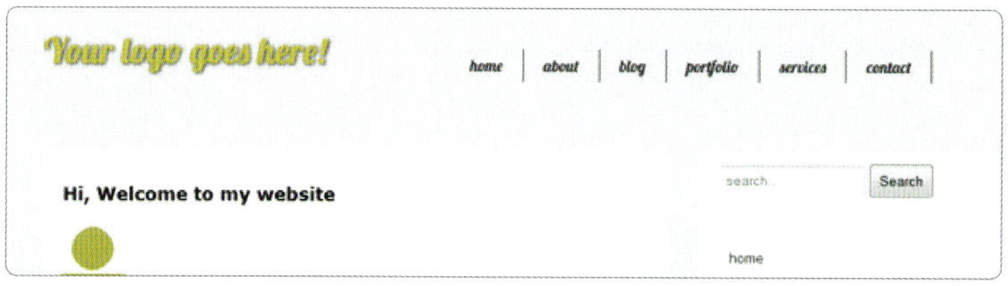

05 Styling our content

Let's open up our 'styles.css' file. We can point to the '#main_content' div and then hock onto the 'p' tag. We can then use multiple selectors here and use the same style properties and values for the<h2> tag.

```
#main_content p, h2 {
        line-height: 22px;
        margin-top: 10px;
        padding: 20px;
        width: 350px;
 }
```

02 Main content header

Now in this step we are going to give our main content area a title that will welcome everyone to the website. We do this very easily by adding in a '<h2>' tag and a nice message within. What we will do is use CSS later to see what we can do to make this look a little nicer.

```
<h2>Hi, Welcome to my website</h2>
```

04 Adding an image

Now we can add in an image within our welcome text. The idea here is to have a small thumbnail image of something that relates to the website. So place your image tag '<img src=' above the welcome text just sitting underneath the header. Then we will use CSS later to float it to the right.

```
<img src="imgs/thumbnail.jpg" height="100" width="100" class="main_
thumb">
```

06 Content image

Now let's float the image over to the right and add some styles to it. We are going to use the same CSS as we did on the sidebar thumbnails. Then we're going to make sure we have enough white space around the image.

```
.main_thumb {
        float: right;
        margin: 40px;
        border: 1px solid #fff;
        box-shadow: 0px 4px 6px #999;
}
```

07 Video

Next we want to add the video to our main content area. Now we can get really technical and use an HTML5 or flash player here, but to keep things really simple, we can shoot over to youtube.com and copy and paste the embed code within our 'index.html' page. Then we want to be able to shift this video about using CSS, so it would make sense to wrap a div around it with an ID of 'video'. For more on this process, check out page 186.

```
<div id="video">
<iframe width="420" height="315" src="http://www.youtube.com/embed/
kNn44gHqanM" frameborder="0" allowfullscreen></iframe>
</div>
```

09 Positioning the video

All we are going to do here is position the video using CSS. Now it makes sense to float the video left. Then we are going to use margin to push it away from the edges and anything that may be surrounding the video will now have a generous amount of white space. Then let's add a black 5px border to finish off our video.

```
#video {
        float: left;
        margin: 20px;
        border: 5px solid #000;
}
```

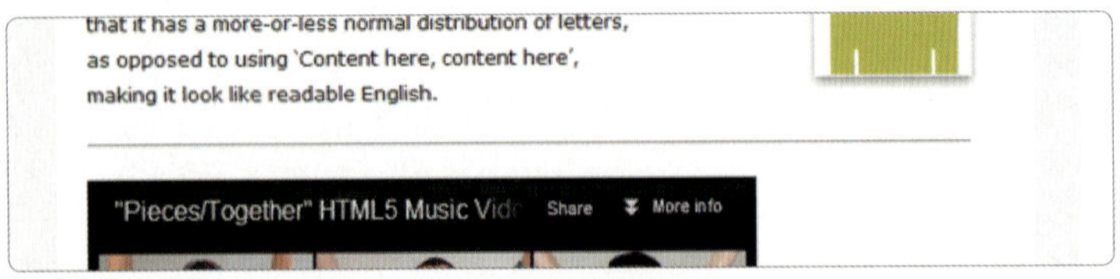

11 Styling the horizontal rule

Styling the horizontal rule '<hr>' is going to be a very simple task, but it can leave you scratching your head at times. For instance, if you want to increase its height, you can't just call 'height: 10px' – we have to instead call upon its 'border' property like 'border: 5px solid #ddd'. But let's keep it simple and decrease its width, give it a grey colour and push it away from the left edge using 'margin-left'.

```
hr {
color: #ddd;
width: 570px;
margin-left: 20px;
}
```

08 The main content height

Now first thing you will notice is that the video is now hanging out at the bottom of our content area. This is because on our '#main_content' rule we specified a fixed height of '500px;' So all we need to do now is locate that rule within our 'styles.css' file and change it from 'height: 500px;' to 'height: 100%';

```
#main_content{
        float: left;
        height: 100%;
        width: 630px;
        background: #fff;
        border-radius: 6px;
        margin-bottom: 40px;
}
```

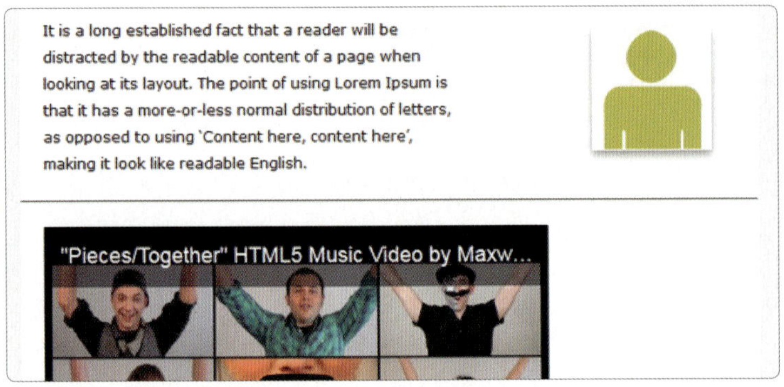

10 Horizontal rule

What we are going to do now is add a separator just above the video. This will be easily styled using CSS, so we won't need to depend on some graphic design software such as Photoshop or Fireworks. It's simply an HTML tag called a horizontal rule '<hr>' and we can add that just above the video div within our 'index.html' file.

```
<hr>
<div id="video">
```

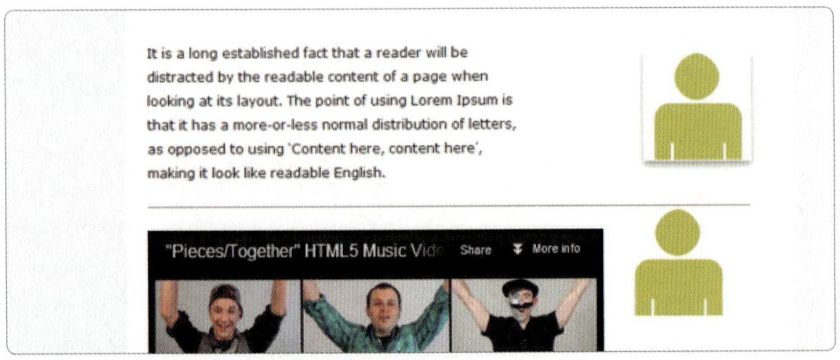

12 Adding more content

So now you should get the idea of how and what we can add for our main content. To get a real feel of it, let's add something underneath our video. What we can do then is add in another thumbnail image. So the best way would be to use the same image but give it a different class name of 'main_thumb2' and place this directly under our closing div of our 'video'.

```
<img src="imgs/thumbnail.jpg" height="100" width="100" class="main_
thumb2">
```

13 More text

So the next step would be to add in some more text that could be used for a summary/excerpt of our video. Underneath our new thumbnail image, place some more dummy text that is wrapped within paragraph tags '<p>' with a class name of 'vid_excerpt' so we can style it using CSS.

```
<img src="imgs/thumbnail.jpg" height="100" width="100" class="main_
thumb2">
<p class="vid_excerpt">It is a long established fact that a reader will be
distracted by  the readable content of a page when looking at its layout. The
point of using Lorem Ipsum is that it has a more-or-less normal distribution
 of letters, as opposed to using 'Content here, content here', making it
look like readable English.
  </p>
```

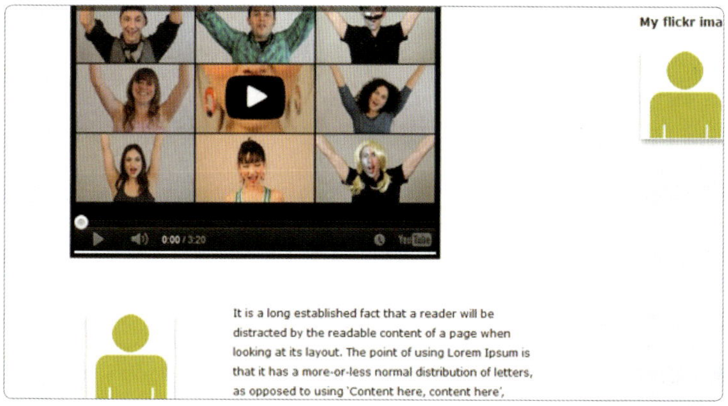

15 The excerpt

Now all we need to do is float our video excerpt to the right and give it some margins with 50px to the right, and 40px to the bottom.

```
.vid_excerpt {
  float: right;
  margin: 0 50px 40px 0;
  }
```

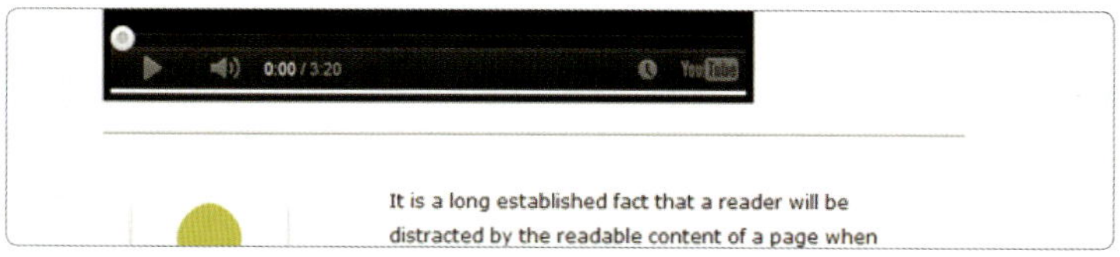

17 Adding another divider

Now what we want to do is add in another horizontal rule '<hr>' above the excerpt text so we can then section out the video properly. So just above the thumbnail image link, place in your '<hr>' tag. But before we view it in the browser, we need to go back into our CSS and float the 'hr' tags left. This will push the bottom one underneath the video.

```
hr {
color: #ddd;
width: 570px;
margin-left: 20px;
float: left;
}
```

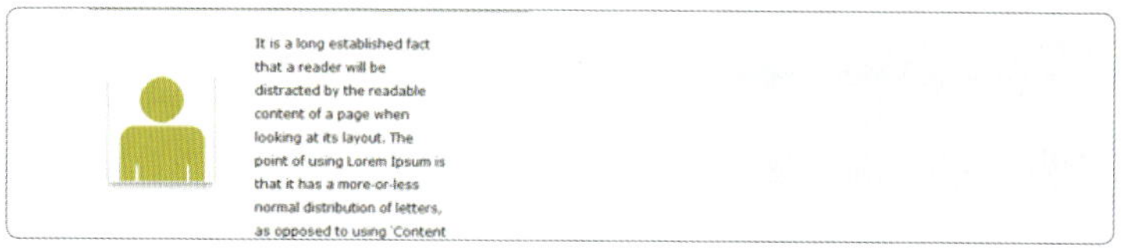

14 Styling the content

What we need to do now is style our new content using some simple CSS. So, open up your 'styles.css' file and position our thumbnail image first. We will float it left and then give it a 40px margin all around. Then to finish it off we can give it the same subtle drop shadow as the other thumbnail we used in the sidebar.

```
.main_thumb2 {
        float: left;
        margin: 40px;
        border: 1px solid #fff;
        box-shadow: 0px 4px 6px #999;
}
```

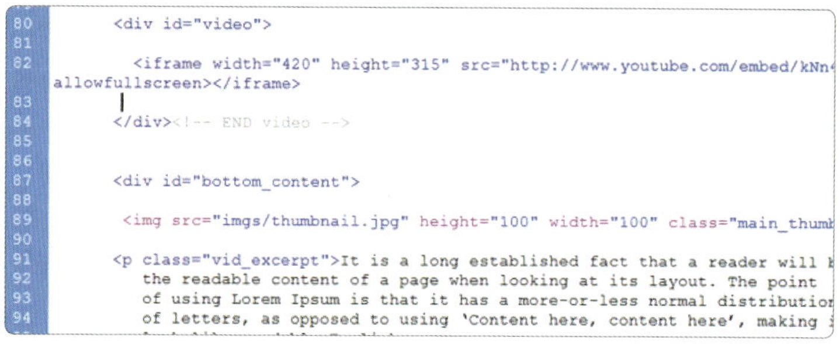

16 Bottom content

When looking at our HTML, it would make more sense to wrap our bottom thumbnail and excerpt content within its own div. That way we can have more control of this section if at all we need to position it further. So, create a div with an ID of 'bottom_content' and make sure you use an HTML comment to mark the ending div '</div><!-- END bottom content -->'

```
<div id="bottom_content">
</div><!-- END bottom content -->
```

18 Going further

As we said in the intro text to this tutorial, it's down to you as to what your content should include. Later in this book we explore adding maps, newsletters, image sliders and more!

Add content to your footer

Finish off your first site with a footer to be proud of

In the past, the humble footer was not much more than a slim strip of colour with nothing more interesting than the copyright text written within. But in many modern websites, we have seen a huge improvement in footer designs and the content held within them.

These days, they are a lot higher and contain all sorts of content which can include contact forms, newsletter sign-up fields, social media integration and much more. Ours for instance, in addition to a newsletter sign-up field and generic About Us text, features another set of links for navigation, so our readers don't have to scroll back to the top or to the sidebar if they want visit another page.

As crazy as it sounds (and this would have sounded incredibly crazy no more than a few years ago), the footer has really taken the modern web by storm and has now developed into an area that needs good planning – like all parts of your website, it is important to offer the right amount of content without confusing the user. So in this tutorial we will build a simple footer and include some useful content that you would most likely see in a modern layout.

> "The footer has taken the web by storm and has now developed into an area that needs good planning"

Dissecting the footer

The most important things to keep in consideration for a good footer

Navigation
Having a list of links for an extra navigation will allow your users to click through other pages without needing to scroll up

The newsletter field
We added this feature because it would make sense for people to learn more about your business/service. A contact form here is also a good idea

The about text
The about text is a great way of letting people know what you are about if and when they are viewing the content within your footer

SHORTHAND CSS

Over the course of this tutorial we have used a lot of shorthand CSS. The reason being is it's quicker to write and decreases your style sheets file size – even if it's only very small. The shorthand is used for margin and padding and there is a lot more you can do with it that we haven't covered. So let's take a margin declaration for an example. It works in a clockwise direction, so 'margin: 10px 20px 30px 40px' would mean 10 pixels top, 20 pixels right, 30 pixels bottom and 40 pixels left. So top, right, bottom, left. Then we can get even more technical by only using two values such as: 'margin: 20px 30px'. Now this means 20 pixels top and bottom, then 30 pixels right and left. And lastly if we just use one value such as: 'margin: 20px' would simply mean 20 pixels all around to whatever element (div) was specified.

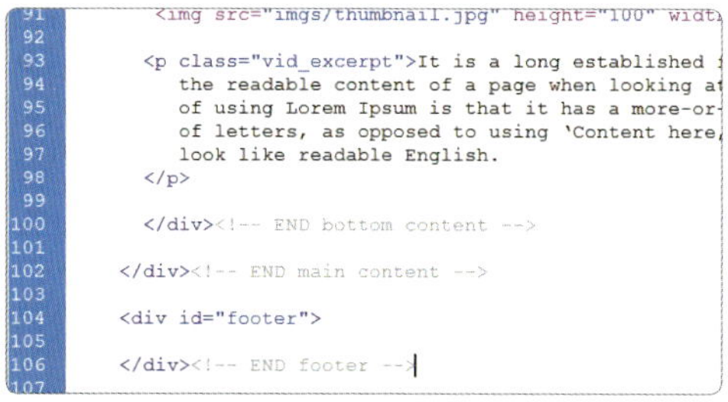

01 Getting started

Open up your 'index.html' file from the last project and scroll down to the very bottom of the document. The first we are going to do here is just underneath our closing 'main_content' div, add in a div with an ID of 'footer'.

```
<div id="footer">
 </div><!-- END footer -->
```

04 Newsletter sign up

Many websites would have either a contact form or newsletter sign up field within their footer. What we will do is keep it simple and add in a newsletter sign up field. We will give it an ID name of 'newsletter' and we will place this straight under the footer links. We can then position this later over to the right using CSS.

```
<form id="newsletter" action="" method="get">
<input id="search_term" type="text"
placeholder="newsletter sign up...." />
<input class="submit_button"
type="submit" value="sign up">
    </form>
```

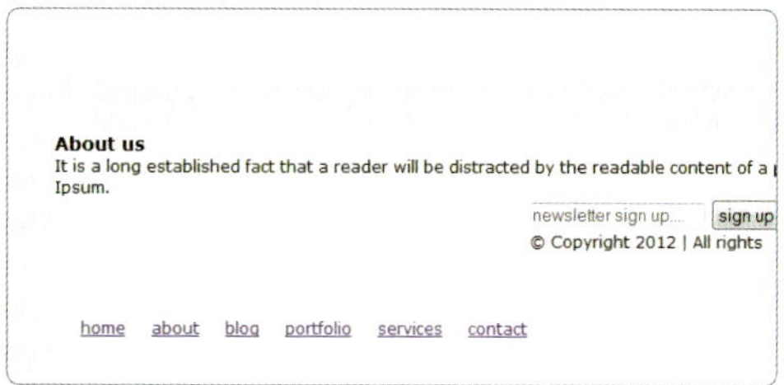

07 List items

Now style the list items'<li>'. Here we are removing the default bullet points and then floating all the items left, which will push each one up and next to each other giving us a horizontal alignment. Then using 'margin-left' we can create some space between each other.

```
.footer_links li {
  list-style: none;
  float: left;
  margin-left: 20px;
}
```

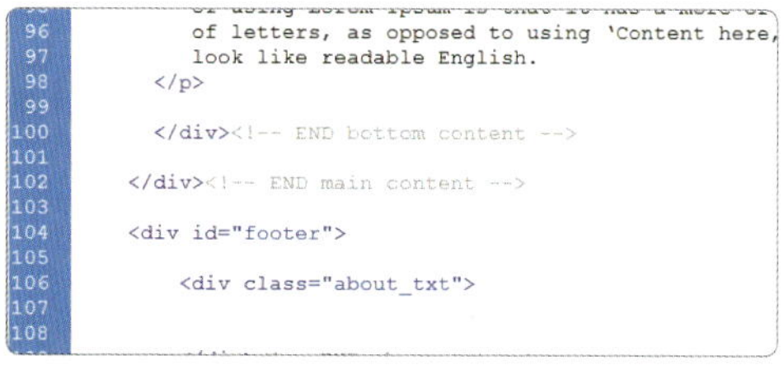

02 About us

In this step we are going to add some 'about us' text that will be positioned to the left of our footer. So first thing to do would be to create a div with a class name of 'about_txt' within our footer ID making sure we add on a HTML comment to the closing div. For content, we will start with a '<h4>' header tag that includes the words 'about us'. Then underneath that we will add in some dummy text that is wrapped within paragraph tags '<p>'

```
<div class="about_txt">
</div><!-- END about txt -->
```

05 Footer background

Now we have finished our HTML mark-up, but if we viewed it in the browser now it would look a bit of a mess! So let's open up the 'styles.css' file, scroll down to the very bottom and start adding some CSS for our footer. First thing we can do is clear the floats so it pops underneath everything above and give it some dimensions and a background colour of white.

```
#footer {
        clear: both;
        height: 200px;
        width: 100%;
        background: #fff;
        margin-bottom: 20px;
}
```

08 Finishing the navigation

Now we're going to finish off our footer navigation. What we need to do is remove the default underline and then give the text a light grey colour. Then for our hover state, let's just change the colour of the text to black '#000', giving us a subtle rollover effect.

```
.footer_links li a {
        text-decoration: none;
        color: #333;
}
        .footer_links li a:hover {
        color: #000;
        }
```

03 Footer links

It is always a good idea to place your site's navigation within the footer so the user doesn't need to scroll all the way up to the top to navigate your site. So let's use an un-ordered list and give it a class name of 'footer_links' and place it just underneath the about text.

```
<ul class="footer_links">
        <li><a href="">home</a></li>
        <li><a href="">about</a></li>
        <li><a href="">blog</a></li>
        <li><a href="">portfolio</a></li>
        <li><a href="">services</a></li>
        <li><a href="">contact</a></li>
</ul>
```

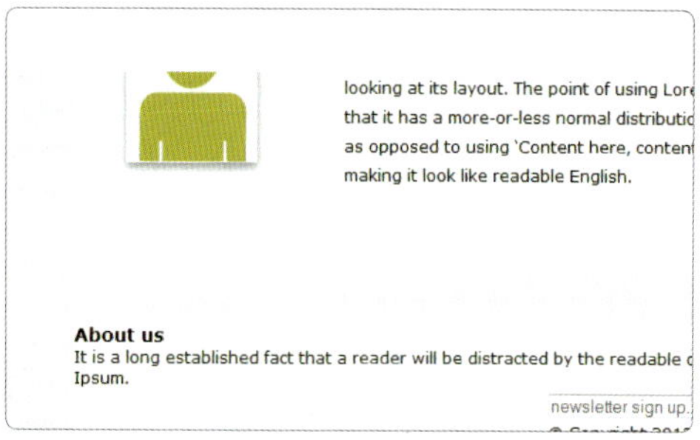

06 The links

Now in this step let's style our footer links so they look more like a horizontal navigation list. We are going to float it left and push it down using margin and give it 20px space at the bottom. Then let's give it a width of 370px.

```
.footer_links {
  float: left;
  margin: 90px 0 20px 0px;
  width: 370px;
}
```

09 About text

Styling the about text is going to be very simple. We first float it left and then give it a width of 250px. We then give it some padding to allow some white space all around. One thing to remember by using padding is it will make the box element ('div') 20 pixels bigger as the padding effects the inner element, not the outer element, and pushes it out.

```
.about_txt {
        float: left;
        width: 250px;
        padding: 20px;
}
```

Find and choose the right host

A decent host is vital to any website's success, so here's how to make sure you choose the right one for you

Choosing a web host should be a task that you spend a lot of time researching and thinking about, and in this tutorial we will give you some pointers to help you make the right decision. There are thousands of hosts that can potentially offer the service you need and many blind you with a multitude of features that you will likely never use, so it can quickly become a very confusing process. Some providers offer services that are specific to blogging platforms, such as WordPress, which can be useful for ensuring that your website remains stable as it grows. Other services host everything and offer very few customisation facilities.

Price is rarely an indicator of quality in the hosting business, as you can purchase great services for minimal monthly fees and have the ability to reach thousands of readers without having to worry about bandwidth. Every site is different and has different needs so before you do anything, take some time to note down your expected traffic and the amount of bandwidth you can expect if things go well.

"Price is rarely an indicator of quality in the hosting business, as you can purchase great services for minimal monthly fees"

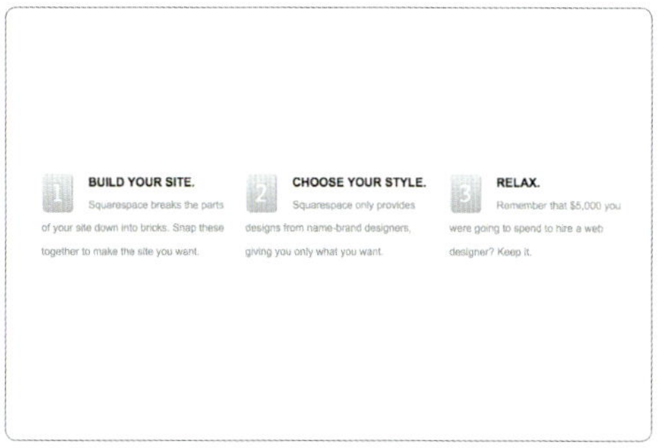

Open or closed?

You'll need to decide first if you require a closed or open solution. Some services offer closed platforms that let you manage only certain aspects of your site, whereas companies like 1&1 (pictured left) offer web space and let you control every aspect of your site via FTP and other means.

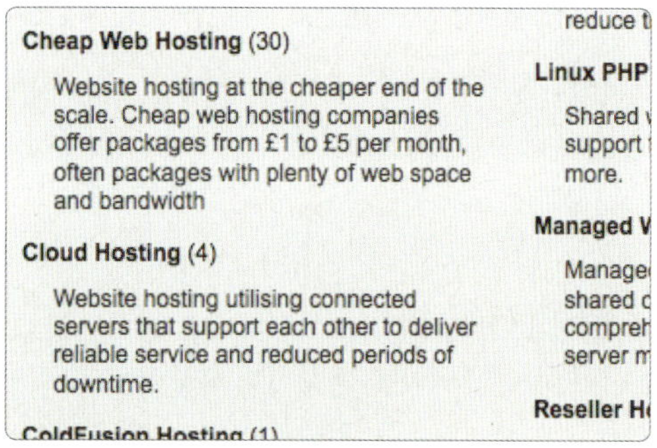

Filter your options

The next place to look will be web host comparison sites that detail many of the options available to you. Even if you don't find a host this way, they will help you understand what hosts can offer. Building up your general knowledge will help you make the right decision.

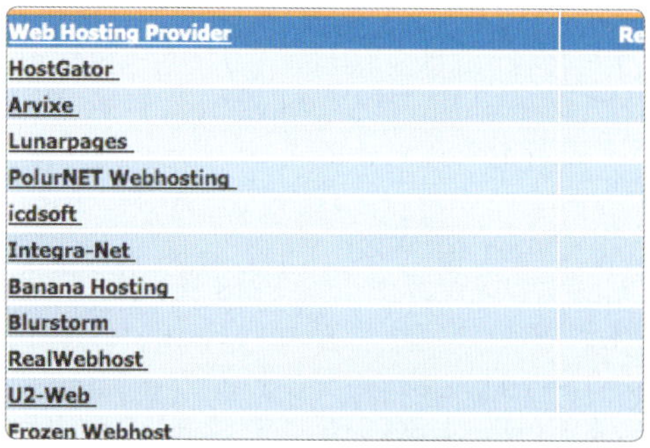

Check out user reviews

User reviews are useful to gauge how reliable a host is, but are not always conclusively correct. The more reviews you read, the more complete a picture you will get on how well a host treats its customers. There are some good and bad hosts out there so take the time to read those reviews.

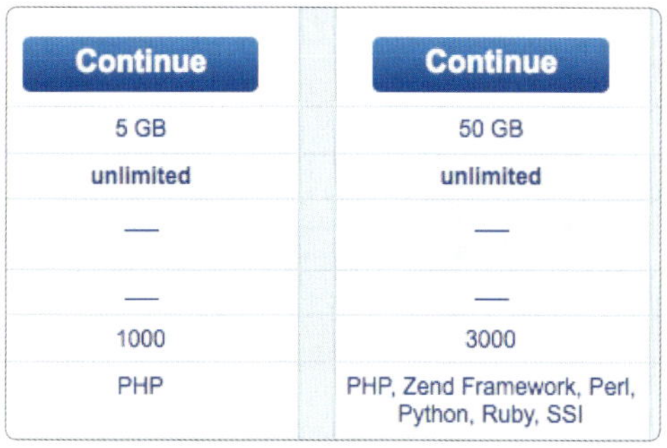

Consider growth

Think about how your site may grow. You will want a host that lets you start small, but offers the ability to upgrade to a more expensive account later on. Moving hosts is a long and hard process, so try to go for one that offers you the ability to change tariffs when you need to.

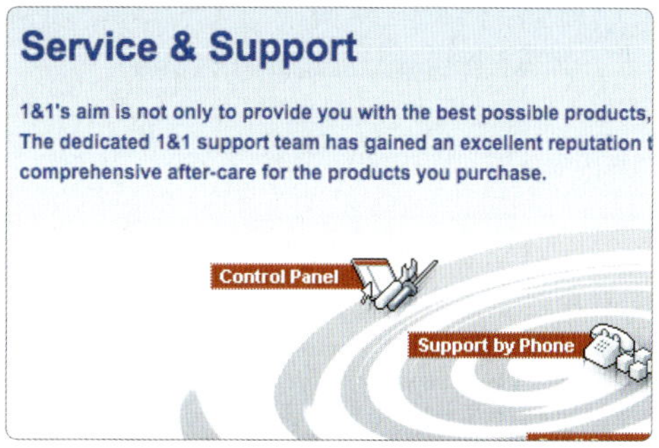

Support is vital

We recommend choosing a host that offers telephone support. Some hosts do offer excellent email support, but for reassurance you should expect to be able to call someone if problems occur. This is no guarantee of good service, but offers a glimpse of the efforts a company makes.

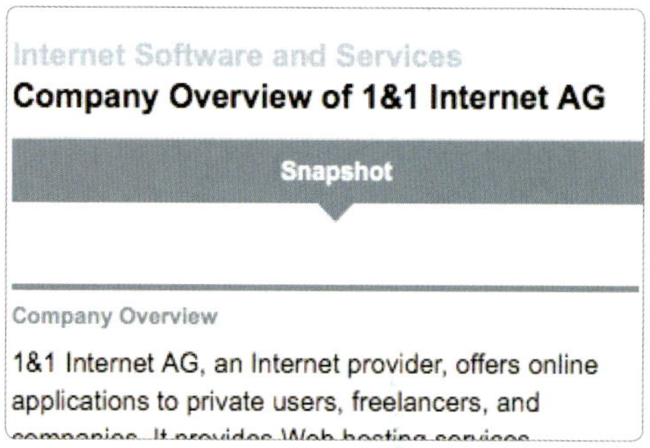

The details

Check how long a host has been in business for and how large the company is. It is of course never a guarantee of a better service, but ideally you will want to host your site with a company that is established and which looks likely to stay in business for the foreseeable future.

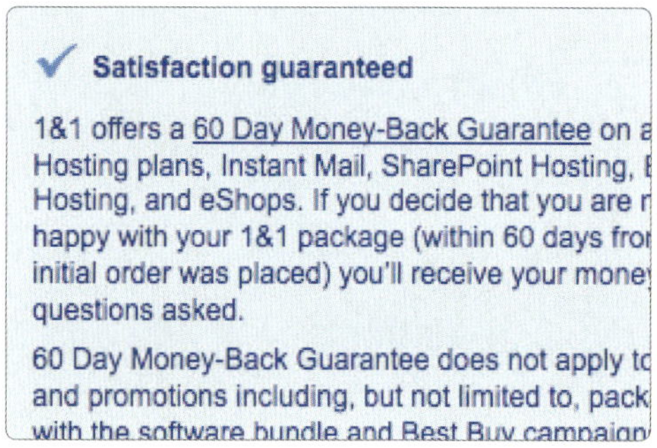

Guarantees

You will want to choose a host that offers an uptime guarantee that is close to 100% and, ideally, a promise that they will keep your site backed up. This is not crucial because you can still save all of your data via FTP, but it's also good to see a money-back guarantee offered as well.

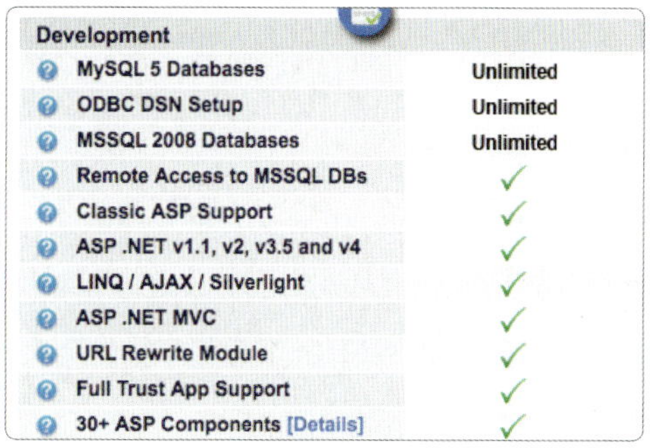

Too many features?

Don't choose a host purely because of the number of features they offer. Many hosts offers scores of features at very low prices that you are unlikely to ever use. While this is tempting, it is rarely worth the money if you won't use the features anyway. Look for reliability above all else.

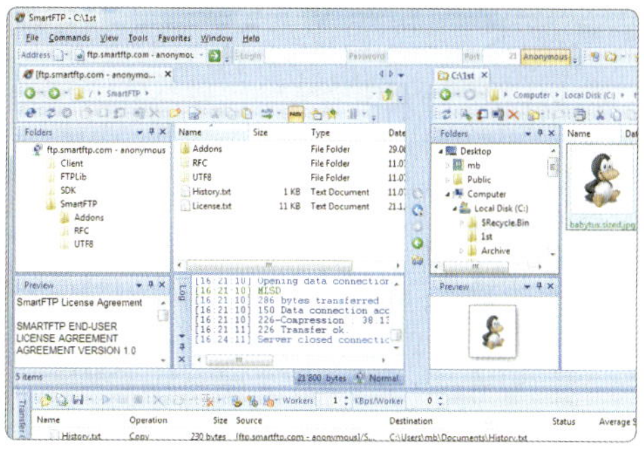

FTP

If a potential host does not offer FTP access, you will need to be sure that there is a very good reason not to do so. FTP lets you back up your site and upload new files and media whenever you want to, and without this access you may struggle to gain complete control over your website.

Build a site

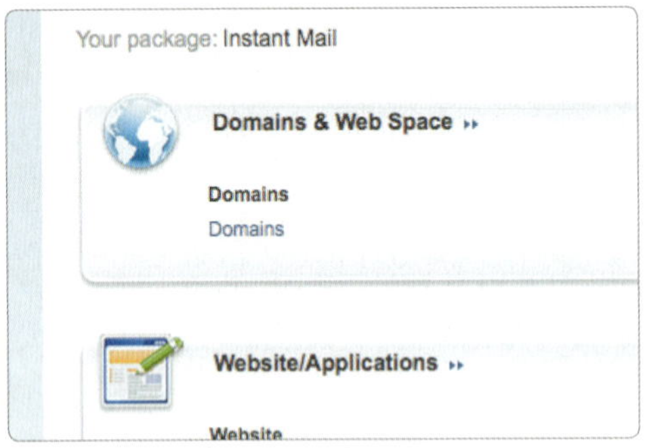

Accurate reporting

Most hosts will offer you access to a control panel that lets you assess your bandwidth usage and other aspects of your website use. You'll want this so you can be sure you're on the right package and not likely to fall foul of penalty charges if your site receives too much traffic.

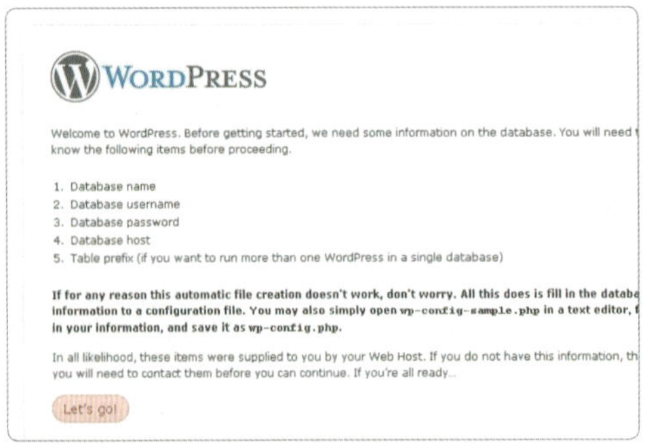

Compatible platforms

Some hosts will quote blogging and website platforms in their marketing and have set up their servers to offer a better service for these software types. WordPress requires dynamic memory in specific areas and a host that understands this will be a better bet if you're using the platform.

Free hosting

The temptations of free hosting plans are obvious, but they are rarely worth using if you are serious about your website. You may receive a slower performance and limited bandwidth and web space, plus the possibility of hosting adverts that will be needed to justify the lack of cost.

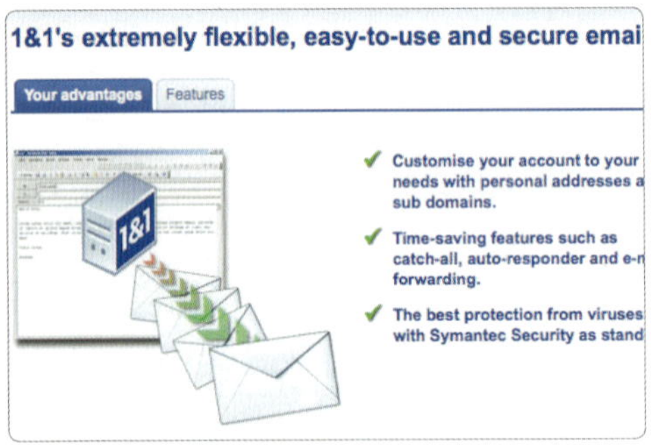

Email is vital

Many hosts will provide email accounts and generous mailbox space with their hosting plans. It makes sense to be able to use your domain name in the site email addresses and you can potentially offer accounts to people who help you update your site and even visitors.

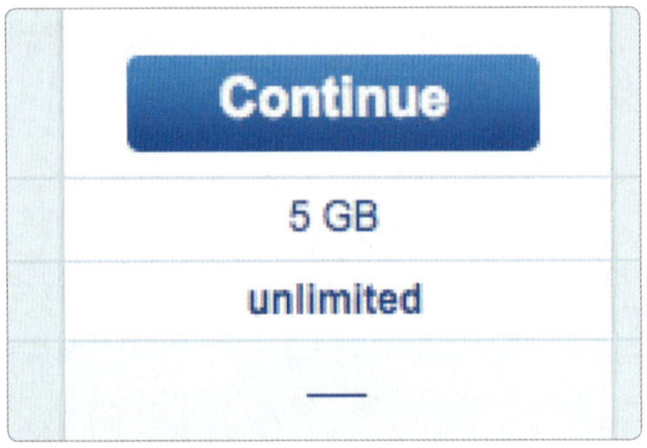

The long game

You can never be 100% sure that a host is worthy, but if you have time to do some testing, try a low-tier plan from a host for a month just to see what their customer service and reliability is like. You can then upgrade when you are ready to launch your site properly. It pays to be patient.

Ongoing costs

Most hosts offer discounts if you commit for longer periods, such as 1 or 2 years. Check to ensure that they will let you sign up for a shorter period initially and that you'll commit for longer if you're happy with the service. You must ensure the service performs before you commit.

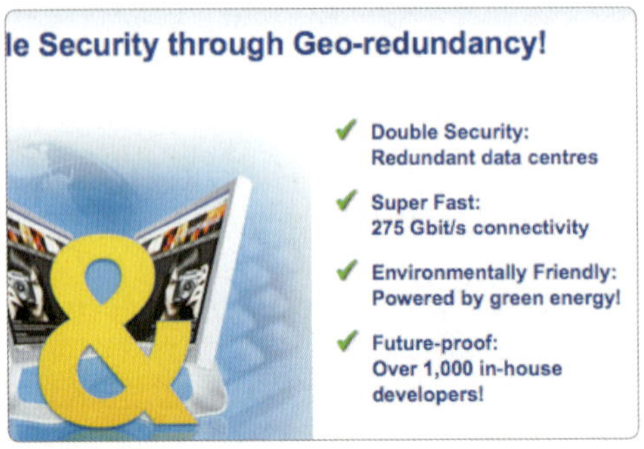

Security

You must research how a host will protect your site and the data held within it. You have the responsibility to ensure that you don't share passwords freely, but your host should also provide protection against those who may want to either take down your site or hack into it.

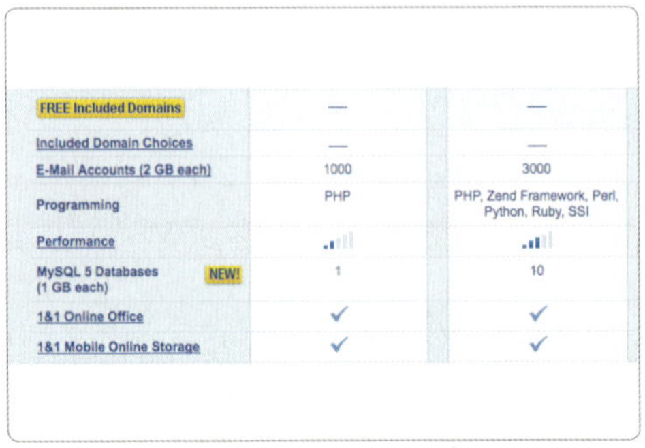

Multiple databases

Ideally you'll want to go for a package that offers more than one database. A database will be required for most content management systems and being able to set up a second one for redundancy or for running two parts of a site is something you will require as your site grows.

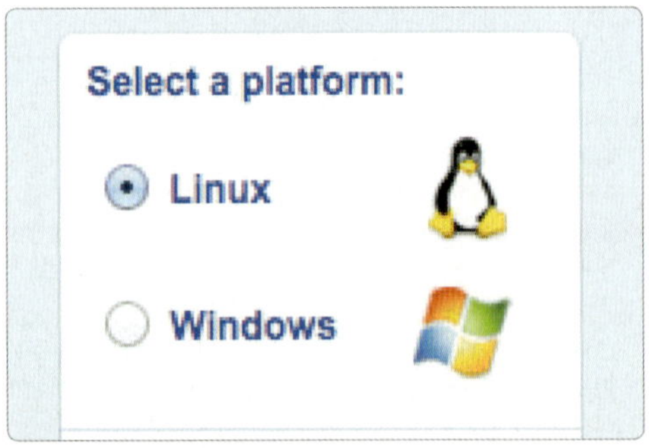

Windows or Linux

Most providers offer Windows and Linux-based servers. Do your research and decide which you require, but for most people a Linux server will be the most suitable. It can ensure that making changes in the future is easier, but check your needs and the pros and cons of both solutions.

Vital hosting features

What should you look for in a host?

Room to grow
You will ideally want to choose a host who gives you room to grow by letting you upgrade your hosting package as your site becomes more popular. It makes life a lot easier

Select a platform: ◉ Linux ○ Windows > Windows vs Linux	1&1 STARTER	1&1 STANDARD	1&1 UNLIMITED	1&1 BUSINESS
	Only £2.49 /month	3 MONTHS FREE!* then £4.99/month	3 MONTHS FREE!* then £6.99/month	6 MONTHS FREE!* then £9.99/month
	Continue	Continue	Continue	Continue
Webspace	5 GB	50 GB	unlimited	unlimited
Monthly Traffic Volume	unlimited	unlimited	unlimited	unlimited
FREE Included Domains	—	—	1	1
Included Domain Choices	—	—	.co.uk, .me.uk or .org.uk	.co.uk, .me.uk or .org.uk
E-Mail Accounts (2 GB each)	1000	3000	5000	unlimited
Programming	PHP	PHP, Zend Framework, Perl, Python, Ruby, SSI	PHP, Zend Framework, Perl, Python, Ruby, SSI	PHP, Zend Framework, Perl, Python, Ruby, SSI
Performance				
MySQL 5 Databases (1 GB each) NEW!	1	10	100	unlimited
1&1 Online Office	✓	✓	✓	✓
1&1 Mobile Online Storage	✓	✓	✓	✓
1&1 Click & Build Applications (65) NEW!	1	5	unlimited	unlimited
Mobile Website Editing Software	—	NetObjects Fusion 1&1 Edition	NetObjects Fusion 1&1 Edition	NetObjects Fusion® 1&1 Edition or Adobe Dreamweaver® CS4
Dedicated SSL Certificate	—	Optional	Optional	✓
	Your data is stored	Your data is stored	Your data is stored	Your data is stored

Windows or Linux
Having a choice between Windows and Linux matters a lot, and each type of site may have a different requirement which suits one server type more than the other

Databases
You will want to choose a package which offers more than one database. This will let you host two sections of your site easily and offer some redundancy if things go badly wrong

Be secure
All good hosts should explain how they will look after your site and all of the work you have put into it. Read the documentation carefully to be sure you're getting what you pay for

Domains and hosting

Think carefully about your domain and hosting setup

There are advantages and disadvantages to buying a domain from your hosting company. If you set up your new hosting plan and then buy the domain at the same time, this will make the setup process much easier.

Your main server can use the domain name rather than a mapped generic URL as the web address and you won't have to worry about redirecting URLs so that your visitors are reaching the right place. Also, many hosting companies offer a domain name for free when you buy a package so you could save some money as well.

However, there is a good argument that purchasing a domain name from a provider who only deals with domains offers you more flexibility in the long run if you decide to change hosts later on. You can simply change how it resolves to your new host and not have to worry about exporting it from one host to another, and you need to be very careful that your domain is still retrievable if it is bundled with a package. You have a choice between flexibility and initial ease of use, so you need to decide which is the most important to you.

Upload your site files using FTP

FTP is a required tool for all webmasters

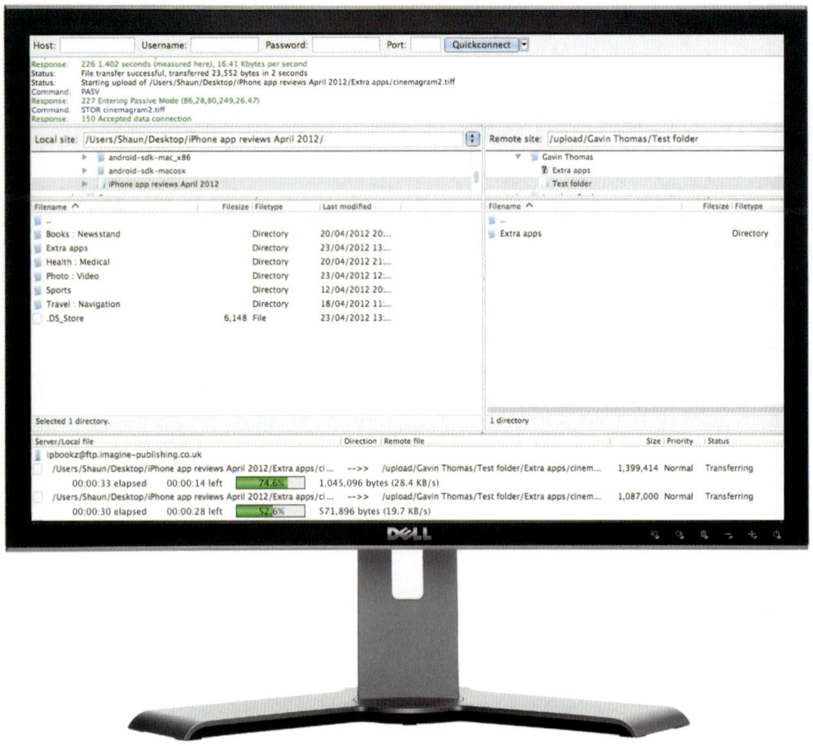

FTP stands for 'File Transfer Protocol' and is a very efficient and secure way to upload files to your own website. When you are setting up a new site, or adding images or media to an established site, it is important to understand exactly how your piece of the web is set up. You will be given an FTP address by your provider and the required login credentials which let you move files to your own space when you need to. The transfer process is no different than moving files from folder to folder on your home computer – it may just take some extra time to complete.

Here we will show you how to get up and running with FTP in minutes and how to manage your storage space in the most efficient way. It is crucial that you treat your space wisely because simply uploading files in no order can slow down and potentially stop a website working completely. If you have any history with desktop computers, you will already know most of what you need to transfer files via FTP, but some extra steps will help you to get up and running quickly.

> "Using FTP is no different than moving files from folder to folder on your home computer"

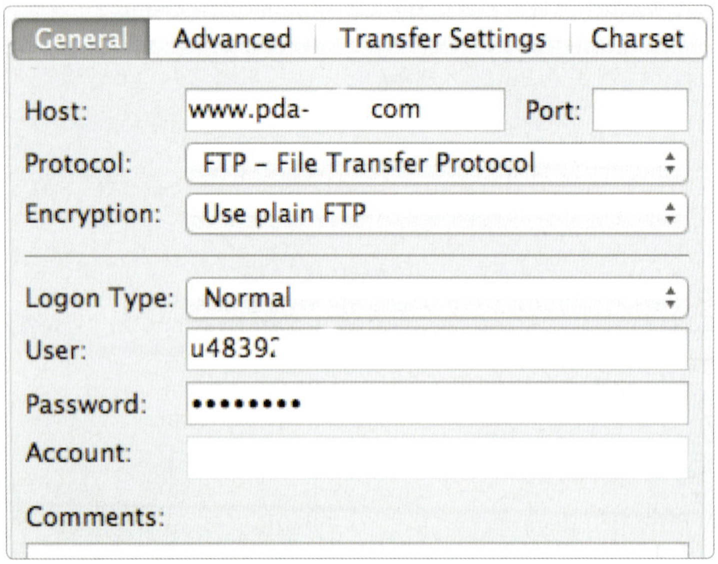

01 FTP credentials

When you set up a new hosting plan, you will be given an FTP address, username and password. These will be used to access your web space and are the only credentials you need to get started.

02 An FTP client

There are many FTP clients available for every platform, but FileZilla is a good place to start. It is free and only requires a quick download to get started. Go to **http://filezilla-project.org** and download the app.

Get to know FTP clients

FTP works almost identically to a standard file manager

FTP ALTERNATIVES

Some web hosts, such as Squarespace, don't offer FTP access at all, but instead choose their own software for uploading files. This is more restrictive than FTP because it takes away a lot of the flexibility, but ultimately it performs the same task. FTP is still preferred by most webmasters, though.

Your space

Your space is shown in the main left-hand panel and follows the standard file manager approach. You can navigate through folders and select multiple files at any time to upload them to your website

Connections

You can connect to multiple sites via this simple button. Once you have input and saved your login details for each site, they will all appear in the drop-down menu when you click this button

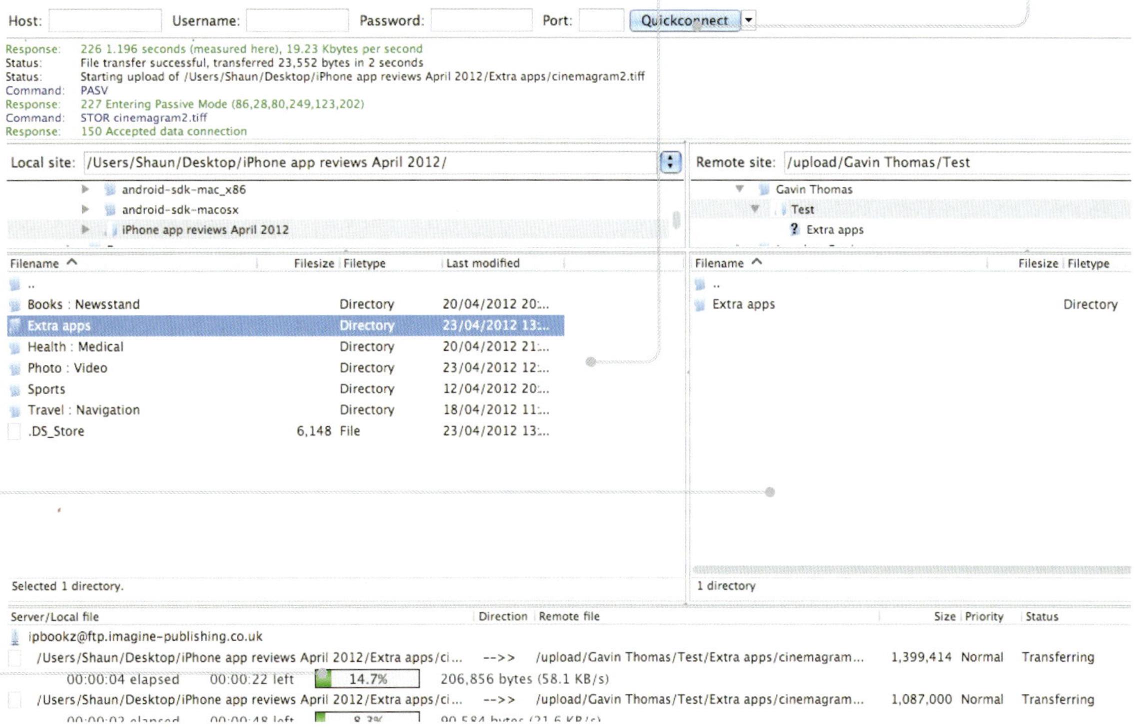

Your remote space

The online space for your website is displayed in the main right-hand panel. You can again navigate to any folder here, but try not to put much in the root folder because this can slow down performance

Transfers as they happen

When you transfer a group of files, the bottom window shows the exact progress as they are being uploaded. This also lets you know that the connection is still active and that the files are being uploaded

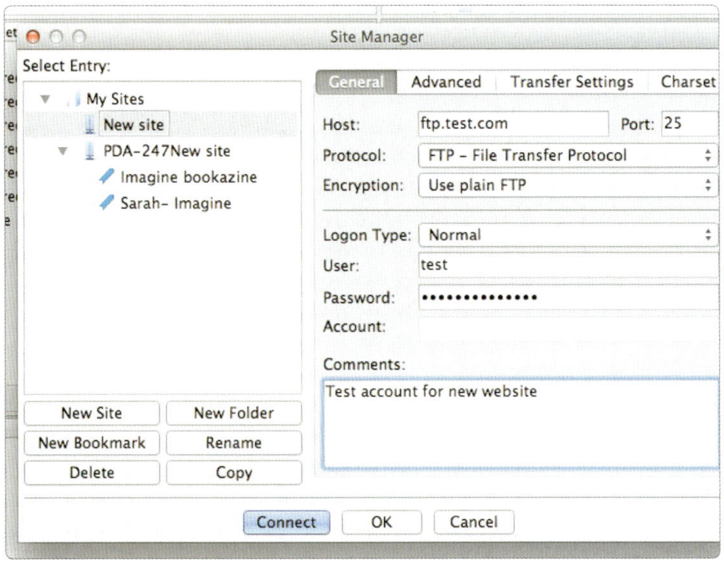

03 Getting started

Open the FTP client and click the File menu. Choose Site Manager from the drop-down and then hit the New Site icon. You can now input your FTP address, username and password and click the Connect button.

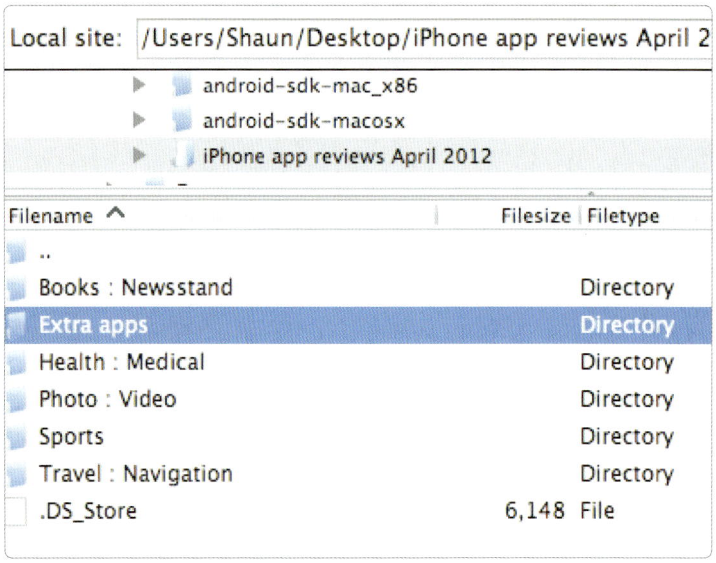

04 Move some files

You will now see two windows. In the left one, navigate to the files or folder you want to upload. In the right one, choose where you want the files to be placed. Now simply drag and drop them from the left to the right.

Buy and transfer a domain name

Setting up your first domain is easier than you may think

Choosing a domain name is easy, but finding one that is available is often very difficult. There are millions of sites on the web and it seems at times as if the majority of names have been taken. If you persevere, however, you will be able to find the domain of your choice and have it up and running very quickly. In this tutorial we will show you how to secure a domain name and how to have it viewable by the world within a few days – you may be surprised at just how simple the process is.

We will also show you how to transfer a domain to a new host if you have reason to change, and even this is now a simpler process than it used to be. There are rules set up which mean that you must be allowed to transfer a domain, and this gives you more control over the process. Think of it as like moving your mobile number from one provider to another. You own it and need to keep it for obvious reasons, and so you should be allowed to take it where you like. It is all very straightforward once you know the process and you will soon be dealing with domains much more efficiently than you expected.

"You may be surprised at just how simple the process is"

Control your domain

Your control panel is the home of your domain management

Transfers
There should always be a transfer option available in your control panel, which will have facilities included that let you export domains to another provider. All good providers will make this facility obvious

New domains
At any time you can use the 'new' option to purchase new domains or add a domain that you own and which has been released by another provider. It only takes a few steps to master

Unlocking
It is likely that you would need to unlock a domain to transfer it to a new provider. This ensures that you have fulfilled the obligations of your current provider and are free to move it

Your domain
The link for your domains is vital for changing other settings such as where it is forwarded to and for finer adjustments to ensure it is working exactly how you want it to

SUBDOMAINS
Subdomains are created to specify a particular part of a website such as an online store. They usually change the format of the domain to subdomain.domain.com and ensure that it not only looks professional, but that the section is available on web searches. For large sections of any site, a subdomain should be used and they are almost always free to set up.

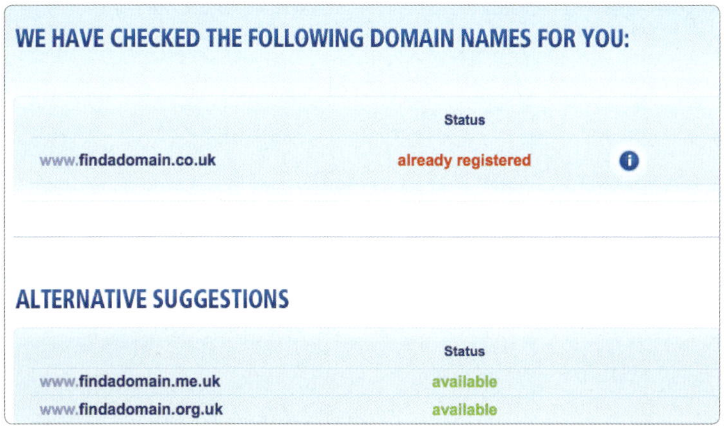

01 Find a domain

The first step is to choose a name and see if it's available. Visit a site like **order.1and1.co.uk/Instant** and type in a name. You'll soon find one to use.

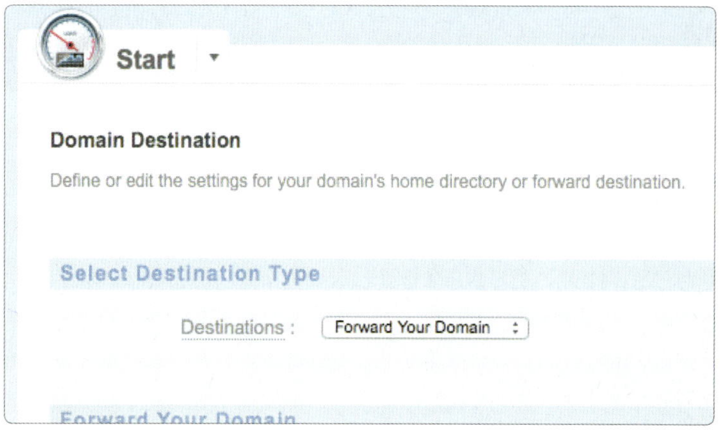

02 Set it up

After buying the domain, you're sent a link for configuring it. The option to forward the domain is useful if you have hosting with a different provider.

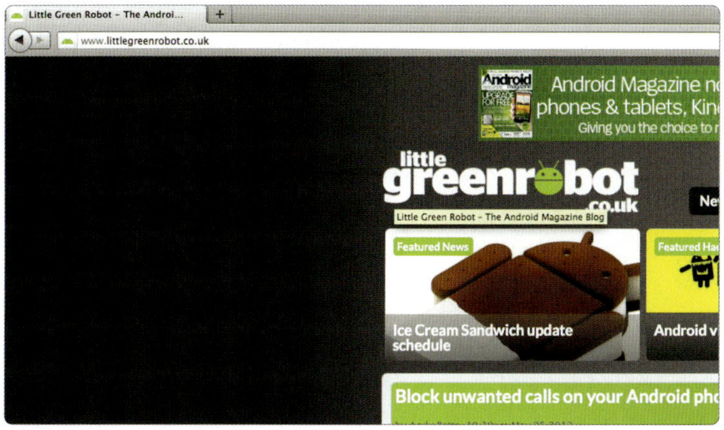

03 Check it's live

Type the domain into a browser. When first set up, it'll be visible to some countries before others. It can take up to three days to become visible to all.

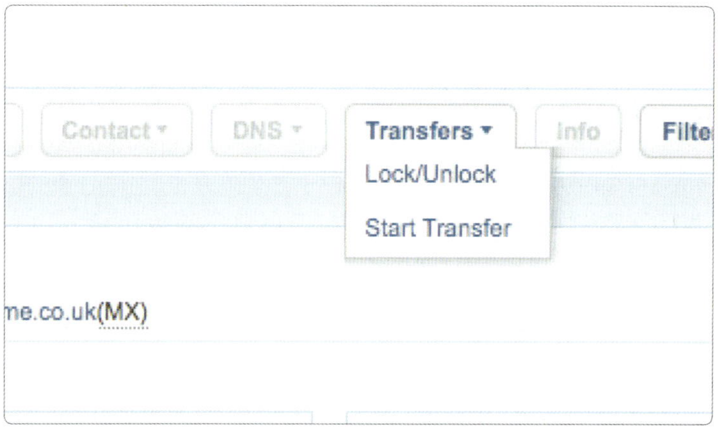

04 Transferring a domain

In your control panel, you should see a 'Transfer' option. You may need to unlock your domain before using this to move it to your new provider.

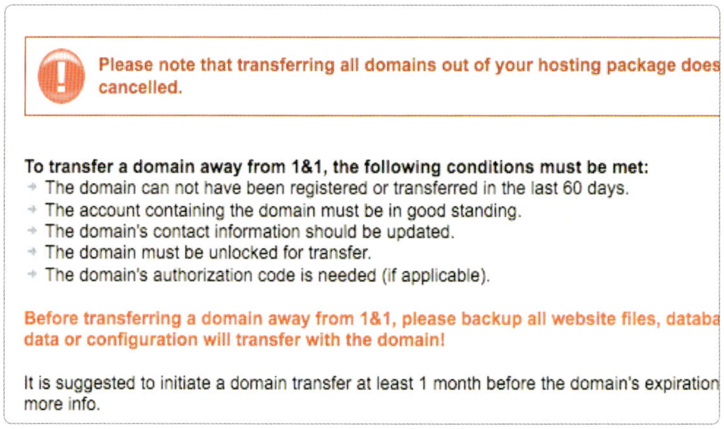

05 Check the terms

Check your current provider's T&Cs to ensure you can move your domain. Your account needs to be in good standing and usually active for 60 days.

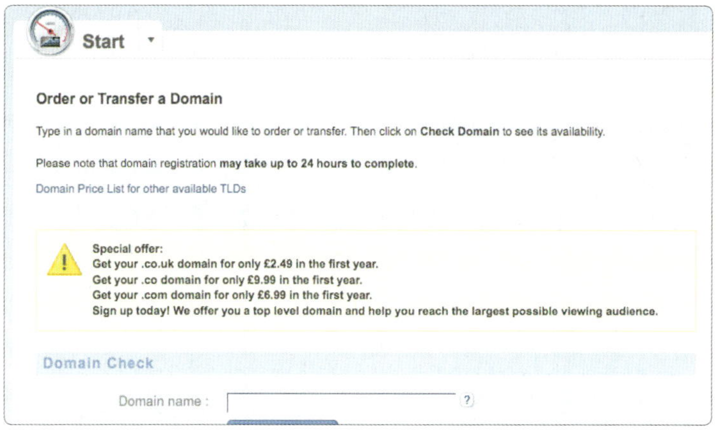

06 Complete the transfer

Now go to your control panel at your new host and choose 'Add domain'. Enter the domain to start the process to move it to the new provider.

WordPress

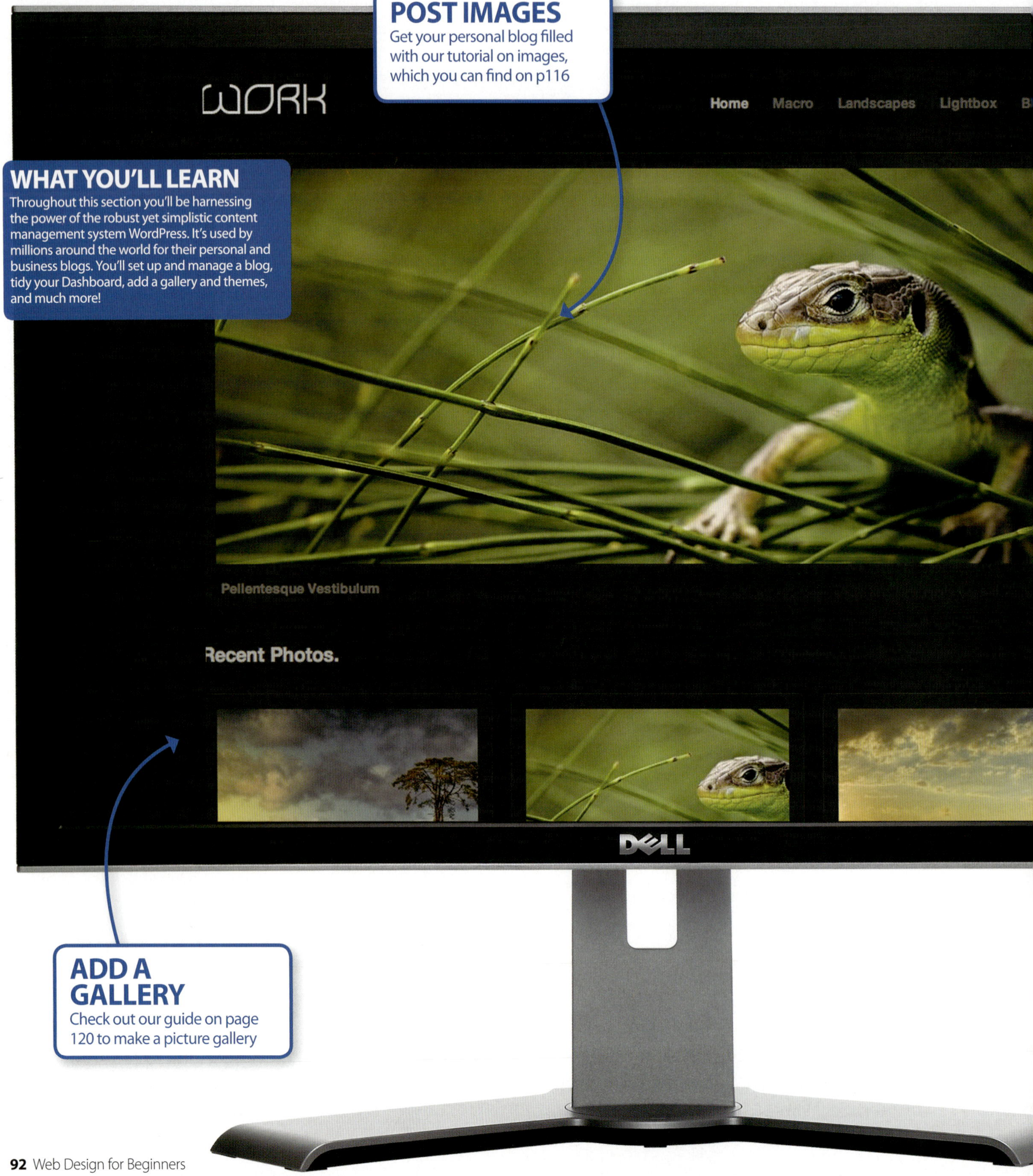

POST IMAGES

Get your personal blog filled with our tutorial on images, which you can find on p116

WHAT YOU'LL LEARN

Throughout this section you'll be harnessing the power of the robust yet simplistic content management system WordPress. It's used by millions around the world for their personal and business blogs. You'll set up and manage a blog, tidy your Dashboard, add a gallery and themes, and much more!

ADD A GALLERY

Check out our guide on page 120 to make a picture gallery

"The appeal of WordPress lies in its combined power and simplicity"

SET UP YOUR SITE
Get your WordPress blog up and running on page 116

128 Manage links

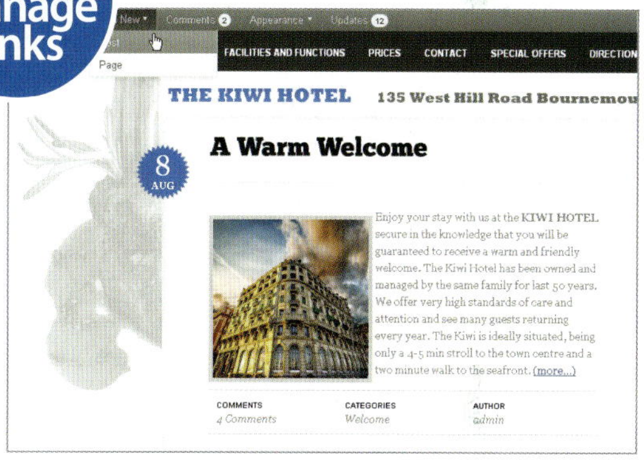

116 Post images

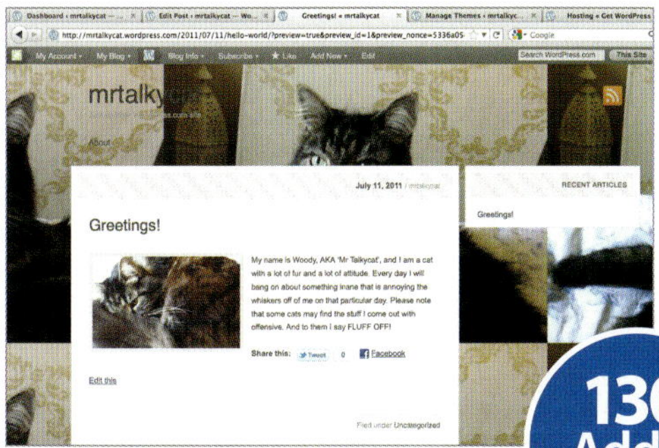

130 Add a theme

WordPress

The Beginner's Guide to WordPress

Whether you're creating a personal blog, business site, fan page or more, we show you how WordPress can be used for all your web design tasks

The appeal of WordPress lies in its combined power and simplicity. On the one hand, it's a solid, fully-featured and extensible Content Management System (CMS) with a huge level of community support (which means you'll always be able to find help and advice if you need it), but on the other it has a very low learning curve. Beginners can get up to speed on how to administer a blog, post new articles and add plug-ins in a jiffy.

As a result, WordPress has become the world's most popular CMS platform, powering websites as diverse as personal blogs and community/society websites, right through to eCommerce web stores and fully fledged fan sites.

One of the core drivers behind its success has been the software's ability to be themed (or 'skinned') to look distinct from the out-the-box appearance, and with a plethora of freely available themes up for grabs for free download, along with a bucket-load of free advice, tutorials (and this bookazine) you'll be able to create a bespoke, tailored design that suits your needs perfectly. Before we get into how you go about creating your own WordPress site though, let's have a look at how WordPress can be used to really get a feel for what's possible. >>

"Set up is, thankfully, a breeze. You don't need any specialist skills, knowledge or experience"

Personal blogging

Got something to say? Let WordPress help you out…

The original purpose of WordPress was, and indeed still is, very much based around the idea of personal blogging. The software gives anyone with access to a web browser the ability to make their voice heard. In a sense, WordPress is partially responsible for the democratisation of the web – no longer is a website the preserve of code wizards and companies with big budgets – now anyone can do it.

At its core, WordPress is a bit like a super efficient online diary. You can upload text, images, sound files and video onto your own digital space and present it as a series of articles (or posts). These are typically arranged chronologically, enabling the visitor to browse back through your posts as if they were paging through the leaves of a book. Of course, some diaries are considered highly private, and if that's the case, WordPress has you covered either directly or through the use of a handy plug-in (extra software that extends the core functionality of WordPress).

Fortunately, WordPress can do a whole lot more than simply save text diaries or articles. You can use it as an online hub, connecting into your Facebook and Twitter profiles, pulling your photos across from Flickr or showing your latest playlist on Last.fm. And it can do all of this without any effort required on your part.

Equally, if you're not looking to share your deepest, darkest thoughts, you can use WordPress to create a website about a subject that interests you, to maintain a recipe database or to apply for a job. The list is almost endless thanks to the flexibility and extensibility of the WordPress platform; it truly is what you make of it.

Set up is, thankfully, a breeze. You don't need any specialist skills, knowledge or experience. In fact, in most cases it doesn't take more than a single click to get your WordPress site up and running, making it very simple for you to start getting your interests, opinions or even funny videos out there and shared with the world.

Of course there will come a time when the software has to be updated, or you want to add some new functionality to your site. Again WordPress has you covered, as updates to the software itself are seamlessly downloaded and applied with a single click in the admin area. Plug-ins are just as simple to install, enabling you to browse through an online catalogue before being installed directly from the web. This means that you can adapt your website over time to meet your changing needs with the minimum of fuss.

Standing out from the crowd is equally important, and once more WordPress makes it very easy to change the way your website looks. The software comes with a couple of default themes and enables you to control the colours, heading text and general settings from within the dashboard admin area. If you want to go for something that looks completely different, however, you can easily add a free or paid-for theme to totally change the visual appearance of your website in seconds.

>>

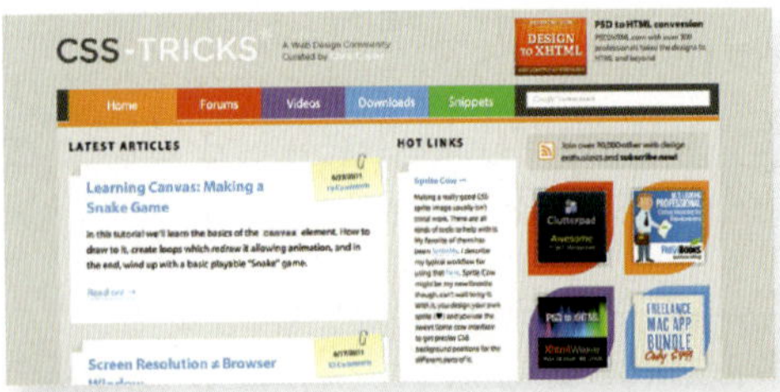

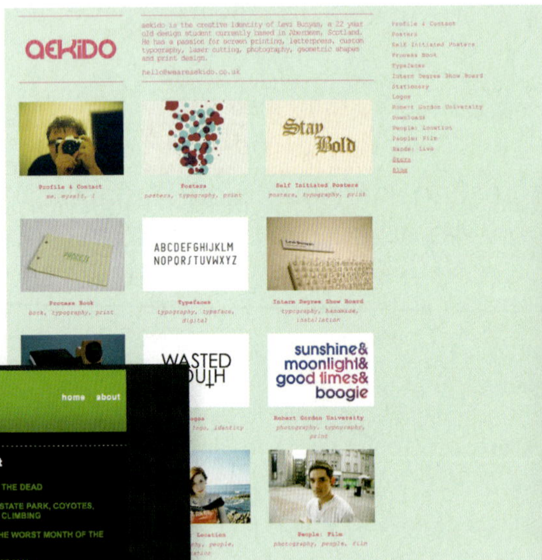

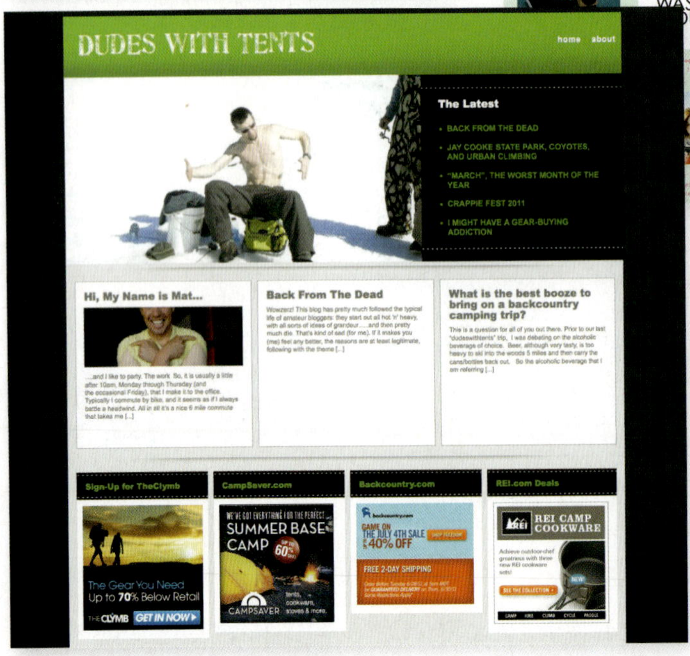

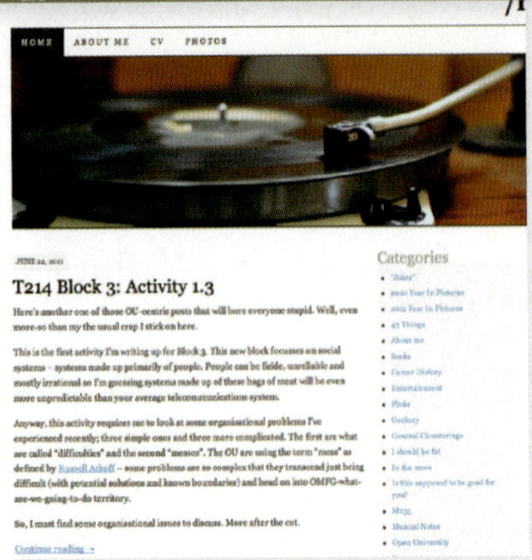

"Set up is, thankfully, a breeze. You don't need any specialist skills, knowledge or experience"

5 ways to use WordPress for your personal site

1 Share photos with friends

With built-in support for media galleries and a massive selection of plug-ins available to enhance this functionality, you can use WordPress to create your own photo-sharing website. Even better, if you give your friends access to the site, they can post their photos directly to your blog, giving you a great record.

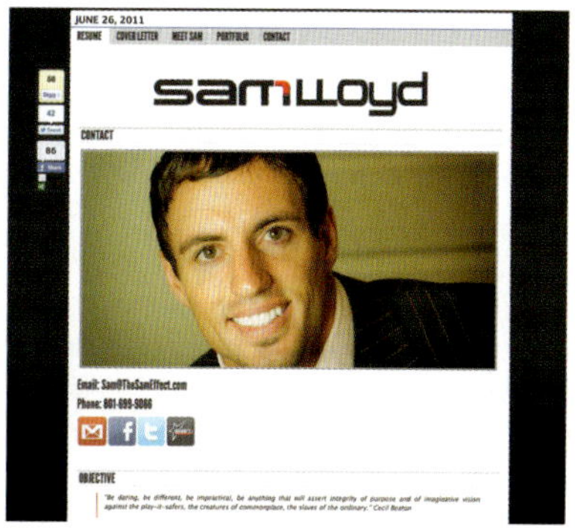

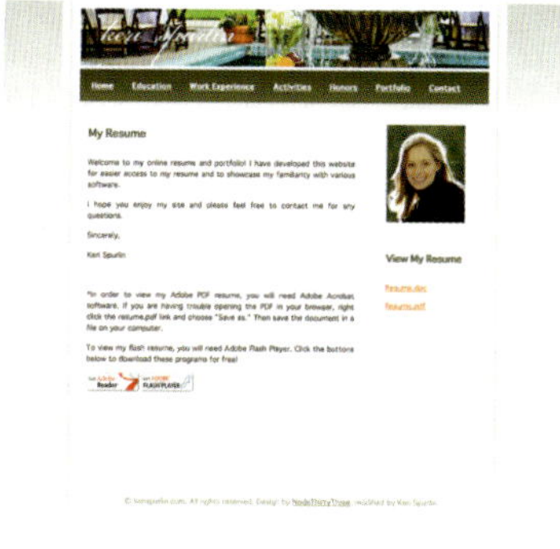

3 Make an online CV

Employers are increasingly looking for potential employees to stand out from the crowd, so why not create an online, interactive CV? You can start off with the standard kind of stuff – employment history, training and personal details. Once your CV is set up, use the post's functionality to keep the site up to date with recent projects, non-work interests and achievements.

2 Keep a movie diary

If you're a movie buff, why not create an online review site? You can tag posts with the names of the actors and director, making it easy to find films by star. Because WordPress enables you to create your own set of categories, it's simple to separate movies by genre, rating, year or whatever works for you.

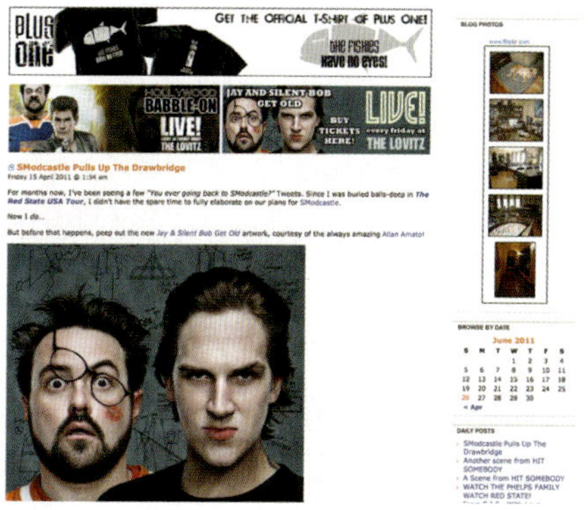

4 Maintain a personal diary

The original idea behind blogging was to keep a diary of what goes on, your opinions and thoughts. That doesn't mean you can't make it personal, though. Using the member's plug-in you can restrict access to view your blog, making it a safe place to post.

5 Report on a subject that interests you

One of the best ways to use WordPress is to become an expert in a field that interests you. You don't need to start off as an expert, but over time as you post more information that you've discovered, you'll soon start to amass a collection of useful content that will bring web visitors interested in the same subject, whether that's cars, football, flags of the world or knitting

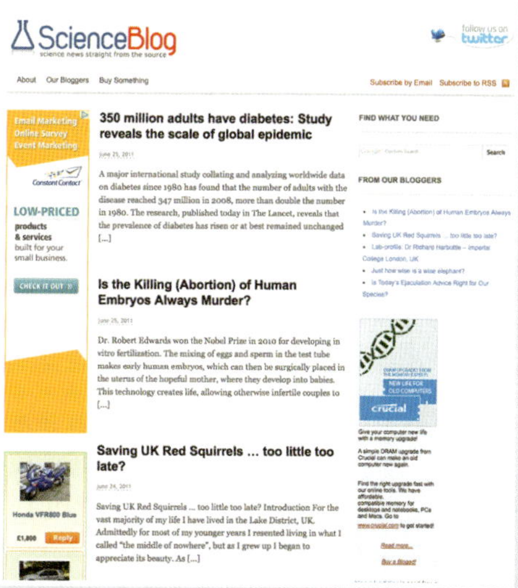

Business blogging

Engage with clients and customers the interactive way

Having a business website is required these days. A good proportion, certainly the majority, of your customers (and more importantly, your potential customers) expect to be able to research suppliers online before making a decision about which business can fulfil their needs. This is true whether you're selling a product or a service and aiming your site at other businesses or consumers.

The downside to running a business website is the cost of setting it up and keeping it up to date, as graphic and web designers have valuable skills and experience that is hard to come by, and therefore they don't come cheap. Keeping your website current is also crucial, as visitors to your page will expect to see that you're live and kicking, and one way they'll judge this is on when your website was last updated. If you're planning to buy something – especially online – you'd normally choose a website that looks well maintained and up to date over one that says "last updated June 2004" in the footer – right?

WordPress offers a great solution to creating a business website because it enables you to deal with both the issues highlighted without any drama. The cost of setting up a website powered by WordPress can be absolutely nothing (although it's still well worth investing in a professional graphic designer if you can, or if money is really tight then you have the option of using an off-the-shelf template to get you started).

Where a WordPress website really comes into its own, however, is in how simple it makes maintaining the page; you can update from anywhere. Simply by logging into the online control panel you can update content, add new pages, images and media files, interact with your customers and respond to enquiries. There's even a WordPress app you can install on your smartphone (free of charge) or tablet device, which enables you to make updates on the move. This all adds up to a really compelling reason to choose WordPress as the Content Management System (CMS) for your business website.

One of the key factors in running a successful business is being able to delegate, and again WordPress is ready and willing. You can set up as many users for your website as desired – so if you have a nominated member of staff responsible for updating the site and they're off sick, someone else can easily step in. Similarly, the administration interface is very easy to understand, so the learning curve is slight even for complete beginners.

For many businesses, that might be enough in and of itself – WordPress is a stable, well-supported and documented CMS that offers a simple way to create and maintain a website. Every business has unique needs, however, so a professional photographer, for example, will want different functionality to a business selling widgets. Specialist needs require specialist tools. Thankfully, WordPress has a highly extensible framework that enables additional functionality to be added to the basic platform. These extensions are known as plug-ins, and there are thousands of them available on the web. Some are commercial, meaning the developer will ask for payment (in recognition of the work required to create the plug-in). Many more are released free of charge, however, meaning there's a chance you'll find something that will meet your needs without having to shell out a single penny. >>

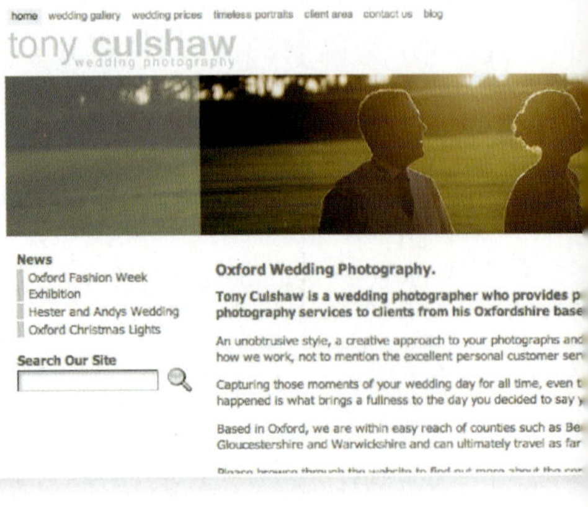

"The interface is really easy to understand, so the learning curve is slight even for complete beginners"

5 ways WordPress can improve your business

Every business needs a website these days, as customers expect to be able to see details of you and your products or services online

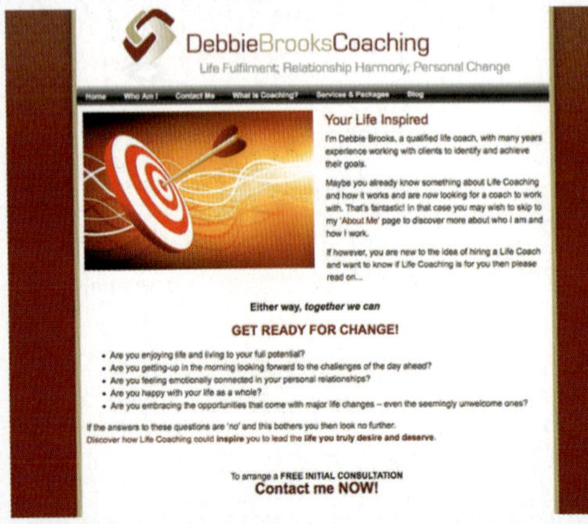

1 Create a basic business site

At the very least, with WordPress you can create a professional-looking website for your business. Stick to the core, basic information at the start: what you do, how much it costs and how to get in touch with the business should all be clear and accessible from the homepage. There are a huge amount of themes available on the web, so you can find one to suit your business.

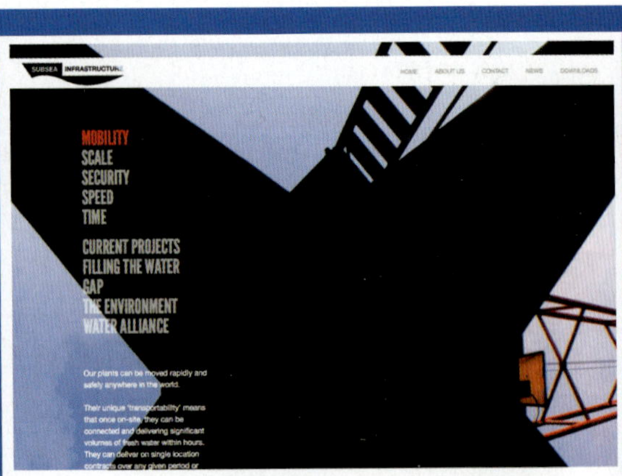

2 Online brochure

If you're ready to go to the next level, WordPress is ideally suited to create an online brochure of your products and services. Think of this as an opportunity to present potential customers with all the details on your core products and services without incurring the cost of a printed brochure. This also means you can change the information whenever you need to.

3 Sell products online

If you've got products or services that are available off-the-shelf, why not sell them online? WordPress has a number of eCommerce plug-ins available, enabling visitors to add products to a shopping cart before paying via PayPal or a Payment Service Provider (PSP) linked to your account.

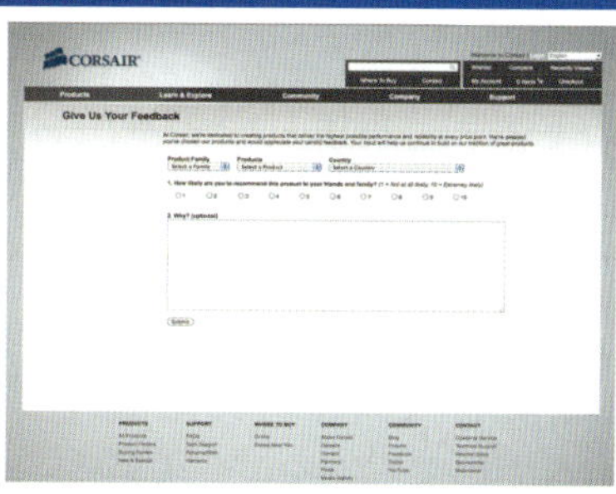

4 Open a dialogue with your customers

Social networks allow businesses to engage with their customers. WordPress lets you take advantage of the opportunities to get feedback from your customers through comments and social media plug-ins, so open up to customer feedback – you might be surprised at the opportunities that present themselves as a result.

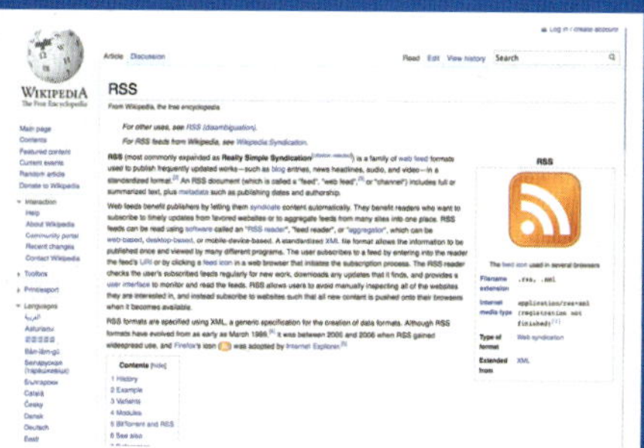

5 Syndicate your content

Performing well in search engines is a crucial part of running a successful business website. Potential customers need to be able to find you when they go searching for your products. One way to achieve this is to allow other sites to use your content as a newsfeed. Write articles about your products and encourage review sites to use WordPress's RSS feed to automatically syndicate your content.

Fan websites

Share the love with a dedicated page for your favourite things

A modern phenomenon, the rise of fan sites on the internet has been huge in the last ten years. Whether it's a celebrity, band, movie or book, you're bound to find a fan site that celebrates it. And if you can't, why not set up your own?

There are numerous examples of hugely popular fan sites, but some of the most high profile in recent years have been based around popular films and books. Take Harry Potter, for example. Fans, not content with JK Rowling's seven books, have created a wealth of content including fan fiction and online encyclopaedias.

Fan sites can also have an impact on the author, musician or television company in question. Brian May's website, **www.brianmay.com**, started off as a fan site before being adopted by Brian as his online home, while fans of The Golden Girls in the UK succeeded in persuading the producers of the show to release it on DVD after an online campaign through a UK fan site.

WordPress lends itself perfectly to creating a fan site because it enables you to engage with your visitors quickly and easily. Giving people the ability to feed back on your views and opinions or submit their own news and articles can really help to create a sense of community. Quite often you'll find cast members, authors or musicians joining in with the conversation too, making it a great way to connect with the people that you admire.

While running a fan site can be a lot of hard work with plenty of time and effort required to succeed, WordPress has a lot of functionality that can make it easier. Firstly, WordPress can be installed with a single click, making it ideal for non-technical users. You really don't need to know anything about websites, computers or the internet to get you on the way to running your own fan hub.

Once your site is up and running, the software is very easy to use, and just as easy to add functionality to. So, if you're looking for a good way to present a gallery of images, you can quickly and easily add this functionality directly from the admin area of your WordPress site by installing a plug-in – and there's no need to download files, FTP them or perform complicated configurations.

One of the key online developments of recent times is the rise of social media – websites like Twitter, Facebook, Ping and the hundreds of alternatives have become the de facto method for interacting, expressing opinions and affiliating with brands, artists and movements. This is crucial from the perspective of a fan site because social media makes it possible, for the first time, to quickly and easily find people who share the same passion.

Once again, WordPress hasn't left this stone unturned, and has plug-ins available for Twitter integration, Facebook content syndication and any number of alternative social media platforms. This means, rather splendidly, that not only is it possible, but you don't even need to spend any of your precious time hooking your website up to these services – you can immediately publicise and promote your fan site across these platforms from the moment you launch. Equally, you can easily integrate a Facebook page or Twitter account so that as you update your WordPress site your new content is pushed over onto Facebook or Twitter, bringing fresh traffic and like-minded visitors.

"The ability to feed back on views and opinions helps to create a sense of community"

5 ways to create a successful fan site

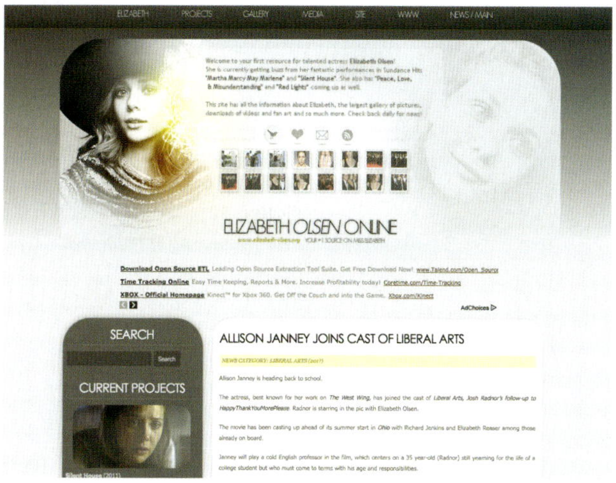

1 Start with a simple news site

WordPress is perfectly suited to creating ongoing news sites. In the context of a specific fan page, this can be as simple as recording the comings and goings of a certain author, reporting some interesting news or rumours about their books or characters, or conducting interviews with people involved in the production of a movie. A simple blog can provide a wonderful wealth of fan information.

2 Make it a multimedia site

Combine news and rumours with picture galleries, downloads and computer wallpapers, and you've got the makings of a fan portal. WordPress has a huge range of plug-ins so that you can include downloadable content, images and video media, audio files and much more.

3 Create a fan podcast

One of the best ways to connect with your audience is to create podcast (audio programme). WordPress fully supports RSS syndication, which means you can connect to iTunes to have your programme automatically download to subscribed listeners. All you really need in addition to WordPress is a microphone and some free recording software.

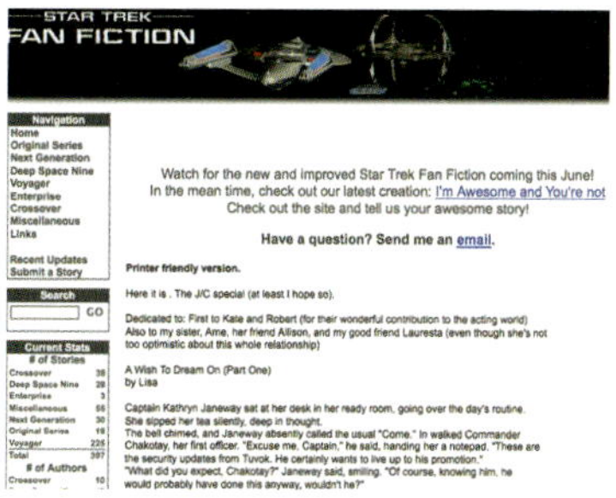

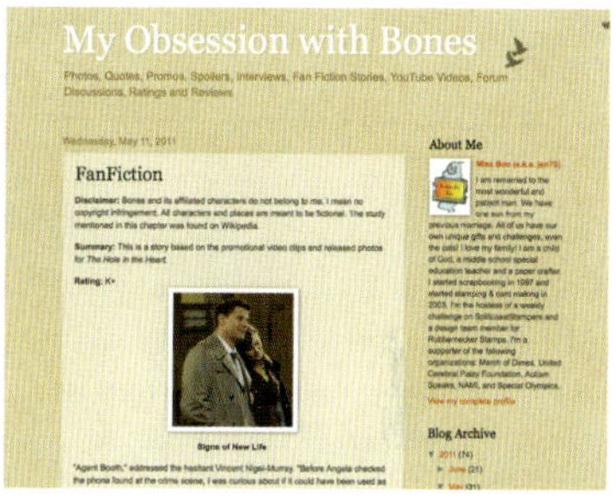

4 Write your own material

If you're following an author it's common for fans to create their own fan fiction based around the characters featured in the work being celebrated. Do note that technically you're breaking copyright law doing this, but many authors are extremely flattered by the fan fiction movement – so ask them!

5 Grab content from other sites

WordPress lets you pull in content from other sites about similar subject matters. Using RSS feeds you can syndicate your own content or integrate other fans' posts into your own site, adding vital information and news to your own. WordPress makes this nice and easy, and it works whether you're including articles, photos from Flickr or audio podcasts. WordPress has lots of plug-ins designed to make it easy to bring in content automatically.

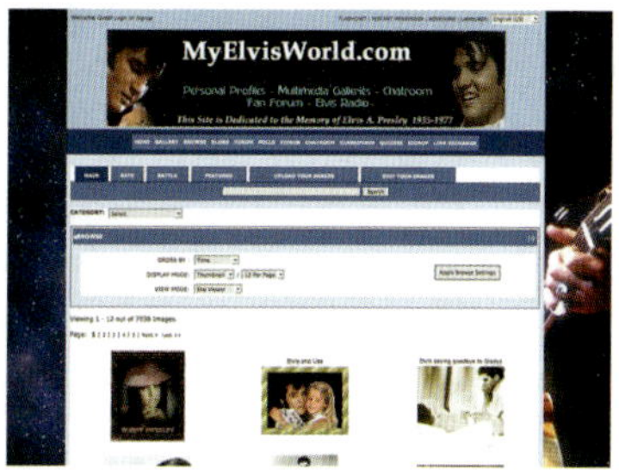

Download, install and set up a self-hosted site

The path to a perfect blog starts right at the beginning. Here we show you how to download, install and set up WordPress

WordPress has become synonymous with the term blog, and with good reason. The web publishing platform is free to download, easy to install and simple to use. Add into this already-appealing mix the fact that there are continual updates and development, a swathe of themes and literally thousands and thousands of add-ons and it's hard to see what's not to like.

WordPress itself comes in two distinct flavours: either hosted via wordpress.com or self-hosted via www.wordpress.org, as we explained earlier. In this tutorial we are focusing on the self-hosting option, which relates to users who already own a domain name and web space.

The WordPress site extols the virtues of its 'Famous 5-minute installation' and undoubtedly

> "It's free to download, easy to install and simple to use"

WordPress can be installed in five minutes, when you know what you are doing. However, for those not so well associated with the WordPress platform the process is a little more in-depth. Here we look at the basics; where to download the latest version of WordPress and how to install.

We also take a more in-depth look at setting up a MySQL database and how to transfer files, ready for installation, via an FTP client. Finally, we run through the installation process and take a peek at how to modify some of WordPress's essential settings.

The WordPress Dashboard

Where you'll be spending most of your time in WordPress

Top toolbar
This toolbar is full of handy links, including access to your WordPress account, where you can change your name, email address and lots more besides

Comments and links
After you start posting, you're likely to get comments from your readers. They, along with people who have linked to your site, will appear here for your approval

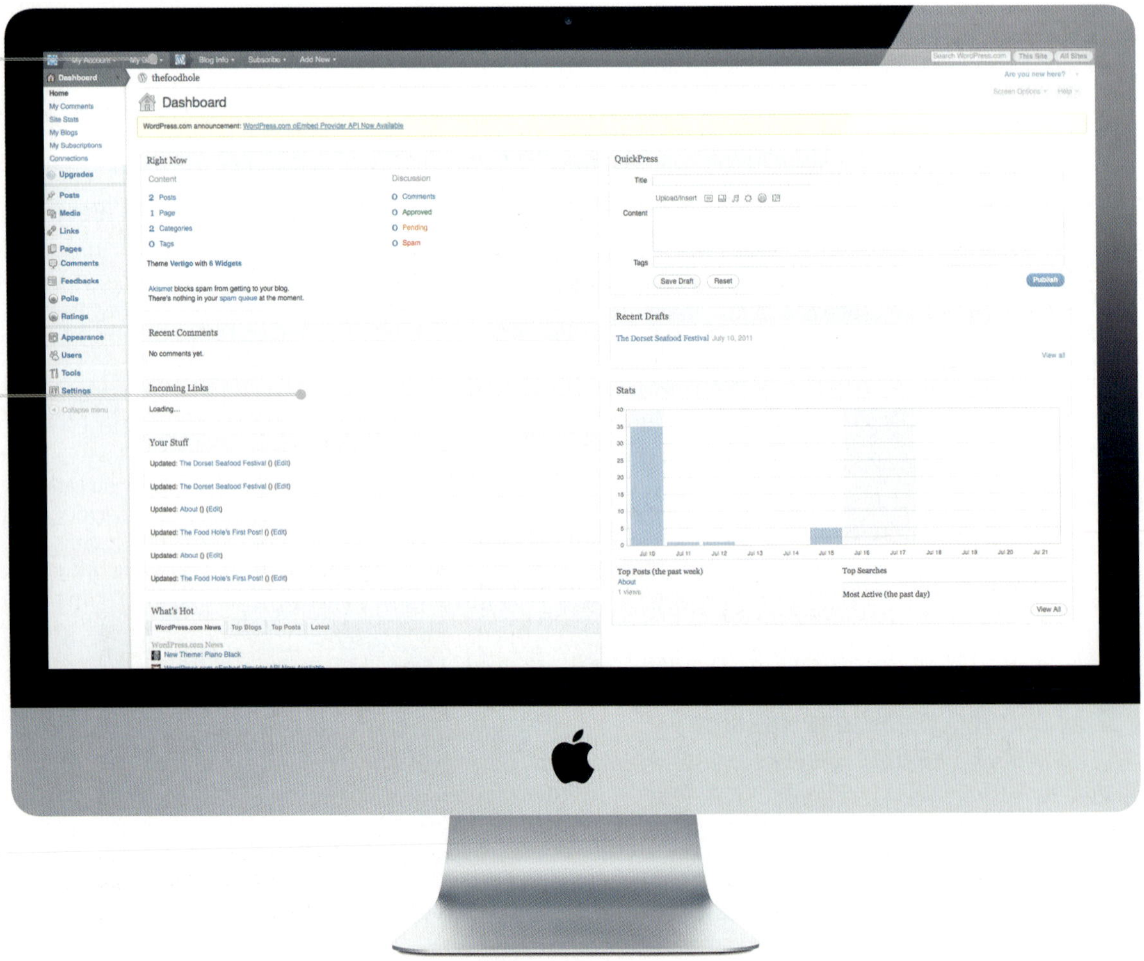

01 Get WordPress

The first step to a great blog is downloading and installing the platform. To download the latest version of WordPress, head to **wordpress.org/download** and click the Download WordPress button and save the file to the desktop.

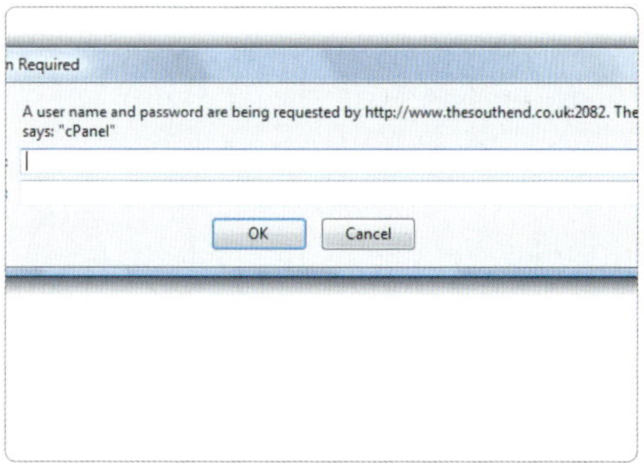

02 Web host account

Before installing WordPress a database needs to be created. We are going to demonstrate a typical setup using cPanel. First of all you'll need to log in to your web host account; these details should have been provided by your web host.

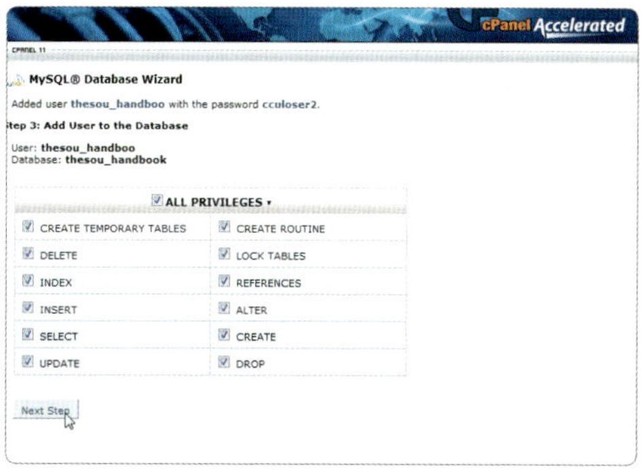

03 Create a database

Locate the Database section and MySQL Database Wizard. Create A Database, add a name in New Database and press Next Step. Now add a Username and Password and press Next Step. Now click All Privileges and Next Step.

04 Database details

Head to the location of the WordPress download and locate wp-config-sample.php. Rename the file to wp-config.php and then open it in a text editor. At the top under MySQL settings is where the database and details need to be added.

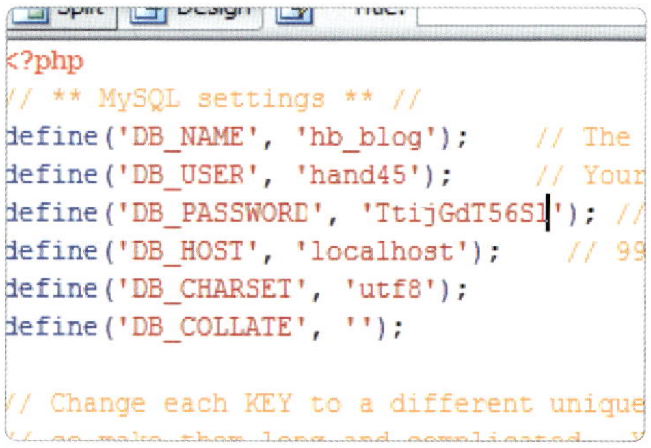

05 Settings

The only settings that need to be changed are 'DB_NAME', 'DB_USER' and 'DB_PASSWORD'. Now substitute the putyourdbnamehere, usernamehere and yourpasswordhere with the appropriate text. Now save the file.

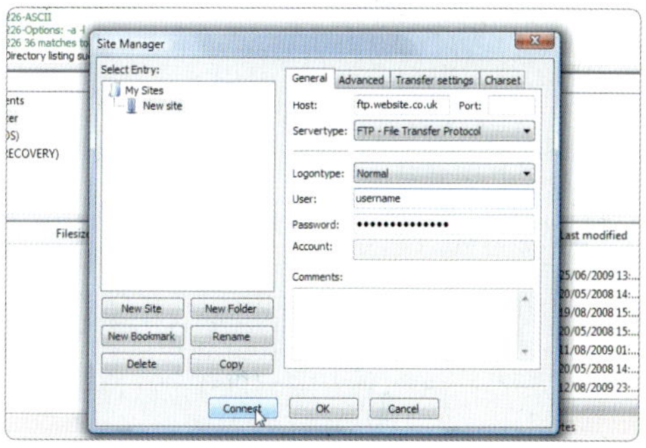

06 Get connected

Now upload all the WordPress files to the desired web space using FTP. Open FileZilla and go to File>Site Manager and enter the Host address, ie ftp.mywebsitename.co.uk and username and password as provided by your host. Press Connect.

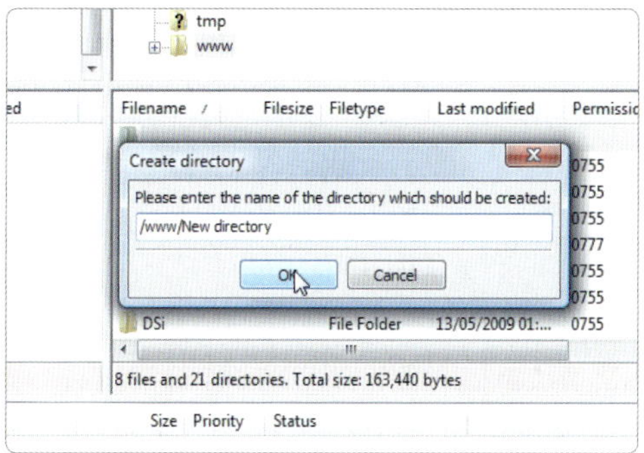

07 Create directory

There will be two windows, the left displaying local files and the right showing files on the server. Double-click the www folder in the top-right pane to get to the root. Right-click the bottom-right pane, select Create directory and name.

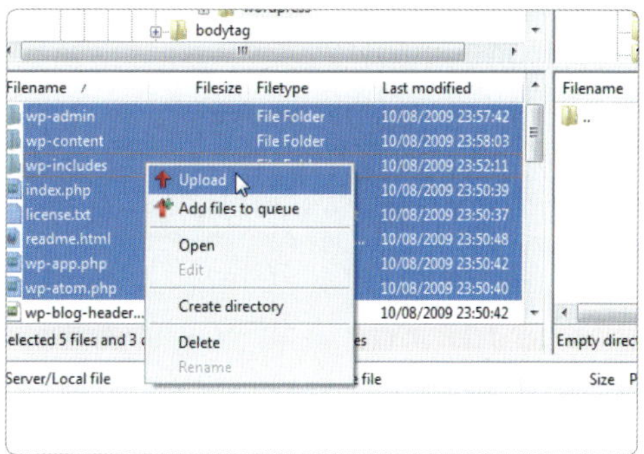

08 Transfer files

Double-click the folder just created. Go to the left windows and use both to locate the WordPress download. Make sure the WordPress folder lowest down the structure is selected. Select all files, right-click and select Upload to transfer the files.

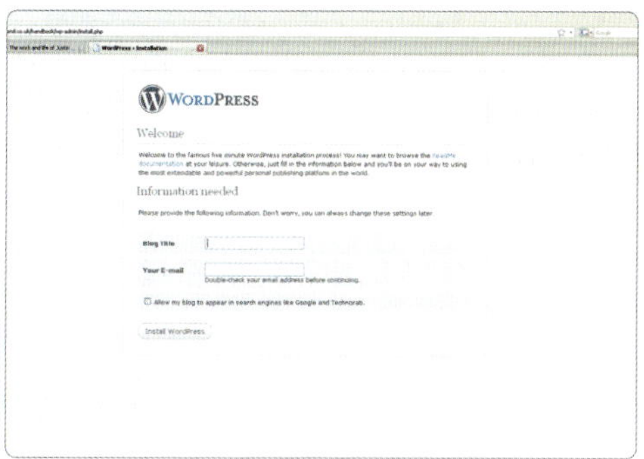

09 Installation script

After all the files have been uploaded, open a browser and enter http://www.yoursite.co.uk/blog/wp-admin/install.php. 'Yoursite.co.uk' is the domain name where WordPress is installed and 'blog' is the name of the folder.

Domain name and web space

To get a WordPress blog online a user needs their own web space and a domain name

The first requirement of any WordPress installation is the need for web space. There are thousands of web hosting companies who will happily supply space for a small fee. However, to determine what sort of web hosting package is needed the user needs to decide how much web space is needed and how much traffic is expected.

Typically, users can get 200MB of web space and gigabytes of traffic for a very small fee. But if more space is likely to be needed, ie a photo blog, go for more. A small UK company that provides cheap and efficient hosting is Z-Host (www.z-host.co.uk). It provides packages from as little as £15 a year (100MB of web space and 10GB of monthly traffic), perfect for first time bloggers. Alternatively, choose 1GB of web space and 40GB of monthly traffic for £60 a year. At the other end of the scale there is a popular choice with web designer Media Temple (www.mediatemple.net). This offers packages from $20 a month (approx £15) but offers gigabytes of storage and 1TB network transfer rates. Other reputable web hosts to consider are Fasthosts (www.fasthosts.co.uk), 1&1 (www.1and1.co.uk) and Heart Internet (www.heartinternet.co.uk).

To host a WordPress blog at a desired URL, ie mywebsite.co.uk, a domain name needs to be purchased. Try www.123-reg.co.uk, this offers .co.uk domain names from £2.99 a year and .com domain names from £9.99 a year. Another well-respected domain name supplier is Easily (www.easily.co.uk).

If the prospect of finding web space and getting a domain name seems like hard work, there is the hosted option. Go to www.wordpress.com, click Sign Up Now and all that's needed is an email address. This gives a new user a unique WordPress URL, ie myname.wordpress.com and hosts the account.

Find a domain name to create an identity for your blog

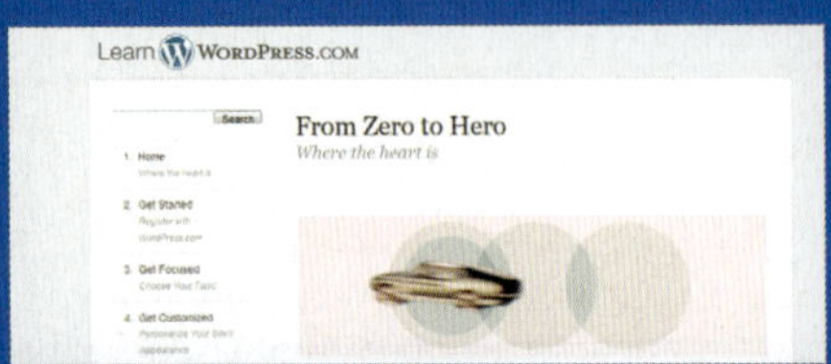

Try the free 'no hassle' option at www.wordpress.com

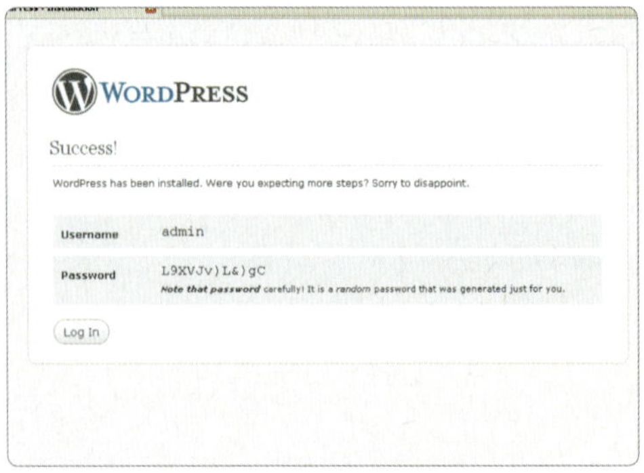

10 It's the Dashboard

Now add a Blog Title, Your E-mail, click the Allow… checkbox and press Install WordPress. Press Log In to skip to the log-in screen, enter the details just given and hit Log In to view the WordPress Dashboard.

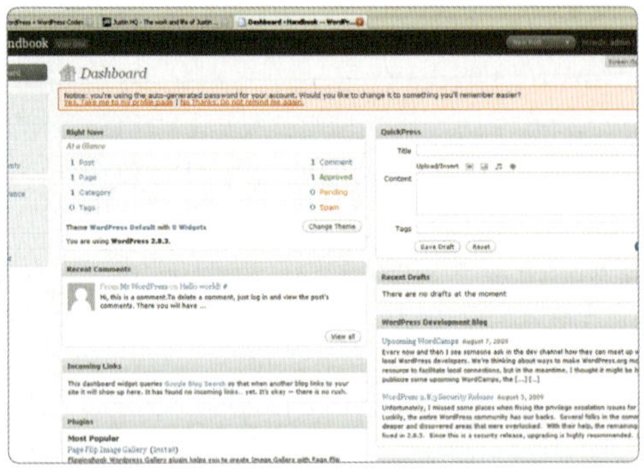

11 New password

WordPress automatically displays a notice telling the user that they are using the auto-generated password. Now add a new password under About Yourself, enter again and then press Update Profile. The new password will now be active.

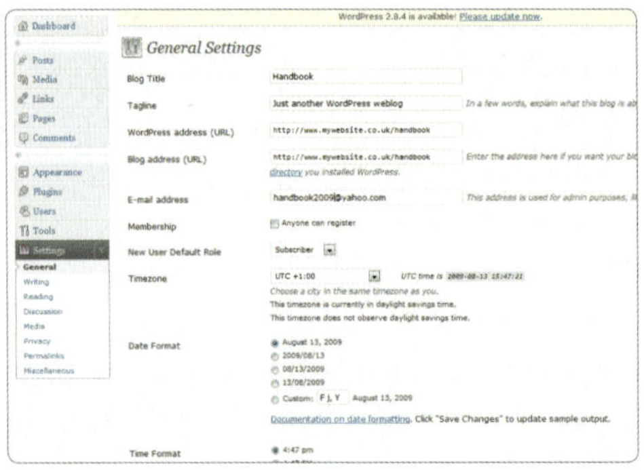

12 General settings

Click Settings to extend the menu and select General. This section allows users to change the Blog title and tagline as seen in the header. There is the option to change the original email address added at setup.

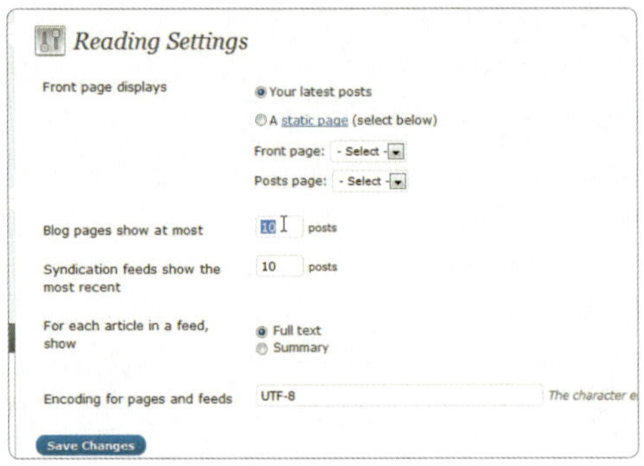

13 Writing and reading

The Writing settings includes the option to choose the default category. This will be applied when a post is not given a category. There's also an option to set up Remote Publishing. This allows users to post from a desktop without logging in.

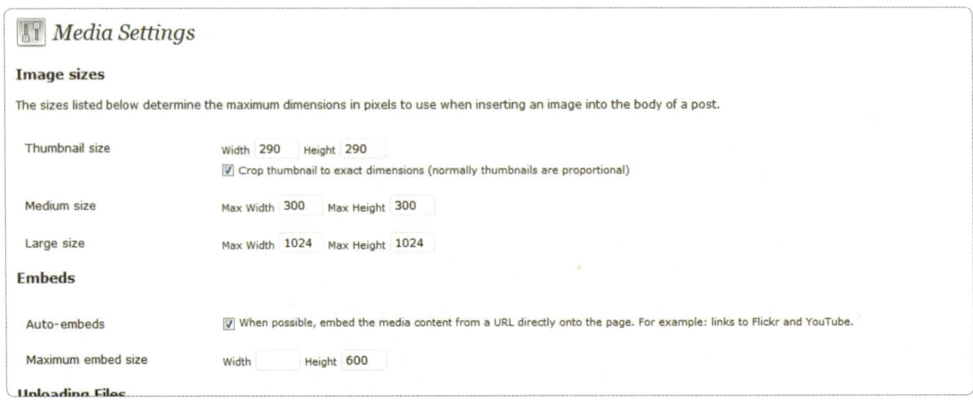

14 Media settings

The Media settings determine the size of images placed in a post. WordPress allows users to select the original size of the image or a pre-defined option set up here. Change the settings to the desired size. This makes sure that when a specific option is selected the image will be a uniform size.

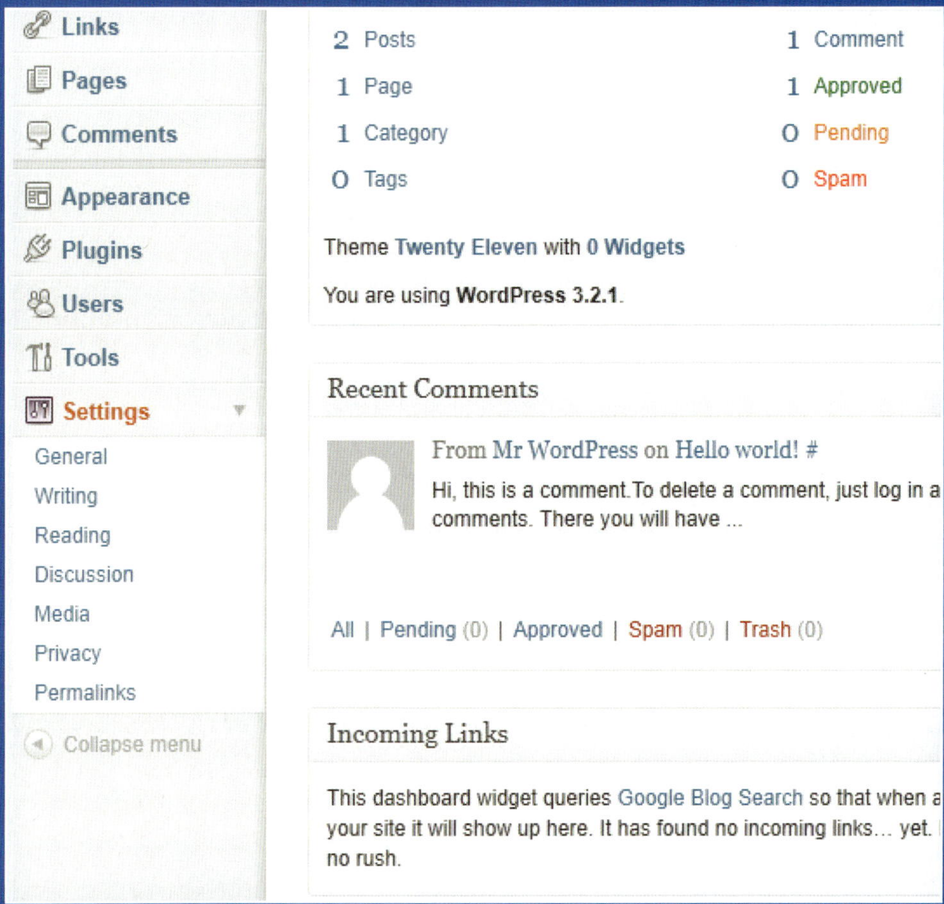

The Settings Panel

Getting to grips with the most common settings for your new install

In this tutorial we are going make some small changes to the settings of our theme. So from a fresh install, log in to the admin panel and within the dashboard you will see the Settings Panel on the bottom left. The Settings panel should be the first place we come to once our initial installation has been done because there are certain things that need to be set up from the off. In here we have seven options that we can make changes to: General, Writing, Reading, Discussion, Media, Privacy and Permalink. However, we only really need to make small adjustments to a few of these settings and some are more important than others, like the Permalink settings. So, let's take it from the top and make the required changes for a solid install.

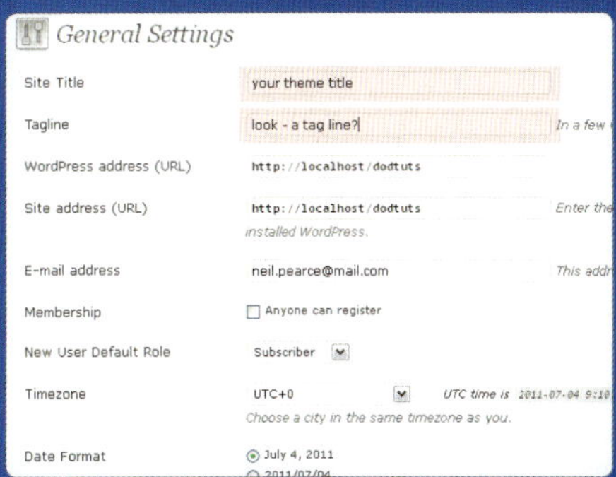

01 The General Settings

At the top of the Settings panel you will find the 'General' settings option. If you click to open that up you will see first and foremost an option to change your theme's title. You will also have an option to include a tagline here. These two options are really all you need to change. Once you have added in your website's title and perhaps your tagline, you can scroll down to the bottom and click the Save button.

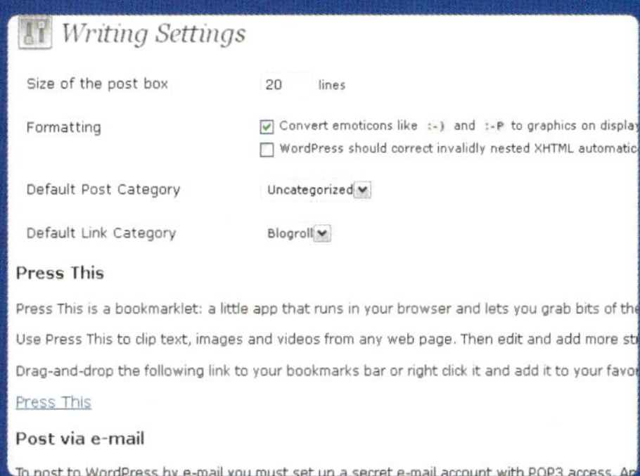

02 The Writing Settings

The next option down in the Settings panel is the 'Writing' option. Click that to open up our Writing panel. In here, among other things, you have the option of changing the amount of lines you have to work in when you're adding a new post to your blog. By default it is set to ten lines, but on a small screen this can seem quite cramped. So you can, for example, set it to 20 lines to allow yourself more space when adding content to posts or pages.

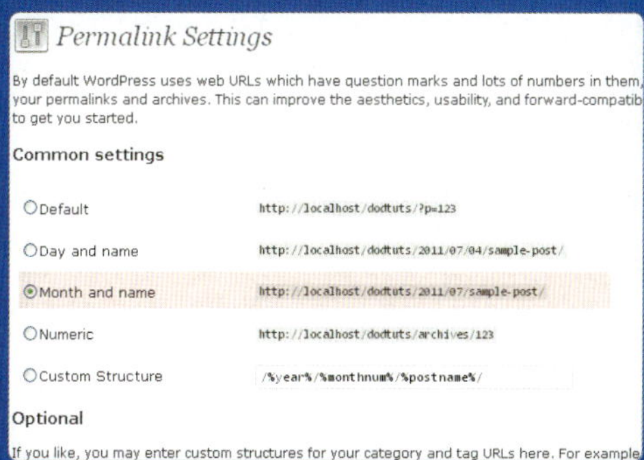

03 The Permalink Settings

The other options in Settings are not really important enough to warrant an explanation and can be left as is. But the last option, the 'Permalink' settings, certainly does, so let's open that up to take a better look. You have different ways your posts will be shown inside the URL and by default the top one should be selected. However, the best ones to use here are the second or third option as these include the 'slug' of your post which is good for SEO purposes.

View and organise WordPress Dashboard modules

Discover how to keep your WordPress Dashboard tidy and useful so you can edit your site, manage comments, post with ease and arrange modules in an order that suits you

One of WordPress's many strengths is its simplicity, and the Dashboard is an area where this simplicity truly shines. Offering everything you need right from the get go, you can quickly get on with the actual work of editing and posting to your site without distraction. As well as a side panel that offers navigation, the Dashboard is made up of modules. These are small widgets that provide you with information from various portions of your site, such as Comments and Links. As with most elements of WordPress, the Dashboard is customisable so you can set it up exactly as you wish and position the most important elements within easy reach.

"You can set your Dashboard up exactly as you wish"

Over the following nine steps we will show you how to determine which modules are shown on your Dashboard, where they are placed and how they are displayed. You will also learn how to save space on your Dashboard by expanding and collapsing your modules, as well as the side panel itself.

Dashboard modules

Keep the ones you like, and get rid of the ones you don't

Comment module
If you don't receive many comments or you don't to see the ones that you do, uncheck its 'Show on Screen' box in Screen Options and you won't have to worry about it

Screen Options
Click here to access all the options for customising your WordPress dashboard. From here you can delete modules or arrange them in a specific order

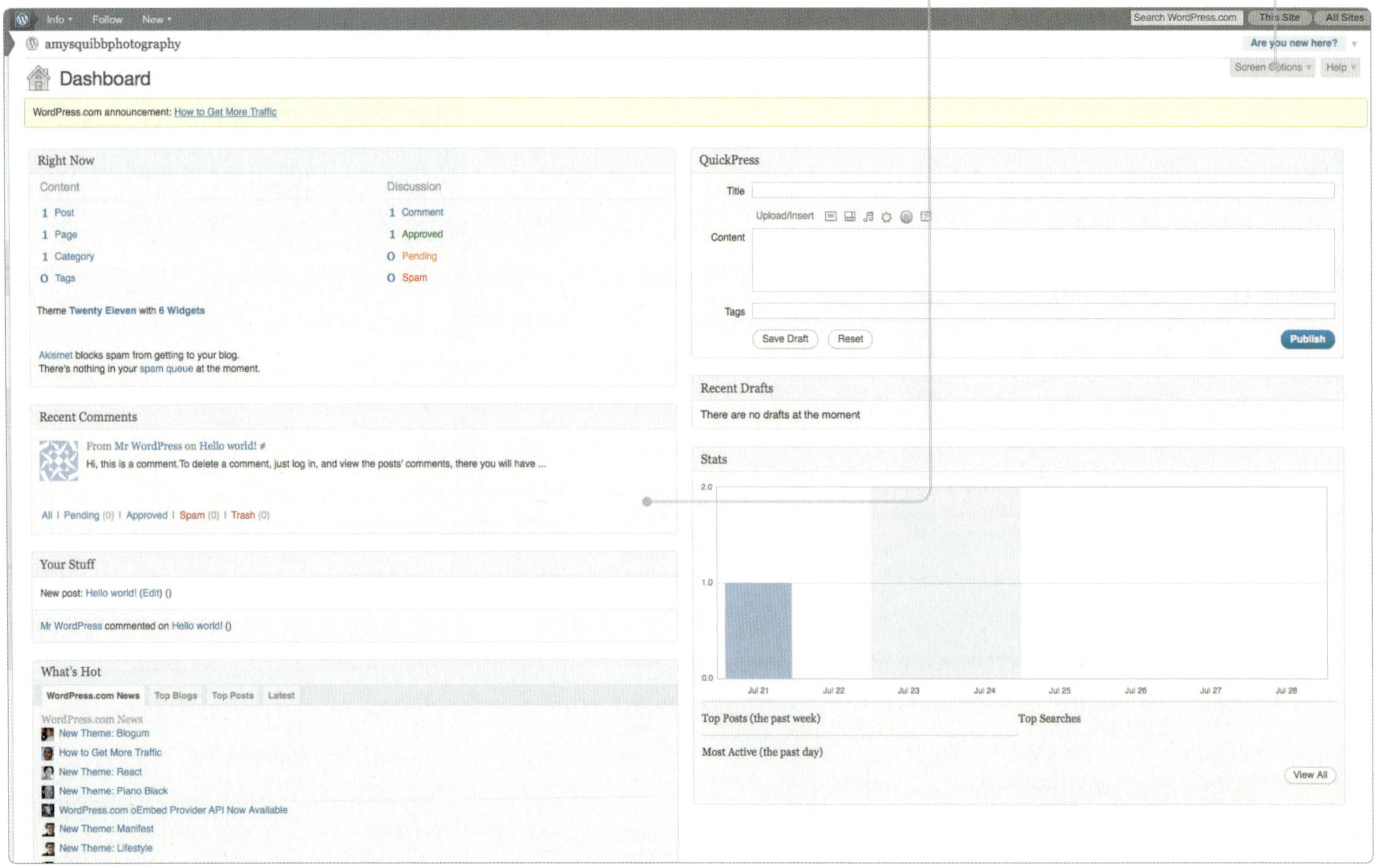

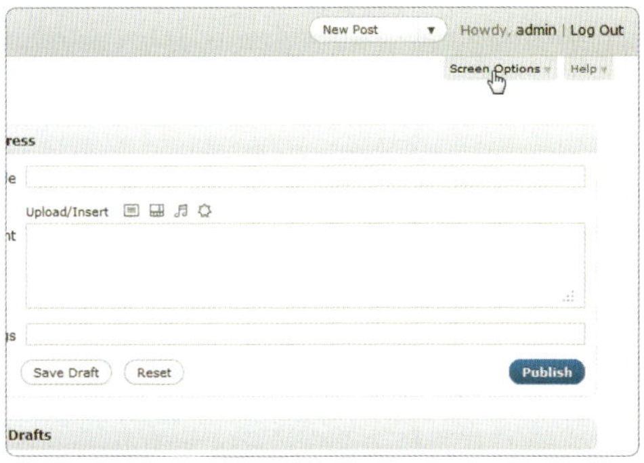

01 Log in to WordPress

Begin by logging in the normal way. The first page you hit will be your Dashboard. At the top of the screen you will see a Screen Options button. You need to click on this button to begin adjusting the way your Dashboard is set up.

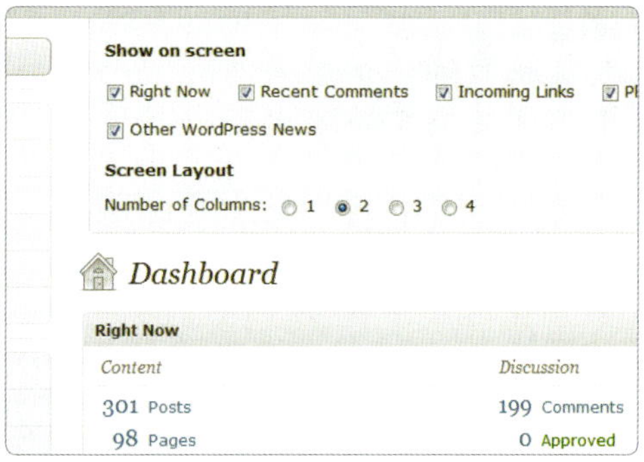

02 Screen options

The checkboxes under the 'Show on screen' section on the Screen Options menu determine which modules will be displayed by default on your Dashboard. Check or uncheck a box to add or remove the module from your Dashboard.

03 Screen Layout

Once you've selected the modules you want to display on the Dashboard you can also choose how they'll be arranged. Under Screen Layout, click on the number of columns you wish to view your modules in from one to four.

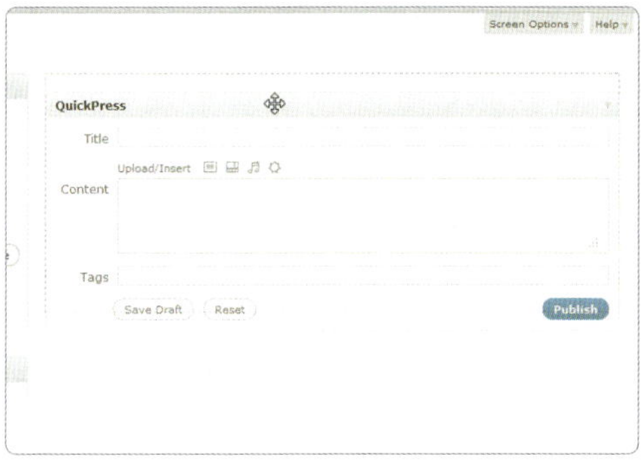

04 Drag and drop

You can now click on Screen Options again to hide the window and return to your Dashboard. With modules in place and the number of columns set, you can organise them. You have to click the title of a module and drag it to a new location.

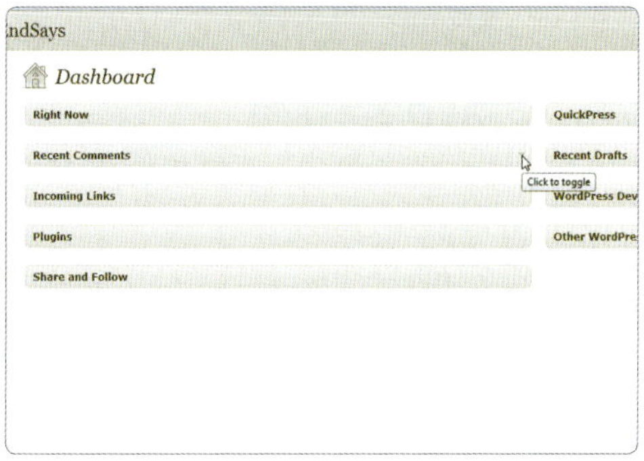

05 Expand and collapse

If you don't need to access a module all the time but you still want it to be available on your Dashboard, you can collapse it until you need it. To do this, hover your cursor over the title of your module and click on the triangle that appears.

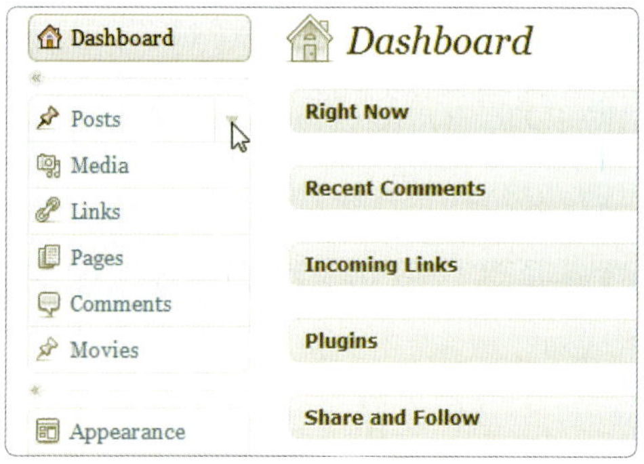

06 Side panel

The side panel, which includes Posts, Media, Links, Pages and Comments, works in the same way as modules when it comes to expanding and collapsing. You need to hover over the title of the side panel element and use the triangle.

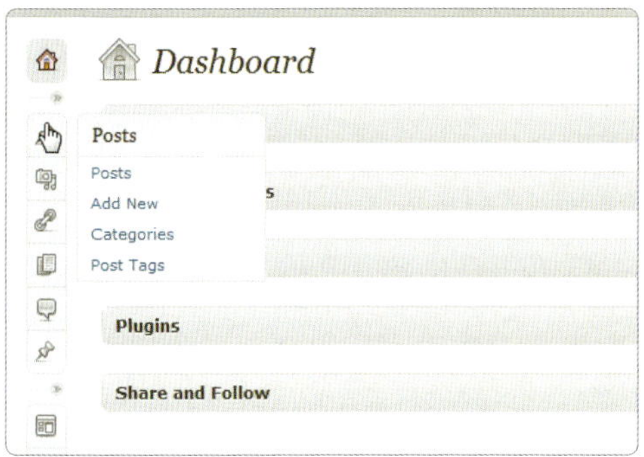

07 Hide the panel

If you want more room to work with your modules you can choose to hide the side panel and see its contents as small buttons. To do this, click on the arrow found above the side panel. Click it again to show the full panel.

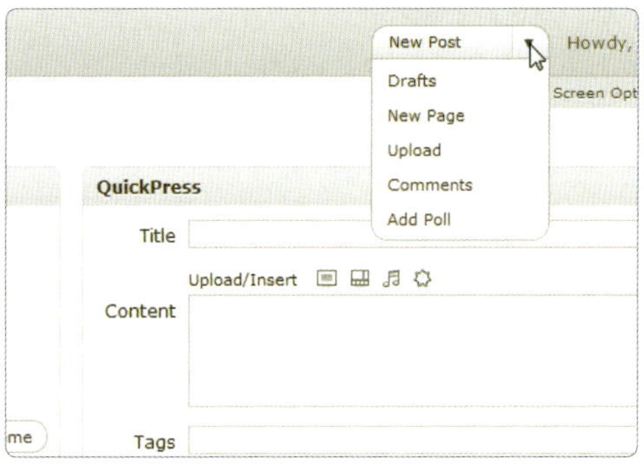

08 Easy access

If you want to jump straight in without using modules on your Dashboard then you can click on the New Post button at the top of your Dashboard screen to begin writing, or click on the arrow next to it to show other locations.

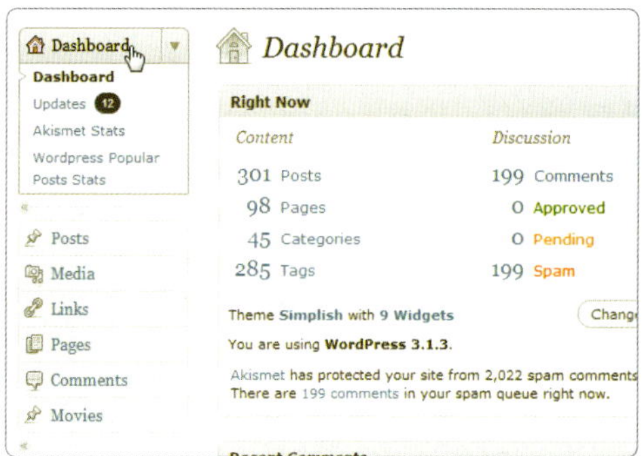

09 Back to Dashboard

The Dashboard button is found on all of the pages you will use in WordPress. If you move into another section of WordPress, such as Comments or Posts, you can always head back to your Dashboard by clicking this button at any time.

Your first steps to creating a WordPress blog

Every good WordPress blog consists of top-quality posts. Here we show how to create well-worked posts with text, images and video

Getting a WordPress blog up and running is much simpler than first time, casual and future expert users might think. Once past the installation process, getting a post online takes literally a matter of minutes.

The base of any blog is its posts and getting these right are paramount to a successful, informative and compelling blog. It is worth noting that the styling of a blog post is predetermined to a certain extent by the current theme. Nevertheless, the Posts window provides enough ammunition to ensure a post is well laid out and neatly styled with engaging content. The title is the first and perhaps most important element of any post; make it relevant and appealing.

Next is the text; again make this engaging and style it so it's readable. Beyond text the more obvious additions are images and video. Finally, before publishing it's time to add in tags and create categories to make posts more search-friendly.

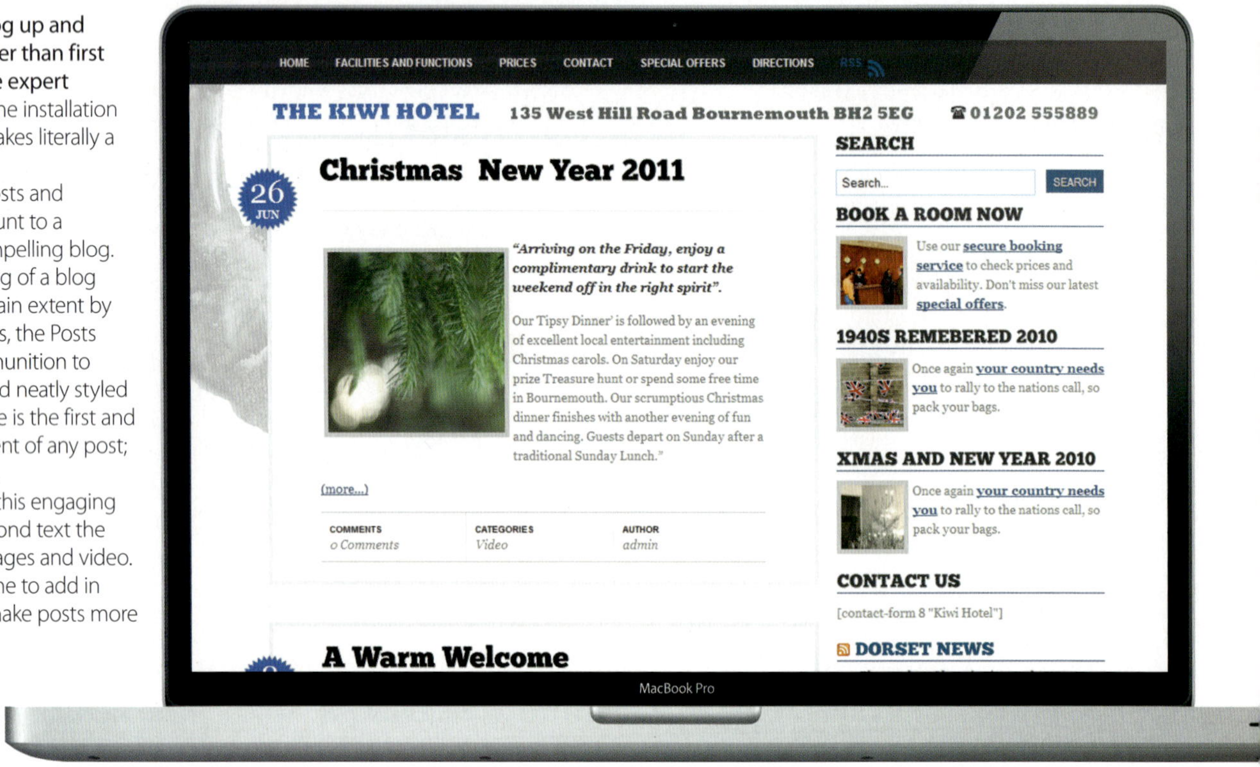

01 Log in

There are two options, first visit the URL of the blog, ie **http://www.myblog.co.uk/blog**. If the default theme hasn't been changed it'll have a Log in link under Meta. Click the link and add your details. Otherwise it can be accessed via **http://www.myblog.co.uk/blog/wp-login.php**.

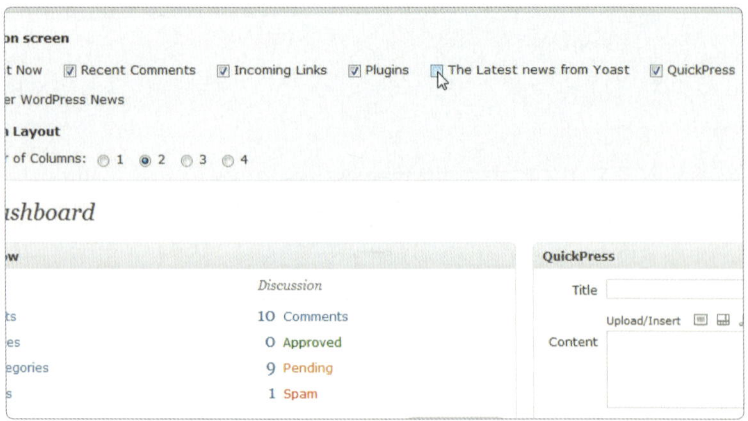

02 The Dashboard

In the Dashboard , users will need to pay attention to the menu on the left and to a lesser degree Right Now and QuickPress. The other modules Incoming Links, Other WordPress News etc can be hidden to free up screen space. Click Screen Options and the checkboxes of the modules you want removed.

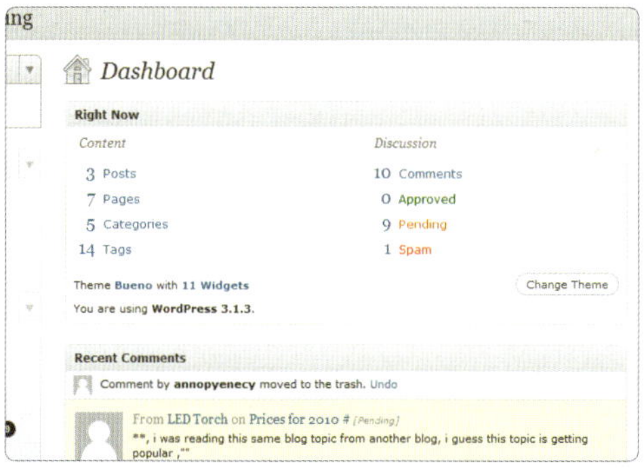

03 Right Now

The Right Now module gives users a quick summary to what the current state of the blog is. All the elements in the Right Now module link directly to its related counterpart. Click the title bar on a module to expand/collapse.

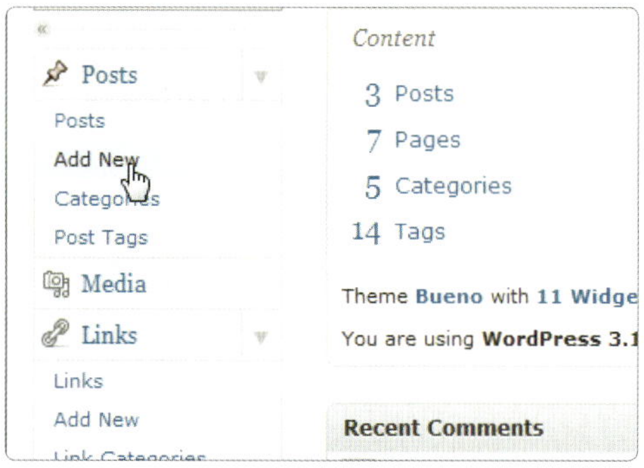

04 The Posts menu

To add or edit posts, the Posts menu is the place to start. Click the Posts title bar and the menu will expand to reveal the post options. To edit a current post click Edit and all the posts stored on the database will be revealed.

05 New post

The new post window is divided into two sections, the title and the body. The first text box in Add New Post is where the title goes. Remember, the formatting will differ from what you see as this is determined in the style sheet.

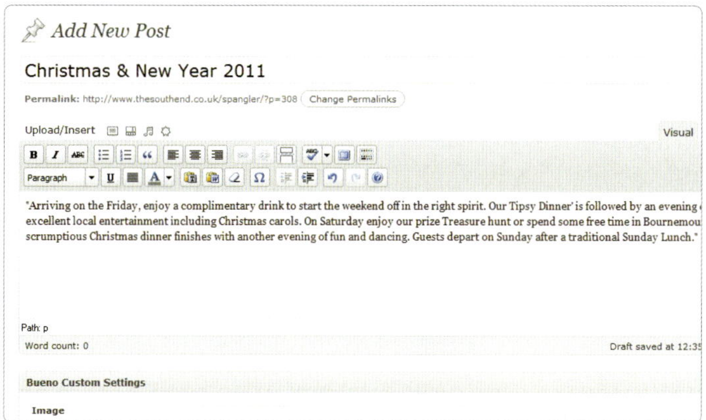

06 Post text

The body of the post is placed in the second text box and this will contain all the text and images found in a single post. To add the post text, type in the desired text like you would do in any other document. Remember to abide by any standard grammar rules, ie paragraphs and so on.

07 Simple styling

The Visual post editor is a simple editor, it is much like using word processing software such as Microsoft Word. Click the last icon on the toolbar, it's called Show/Hide Kitchen Sink, to view all options. To bold the first sentence, select the text and press B, alternatively use the keyboard shortcut Ctrl/Cmd+C.

08 More styling

To add more styles to the text, select the appropriate button. 'I' adds the italic effect, 'ABC' adds the strikethrough effect, 'U' adds an underline and 'A' allows users to choose a new colour for the text. Use the Align buttons to place your text left, right or centrally.

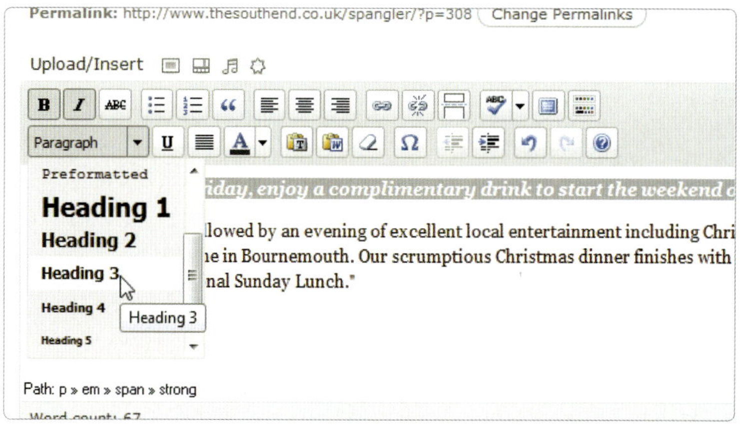

09 Resizing text

The text in a post can't be resized in the traditional sense. The text size is predetermined by the theme in use. However, the Paragraph drop-down list has a number of options, ie Paragraph, Heading 1, Heading 2, etc. Heading 1 is the largest, 6 the smallest and Paragraph normal.

Learning how to manage your blog

Here we include a few more tips and techniques you will need to know

Getting posts on to a blog is the main priority for many bloggers and the WordPress (2.7 onwards) Dashboard provides a quick and easy answer. QuickPress allows users to create and publish a post directly from the Dashboard. This is a slimmed down version of the standard Add New Post page and provides all the essentials without the need to go beyond the opening page. Users can add a title, text, insert images, video, audio etc and add tags.

Editing and updating posts is a simple but essential task and a visit to Edit>Posts will reveal all the posts in a blog. Each post is assigned a number of quick access options that only appear when the cursor is placed over the post title. The options on offer are Edit, Quick Edit, Delete and View. Edit takes a user to the standard post allowing users to edit as normal. Remember, when you've finished editing a post, hit Update Post to save any changes. The Quick Edit option works within the Edit Posts window and allows for users to neatly and quickly change categories, tags, title, etc. The Delete and View options do exactly what they suggest.

Beyond editing a post there are a few additions that we have yet to mention. Links are a key component of a website, and WordPress is no different. The standard toolbar includes two link options, Insert/edit link and Unlink. To add a link select the desired text and press the Insert link button (top row). In Link URL add the URL to link to (needs http:). By default, WordPress includes http://, so if copying in a URL remember to check that the http:// has not doubled up. Target allows the user to choose if the link URL opens in the same window or new window. There is the option to add a title, and to add a class. This effectively styles the link using a pre-determined style.

Use the Quick Edit option to quickly change categories, add tags and modify the title

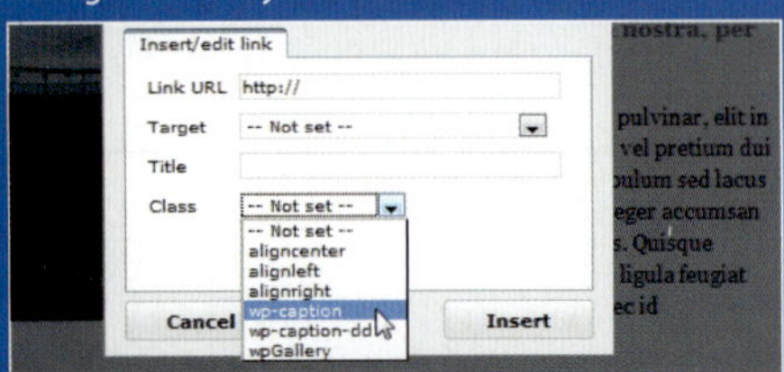

The Class drop-down list within the Insert/edit link window offers a selection of style option

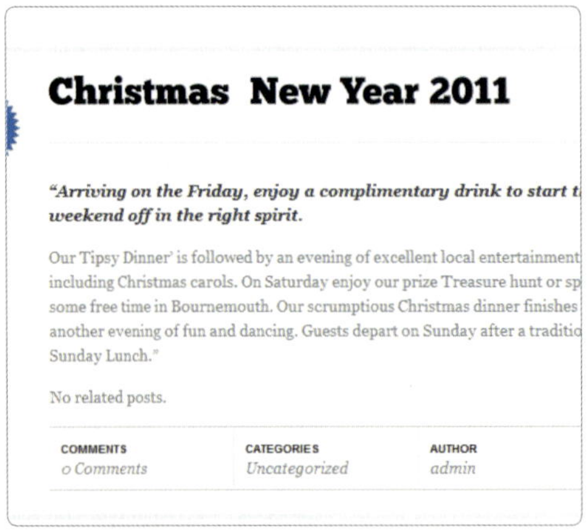

10 Preview post

The post is now beginning to take shape. Click Preview in the Publish module, this will open another window to display the selected post. Keep the window open and refresh when more has been added to the post.

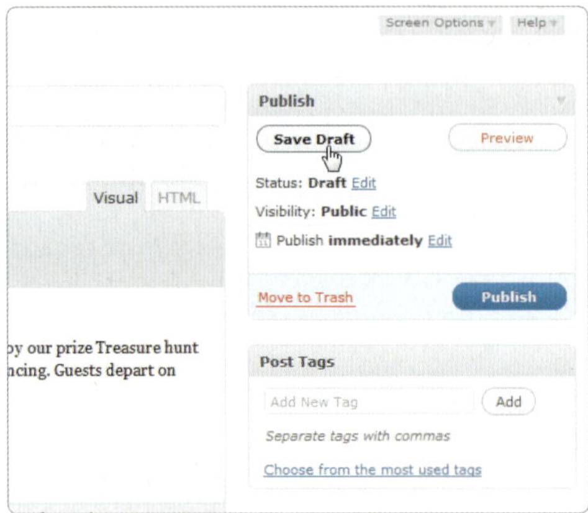

11 Save Draft

If the post is in good shape save a draft of the post by pressing Save Draft. This will save the post and reload the page allowing the user to continue adding to the post. The draft of the post can be found via Posts>Edit.

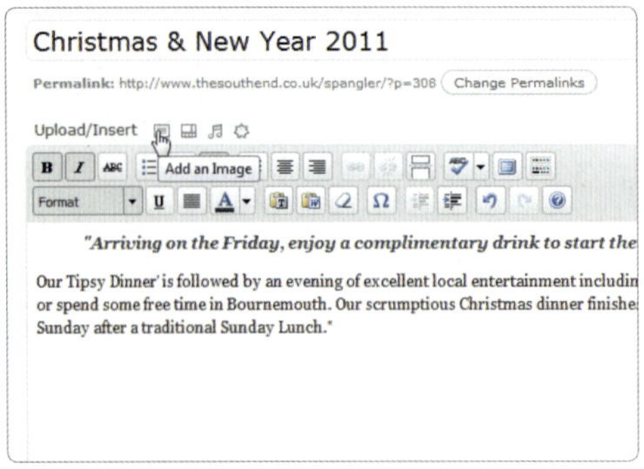

12 Upload an image

Post text is often accompanied by an image. To insert an image, place the cursor in the position where the image is set to appear. Click the Add an Image icon, then Select Files, browse to the location of the image, select it, and press Open.

13 Insert options

There are a whole host of image options. The name of the image is used as the title, this is the text that will be seen in the browser when the cursor is placed on the image. Caption text will appear directly underneath the text.

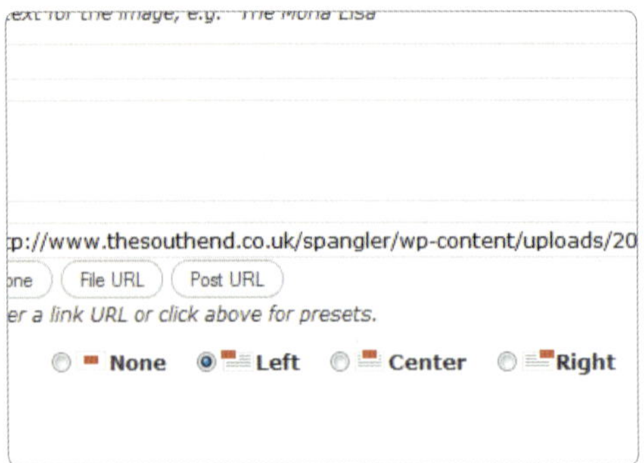

14 Image alignment

Before inserting an image the Alignment options need to be determined. If the Alignment option remains as the default (None) all text will be placed above and below the image. Left, right and centre will wrap text around the image.

15 Image size

Users can choose to select an image size before adding to a post. Full Size is the actual size of the image. The remaining options – Thumbnail, Medium and Large – are predetermined by the current theme.

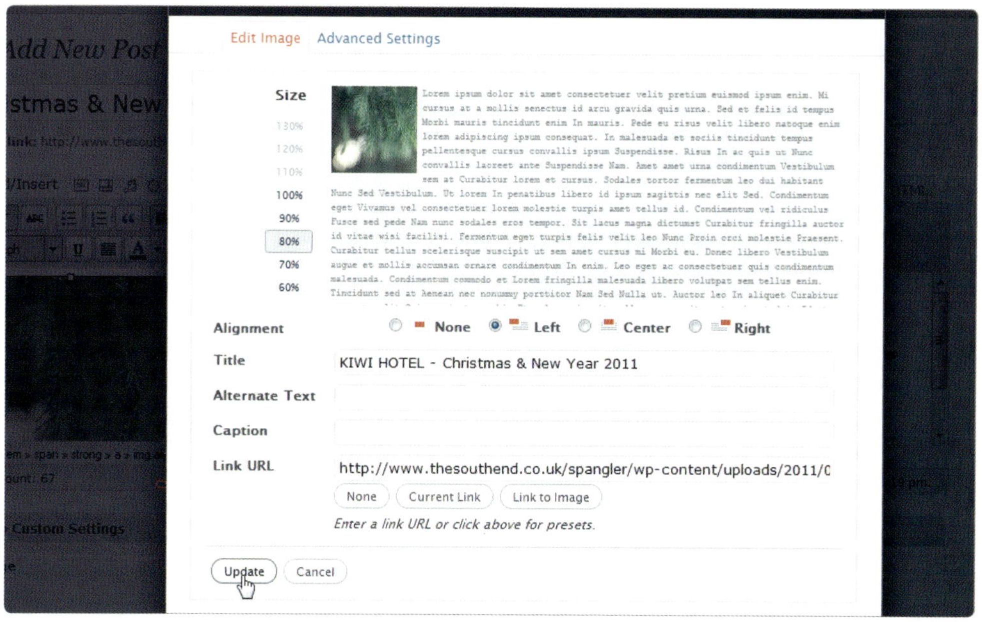

16 Edit image

An image in a post is still open to editing. Click the image and select the icon to the left to open the Edit Image window. Here users can choose to resize and more. Press Update to initiate any changes.

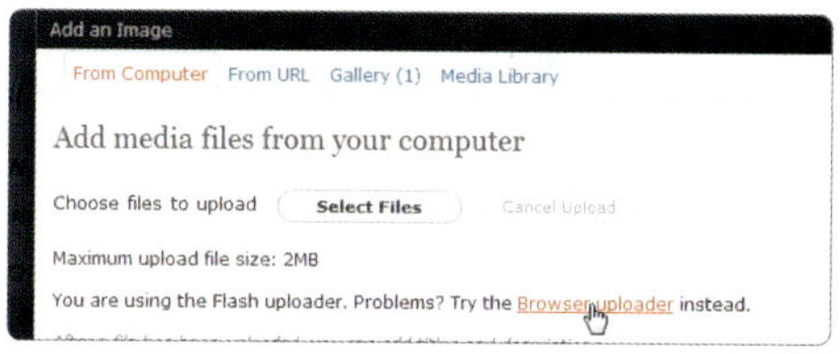

17 Browser upload

WordPress uses a Flash uploader to insert images into a post. If this isn't working users can try the Browser uploader. Click the relevant link and click Browse, locate the image, select and press Open. Press Upload to go to the Add an Image window.

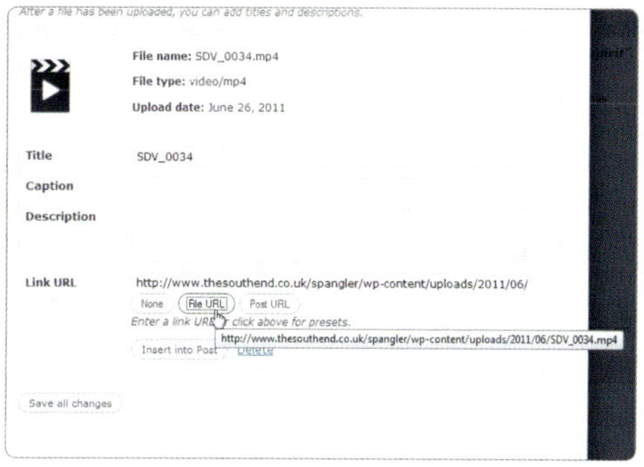

18 Link to video

Place the cursor in the position where the video is to be added. Click the Add Video button, select the video and wait for it to upload. Click the File URL button. This will add the link address to the Link URL text box. Click Insert into Post.

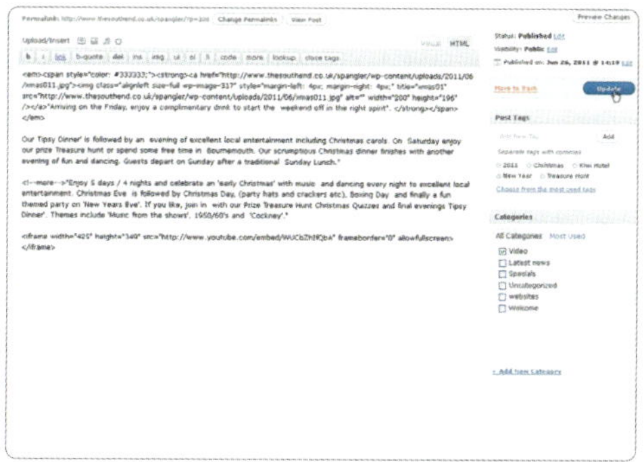

19 Add a YouTube video

Head to YouTube (www.youtube.com) and search for a video. Underneath the video is a Share button, click to reveal the Embed button. Copy the code, head back to WordPress, switch to the HTML view and paste the code into the post.

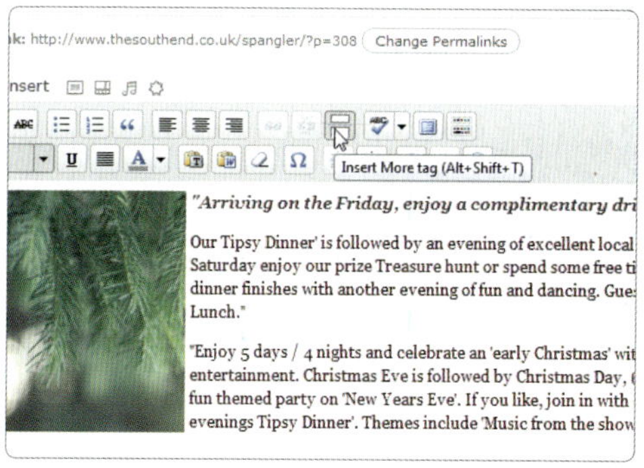

20 Read more

A post will display all the text and images on the front page of a post. To reduce the amount of post text on the front page the More tag can be inserted. Place the cursor in the desired position and press the Insert More tag button.

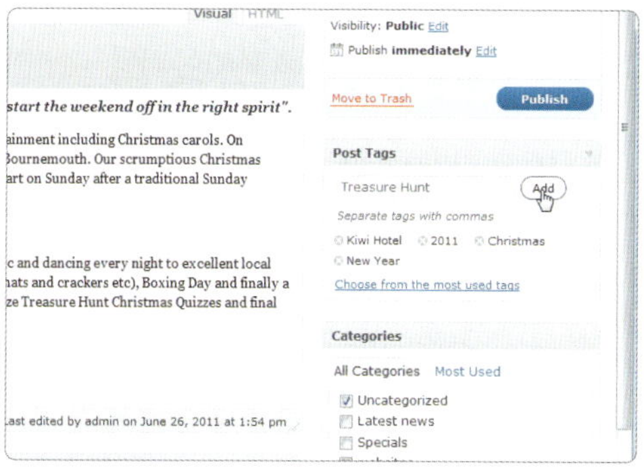

21 Tags

Adding tags helps identify the content of a post and help visitors find a specific post. To add a tag simply enter the descriptive text in the Post Tags text box and press Add. Repeat to add more tags. To remove a tag click the x button next to the tag.

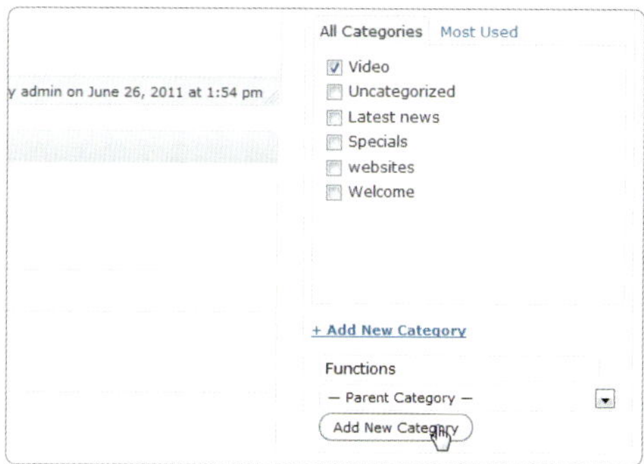

22 Categories

Categories help define where a post can be found. Create a new category by clicking + Add New Category, adding the title and pressing Add. By default all new categories are selected. Choose the relevant category or categories for the post.

23 Publish

Finally, the time has come to publish the post. Check the post via the Preview button, make any adjustments and hit Publish. The post will now appear on the blog front page. Head back to Posts>Add New and start populating your blog.

Edit your WordPress blog posts with ease

Whether you are updating some information or correcting a mistake, you will always need to edit your posts. We guide you through the various ways you can do it

WordPress is designed in such a way that creating a new post for your blog is as simple as typing it in. You won't, however, always get it right first time. If you've got a news-based site then you might need to update a post with new information as it becomes available, or sometimes you will simply need to go back and correct a typo. Thankfully this is not a task to challenge anyone. A WordPress blog is a dynamic site where nothing is ever fixed and final, and every word and image can be tweaked and adjusted until it is right.

In this tutorial we will guide you through the various ways in which you can edit your posts, from that simple typo correction to more advanced functions that enable you to batch edit your posts in order to help keep your site organised and make it easily searchable for your visitors. We also detail how you can sort your categories, so those readers who are only interested in one topic can easily get to what they want to read.

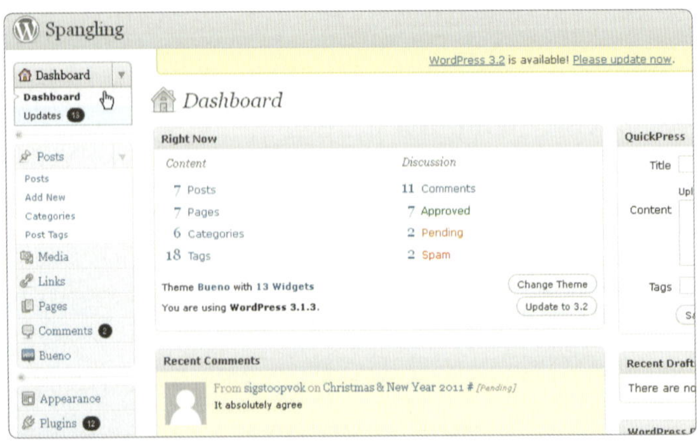

01 A quick check over

Once you have finished composing a post and have published it on your blog it is always good practice to go to your site and give it a quick once over – if you haven't got someone checking your text, simple mistakes can be easily missed. Click View site to preview it.

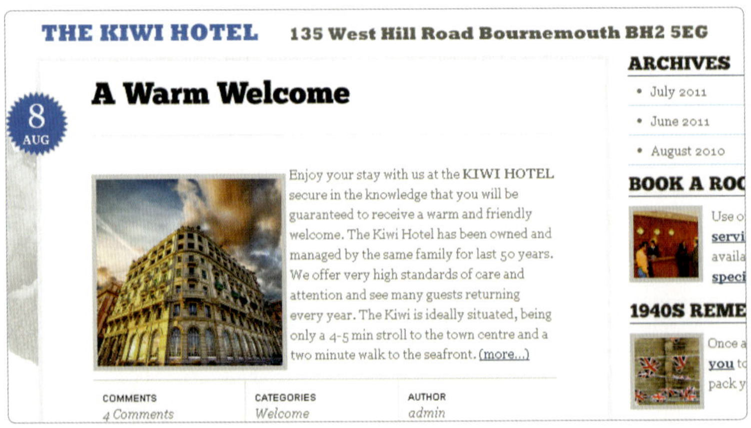

02 Editing shortcut

To edit your words, you need to click through to the post you have just published. If you are still logged in to your WordPress account then you will see a little red icon called Edit Post at the top of the post. If you click on this, you will be taken straight through to the edit post screen.

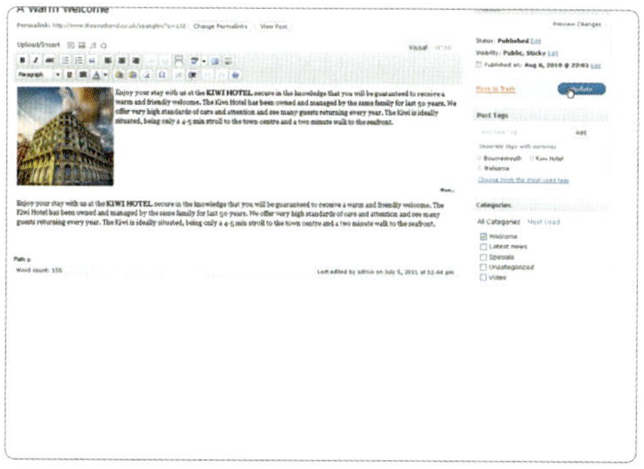

03 Begin editing

You will be back at the editing screen where you created the post in the first place. Use it as you would when creating a new post from scratch – text, images, URLs, tags and categories are all editable too. Click 'Update post' when done.

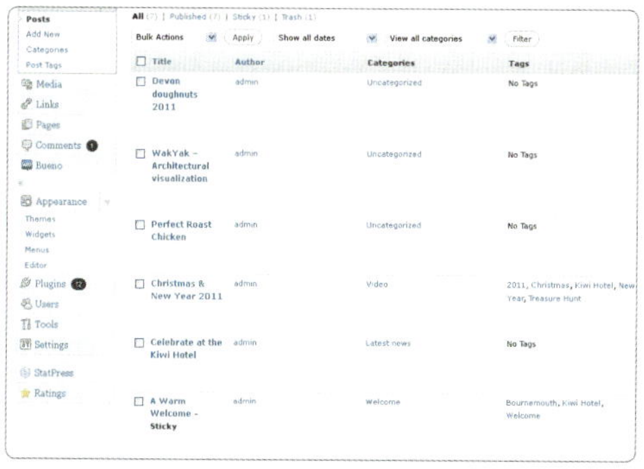

04 Post management

For much wider editing purposes, open the control panel and click on the Posts menu option found over on the left-hand side of the screen. This will now open a new screen showing every post you have published on your site.

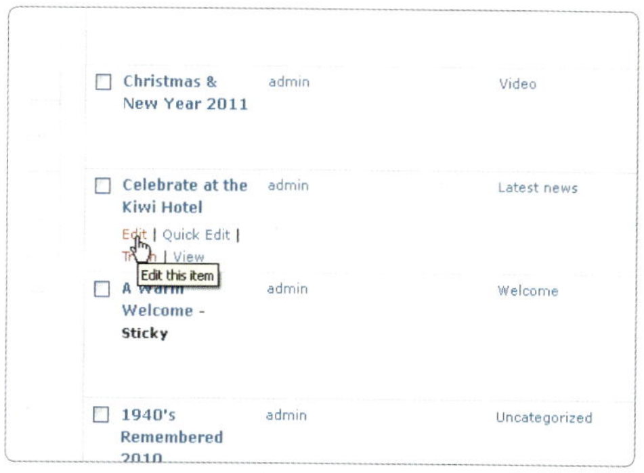

05 Editing options

Hover your mouse over a post and some options will appear, including Edit and Quick Edit. Edit is the same as the Edit Post option from step two, taking you to the regular post editing screen. Choose this option if you need to change the text.

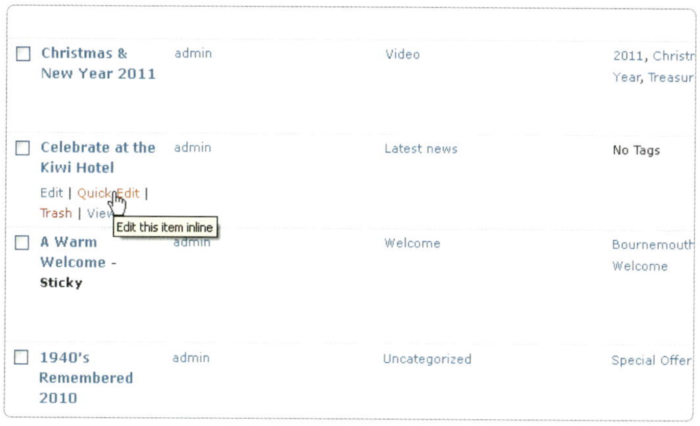

06 Quick Edits

If you are happy with the content of a post but still need to edit it more for housekeeping purposes, for example to add it to a new category or change its tags, you can simply select the Quick Edit option. The box will now expand to give you a range of admin options.

07 Changing the slug

One interesting – and useful – change you can make to a post is the slug. This is the part of the URL that is automatically generated from the title of your post. For ease of use, especially if your post is a sticky, you can change this to something more memorable.

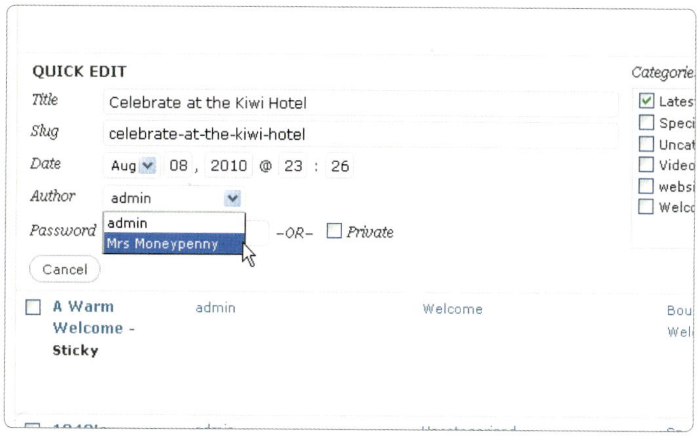

08 Author name

Likewise you might need to change the author name assigned to the post. Even if you are the only person posting on your site you might want to post site announcements under 'admin' or similar to keep them separate from content posted under your own name.

09 Categories

If you forgot to add your post to relevant categories initially then you can do that under the Quick Edit function here. However, if you want to create a new category you will need to either go into full editing mode or click on the Categories option in the left-hand menu in order to create it.

Updating RSS feeds

Keep people coming back to your site and updated thanks to RSS feeds

When you edit a post and click the Update button the changes will be instantly applied to your site, but your avid readers will not be immediately aware of the fact that you have changed the story. It won't be placed at the top of your front page, neither will your RSS feed be updated with a new entry. Of course, if you are only correcting a typo or tweaking an image this is exactly how you would want it to be, but if you have made a significant change to one of your posts then you need to be able to alert readers to your changes so they can find out all the latest news on stories available on your blog.

The way to go about this is by adjusting the date the blog entry was posted. If you change the date to something later than your last entry then it will automatically move the post back up to the top of the front page (where it will stay until you get round to posting again). In order to update your RSS feed you should change the date to something in the future. Schedule a new posting date of, say, one minute from now, then in a minute's time the story will be posted again (but not duplicated) and the RSS feed will also be updated. Users who subscribe to your feed will see the story back in their newsreading software, and the post will be marked as 'Updated' in order that they know they have already seen the post before and should be on the lookout for changes.

A final piece of good practice is to clearly mark the edits you make to a post so that your readers can find them easily. This especially applies if you have more information to add to a news story, or are making a change based on readers' comments. Rather than writing in the lines, add a new paragraph at the bottom of the post, marked Update. If necessary you could also add the word (updated) to the post title as well. Your readers will be grateful for this as it'll save them searching for the new content.

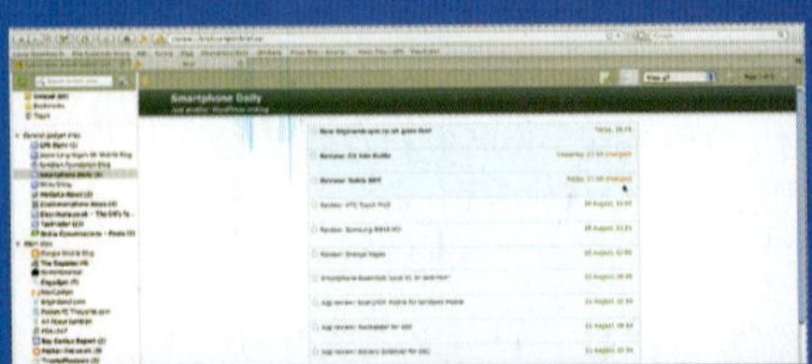

Updated RSS feeds will be clearly marked so your readers can look out for changes

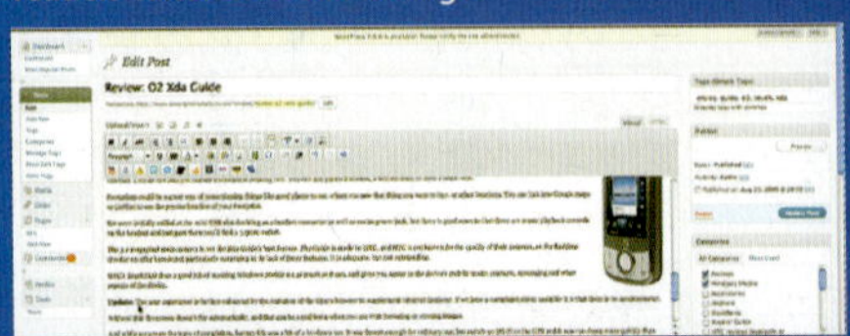

Mark the changes you make to your posts clearly so your readers can find them easily

10 Changing status

After making any of these changes, or indeed any others you may wish to, you need to make sure you click the Update Post button in order to apply them to the post. If you open another post before doing so then your post will not be updated. If you want to undo any changes then click the Cancel button.

11 Make it stick

Quick Edit is extremely useful for making minor changes to single posts but sometimes you will want to make similar changes to multiple posts, for example, when you are cleaning up your tags to ensure consistency throughout your site. Click the Posts option to view all the posts on your blog.

12 Update your post

After making any of these changes, click the Update Post button in order to apply them to the post. If you open another post before doing so then your post will not be updated. If you want to undo any changes then click the Cancel button.

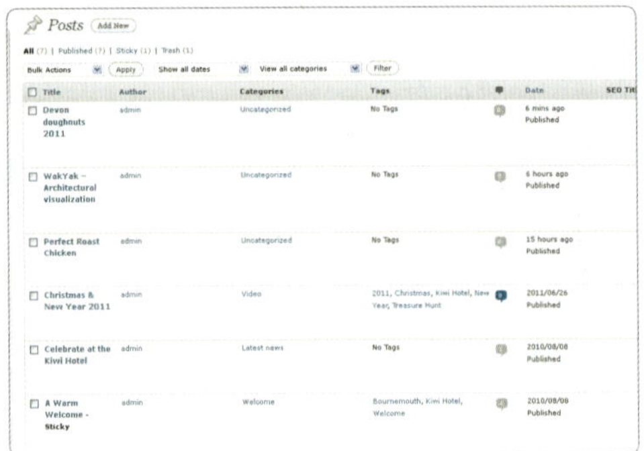

13 Bulk editing

Quick Edit is useful for making minor changes to single posts but sometimes you will want to make similar changes to multiple posts, for example, when you are cleaning up your tags. Click the Posts option to view all the posts on your blog.

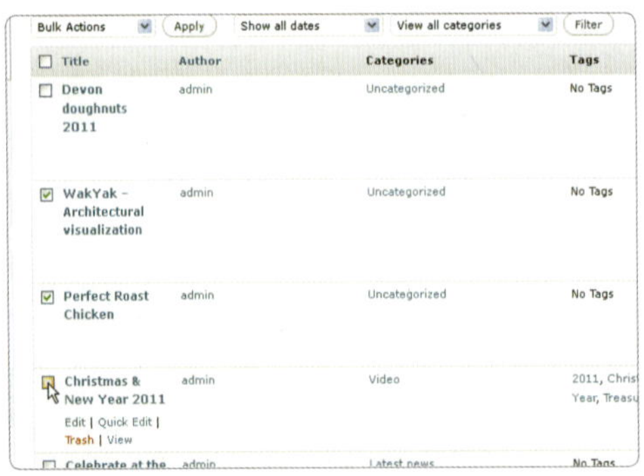

14 Choosing your posts

There is a checkbox next to every post, so tick the ones you want to edit in bulk. If some of the posts are listed on another page you will need to use the Search function to find them – clicking through pages will lose your previous selections.

15 Getting ready to edit

With your multiple posts selected, click on the drop-down menu at the top of the window that is marked Bulk Actions and choose Edit from the list. Click 'Apply' to open the bulk editing menu options. This feature can save you a lot of time.

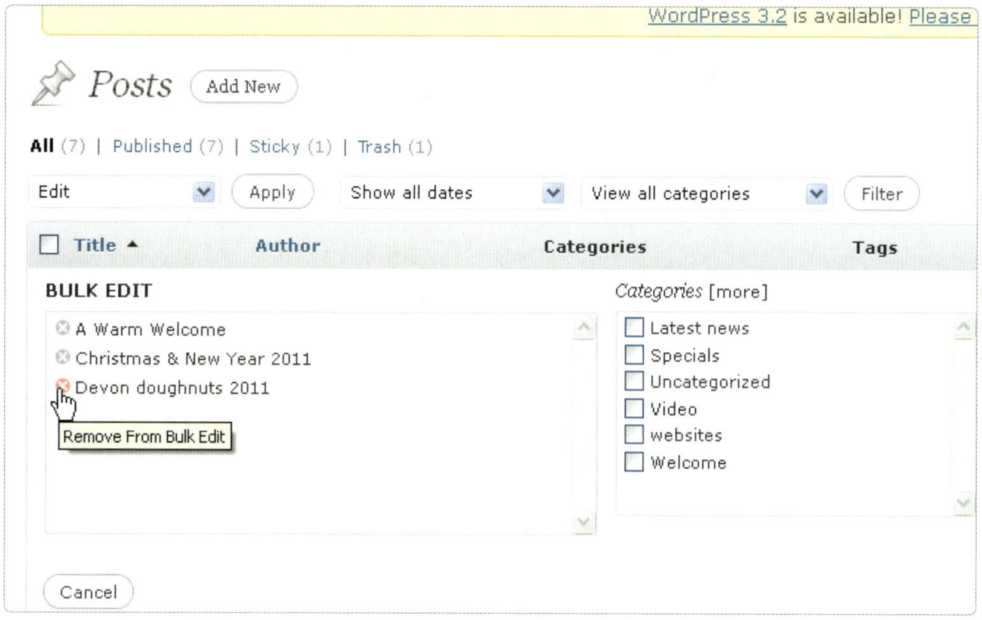

16 Removing posts

The left-hand box displays the posts you will be editing in bulk. Each one has a small X next to it – if you decide you don't want to apply your changes to any specific post you can click the X at any time to remove it.

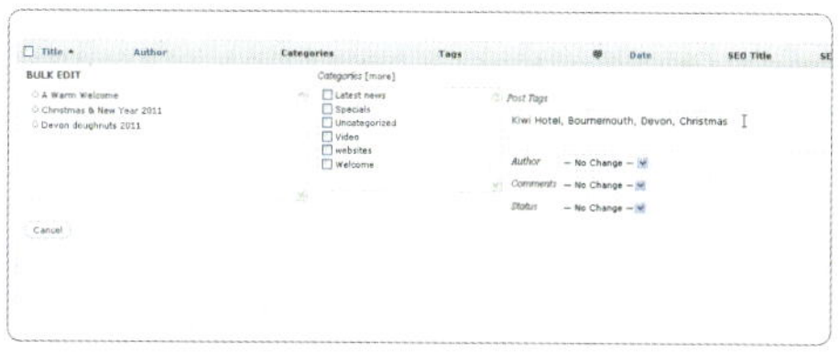

17 Adding tags

The most likely use for editing several posts at one time will be to assign new tags to them. Enter your choice of new tags in the box, separating each one with a comma and space. You cannot remove existing tags in this way.

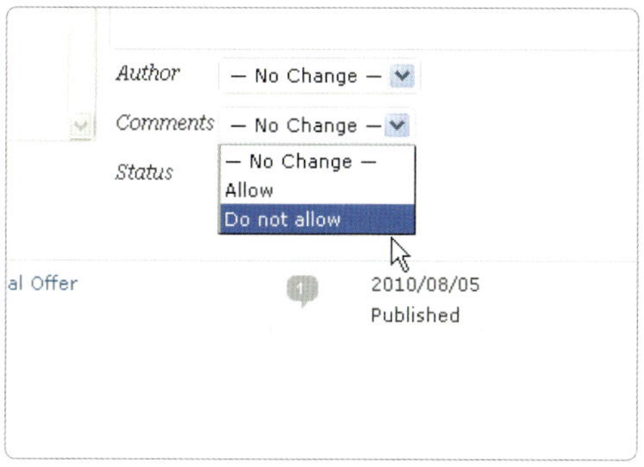

18 Closing comments

Another good use of batch editing is for closing comments that may appear on older posts. These are the ones that are likely to attract spam so you can prevent more comments by selecting the 'Do not allow' option from the Comments menu.

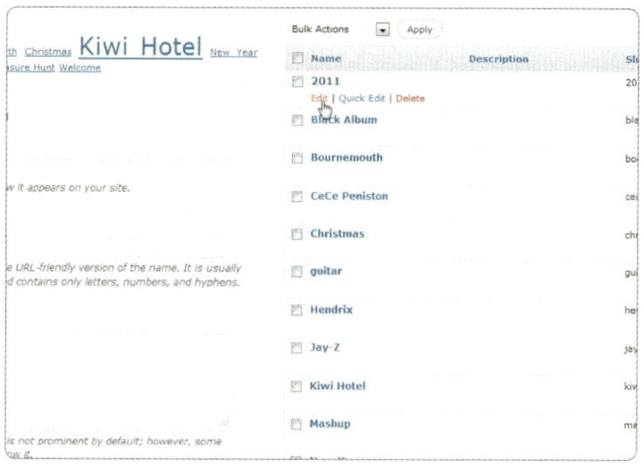

19 Managing tags

Under Posts is the Post Tags option, click to open. Here a new tag can be added by adding a tag name, slug and description and pressing Add New Tag. The available tags are listed to the right, hover the cursor over a tag and press Edit.

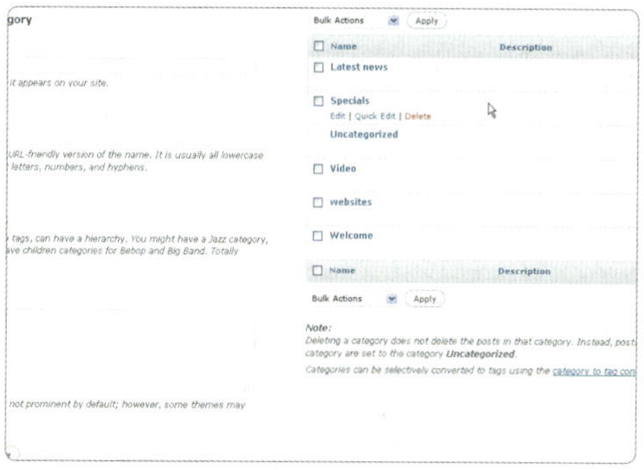

20 Editing categories

Categories are the most important way of keeping your site organised and its content manageable. As with posts you can edit them in bulk by ticking the box next to them, although in this instance they can only be deleted.

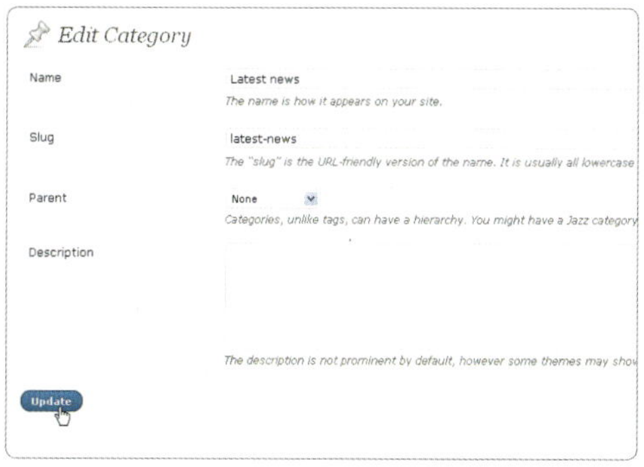

21 Tidying your categories

Hover your mouse over a category in order to see the Edit option. Click this and you can fill in additional details about the category, for example a description which can be shown in your blog's theme to give users more info.

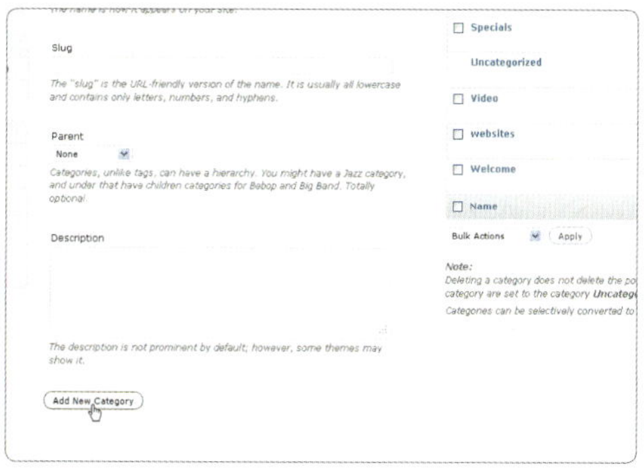

22 New categories

To create a new category enter a name and click on the Add New Category button. You can now assign posts to this category using the Quick Edit function explained in step nine. Try to keep categories to a minimum though.

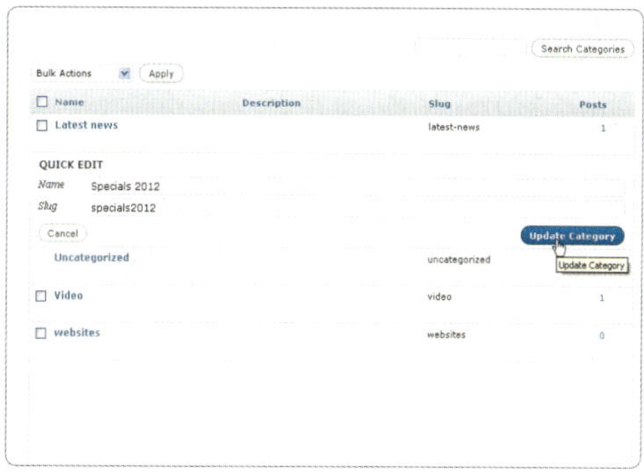

23 Category slugs

Finally you can change the slugs for each category. By default the category URL will be derived from the name, but if there are multiple words in it you might want to give it a shorter, friendlier name.

Post images into your WordPress blog

Every blog post needs an image to illustrate it, and WordPress provides no fewer than four methods for doing this

It almost goes without saying that good images are a crucial part of any blog – yours or anyone else's. Even if your site is not particularly visually oriented (ie you're not running a photography business!), a well-chosen image displayed on the front page of the blog is second only to post titles in encouraging visitors to click through to read your content.

They can also be used to help pace longer posts, breaking up large swathes of text into more digestible chunks. If you want to drive traffic on your blog then you need to make it look good – text-only pages will drive people away, and that's the last thing that you want to happen.

Adding images to posts is actually quite a simple process in WordPress, but the site does give you a number of different ways of not only adding but also managing images you've used. In this tutorial we will take a look at each of these techniques, and show you how to get the most from what will be one of the common tasks you will perform on your blog.

> "Images can also be used to help pace longer posts, breaking up large swathes of text into more digestible chunks"

Effective images

How well-placed pictures can improve your blog dramatically

Header
A vital part in any website design, the header is often the first thing viewers will see. If they see something as eye-catching as this, they're sure to stay

Breaking it up
Dividing your text up with a few cleverly placed pics will increase your site's readability no end. Most web users don't want to read endless blocks of text

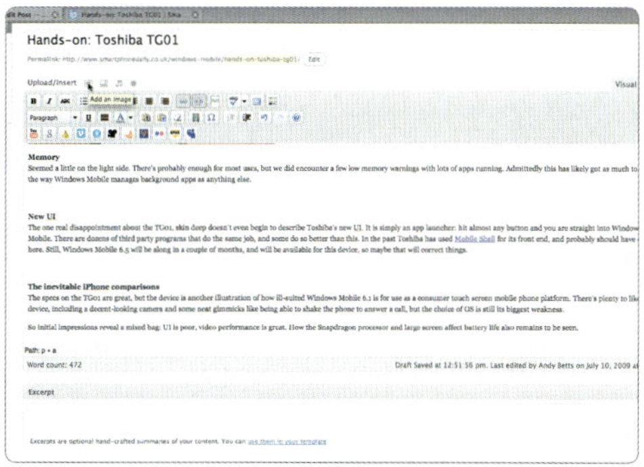

01 Position the cursor

As a general rule, it's easier to add your images either before or after you have added your text. All you have to do is position the cursor where you would like your first image to go then simply click the Add an Image button.

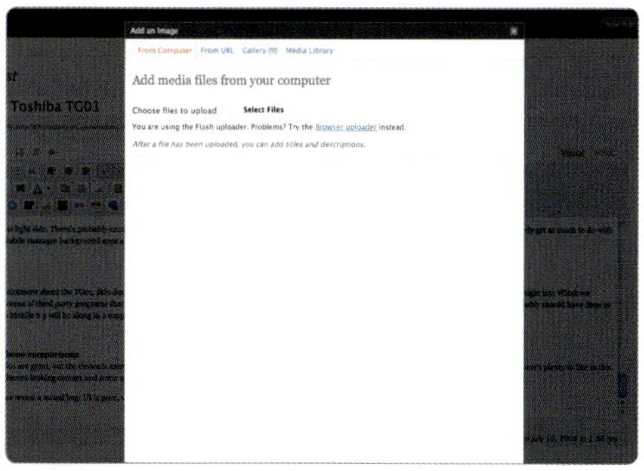

02 Find your images

From the window that opens you will see that you have four methods for finding and adding images to your post. The one you will probably use most often is From Computer, which refers to an image that is stored locally on your PC or Mac.

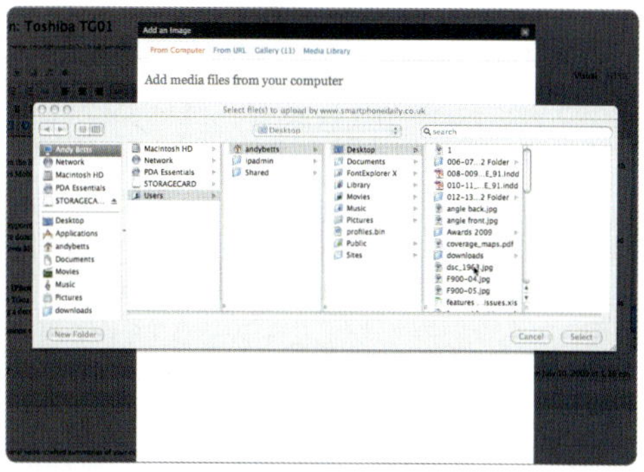

03 Uploading images

Now select an image, or images, to upload to your site. It's a good idea to group all your images together into a folder before you begin Ensure your files are JPEG, GIF or PNGs – WordPress will upload other formats but won't display them.

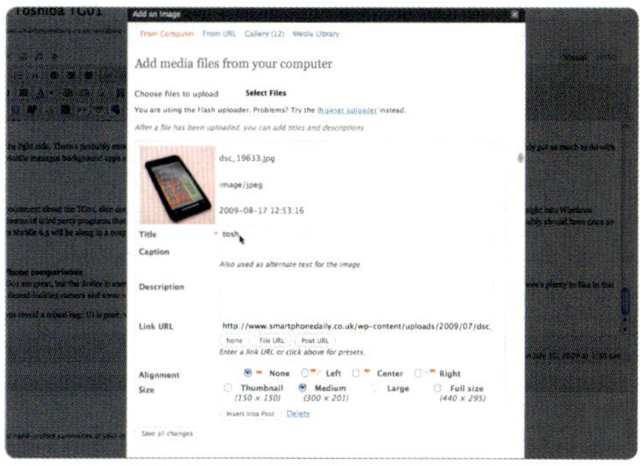

04 Pick a name

The caption serves as caption and alternate text if the image is not displayed, and a relevant name will help you find an image you later wish to reuse. Be aware that some templates might have problems displaying captions on the front page.

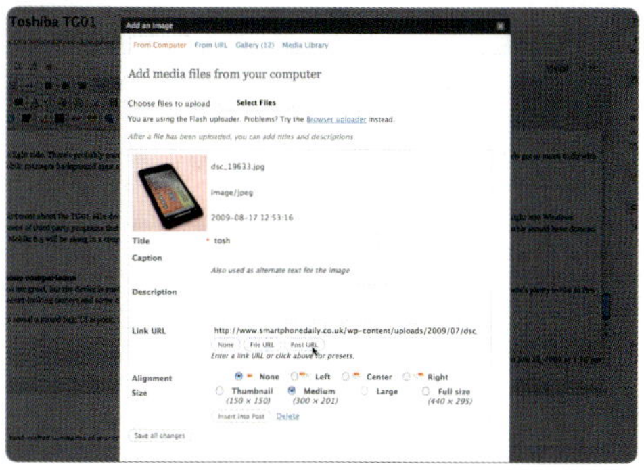

05 Adjusting links

You have three options on what you link an image to. Choose File URL so that when the image is clicked the full-sized version is displayed separately; or Post URL so that clicking the image displays the full post. Click None to remove all links.

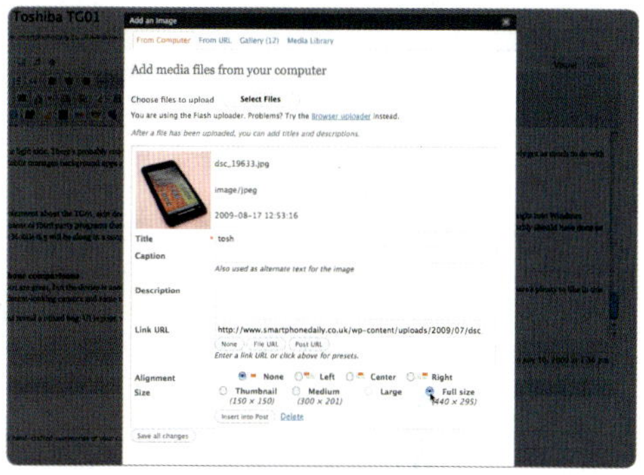

06 Resize the image

If your image is large you should resize it before uploading to WordPress. The Medium option will resize an image so that it is usable within most templates. Thumbnail crops an image down to 150x150. Full size may require resizing.

07 Alignment options

When you've selected the image size you need to choose how the image is aligned in the post. Align Left or Right will wrap the text of your post around the image. Your post needs to be long enough to cover the height of the image.

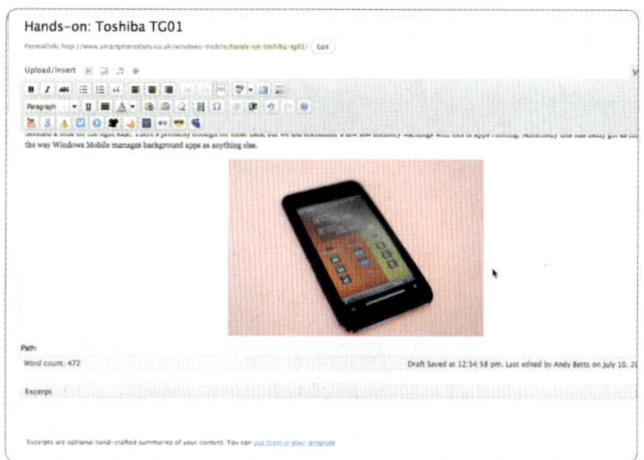

08 Inserting the image

In most cases you may choose None and use the default alignment. Once you have done this, click the Insert into Post option and the image will now be placed at the position of your cursor in step one, or you can just drag it to a new position.

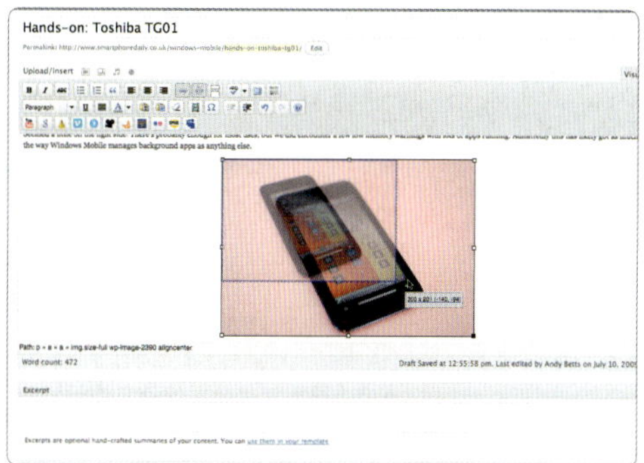

09 Manually resizing pictures

If you selected Full Size in step six your image might now be too wide. If this is the case you can resize it. Click on the image then grab one of the handlebars and drag inwards to make it smaller – the new dimensions are shown.

How to resize your images to fit your post

Taking the time to prepare your images can make your blog look more professional

When working with images on your blog it is vital that you consider the importance of resizing those images as a way of enhancing both the look and usability of your site. Dragging the image handles, as we showed in step nine, will change the physical dimensions of an image as it is displayed on a webpage, but will have no effect at all on its file size. If your site is image-heavy, and if you are working with photos especially, your original image files might run into several megabytes apiece. Put a handful into a single post and the size of the page – and the associated bandwidth requirements – will mount up. You might find that even with a fast connection your site's visitors won't appreciate having to load 10MB pages as a matter of course. When resizing your images you also need to be aware of the width of the main column in your blog template in order that it fits in properly.

As a general rule, unless you need to provide your site's visitors with higher-res versions of your images you can resize them so that they are no wider than that column. If you do need to provide higher-res images then resize to around 1200-1800 pixels then use the File URL option as in step five and manually resize the inserted image so that it fits into the column properly. When you do this the image will be displayed neatly embedded in your text, but clicking on the image will open it in a new window, displaying the full high-res version.

Remember that high-res images can easily be acquired and used on other sites, so if you have any that are especially unique to you then it is a good idea to watermark them, something you can do simply by adding your site's logo in the corner of the image in Photoshop. To the same end, if you use images found on other sites always be sure to credit them and to link to the page where you found it.

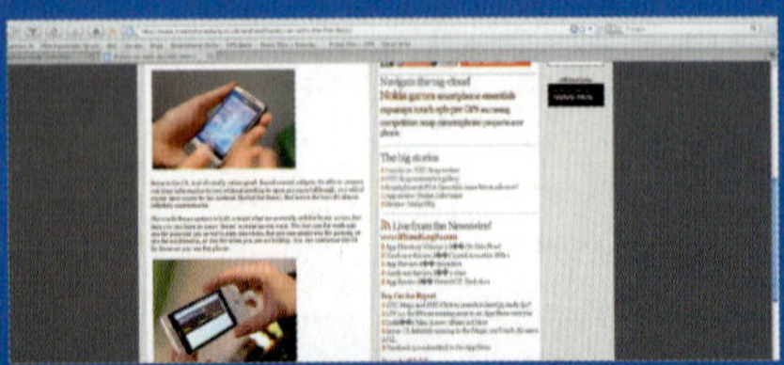

Size your images to fit neatly into the main column of your blog template

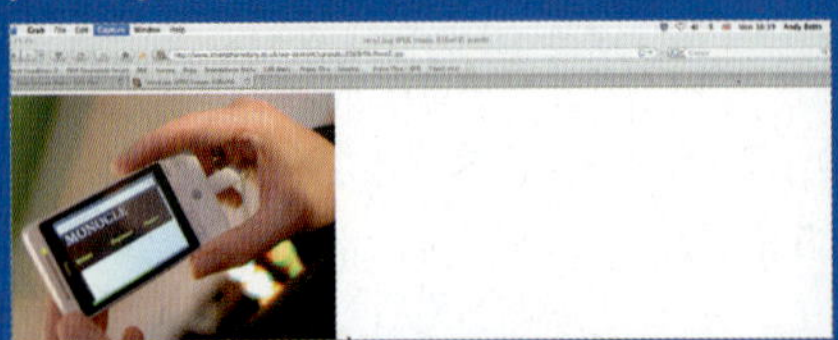

Linking to the file will also ensure users can view a higher res version if they need to

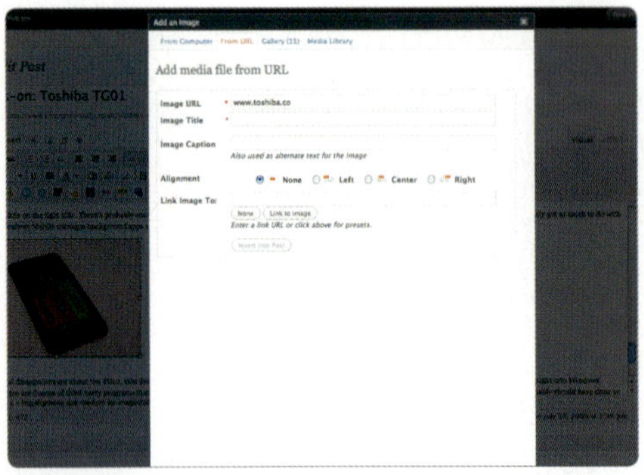

10 Images from URLs

The other options for inserting images include 'from URL'. This requires you to enter the URL of an image hosted on another site. . You should use externally hosted images very sparingly, since displaying the image on your site will use the other site's bandwidth.

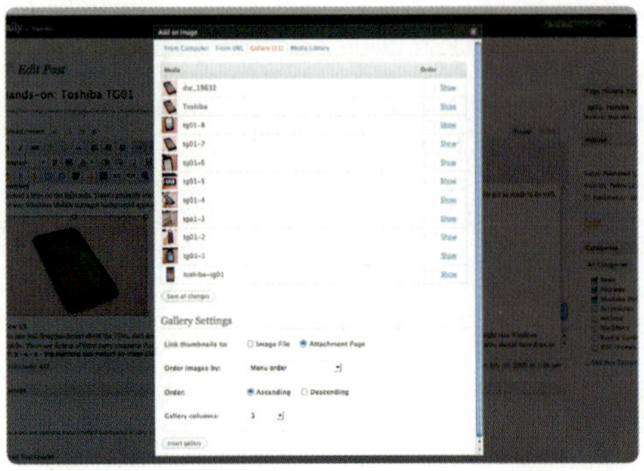

11 The gallery

The third image option is Gallery. What this does is show all of the images associated with the post you are editing. If you uploaded multiple images in step three then they'll all be listed here, ready for you to edit and insert them into the post. It's not possible to batch edit all of your images.

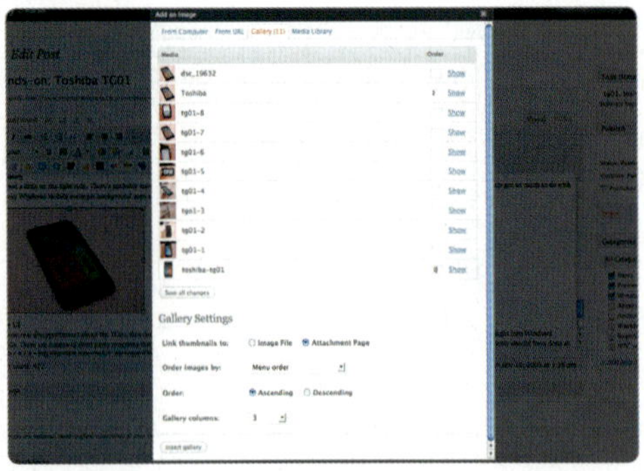

12 Create an image gallery

If you want to insert a thumbnail image gallery into your post, view the bottom half of the gallery screen. The Gallery Settings enables you to post an entire group of images in one go. To manually order them you need to enter a number in the Order column, then just click Insert Gallery .

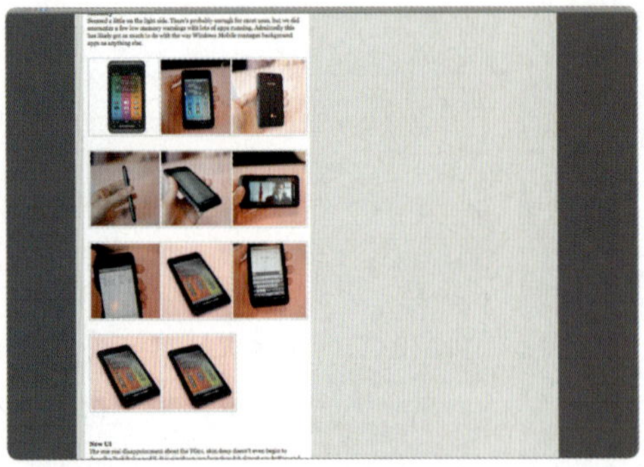

13 The Media Library

The final option is the Media Library, where you can access every image you have uploaded to your site. This is where you come when you need to reuse images already posted. So long as you've given them sensible names they will be easily searchable. Click Show to see the usual options.

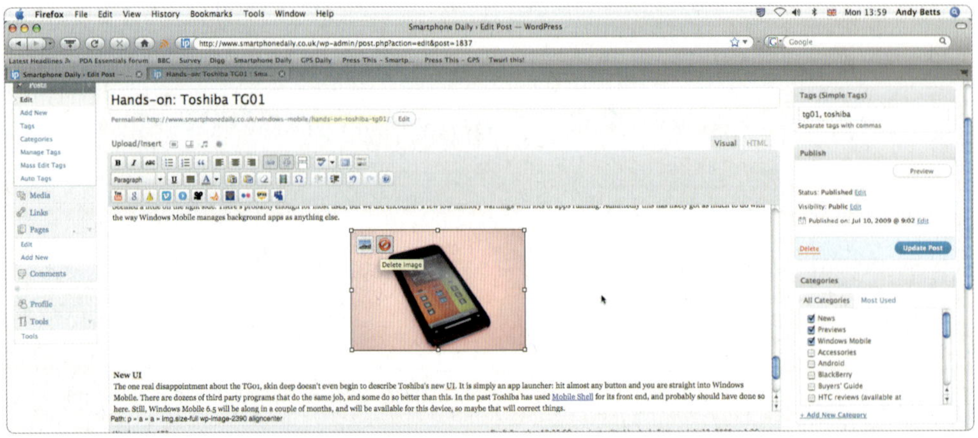

14 Editing and deleting

If at any point you want to make changes to the way an image is displayed on your blog to simply click on it in the edit window and then choose the Edit Image button. This will take you right back the settings screen where all options are full tweakable. To remove an image click the Delete button.

Using the Featured Image option

How to use the Featured Image option for your blog posts

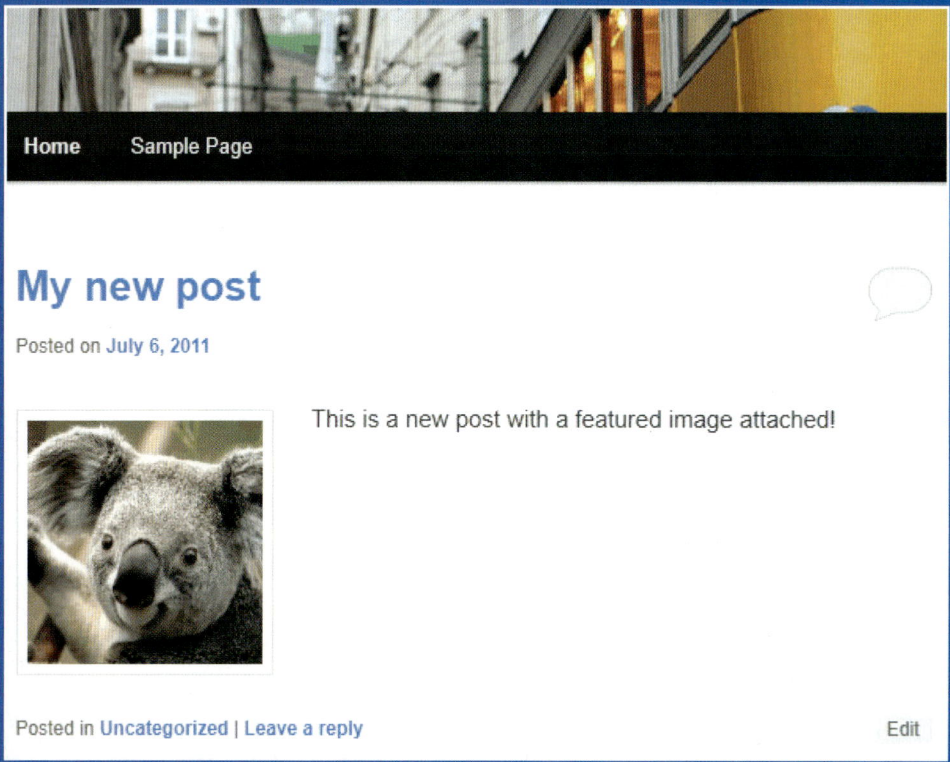

One of the greatest things about WordPress is the way it takes care of things that would take an experienced designer/developer a while to achieve. It just makes things easy and the Featured Image option is no exception. The basic idea behind the Featured Image function is that many bloggers, on their homepage, want to display an image that is associated with a post. However, implementing this has always been tricky. Previously, users had to take advantage of custom fields, which would allow users to specify additional information about a post, in this case the location of a thumbnail image. So since the introduction of version 3.0 the user simply uploads a single image, designates it as a featured image and then WordPress resizes it as appropriate and places it into the theme where desired. So, let's take a look how this is done.

"Since the introduction of version 3.0 the user simply uploads a single image, designates it as a featured image and then WordPress resizes it as appropriate and places it into the theme"

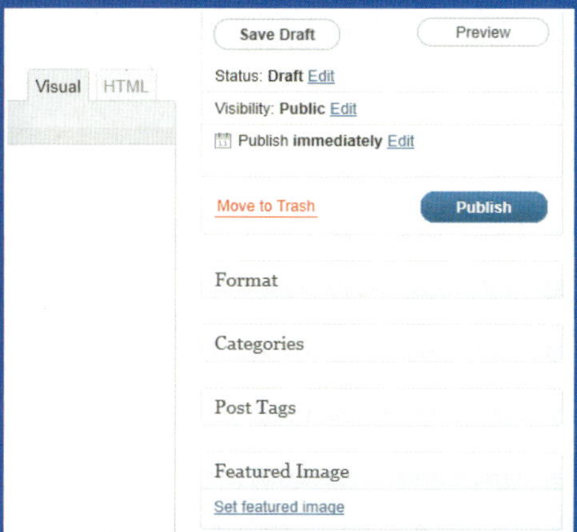

01 Use the Set Featured Image link

Once logged into your dashboard you should see a Featured Image box on the right-hand side of the post page. Initially it will only include a link to "Set Featured Image". Clicking the link will open up the usual WordPress image uploader where you will upload the image as usual.

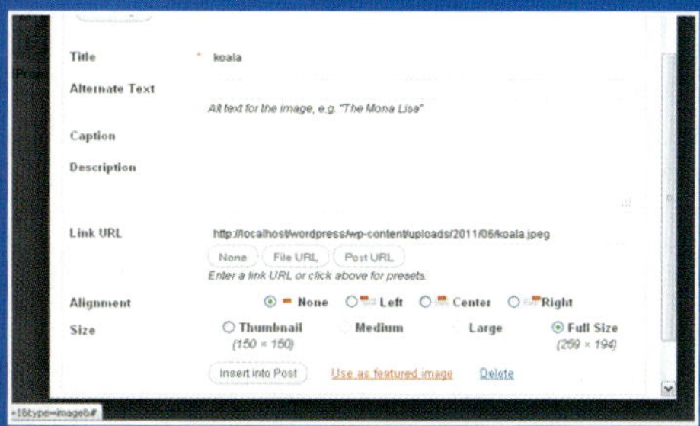

02 Once uploaded

Once you have finished uploading, a preview of the image should appear in the pop-up dialog box and you are free to insert the image into the post as with any other image. WordPress should take care of the rest, including resizing, cropping and ensuring that the image is in the right places.

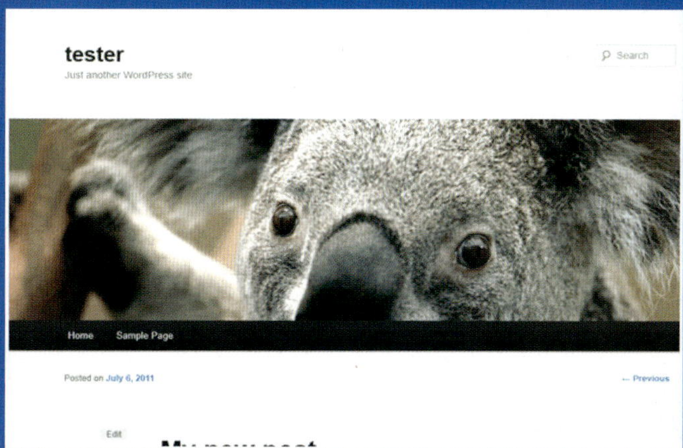

03 Twenty Eleven theme changes

If you have been using the Twenty Ten theme up until now, you'll see that once the featured image has been uploaded and saved, it is found on the post page. But the Twenty Eleven theme actually adds it to the header of that post.

Add a gallery of images in WordPress

Discover how to upload multiple images, create uniform image dimensions and choose the number of columns to create the perfect image gallery

When using WordPress the typical scenario for adding images is to insert a single instance, a simple and effective scenario. However, if more images are needed for a single post, or page, then the WordPress Gallery feature is the perfect solution. Users can upload multiple images, which WordPress puts into a gallery, making a nice visual element that allows you to display a multitude of images all in one go.

The images can still be added individually or there is the option to upload the whole gallery in one fell swoop. Adding the entire gallery of images is nothing more than a single click, but there are a number of options to set up before you actually get round to inserting. Users have the option to define where the thumbnails link to, what order they are displayed in and how many columns they want across a post or page.

Once the gallery is finally in place it's a quick click of the Edit button and the settings can be modified as desired, giving you the option of adding that personal touch and fitting in with your theme. There is also the option to change the dimensions of thumbnails in the gallery to suit any post or page.

"Adding the entire gallery of images is nothing more than a single click"

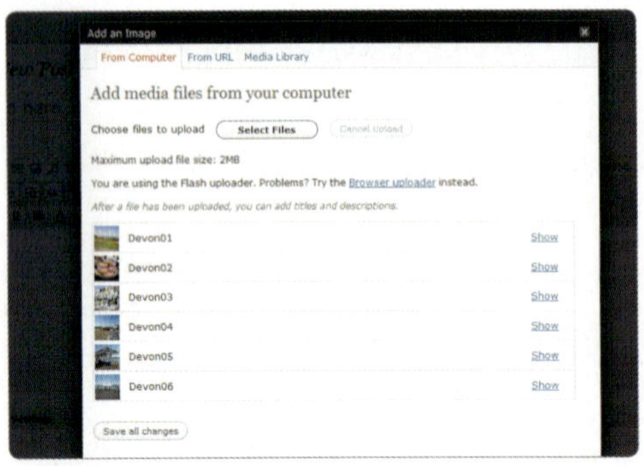

01 Add images

Upload all the necessary images. Create a new post and click the Add an Image icon that resides next to Upload/Insert. Now click Select Files, locate all the necessary files, use Shift + arrow keys to select multiple images and press Open to upload all the images.

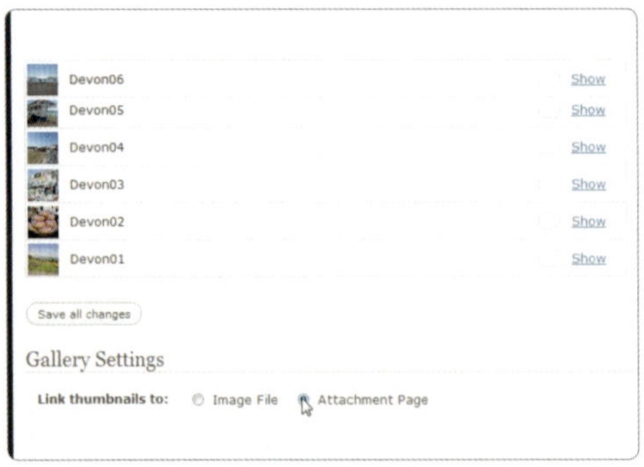

02 Gallery settings

All images are placed into the gallery. Under Gallery Settings there are some options. The first is Link thumbnails to: which is set to Image File. This links all gallery images to the full size image when clicked. Select Attachment Page and the images are placed into a page, like a mini gallery.

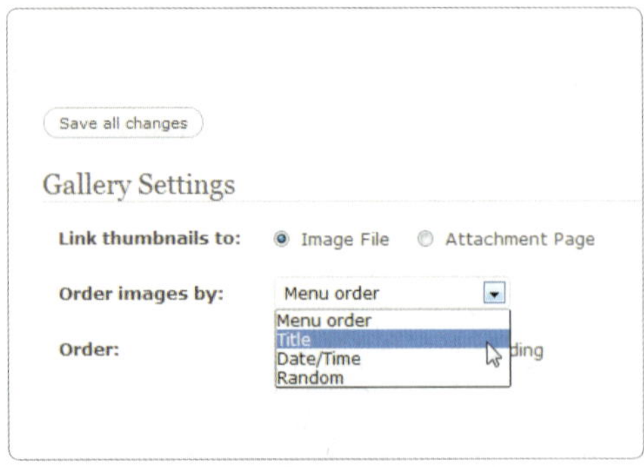

03 Image order

The image order is determined by 'Order images by' and 'Order'. By default, these are set to Date/Time and Ascending. To re-arrange the order, select Title and combine with Ascending or Descending. To customise the order further select Menu Order from the 'Order images by' list.

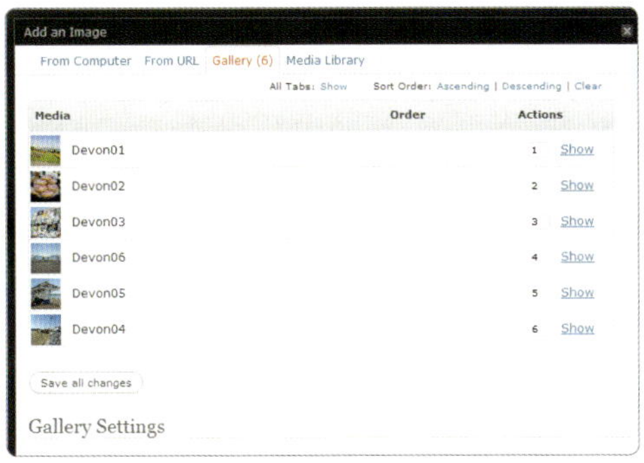

04 Customise image order

To create a custom order, ensure the Menu Order is selected from the list. Adjacent to each thumbnail in the Gallery tab is the Order column. Enter a digit to place the image first in the gallery. Add the appropriate number for each image in the gallery and press Save all changes.

05 Title and caption

Each image is assigned a Show link, click this to view the image options. By default the image Title is the image name. Add a more SEO-friendly title. This is the text that will be seen when the mouse hovers over the image. Adding a caption will add a styled caption.

06 Link URL

By default the Link URL field is empty. There are two presets which can be applied: click File URL to add a link to the image or click Post URL, which will redirect to the image displayed as mentioned in step two. Alternatively, add a custom URL to link to an external image post, site or resource.

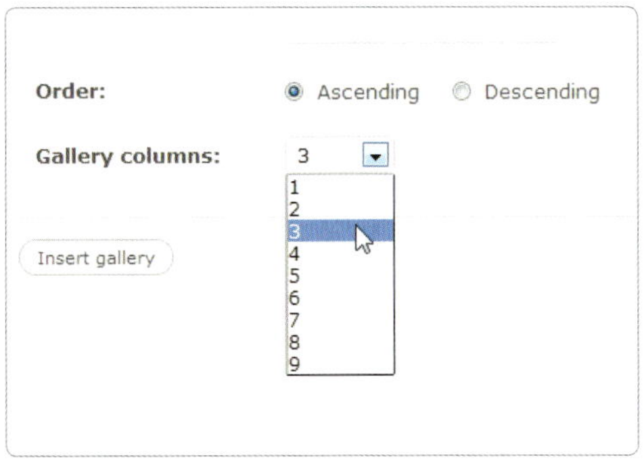

07 Gallery columns

Click Hide to close the image window and repeat step five to change each image title etc. Tthe Gallery columns drop-down list defines how many columns – in this case images – will appear across the page before moving onto another line. Select from the list and click Insert gallery.

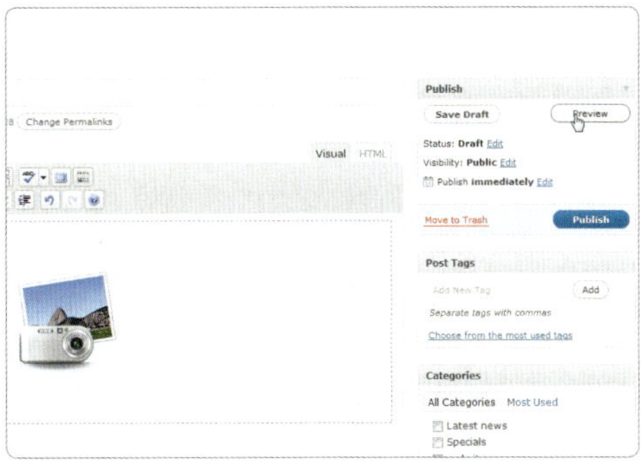

08 View gallery

The gallery is displayed with a blue background and a camera and photo icon. To view the gallery in its current state, you need to head over to the Publish pane and then simply click Preview. This will now open up a new window and display the gallery as it will appear in the page or post itself.

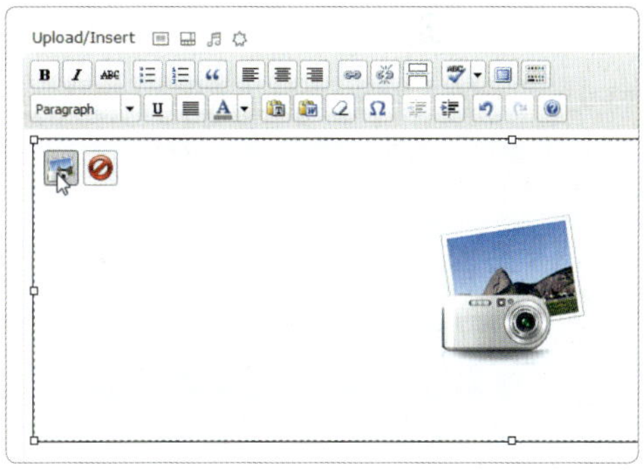

09 Edit gallery

To edit the gallery click on the gallery outline in the edit window and two icons appear in the top-left corner. The red icon deletes the gallery and the icon to the left edits. The Edit icon will display the Gallery tab as seen previously. Make any adjustments and click Update gallery settings.

10 A perfect fit

How the gallery displays is determined by the size of the thumbnails, width of the post body and column number. If the post width is 600 pixels, the thumbnail width and number of columns need to match (eg, four columns multiplied by a thumbnail width of 140px equals 560px, plus padding).

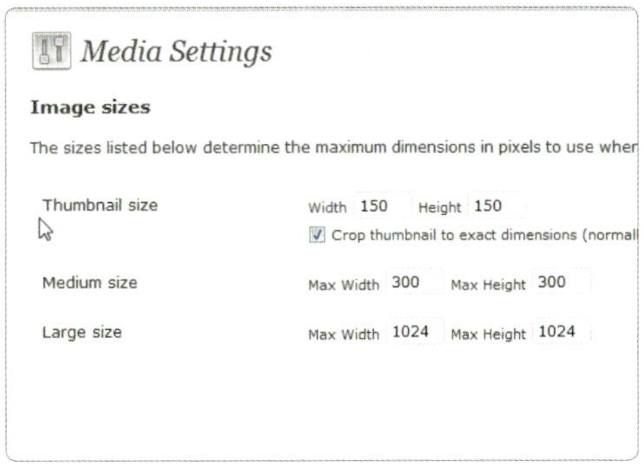

11 Thumbnail dimensions

The gallery displays all images as thumbnails with the size determined by the theme. To modify the dimensions go to Settings in the left column (WordPress 2.8+) and select Media. Add Width and Height dimensions in Thumbnail size and ensure the Crop thumbnails… checkbox is selected.

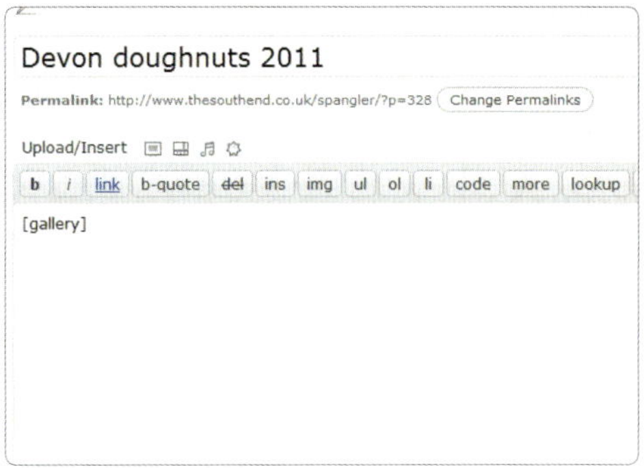

12 Shortcode

Once a gallery's been created, WordPress inserts the code to display the images, or users can insert the gallery into any post or page using the shortcode [gallery]. To insert, open a post or page, switch to HTML and add. To keep the same styling switch to HTML in the post and copy the code.

Add video and audio to your WordPress blog

Your blog will truly come alive with the addition of some multimedia content. Adding videos from YouTube or elsewhere is easy when you know how…

There's no better way of drawing users in to your blog than with some well-chosen multimedia content. Whether you are creating your own video tutorials or sharing the latest craze sweeping the nation, giving your readers something extra to look at beyond static words and pictures is a sure-fire way to keep them clicking through your site – and then coming back for more.

The easiest way to add a video is by using one of the freely available Flash video services available online. The most famous, of course, is YouTube, and that is the focus of this tutorial. By using YouTube you can use videos in high definition, so there are no worries about quality, while the phenomenal popularity of the site will also help you promote your blog to a wider user base. We'll also show you how you can enable users to share videos embedded in your pages, as well as how to add other kinds of media content to help bring your blog alive.

"The popularity of YouTube will help you promote your blog"

Embedding videos

It's easy to add a video to your blog by embedding one from YouTube

YouTube content
Although there are many video sites out there that you can embed from, YouTube is by far the most popular and the easiest. Make sure you choose the right dimensions

Description
Although a video will undoubtedly get visitors interested in your site, it's good practice to write a description underneath to add some context to the media

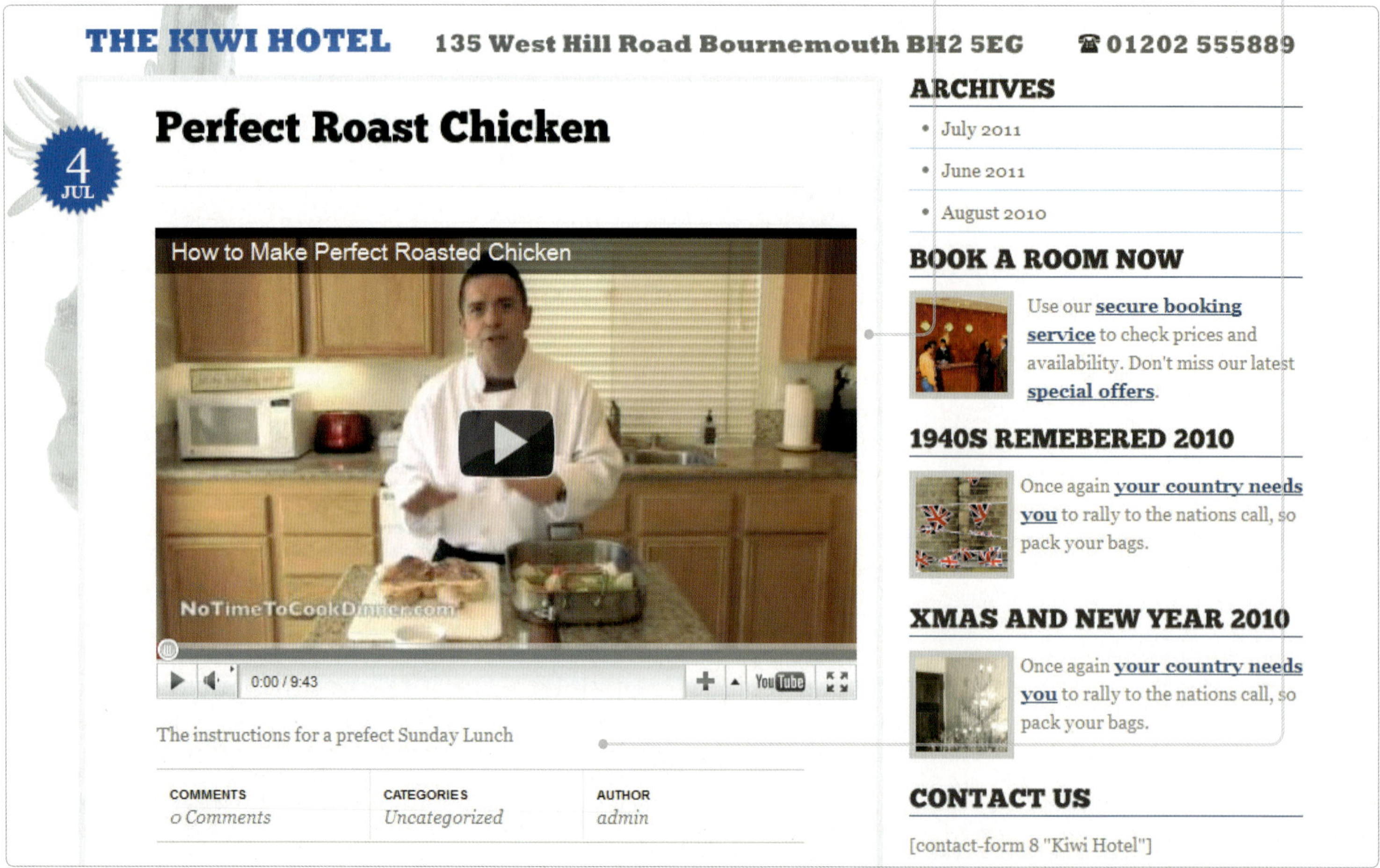

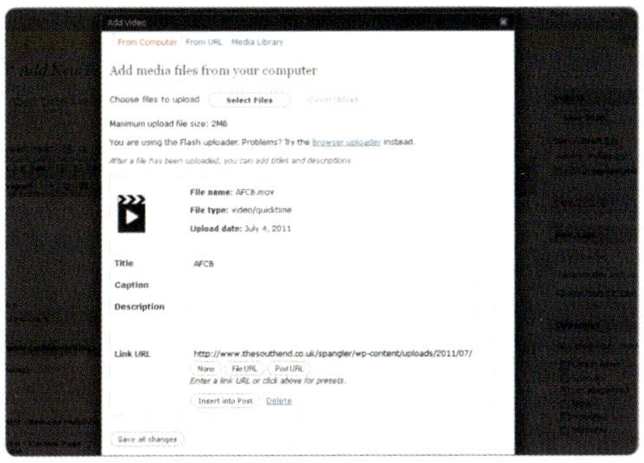

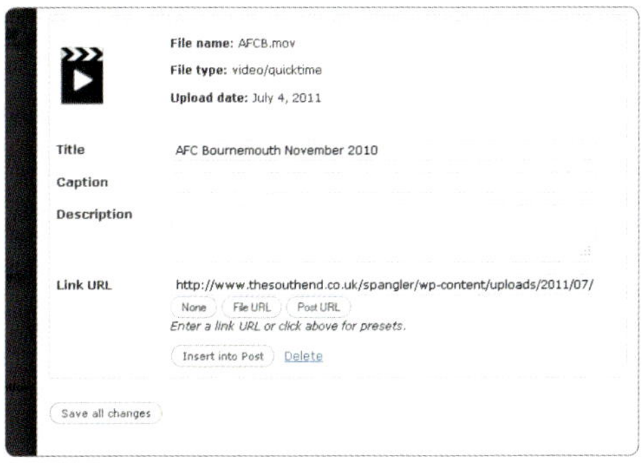

01 Upload a video

To start, select a post or create a new one. Just below the title box are the Upload/Insert options. To quickly add an existing video, click the second icon from the left, Add Video, to open the Add Video window. Click Select Files and choose a video from your computer.

02 New title

One you've chosen a video, the screen will display the file name of the video, the file type, the title and the Link URL – this is the web address where the video is stored. To change the title to something more relevant, simply click inside the Title box and type in the new title.

03 Include details

The Add Video window offers the option of adding a Caption and a Description. To add, type in the appropriate text in the Caption and Description boxes. When complete, click 'Insert into Post'. This will add a link to the video which, when clicked, will play in the default video player.

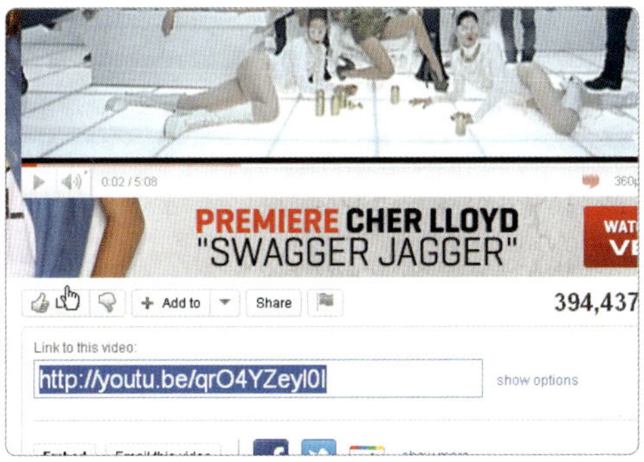

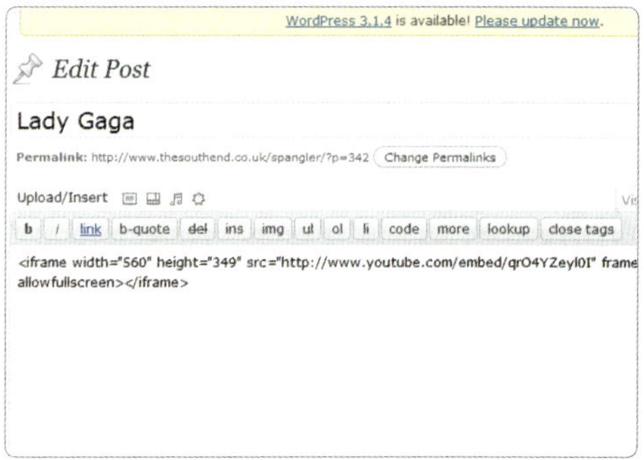

04 YouTube link

To add a video to a new or existing WordPress post, first head to YouTube. Search for the desired video using the Search box at the top of the page. This will display a list of videos. Click on the video image or title to go to the video. Now click the Share button and copy (Ctrl+C) the link.

05 Automatically add video

Now head to WordPress and the post to which the video is going to be added. Click the cursor in the appropriate position in the post where you want the video to be placed. Now press Ctrl/Cmd+V to add the link to the post. This should automatically embed the video in the post.

06 Manually insert video

A YouTube link is not always embedded automatically. To add a video manually, click Share under the chosen YouTube video followed by the Embed button. This will display the embed code. Copy the code, go back to the post, switch to the HTML editor and paste the code.

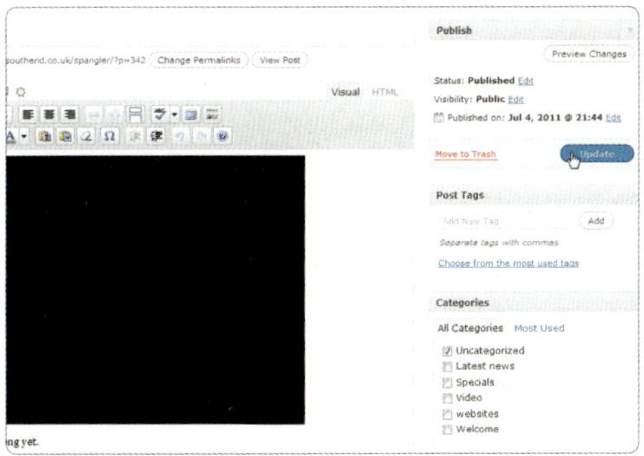

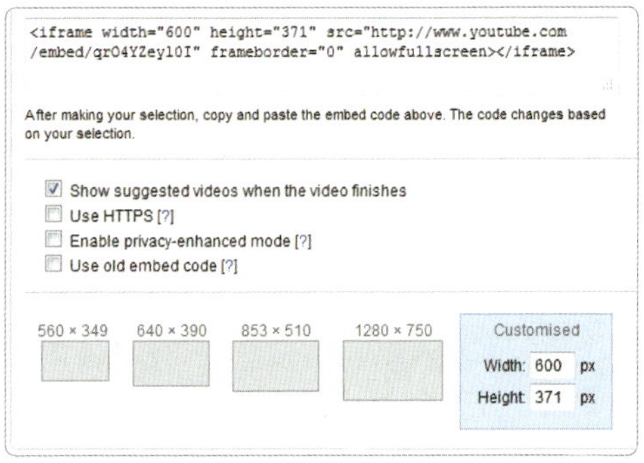

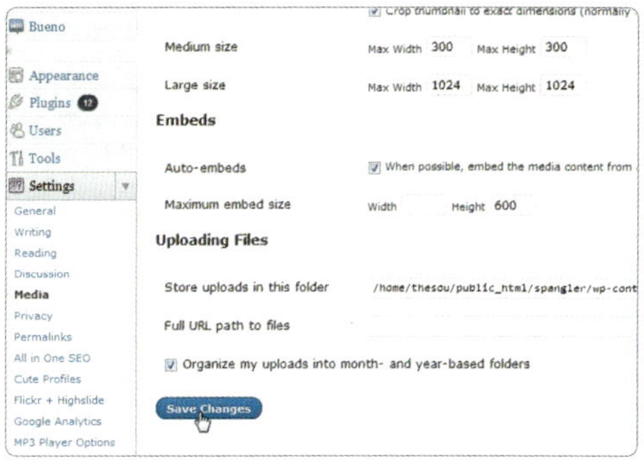

07 Publish post

Now switch back to the Visual editor, which will display a black box where the video will be shown. Add in any text to accompany the video and click the Publish button to display. WordPress may remove the link; if so, go back and add it again then hit the Update button.

08 Video size

By default a YouTube video will be assigned the dimensions 560x349 pixels. Alongside the default option are a number of common sizes. These keep the video at the correct aspect ratio. If none of these matches your requirements, you can enter a custom width and height for the video.

09 Maximum video size

As mentioned in step 5, a YouTube video link should automatically embed into a page. This option is switched on by default and can be found via Settings>Media on the Dashboard. This setting also allows a user to include the maximum width and/or height.

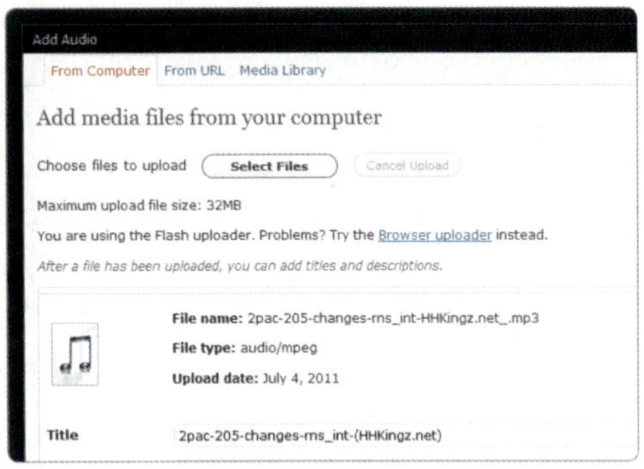

10 Add audio

Sitting next to the Add Video button in the Upload/Insert collection of buttons is the Add Audio button. Select the desired file from your computer and click Open to add. The file will upload and present the window shown in the screenshot above.

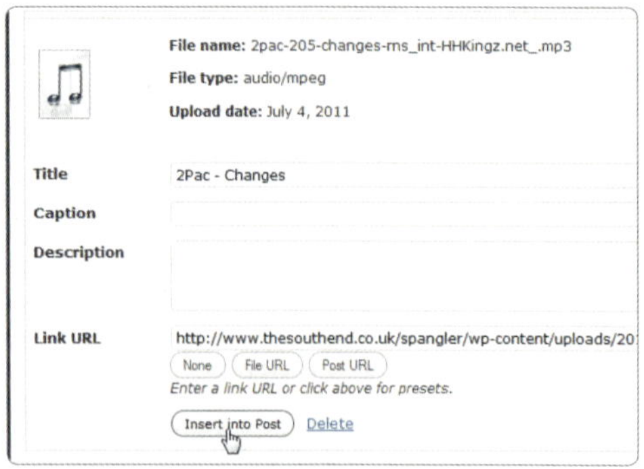

11 Audio details

By default, the Title of the audio clip will be the name of the audio file, which may not help identify the track. To add a new title, simply select the current title and type in the new title. To complete the audio details, add a caption and description and press the 'Insert into Post' button.

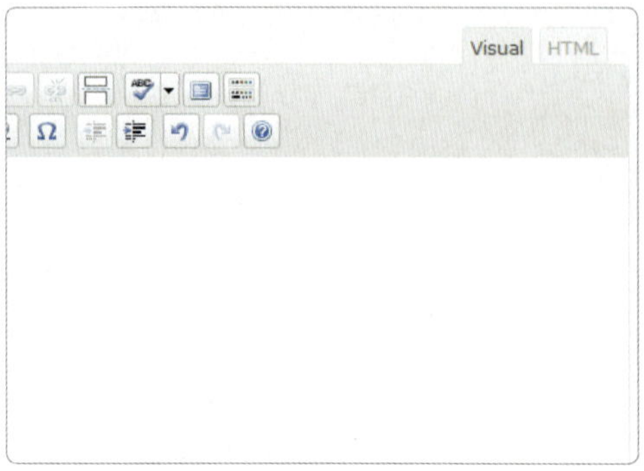

12 Audio playback

The previous step will add a link into the WordPress post using the audio clip title as the link text. The latter can be modified to something different. Simply select the text and type in the new link title. When the post is published the link, when clicked, will open.

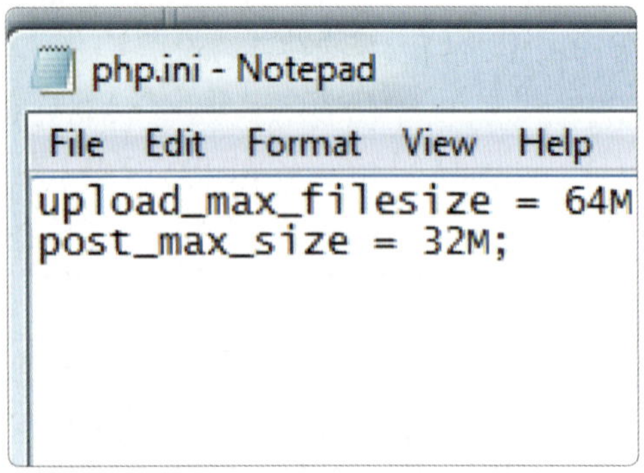

13 Maximum upload file size

WordPress limits the upload size of a file to 2MB, which restricts what video and audio can be added. This can be modified with an addition to the wp-admin folder. Open a text editor and type 'upload_max_filesize = 32M; post_max_size = 32M' and save the files as php.ini.

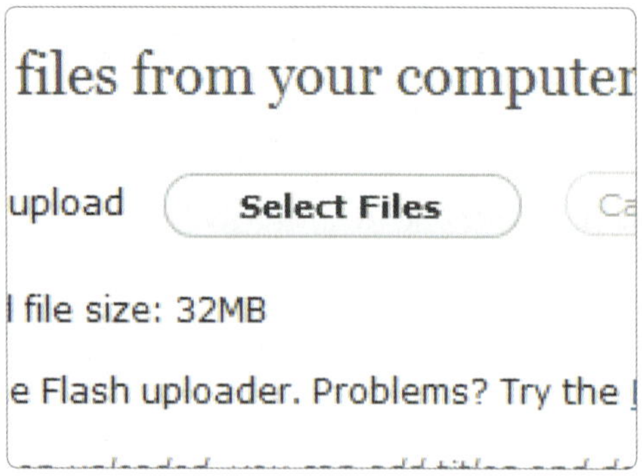

14 Upload php.ini

To upload the php.ini file, a FTP program is required. If you do not already have one, try FileZilla. Now connect to the server where your WordPress install is located. Locate the wp-admin folder and upload the php.ini file. Now, the maximum upload file size will have changed.

15 Add Media

The Upload/Insert section also includes the Add Media button, which works the same way as Add Video and Add Audio. However, the Add Media option allows for a more generic selection of content to be added. Click the Add Media icon, select the file and click 'Insert into Post'.

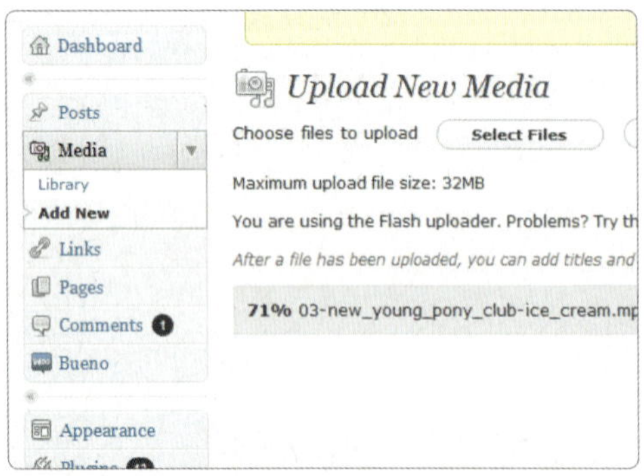

16 Media Library

Any media content uploaded to WordPress is stored in the Media Library, which is found via Media in the Dashboard menu. From here users can upload new media by clicking Select Files, selecting a file and uploading. This will add the media content to the Media Library listing.

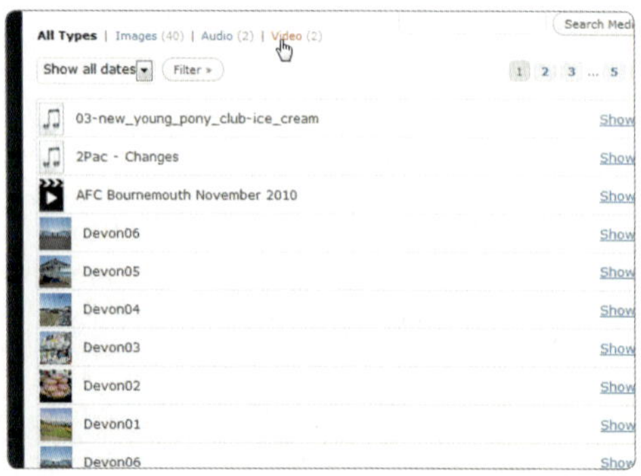

17 Select media type

Adding media content to the Media Library allows users to add already uploaded content – into a post. Click the Add Media icon, or Add Video or Add Audio, and click Media Library to view all uploaded media content. You can use the filters to select the desired media.

18 Show media content

The media content is displayed as a list with an icon to help identify the type of content. To display the media content, you need to click the Show link. This will display details such as Title, Description etc, as seen previously. To add media to a post, simply click the 'Insert into Post' button.

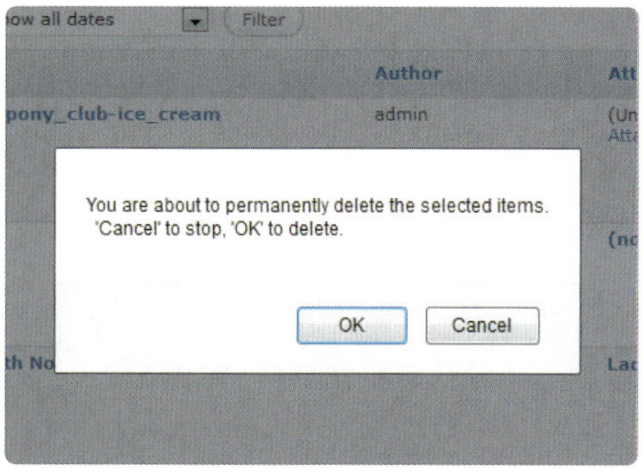

19 Managing media

The Media Library allows users to edit, delete and view content from the Library. Roll the mouse cursor over a file to display the available options. To delete a file, click Delete Permanently, then click OK. The Edit option allows a user to edit details, while View shows the media in a post.

20 Attach video

Video and audio uploaded via the Media Library is not attached to a post and will be assigned as Unattached. To attach a video (or audio) to a post, click the Attach link and search for a post. Choose the desired post and click Select. The media will now be included in the Gallery section of a post.

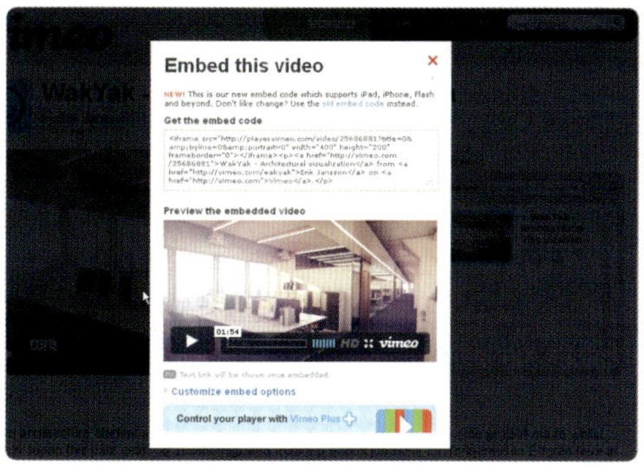

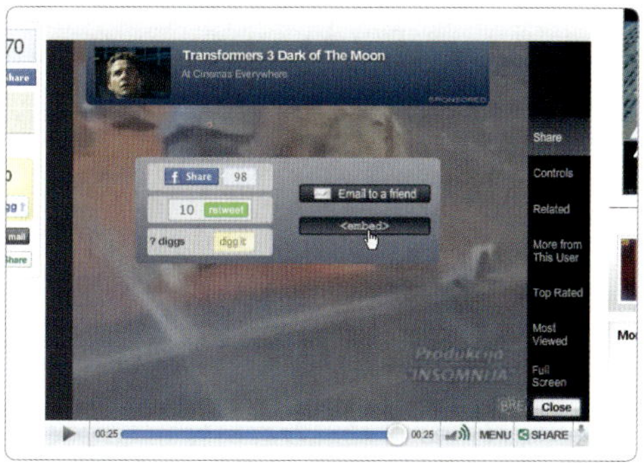

21 Vimeo video sharing

Vimeo is another video-sharing site that is similar to YouTube and allows users to share video. Head to the site (www.vimeo.com), search and select a video and within the video you will find an embed button. Click this to get the embed code and then copy and paste it into a post.

22 Video-sharing sites

There are a host of other video-sharing sites. Ones worth checking out are Break (www.break.com), Daily Motion (www.dailymotion.com), Viddler (www.viddler.com), Google Videos (http://video.google.com). All offer similar options where users can copy an embed code to add to a post.

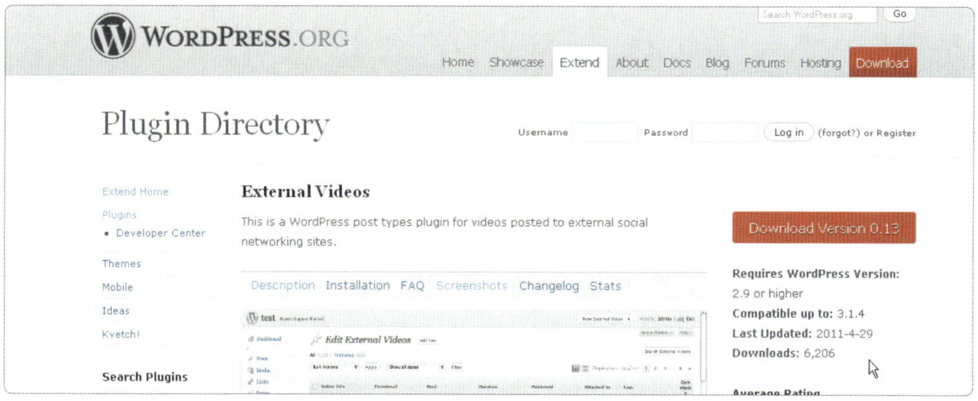

23 WordPress plug-ins

WordPress is a powerful platform and there are numerous plug-ins available that may prove useful for adding media content. To assist with adding and managing media content, there a number of plug-ins found via the official WordPress Plugin Directory – point your browser to http://wordpress.org/extend/plugins. A couple that are well worth trying out are External Videos and WordPress Video Plugin.

Understand media file formats

With so many different types of video and audio file, how can you be sure the one you're using will play?

The reason we have given so much attention to using YouTube videos in this tutorial is not only a result of the popularity of the video-sharing service, but also that it delivers the simplest method of adding media content to your blog without the need to worry about things like file formats. Indeed, while many common video formats (such as .avi) are not suited to playback on the web, uploading the same file to your YouTube account will make it perfectly accessible to everyone on pretty much any computer. Users visiting your site will not need to worry about codecs when trying to view it either – and there's nothing more likely to turn people away than serving up media that they can't view.

If you want to go it alone, though, you should be aware that some video file types are better than others. As mentioned, .avi files may well play in a browser but cannot stream, so the entire file will need to be downloaded before it can be played. Other formats like .mov (the QuickTime format), .mpg and .wmv can be streamed within a browser window. The latter is a good bandwidth-friendly option, although Mac users will need a plug-in to be able to access it.

For audio you are unlikely to go beyond either .mp3 or .wav files as your formats of choice. Either of these is fine, although .wav is uncompressed so will take longer to download and use far more bandwidth, so .mp3 is preferable. Either way, if you are dealing with files that are large it is good practice to maybe mention it somewhere so that the user knows what to expect. Steer clear of older formats that were once popular, like Real Audio, as users may not have a compatible codec installed; likewise Windows Audio which, even though fairly universal, still causes some problems for Mac users.

Flash video services provide a worry-free method of ensuring your video is viewable by everyone

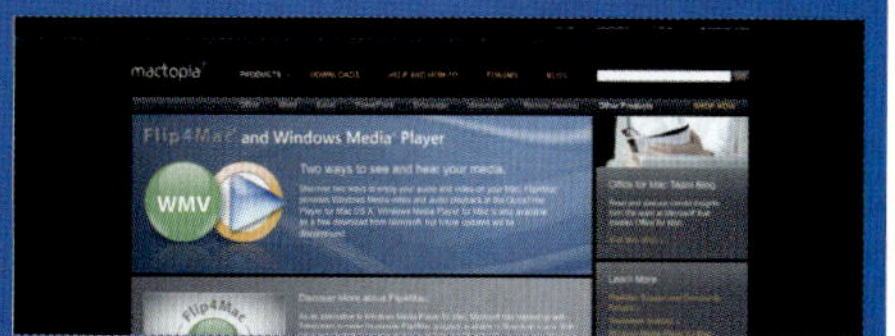

Try to ensure your audio files are totally accessible, and spare a thought for Mac users when using Windows files

Create, apply and manage tags in your posts

In this tutorial we will cover how to create and manage tags efficiently and the benefits of having them in your website projects

Tags are something that quite often can be passed over in WordPress websites, with a lot of people under the misconception that a tag and category are the same thing. A tag is something that is used to improve site navigation and group similar posts together. Tags are unique names of reference but do not work in a hierarchy like categories, as they are just used to cross reference posts. When posts have been tagged depending on your theme they will be displayed either within the post or in a tag cloud. If the reader enjoys the post they have just read then they will have the option to click on the tags to discover more posts of the same subject.

A tag cloud will accumulate all the tags or a certain number into a section of the site where they can always be accessed. Tags are simple to create and using them correctly can benefit site navigation and usability hugely. Follow these simple steps as we show you how to use tags properly.

"A tag is used to improve site navigation"

Managing tags

These are vital to improving your site's usability

Edit tags
Hover over a tag and you have the choice of editing its name, the tag slug and the description. Alternatively, you can just delete it from your site

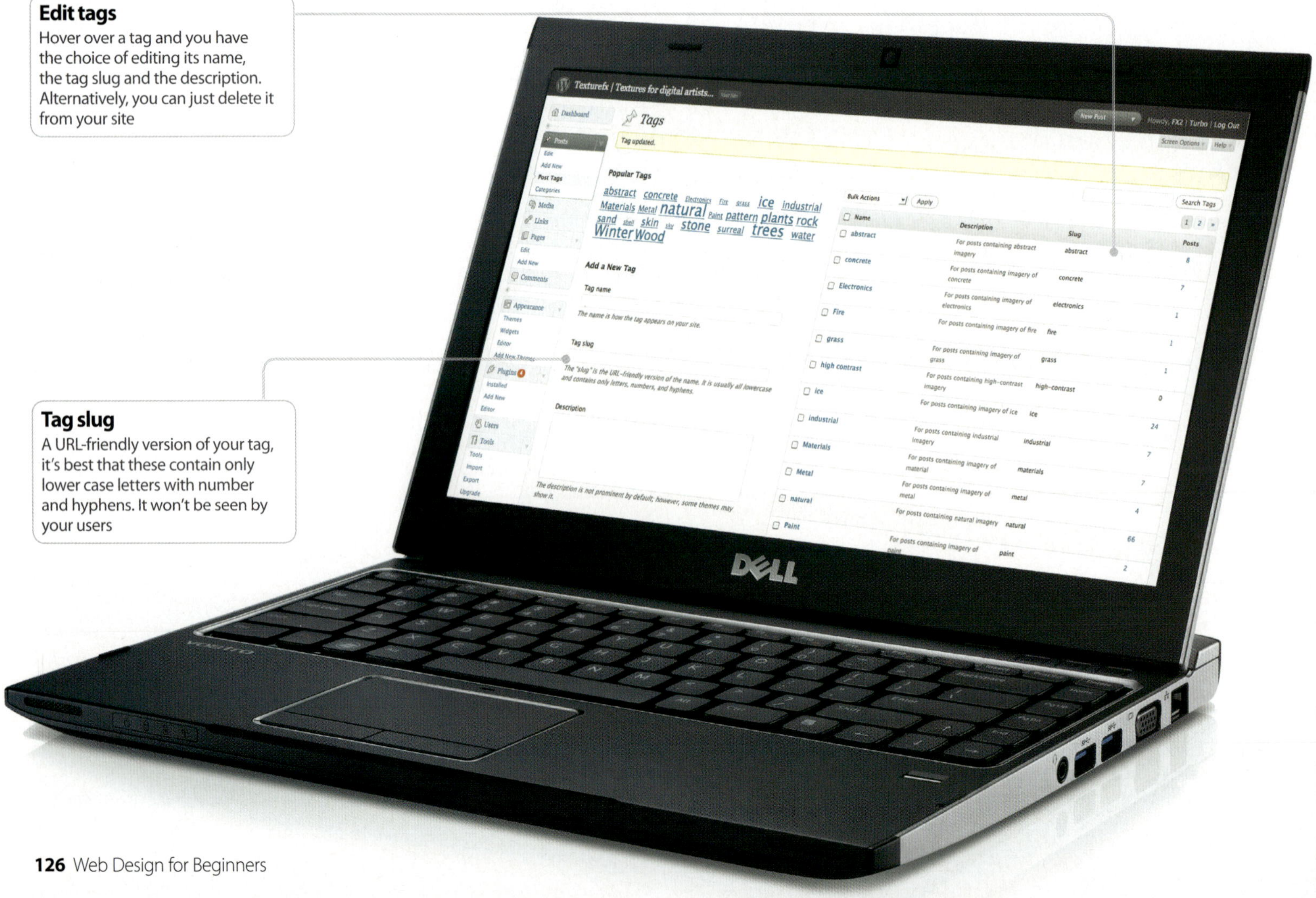

Tag slug
A URL-friendly version of your tag, it's best that these contain only lower case letters with number and hyphens. It won't be seen by your users

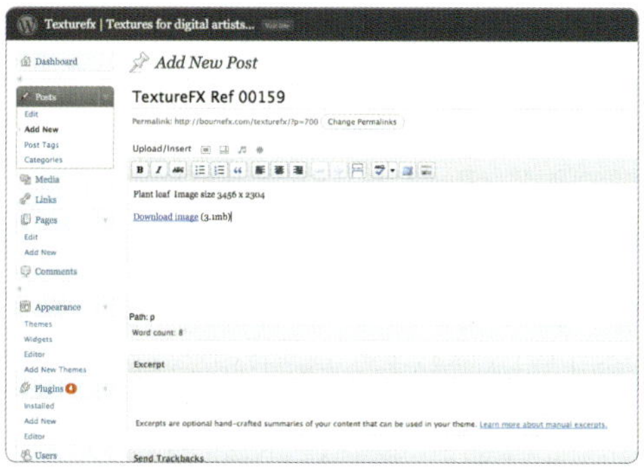

01 Getting started

If you haven't created any posts yet, create a few test posts for the purpose of this tutorial. Your version of WordPress may look somewhat different to what is shown here, depending on which version you're using.

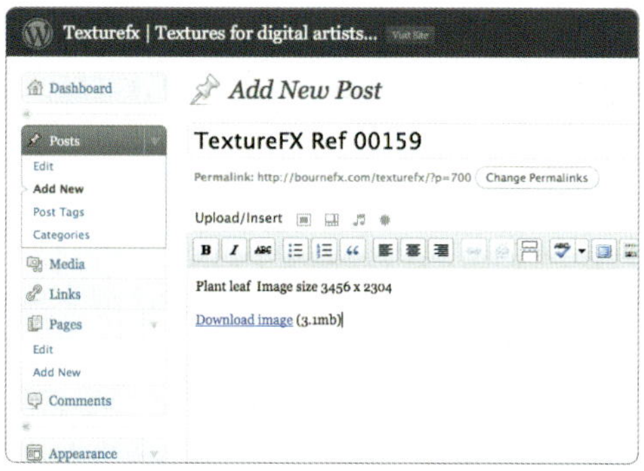

02 Naming tags appropriately

The first step to creating a tag is choosing a name for it. It is best to think about how the tags will work as a whole when you do this, although you can actually change them further down the line if you wish to.

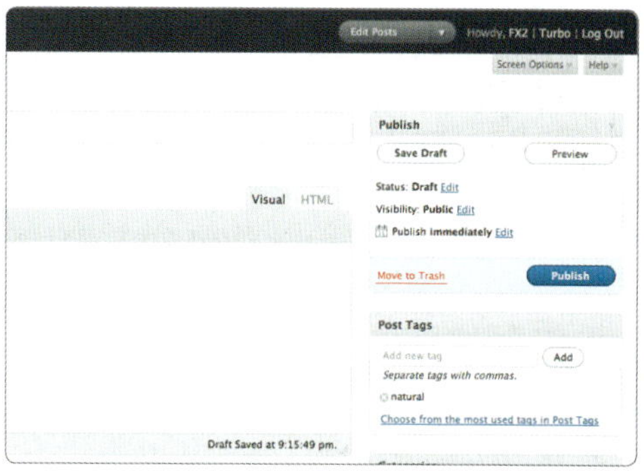

03 Post tags section

With a post open, the 'Post Tags' section is accessible from the right-hand side column. To add a new tag, you will just need to type in the name and click on the 'Add' button. Once the post is updated then the tag will be applied.

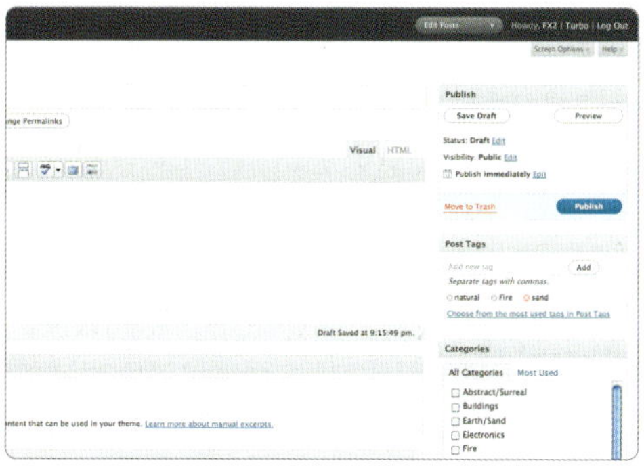

04 Adding multiple tags

You can enter as many tags as you like, as multiple tags can be added by using a comma and space. To remove a tag you have entered, you need to click the cross next to it and it will disappear – it really is a simple process.

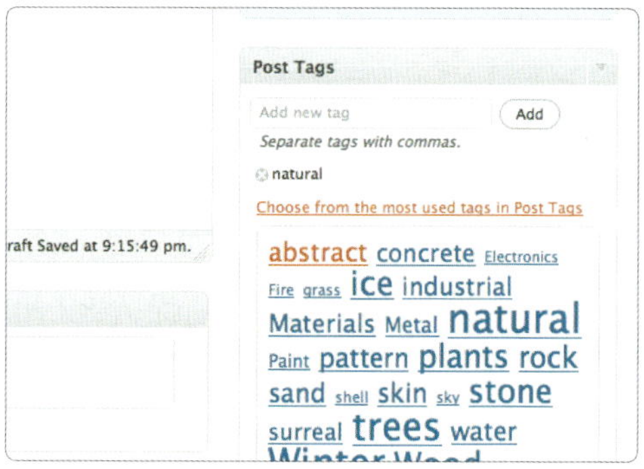

05 Most used tags

The tags added are now accessible under the 'most used' section. Tags can be added through the Post tags menu, but if it has not been applied to a post first it will not be added to 'most used'. This means you will need to manually type words.

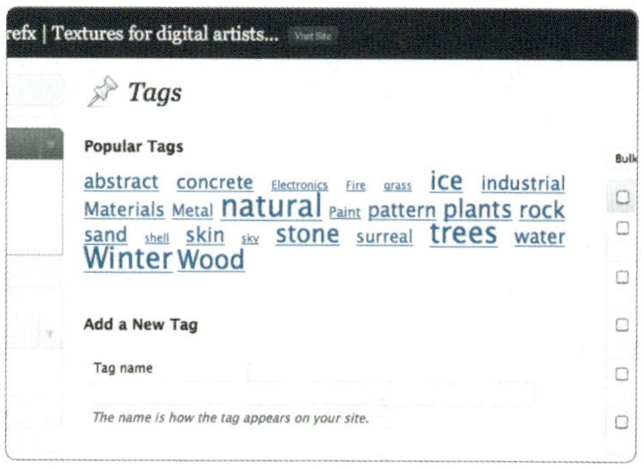

06 Post tags menu

Click on the 'Post Tags' button under the 'Posts' section to access the Tags page. This is where tags are managed. The posts column displays the number of times they have been used. Clicking on it will reveal which posts it is applied to.

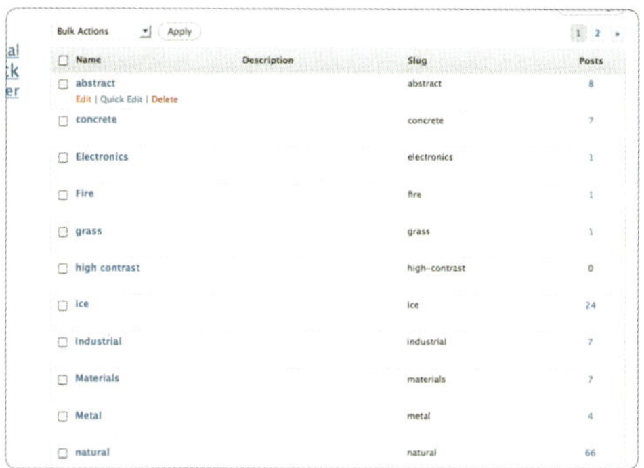

07 Editing tags

To change a tag, hover over it and the options of Edit, Quick Edit and Delete will appear. Quick Edit allows you to change the name and tag slug, with the Edit mode giving you the option to change the description as well.

08 Tag slugs

Tag slugs are simply a URL-friendly version of the tag name. A slug needs to be formatted to web standards, though, but this will not be seen by site users. It is best to have it all lowercase letters and it can only contain numbers and hyphens.

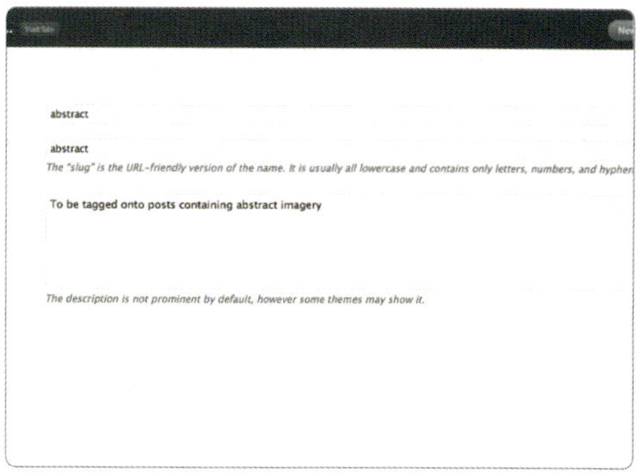

09 Tag descriptions

The tag description is optional and it's not shown in most themes, so generally this is only for your own reference. This is a good opportunity to make some notes, so that you understand everything and it is explained to other admins.

Manage links in your website's sidebar

Using the Links functionality in WordPress is a good way of tidying up and categorising one or multiple sections of links within the website sidebar

With the release of WordPress version 2.5, Blogroll was renamed 'Links', which promoted Links to a content type to sit alongside Pages and Posts. Initially when the WordPress platform was created, it was specifically aimed at bloggers; this fact is evident within the Links section of the admin Dashboard, where the default category is called 'Blogroll'. WordPress was intended to allow bloggers to create communities between friends' blogs, their favourite websites or interesting stories that they might have found – much like a roll of honour, hence the name.

The flexibility in the Links section, however, means you may want to set up links for alternative means. For example, it could be used to simply tidy up a collection of links by organising them into categories. Or you may wish to offer affiliate links to other websites, which could generate revenue for your site.

In this tutorial we will take you through all of the basic methods for adding and editing links in the WordPress Dashboard, along with adding and managing the different categories you make for your links. Also, if you accidentally make a mistake, we'll show you how to easily remove unwanted links or categories.

Sidebar links

This feature is incredibly important to your site's navigation

Content above all
No matter how many links you've got and how nice they look, if you don't have the content to back them up, you won't get many returning visitors

List of links
The right-hand side of your blog page contains your links that you can set up using the tutorial on the opposite page. Be careful not to overdo it!

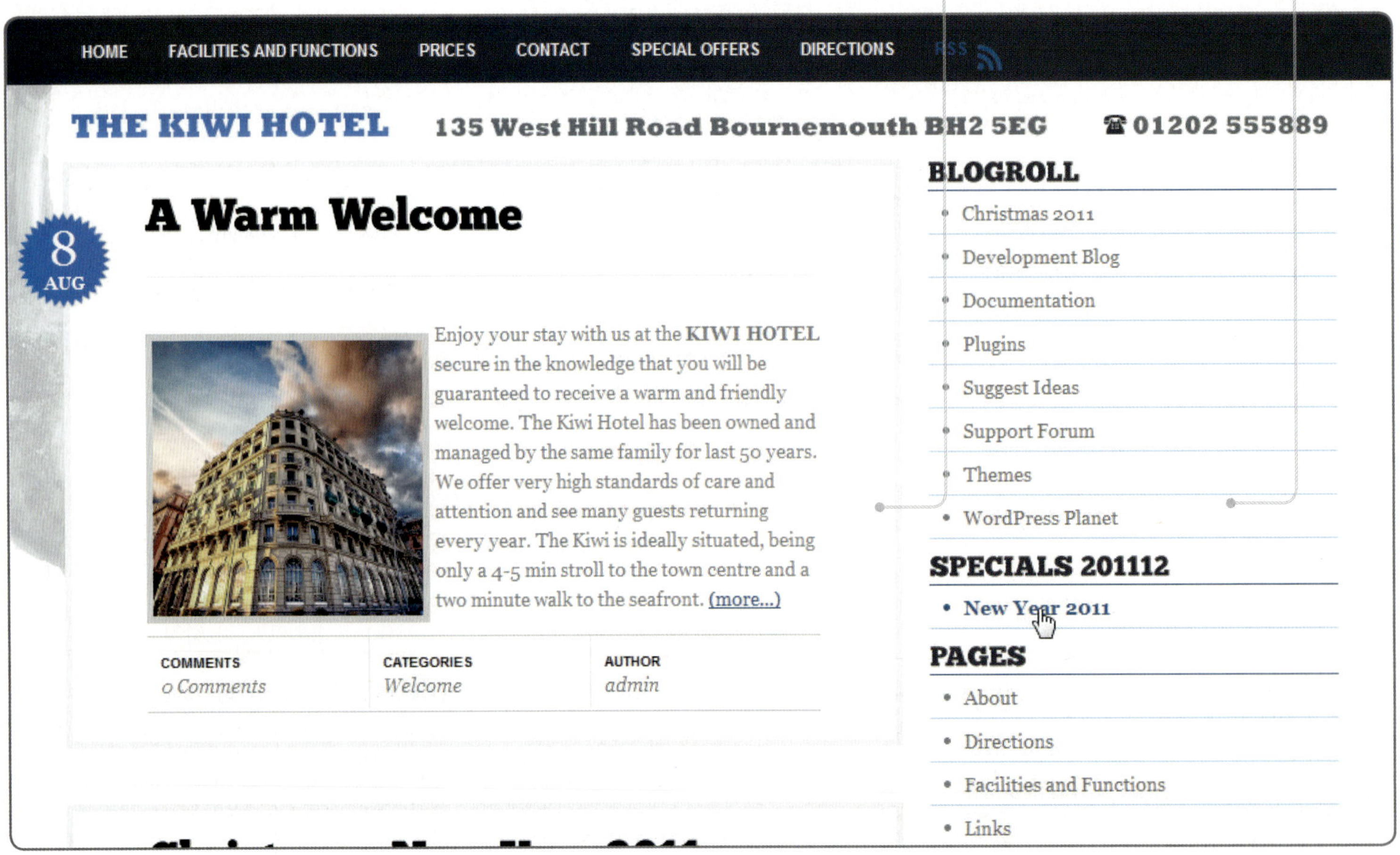

01 Adding links

In the 'Links' menu, click on 'Add New' option to open up the Add New Link interface. In here we can enter a name for our link, enter the web address, provide the link with a description, select a category and provide a target window.

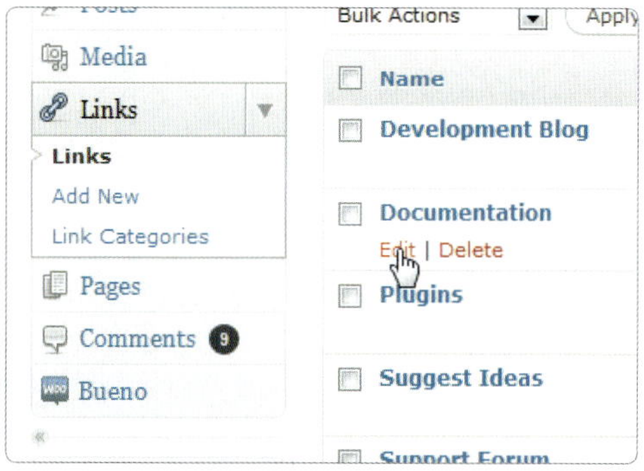

02 Editing existing links

To edit an existing link, first click Links in the Links section. This will list all the links that have been set up for the site. When a link is rolled over, the options Edit or Delete appear. Select Edit to view the Edit Link interface and make any changes.

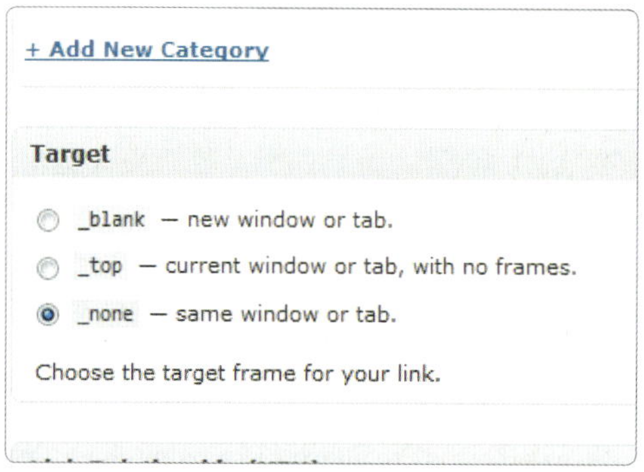

03 Setting a target

In the Add New or Edit Link interfaces you might have noticed the 'Target' section. Here are three options '_blank', '_top' and '_none'. All three options have an explanation as to what each option represents next to them.

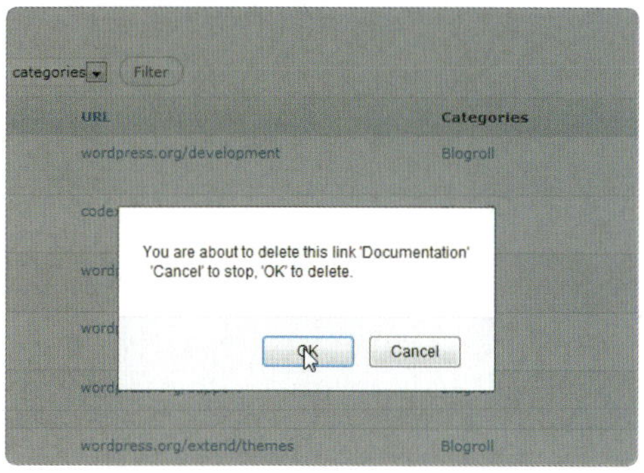

04 Removing links

If you have created a link that you no longer require, open the Edit Link interface and roll over the link you'd like to remove. The option 'Edit' or 'Delete' will again appear. Click Delete and a pop-up box will ask you to confirm this selection.

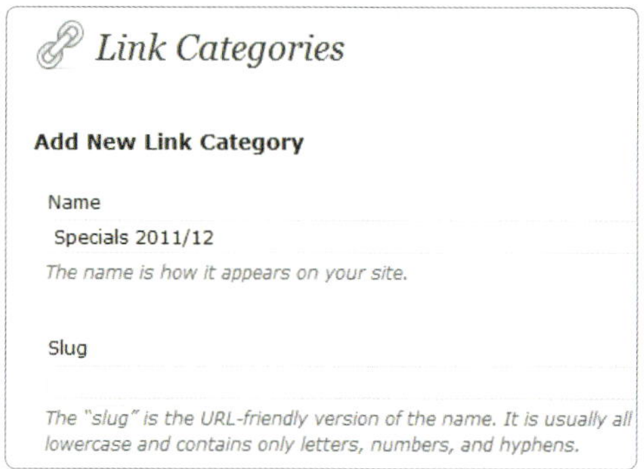

05 Creating new categories

Click 'Link Categories'. Here you'll find a form, providing the opportunity to add a new category. Simply fill out the Category name, enter a Description (this part is optional) and click the 'Add Category' button at the bottom of the page.

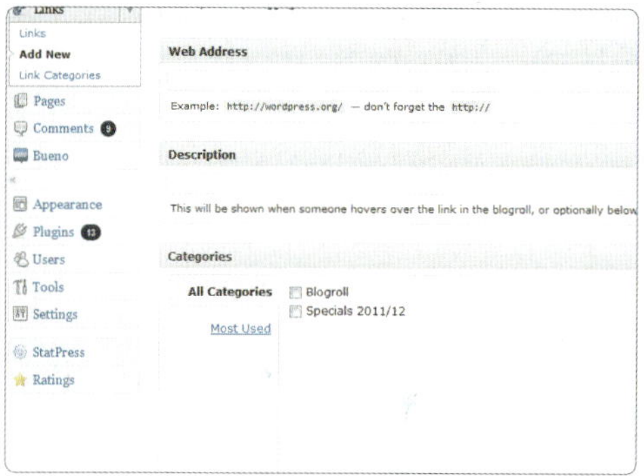

06 Add a category differently

You will notice in the 'Categories' section of the Add New Link interface the option to '+ Add New Category'; this is a different and quicker way of adding an extra category. When this has been clicked a 'New category name' box will appear.

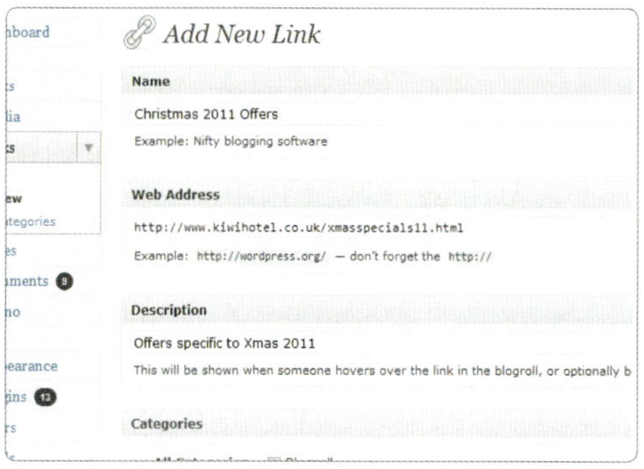

07 Add links to the category

By following the same process as the 'Add New' link, you'll see that your category is available to select in the 'Categories' section. As before, enter the info and then select your category by clicking on the tick box next to the category name.

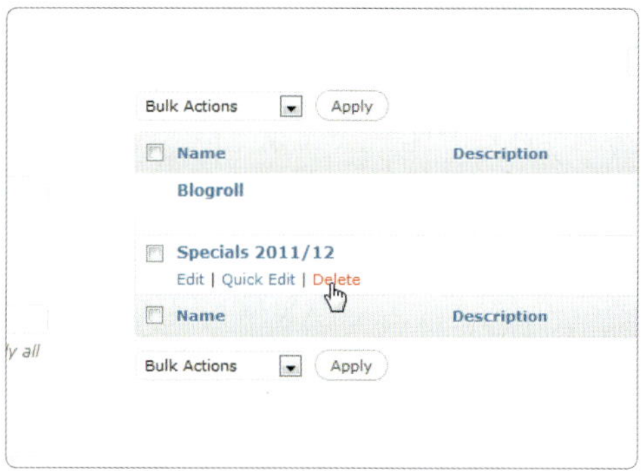

08 Removing a category

If you've created a category that you no longer require, open up the Link Categories interface and roll over the category you would like to remove. An option to 'Delete' will appear; when clicked, you will be asked to confirm your action.

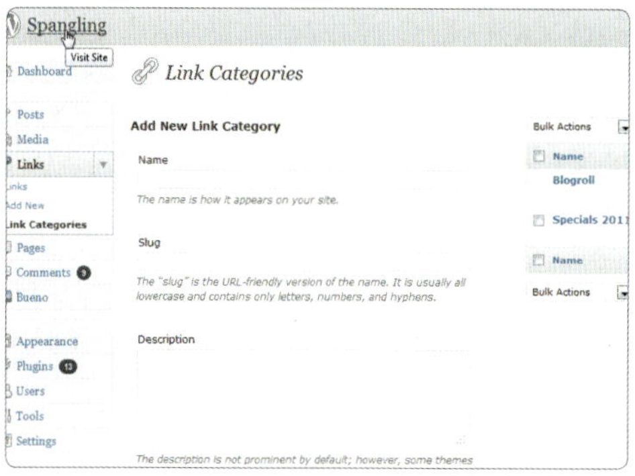

09 View the site

To view any newly created links, click the title of the blog in the top-left-hand corner of the window. The links will open in a new or the existing browser window depending on what target has been chosen.

Add a new WordPress theme to your website

A blog tends to be a perfect outlet for creative expression and conveying personality, which you can enhance by using a new theme

Themes are a great way to not only change the look and style of your weblog – in relation to the various pieces of page furniture – but also provide greater control over how the information is presented. A theme is essentially a group of files that work in unison to produce a new graphical interface. Mercifully, finding and installing them is relatively quick and easy – especially as since WordPress 2.8 there is the option to search for and add themes within WordPress itself.

This feature allows users to search, preview, download and install themes directly from within the dashboard, making the whole process quick and easy. However, the 'Add New Theme' feature is restricted solely to the WordPress Theme Directory and so themes outside of the directory will need to be downloaded and installed manually – which provides a lot more variety, but requires slightly more effort. In this simple tutorial we will show you how to do both.

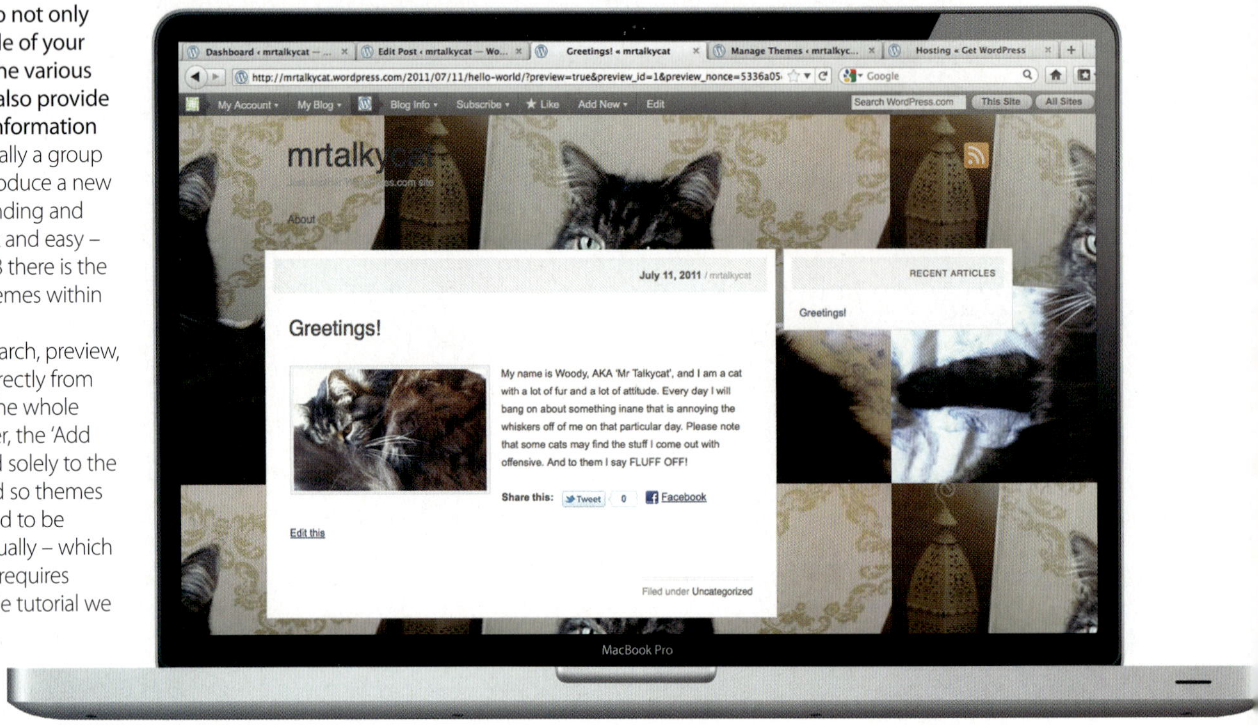

01 Finding a new theme

When you first start using WordPress, two themes will be available to use as standard: 'WordPress Default' and 'WordPress Classic'. However, more themes can be searched for and installed from within the app. To start looking, click on the Appearance menu and then click on Themes.

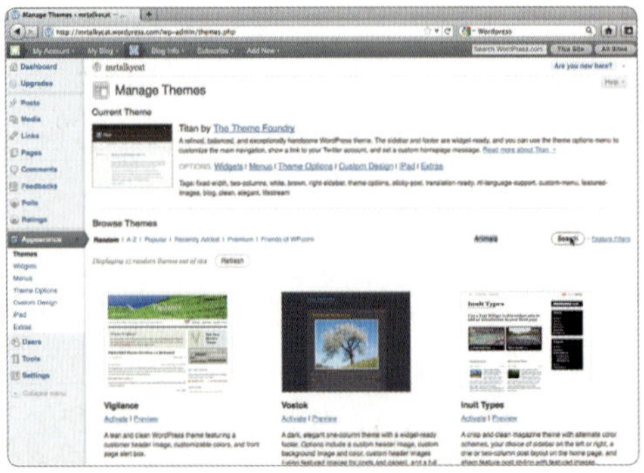

02 Previewing a theme

You can browse themes by category, or trawl through an A-Z. If you're after something more specific, enter keywords into the Search window. When you have a list of options, click the Preview link beneath the image to get a zoomed-in view of that theme so you can gauge if it is right.

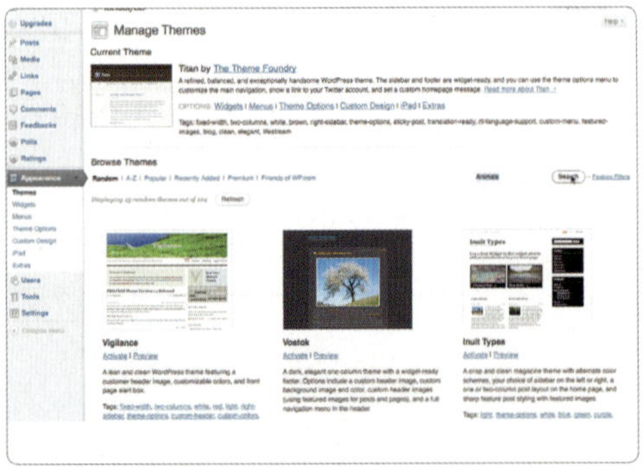

03 Installing a theme

Once you've found a suitable theme, click the Install or Activate link and your chosen theme will be downloaded and installed to the Themes section. Click on Themes and when the page has loaded, your new theme will be visible at the top of the page under the Manage Themes header.

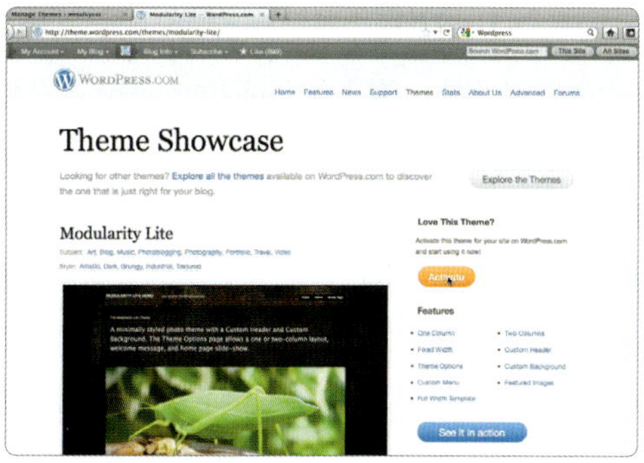

04 Activating a theme

Once your theme has been installed, a number of actions are available. It you click on the 'Read More…' link in the description that accompanies the theme on your Manage Themes page, you'll be shown the theme in action and provided with the option to Activate.

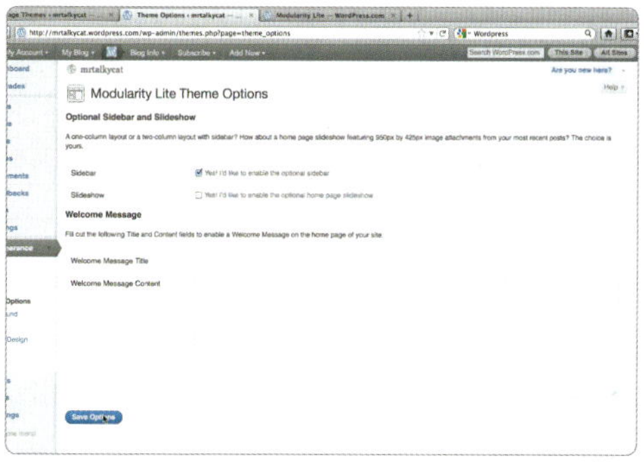

05 Theme options

If your chosen theme has specific options that you can tailor, a new link will appear in the Appearance menu. Click on the link to show the options and make any changes needed. The options you will be presented with vary depending on which theme has been selected.

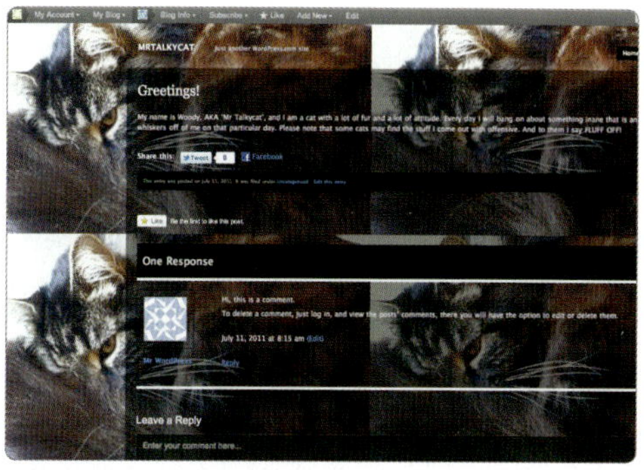

06 Your theme in action

Once a new theme has been activated and its options set, you can start adding posts to your page to see how your theme looks. Go to Posts, highlight any added posts and click on View. You'll now be able to see how your posts look in your new theme.

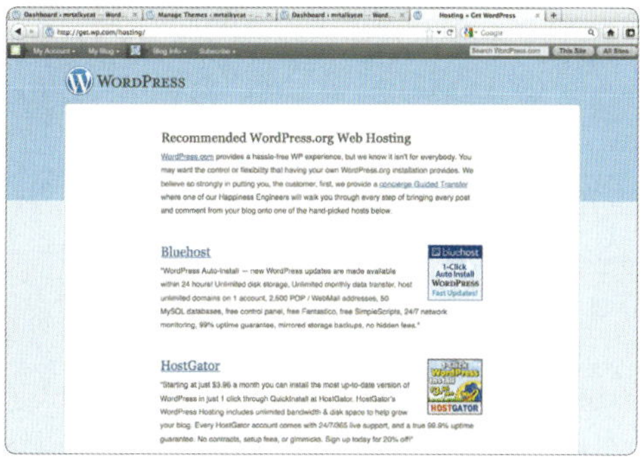

07 Adding an original theme

You can no longer add original themes to your WordPress page, so if you wish to apply new custom themes then you will need to move your Wordpress.com blog to a web host that allows editing and uploading of completely custom themes.

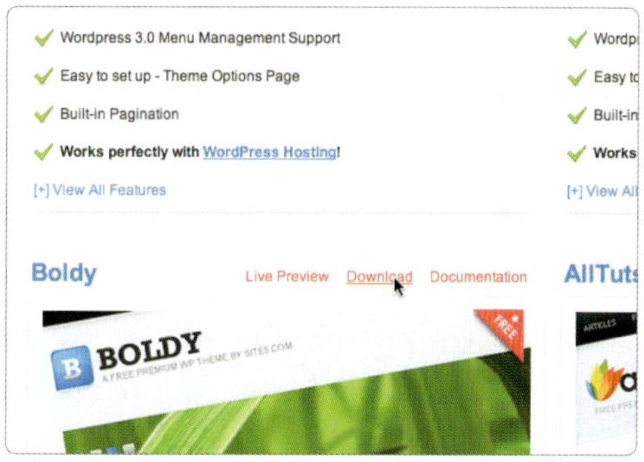

08 Other theme sites

If you can't find the theme you are looking for in the WordPress catalogue, you can always search online for suitable options. There are many sites offering free themes, so take time to browse and when you find one you like, locate the Download link and save it to your desktop.

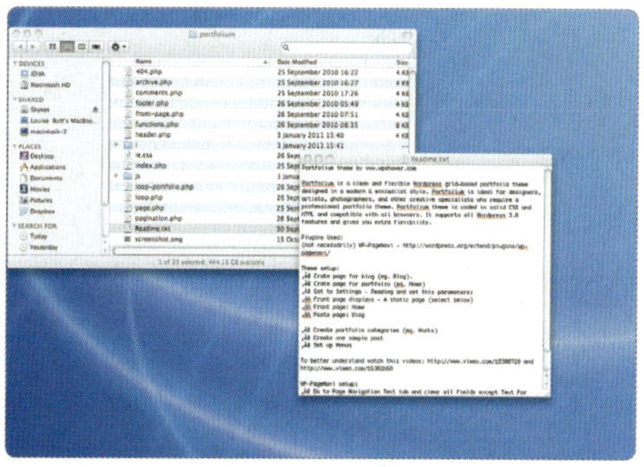

09 Decompress and read

Most themes are downloaded as ZIP files to reduce the time they take to download. Locate the downloaded file on your computer and unzip the folder, then check the contents for a 'ReadMe' file. Open this and study it to find out how the theme is allowed to be used.

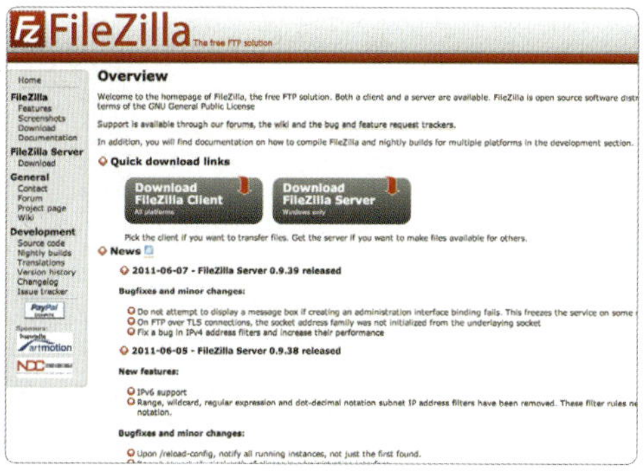

10 Uploading new themes

Once a theme has been downloaded, it needs to be uploaded to the correct folder on your weblog account. For this you will need an FTP client such as Fetch or FileZilla, both of which can be downloaded for free; to do so, just perform a web search and then follow the relevant instructions.

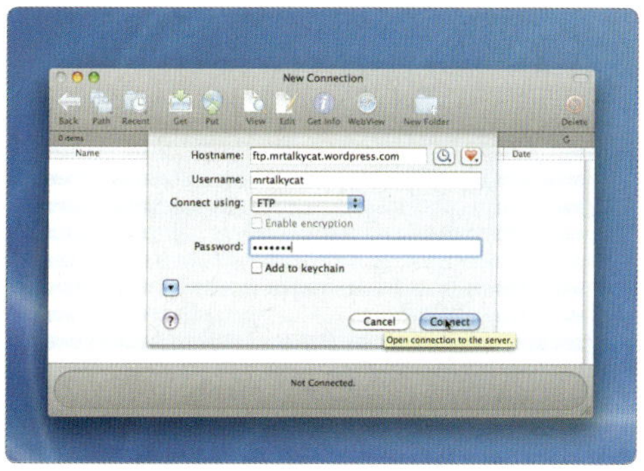

11 Transferring themes

Obtain the FTP details for uploading content from your web host account details and locate your downloaded WordPress theme folder on your computer and upload it to the wp-content/themes folder. Check your Dashboard and select Appearance>Themes for the new content.

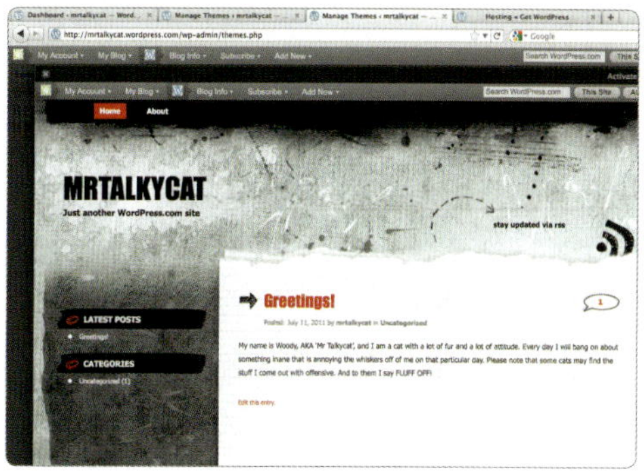

12 Activate new theme

To change the current theme to the installed theme, you need to click Activate. Doing so will switch your current theme to the new theme. Now view your new theme to make sure that everything is in working order. Also, clear out your old themes to keep your directory in order.

Customise your blog's theme

With a little patience, knowledge and guidance, a WordPress theme can be modified to create a new look in less than an hour

Themes are the style icons that drape themselves across the underlying framework of WordPress, making them exactly what the users see. There are thousands upon thousands of them available on the web, whether premium or free. Typically, premium themes offer more features and style, but there are plenty of free themes that make the grade, it's just a matter of finding them.

Once a theme has been found and installed it can be used immediately. However, the colours, fonts and background images might not be exactly what is wanted. For a quick fix makeover, the simple answer is to modify the style sheet (style.css). This is common across all WordPress themes, but the naming conventions, apart from HTML tags, are almost guaranteed to be different. Thankfully, a browser and a visual HTML authoring tool can assist with the identification process. With tags identified and styles in mind a theme can be changed very quickly.

Custom colours
You're able to customise the colours of the standing elements of your web page, including the search box, with some tinkering in your style.css file (see step 11)

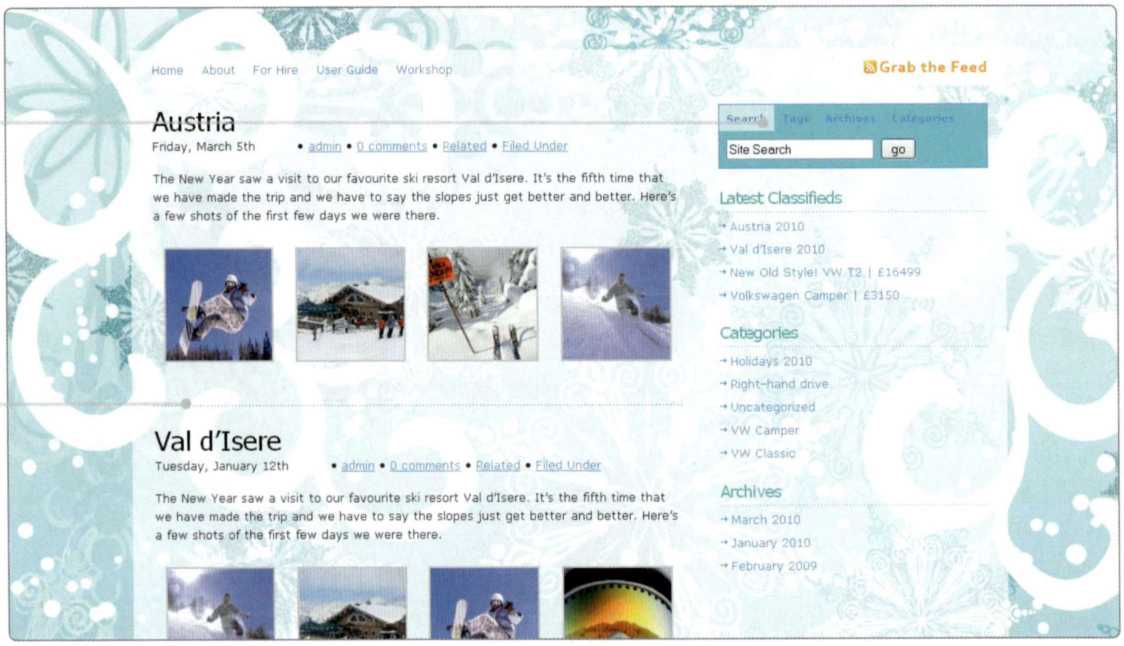

Plenty of choice
There are many WordPress themes to choose from, and they're easily found by browsing the web. We're using the Killian theme from Solostream (www.solostream.com)

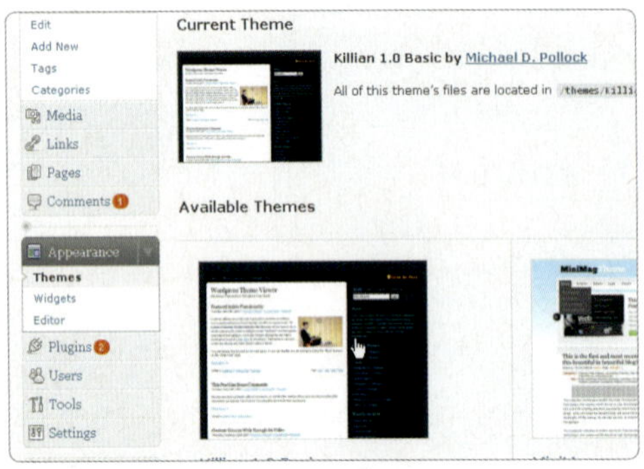

01 Select a theme

There are loads of themes out there, ready to be used. We're using the Killian theme from Solostream (www.solostream.com). Install the theme, head to the Dashboard and activate the theme. Now click Appearance>Editor and select Stylesheet (style.css) from the Edit Themes screen.

02 Easy to identify

To help identify the different elements of the page, head to the URL and save the page. Now open this in your text editor, and start identifying the different tags. Now copy all the text in style.css and paste into a text document as a backup, and reference if something goes wrong.

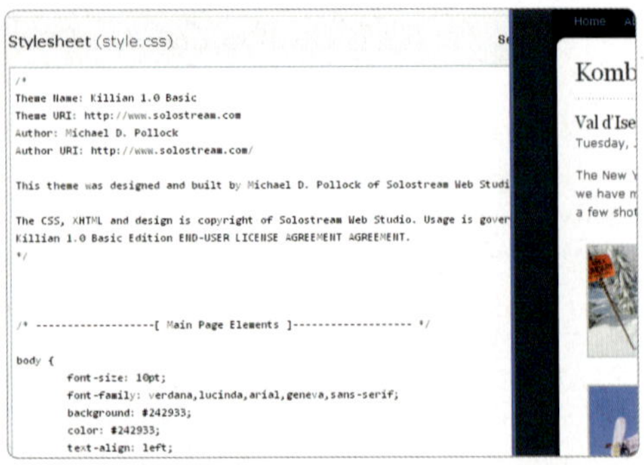

03 Body text

To view changes immediately, open two browser windows, one code and other URL, and place side-by-side. Alternatively, open two tabbed windows. The body tag contains the default font and font size. Change font-size to 10pt and font-family: Verdana, lucinda, arial, geneva, sans-serif.

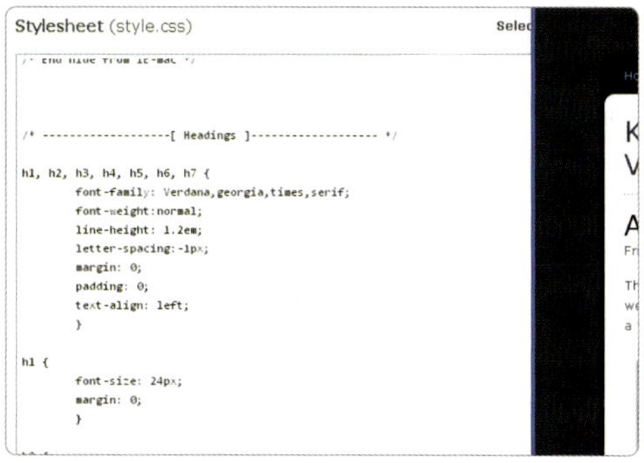

04 Post title

To modify the post title text head back to styles.css and locate Headings. The first class, h1, h2, h3, h4, h5, h6, h7, determines the font. Change font-family: georgia, times, serif; to font-family: Verdana, georgia, times, serif;. Now head to the h2 tag and change the font-size to 24px.

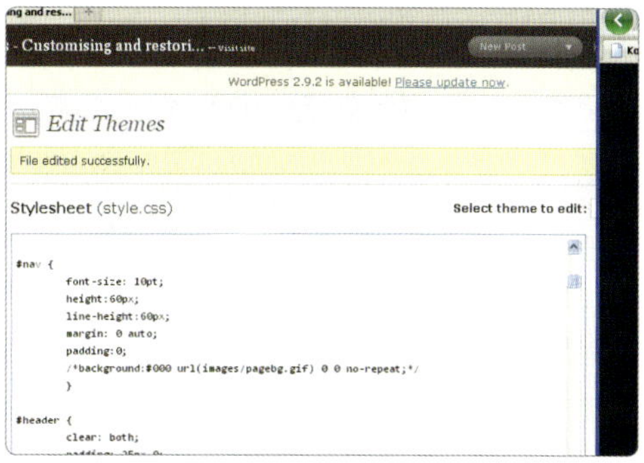

05 Remove backgrounds

The theme uses a selection of background images to add the curved corners. Head to the #nav tag and comment out the background by adding /* before and */ after. This leaves the text there should it need to be put back into place, but also means it doesn't display in the live page.

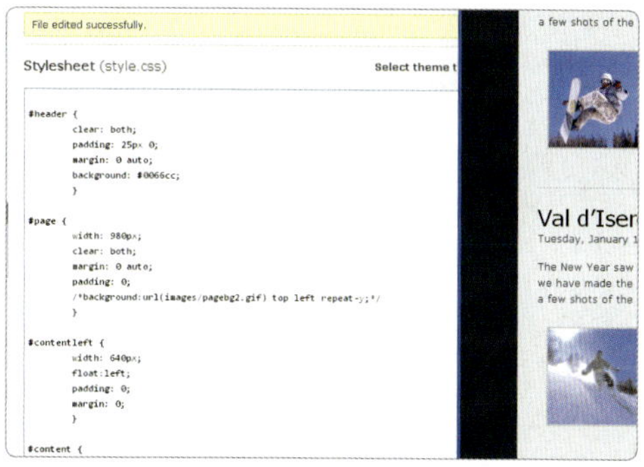

06 More backgrounds

The previous step gets rid of the background image at the top of the page. To remove the other background images scroll down to #page and comment out the background. Finally, head to #footer and comment out the background image here, giving you a clean slate to work with.

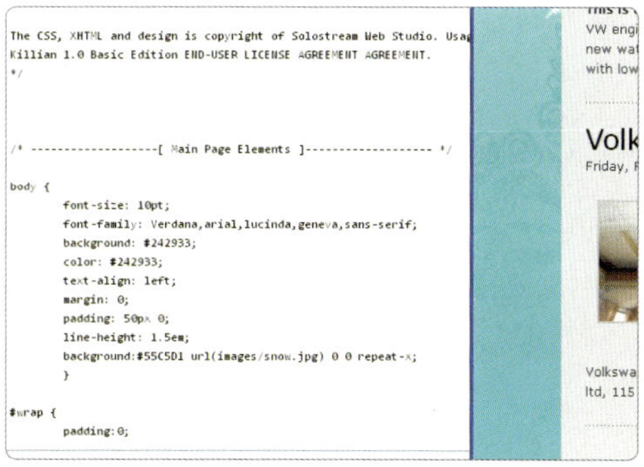

07 New background

Here we have chosen a vector-style winter-themed image at 1500x1500 pixels to help compensate for different resolutions. Add background #55C5D1 url(images/snow.jpg) 0 0 repeat-x; – this will add a horizontal repeating background image and a coloured background.

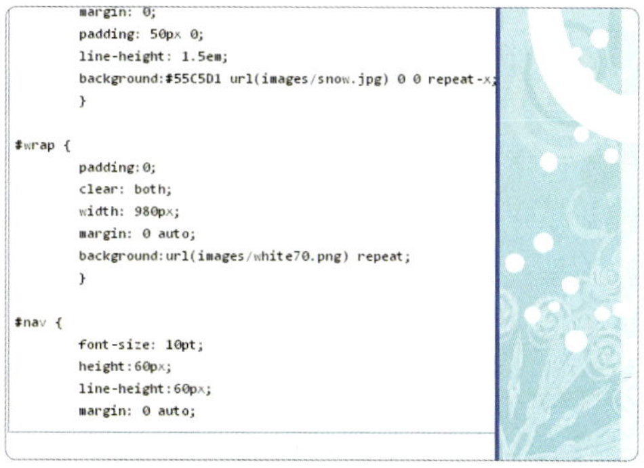

08 Transparent background

The main area theme is all one colour, but not a complementary one. Change it to a transparent white to make the background visible. Create a 10x10 pixel image with a transparency of 70-80% and save as a PNG-24. Now add: background:url(images/white70.png) repeat;.

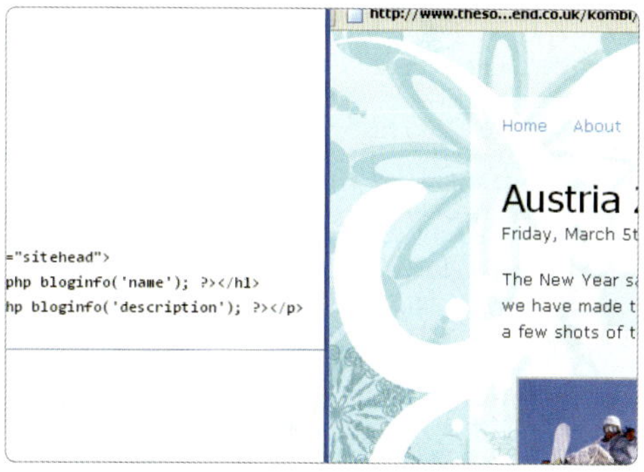

09 Big head

The default blog theme has the title at the head of the posts. To remove it altogether, open the Header (header.php) template, scroll down and locate the <div class="sitehead">. Add the following <!-- before the opening tag and --> after the closing tag.

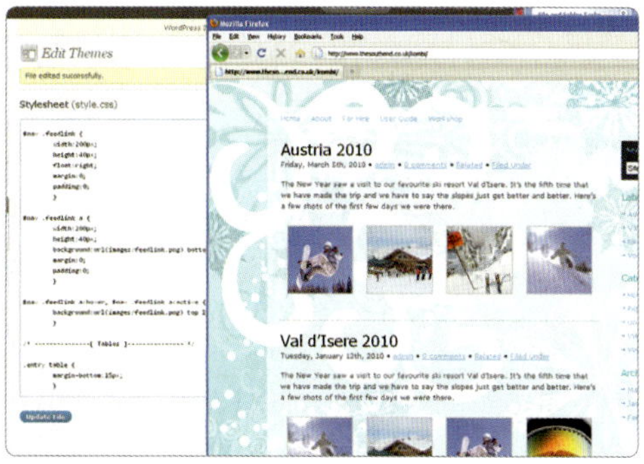

10 RSS feed

The RSS feed is a single image (called feedlink.gif) that repositions itself when the hover state comes into play. You can now create a matching image for the new-look theme, then save it as a PNG-24 and give it the same name. Now upload it to the theme images folder, then scroll to navigation.

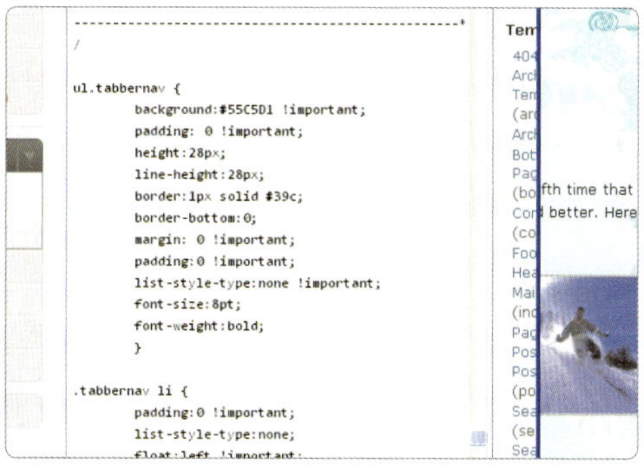

11 Search bar

To modify the search bar colours, scroll down style.css and locate ul.tabbernav under the Tabber section. Change the background to #55C5D1 and the border:1px solid #39c;. This will change the tab section. Now go to .tabberlive .tabbertab and set the background and border.

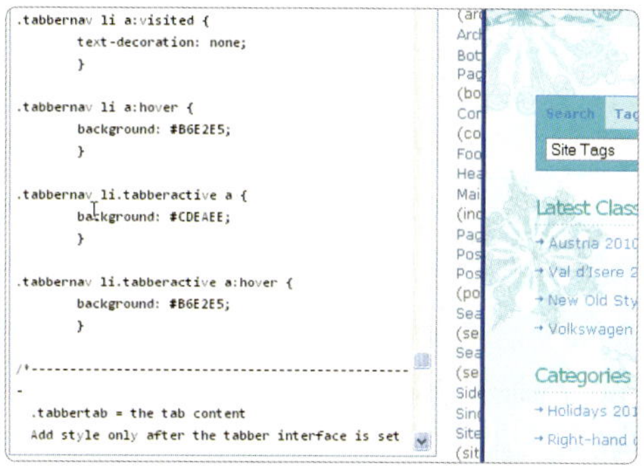

12 Link styles

To modify the link styles, locate .tabbernav li.tabberactive a and change the background colour. Do the same to .tabbernav li.tabberactive a:hover. Change the background colour of .tabbernav li a:hover to the same colour as the hover state. That's it!

Understanding SEO

146 Promote via Twitter

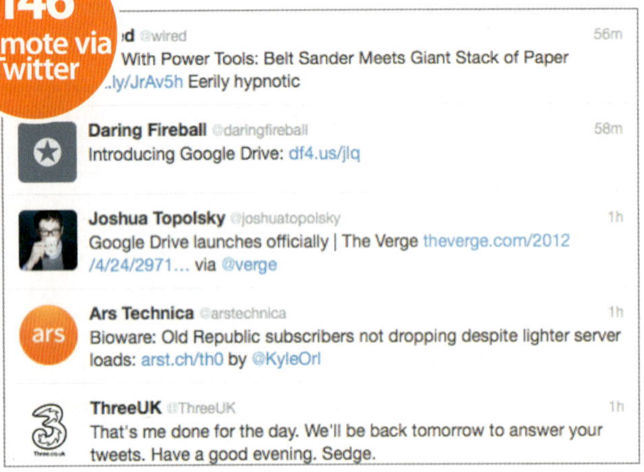

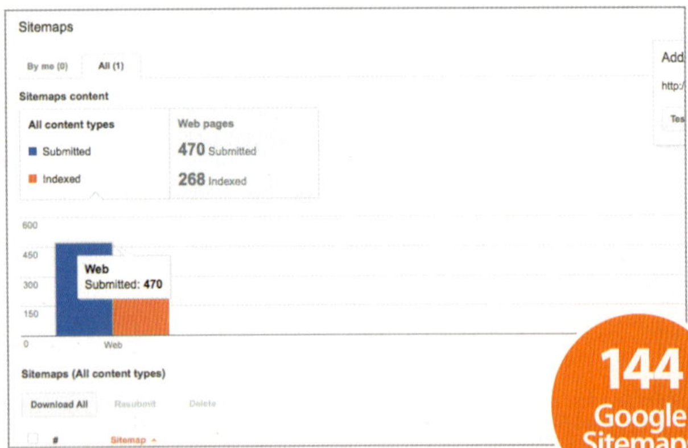

144 Google Sitemaps

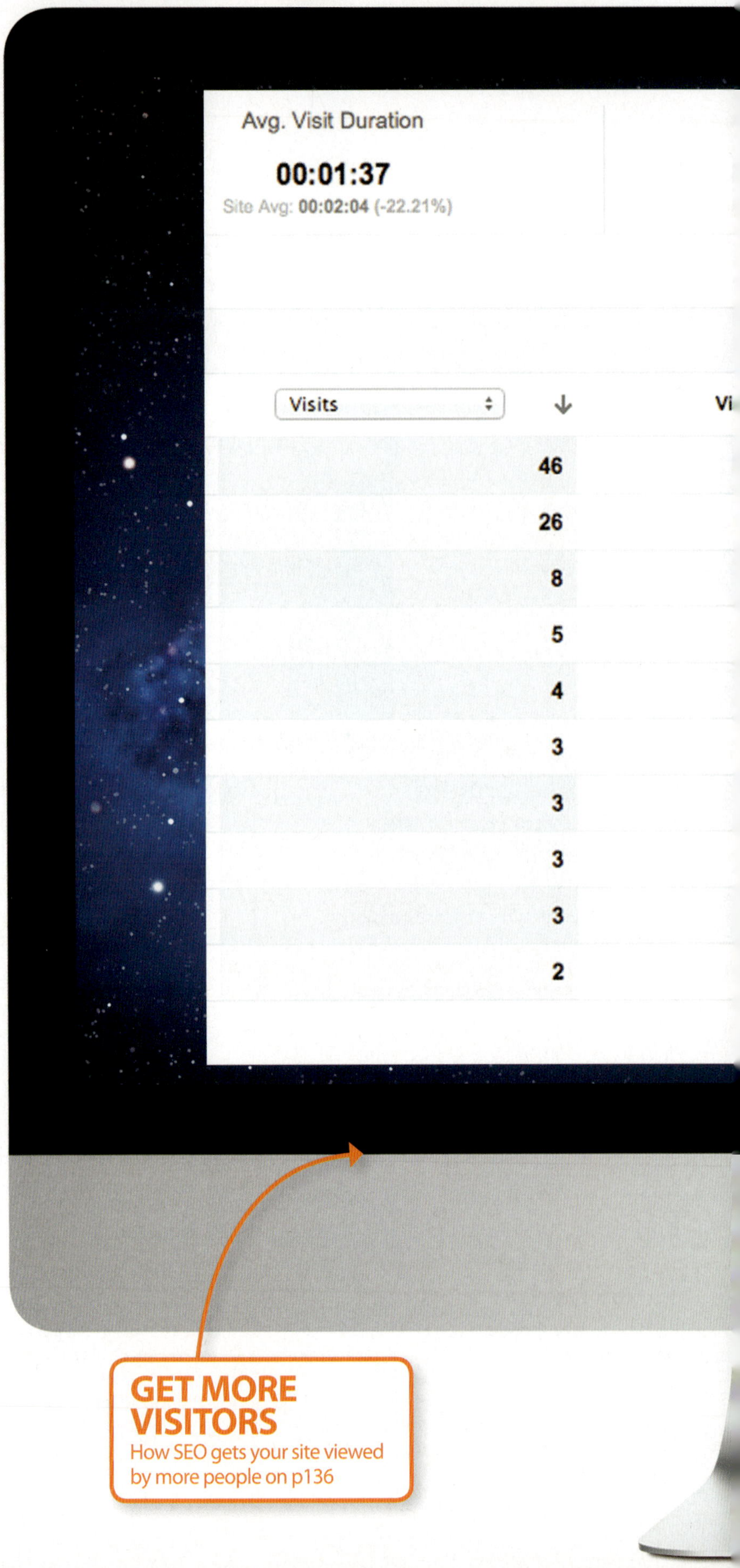

WHAT YOU'LL LEARN

It's the smallest section in our book, but it may well be the most important. Understanding SEO will help you get people visiting your site – hopefully over and over again. After all, your website could look amazing and function perfectly, but if no one knows that it exists, then there's no point in it being there. You'll learn key things to help improve your SEO (Search Engine Optimisation), how to make the most of Google Analytics, and promote your website via social networking services.

GET MORE VISITORS

How SEO gets your site viewed by more people on p136

GOOGLE ANALYTICS

Make the most of this powerful tool with our guide on page 140

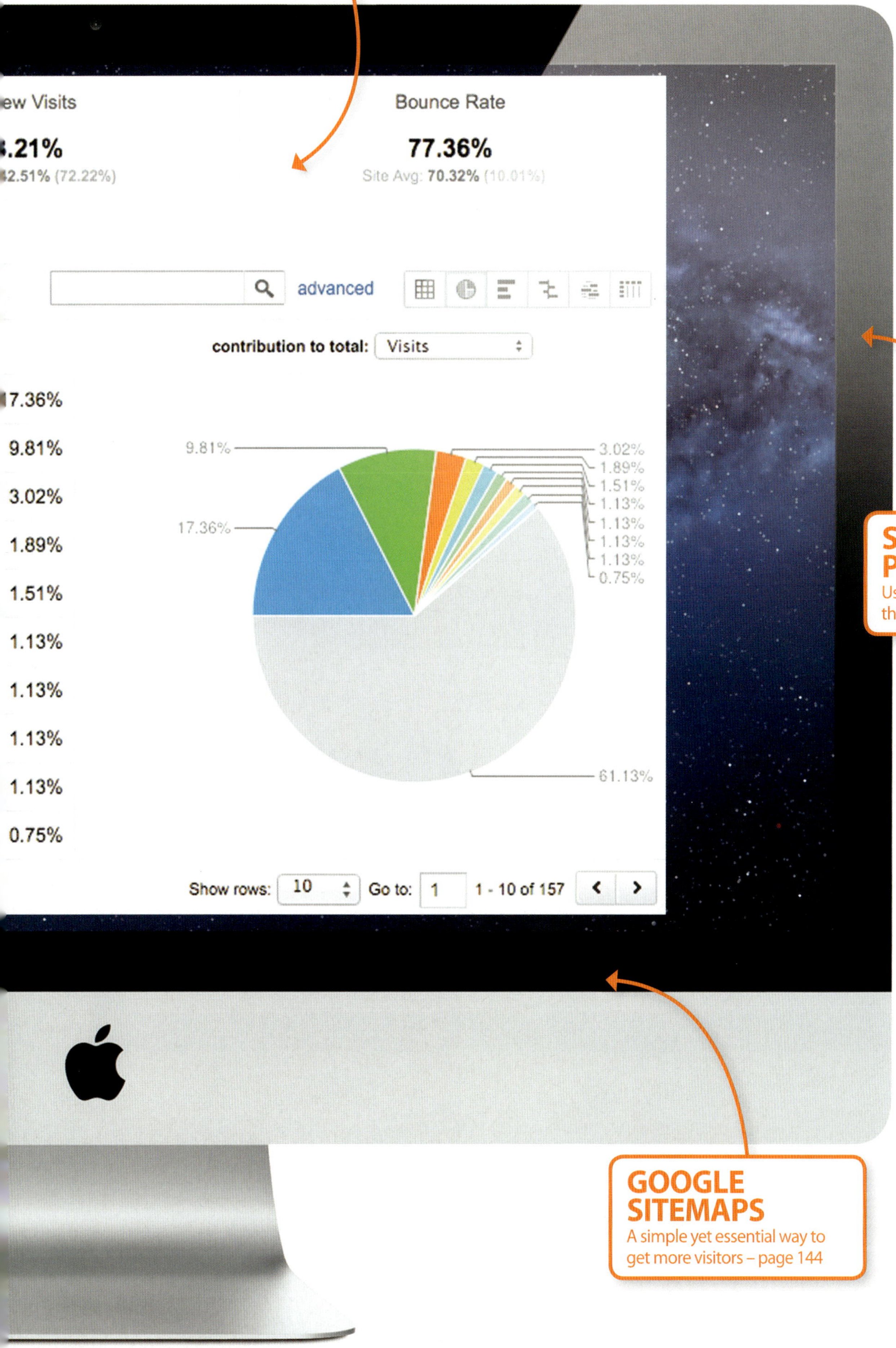

SOCIAL PROMOTION

Use social networking to get the word out on page 146

GOOGLE SITEMAPS

A simple yet essential way to get more visitors – page 144

Get more people to visit your website

SEO is incredibly important for building a high-traffic website

SEO (search engine optimisation) is not a feature that you may be aware of when first setting up a new website, but understanding how it works can make the biggest difference of all to ensuring that you drive as much traffic to your site as possible.

The quality of your website's content must always be paramount, of course; but no matter how good the quality, you still need to make sure that your website stands out and competes against the millions of other sites that are also trying to attract the same visitors. There is no guaranteed way to ensure lots of traffic, but to not make use of SEO techniques is probably to ensure that your new site takes a long time to get off the ground, with the possibility that it will never gain more than a handful of visitors. The consideration of how internet search engines work and what people are looking for will ensure that you are targeting your content to the right people at the right time and give you a better chance of making your site a success within a relatively short time period.

"Ensure that you are targeting your content to the right people at the right time"

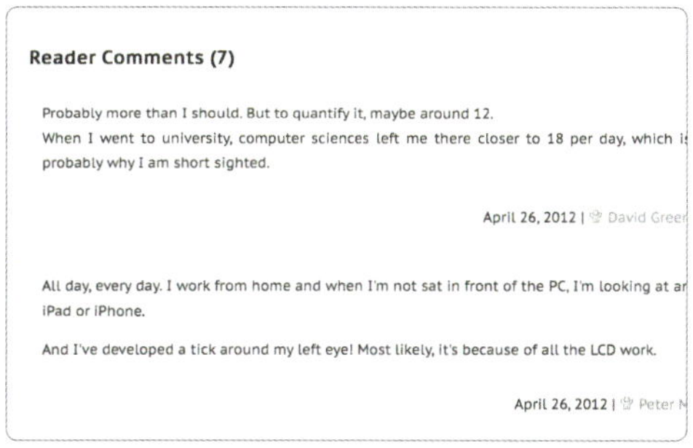

Encourage interaction

If you allow readers to comment on your content, they are likely to add info that search engines will pick up on. This means your readership is doing some of the work for you and increasing the amount of information that search engines will list. It is also ideal for encouraging repeat visits.

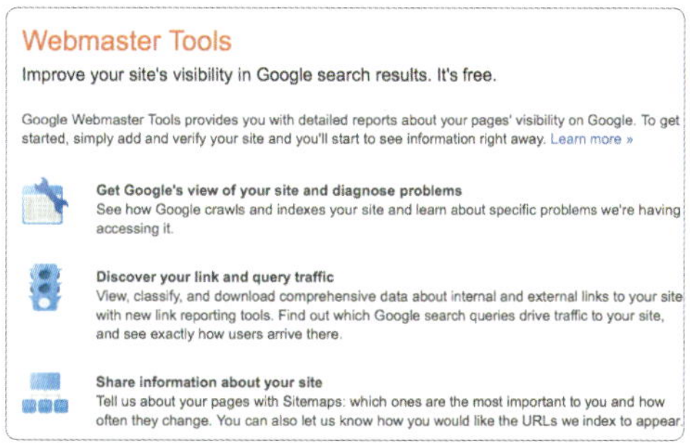

Google Webmaster Tools

Sign up for Google Webmaster Tools. Google provides a great deal of information on how to use keywords correctly and how to potentially increase the number of web searches that will end up at your website. Google is still the biggest search engine and you will ignore it at your peril.

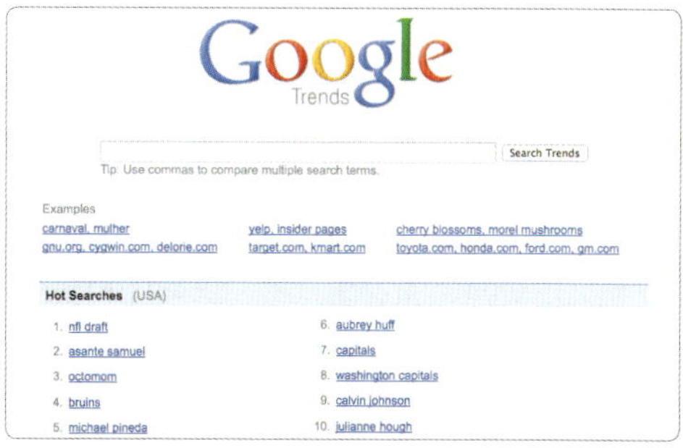

Know the trends

Since they change so quickly, it makes sense to know what the trending topics of the moment are. Keep an eye on **www.google.com/trends**, which shows the top searches in real-time – if you can tap into these topics, provided they're relevant to your site, you may increase traffic.

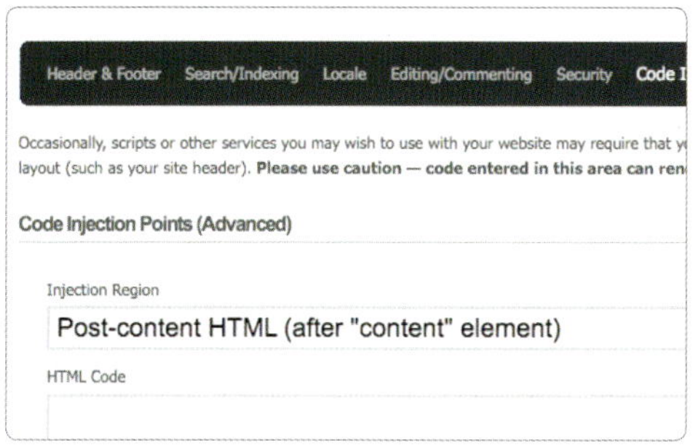

Avoid the bloat

As you get more experienced with your website, try to cut down the code as much as possible. You are at the mercy of search engines and unnecessary code will only get in the way. Keeping everything trim will also speed up the site for your visitors and the search engine robots, so everyone's a winner.

Meta tags

Your website should have a meta description at the top of the page. This is not visible to the reader, but does tell search engines what the site is about and is also displayed in search engine results. Written effectively, it will entice people who receive results from your site to visit above the other results that are returned.

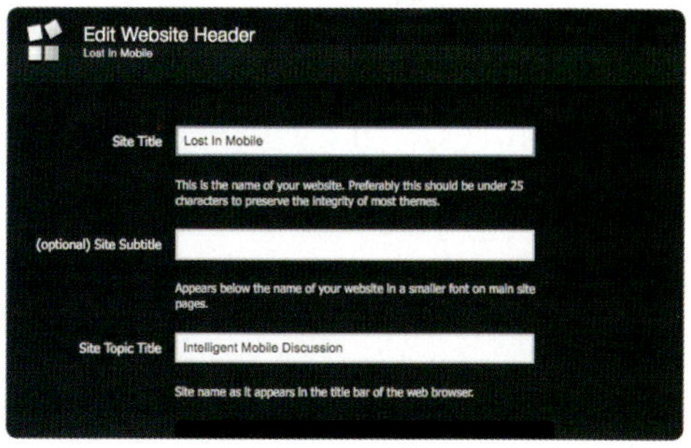

Keywords

Keywords are possibly the most important way to generate search engine traffic and using them for your daily content makes a lot of sense. Do not forget, however, to include keywords in your site's meta description, because these will work over longer periods of time to drive traffic to your site from those interested in the subject matter.

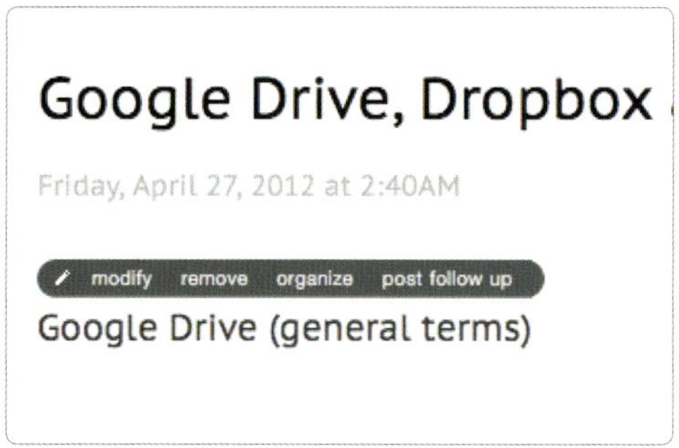

Title tags

Keywords should be used in title tags for each page as well, because this creates a larger swell of content for the search engines to find. If every page has the same keywords and tags, you are effectively greatly reducing the number of pages that will be found by search engines.

Try to be unique

Simply copying headlines and content from other sites is not a good idea. It not only shows a lack of originality, but also means that you will receive very low search ratings for that content. Search engines rate unique content above everything else, so try to be original as often as possible.

Avoid duplication

You also need to be careful to avoid repeating phrases or content on your own site. This can trick search engines into believing that the content is not justified and you will rank lower through penalisation. It is good practice anyway to not duplicate your own content on any site.

Understanding SEO

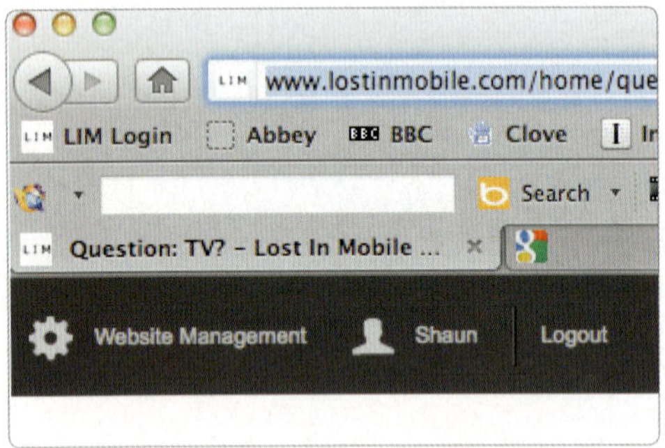

Be search engine friendly

Most CMSs offer a choice of how URLs for each page will be displayed. Try to use the 'search engine friendly' format which uses the title tag of the page in the URL, eg '/www.domain.com/article-title'. This also makes it look much cleaner and more professional to the reader.

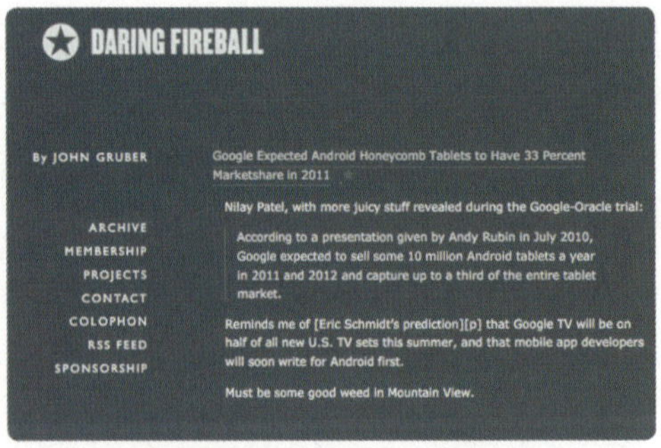

The website structure

There are tricks to how content should be displayed on any website and there are some rules that are worth following. It has been proved that people tend to read in an 'F'-shaped format, so try to keep as much of your important content near the top and in a left-hand bar as is feasible.

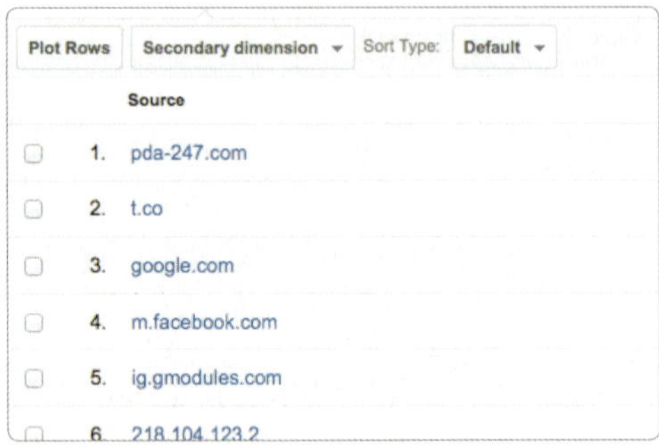

Build links

One very important factor in increasing your traffic rank is to build links with other sites. The more incoming links you have, the better, and this can also improve your page rank with Alexa, Google, etc. Links build your reputation as well as your traffic – and you need both for success.

Automated SEO plug-ins

If you use a CMS like WordPress (see page 108), there are many plug-ins available that automate much of the process of improving your site's SEO. If you have little knowledge of how SEO works, you should try one and then start working out your own solutions as your knowledge increases.

The hard work

Tricks to build links back to your site include posting comments on popular websites with your link in the signature and increasing your activity on social networks. This can take time to pay off, but will almost certainly increase your traffic if you persevere and keep plugging away at it.

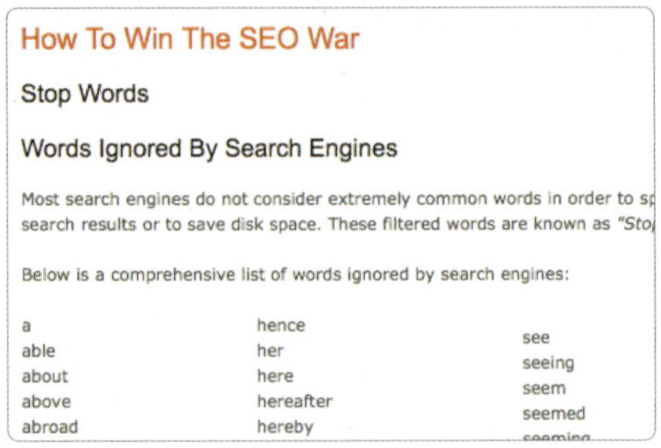

Stop words

If you have your URLs presented using the titles of each article, you need to be aware of stop words. Search engines ignore commonly used words such as 'I', 'the' and others, so using them can confuse the searches. There are plug-ins available that will automatically remove these for you.

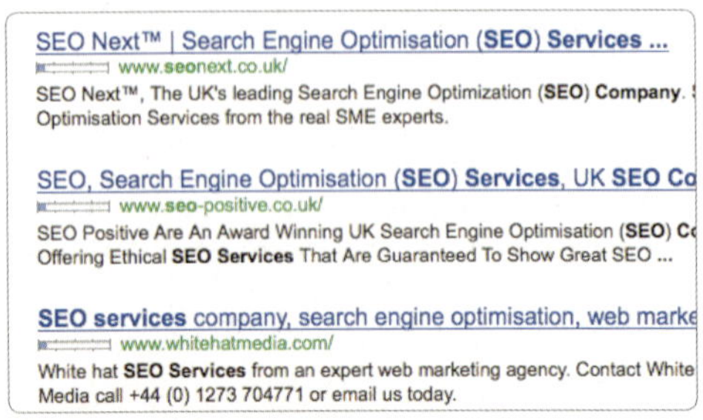

Paying for help

A simple search for 'SEO' on the web will bring back many companies offering to improve the SEO on your site. You should research these carefully before you decide to pay for help, but they can at the very least offer advice and arm you with invaluable knowledge that you can use in the future.

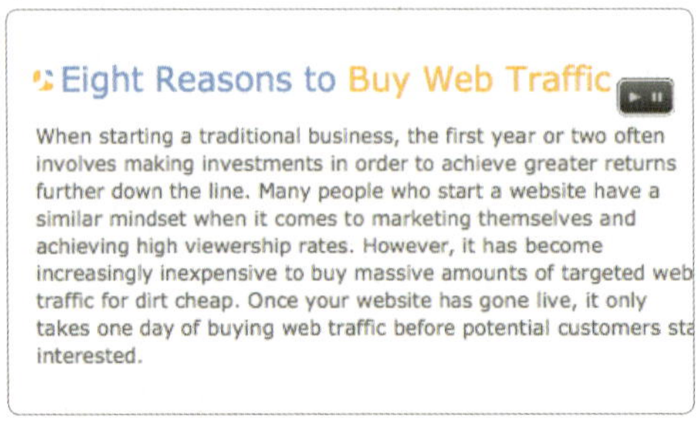

Don't buy traffic

There are many services available that offer the chance to buy links, followers and all sorts of other mechanisms that claim to improve your traffic. Be aware that some search engines will avoid known services and in some cases will blacklist them completely. This could undo all of your hard work in a matter of days.

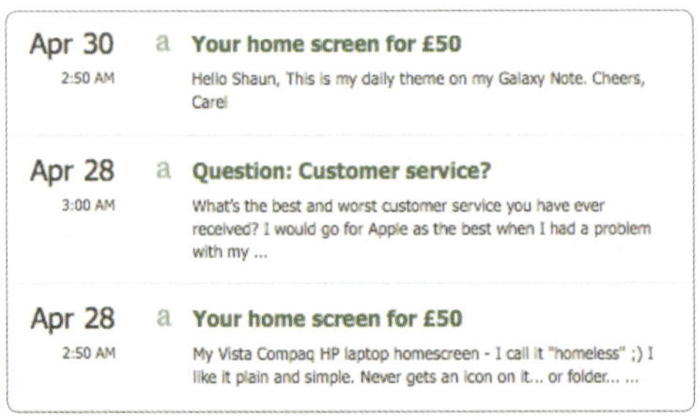

Don't obsess

The main thing with SEO is to understand the tricks you need, but to not obsess over them. Most of your time should be spent creating a web experience that brings readers back repeatedly and the SEO side should be seen as topping up your core audience. For businesses, SEO is much more important to gain new customers.

Important SEO factors

Make your site SEO friendly

SEO-friendly URLs

Make sure that your URLs are SEO friendly. Using the right format will greatly help search engines index your content and it also looks much cleaner to visitors

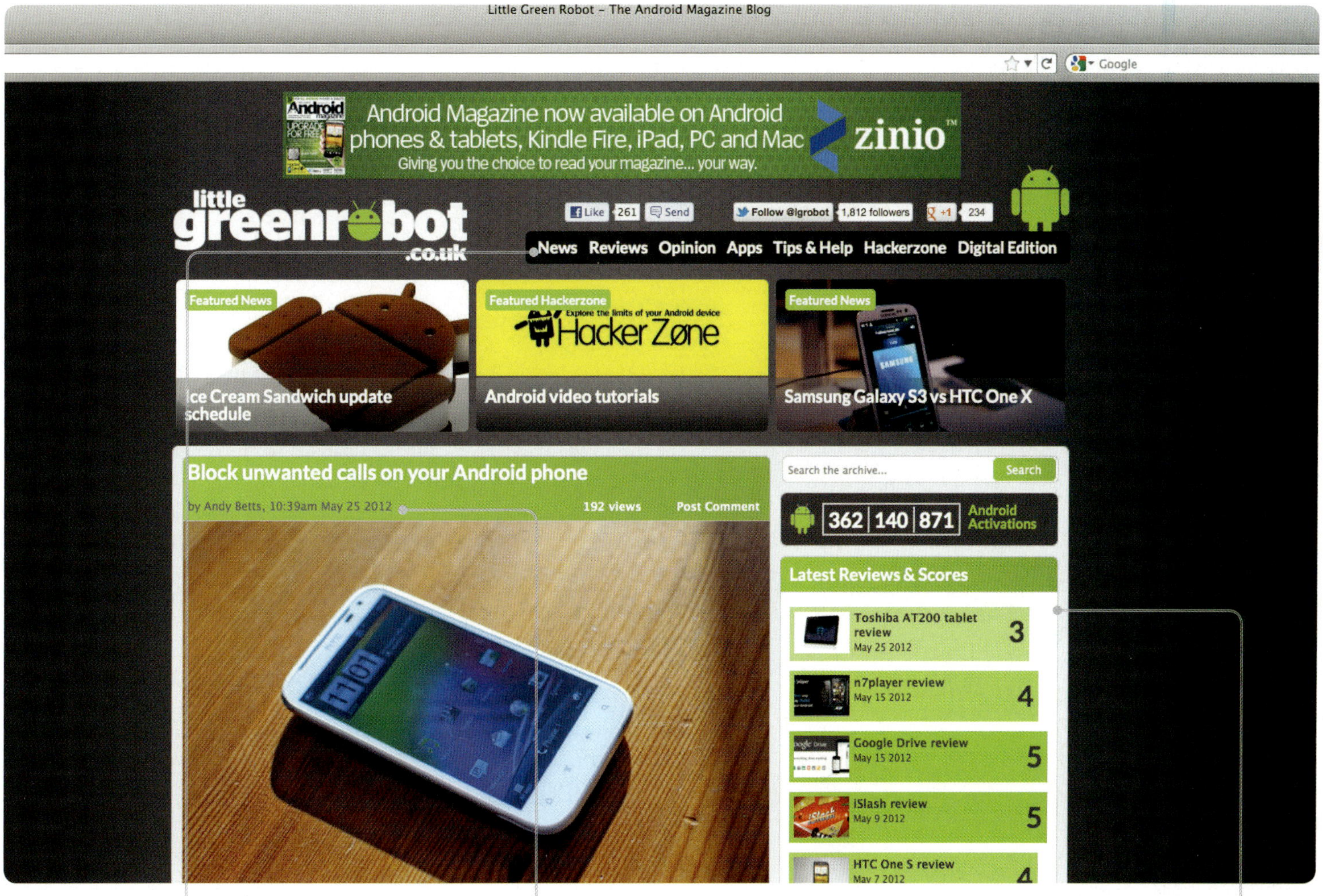

Meta tags

Try to ensure that your header code includes meta tags and keywords that let search engines know what your site is about. This is vitally important for ranking higher on web searches

The right format

Websites should be displayed in a form that is easy to read by anyone who visits. This will make it easier for them to understand the content and increase the likelihood of them returning

Content above all

Don't concentrate on SEO above the most important aspect of your site: the content. The majority of your time should still be spent creating interesting content worth reading

Judging SEO success

It's not easy to judge how effective your SEO strategy is

We said in the final step of this tutorial that SEO should not be obsessed about and that the content is the most important, but you still need to understand how your statistics show your success. We can break down your visitors into two broad categories: those who repeatedly visit your site and those who have recently visited. In general terms, you can analyse how many are from each group by checking your stats and seeing who has come direct to the site, who has been referred by another site and which readers have come via search engines. The direct visitors are likely the loyalists who enjoy your content, while the one-time or referrals have most likely come from searching for specific information. To add complexity, even your loyal readers will likely have come via search in the first place so they could still represent a good example of SEO working effectively for you. The best advice is to keep an eye on your stats and to check for shifts in the numbers. Ideally, you want a loyal base of readers who may spread the word, but with a healthy number of new readers continually dripping through.

Use Google Analytics to understand your audience

You need to analyse your traffic to see what you are doing right

No matter how much effort you put in to a website or how great your content is, you need to understand what your audience is looking at and what they are interested in to keep growing your site.

You can use web services that claim to understand your traffic, but by far the most recognised service is Google Analytics. It can show you, in great detail, which parts of your site are successful and which parts require extra effort to receive attention from the masses. You can monitor all aspects of your site, from social networking impact to the number of people visiting on mobile devices, and more general statistics including visitor numbers and when they visit.

The basic Google Analytics service is free and includes all of the features most webmasters will need, but there are premium options available should you need specific features to take your analysing further. In this tutorial we will teach you how to set up Google Analytics for your site and how to make the most of the service to understand and increase your traffic.

> "The basic service is free and includes all of the features most webmasters need"

Highly analytical

So many stats and so much helpful information

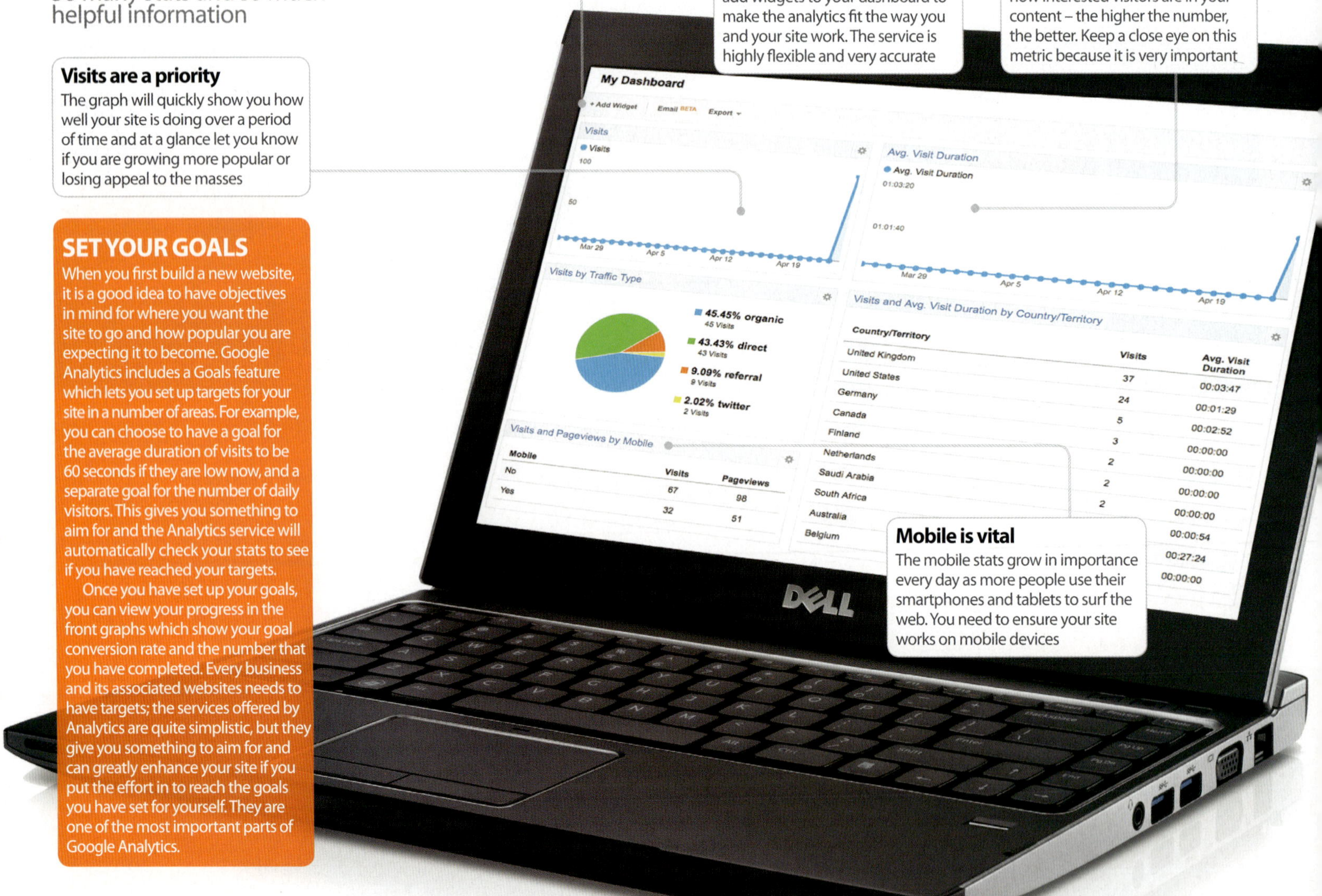

Visits are a priority

The graph will quickly show you how well your site is doing over a period of time and at a glance let you know if you are growing more popular or losing appeal to the masses

Customisation

You can create custom reports and add widgets to your dashboard to make the analytics fit the way you and your site work. The service is highly flexible and very accurate

Time counts

The average visit duration shows how interested visitors are in your content – the higher the number, the better. Keep a close eye on this metric because it is very important

Mobile is vital

The mobile stats grow in importance every day as more people use their smartphones and tablets to surf the web. You need to ensure your site works on mobile devices

SET YOUR GOALS

When you first build a new website, it is a good idea to have objectives in mind for where you want the site to go and how popular you are expecting it to become. Google Analytics includes a Goals feature which lets you set up targets for your site in a number of areas. For example, you can choose to have a goal for the average duration of visits to be 60 seconds if they are low now, and a separate goal for the number of daily visitors. This gives you something to aim for and the Analytics service will automatically check your stats to see if you have reached your targets.

Once you have set up your goals, you can view your progress in the front graphs which show your goal conversion rate and the number that you have completed. Every business and its associated websites needs to have targets; the services offered by Analytics are quite simplistic, but they give you something to aim for and can greatly enhance your site if you put the effort in to reach the goals you have set for yourself. They are one of the most important parts of Google Analytics.

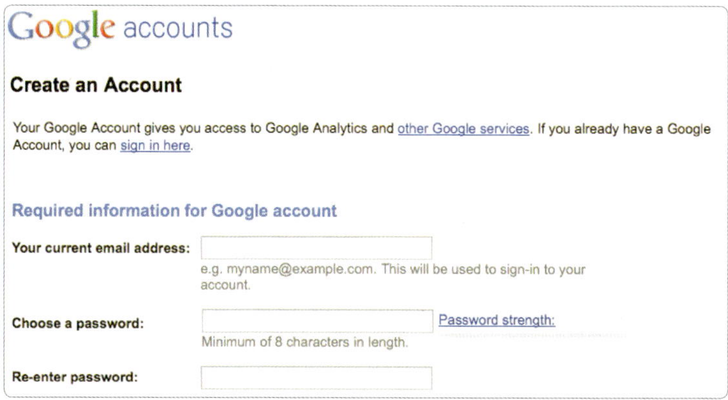

01 The first step

Go to **www.google.com/analytics**. If you don't already have a Google account, click 'Create Account'. Tap 'Sign up' and enter the required details – try to make the password as secure as possible. Then click 'Create my account'.

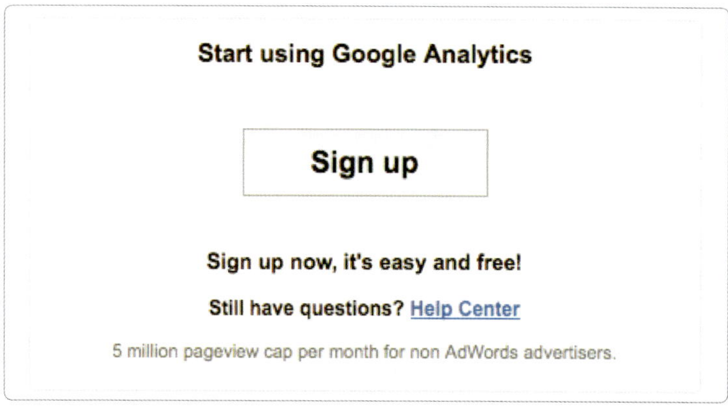

02 The second step

Now you have a Google account, you'll be asked to sign up to Google Analytics. Tap the 'Sign up' button and proceed to the next page. You now need to input your website URL and choose an account name.

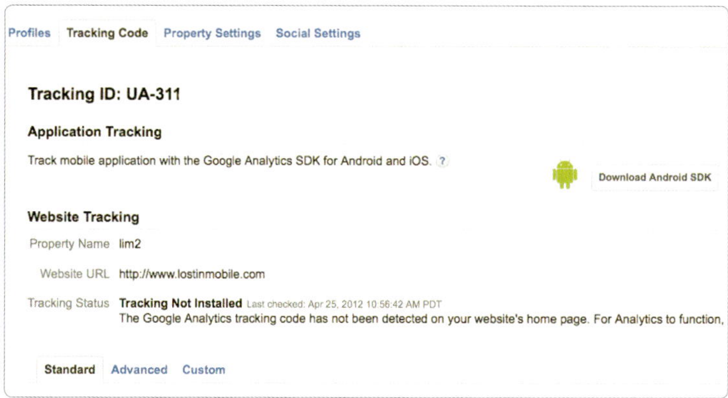

03 Starting the setup

On the next page, scroll down to the 'What are you tracking?' section and choose the correct option for your website setup. Most people will require the 'Single domain' option, but choose 'Multiple subdomains' if applicable.

04 Time to jump

Now to find out how to insert the Analytics code for your site setup. Each service is different and you'll need to find the correct process for yours, whether it is WordPress, Squarespace or another web publishing platform.

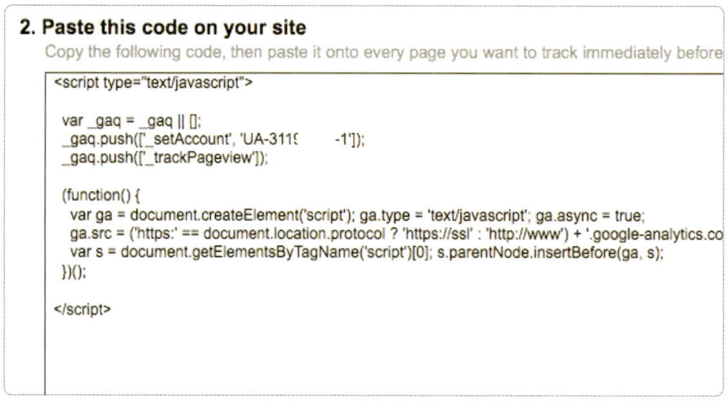

05 Use the code

Return to the Tracking Code section and copy the code under 'Paste this code on your site'. Paste it into the required place on your site. Then, when you click 'Save' at the bottom, you should see a 'Success' button appear at the top.

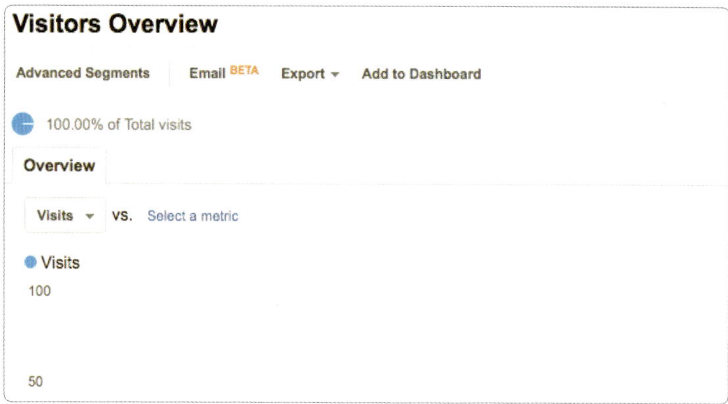

06 No traffic

Click the Home button at the top to see a series of windows which will all show 0 hits. Don't panic: it takes some time for the code to start showing traffic. Leave it for 48 hours before you come back and check your stats.

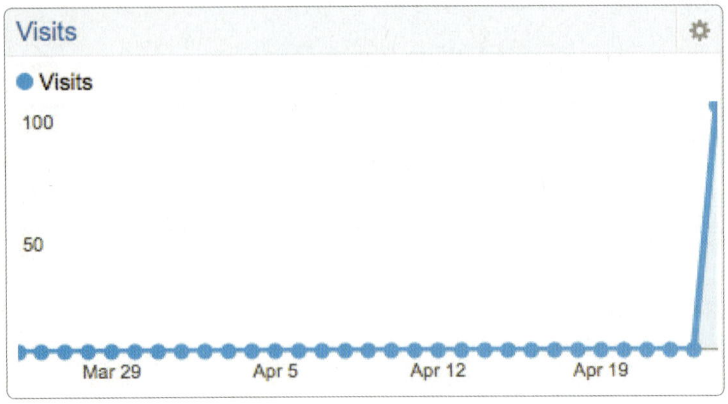

07 Your first stats

When you come back, you should see a series of graphs showing the traffic for your site. Don't worry if it's low, since Analytics tends to get more accurate over time, but you will need to spend some time looking at the graphs.

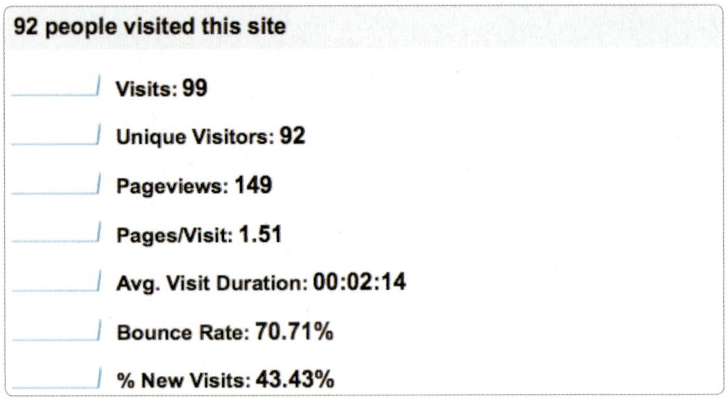

08 Check your visits

Click 'Visits' at the top of the box and a new page will pop up. The graph at the top shows the number of daily visitors and the boxes below delve deeper into the operating systems used and geographical locations of your readers.

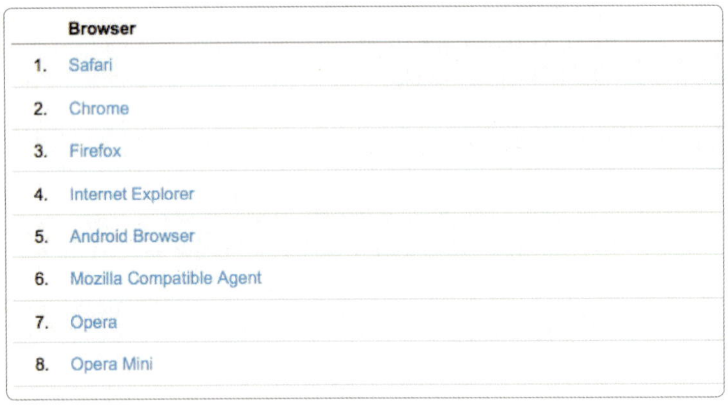

09 Study the data

It makes sense to check the 'Browser' stats first, showing which browsers visitors are using. You should ensure that your site presents correctly in each, putting emphasis on the most popular browsers within your readership.

10 Check the screens

As well as the OS, check the screen resolutions used by visitors. If low ones are at the top, you'll need to ensure your site works on mobile devices. Either let it scale down or use a plug-in to change it to a mobile version automatically.

11 Build the interest

The 'Avg. Visit Duration' box details how long visitors stay on your site. Very short visits are classed as 'bounced' and can be ignored. The longer the average, the more interesting your content is to the readers – a good sign!

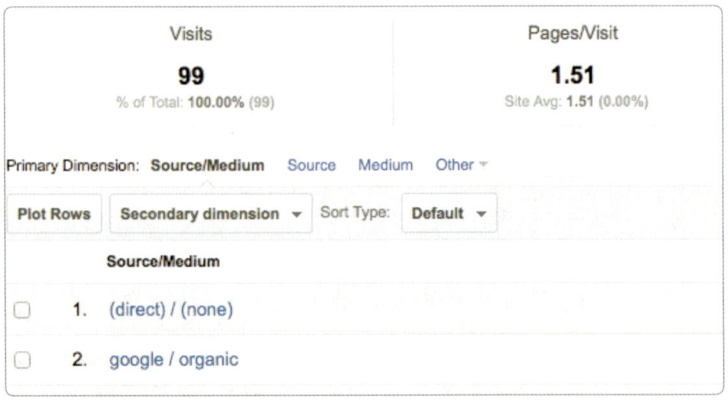

12 Delving deeper

Standard Reporting>Traffic Sources shows the keywords searched for to get to your site. It also shows how much traffic is direct to the site and how much comes from search engines – ideally, you'll want to see the latter grow.

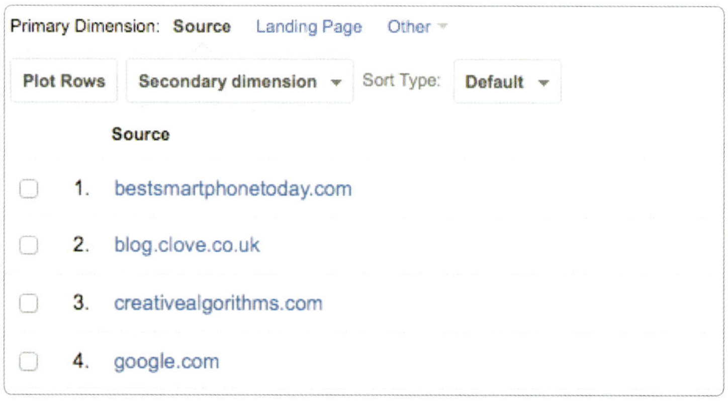

13 Referrals

Also check the 'Referral' stats which show sites that are linking to you. This will show high-volume links and also sites that have completely copied your content with a link back. This is not good practice, so ask them to stop.

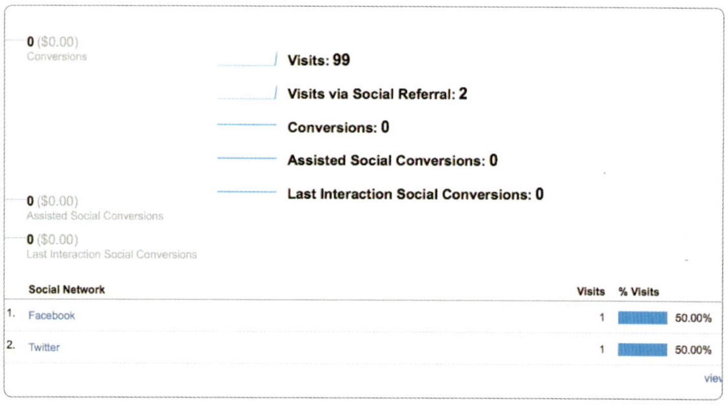

14 Social stats

'Social' shows traffic from social networks, which will help you analyse how effectively you're using Facebook, Twitter, etc. It's not too hard to make these stats grow to form a decent percentage of your traffic (see p104-105).

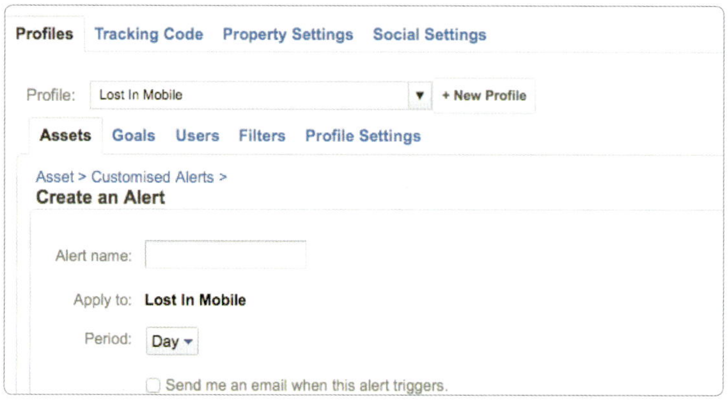

15 Custom alerts

You can create custom alerts by selecting 'Intelligent Events' on the left, then Overview>Custom Alerts. Alerts can be set up to advise you immediately if you receive a lot of traffic or if it drops below a certain level.

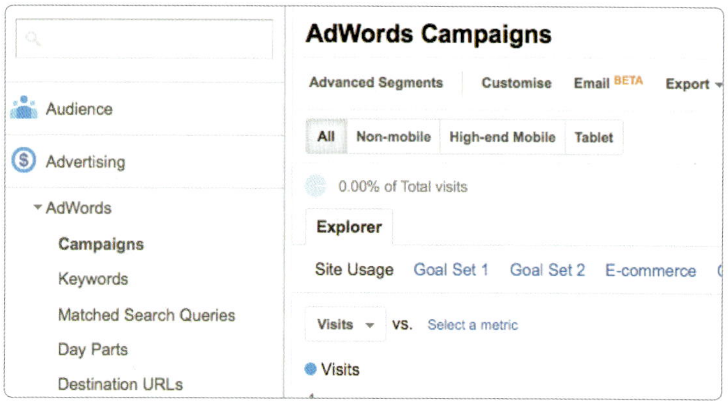

16 Advertising

Google Analytics also offers detailed AdWords reporting. This helps you to see if your money is being well spent or if you need to change your methods. Well-targeted ads can make a huge difference to incoming traffic numbers.

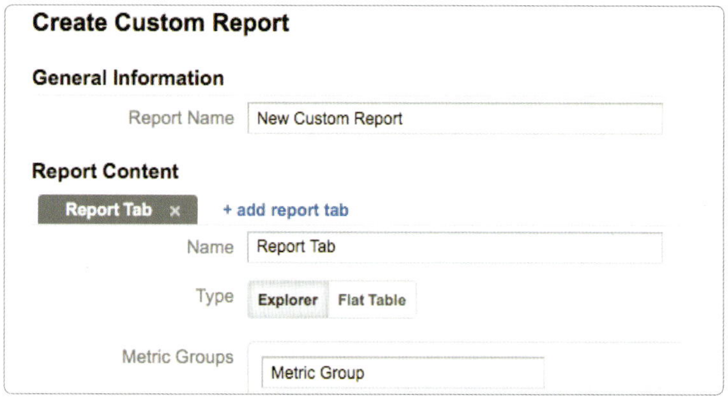

17 Custom reports

'Custom Reporting' lets you build reports tailored to your goals and the way your site is set up. You can create reports that cover all of your specific needs and this could potentially greatly speed up your traffic analysis in the future.

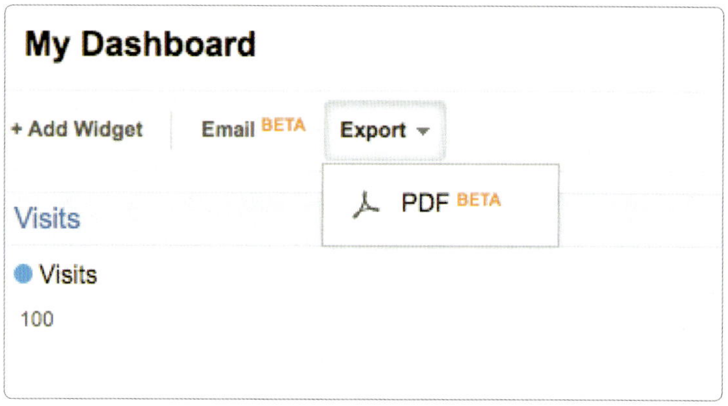

18 Export your data

Use the 'Export' option at the top to export your data in PDF format. This can be useful to share with potential advertisers or for data analysis – you can send it to specialists for advice on the best methods to grow your site

Create a Google Sitemap for easier searching

A Google Sitemap will make a huge difference to your site's recognition

A Google Sitemap is important for a variety of reasons. Firstly, it tells Google how your site is structured and ensures that the search provider is aware of every page on your site. This ensures that new sites with lots of varied content are properly structured in the Google mechanism as well as on the site itself and greatly increases the chances of search results coming your way. In fact, a Sitemap is more important for new sites because Google is less likely to be aware of your content if few other sites link to it, and this can mean a long road to recognition from the biggest search provider of all.

A Sitemap offers a short cut to Google recognition. While it offers no guarantee of success, the process to upload one is quick and simple, so you have nothing to lose by following the steps here. Once you have completed the process you should be able to leave it there, but it can be beneficial to update it from time to time. The most important factor, however, is to ensure you have uploaded one initially. Anything you can do to make Google aware of your site is a very good thing.

> "A Sitemap offers a short cut to Google recognition"

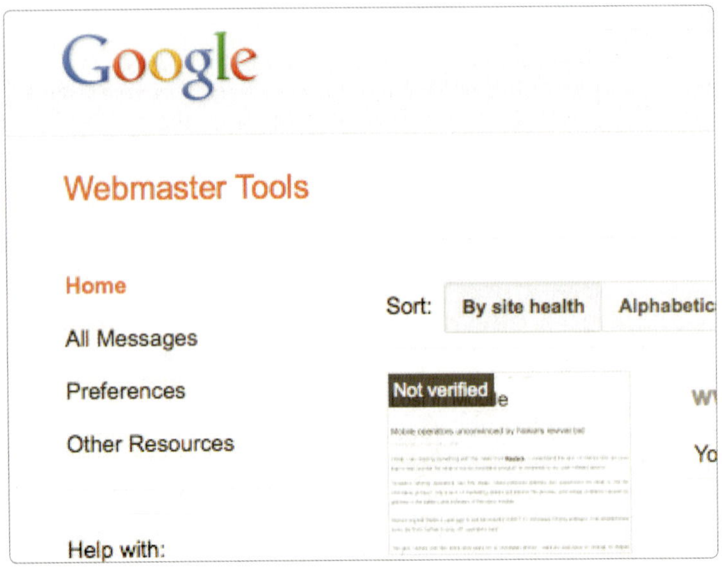

01 Sign up with Google

Go to **www.google.com/webmasters/tools/** and create a new account via the 'Sign up' button. You then need to input your site URL and verify it by following the instructions provided on screen. You need to do this to prove that the site is yours.

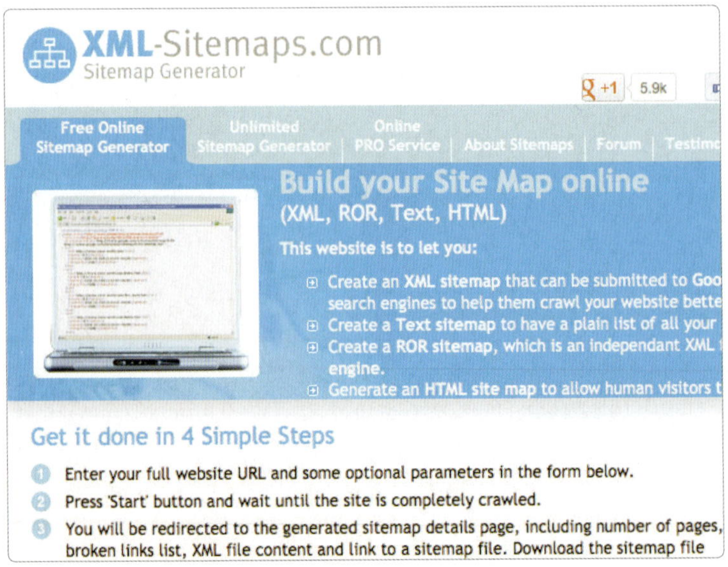

02 Create your Sitemap

Go to **www.xml-sitemaps.com**, which is a site that lets you automate the process of creating a Sitemap. Simply enter your URL and tap the 'Start' button. When completed, you will be presented with an XML file to download.

Your site's Sitemap

A look at your personal Sitemap

How many pages?

You can check to see how many pages are included in your Sitemap against the number of pages you can see on your site using FTP. They should ideally be identical

Regular updates

You will be able to see when the Sitemap was last processed, which will help you to ensure that the data being scraped is recent and accurate. Try to update every quarter if you can

Multiple Sitemaps

You can upload multiple Sitemaps to Google to keep your site information fresh and up to date. Try not to upload them too often because that will add little benefit and could cause problems with Google searches

Know the location

The Google Sitemaps page will show which file it is looking at and you should ensure that this matches where you believe the file to be on your own server. A single '/' means it is in the root folder

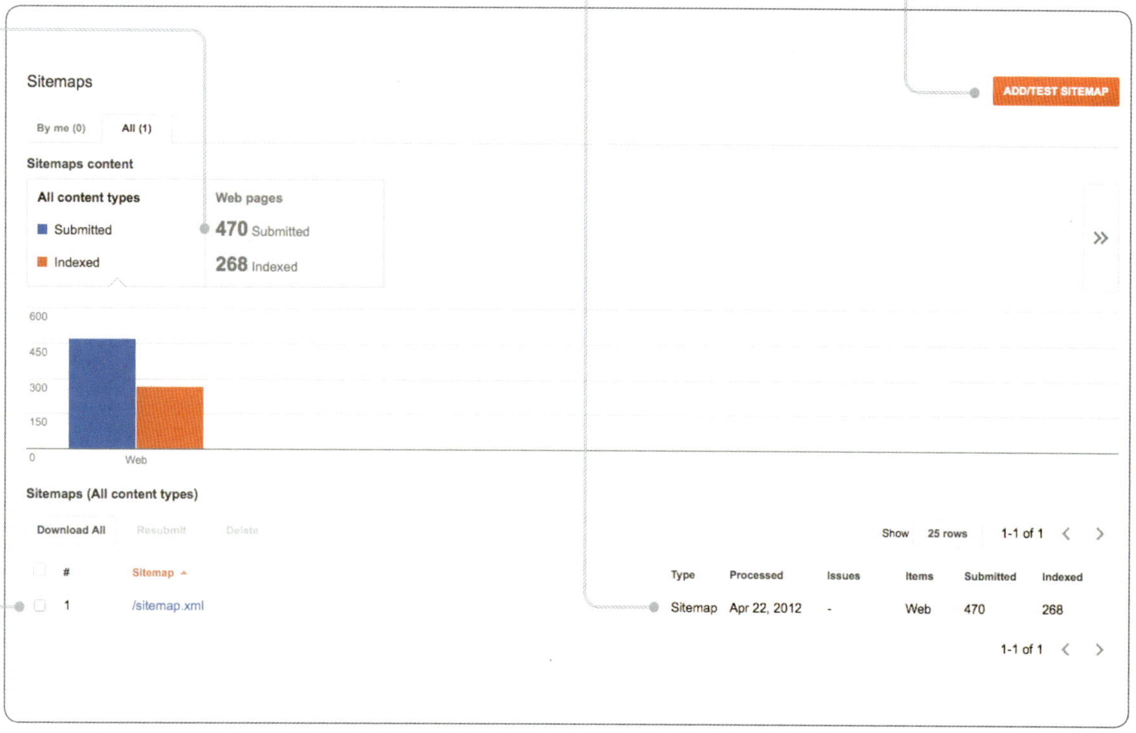

NOT JUST GOOGLE

You can submit sitemaps and other site-related data to other search engines as well. For example, there are webmaster tools available for Bing at **www.bing.com/toolbox/webmaster/** and these work in a very similar way to the Google process. If you have the time, try to submit sitemaps to all of the large search engines to increase your visibility to everyone.

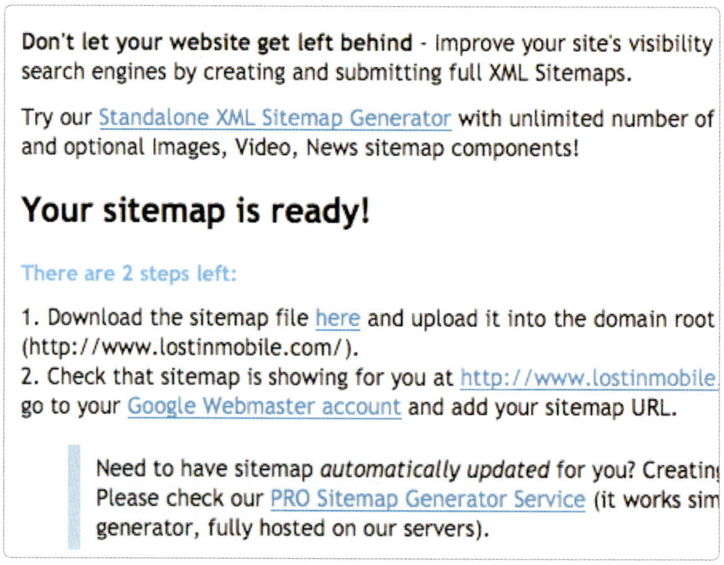

03 Upload the Sitemap

You now need to upload the Sitemap file to your root folder via FTP. Simply upload it and check that it is visible by navigating to **<your domain>/sitemap.xml**. You should see the file displayed and if present, you can move to step 4.

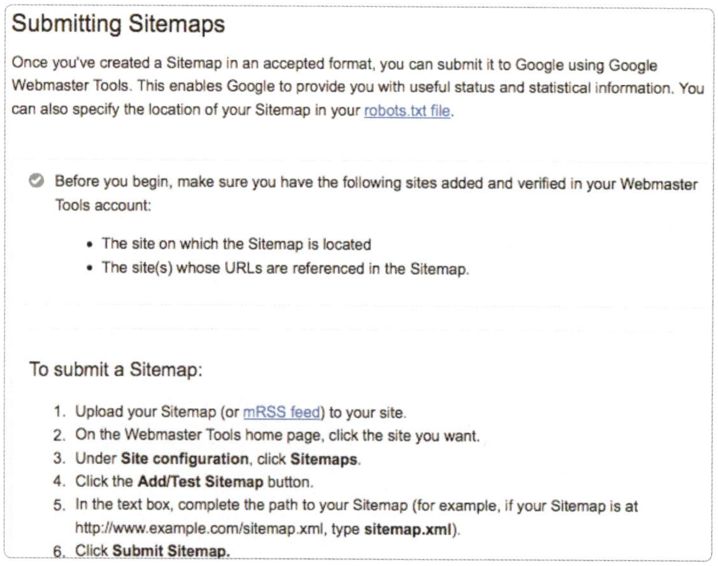

04 Submit your Sitemap

You now need to go to Site Configuration at Google Webmaster Tools and choose 'Add/Test Sitemap'. Simply enter the URL of your Sitemap and submit it. Google will then analyse the file and index your site accordingly. It's a painless operation.

Promote your website through social networks

Social networks are incredibly important when spreading the word

Social networks, like Facebook and Twitter, are now used by millions of people every day and it has become standard for websites to interact with the more popular networks in a very public manner. You can add links to site-related accounts from social networks and also ensure that your readers are aware of your social networking presence by adding links from your site as well. However, you need to be careful not to overdo your social networking presence because this can actually drive traffic away from your site and onto the social networks. So you must use them to your advantage and only to increase the traffic *you* are getting on your site.

It makes sense to start with the bigger services such as Twitter and Facebook and there are many tools available that will automate the process of sharing your site content with readers and to alert them to new links. The trick is to entice people using social networks to access your site with intriguing descriptions that make them want to read more via links back to you. Social networks let you inform people directly of new content rather than relying on a chance visit and can make all the difference between success and failure for a new site. You really can make social networks work for you.

"Social networks let you inform people directly of new content"

Share your site

Social networks can account for much of your daily traffic

Who to follow
You should make efforts to follow select people from your website's social network account. Try not to follow everyone, but carefully select those who may be beneficial to your site

Important links
The links placed on social networks can become a large part of your incoming traffic if they are shared by other people on the networks who find your work interesting. Every click counts

Tempt the reader
Try not to make headlines completely obvious, but to tempt the reader to read more. If it says everything in the title, they will have little reason to visit your site

Describe your site
If you set up a Twitter account for your site, make sure you describe its aims succinctly and clearly to attract more people to follow your articles. This can make a huge difference to your success

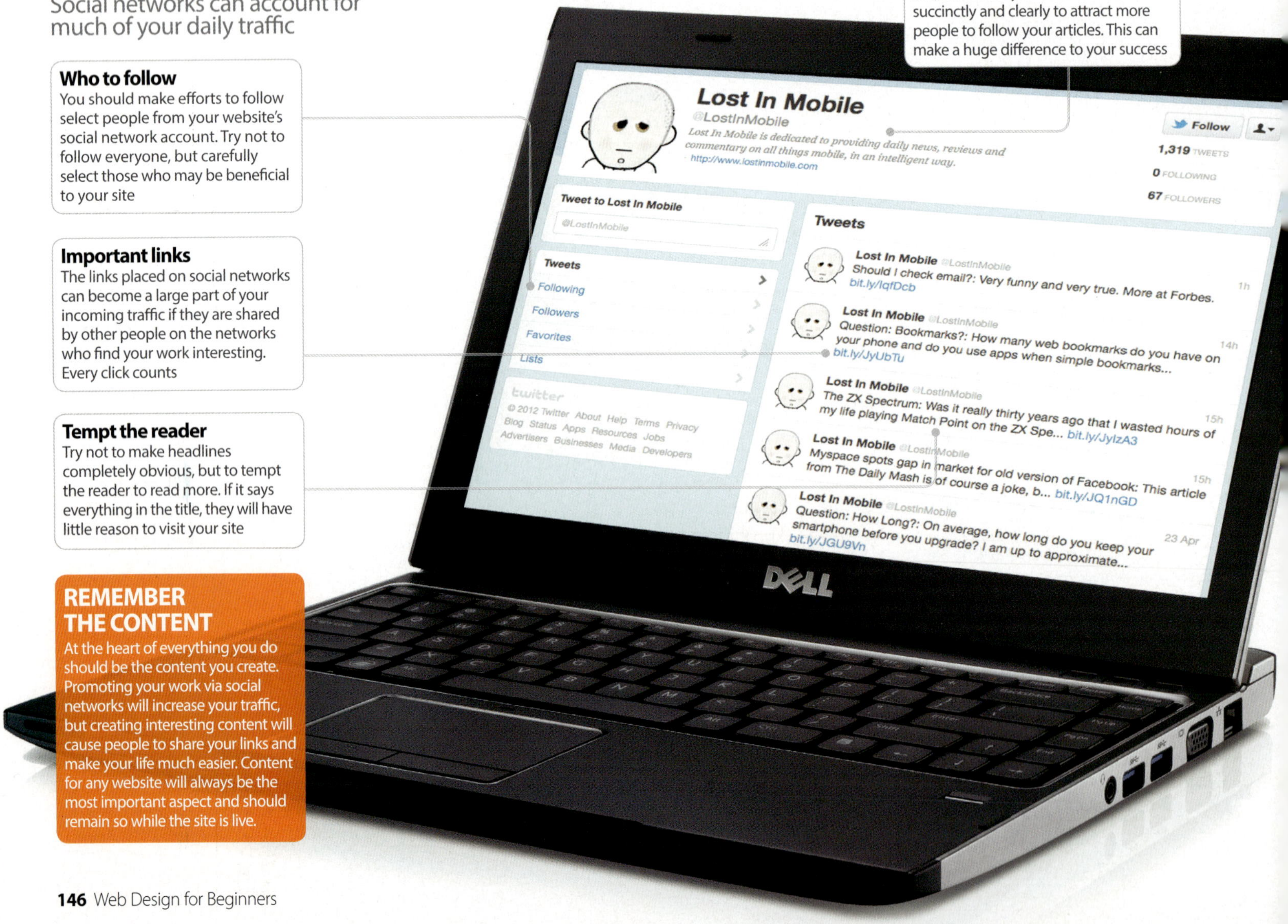

REMEMBER THE CONTENT
At the heart of everything you do should be the content you create. Promoting your work via social networks will increase your traffic, but creating interesting content will cause people to share your links and make your life much easier. Content for any website will always be the most important aspect and should remain so while the site is live.

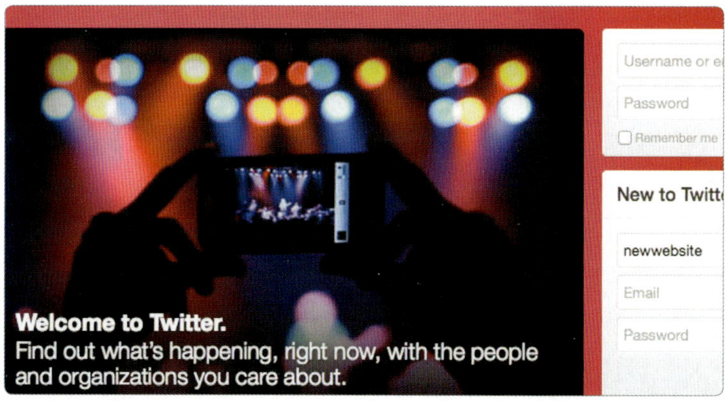

01 Build an account

Go to **www.twitter.com** and set up a new account with the same name as your website. Do the same at **www.facebook.com** as well. Make sure you add informative and full descriptions of the site's purpose to each profile.

02 Automate your content

Whatever CMS you're using, you should be able to find plug-ins that automatically push updates on your site to Twitter or Facebook. Then anyone following your account will see multiple links each day for your site.

03 Obvious links

Set up an obvious link on a sidebar of your site to the Twitter account. This pushes readers to it, where they can follow you and be presented with website updates as they happen. The click rate for this type of account is high.

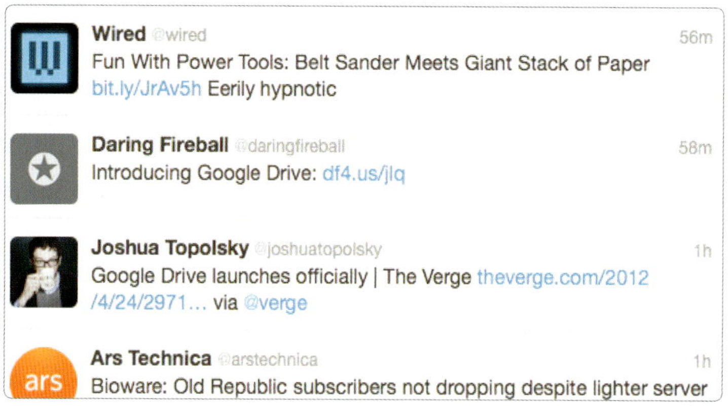

04 Make it personal

It is also advisable to set up an individual account where people can follow you on a personal level. You can then occasionally add tweets with links to your site, which should prove popular. Remember not to tweet every article, though.

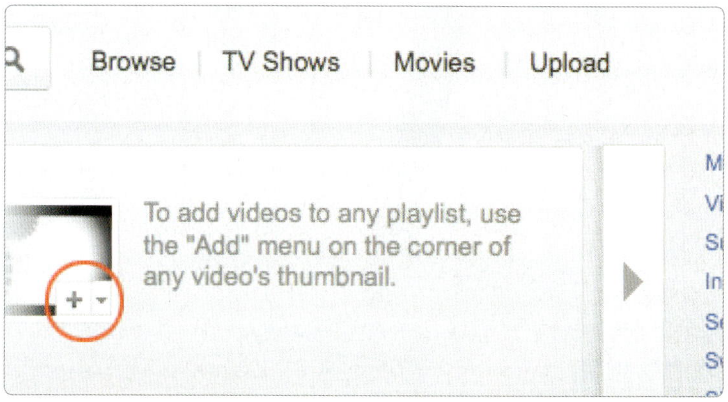

05 Use YouTube

Videos are the most popular form of content. Set up a YouTube account in the site name and publish as many videos as you can. You can then embed them into your site and also share the links via Twitter and Facebook.

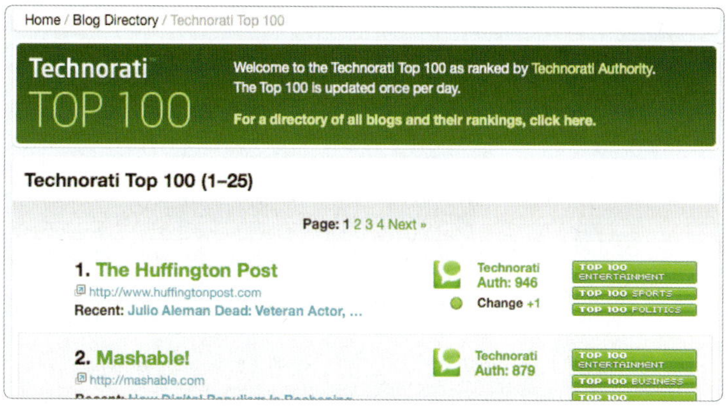

06 Use directories

Use services like **technorati.com**, which let you list your site alongside others to help you judge how popular it is. This can bring in extra traffic because sites are placed in categories, which should polarise interest from potential readers.

Photoshop and graphics

156
Optimise images

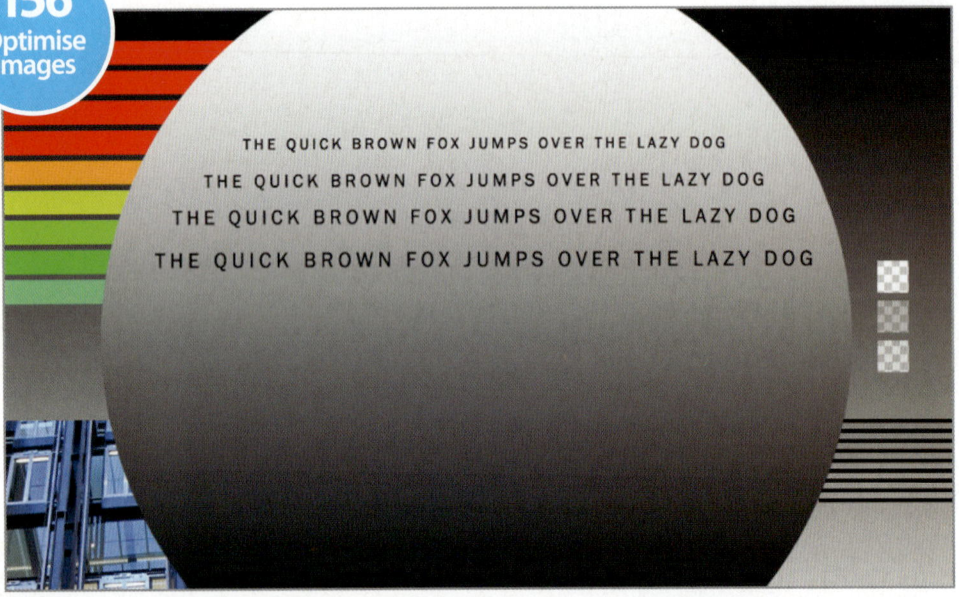

WHAT YOU'LL LEARN

Although you're more likely to hear about it being used to retouch models or enhance landscapes, Photoshop is used a lot in modern web design. Although you can get a website online and viewed by many without even touching the software, well-realised graphics made in Photoshop will enhance every website. We take you through its role in web design, and you'll learn how to get your images ready to go on the web, as well as how to design a great background, header, and footer.

PORTFOLIO THEME

Create a great place in which to put all your images on p176

HEADER & FOOTER

Effective header and footer art can make the difference – p164

150
Photoshop feature

PHOTOSHOP IN WEB DESIGN
Learn how the image-editing software is used in web design

"While Photoshop won't sling code for you or troubleshoot server protocols, it can be your best friend during the initial design phase"

164
Header & footer

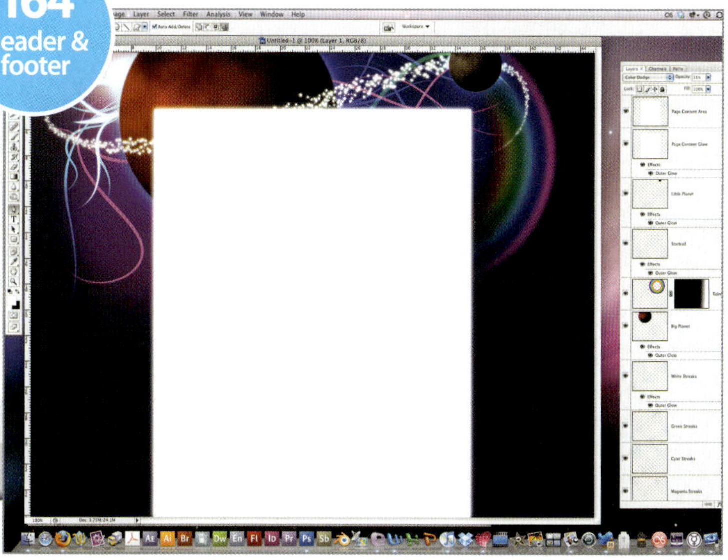

160
Create a background

Photoshop in web design

Photoshop puts the 'design' in web design. Learn the basic concepts needed for solid design and the techniques used to produce backgrounds, buttons and mockups

Almost all custom designs start out in Photoshop in the wild, wacky and wonderful world of web design. While Photoshop won't sling code for you or troubleshoot server protocols, it can be your best friend during the initial design phase of the project. It's also invaluable for the development phase of crafting the endless stream of graphics files used to build the site. Over the next several pages, we'll take a look at some of the web design concepts you will need to know and then a few basic techniques to get you started.

Size matters

Screen size and print size are two completely different animals. Computer screens are made up of tiny dots of coloured light called pixels. These pixels are what comprise the images seen on the screen. There are 72 of these pixels per inch. This is actually a relatively low resolution when compared to printing (which is often around 300). A common tendency is to take a high-resolution photo (created via scanning or a digital camera) and shrink it down just by specifying a smaller size in the html or CSS. This doesn't actually shrink the file, it just displays it smaller. So the entire large high-res file is still loaded, but most of the pixels are not displayed and therefore wasted. Repeating this process will drag out load times, but provide no benefit. The better solution is to use the Image>Image Size command in Photoshop to size an image to be the exact dimensions you need. Just be sure to specify the resolution as 72 dots/inch.

The resolution of images aren't the only size-related concern when considering web design in Photoshop. One of the very first design decisions you will need to make is how big a screen you intend to target. Keep in mind that technology never stands still; what was true for screen sizes five years ago is no longer true now. What is true now will likely not be true even a year from now. But we need to start somewhere. Current web design trends target a minimum screen size of 1024x768. This is a common enough monitor setting that you can expect a good portion of web viewers will use. A significant portion will actually use larger, but that's no worry as having an extra bit of space around the design won't hinder the use of the site in any way. Your first instinct might be to immediately just create a >>

Properties
Levels
Preset: Custom
CMYK
Auto
3
1.00
253
Output Levels: 0
255
Layers
3D
Channels
Kind
Normal
Opacity: 100%
Lock:
Fill: 100%
Levels 1
Lighting
Model texture
King texture 6
King Texture 7 copy 2
King Texture 7
Layer 7 copy
Tatoo 1
Effects
Color Overlay

Photoshop and graphics

new blank document sized at 1024x768 and start designing. But just because the monitor is set to display that many pixels, doesn't mean you get to use all of them for your design. Several pixels are already claimed with the operating system and browser interface.

The generally accepted guidance is to use a width of 960. In fact, for ease of use and to save yourself headaches later on, we would recommend using some of the templates and sketch sheets freely available at **http://960.gs**.

Construction

Okay, so say that now we've got our template interface document, and we've put in our menus and nav bars, we've got our front page content all groomed up in Photoshop and it looks spectacular. What's next? Is there a 'publish to web' export option? Well, no. Not quite. All we've done here is draft up the overall look. In order to make this into a website, we have to build the site using HTML and CSS. So in Photoshop, we create the small graphic elements that will be used to assemble the pages. Each individual element will need to be cut up, optimised, catalogued and saved.

> "In Photoshop, you create the small graphic elements that will be used to assemble the pages"

For example, if you have a content box with an attractive border treatment, you might think you could simply create the box as a single image and layer the text in front of it. But what happens when you need to change the content and it has twice as much text? Or if the reader sets their viewing text size to extra large? Then the text is going to overflow the graphic and spill over into

Mobile graphics

Designing interfaces has always been a challenge because you can't know what screen size and resolution your reader will be using. You can design and test for the most common ones, but it's impossible to know and prepare for every combination of platform, operating system, browser, browser version, screen size, screen resolution, and screen colour depth. And that's just thinking about monitors and laptop screens. Add the assortment of different mobile devices to the mix and you've got a Herculean task on your hands.

Photoshop 5.1 provides a substantial weapon in this fight, and it is called Device Central. The Device Central can be activated through the New Document dialogue Box, or the save for Web and Devices dialogue box. The general idea is this mini-app calls upon an online library of mobile devices and allows you to customize your designs to fit that device's screen size, resolution and colour depth. This can range from the tiny early smartphones with 240x320 screens, to the iPhone 4S at 640x960 all the way up to the new iPad at a whopping 2048x1536 screen!

Anatomy of Photoshop

Photoshop is a powerful graphics program with features that run deep. The program is equally at home in creating logos, movie posters and magazine covers as it is creating web graphics. Due to its maturity and wide range of features, it can seem a bit overwhelming to the beginner. The anatomy of Photoshop is fairly logical, once you know what to look for. There's the general workspace that is in the middle of the screen, and then everything else roughly falls into one of the major categories of tools, options, menus, panels and dialog boxes. In this section we will take a closer look at each of those and help you understand what makes Photoshop the program that it is.

Options Bar This bar contains tool-specific options. This changes according to the tool selected. Changes made here are seen in the next use of the tool

Menus These house the features for file handling (save, print, etc) and those that are applied to the layer or canvas as a whole such as filters and canvas sizing

Panels These contain operations that aren't performed by the tools. Including the Layers Panel where you control stacking and styling of the elements in your composition

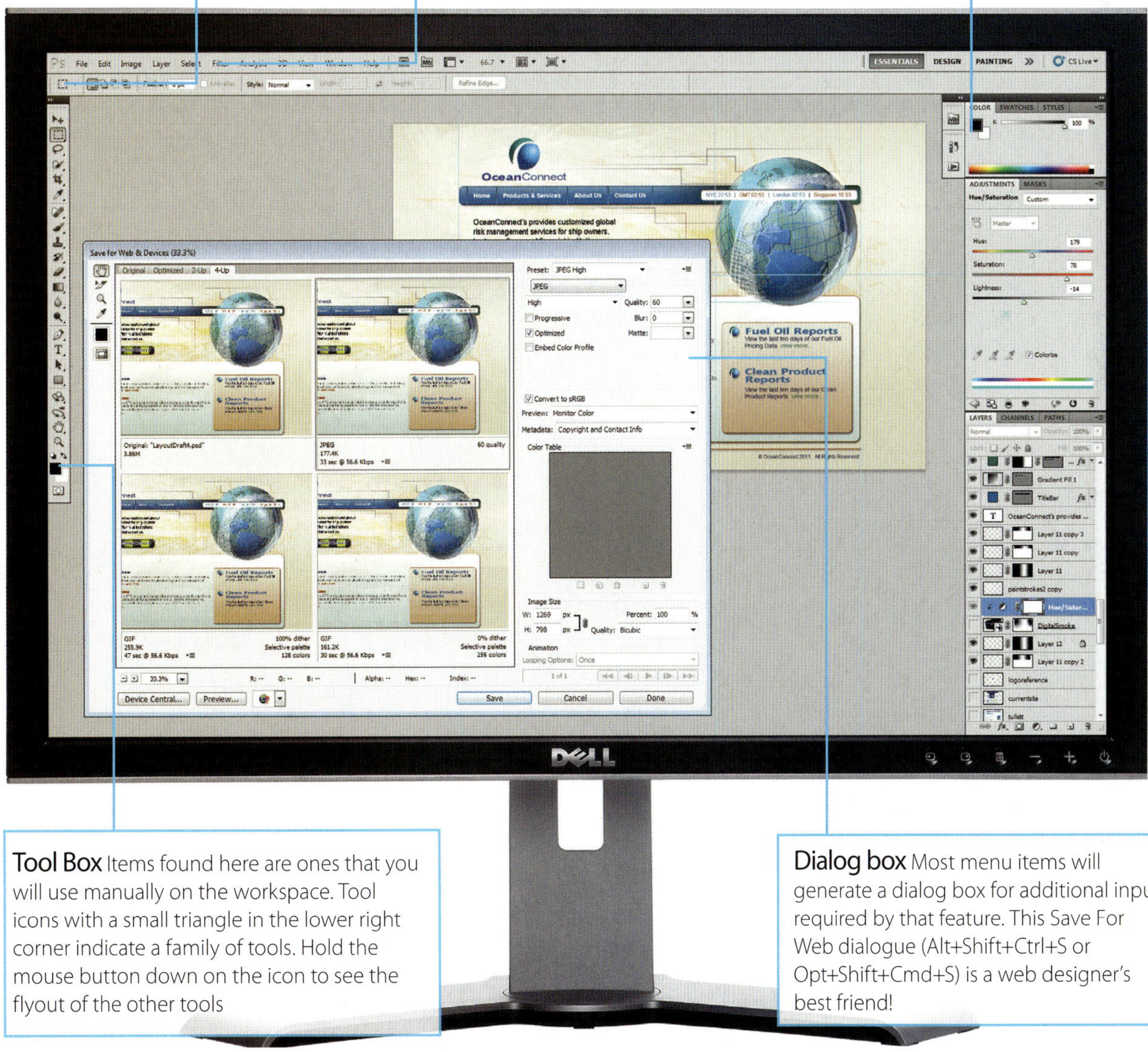

Tool Box Items found here are ones that you will use manually on the workspace. Tool icons with a small triangle in the lower right corner indicate a family of tools. Hold the mouse button down on the icon to see the flyout of the other tools

Dialog box Most menu items will generate a dialog box for additional input required by that feature. This Save For Web dialogue (Alt+Shift+Ctrl+S or Opt+Shift+Cmd+S) is a web designer's best friend!

other parts of your design. Instead of creating such a mess, the accepted practice is to construct the box from several smaller graphics, ie top graphic, middle content graphic that can be repeated if needed, and a footer graphic. Keep this in mind while designing a site. It's much easier to work around the construction limitations on the design side than it is to figure out a code hack to force an arbitrary design element to work correctly on the development side.

The best method of cutting up graphics in Photoshop is to use the Slice Tool. Hold down the mouse button on the Crop Tool until you see the tool flyout. The Slice tool will allow you to tell Photoshop where to slice up the graphic, then the entire lot of slices can be exported at the same time instead of individually.

Pixel perfect

We previously discussed how monitors display 72 pixels per inch and how that's a relatively low resolution, meaning the pixels are relatively large. So even a single misaligned pixel is visible at this scale. When using the drawing tools in Photoshop, like the pen or shape tools, Photoshop will allow you to create lines that don't line up exactly with the pixel rows. It displays these lines by 'anti-aliasing' or having the edge smoothed over adjacent pixels. This behaviour is recommended for high-resolution broadcasts and print, but for web displays it usually comes off as looking blurry. The better approach is to create sharp lines by tending to the pixel boundaries. If dealing with shapes, open the additional options area found in the options bar. Engage the Snap to Pixels checkmark to ensure the shape edges are always aligned with the pixel grid.

An additional method of creating sharp, crisp edges of your web graphics is to use the Single Row Marquee Tool and the Single Column Marquee Tool. These can be found by holding the mouse button down on the default Rectangular Marquee Tool until the tool bar flies out revealing the other tools in that family. Use the single row/column tool to select the very edge pixels of a shape. If the shape was badly anti-aliased, this selection will allow you to delete the blurry pixels. Another common technique is to use these tools to fill the very edges of pixels with solid white or black, which increases the contrast of the edge and creates a visibly sharper line.

Use Photoshop to create eye-catching graphics, images and buttons that will make your website stand out.

Mockups

The primary benefit to first designing a site interface in Photoshop before building the live site is the ability to create changes quickly for evaluation purposes. This saves time and money on revisions while nailing down the exact appearance before entering into the long and costly production phase of the project. It's much easier to change the background colour by adjusting a single slider bar in an adjustment layer than it is to completely write over the old background file and reload the page with the new coloured background.

Part of the toolset that makes Photoshop so versatile in this way is Layer Comps. Found by opening the panel of the same name (Window>Layer Comps) these are essentially bookmarks of the visibility, position, and layer style appearance of all the layers within the document. Use Layer Comps to capture variations

Jargon buster

Opacity

The opposite of transparency. Opacity describes how visible each pixel of that corresponding layer is. 100% opacity means every pixel contained on that layer is completely visible, while 0% opacity means the pixels are totally invisible. Opacity can be set overall for a layer by a setting found in the top of the Layers panel or can be defined by a mask.

Masks

Masks are means of determining areas of visibility on a layer, as opposed to the Opacity setting which determines it globally for the entire layer. The most common form is a Layer Mask which uses a greyscale file to assign pixel visibility. White areas of the mask show the corresponding pixels as fully visible, while black areas render them entirely hidden.

Vector/Raster/Bitmap

Images in Photoshop are created as either vectors or bitmaps (known as rasters), vector-based elements like shapes, text and items created with the pen tool are defined by mathematical equations and are resolution independent. Elements created by photos, brushes and gradients are defined pixel by pixel and known as bitmaps. These elements are dependent on their source resolution.

Selection

The official term 'Selection" in Photoshop means areas of the canvas that are isolated or focused upon by using one of the many selection tools. The current selection is shown by a blinking dotted grey line known as 'marching ants'. Selections restrict editing operations to only the selected pixel of the current layer, thereby protecting the rest of the pixels.

of a design and easily present them to a client without having to juggle multiple files.

Buttons

Buttons are the bread and butter of most web designs. The most basic way to create a button is to use a shape tool such as the rounded rectangle. First select the foreground colour you wish for the button. Then draw out the button and place a layer of text above it. To style the button, be sure the button shape layer is the active, targeted layer. Then press the small 'fx' icon at the foot of the layers panel. Select a style from the list, such as Bevel and Emboss, and make the setting adjustments as you see fit. You've created your first web button!

To create the popular rollover effect on your button, it's as easy as changing up the Layer Style. However, implementing the effect requires a bit more work. There have been several techniques over the years for doing this, most used to involve JavaScript and preloaders. Today, it is mostly done with a single combined image that is repositioned with CSS upon rollover. So once your button is created, generate a copy of the button layers by selecting both the text and shape layer and pressing Ctrl/Cmd+J. Then move the copy down below the original just so the two edges are touching. Adjust the copy to display the rollover effect and save the entire file out as a single button image. When building your page, the container to hold the button should be half the height of this image. Then a rollover:hover class assignment can be created in the CSS to reposition the button image within the container. This technique eliminates the need for both JavaScript and preloaders. It also reduces the total number of graphic files that need to be loaded because the button and its rollover are now a single image instead of two.

As a final piece of advice: Photoshop can be used to create a wide range of amazing visual effects. We encourage you to wield this power with the greatest of your strength, but remember the cardinal rule of web design: Form follows function. Never let your design get in the way of the site content. The interface design can't make the site; only the content can do that.

Image Formats

.gif

The original Graphic Interchange Format. GIFs are limited to a maximum of 256 colours, so they are better suited for line art than for photos. GIFs can support a binary transparency, each pixel is either fully opaque or fully transparent. GIFs also support a frame by frame animation capability.

.jpg

JPEGs are the most common choice for digital images with rich colour depth such as photographs or any artwork with gradients and a high range of colour tones. The primary strength of JPEGs is the compression, which is a 'lossy' compression. Each time a JPEG is compressed, more and more data is discarded.

.png

Portable Network Graphics files (PNG) were an answer to the restrictions on GIF files. PNGs support an 8-bit transparency, which means there can be a fade to the transparent edge. PNGs also support more colour depth than GIFs and a lossless compression.

.pdf

Portable Document Format files (PDFs) are commonly used for downloadable documents, not frequently for display images. PDFs hold several advantages in that they support multi-page documents and embeddable files. The primary drawback is that they are not displayed in-line like other image formats.

WBMP

Wireless Bitmaps are monochrome images (strict black and white) that are optimized for display on monochromatic mobile devices. A very efficient and small format that comes at a price of blocky black-and-white pixellated images. As mobile devices have matured to use better displays, this format sees less and less use.

Optimise images for use on the web

Saving images in the appropriate format needn't be difficult

One of the things people struggle with when learning how to design for the web is choosing an appropriate format in which to save their images. It's a minefield that requires a basic understanding of both image formats, type and compression.

Back in the 1990s when the worldwide web was young, the most commonly used formats for images were BMP and TIFF files. BMP (short for bitmap), was the native format for images created in Microsoft Paint and other simple image editors of the time, while TIFF (originally short for Tagged Image File Format) was – and continues to be – a high-quality format used in the production of printed material such as this bookazine. Both formats suffer from a problem, however: they are not exactly skinny.

While internet connections have grown much faster in the last couple of decades, it's still important to ensure that your file sizes are as small as possible to achieve a fast-loading webpage – most visitors are not prepared to wait very long. In this tutorial we'll examine the different formats that work on the web, and show you how to choose the most appropriate format for your images.

> "It's still important to ensure that your file sizes are as small as possible to achieve a fast-loading webpage"

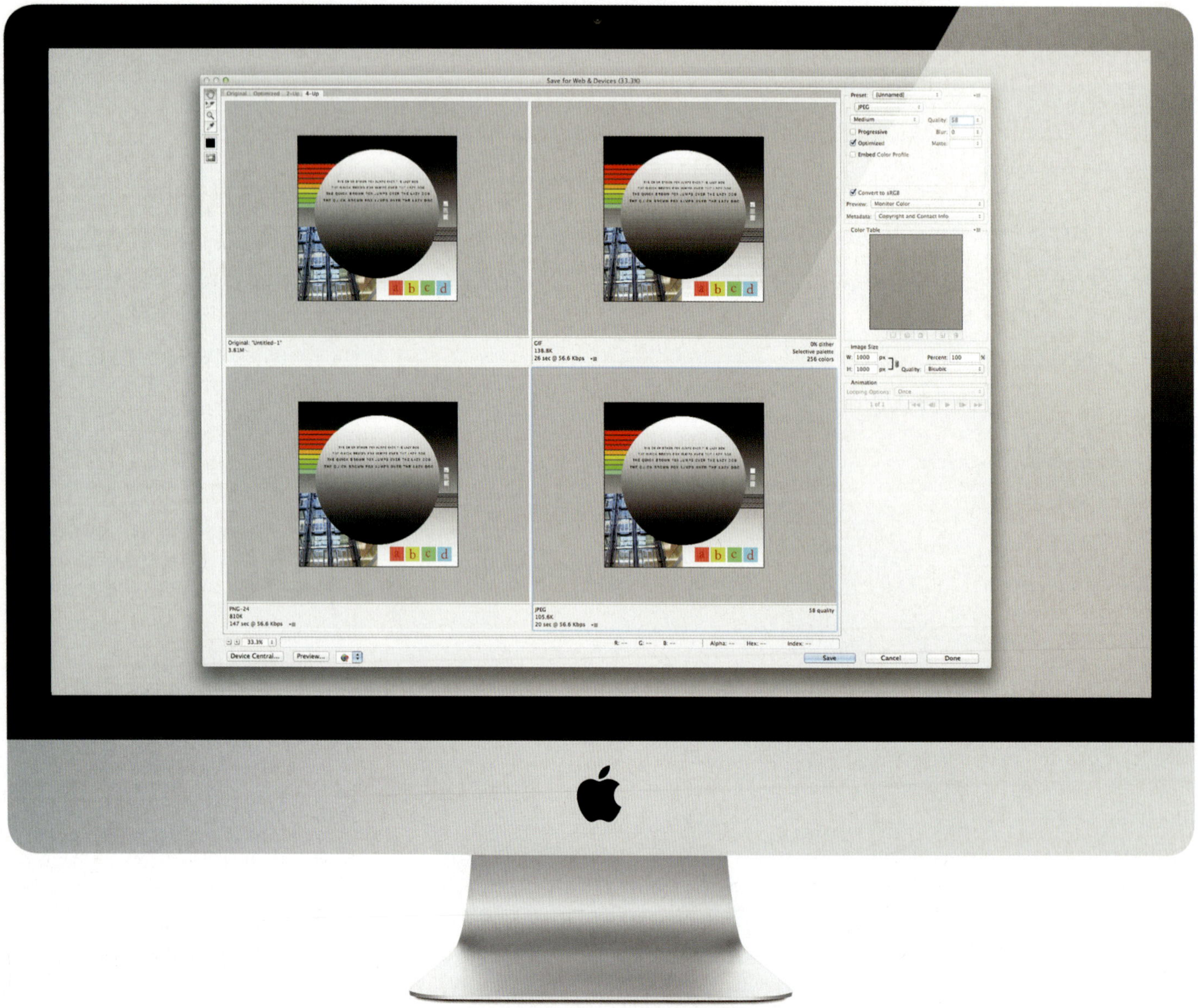

01 Create a test graphic

We've created a test graphic (supplied on your free CD) that'll allow us to examine the various characteristics of the three primary web formats (plus a rarely used fourth). This image comprises several layers arranged to provide an example of each format's strengths and weaknesses.

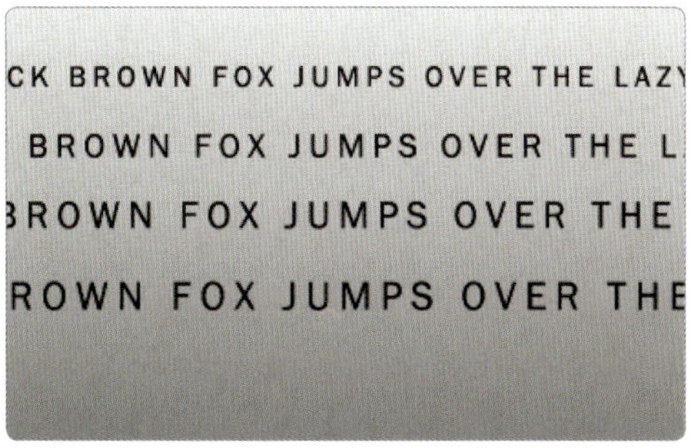

02 Text

We've added some regular text in various sizes to compare how different formats and compression settings affect legibility. This is becoming less important as more sophisticated effects can be added to HTML-rendered text, but is still worth considering when choosing a format to save in.

03 Bands of colour

Bands of flat colour will help us check for image artefacts according to the compression method applied. As you'll see later on, JPEG files will make these areas of flat colour render as patches of different colours when we apply too much compression to our image.

04 Detailed photograph

We've included a detailed photo in the bottom left corner of our image so you can see the effect of a limited colour palette on photo-realistic images, and how this creates a posterised effect which can be used for artistic effect.

05 Text on background

We've added some large letters on different coloured backgrounds, including a dark red on light red combination that will test the 8-bit format's ability to distinguish between colours that are close to each other tonally or in hue.

06 Variable transparency

Each of the three squares has a different level of transparency. The top one is entirely transparent, the middle 50%, and the bottom one 30%. This allows us to check to see how each format handles transparency accurately or otherwise!

07 Narrow bands

The narrow bands of black against a gradient will help illustrate how restrictive colour palettes will shift colour and tone to try to minimise file size and number of colours. This also adds complexity to the file, making for a more challenging compression when saving for the web.

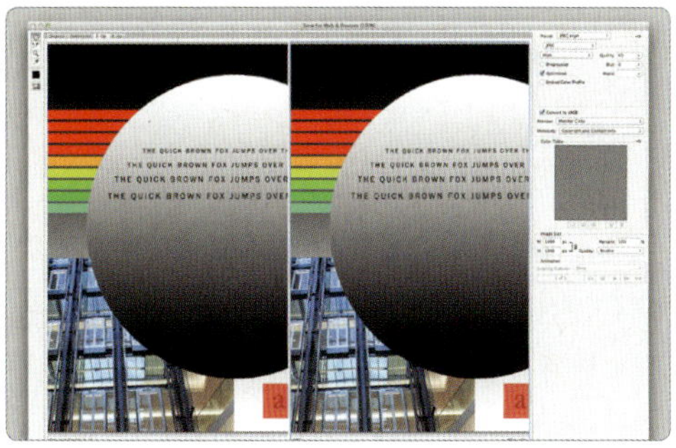

08 Save for web & devices

Now let's bring up the Save for Web & Devices dialog box, found under the File menu. Note the tabs at the top-left corner of the dialog box which allow you to switch between 1up, 2up and 4up views. Start by switching to the 2up view so you can compare formats side-by-side.

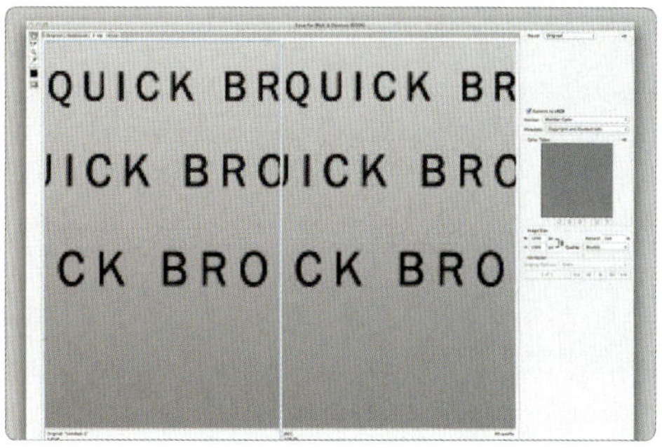

09 Check the text

If you set the right side to use JPEG and the quality to medium, you can see by zooming in that the compression algorithm is adding some strange blockiness around our text. This reduces the legibility of the text and is a particular problem for smaller text rendered in an image.

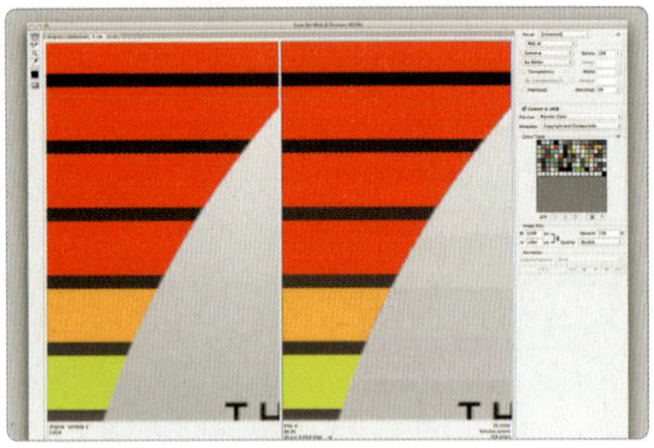

10 8-bit formats

There are two 8-bit formats available here: GIF and PNG-8, both limited to a colour palette of just 256 colours. See how this makes our gradient in the circle render as a series of jaggy bands when we apply the PNG-8 format. 8-bit formats are not a good choice for finely graduated colour.

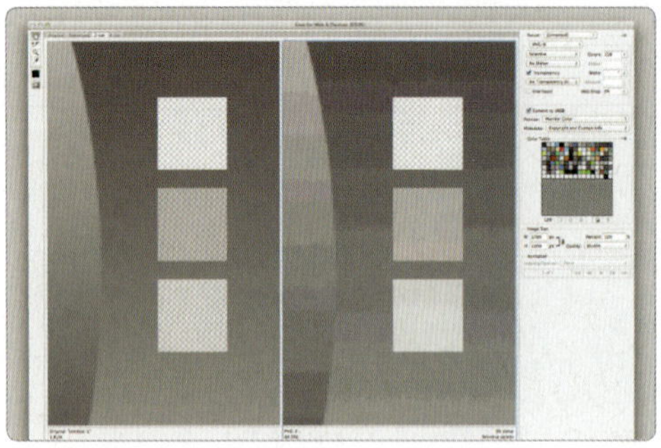

11 Transparency check

You'll also notice that these 8-bit formats support 'binary transparency'. This means a pixel is either considered to be transparent or not transparent. Anything other than fully transparent is rendered in a colour based on the blend of the transparent pixels and the matte (background) colour.

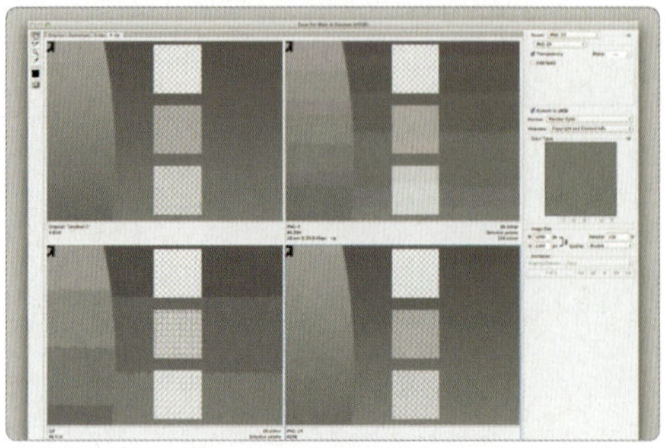

12 More transparency

Only the 24-bit PNG file supports multi-level transparency. It comprises four channels: RGB (for up to 16.7 million colours) and a transparency channel supporting up to 256 levels of opacity. JPEG doesn't support transparency at all. If you need variable transparency, PNG-24 is required.

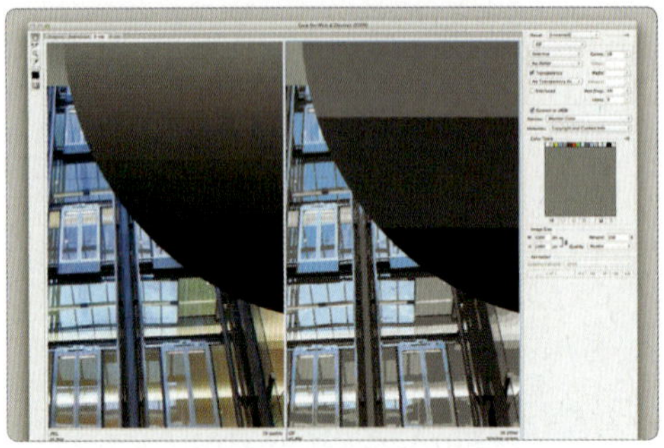

13 Posterising photographs

In the photo section, you can see that the 8-bit formats will reduce the image to a few colours. This can be used for creative effect, but if you want a realistic photograph you need to save as JPEG, or at a push as PNG-24 – although, as you'll see, the file size for PNG-24 will be much bigger.

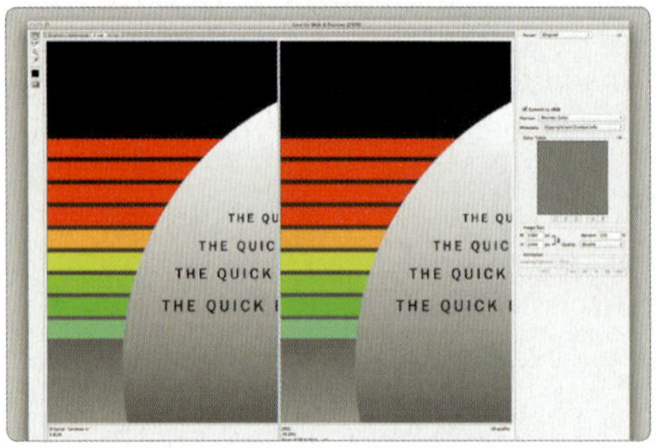

14 Over-compression

JPEG is solid for fine gradient detail, but it's not so good for areas of solid colour such as a logo or repeating background. This is due to the way the compression system works: it divides the overall image into tiles that don't reference each other, which can lead to strange patchwork effects.

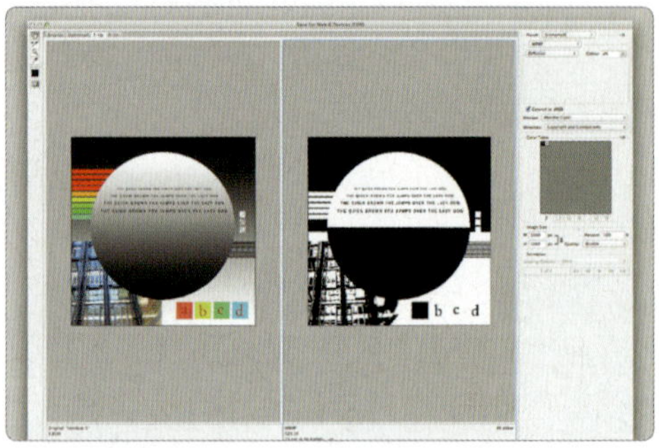

15 A lonely format

You'll notice an option for WBMP. This is a 1-bit format that only supports black and white – not even grey! It was used for mobile phones back when screens were monochrome, and mobile data hugely expensive. It's pretty redundant now, so you can safely ignore this option altogether!

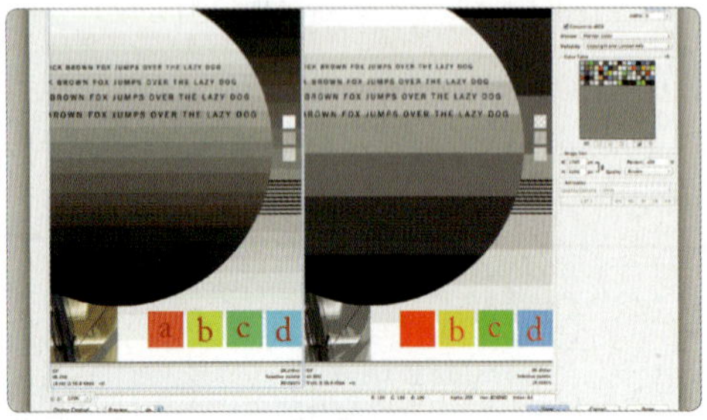

16 Close colours

Observe how the text in our red box has disappeared because the red colours were too close to each other. This has happened because we've got more than 80 colours in our image, and the GIF format has had to consider similar colours as the same. Beware having too many colours when saving in GIF or PNG-8 format.

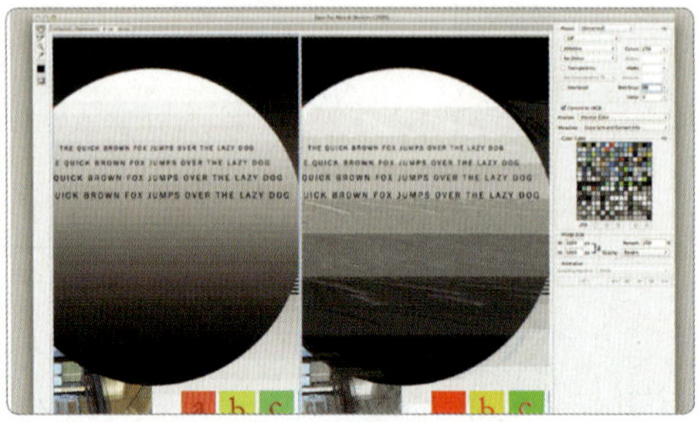

17 Lossy compression

All these web formats are 'lossy' – that is to say that information is thrown away when the file is saved. To illustrate the point, you can apply extra compression to the GIF and PNG formats to offset accuracy against file size. The more lossy, the less the image looks like the original, but the smaller the file will be.

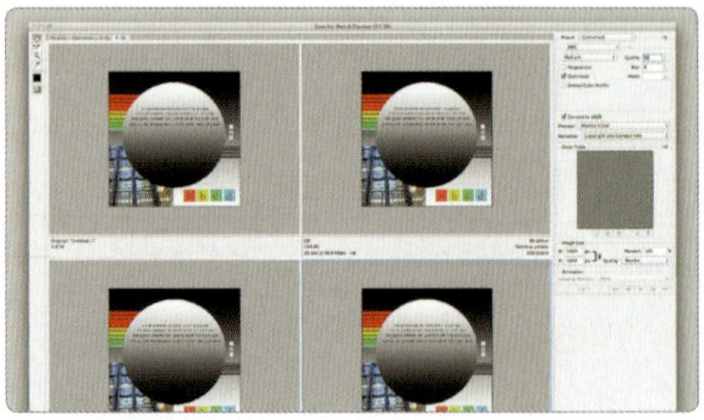

18 File sizes

One of the most useful tools found within the Save for Web & Devices dialog box is the file size display in the bottom-left corner of each image preview. This enables you to compare file sizes between different settings, and therefore make an informed decision over how to treat a particular image.

Testing the limits

We've designed this image to make life difficult for the different web formats, and show their weaknesses. This will help you understand what limitations you have to work within

Text

In general, text is best saved in GIF or PNG format. JPEG will tend to add muddiness around text as a result of the way it compresses images. Text on a photo is better saved as a JPEG, however

Logos and flat colours

GIF and PNG files are best for logos and images with flat colours. The compression works so that all flat colour is faithfully reproduced (but beware restricting the palette too much as that colour may not match the original if you do!)

Photos and gradients

Anything with fine graduated colour, such as a gradient or photo, will be best represented by the JPEG format. JPEG is designed to look for areas of similar colour nearby and aggregate them into patches, saving file space. It's good for images with lots of detail and colour

Transparency

If you need variable transparency, you only really have one option – PNG-24 is the only format that allows you to set transparency at a level other than off/on. JPEG doesn't support transparency at all, while GIF only has a single bit assigned to it, making it not very useful for this application

Bitmap versus vector

Images can be created in two ways, but which is which?

When you take a photo with your digital camera or mobile phone, the chip that records the light saves each point of light as a pixel in a large grid. When viewed from a distance, the differing levels of brightness in each pixel describe an image that's recognisable to the human eye. This is called a bitmap image, and it's both the most common format and the one we mean when we're talking about JPEG, GIF or PNG files. However, there's another system that doesn't rely on having a grid at all!

The problem with a bitmap image is that when you want to resize it, the computer has to either throw away information to make the grid smaller (as nothing can be smaller than one pixel), or make information up when you want to enlarge your image. The alternative is to use a different approach altogether. Vector images use mathematics to describe the relationship between different points, drawing a line between the points and applying effects such as colours, fills and gradients to build up an image based on many points. This means that they can be resized to any level without any pixelation or loss in quality.

If this has you confused, don't worry – as a general rule of thumb, when you save an image in Photoshop it will always be output in a web-friendly bitmap format.

Create great backgrounds for your website

Create a rich, original image that tiles perfectly in Photoshop

Background images are an essential part of designing a website, and being able to create a tiled image – one that repeats without seams – is especially important when you don't know how long your pages will be.

We can find inspiration all around us for repeating patterns, whether it's a bee's honeycomb, parquet flooring or some vintage wallpaper. While it's true to say that styles and fashions come and go (often at an alarming rate), there are those that are always in vogue – timeless designs that work whatever the era. 'Vintage' suggests age, refinement, sophistication and experience.

In this tutorial we're going to create a classic fleur-de-lys in Photoshop, starting from a sketch, and work it up into a fantastic vintage wallpaper tile that will repeat perfectly for use on your website. We'll weather and age our design to help create a time-beaten look, and save it in a format that will work on the web. If you don't fancy using a fleur-de-lys, sketch an alternative motif, scan it and follow along from step 3; this approach works for any kind of repeating pattern element.

"We can find inspiration all around us for repeating patterns"

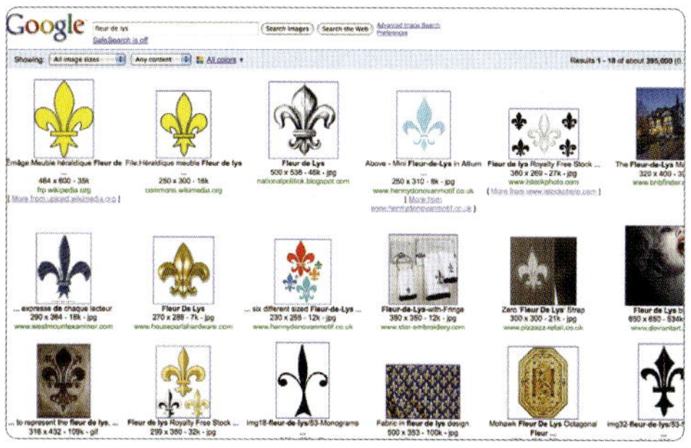

01 Do your research

It really is worthwhile doing your research and getting some real-world reference material. You can go to the library and get a book of interior design, visit your local wallpaper shop, or take the easy option and use a search engine to find images of the motif you have in mind.

02 Sketch your design

Sketch out your design elements on a sheet of paper. Don't worry about getting all the fine details right at this stage – this is more the idea generation stage of the process, so experiment with different shapes and forms. Consider how the design might sit in a pattern.

03 Scan your artwork

Scan your sketches into your computer. Open the sketches in Photoshop and choose your favourite design. If you'd like to incorporate elements from two sketches into one final design, that's also fine: identify which part you want to start drawing first and zoom in close around that object.

04 Select the Pen tool

We'll use the Pen tool to create a path; it's ideal for areas with clearly defined edges. Click to create a point on one corner of your motif, then click again further along the same edge to create another. A straight line is drawn between them.

05 Paths and the Pen tool

To create a curved line, hold the mouse button after clicking, then drag to either side. Work your way around the motif, adding points, until you can click on the original point. Double-click the work path in the Paths panel and name the path.

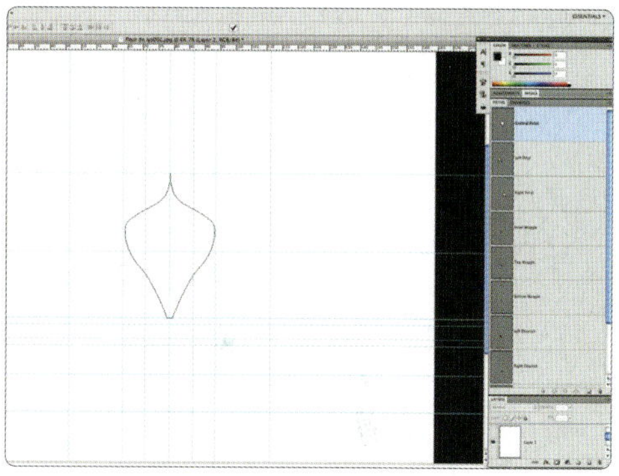

06 Finish paths

Work your way around each object in turn. We made a total of ten paths: one for each of the top and bottom petals, three for the central bands, and one for the central flourish. Now turn off your scan layer by clicking on the eye icon in Layers.

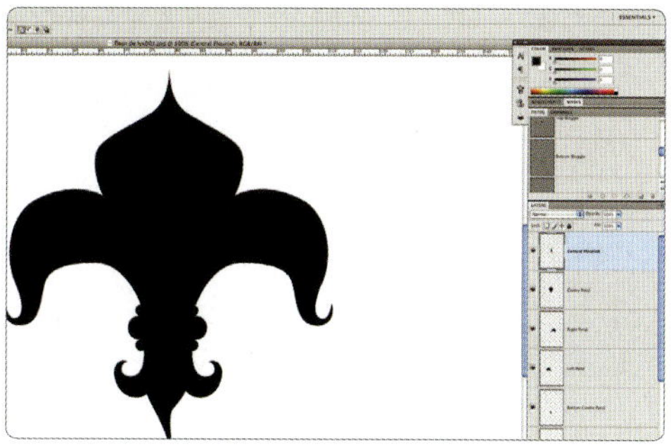

07 Fill each path

Create a new layer then Ctrl/Cmd+click on the first path in the Paths panel to load it as a selection. Fill it with black by using the Paint Bucket tool or using the shortcut keys Alt/Opt+Delete. Repeat for each path in turn, making sure each new path is filled on a new layer.

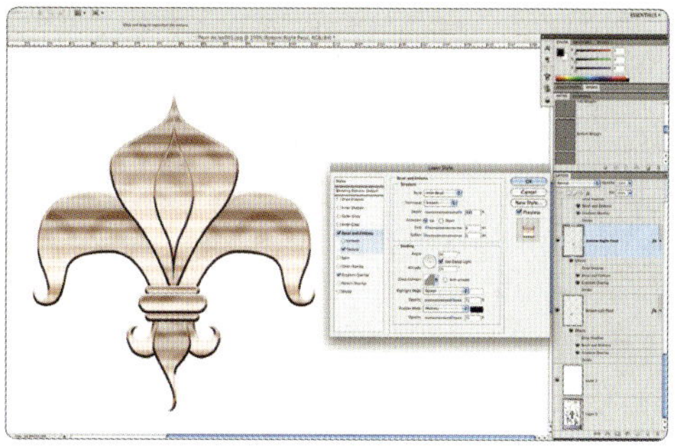

08 Add layer styles

Choose a layer and select Layer>Layer Style>Gradient Overlay. Choose Copper. Tick the boxes for Bevel & Emboss and Texture, then play with the settings. Right-click on the layer in the Layers panel and choose Copy Layer Style. Right-click and paste the layer style onto each layer in turn.

09 Merge and decorate

Turn off any background layers, then choose Merge Visible from the Layer panel pop-out menu. Using the Burn tool, burn shadows across the motif for a lightly distressed look. Add a Hue/Saturation adjustment layer and reduce the copper to silver by desaturating the image.

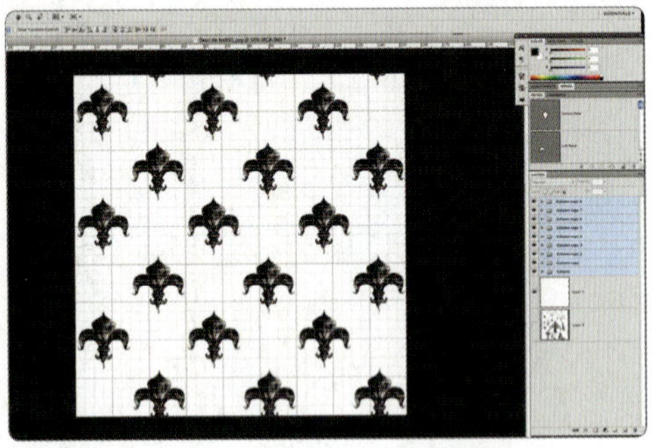

10 Lay out the pattern

Highlight the fleur-de-lys and Adjustment Layer layers and then Convert to Smart Object. Increase canvas size to 1800px square and change Grid options to show gridlines every 200px. Copy and position the motif across the canvas at even intervals, using the Grid to aid placement.

11 Add texture

Pick a blue for foreground, with a darker version for background. On the background layer go to Filter>Render>Clouds. Duplicate this and put it at the top of the layer stack. Set blending mode to Exclusion. Put a copy at the top of the stack; Filter>Render>Fibers, blending mode Overlay.

12 Add extra distress

Download a free concrete texture from **www.bittbox.com/freebies/free-texture-tuesday-concrete/** and add it to your image. Set it to blend using Darker Color and reduce the opacity to 20% so that there's some general additional distress to your image.

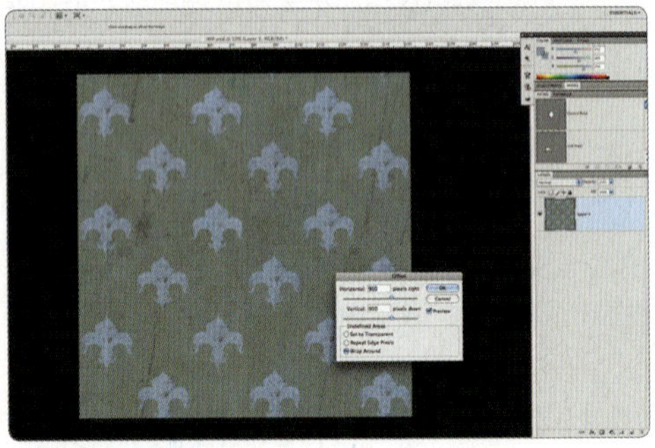

13 Create an offset

Merge all visible layers into a single one, then choose Filter>Other>Offset. Enter values of 900px for both Horizontal and Vertical; this is half the canvas size. You'll probably see a slight seam across the middle of your image. Use the Clone Stamp tool to blur this seam.

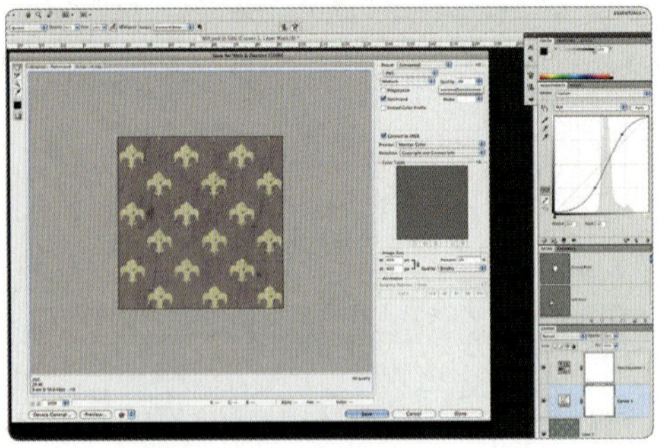

14 Offset, tweak and save

Your image will now tile perfectly. Add a Curves Adjustment layer and Hue/Saturation Adjustment layer to increase contrast and recolour the artwork if desired, to suit your website. Save your document as a PSD file to ensure you retain the original source material for later reuse!

15 Save for the web

We'll use Photoshop's 'Save for Web and Devices' function to output a web-ready version of our artwork. Choose File>Save for Web & Devices and select Medium JPG – it'll work well for the subtlety of texture we've created. Save the image with a name with no spaces, eg 'background.jpg'.

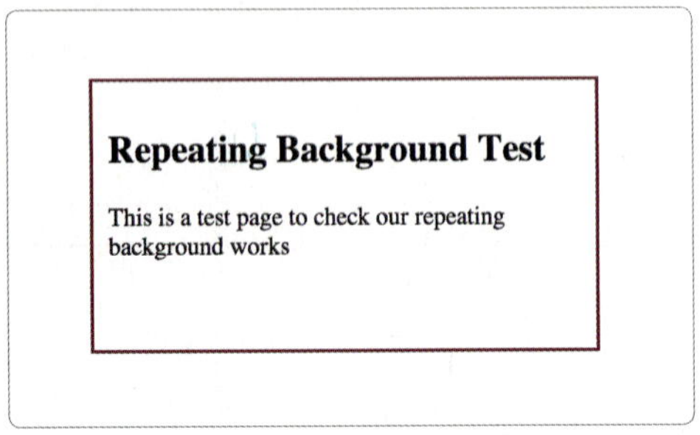

16 Use your image

Once you've successfully saved your image, it's time to use it on your website. To do this you'll need to have a webpage lined up and ready to go, with a CSS stylesheet and an element you're going to apply your repeating background to. If you haven't already got these in place, come back to this section later on!

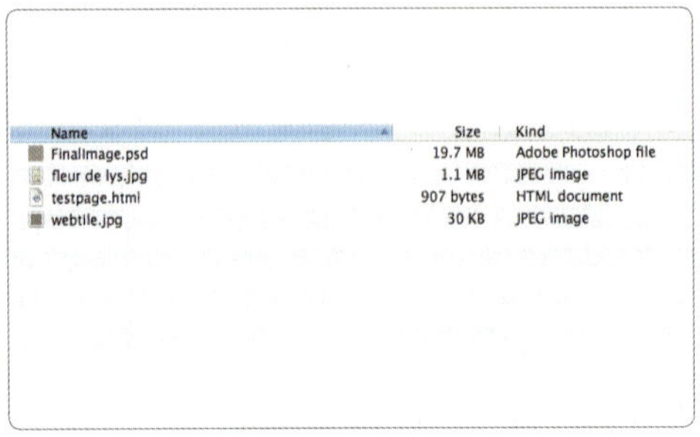

17 Import your image

Adding a background image to your website using CSS is very simple. First you define the element you'd like to create the CSS rule for – this is achieved by naming the element either through its tag name, class or ID. Next, add a rule for background-image and specify the image you'd like to use as a background.

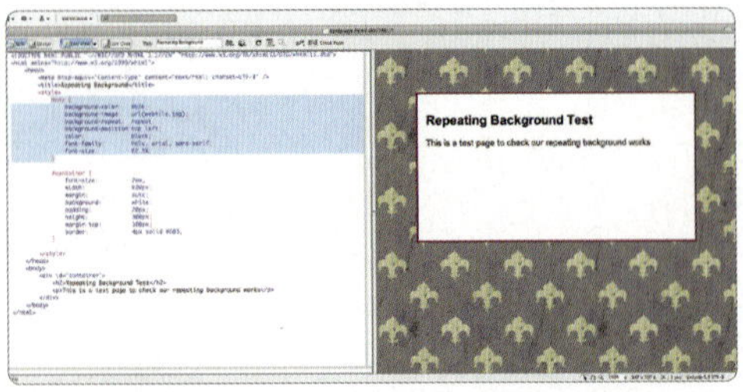

18 Other properties

Your image will need to be in the same folder as your stylesheet. You can set the position of your repeating image using the background-position property, how it repeats using background-repeat, and a fallback colour to be used using background-color.

```
body {
background-color: #ccc;
background-image: url(background.jpg);
background-repeat: repeat;
background-position: top left;
}
```

Repeating background images

See how we constructed our repeating background image

Added grunge

We've used a concrete texture to add extra grunge and character to our background tile. This is the antithesis of the modern, clean web look but it's often good to go your own way and avoid following fashions on the web – especially if you want your site to stand out!

Save as a JPEG

Because our image has lots of colours and fine textures, a JPEG file is the best format to use for this particular background tile. We've created quite a large tile, but you could have used just two motifs arranged diagonally to get a similar effect

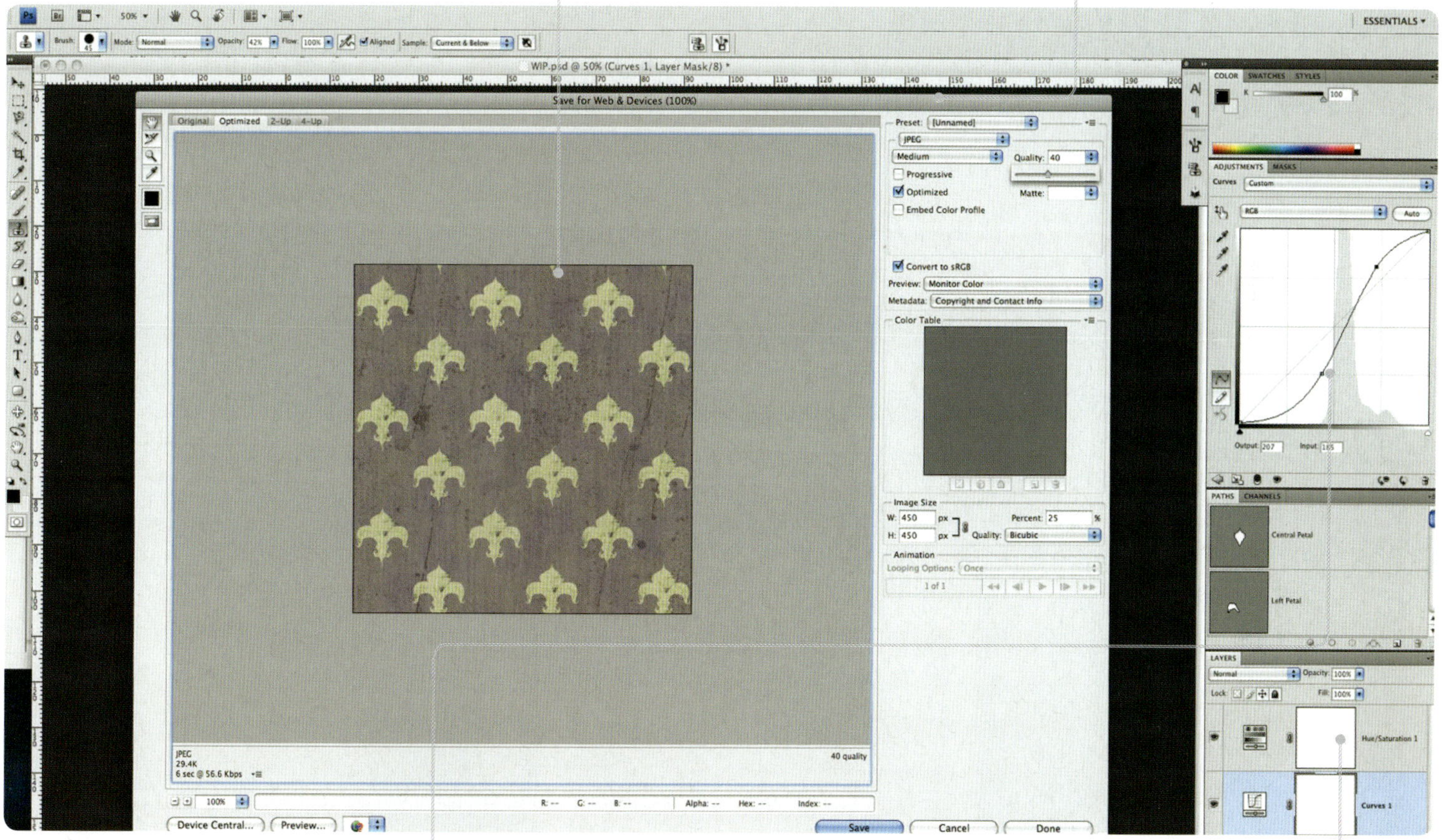

Curves for contrast

We've used a curve adjustment to increase the contrast of our design. Our curve has an S shape which darkens the dark pixels and lightens the light pixels to create more dynamics in our image

Adjust hue and saturation

The colours have been adjusted before we saved our image using a Hue/Saturation adjustment layer. This allows us to control the overall colour balance without having to manually alter each layer individually, and allows for experimentation!

Repeating backgrounds

The background tile is a great web design tool

Because you never quite know in advance how long a typical webpage may be, it's often very useful to be able to create a background that is capable of scaling to fill the space, no matter how big or small that space is. This is why repeating background tiles are such a mainstay of web design – they can be quite small but cover a large area of screen without the need to create a different version of your background for each page. The offset filter in Photoshop makes it easy to check that your image tiles perfectly, and correct any issues if it doesn't.

When trying to decide on a background to incorporate into your website design, it's worth having a look at what other websites are doing. A combination of a partially transparent image (saved as a PNG file for variable transparency) and a background colour set to use a CSS3 gradient can give the impression of an image that's much bigger than it really is. CSS3 also allows you to apply more than one background image per element, opening up a whole series of possibilities that didn't even exist until quite recently.

Design effective header and footer graphics in Photoshop

Make your website memorable with a custom header and footer

Have you ever browsed the web and come across a website that has a really beautiful header? Do you wish you had something equally stunning sitting at the top of your website? Having a unique, memorable identity on the web can be the difference between a user remembering your site and the same user instantly forgetting it. The most important rule on the web is to ensure your site has great content that compels return visits; but, given the choice, most people would also like their site to look nice.

Of course this can present a challenge, especially if you feel you're lacking inspiration, artistic ability, or both. Fortunately, you don't really need either! Some basic Photoshop techniques can be used to take a very simple concept and make it into something really special. The same techniques we use in this tutorial will work with many different types of subject matter, so follow the steps below and then apply the principles to your own project. Once you've created your header, you can do the same for the footer of your design too, creating an integrated, consistent design.

"Some basic Photoshop techniques can be used to make something really special"

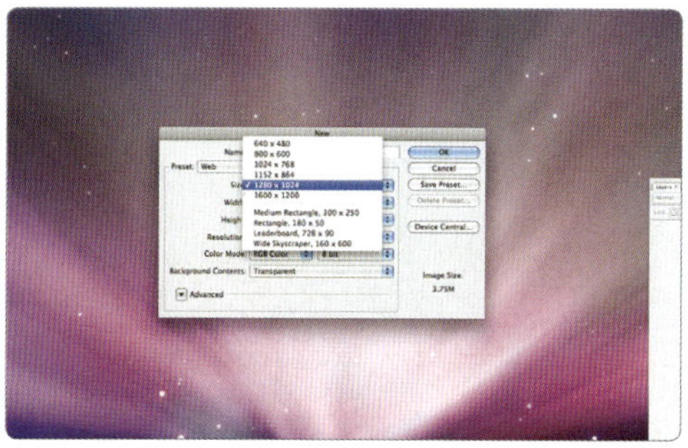

01 Create a document

Create a new Photoshop document. If you have a recent version, choose one of the web presets; if not, choose a document size of 1280x1024px at 72dpi and a transparent background. If you create a document with a background layer, double-click on this to convert it to a normal layer.

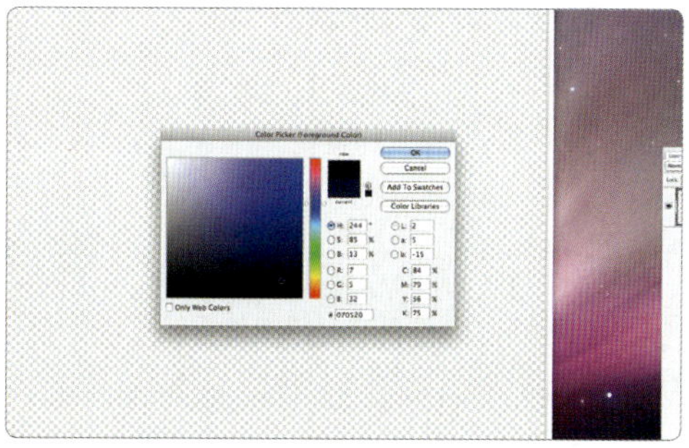

02 Create the base colour

We need to create a base colour to work over. In this tutorial we're creating a graphic that includes planets and stars, so it makes sense to choose a dark background base colour. Double-click on the foreground colour well on the toolbar and select a dark blue. We've used #070520.

03 Organise your layers

Fill the layer with the colour you've just selected by using the Paintbucket tool (or use Alt+Delete on a PC; Option+Backspace on a Mac). Let's name our layers appropriately. Click twice on the name of the layer you've just filled, then type 'Page Background' over the existing name.

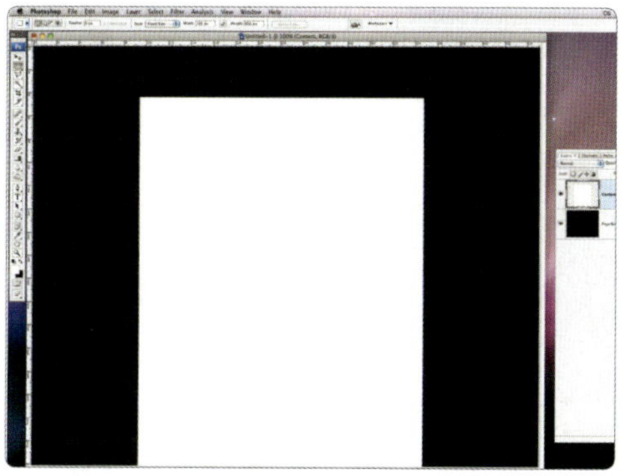

04 Add the content area

Select the Rectangular Marquee tool and change the style to 'fixed size'. Enter a width of 720px and a height of 900px. Click once near the bottom of the document to create a selection. On a new layer, fill this selection with white.

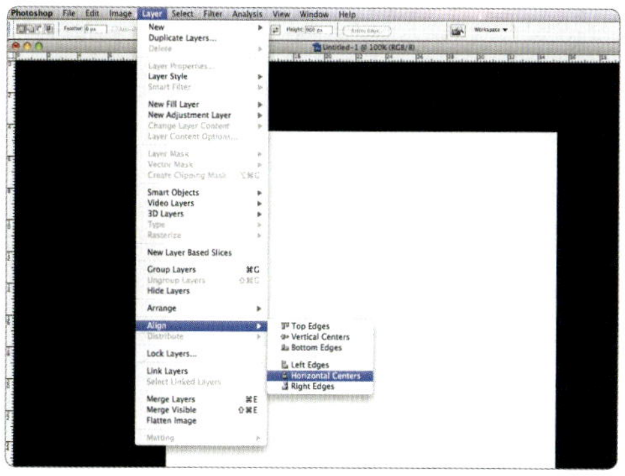

05 Align your content

We want our content area to be centred. Select both layers by clicking on one, then Shift-clicking on the other, then use Layer>Align>Horizontal Centers. This will position your 720px content area perfectly in the centre of the design.

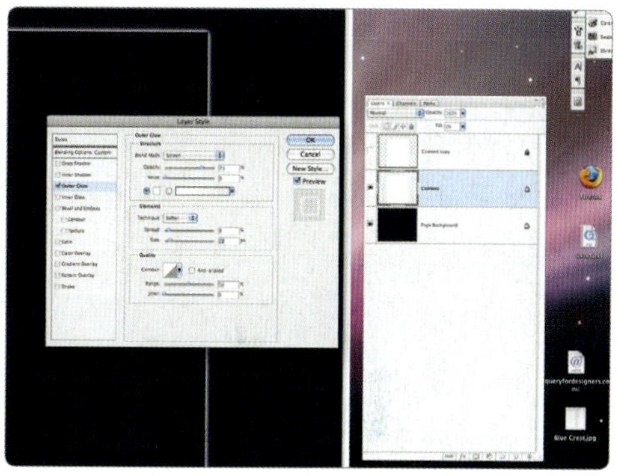

06 Create a glow

Duplicate the content layer and select Layer> Layer Style>Outer Glow. Set the colour to white, spread 8% and size 13px. Click OK, make the other content layer invisible and set Fill to 0% for this layer. This should leave only the glow visible.

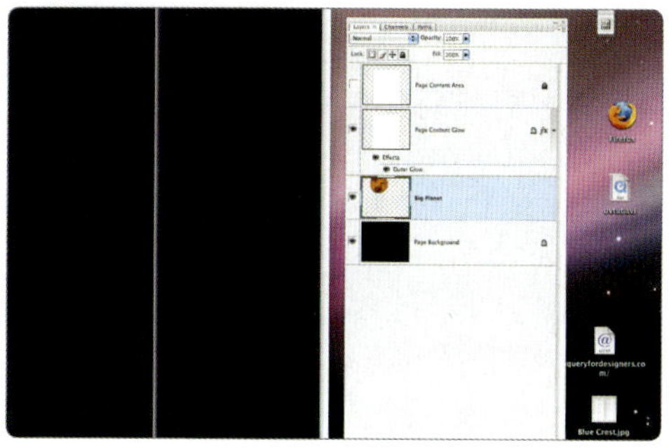

07 Create a planet

Create a new layer, 'Big Planet'. Select an orange for the foreground colour, dark red for the background. Using the Circular Marquee tool with Shift held down, draw a big circle then Filter>Render>Clouds. (Hold Alt/Option when selecting this to get a higher-contrast result.)

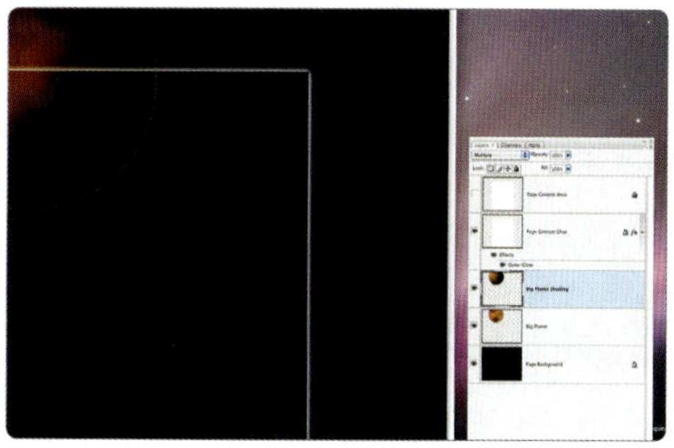

08 Add shading

The planet needs shading. With the selection still active (if you lost your selection just Ctrl/Cmd-click on the planet layer), create a new layer and use the Gradient tool to fill the selection with a radial gradient from orange to black. Set the layer to use Multiply as the blending mode.

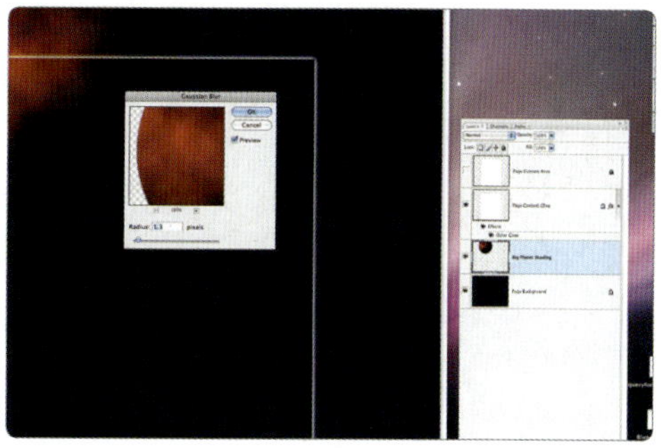

09 Merge and blur

Select the planet layer and the shading layer then, using the fly-out menu at the top right corner of the Layers panel, select 'Merge layers' to convert these two layers into one. Add a small blur: Filter>Blur>Gaussian Blur. Enter a value of 1.3px and click OK.

Using Photoshop's brush engine

Using brushes in Photoshop, you can achieve a wide variety of effects

Photoshop comes with a variety of brushes built in. Selecting the Brush tool opens up a range of options in the toolbar allowing you to choose style, size and hardness. You might be forgiven for thinking that this is the beginning and end of brushes in Photoshop, but there's so much more.

For starters, the set of brushes that appears by default is only one of many sets Adobe thoughtfully provides. To load other brush sets, click on the flyout menu when selecting a brush style. You'll see a whole bunch of brush sets just waiting for you to activate. Choose one you like the sound of and Photoshop will ask you if you'd like to append or replace the current brush set. Appending simply adds the new brushes you're loading to the existing set. If you'd rather keep it clean, replace the set and you'll just have the set you last loaded.

In addition, you can download and load in whole new brush sets from the web. A quick internet search for 'free Photoshop brushes' yields thousands of results. Every kind of brush you can imagine can be found, ranging from simple shapes to entire illustrations in a brush. To install, simply download the brush set of your choice, then click Load Brushes from the Brush flyout menu.

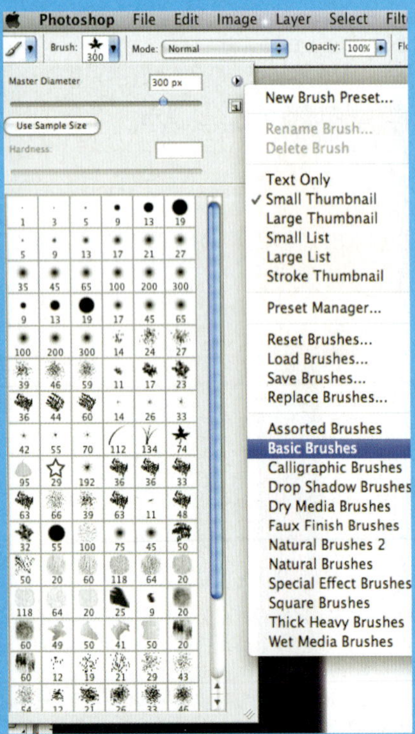

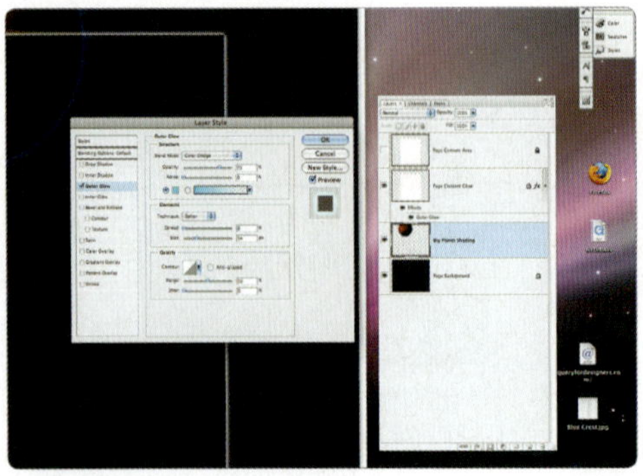

10 Give it a glow

It would be nice to have a light-distorting atmosphere on the planet, so let's add another outer glow to simulate this. Select Layer>Layer Style>Outer Glow. Choose a bright cyan as the colour, and set the blending mode to Colour Dodge. Play with the other settings to suit.

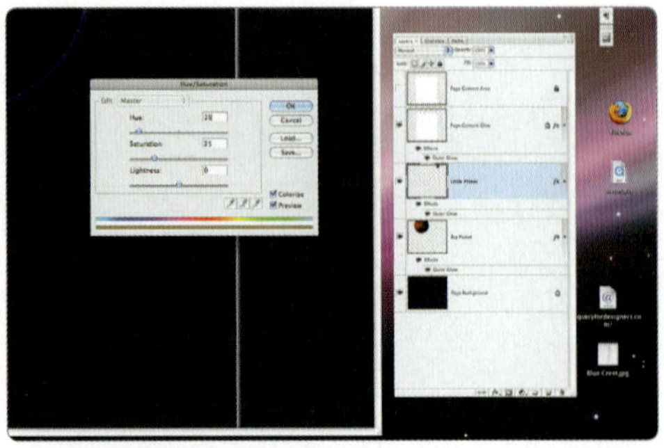

11 Copy and recolour

Let's quickly create a second, smaller planet. Make sure you have the planet layer selected, then select Layer>Duplicate Layer. Select Edit> Transform>Scale and reduce the size. Finally, choose Image>Adjustments>Hue/Saturation and tick Colorize. Play with the settings to find a nice result that suits.

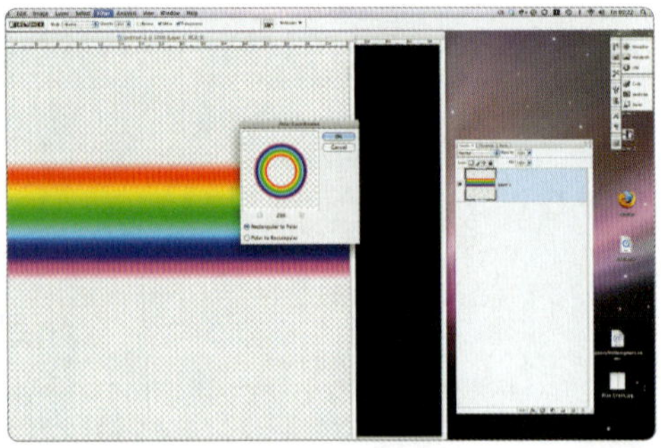

12 Create a rainbow

Create a new document at 1024x1024px, 72dpi and transparent. Select the Gradient tool and, from the tool presets, choose the 'Transparent Rainbow'. Draw a linear gradient top to bottom, covering the middle third of the canvas. Select Filter>Distort>Polar Coordinates. Ensure 'Rectangular to polar' is selected and click OK.

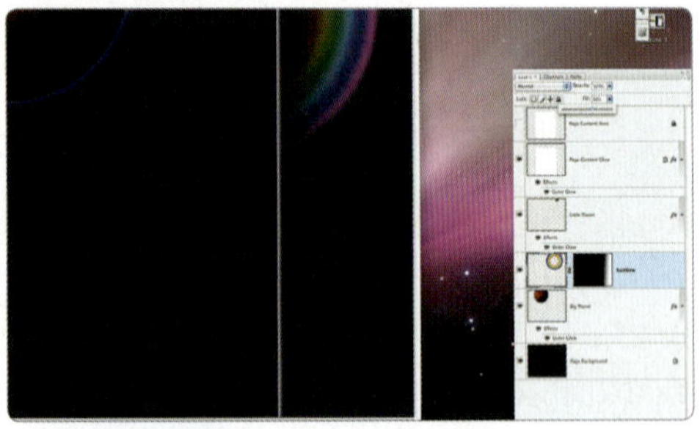

13 Bring the rainbow into your scene

In the rainbow file, select Edit>Copy Merged (shortcut: Shift+Ctrl/Cmd+C), then return to the main document. Select Edit>Paste (shortcut: Ctrl/ Cmd+V). Add a layer mask to the rainbow layer, and draw a black to white gradient onto the mask to hide the left-hand side of the rainbow. Position the layer to the right of the canvas.

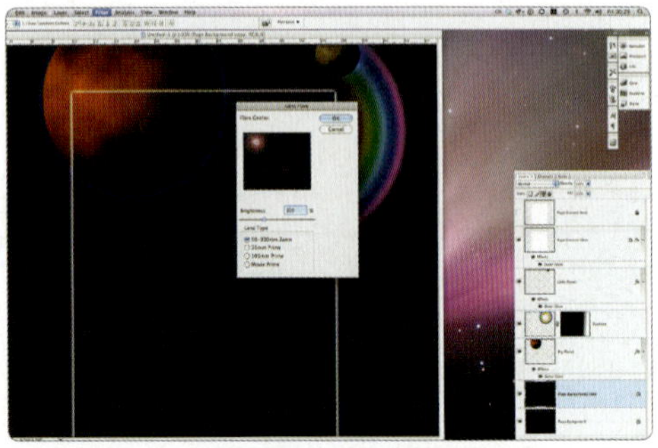

14 Add a lens flare

We'll simulate a bright sun appearing behind the planet. Duplicate 'Page Background' layer. With the duplicate selected, Filter>Render>Lens Flare. Click on top left corner of filter preview window to set flare position, then click OK. You can use the Eraser tool to remove unwanted bits of flare.

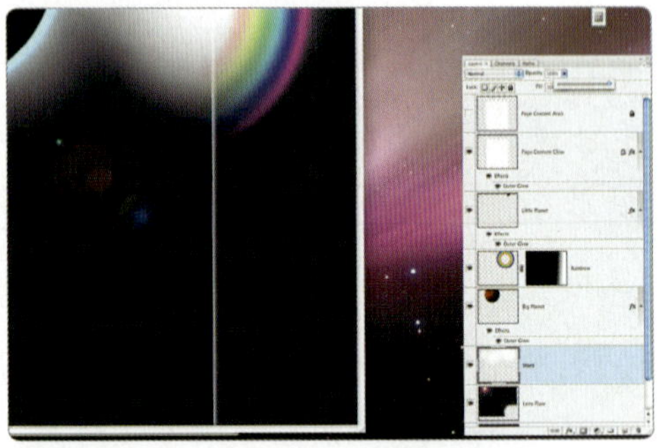

15 Add stars to the space

Add stars to a new layer. Select a foreground colour of white. Using the Gradient tool set to use a radial foreground-to-transparent gradient, draw small overlapping gradients covering the top third of the canvas. You can always add more later, so don't overdo your gradients.

Creating our custom header design

After creating basic planets, we use various effects and techniques for the design

Shooting stars

The shooting stars effect is achieved using a stroked path with simulated pressure. The brush is set to use a scatter effect so that the individual elements look like a meteor or comet trail. We've added an outer glow layer style to complete the look

Rainbow a go-go

The rainbow effect is created using a simple gradient and the polar co-ordinated filter inside Photoshop. This, when combined with the stars, planets and tentacles, helps to create a coherent whole design

Planets

The planets were created using nothing more sophisticated than the Cloud filter and a circular selection. Shading helps to create a sense of mass, and an outer glow layer style ensures that the planet fits into the scene nicely

Fancy tentacles of colour

The tentacles of colour have been created using a stroked path, with simulated pressure. Each colour is chosen from the rainbow to complement and set off against the other elements nicely

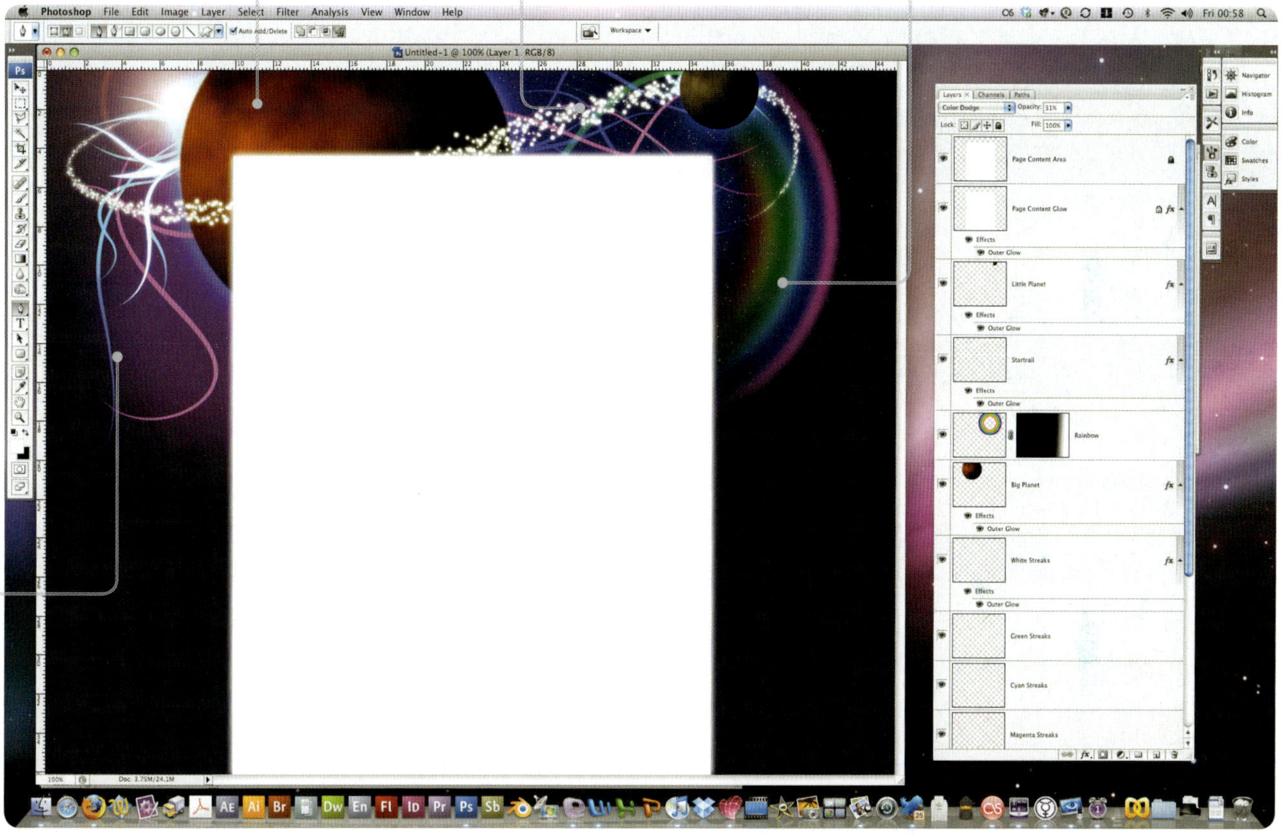

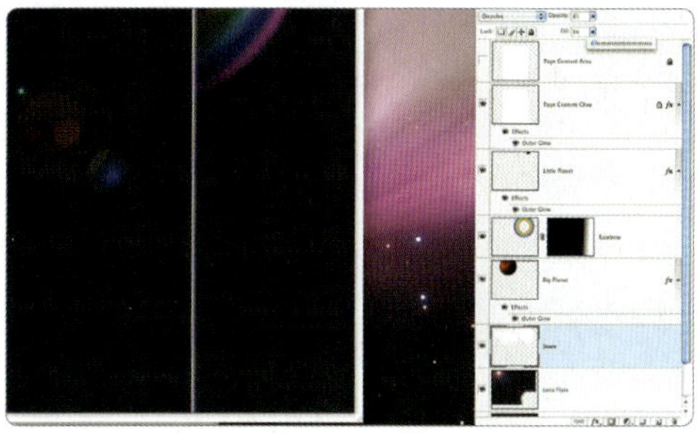

16 Set the stars free

With your gradients in place, it doesn't quite resemble a star field. To get the star effect, change the layer's blending mode to 'Dissolve'. This gives an instant star effect, but there are way too many stars. Reduce the number by adjusting both the layer's opacity and fill values to something around 5% for each.

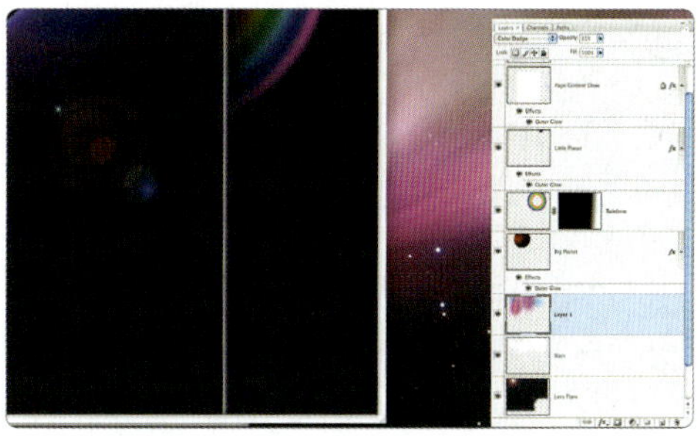

17 Create an aurora

Create a new layer and set the blending mode to 'Color Dodge'. Using the Gradient tool, again set to foreground-to-transparent, draw magenta and cyan gradients around the top third of the canvas to create a nice aurora effect. You can adjust the opacity of the layer to control the amount of aurora visible.

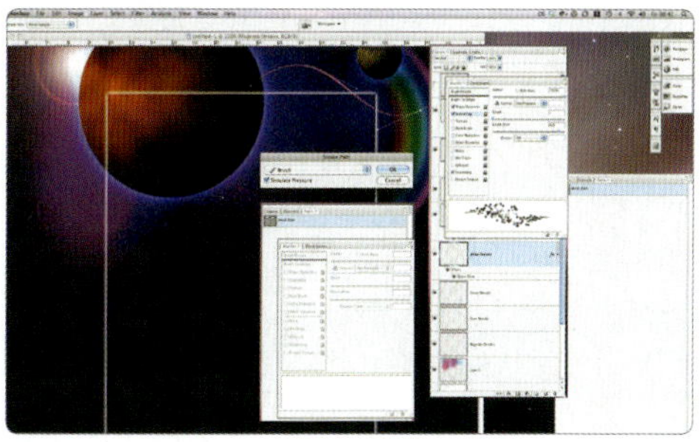

18 Add streaks of light

Create a new layer; foreground colour magenta. In Brush tool, select a small round brush. Select Pen tool. Create a curved path by clicking and dragging in three positions. Select Paths panel, right-click on work path and select 'Stroke Path'. Ensure 'Simulate Pressure' is checked. Repeat with different brushes to complete the effect.

Make a logo for your website

Learn how to use Photoshop to create a stylish logo for your website

Branding is a key part of making your website stand out from the crowd of competing sites on the web.

If you spend some time thinking about your favourite websites, they most likely each have a distinctive feel about them, with a colour scheme and logo design that's simple, clean and memorable. Many of these websites' logos might simply consist of some well-chosen type (using a font that suits the style of the website and its content), while others will likely feature a small graphical icon in addition to the type.

In this tutorial we're going to take a look at what makes a logo work well, how you can use it to set the tone for your website and how to use colour effectively to design a logo that will be both memorable and easy on the eye – the two don't necessarily go together!

Now, you shouldn't worry if you're not a Photoshop expert, as we will also be using the tutorial to introduce some of the most common features of Adobe's seminal graphics software and explain how they work.

Therefore, by the time you've worked through the steps in this tutorial, you will have a clear set of guidelines for what makes a great logo, and how to go about designing your own to complement your website's design.

CHOOSING AN EFFECTIVE COLOUR SCHEME

A wise choice of colour scheme can be the difference between an effective, memorable logo and a forgettable design. When deciding on a colour scheme, there's a lot of theory you can use to help you. For example, red usually represents danger or passion, while green means fresh, safety or jealousy. If you need help finding a starting point, look at other websites covering similar content to see what they're doing with colour, or visit an online tool such as Kuler (**http://kuler.adobe.com**) to get some ideas. Keep in mind that different shades of the same colour can present an entirely different feel to your design!

Breaking it down

How we designed our logo

Add an icon
We've used an icon that's quite recognisable – the bass clef – to help explain what the brand is all about without the need for any prior knowledge. This is quite an obvious choice, but sometimes obvious is good!

Choice of font
We've used a serif font to suggest dependability and tradition. The two words of the logo have been joined together but differentiated with different weights of type

Colour scheme
We opted for blue after some consideration – largely because in the markets this business is operating within, the colour blue suggests safe, calm and reliable

Kuler
We used Adobe's Kuler system to help find colours that would work well with our choice of primary colour. Ordinarily we'd stick with just two colours, but here we've pushed the boat out and gone for three

"A logo is a key part of making your website stand out from the crowd"

01 Create a document

Create a new Photoshop document, bigger than you'll need for your logo. Our design will consist entirely of type and a couple of vector shape layers, but keep in mind that bitmaps don't scale up well.

02 Create a background

We'll create a background layer to work on. If you know you'll always be displaying your logo on a particular colour, use that as your background, otherwise plump for white or black. Type the name of your business/brand.

03 Choosing fonts

For a business logo, the font shown would be completely inappropriate. Think about the values you'd like the logo to convey and choose a font accordingly. Avoid clichéd fonts such as Papyrus and Comic Sans altogether.

04 Size it up

Size up your text to fill the canvas sufficiently. Ours is over 100pt, but we can scale the document down later. Consider how different words interact with each other – we'll remove the space and make the second word bold.

05 Deal with tracking

Logo text is usually 'tracked in'. Try setting the tracking to -20 or less in the Character panel – maybe as low as -50 depending upon your choice of font.

06 Look for shapes

We'll create an icon that complements our typography. Choose the Shape Layers tool and look at the available shapes in the drop-down.

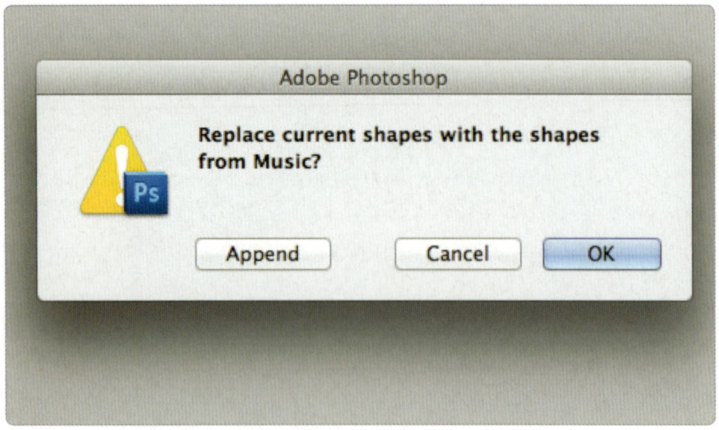

07 Load more shapes

In the fly-out menu is a set of shapes we can load that are music-centric – perfect for our needs. Click on the library to load it into Photoshop, and choose to Append or Replace the existing shapes, as suits.

08 Draw a shape

Select a shape from the set and click-drag to create your shape. Holding Shift will ensure the shape remains in proportion. Consider the size of the icon in relation to the text, ensuring both sit comfortably together.

09 Fill your layer

Shape layers are easy to re-colour. Select the layer, then choose a colour and use the Paint Bucket tool to fill it with a colour. Here we've changed the colour of the bass clef to black, though we may well change it later.

10 Add a strapline

Now it's time to add a strapline to describe your business. Ours is 'sheet music for serious musicians'. We've used the same font as the main logo, and right-aligned the text to sit neatly underneath the main text.

11 Apply kerning

There are some uncomfortable gaps between letter pairs. Using the Text tool, position the cursor between two letters in the logo. Hold Alt/Opt and use left/right arrows to alter the space between them. This is called 'kerning'.

12 Think about colour

We didn't intentionally choose the red colour that's been in use up until this point. Take the opportunity to experiment with a few different colours, just to get a feel for how they change the poise and impact of the logo.

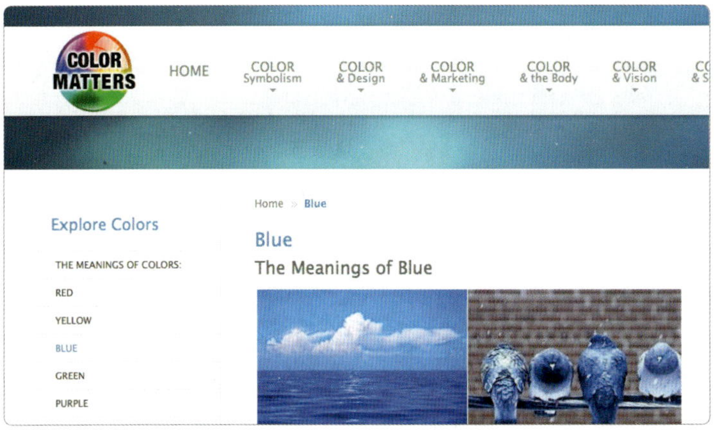

13 Do some research

A quick web search brings up thousands of results for 'colour association', including this site which lists blue as suggesting trust, integrity, dignity, intelligence and authority – perfect for our business. We'll try blue next!

14 Make it blue

We've applied a medium blue to our primary text and a lighter blue for the bass clef. This almost works, but the colours don't quite sit together perfectly and the strapline is now overpowering with its black type.

15 Recolour the strap

Experiment with the strapline colour. You might want to use the same colour as the logo, or not. We've taken the safe route and used a middle grey to avoid overpowering the logo, but still provide strength.

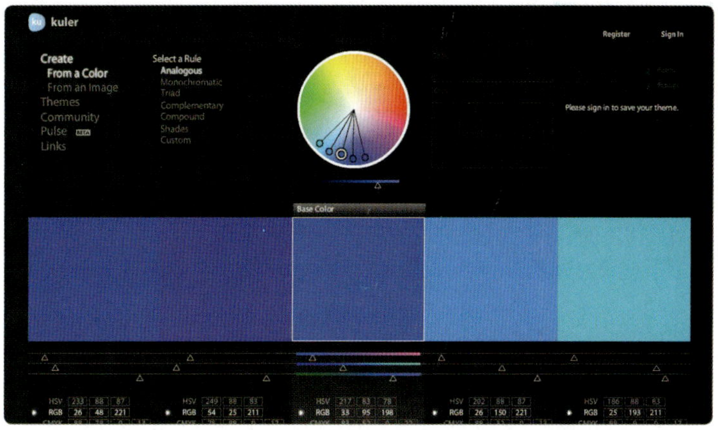

16 Use Kuler

Let's see if we can get a better set of blues that will work in harmony. Load up Kuler (**http://kuler.adobe.com**) and input your base colour. Select a base rule to work with and see the colours Kuler recommends.

17 Be bold!

We're using a colour from the triad scheme on Kuler to create an accent over the letter 'i'. This works well but makes the bass clef look a little weak, so it's back to the drawing board to try another iteration.

18 Complete it

We ended up using the other colour from the triad Kuler generated for us. The end result is bold and distinctive. The semiquaver added to the letter 'i' is perhaps a step too far, but don't be scared to experiment!

Design a clean and modern navigation box in Photoshop

Create a stunning high-gloss navigation panel from scratch

Most of the sophisticated designs that you will see while browsing the web are constructed very simply. Rather than using some magical CSS technique and hidden HTML knowledge, the majority of the web comprises basic HTML and CSS, with clever graphics used as background images to individual elements to make the design appear to be more complex than it really is – a bit of smoke and mirrors, if you like.

The basic concept is that every element in an HTML document is a box. If you imagine piling a series of cardboard boxes up to form a wall of cardboard, you could then use a marker pen to draw a fancy curve that moves across multiple cardboard boxes. Although the boxes themselves aren't curved, by drawing a curved design onto your boxes you can give the impression of a curved element.

In this tutorial we are going to use the same concept to create a highly polished black lacquer effect navigation box. We will design this as a single graphic inside Photoshop, and then split it up into multiple pieces, each of which will be applied to an individual element (or box) inside an HTML page. The end result will be a design element that looks fancy, but is really very simple to construct!

> "A design element that looks fancy, but is really very simple to construct!"

PHOTOSHOP'S BLENDING MODES

One of the best, and most used, features in Photoshop is its ability to change how two different layers interact with each other. By now you'll be familiar with the idea of lowering the opacity of one layer to make it partially transparent, and thereby allowing a layer beneath to shine through. In addition to this most basic interaction between layers, we can also use the colour, tone and opacity properties of one layer to actually change the appearance of layers beneath. This is called a 'blending mode' inside Photoshop, and there are lots of different options to experiment with!

The most commonly used blending mode is 'Normal'. By default, new layers inside Photoshop use the 'Normal' blending mode and don't directly affect the way layers beneath are displayed. If you try changing a layer's blending mode to 'Multiply', however, you'll see that the overall result is a darker image. This is because Photoshop is taking the colour and tone values from both layers (the one you set to use Multiply, and the layer(s) beneath) and multiplying the colours together. This creates a useful effect where you can use one layer to effectively mix in and darken a second. Other layer blending modes divide the colour values, use one set of layer pixels to mask another or add/subtract. Experiment to see how blending modes work, and use them on your next image!

Deconstructing our navigation box

Our smoke and mirrors hide a simple piece of artwork!

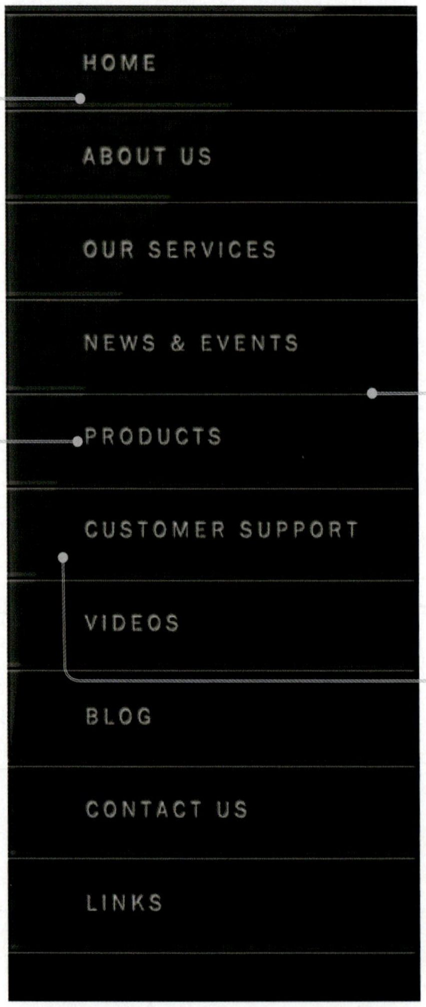

Gloss effect
We achieved our gloss effect by using the elliptical marquee tool to draw a large oval, then filling the selection with white pixels. Reducing the opacity made the white look like a glossy reflection on the surface of our navigation panel

Separation of buttons
Each button is separated from the next with a sophisticated border. This is composed of layer styles and a separating black sliver. The border is essential to help sell the idea that you're seeing individual buttons rather than one big graphic

Text labels
The text you see here is rendered inside Photoshop with a bevel and emboss effect applied. However, keep in mind that for accessibility reasons you should ordinarily output text using HTML and CSS, positioned over the top of a background graphic

Extra shine
Each button has a very subtle additional bit of shine applied to the left-hand edge. This, in combination with the other lighting and reflection effects, helps to cement the optical illusion that you're looking at individual buttons

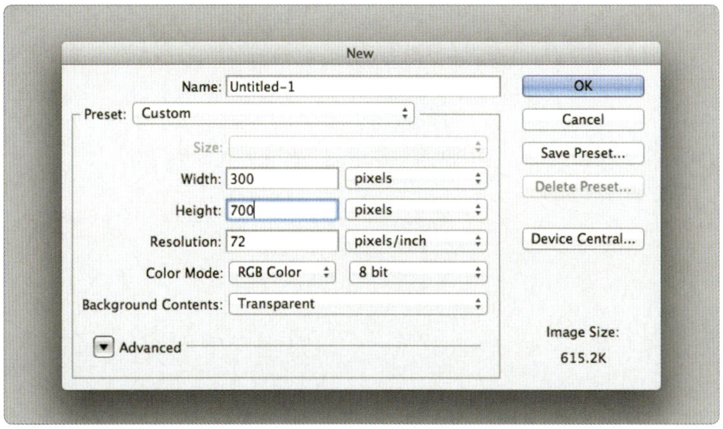

01 Create a document

As this is a web graphic, we'll create a document that's 300x700px. This will be the primary dimension of our navigation box, but should our box need to be taller we'll either repeat our graphic, or use a flat background colour.

02 Fill the layer

If you already have a background layer, double-click on it in Layers to turn it into a normal layer. Using the Paint Bucket tool, fill the layer with black. We'll also use black as the background colour in our HTML document for the box.

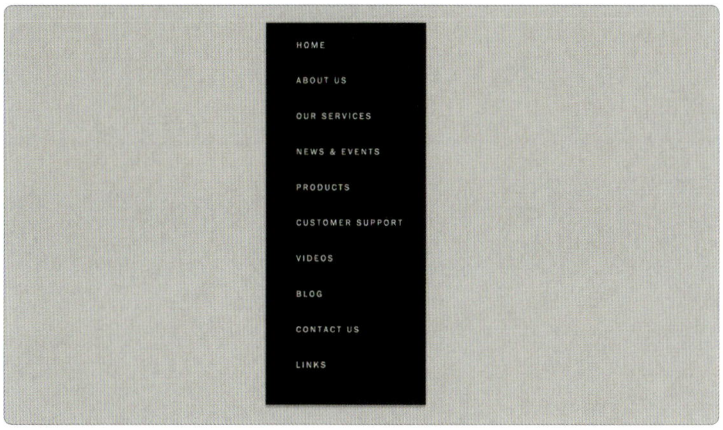

03 Create your text

Use the Text tool to create labels for the box buttons. You can render this text using HTML later on if you want. Select all your text and press Alt/Opt while pressing the up/down arrow to adjust the line spacing ('leading').

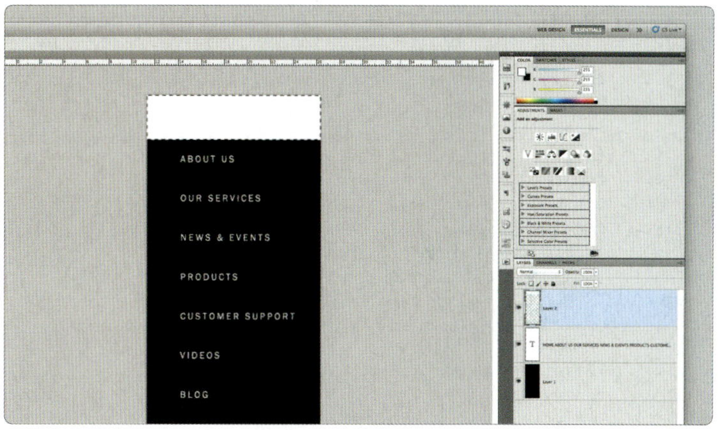

04 Create the threshold

Create a new layer and use the Rectangular Marquee tool to draw a box around the top item in your list. Fill the selection with any colour (we used white). Now reduce the Layer Fill value for this box to zero.

05 Layer styles

Choose Layer>Layer Styles>Bevel and Emboss. Experiment with values to find a nice dividing line effect between the two buttons.

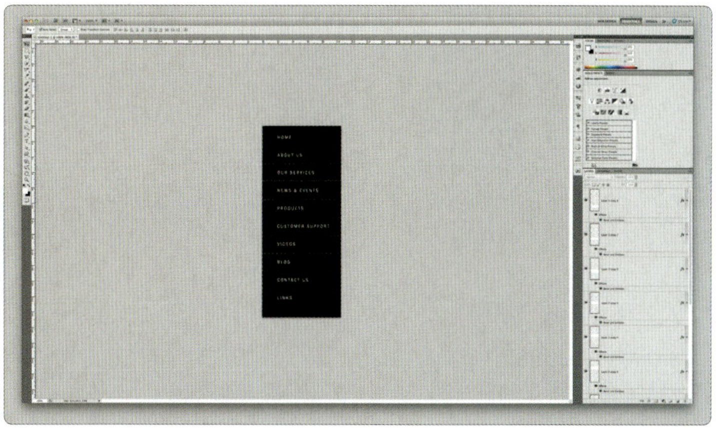

06 Step and repeat

Duplicate white box layer and place between the second and third buttons. Repeat this process until you've created a border between every button.

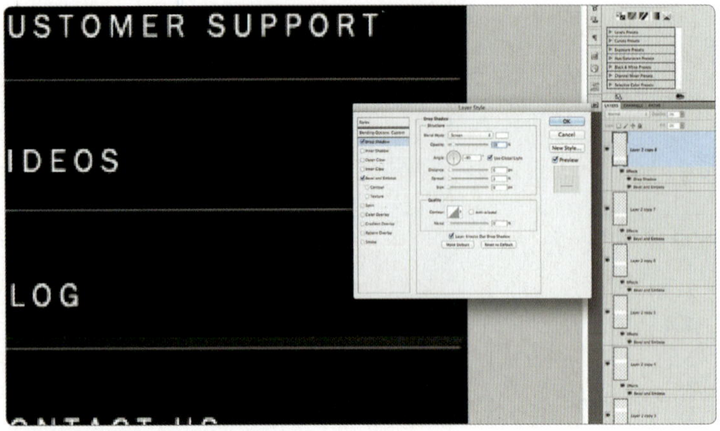

07 Adjust the effect

Choose a white box layer, add a Drop Shadow effect (under 'fx' in Layers panel) and experiment with settings to find a nice sharp shadow. Set the colour to white, the blending mode to screen, and opacity to around 15%.

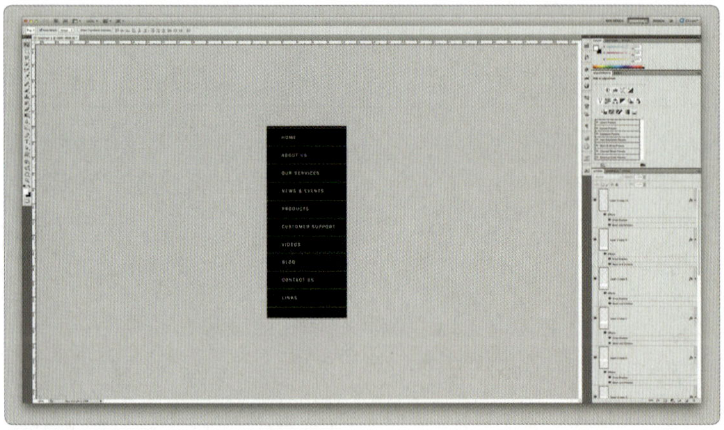

08 Copy and paste

Now you have your adjusted style set up, right-click in the Layers panel and choose Copy Layer Style. Next, right-click on each of the remaining white box layers in turn and choose Paste Layer Style from the pop-up menu.

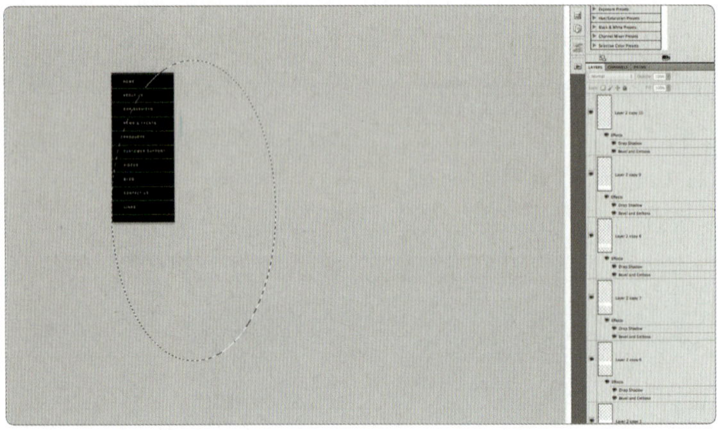

09 The big reflection

We need a big reflection to cover the whole panel. Zoom out and draw a big oval with the Marquee tool to select the bottom-right half of the image. Make sure only one curve segment is over your image for best results.

10 Invert and fill

Choose Select>Inverse (or Cmd/Ctrl+I). Create a new layer and fill your selection with white. Make sure this layer is at the top of the stack of layers, above everything else. Next we'll make this look more like a reflection.

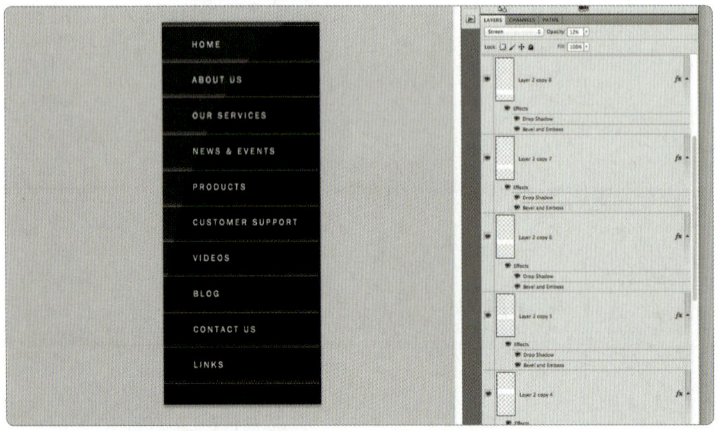

11 Blending modes

Set the blending mode for the reflection layer to Screen. Experiment with the opacity so that the white area looks like a reflection – you may have to take it right down to between 10 and 20% to get the right effect here.

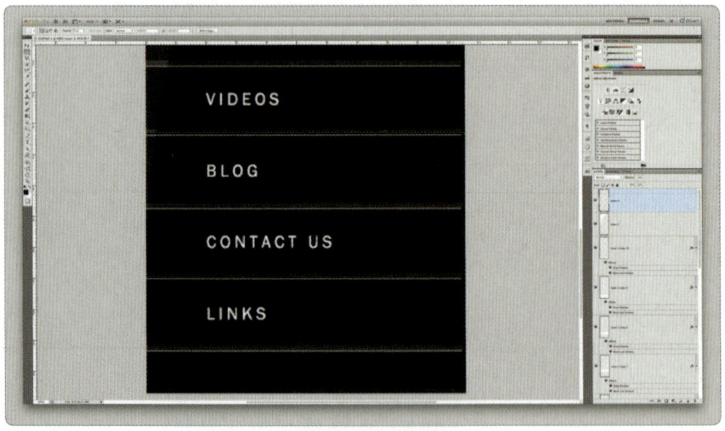

12 Add a void

We can simulate a shadow beneath each button by adding a sliver of black. Use the Marquee tool to select a few pixels in height, and the entire width. Now create a new layer and use the Paint Bucket to fill with black.

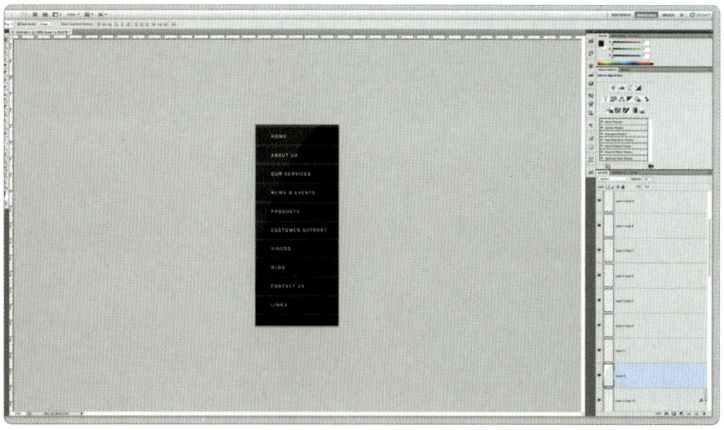

13 Step and repeat

Duplicate the black sliver layer and position at the top of the white box reflection. Repeat for each button so that the edge is light, a dark void appears above, and the light reflection for each button shows above that.

14 Add another reflection

Create a new layer, then use the Rectangular Marquee tool to select a small vertical slice at the left side of a button. Use the gradient tool to draw a white-to-black gradient, then reduce the opacity of the layer to around 10%.

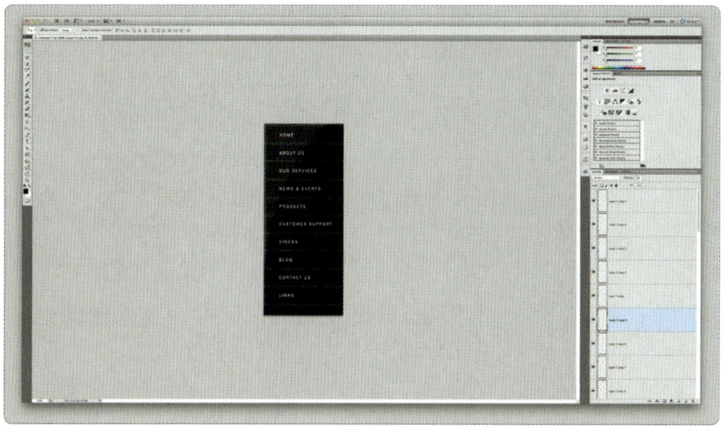

15 Copy and paste

Copy and paste this highlight to each button for a slight reflection. You could repeat this process for the right edge of each button, but we felt this was enough to give the suggestion of high gloss and so we left it at that.

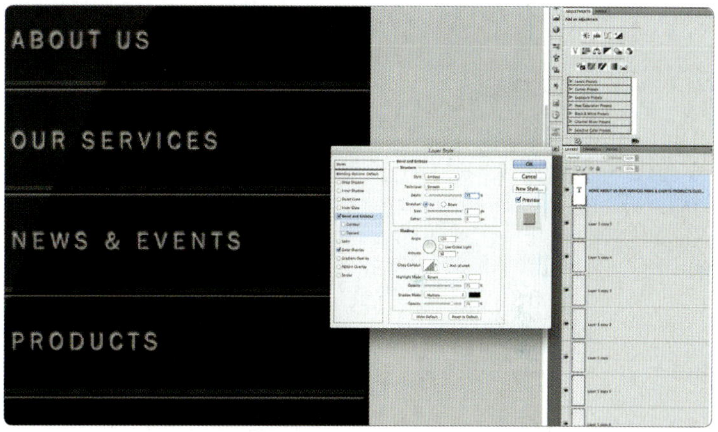

16 Bevel and emboss

If you want to render your text using HTML, hide the text layer and go to the next step. If not, you can add any special effects you like to the text in the graphic. We added a bevel and emboss effect to ours using Layer Styles.

17 Slice and dice

Using the Slice tool, draw a rectangle around each button in turn. If you make a mistake while drawing, either undo (Cmd/Ctrl+Z) it, or use the Slice Select tool to adjust the dimensions of your slice.

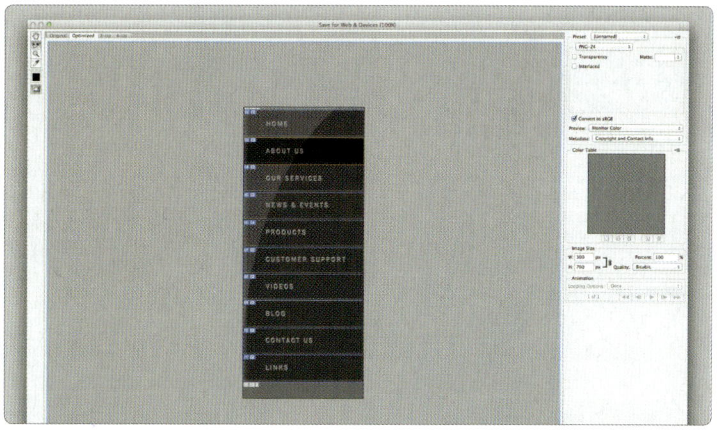

18 Save for web

Choose File>Save for Web & Devices, and select every slice. Save it as a PNG file. Photoshop will automatically output each graphic separately, ready for assembly using CSS and background images!

Create a portfolio theme

Create a clean, professional site design perfect for showcasing your creative work with genuine style

In this tutorial you will learn how to create a clean-cut portfolio website from scratch, which will focus all the attention on your work, rather than distract with over-the-top graphics or a surplus of text.

The notion of clean portfolio websites comes from top industry agencies that mostly use simple and minimalist layouts to showcase creative work. The easier the browsing experience is for your clients, then the more inclined they will be to stay and search through your work, which in turn boosts the probability of them deciding to hire you for the job.

Combinations of white, black and grey never go out of fashion, and a simple layout with clean design can give you an edge when it's time to give your portfolio a facelift.

With the arrival of Web 2.0, it became very popular to use massive headers and long-winded introductions; indeed, the majority of Web 2.0-style portfolios focus on copy and the design of the site, rather than the artwork. But if you consider your portfolio from a client's point of view, the biggest emphasis should be placed upon your work and straightforward navigation, rather than big, bold graphics or excessive greetings on the welcome page.

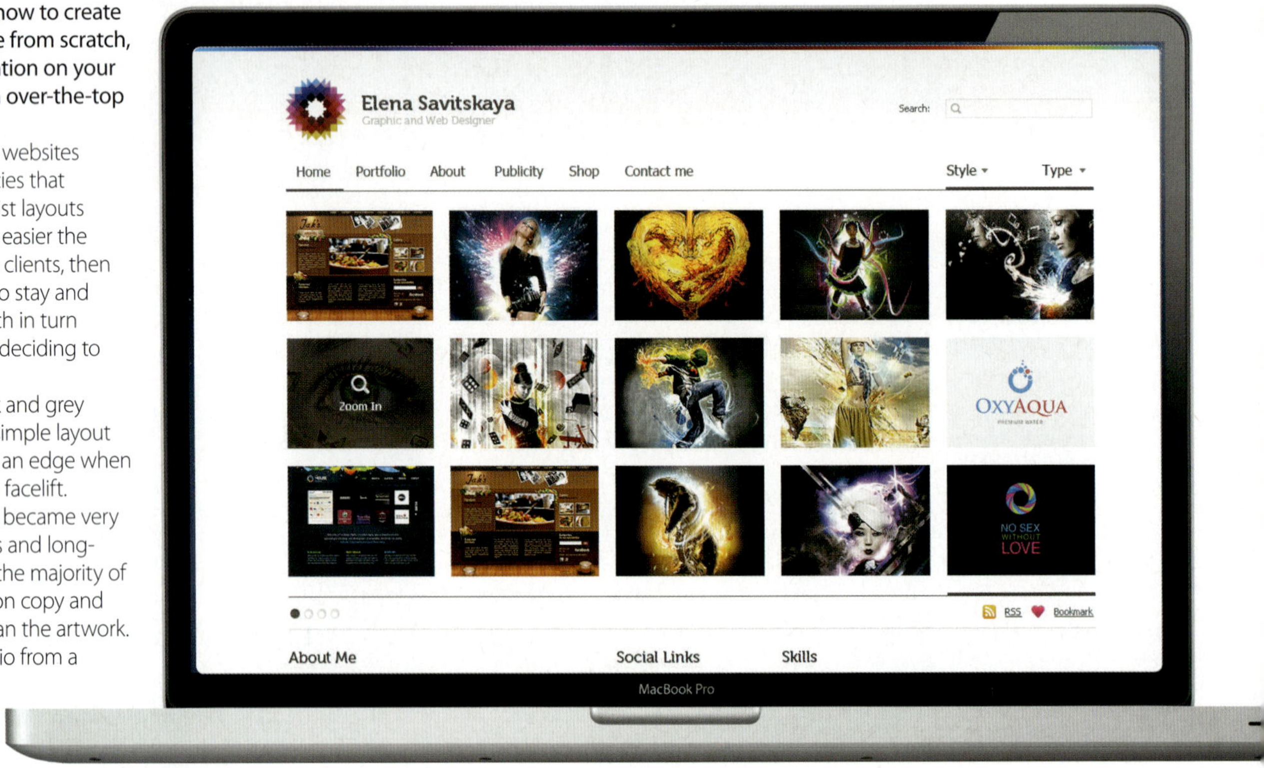

"The biggest emphasis should be on your work"

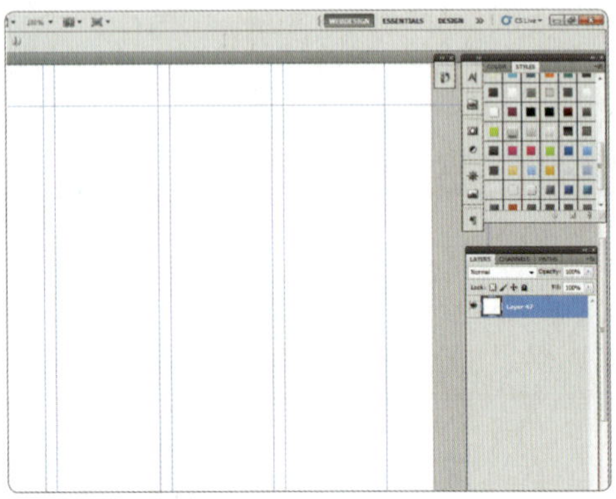

01 Prepare the workspace

First, we need to build a grid, upon which the website will be based. This is determined by the number of thumbnails desired on the homepage. In our case, it's five thumbnails.

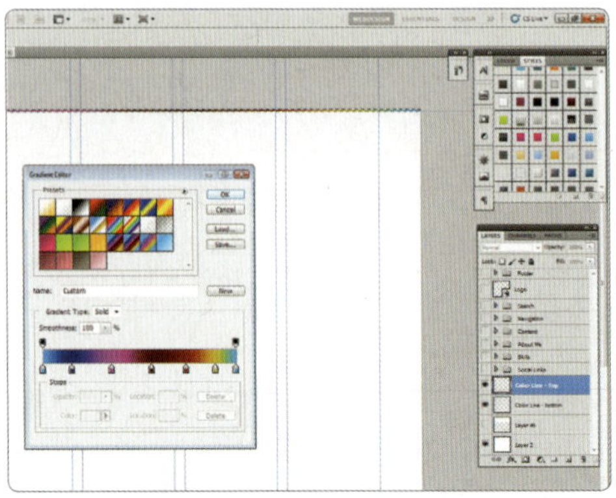

02 Create gradient lines

Select the Rectangular Selection tool and create a 5px-high selection at the top. Create a new layer and fill with a gradient that starts and ends the same. Repeat with a 3px-high selection for the bottom.

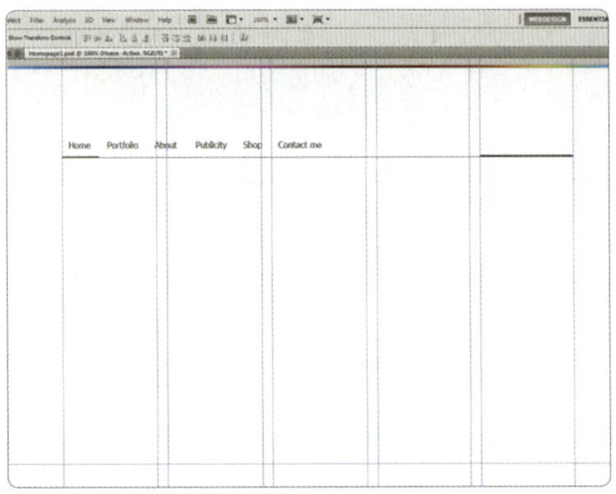

03 The main navigation

With the Pencil tool, pick a dark-grey colour and draw a line. Go to the Type tool and create sections, then set a font Under the Home tag, create a 2px active state line; this will highlight the current page.

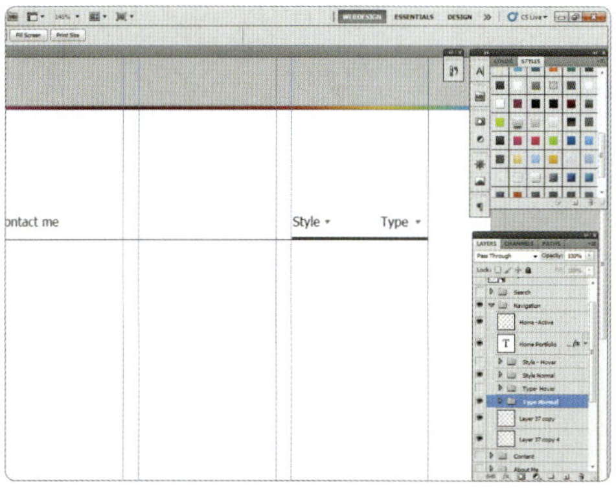

04 Navigation continued

In the last column, create a 3px-high line; ensure the line is the same length as the last column of the grid. Write 'Style' and 'Type' into the navigation and create little drop-down triangles.

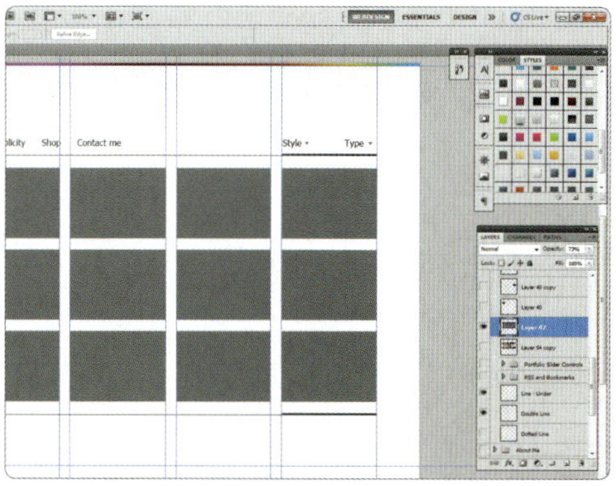

05 Showcase area

Copy the thin navigation line and the thicker line on the right-hand side and move it down the page for the showcase. This will be the focal point of the site. Create 175 x 125px thumbnails and spread across.

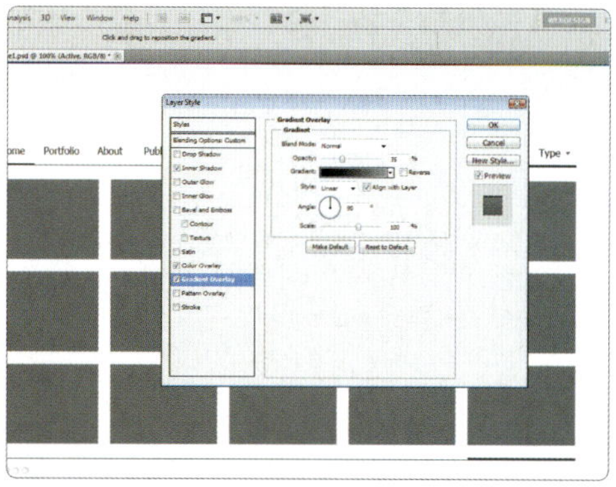

06 Showcase navigation

Create a circle. Create four duplicates and spread them evenly on the left-hand side under the showcase. Set the colour to '#222222', double-click the layer and set Color and Gradient Overlay styles.

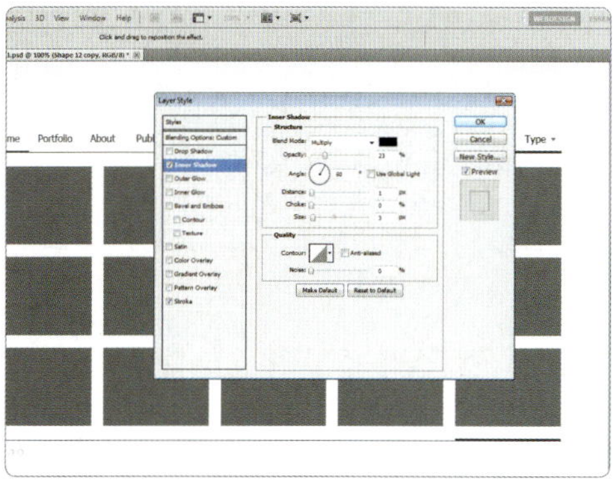

07 Showcase navigation 2

Now let's style the inactive state. Set the circle's Layer Fill to 0% and give it a small Inner Shadow and a tiny Stroke. Follow the screenshots for setting the style or feel free to experiment.

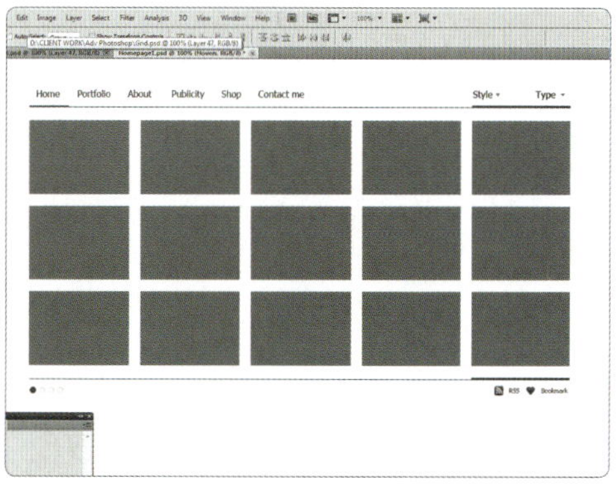

08 Bookmarks and RSS

On the right-hand side beneath the showcase area, create two icons. Add text in a grey colour, set it to Tahoma, Regular, 11pt, with Anti-aliasing turned to None. Put the buttons in the folder.

Quick tip

The right width

Figuring out the best width for your website can be a bit of a nightmare. The current standard is something between 940-960 pixels; in our case, we used 955px width for our grid, which is perfect for 17-inch screens. Always leave some space outside the grid, so you can better see how the website will look on larger screens.

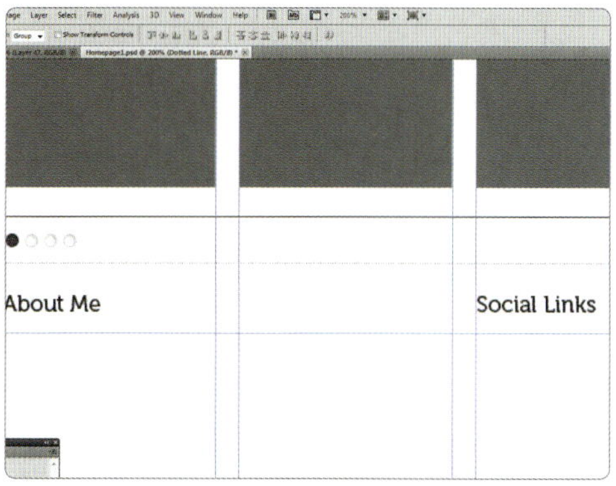

09 Design on the dotted line

Create a slightly brighter grey 1px dotted line under the showcase navigation to divide the area. Now pick up the Type tool and create headings, such as 'About Me', following the grid.

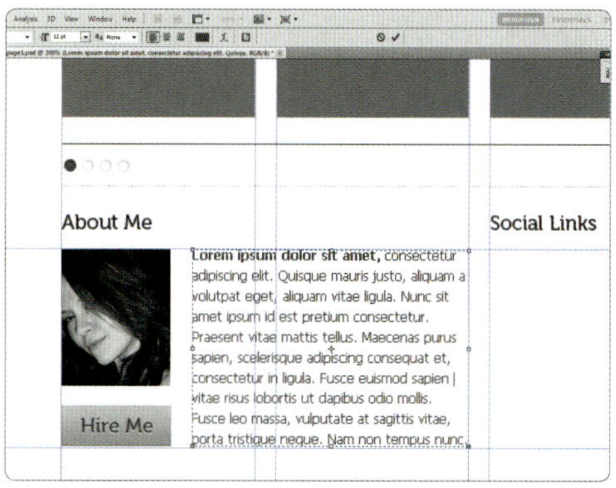

10 About Me area

Find a picture of you to place on the homepage, make it greyscale and place it on the left of the About Me area. On the right, create a text area, then create a Hire Me button.

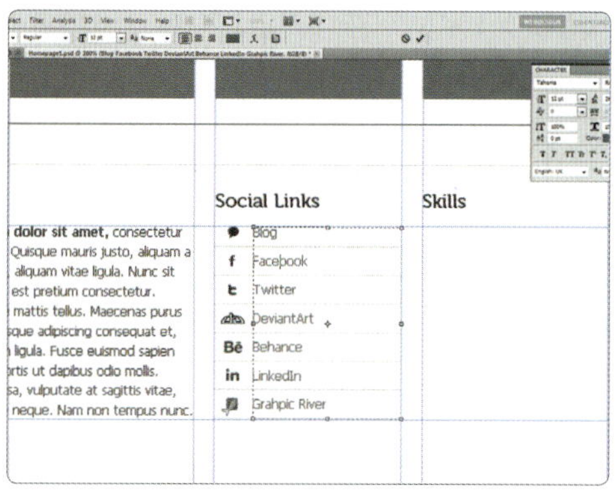

11 Social networking

Under the Social Links header, create a list of links to social media profiles and add icons. Separate lines with the dotted line. Create a Hover folder on top of the text and make the text's hover state black.

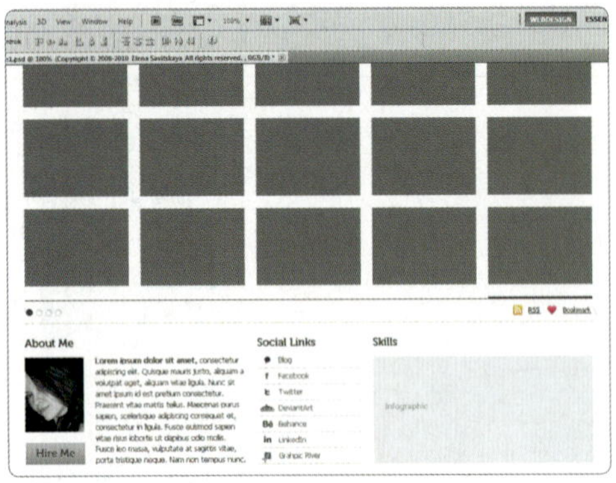

12 Footer layout

For the Skills, add a grey placeholder using the grid; this can become an image link to your CV, a skills infographic or project. Duplicate the dotted line and move it under the areas to divide the space.

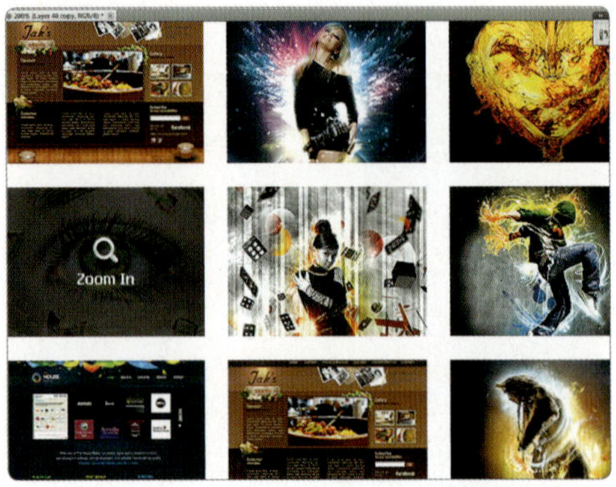

13 Showcase area: details

When designing, it's very helpful to use as much real content as possible, so let's add thumbnails. Pick a thumbnail, create a rectangle of the same size and fill with black (70% Opacity).

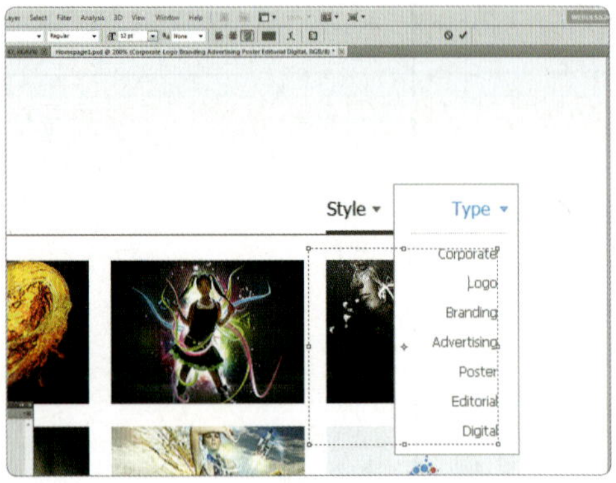

14 Hover style and type

Using the Rectangle tool, create a white rectangle and give it a 1px grey Stroke style. Duplicate Type and its triangle, putting all layers in a 'Hover' folder. Add a 1px dotted line beneath the heading.

Quick tip

Folders

Before submitting any work for programming, it's good to ensure you have hover states for all parts of the site that will need them when coded, to save you explaining every bit to the programmer. It's also helpful to keep your layers organised in the correct folders, named logically. Create folders before you start; these will help to focus you as you go along.

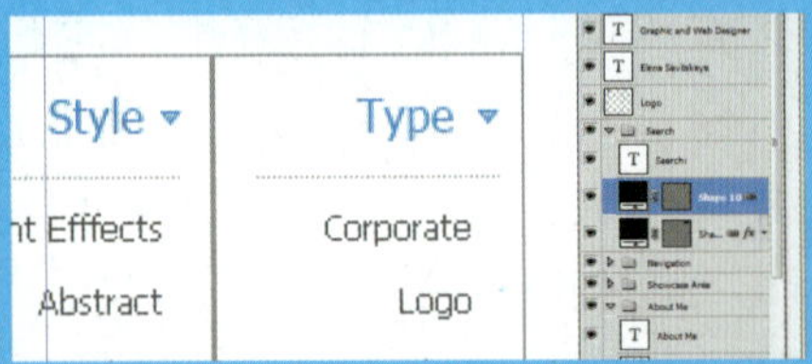

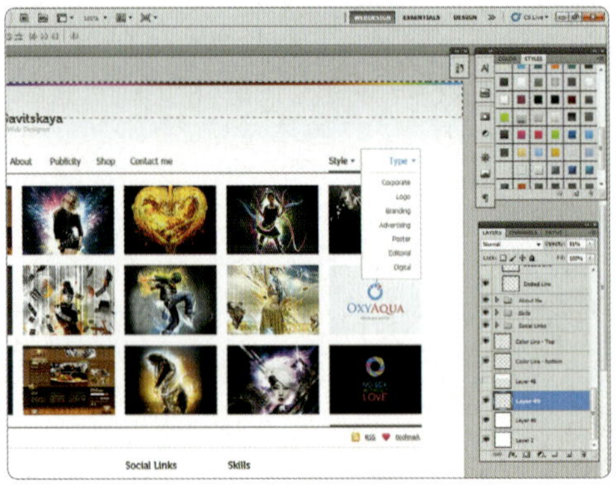

15 Add the logo

In the top-left corner, add your logo and tagline. Go back to the first layer and create a new one on top, apply a grey-to-transparent gradient and add that to the top to give it a bit of depth.

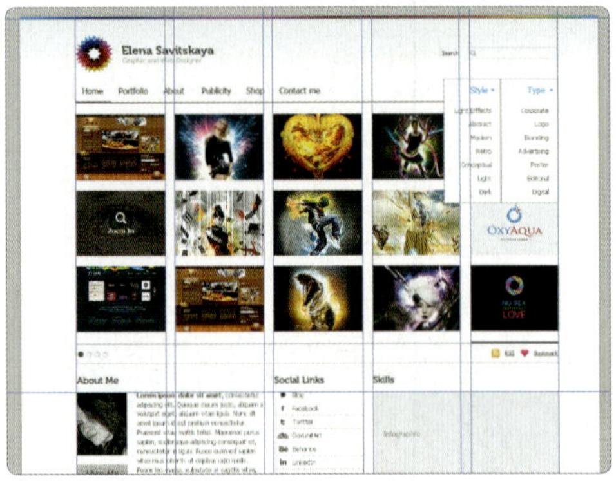

16 More details

Tweak the grey gradient opacity until you're left with a hint of grey; we used 34% Opacity. Now it's time to double-check. Bring back the grid and ensure that nothing goes outside the edges.

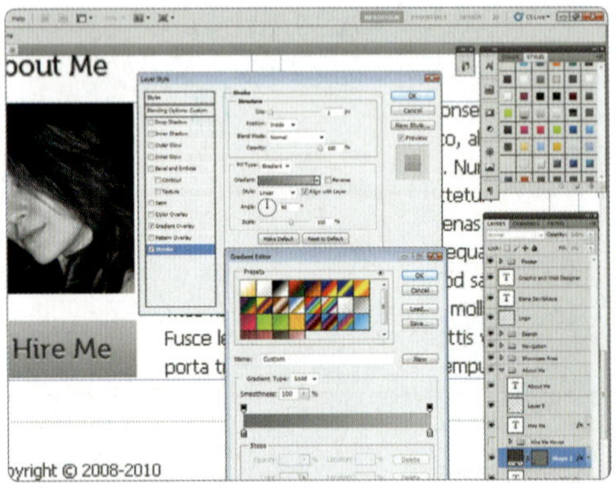

17 Hire Me button

To give the Hire Me text a pale shadow, double-click it, activate Drop Shadow then set blending mode to Normal, colour to White. Set Distance to 1, Size to 0, Spread to 0, Opacity to 1px and Angle to 90°.

18 Hire Me button hover

Duplicate the button layers, create a folder called 'Hover' and put the duplicates in. Create a new layer on top, then right-click on the background thumb in Layers to create a selection of the same size.

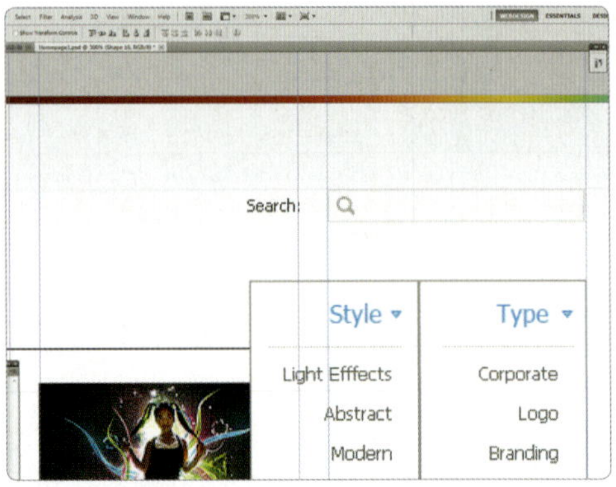

19 Add search bar

Create a rectangle, set Fill to 0%, double-click the layer and add a Stroke: Size 1px, Position Inside, Color Black and Opacity 10%. Check the Inner Shadow box and change Opacity to about 4%.

A photo portfolio

The finished project, complete with images

The header
Your header still needs to be clean like this. Your images may grab the user's attention, but if they can't navigate the site they won't come back

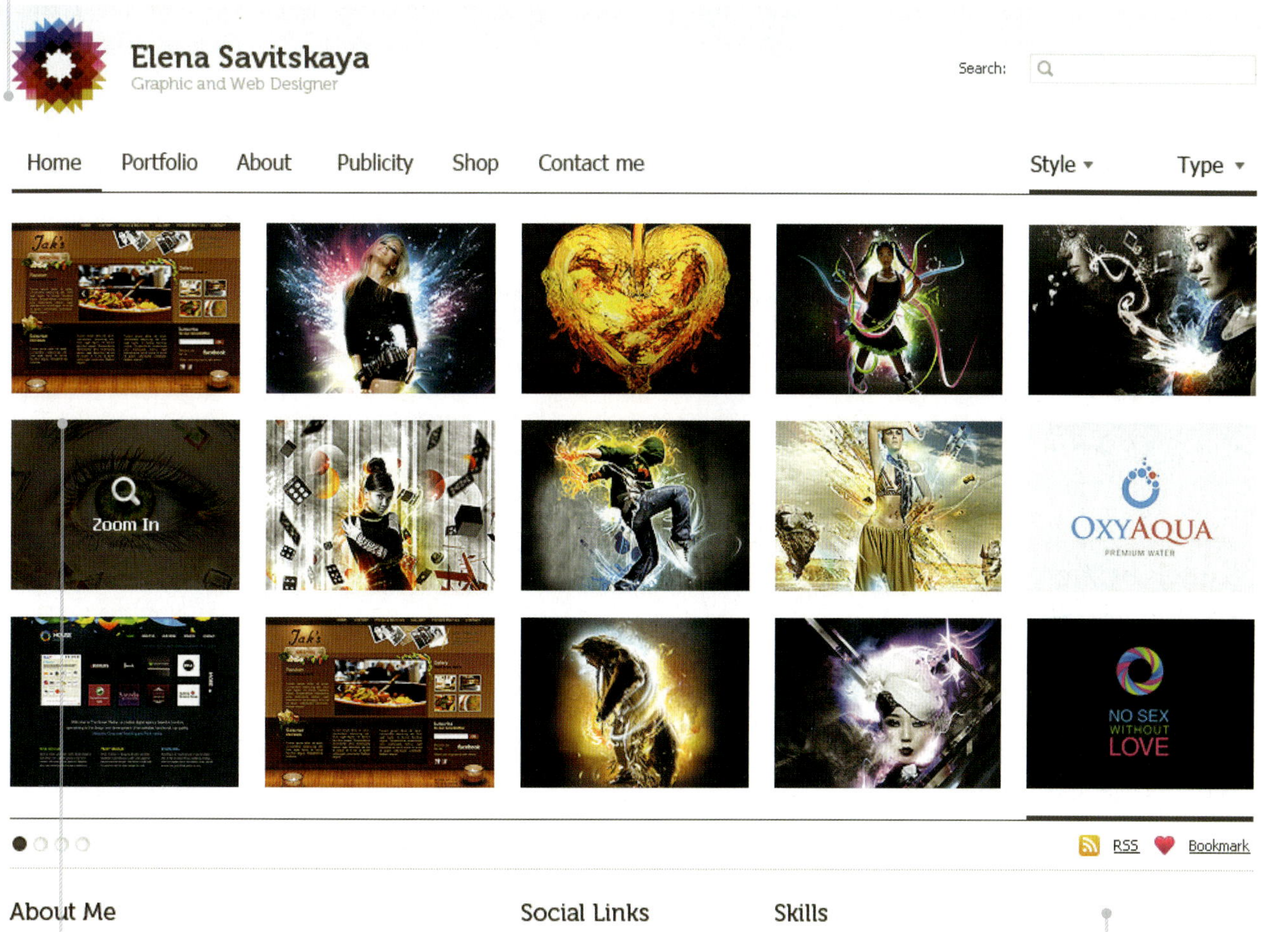

The content
Much like the header, the images must be presented in a clean and clear style. This gives the site a professional look, and also ensures all images are viewable

Continue
Of course, the images at the top of the screen will capture attention, but scrolling down will reveal more content about yourself

Using styles and palettes for web design projects

It's very helpful to develop a habit of sorting your styles and colour palettes for every web design project. Prior to starting the work, clear all the colours in your colour palette and clear all layer styles as well (or save them somewhere safe if you have a massive amount of styles saved from previous projects). As you progress with your design, keep creating palettes and styles, saving them separately. This will keep your workflow very clean and will prevent you from using too many effects and colours within one project, as that's not always a good thing. The same rules apply to gradient palettes. All the effects and settings we used in this tutorial can be found in the source files on the disc. If you don't know where a particular style belongs, double-click it in the palette and the name will indicate where it should be used.

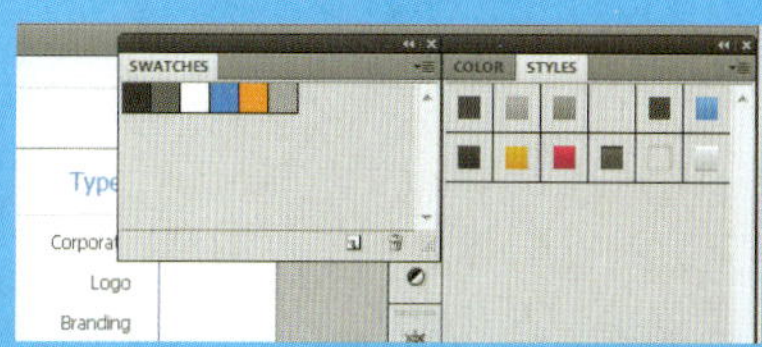

Customise your site

188 Add maps

WHAT YOU'LL LEARN

Although by now you'll have learned lots of code and designed lots of graphics, there are still plenty of things you can do to make your site special. In Customise Your Site you'll learn how to create your first script, add social network interaction, maps and videos to your pages, as well as how to create feedback forms so your users can feed back what they think of your site.

"The options available for each button mean you can tailor the settings for a bespoke finished result"

192 Add Twitter links

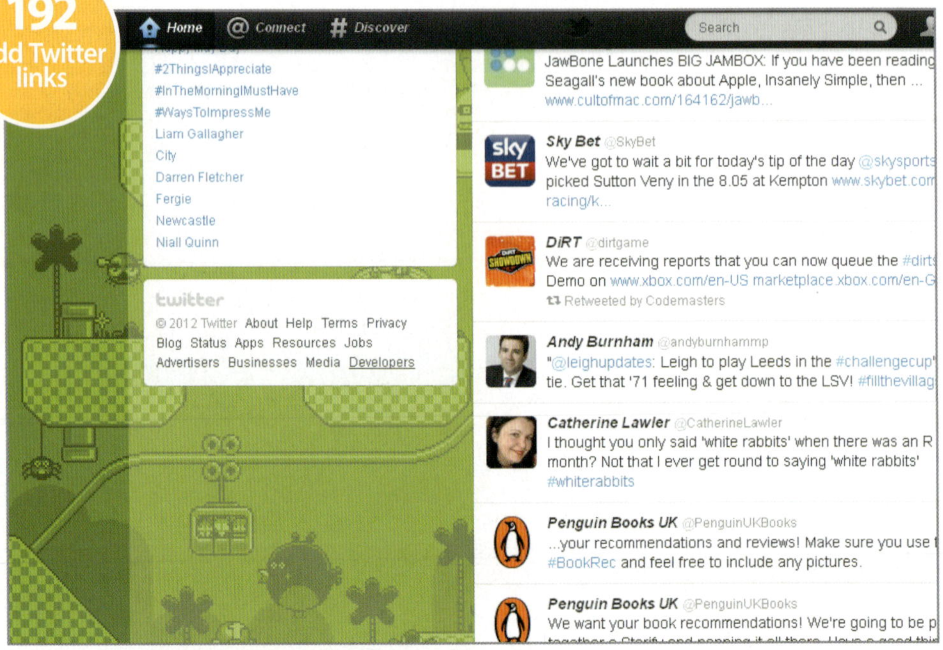

206 Create newsletters

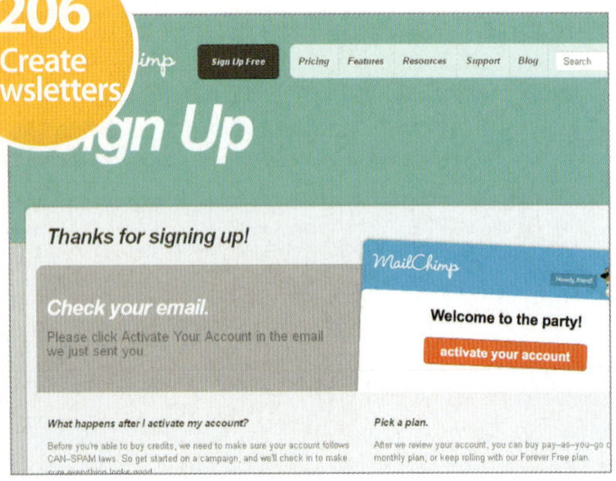

EMAIL NEWSLETTERS

Get in touch with your visitors with a newsletter on page 206

GOOGLE FONTS

Add some style with free Google fonts on page 200

GOOGLE SEARCH FORM

Harness the power of Google with a search form on page 198

Create your first script with JavaScript

JavaScript is a great tool for adding interactivity to your website

The modern website consists of three primary elements: the HTML code that provides the structure and content of your page; the CSS that brings design and form to your structure, creating the visual aesthetics and overall layout; and script to add interactivity to the page.

Scripts are little programs that run inside the web browser, allowing the developer to talk to different elements on the page, reacting to user input and making something happen. Sometimes this is as simple as changing the colour of an item on the page, while other times it might be creating the logic for a game, validating that a form has been completed correctly, or even loading new content into the page.

The most common scripting language currently in use on the worldwide web is JavaScript. The name is really a bit of a misnomer as it bears no relation to the (much more scary) desktop programming language, Java. In this tutorial we're going to examine the basic structure of JavaScript, and experiment with it a little to get an understanding of how it works.

"The most common scripting language currently in use on the worldwide web is JavaScript"

USING JAVASCRIPT LIBRARIES

While the ability to code in JavaScript is admirable, the modern web designer doesn't really need to understand all the ins and outs of JavaScript programming to be able to add interactivity to their website. In recent years, the JavaScript library has grown in popularity, making it really easy to interact with elements on the page and make them do things in response to user input or timed events.

The most popular library by far is jQuery, found at **www.jQuery.com**. By adding a simple line of code to the top of your HTML document, you can include the jQuery library in your page. Once the library is available, any script you write can employ the many pre-built bits of functionality that jQuery provides, allowing you to easily animate elements, hide and reveal content on your page, set the CSS properties or even load content directly into your webpage. It really is a great time-saver.

The web is full of useful resources on the jQuery library, but the best place to start learning about the possibilities is at the jQuery website itself. Another resource of note is Remy Sharp's excellent jQuery for designers website, found at **www.jqueryfordesigners.com**. This site includes in-depth video screencasts showing how to construct your interactions with clear instructions.

Getting to grips with JavaScript

JavaScript is a powerful tool, but it's easy to pick up

Talk to the user

The alert() method allows you to create a pop-up message that is displayed to the user with an OK button to dismiss it. This is useful for letting users know when something has gone wrong, or simply to say hello (although beware – people don't like pop-ups, so use with caution)

Store data

Data can be stored inside variables for later reference. Here we've assigned the string 'apples' as the value of a variable with the name 'fruit'. Each time we use the variable name 'fruit' in our commands, the value 'apples' will be automatically substituted in

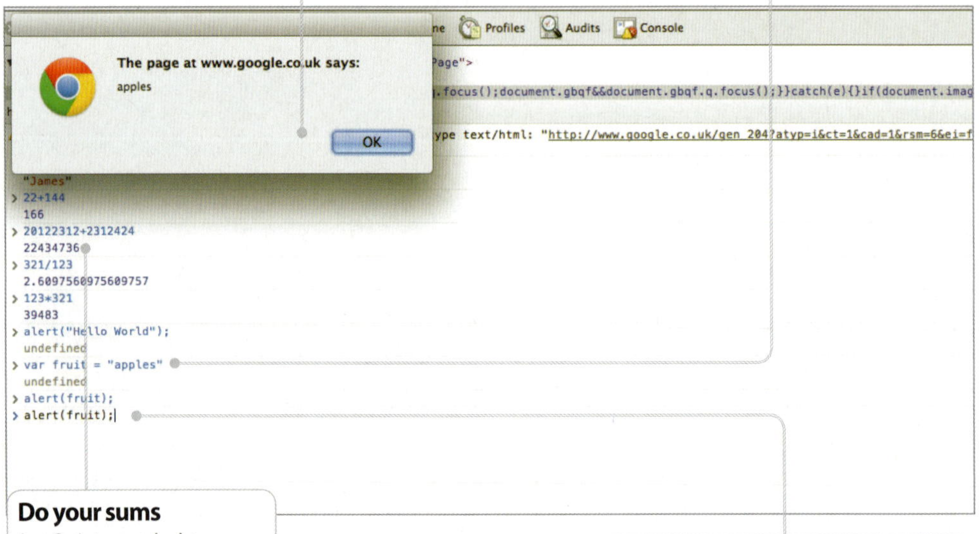

Do your sums

JavaScript can calculate mathematical equations for you. Enter a sum at the console and JavaScript will return the result immediately, without hesitation or the need for fingers and toes!

Alert with variables

You can also parse in variables as an argument to the alert() method. Here we've parsed in our fruit variable, and JavaScript has automatically substituted in the value we assigned to the variable – 'apples'

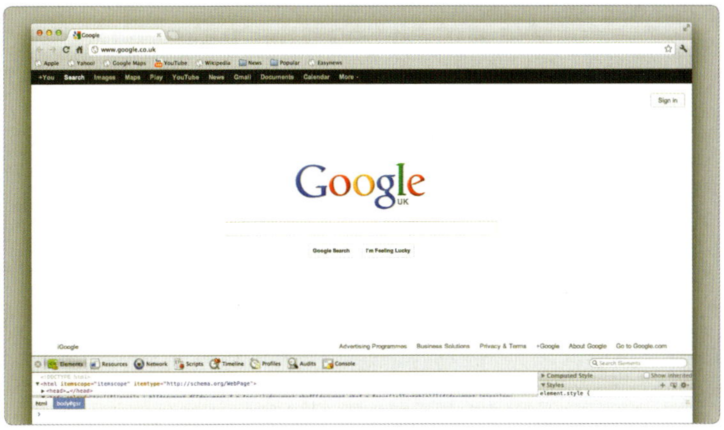

01 Get the tools

You need a console that lets you interactively test scripts. Download Firefox & Firebug, or Safari/Google Chrome. Open Firebug, choose Develop>Show Error Console in Safari, or View>Developer>JavaScript Console in Chrome.

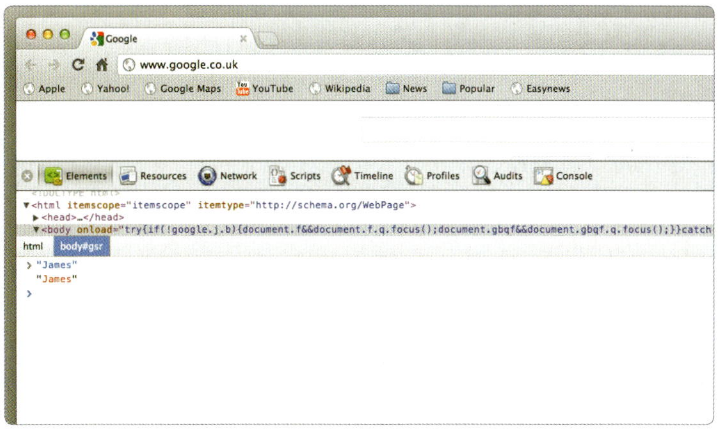

02 Enter your name

Enter your name at the console prompt, inside quote marks (" "). The console returns the same value. You've entered a string and JavaScript has responded with the same string. Strings must be enclosed with quotes.

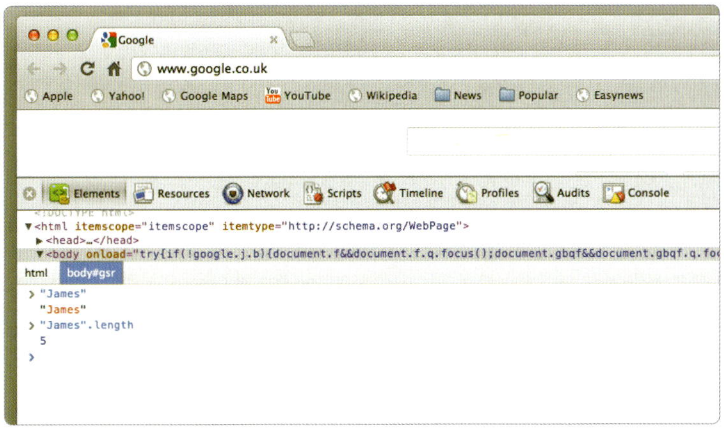

03 Make it work

Type your name in quotes again, but this time append .length to the end of the command. JavaScript will examine the string and determine how long it is, returning a value for the total number of characters in the string.

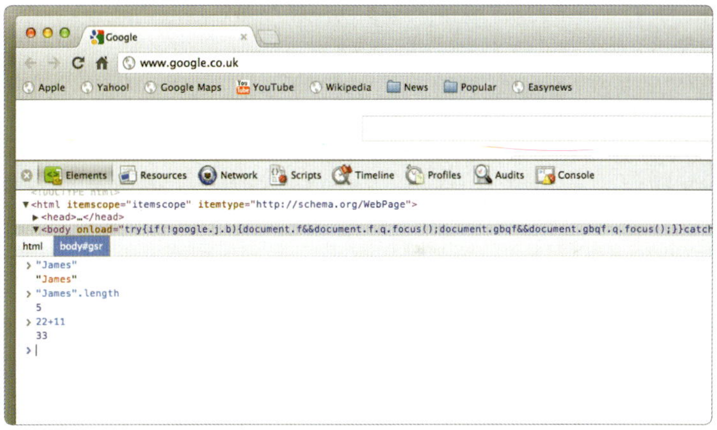

04 Do some maths

You can also use JavaScript to do maths! Enter 22+11 into the console and press Enter. JavaScript will calculate any mathematical equations for you automatically. In this case, the returned result will be 33.

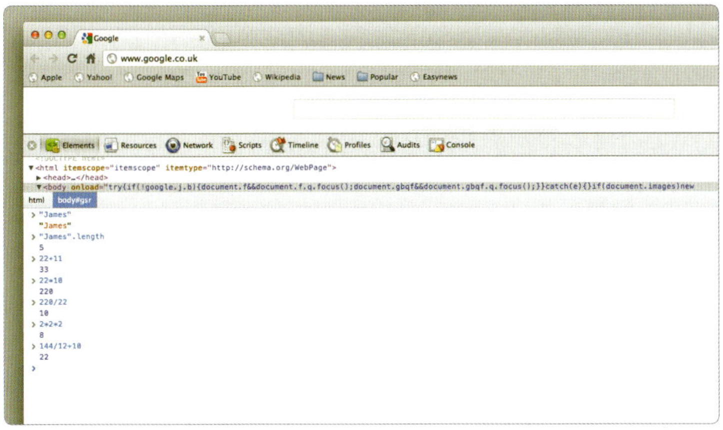

05 More complex maths

You can also multiply (*) and divide (/) using JavaScript. Try entering some equations using these to check that JavaScript returns the right results.

06 Send a console message

The alert() method presents a pop-up window with a message and an OK button for the user. Try entering alert("Hello world") in the console.

Customise your site

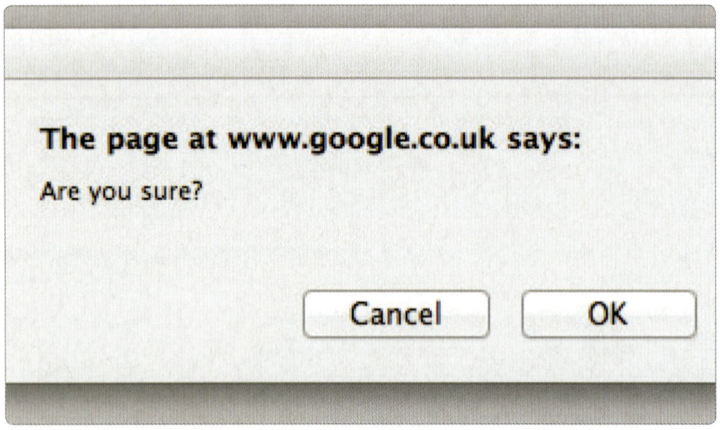

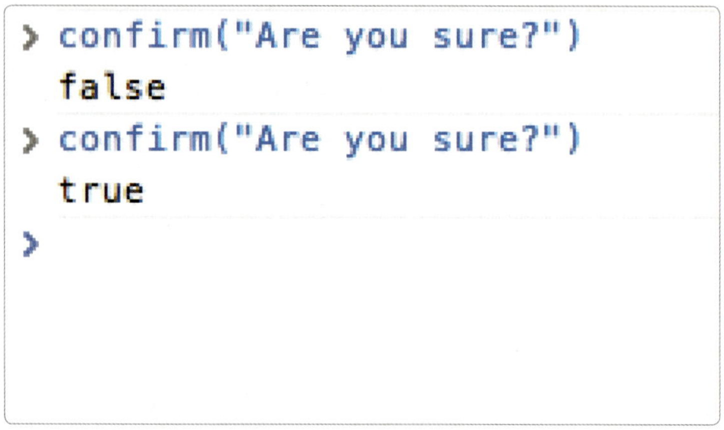

07 More messages

JavaScript returns a result of undefined after you dismiss the alert box. This is because the result of the alert wasn't optional. Some outputs give a choice of response. Try typing confirm("Are you sure?") and pressing Enter.

08 True or false?

If you pressed the Cancel button, JavaScript will have returned a value of false. If you pressed OK, JavaScript returned true. This is useful data that JavaScript is providing – we can tell which button the user pressed!

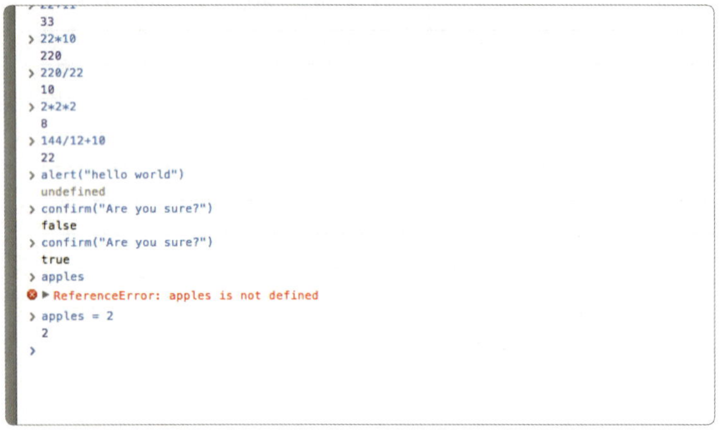

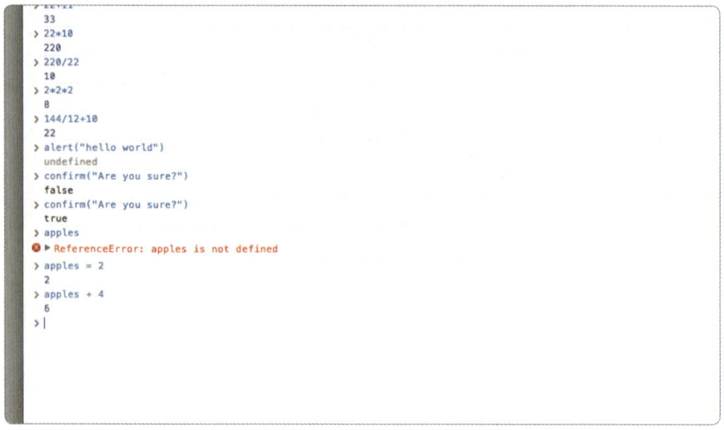

09 Store data

Variables are special areas designed to keep hold of bits of data. Try entering apples = 2 and pressing the Enter key to create a variable called 'apples' with the value of 2 assigned to it.

10 Return the value

Each time you type in the variable name apples from now on, JavaScript will substitute in the value you've stored in it. Try entering the following code and pressing the Enter key to see what happens: apples+4

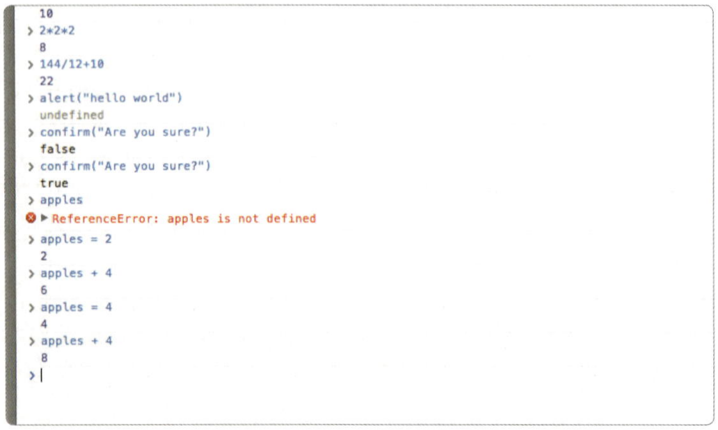

11 Reassigning values

JavaScript returned a value of 6. When you asked it to add apples and 4, it substituted in the value 2 in place of the variable name. You can reassign values. Try entering apples = 4 and pressing Enter. Next, try apples+4 again.

12 Strings and numbers

You can also store strings inside variables. Create a variable 'yourName' and assign your own name to it as the value. Remember that strings must have quote marks around them or you'll get an error message from JavaScript.

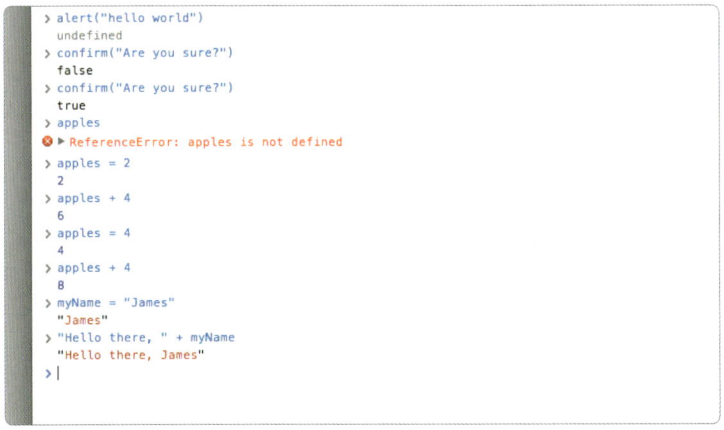

13 Add strings

You can chain two strings together to output a single string. Use the + symbol to join together two strings as follows and press the Enter key when you're done: "Hello there, " + yourName

14 Bringing it together

Now you know about variables, strings and alerts, let's use a special alert that asks the user to input some data – the prompt() method. Enter the following code and press Enter: theirName = prompt("Enter your name");

15 Reacting to input

You've just stored the value of the prompt box in the variable 'theirName'! You can now create an alert that outputs that value, or an alert using a prompt box as the message itself. Try: alert(prompt("Tell me your name"))

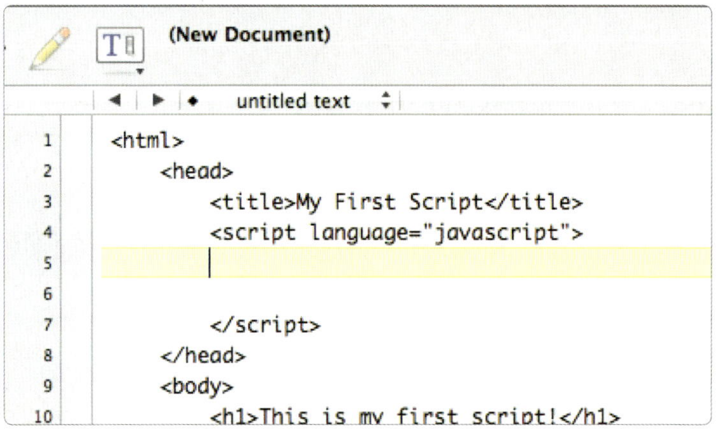

16 Use your learning

You've just learnt the basics of JavaScript and know enough to create an interactive script to include in your page. To add it to an HTML page, you use a <script> tag, which should normally sit inside the <head> section.

17 Create your first script

For scripts inside a document, add a ';' symbol at the end of each instruction. Try creating a script that asks a user for their name, stores the value in a variable, and outputs a message including their name using an alert box.

18 Test your script

Try loading your webpage. All being well, you should see a prompt pop up asking you to enter your name. Once you enter your name, an alert should pop up with the message you entered, along with your name.

Embed a video on your website

We look at embedding compelling movies in your website

Adding a video on your website is crucial nowadays and in many cases almost expected. People want dynamic content and a video can really lift a website, providing great visual impact to any page. Since the days of Web 2.0 – that is, when the web became a caring, sharing community – creating and uploading a video has become much easier. It used to be that you had to do fiddly stuff such as uploading via FTP and ensuring your content had all the right formats. Well, thankfully, those days are over. Send it to YouTube and you can not only let millions admire your work but you can then grab some code and embed the video into your website.

All of the software that you need to run a video is provided for you since you are, in effect, creating a link back to the YouTube website even though the content is playing right there on your own page, complete with all of the stop, rewind, forward and play functionality that you would expect your visitors to be able to enjoy. There are other websites that are also great to stream videos such as Vimeo, but YouTube is a good option that is popular and also ideal for beginners.

"All the software that you need is provided for you since you are creating a link back to YouTube, even though the content is playing on your own page"

Embed a YouTube video

Click a few buttons and obtain a piece of code!

The code

After clicking 'Embed' you'll see this code appear. Hit Ctrl/Cmd+C to copy it, and then paste it into your website code. The code will change depending on your size selection

Alternatives

You don't have to use your own videos; YouTube provides a list of similar videos to the right. You may wish to ask permission to use it and you should credit the author

YouTube URL

This truncated web address could be all you need to copy if you're running a WordPress blog. If you copy and paste the address, it'll do all the embedding work for you

Sizes

YouTube provides you with a few preset sizes of video to embed, but you can also create your own custom size using the text boxes to the right

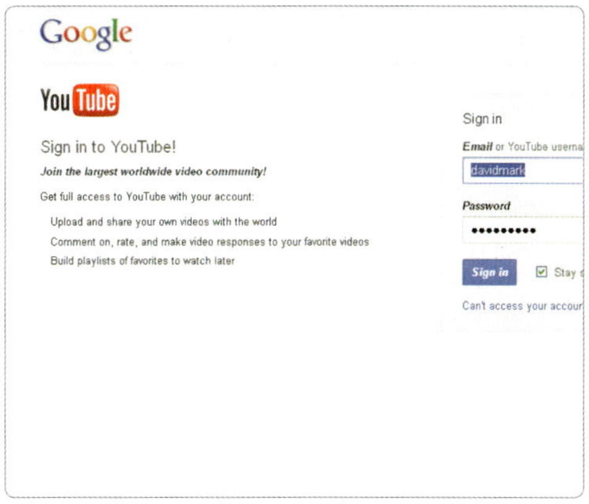

01 Logging in

Log into YouTube using your Google username and password. If you do not have one, click the Sign Up icon and go through the steps.

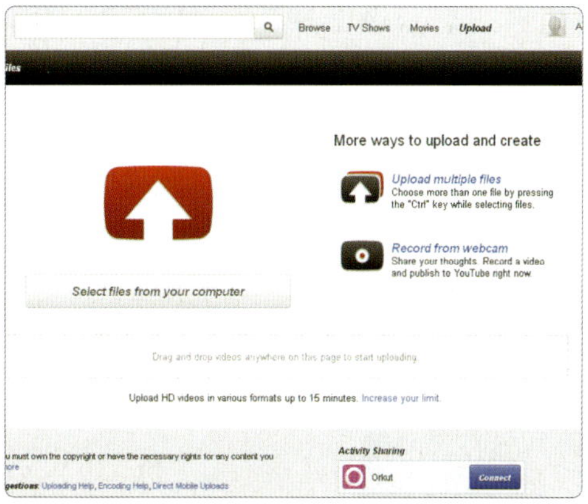

02 Add a video

At the top of the page there is an option to Upload. Click on this. Clicking the white-on-red arrow will allow you to browse for a video.

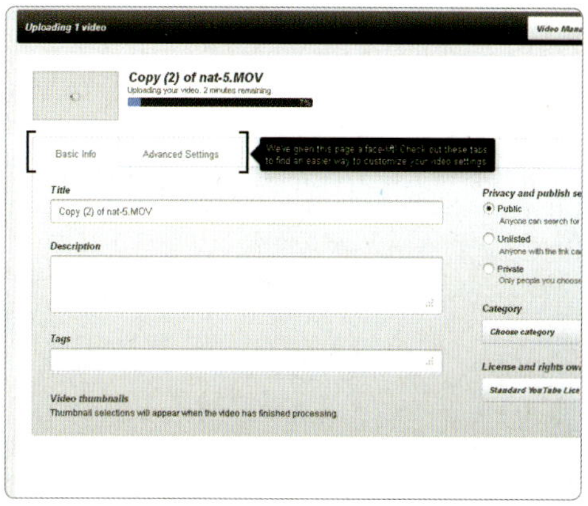

03 Fill in details

Your video will now upload. Click the title and replace the text with a snappier one, write a description, insert tags and choose a thumbnail.

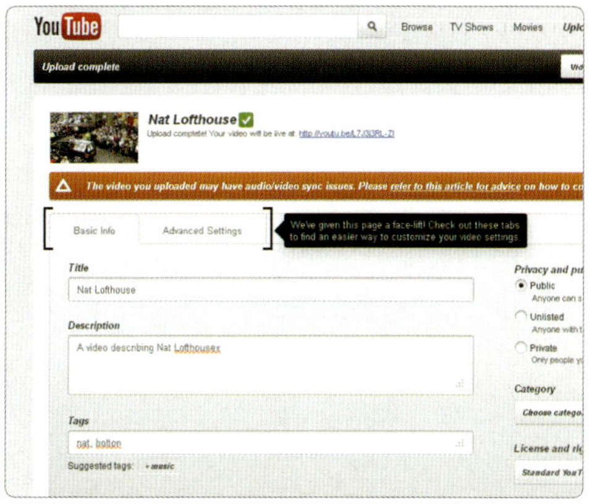

04 Save the video

Changes are automatically saved. The key piece of information is the YouTube link next to your video. This is where your upload will reside.

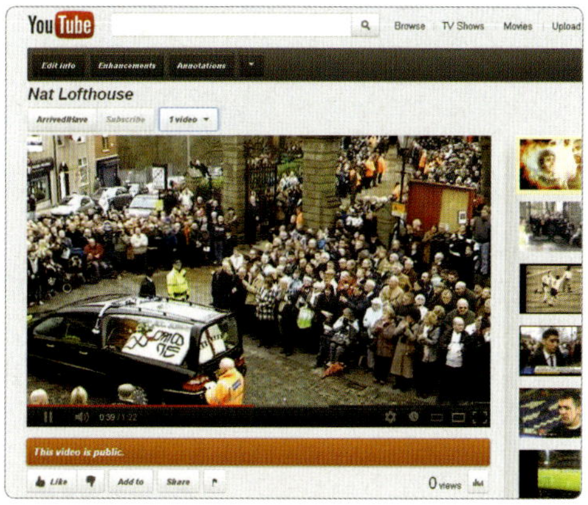

05 View the video

Click on the link from step 4 and view your video. If all is well then it's time to start embedding. You can also use other people's uploaded content.

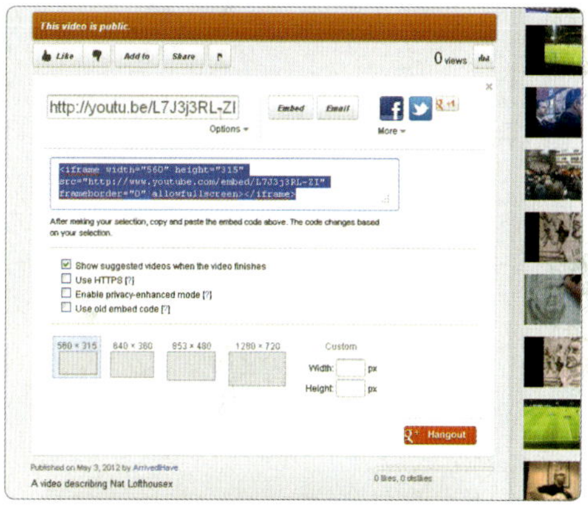

06 Get the code

Underneath the video, you will see a button called Share. Select the Embed button in order to call up some code to make embedding easy.

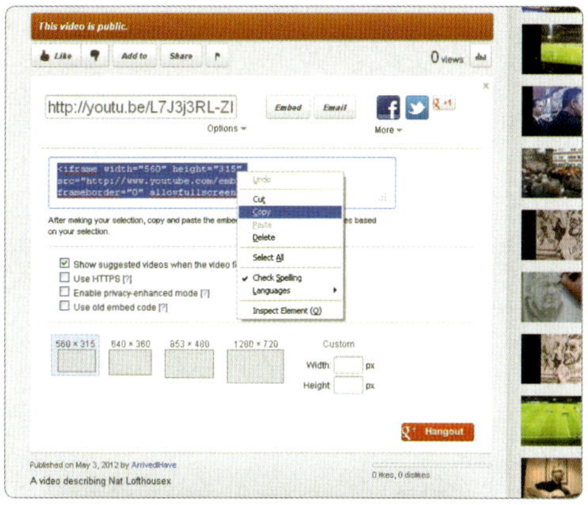

07 Copy and paste

The code starts with <iframe. Highlight this text and Ctrl/right-click. A drop-down menu will appear so scroll down to the Copy option.

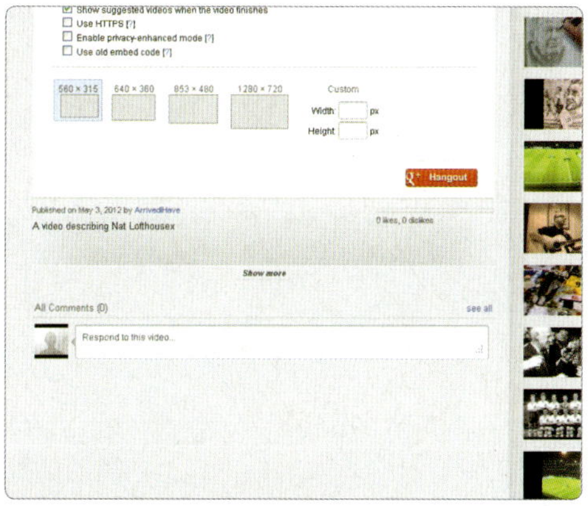

08 Check the size

You may not want to use the default size, so click on one of the size options or input the values. Highlight the code, Ctrl/right-click and Copy.

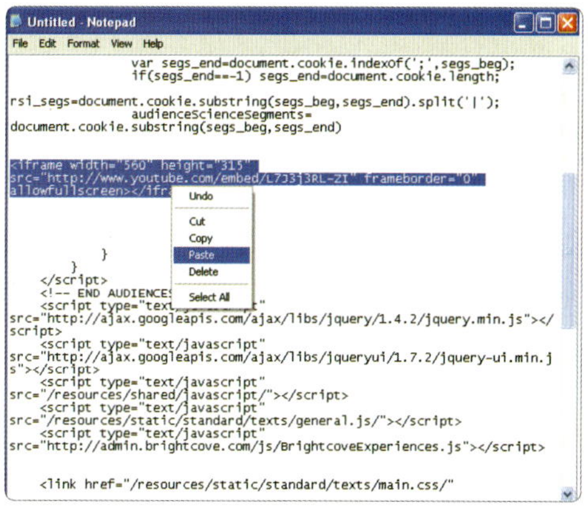

09 Pasting the code

Decide where you wish to place your video in the code. Select Paste, save the changes and upload your file. The video will now be on your site.

Get a map on your website

Use Google to generate embeddable maps for your pages

There are many reasons why you may want to embed a map onto your website. Perhaps you are running a business and you want to let people know exactly where you are based and show them how to get there. Or maybe you are writing about a specific location and you'd like to pinpoint to people the exact spot that you are referring to in relation to other local landmarks.

Having a map is a great way of taking an address and making it even more useful and, thanks to Google, it is very easy to do. Although other mapping services are available, Google Maps is user friendly and feature packed, giving you customisable options that extend to size and looks, from a normal street map to a satellite view.

With only a few clicks, you are able to not only generate your map and position it to your exact liking but also to have Google generate the required HTML code that makes embedding the map easy.

There are some restrictions that are worth bearing in mind. You can't embed Traffic maps and some Maps features such as Street View are not available to you. But it is hard to complain when the process is so straightforward, not to mention free.

> "With only a few clicks Google [can] generate the required HTML code"

Customise your map

Have your map just the way you want it to fit your site

The code
This code changes as you alter the attributes for your map. Just copy and paste this code into your website using the method you usually utilise to build it

Map options
You can click on these buttons to cycle between different map views. It is possible to have a satellite image, for example, or even make use of Google Earth

Map size
Alter the size of your map by using the options here. If you know the exact width and height you want, enter the dimensions in pixels in the number boxes

Zooming
You can zoom in and out on your map in order to precisely get the spot which you wish to embed. Place your cursor on the map and click to move it around

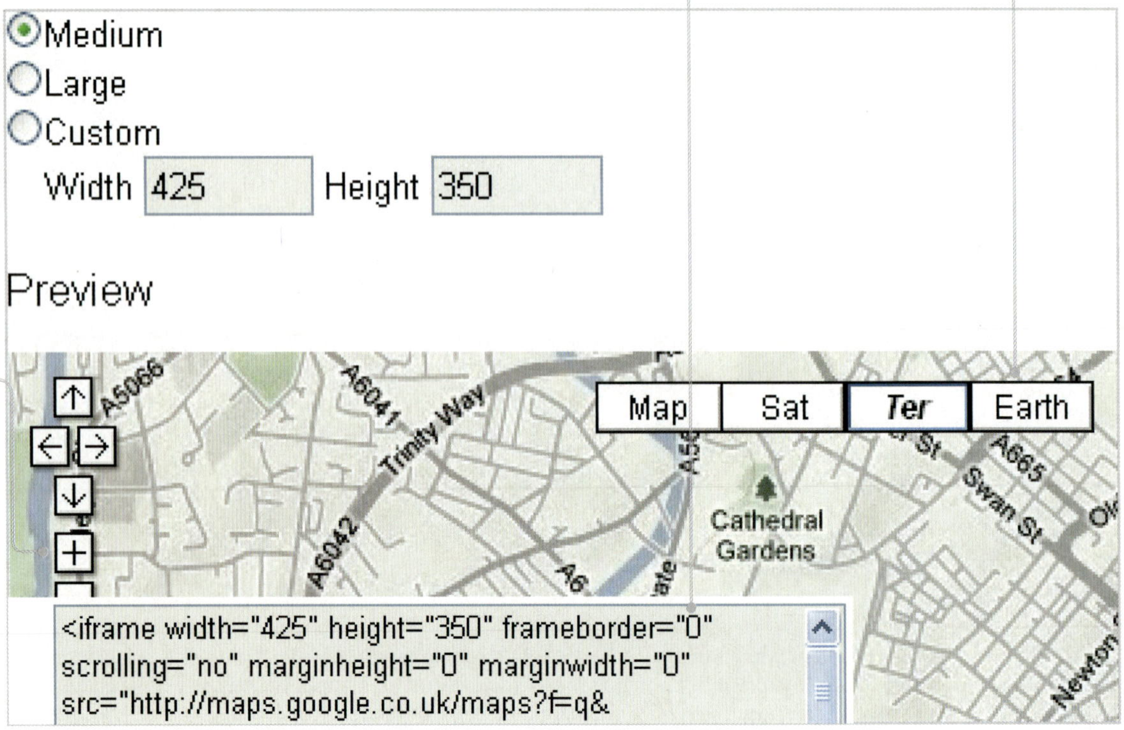

USING WORDPRESS
To embed a map into a WordPress blog, you need only follow the instructions on this page. The generated code can be pasted directly into WordPress's HTML editor which can be accessed by clicking the tab next to Visual. You can switch to Visual to see how it looks. Once you are done, just click on Publish to complete.

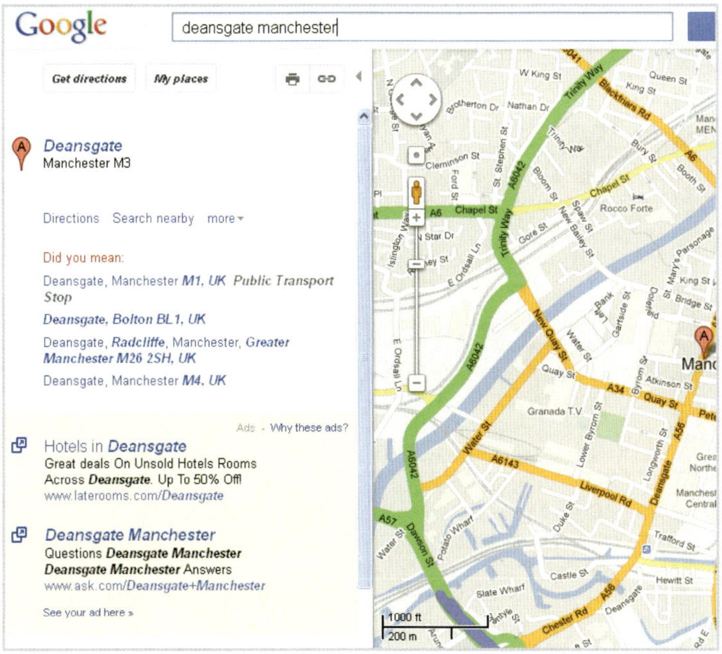

01 Creating a map

You can produce a map using Google's excellent mapping feature, so go to **http://maps.google.co.uk** on your browser. In the address bar at the top, type in the location that you wish to centre your map on (by address, postcode or landmark) and click on Search.

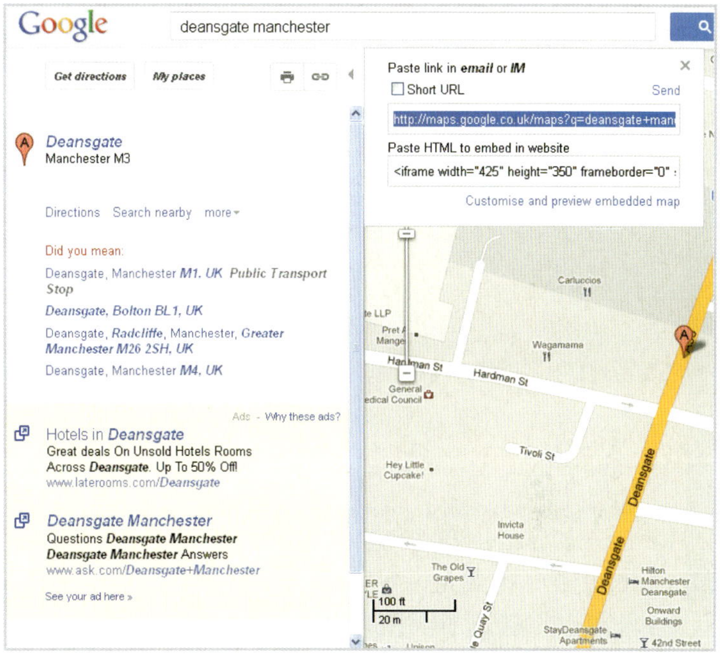

02 Getting the code

Click on the embed icon which looks like two joined circles next to the print option. This will bring up a box which has a direct URL to your map as well as some HTML code. Ctrl/right-click on the HTML code and select Copy. You can now paste this into your website.

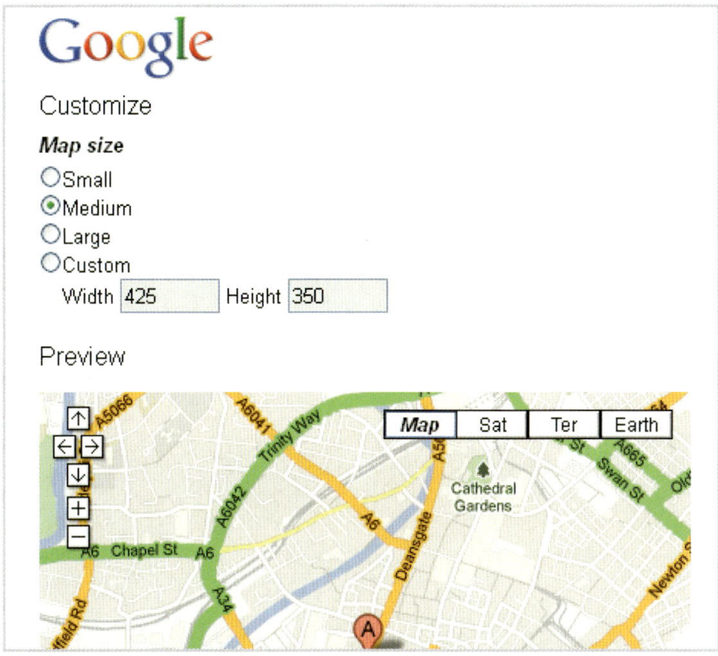

03 Advanced options

By clicking on Customise and Preview Embedded Map you can view some advanced options. The first is the size of the map. You can choose from small, medium or large, or you can customise the width and height by inputting the values in exact pixel numbers.

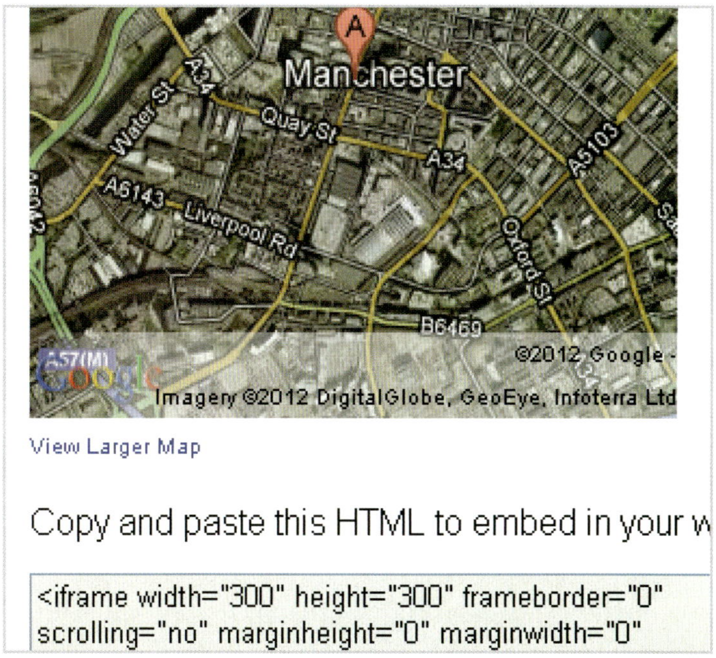

04 Change the view

It is also possible to alter what you see on the map. You can select a normal map or you can choose a satellite view, terrain or earth. When you alter an attribute, the code below alters. When finished, copy, paste and embed the code in your site.

Add links to Facebook

Show images of your fans and add a Like box

You will probably have seen Facebook 'Like' boxes on websites before. They enable visitors to click a single button in order to Like or Recommend a particular article on the site. This will then appear within their Facebook profile, thereby helping to spread the word. It's a very simple way to share content that makes good use of the largest social network on earth.

Having one on your website makes perfect sense and luckily it is easy to make use of a Like button. Facebook has a developer area of its website which gives you a form to fill in. Once you are satisfied with the look of your button, you are then able to generate some code which you can paste into your website using your text/HTML editor of choice.

There are other options too. You could have a simple Send button or a comments form, and there's also a Live Stream to experiment with. But the most effective plug-in is the Like button, and when you are just starting out it's a good one to get to grips with before you move on to more advanced options.

> "You could have a Send button or comments… but the most effective plug-in is the Like button"

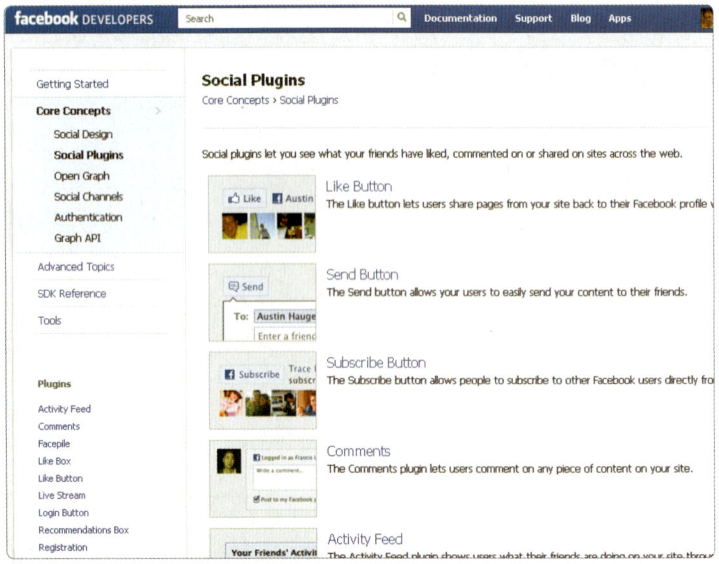

01 Log in to Facebook

Go to **http://developers.facebook.com/docs/plugins** and log in to your account via the Login option in the top-right corner of the screen. This will take you to the social plug-ins section of the Facebook Developers website where you will generate some code.

02 Add a Like button

Click on the Like Button option. Scroll down to Step 1 – Get Like Button Code and fill in the form as required. Add the URL of your webpage and decide if you want a Send button as well, which allows your page to be posted on Facebook.

Understanding the form

We look at the various options available to you when creating a Like button

Colour scheme

You have a choice of making the button light or dark. Dark puts the button on a black background, a good choice if this is the colour of your website's background

Getting the code

Once you have made alterations to the width, chosen whether or not you want it to say Like or Recommend and altered the font, click Get Code

SHOWING FACES

The Like button allows a user to share your content with other friends on Facebook. One of the options available is the ability to Show Faces. When this is ticked, the Facebook profile picture of users who click Like on your website will appear on your page. It's a quick and easy way to encourage interactivity on a more personal level.

The form

You can opt not to have the Send button. Just untick the box. As well as the Standard layout, you can opt to just have the Like button with the number of likes, or rearrange the button into a box

The preview

This section shows how your Like button will look. Here we see that the user can click Like and Send (adding your page on their Facebook profile) and it tells you how many like it

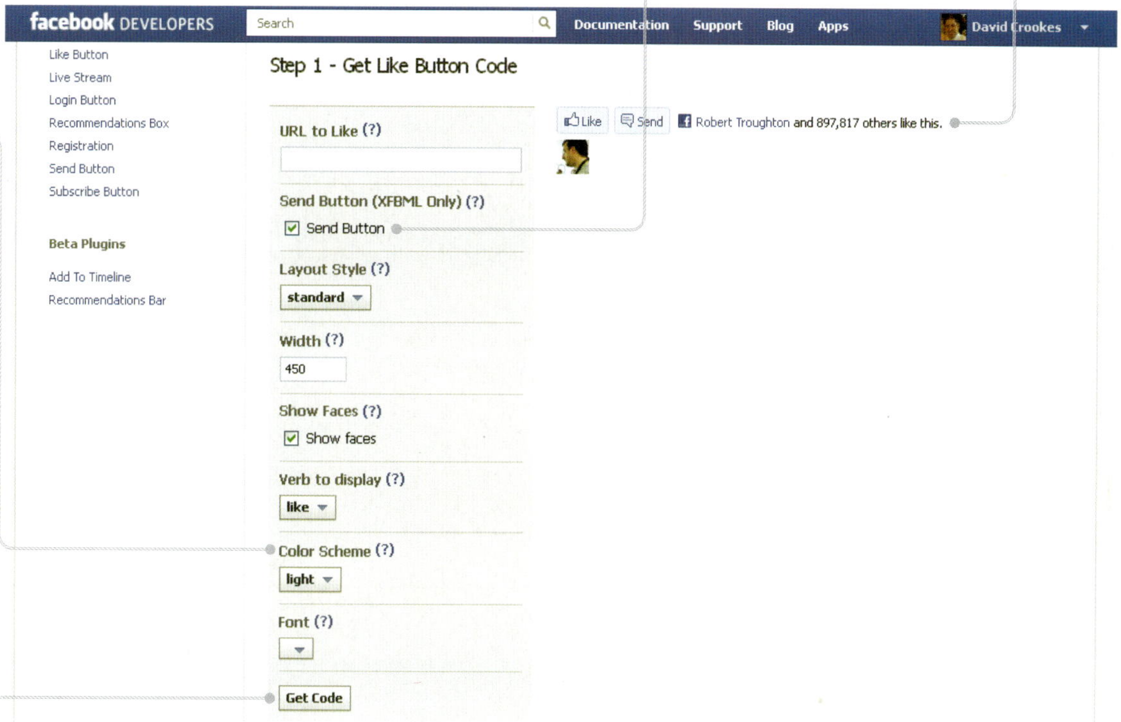

03 Choosing the options

Alter the layout style and width. You can select to have small images of Facebook users posted within the Facebook button. You can also change Like to Recommend and alter the font. Changes can be seen to the right. When finished, click Get Code.

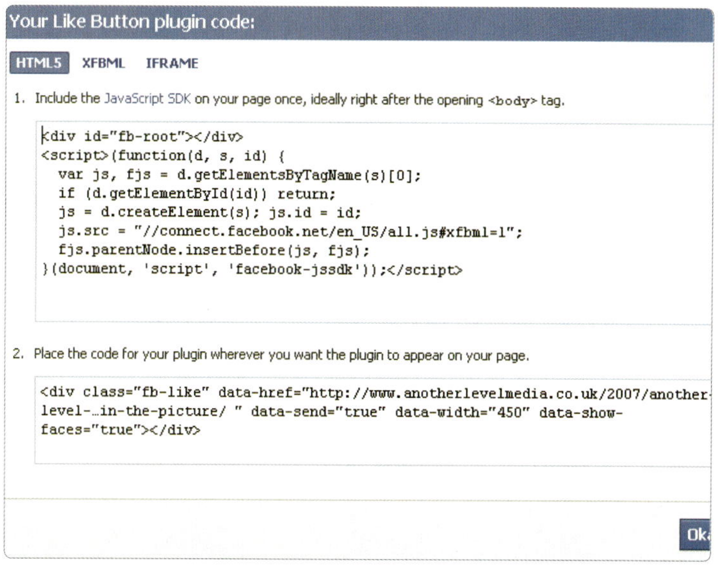

04 Using the code

A window pops up showing three HTML5, XFBML and iFrame codes. Typically HTML5 will be the one for you. Highlight the top box text and copy it. Paste it at the top of your website code. Copy the bottom box text and paste within your code in the required spot.

Add links from your site to Twitter

Display your social media account on your webpage for more followers

Twitter is an important aspect of the web nowadays. It is always a good idea to link from your website to your Twitter account. This way you can build up extra followers and give visitors a flavour of what you are posting about.

It is possible to add buttons to your site and embed interesting tweets. Twitter makes this easy with development tools built into its website. They are rather hidden but are extremely easy to find.

When creating buttons, there is a good deal of flexibility with a wide choice of looks. Some of them make use of your username while others allow you to include hashtags. And you can let people directly link to your individual pages so that any content that you have included can be tweeted.

Code is then generated which can be pasted into your website. The options available for each button mean you can tailor the settings for a bespoke finished result. It is worth playing around with these until you find the perfect link for your website. Each button gives you an example of what it will look like at the end.

> "The options available for each button mean you can tailor the settings for a bespoke finished result"

Integrating Twitter

Make the most of the social networking giant

Embed
You can also embed your own or someone else's tweets with ease. All you need is the HTML code, which you can get by double-clicking a tweet and selecting 'Details'

Twitter button
You can choose from a range of buttons, including ones with a hashtag. We've gone for a 'Follow' so users are one click away from following our tweets from our site

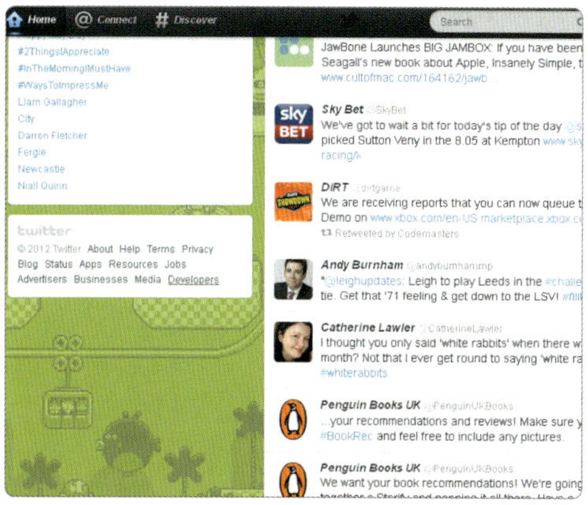

01 Log in to Twitter

Go to **twitter.com** and log in to your account. Click on the Developers link on the left-hand side of the main page to navigate to this site.

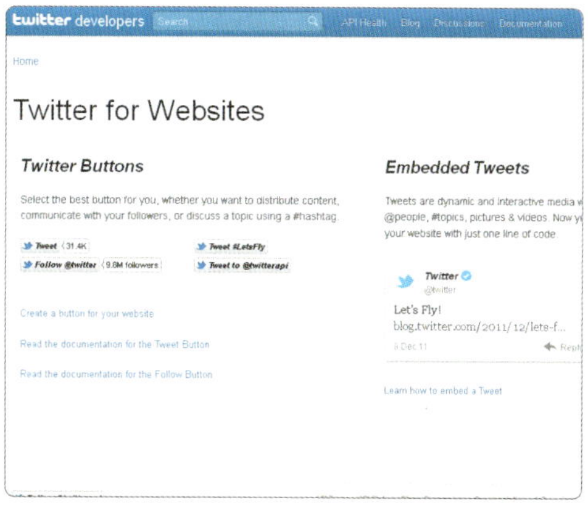

02 Using Twitter Developers

The front page of Twitter Developers has a large box which says 'Add Twitter to Your Website'. The options are Twitter Buttons or Embed Tweets.

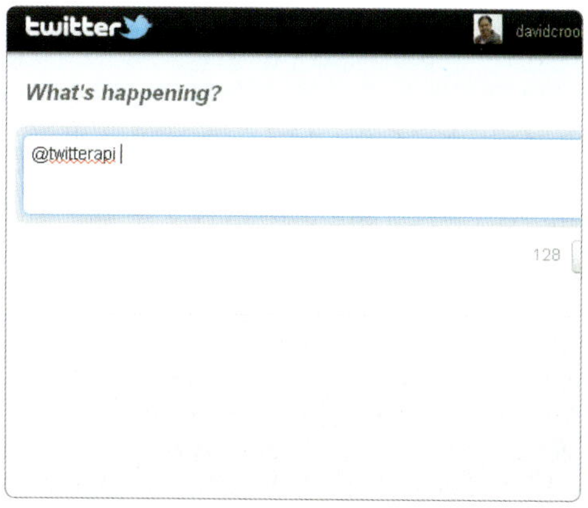

03 Choosing Twitter buttons

If you click on one of the four buttons, you will be shown an example of how it works. For example, Share a Link will let visitors share a specific page.

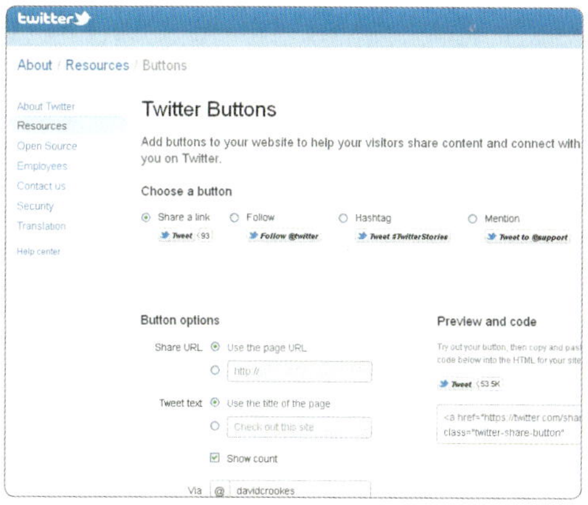

04 Creating a button

Click 'Create a Button for Your Website' and choose one to use. Start with Share a Link. Click the button next to it and pick an option.

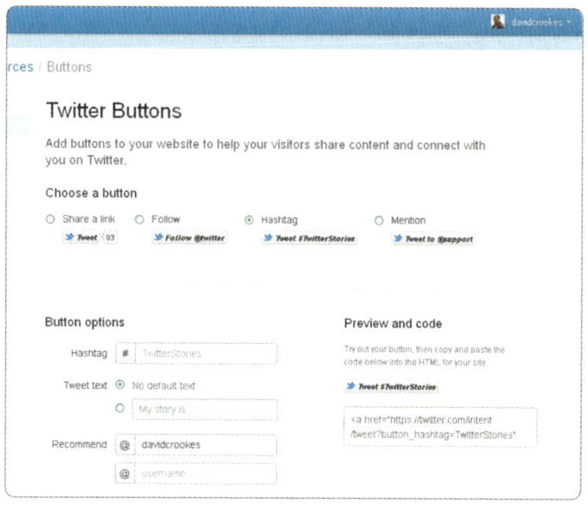

05 More buttons

Under the Follow option, you just need to specify your username. Fill in the various options corresponding to the button that you wish to use.

06 Get button code

To the right of the options, you will see an area called Preview and Code. Beneath this will be the button code you need to copy.

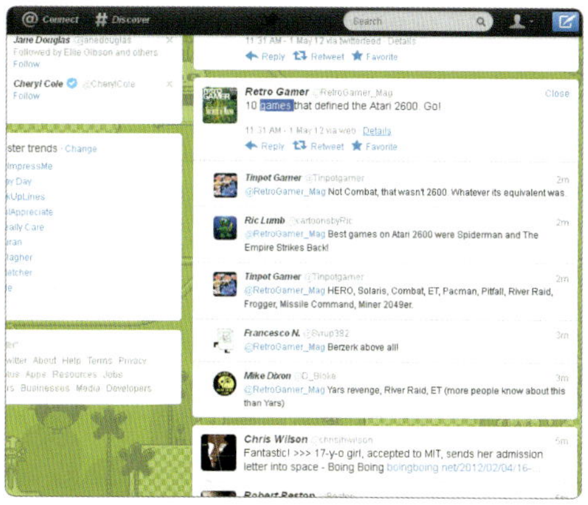

07 Embedding tweets

Go to **twitter.com**, log in and look for a tweet that you want to embed. Double-click on it and look for Details. Click on this word.

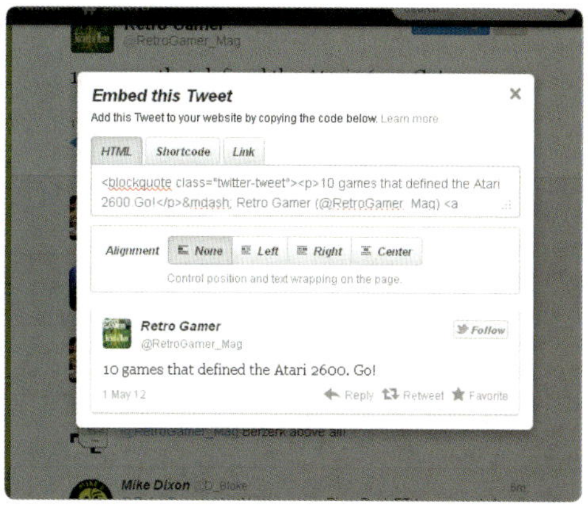

08 Getting embed code

This will show the tweet on its own page with a link to Embed it. Click and a window will appear. Copy the code in the HTML tab.

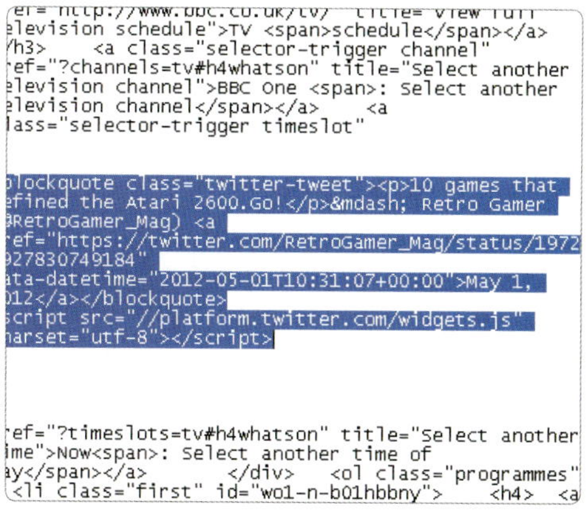

09 Pasting code

Access your site's HTML code and find a suitable position for you new code. Paste it in and when it's published your Twitter link will appear.

Create a web form

Use Wufoo to produce free forms to embed on a page

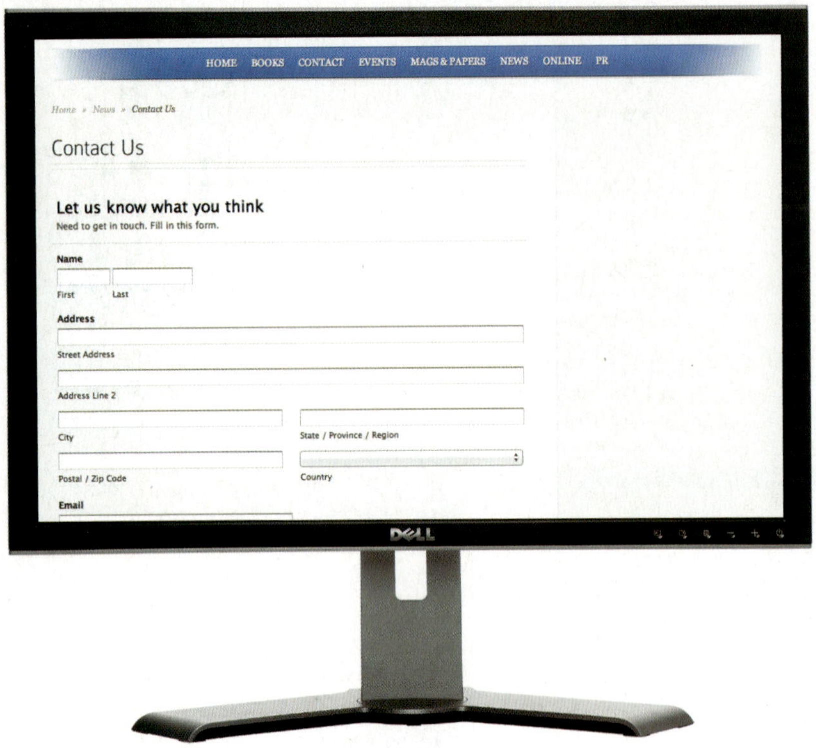

Although you can create a form by coding it in HTML, if you are only looking to produce a small number of forms, it is wise to use a free web-based service to build them. One of the best is Wufoo, which gives you access to many different fields from name and address to input text boxes. Even better, it is possible to then embed this form into your website, creating a seamless experience for your visitor.

With Wufoo, you can alter the names of the text entry fields and play around to ensure the forms work just the way you want them to. If you want to go for a more advanced, bespoke option, you can also click on Themes which enables you to add a logo, include borders and shadows and have buttons. It's much easier to use Wufoo than if you coded it yourself. This is because you would have to produce a contact.php file to process your file data. Wufoo will do that hard work for you.

The forms have a Wufoo Powered stamp at the bottom but this is no great hardship. You can be notified when a form is filled in by text message or email, and you can go back and edit forms whenever you want. It's highly recommended.

"Wufoo gives you access to many different fields, creating a seamless experience"

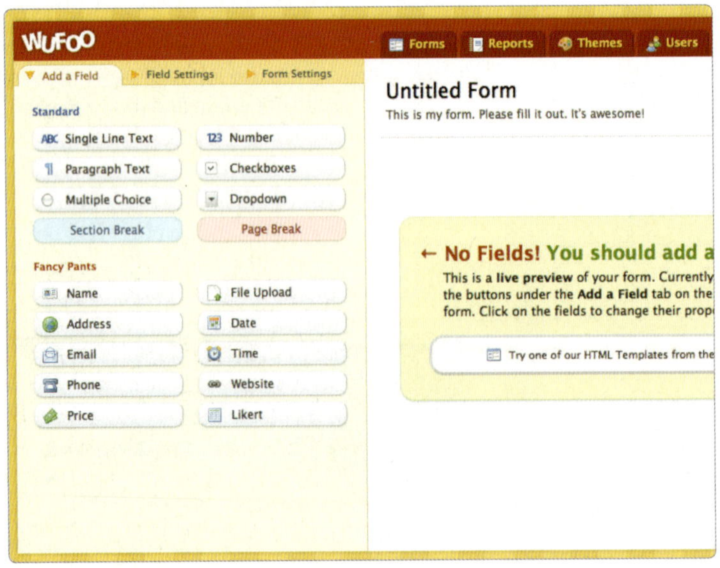

01 Launching Wufoo

Sign up to Wufoo at **wufoo.com** if you haven't done already. The free account allows you to build three forms. Click on New Form. On the right of the screen will be a preview of your form. To the left are the elements which make it up.

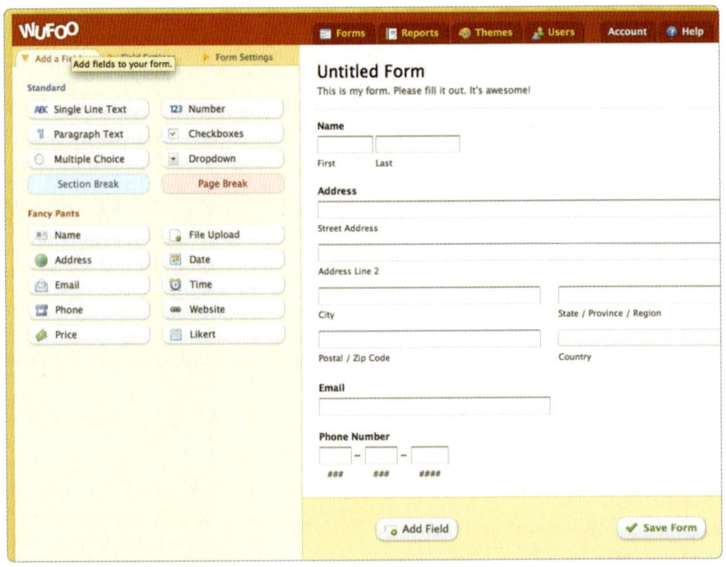

02 Add the fields

We are going to create a basic contact form for our site, so that will include a name, address, email and phone number. Click on the respective buttons on the left of the screen (under the term Fancy Pants). The fields will be added to the right.

The Wufoo interface

We look at how the site makes form building easy

Add a Field

Clicking on the Add a Field option allows you to pull in the fields you want when building your form. Field Settings enables you to further customise your form for each field you enter

Form building

Your form builds and appears in the right-hand pane. Highlight a field to alter it. You can also delete a field by highlighting and clicking on the small red – icon in the bottom right of the box

CAPTCHA

One of the dangers of having a form on your website is that internet bots can pick up on them, fill them with garbage and submit. You then end up with lots of rubbish that hasn't been generated by a human. A Captcha is one of those distorted images that you often get at the end of forms that require you to figure what they are trying to spell. A bot will never get it right so you cut out any spam.

Form Settings

Give your form a name and describe it if you like. This information will appear on your embedded form. You can also alter the text which appears to a visitor after they submit your form. You can even have a Captcha

Notification Settings

Click on Forms, then select Notifications on the line of your new form. You can now specify whether you want to be told via SMS or email when a form is filled in

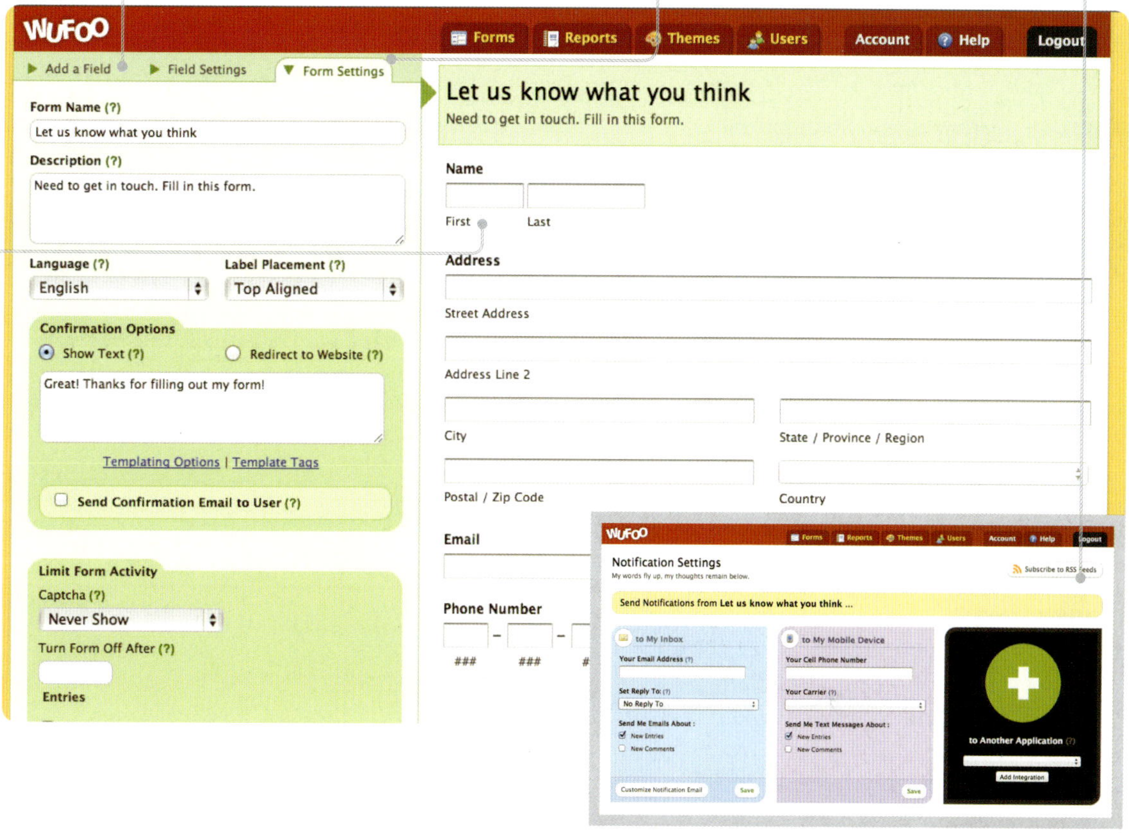

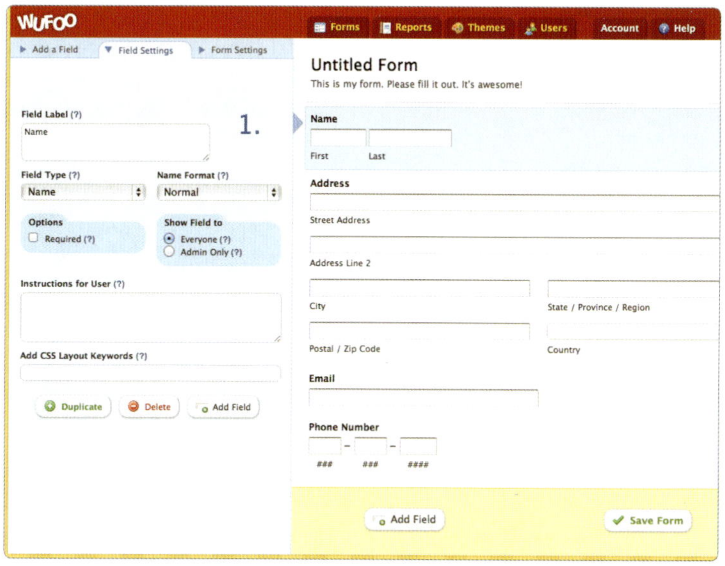

03 Field settings

Click on a field to the right of the screen to see the settings. This enables you to alter the label, select a field type, instructions and so on. Keep building your form, inputting the relevant settings and text, and when you have finished, click Save Form.

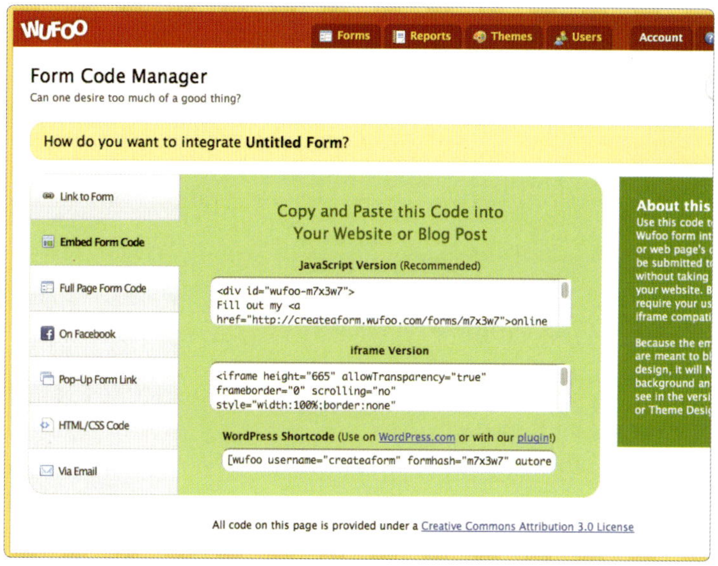

04 Form Manager

Click to go back to the Form Manager. Look along the line of the form you have just created and click the icon for Code. In the Form Code Manager, choose the Embed Form Code. Copy and paste one of the codes into your webpage HTML so it appears on your site.

Add a shopping cart to your site

Allow people to stack goods high and pay for them

There are many ways in which you can sell items online. You could use eBay or Amazon Marketplace. You could sell direct to companies which buy specific items. Or you could go it alone and set up your own store via your personalised website. Maybe you want to be able to control the user experience or perhaps you have just one item for sale and want to centre an entire web offering around that specific product. Whatever you want to do, it is easy to create a shopping cart for your website.

We will be using PayPal for this tutorial. PayPal is an accepted standard for online payment transactions and people are familiar with it. It means you have a solid name behind you and also the higher likelihood that someone will be willing to buy. And, as luck would have it, PayPal offers a very simple way of creating a cart which means people can shop and buy items from you.

All you have to do is create a button. You could have just one, Add to Cart, or you could combine that with another – View Cart. Whatever method, your page will look inviting and professional.

> "PayPal is an accepted standard for online payment transactions"

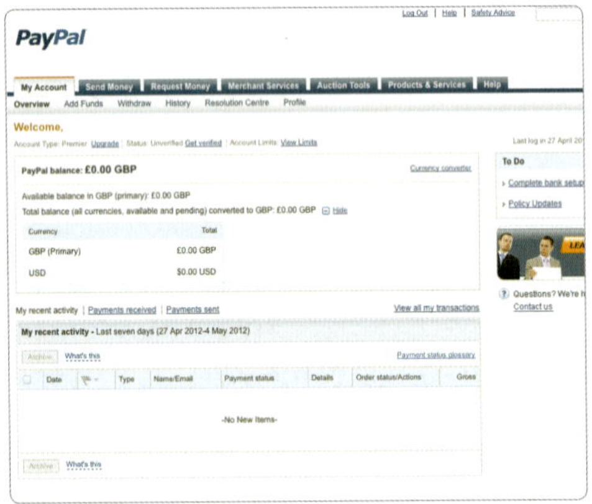

01 Go to PayPal

You will need a Premier or Business PayPal account. When signing up, you can specify a Premier account from the start or upgrade.

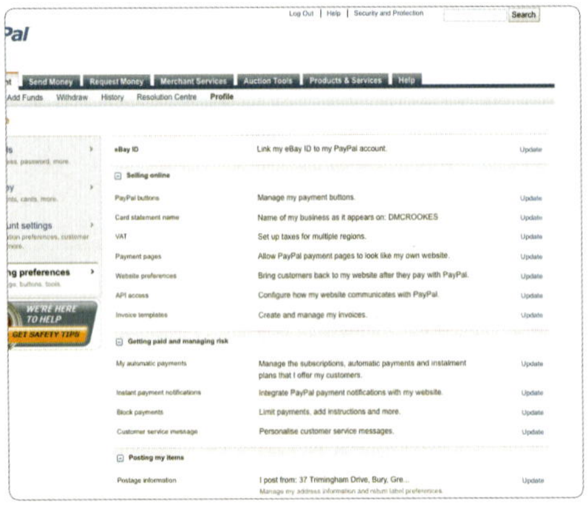

02 Create a button

We are now going to create an Add to Cart button. Click on Profile>My Selling Preferences. Click Update (next to PayPal Buttons).

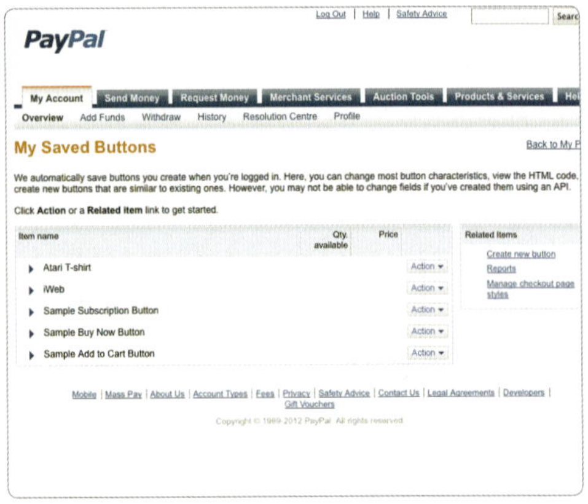

03 My Saved Buttons

You will now be taken to My Saved Buttons. Assuming you have not created any before, click Create New Button under Related Items.

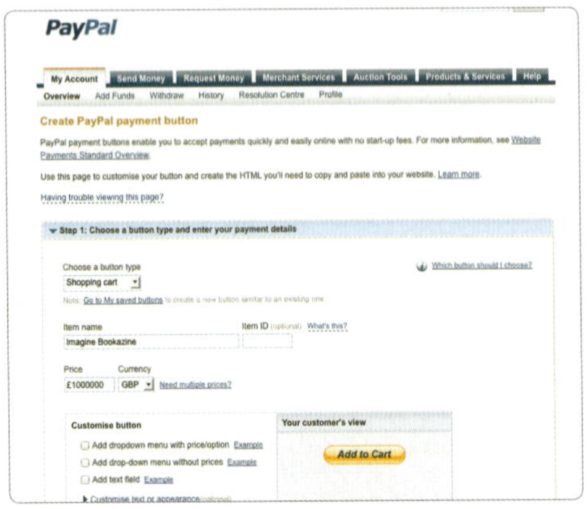

04 Creating a button

On the Create PayPal Payment Button page you will see a series of steps. Ensure the button type is Shopping Cart by using the drop-down menu.

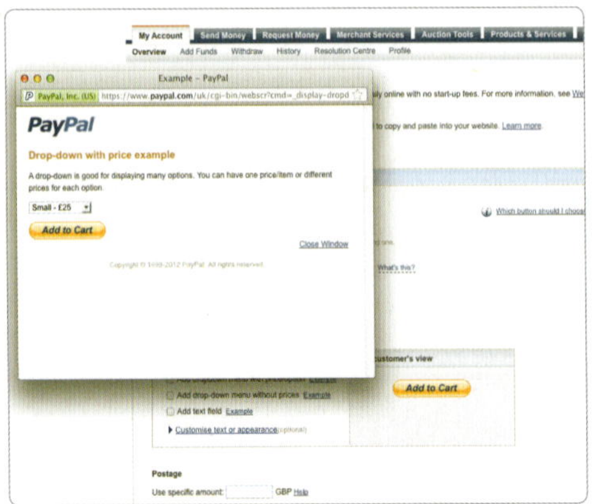

05 Customise your button

Choose one of three customised Add to Cart buttons. Click the examples to see what they are like and what additional functions they offer.

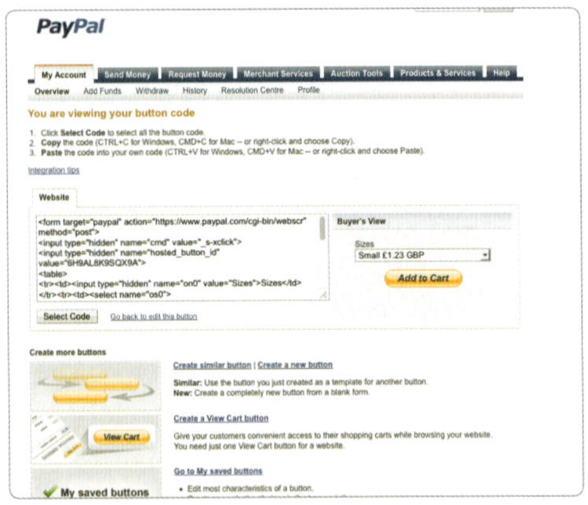

06 Generate the button

You can add postage information or skip straight to the bottom of the screen and click Create Button. This will generate code to copy and paste.

Create a PayPal button

Monetise your site with a little help from HTML

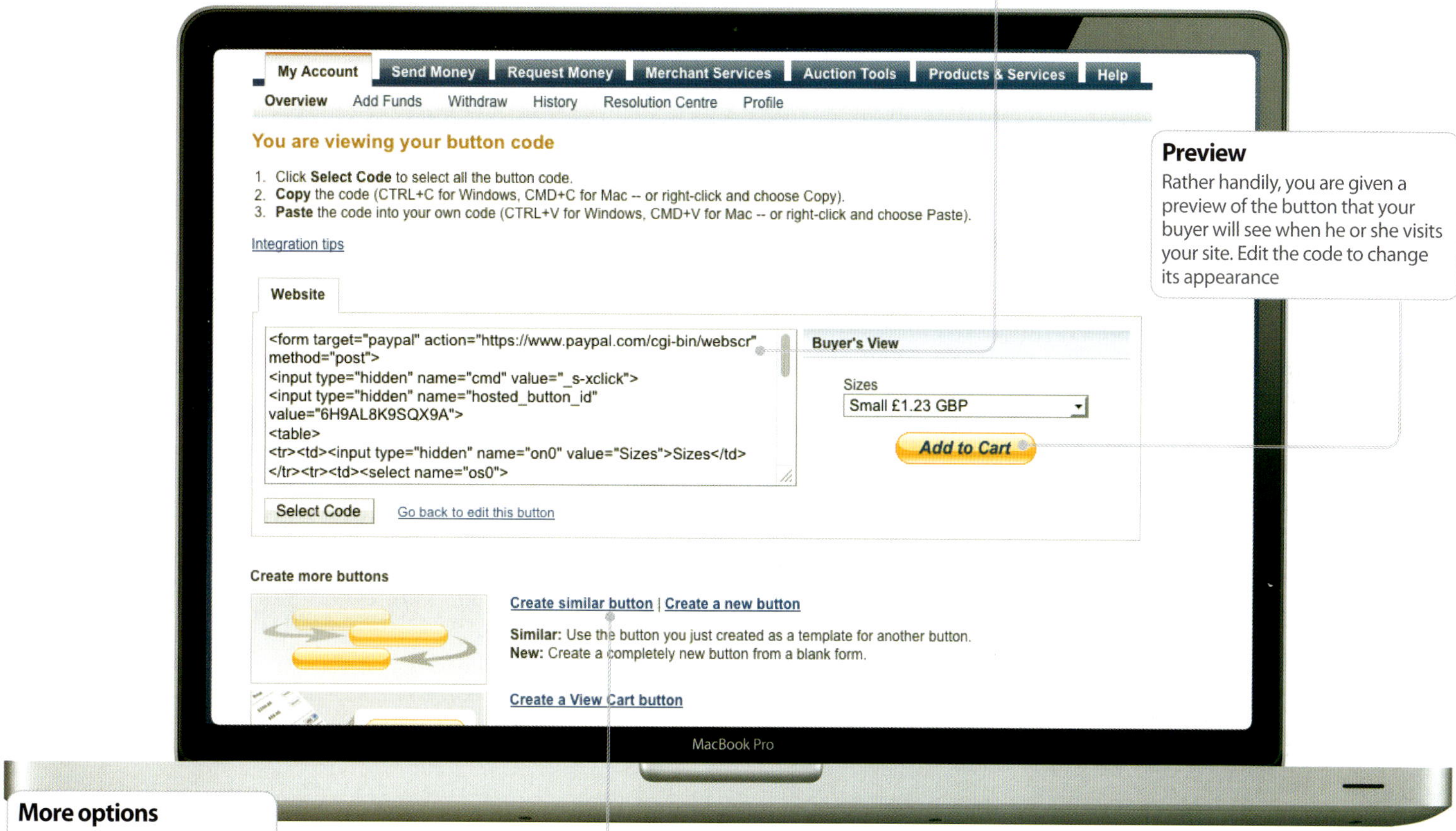

The code
After you've customised your button, you will be presented with this code that you can put into your website. Click 'Go back to edit this button' if you're not happy with it

Preview
Rather handily, you are given a preview of the button that your buyer will see when he or she visits your site. Edit the code to change its appearance

More options
If you don't like the button you're using, just create another button via this link. You can also keep the code and use it as a template for a similar one

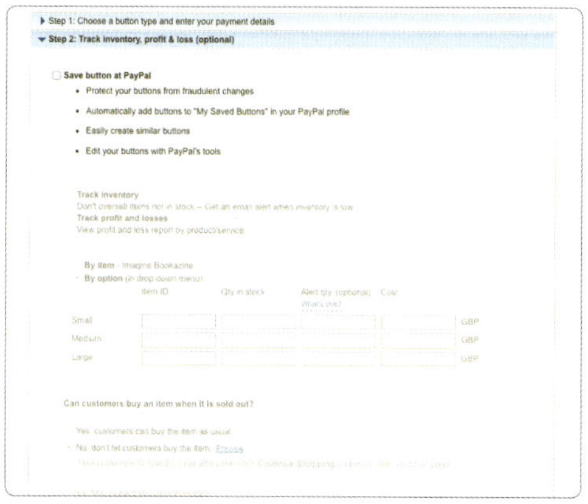

07 View Cart button

You will want a View Cart option as well. Ensure that you go to the Track Inventory and clear the Save Button at PayPal box. Click Create Button.

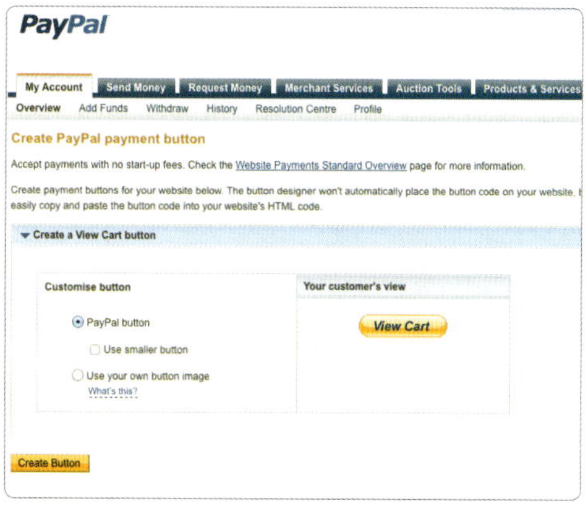

08 Seeing options

Now you will see an option to Create a View Cart button. Unless you want a small button, click Create Button. The process is now complete.

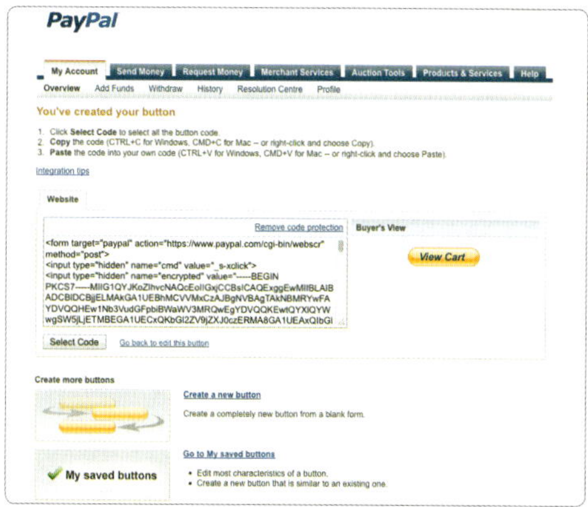

09 Pasting the code

Once again you will be given some code to copy and paste into your website. Now your visitors can add items to their cart, view the cart and buy.

Create a search engine form

Harness the power of Google to scour your own pages

If you have a lot of content on your website, then you will want to make searching through it as painless as possible for your visitor. Having a search engine on your site is the answer and it is not as difficult as you may imagine.

The king of search engines is undoubtedly Google. Not only does it allow you to search through the entire web, but you can also search within websites too. Try it. Go to Google and type site: **www.bbc.co.uk** and tap in a search term. Google will search through the pages of that site alone.

You can harness this power by using Google's custom search engine form. All you have to do is fill in a variety of fields and it will generate code that you can then paste into your website. When visitors fill in the search box, the results for your website will appear. The downside is that this also contains advertisements but it's a small price to pay for such versatility and ease of use.

People are familiar with Google, it's functional and practical, so it's a step in the right direction to make your site more user friendly. It is quick and painless, and there is a whole raft of controllable features at your fingertips.

"The king of search engines is Google and now you can harness its power"

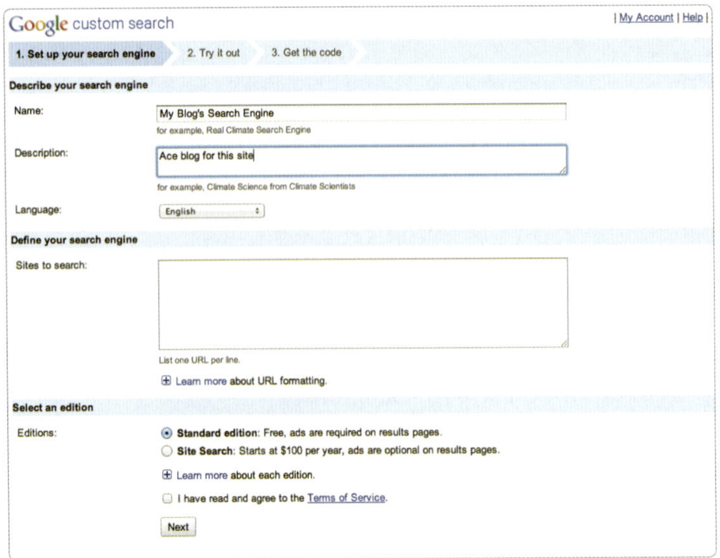

01 Getting started

Go to **www.google.com/cse** and click on the button for Create a Custom Search Engine. You will be presented with a form and a range of options. Fill in the name you want to give your search engine, describe it and choose the language that your visitors will be searching in.

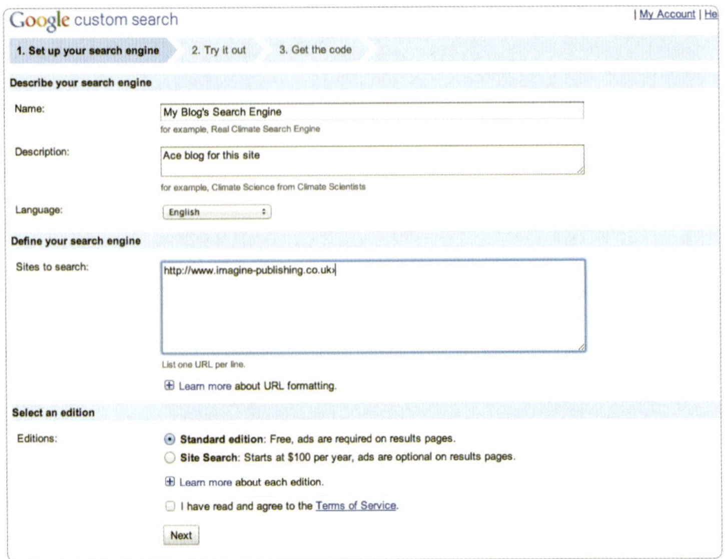

02 Define the engine

Within the box for Sites to Search, type in the name of your website. You do not have to stick to just one URL for this, but instead can list separate URLs on a different line. This is handy if you also want to pull relevant material from another site.

Change the look and feel

After creating a search engine, you can alter the look and feel of it

Choose a style

You can choose from different styles. Clicking on these boxes explains how they are distinct. For example, green sky has a dotted rule separating search results and uses the Trebuchet font

The layout

There are different ways of presenting your search engine results. You can have them on a full-width screen, make it compact, have it over two columns or two pages, just show the results or see a Google-hosted layout

Control panel

Running down the left-hand side of the screen is a list of options. You can alter the basics of your search engine, delve into Google Analytics and alter the way the engine indexes

Preview the search

At the bottom of the screen, you can see a preview of how the results will look for the various options that you go for. Just type in a search term to view them

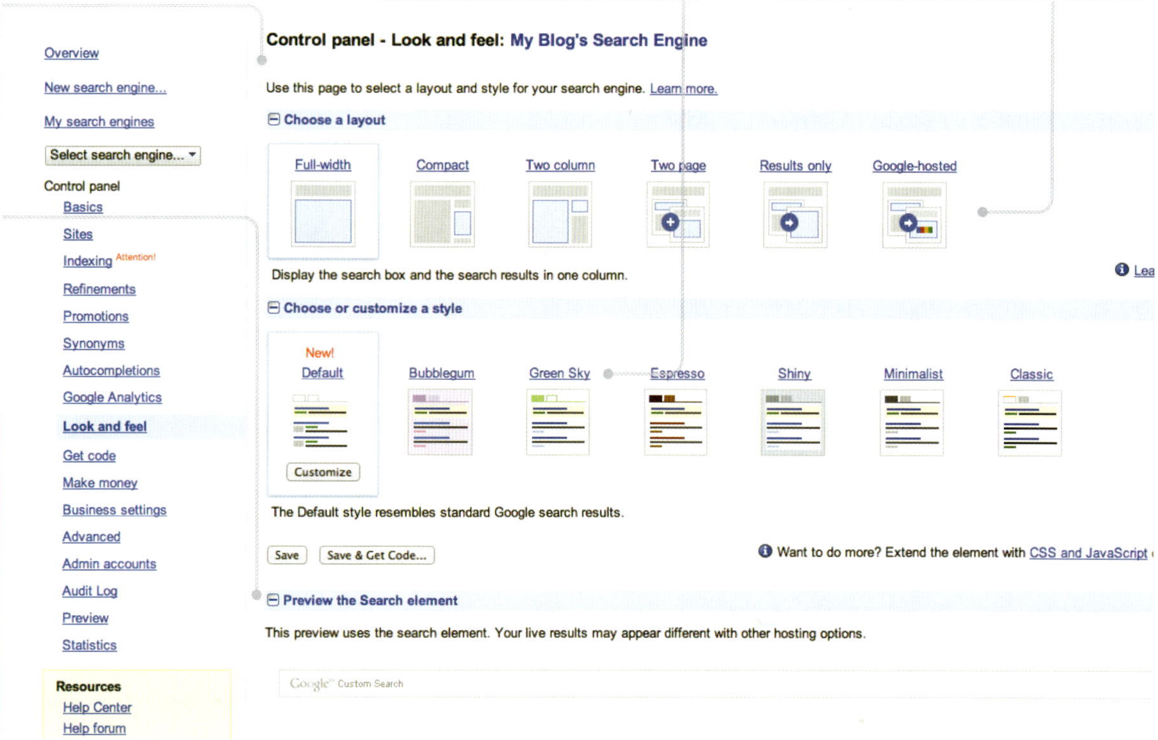

WHY HAVE A SEARCH ENGINE?

The key to a good website is its navigation, so it makes sense to enable people to get around your site with the greatest of ease. A search engine will ensure your site is more useful so that they will be more likely to return. Since it is free to use a search engine such as Google, it would be silly not to take advantage.

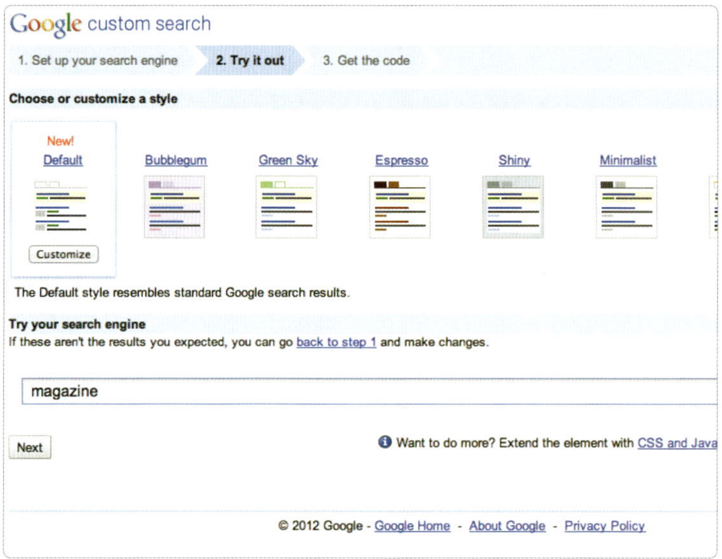

03 Testing the engine

Tick the Standard edition of the free version and agree to the terms of service. Now click Next on your browser. Choose from the search engine types on offer and type a term into the search box. If the results appear correct, hit Next.

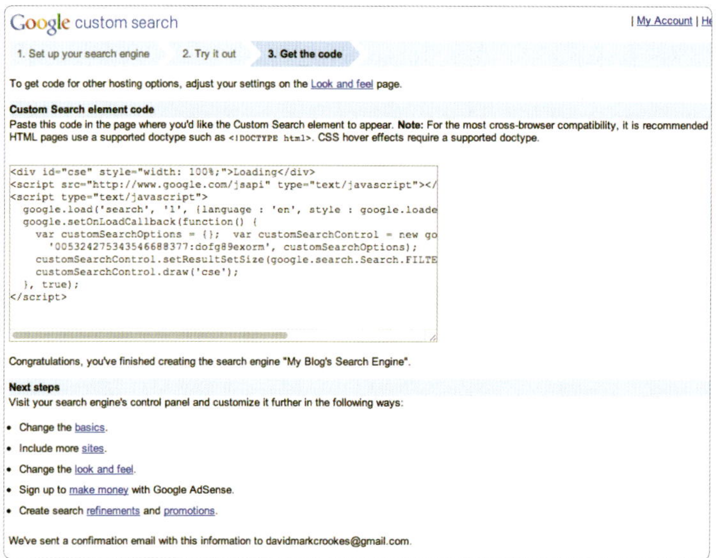

04 Grab the code

You will be presented with some code. Copy and paste the code onto your website in the appropriate spot. Now when you go to your website, you will see it has a Google search box that only searches the pages or sites that you have specified.

Add Google fonts to your site

Bring quality, professional typography to any page with ease

If you have become fed up of using the same fonts over and over again, then it is possible to ditch your Arials and Times New Romans and instead choose something that is fresh and cool. How? Via Google Web Fonts, a brilliant service by the search engine giants that provides any developer with a host of fonts, all of which are perfectly compatible with web browsers ensuring you won't have any issues of people being unable to view your content.

The fonts are pulled not from your own computer or that of the visitor to your site, but from Google. These are then served to your website which is why they can be compatible with all browsers. And it's easy to do, requiring little more than finding the right font and then using a small piece of provided code and embedding it within the existing code of your website with a simple copy and paste.

Of course, if your site is pulling in items from another website, then it could cause some speed issues. Luckily, Google has gone some way to helping with that by showing you how much of a load a particular font will have so that you can assess whether or not it is worth using.

"Ditch your Arials and instead choose something that is fresh"

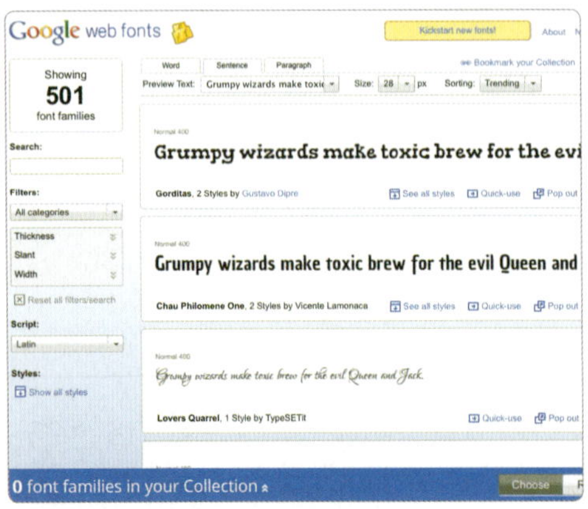

01 Getting started

Go to **www.google.com/webfonts**. You can see how many font families there are to choose from by looking in the top-left corner of the screen.

02 Browse the fonts

Use the scroll bar to the right of the screen to navigate. It is possible to browse every single font family in this way with previews in the boxes.

03 Font weights

Within each box is a number typically preceded by the word Normal. This can make a major difference to the way you approach a font.

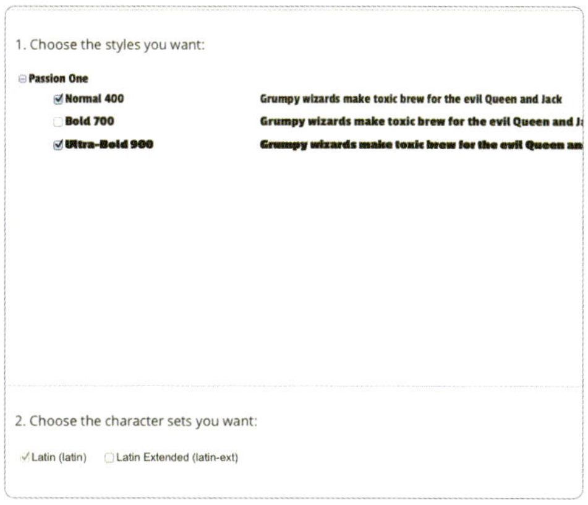

04 How heavy?

So what do these numbers mean? Well, 100 is ultra light and 900 is ultra heavy. Normal is 400 and Bold is 600. Filter out those you don't need.

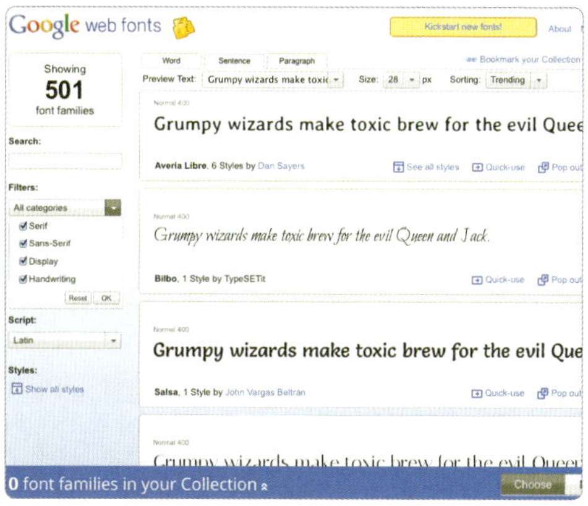

05 Let's search

In the left-hand menu, you can see a set of filters. Click on All Categories and tick if you want Serif, Sans-Serif, Display or Handwriting fonts.

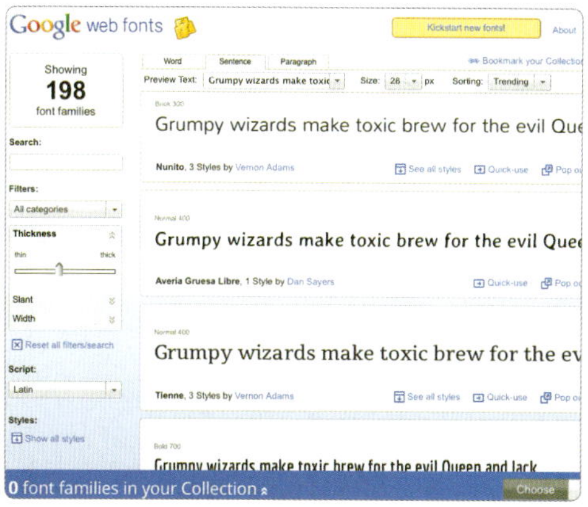

06 Thickness of font

We now want to tell Google how thin or thick we want our fonts. Click on Thickness and move the slider for the right level of weight for your font.

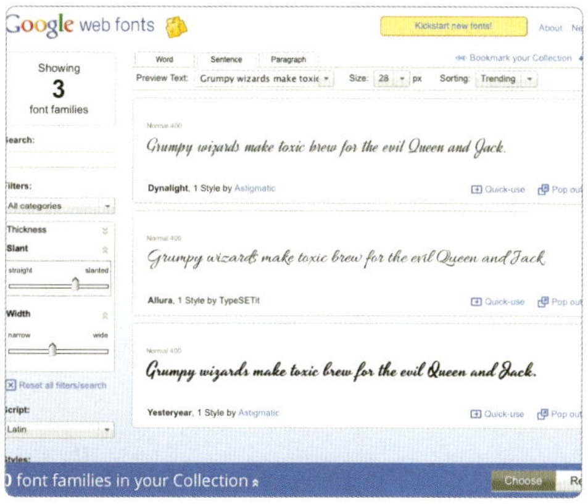

07 Slant and width

These are two more options. Simply move the slider to suit and the results will show on the right. Reset all filters by clicking the X.

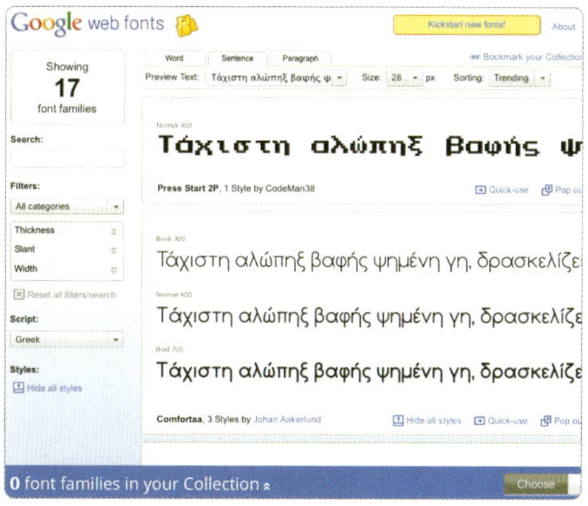

08 Read the script

It is also possible to narrow down your font search according to the script. Latin is best for the English alphabet, but play around a bit.

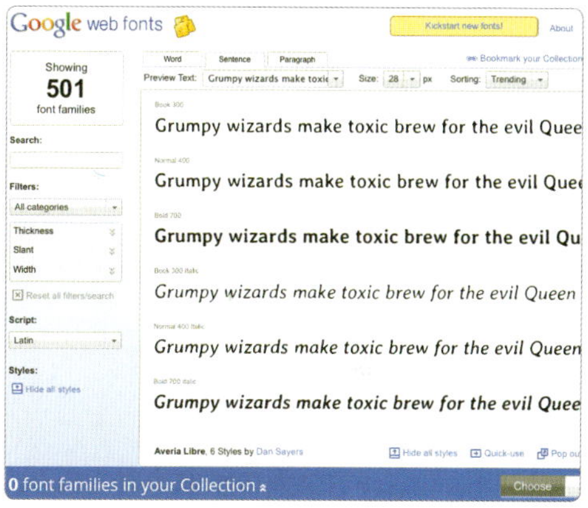

09 Font styles

Under Styles in the left-hand menu it is possible to tell Google whether or not you want to show all of the styles for a given font or hide them.

10 The search results

There are three ways to display the fonts. You can see them as single words, a sentence or a paragraph. Use the tabs to make your choice.

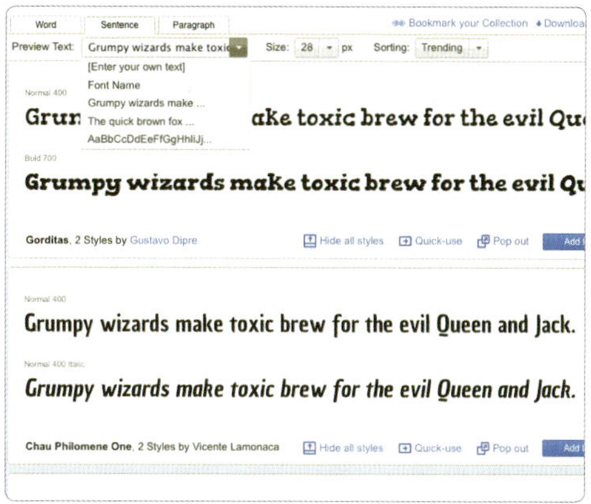

11 Preview text

You can tell Google what text you want displayed. Click the drop-down next to Preview Text and you can have it display different words.

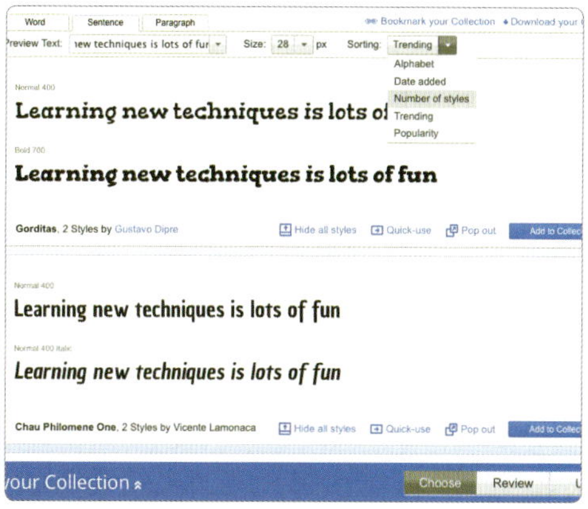

12 And there's more

Change the font size by clicking on the drop-down menu next to Size. You also have a list of options to explore for sorting your font.

Customise your site

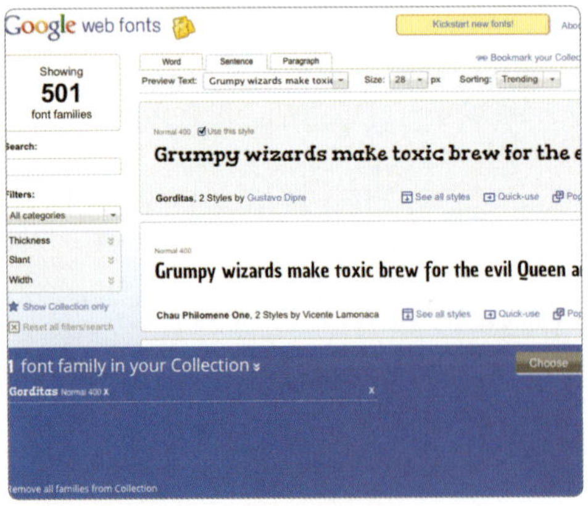

13 Add to collection

If you like a particular font, you can save it. Click Add to Collection and it will appear at the bottom of the screen. Click the X if you want to delete.

14 Pop-out

You can also see the fonts in full by clicking on Pop Out. You get to view the different styles and can also see the letters mapped to the keyboard.

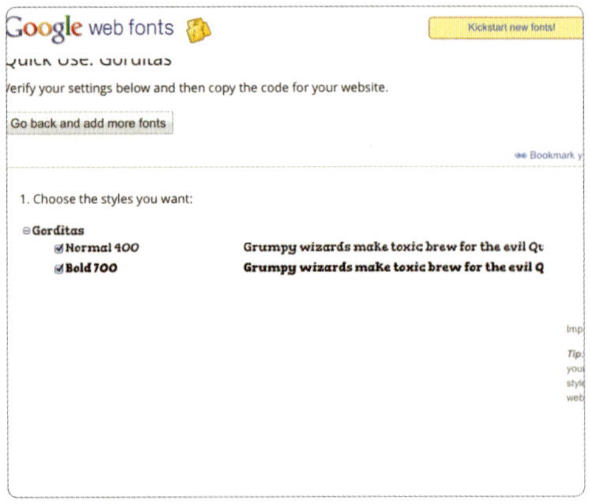

15 Use a font

Now to use the font on your website. Click on Quick Use and tell Google what you want. A meter tells you the impact on your load speed.

16 Make your choice

The first step is to choose the style that you want to use for your font. If there is more than one, you have to put a tick in the relevant box.

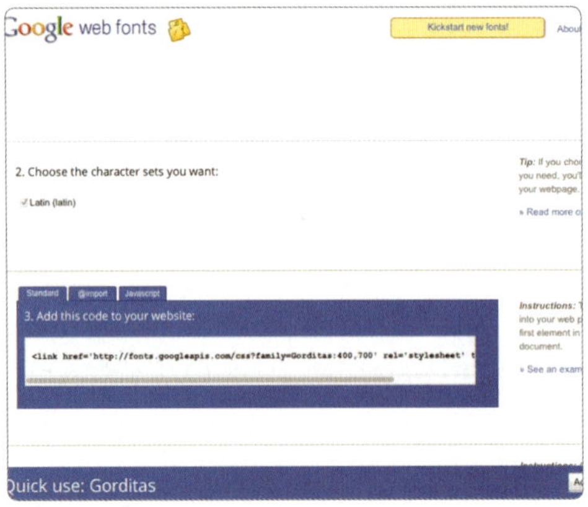

17 Character sets

You will then be asked which character set you want to use. You are ready to grab some code for your site so the font can be used on any page.

18 Adding code

Ctrl/right-click the code and select Copy. This will be embedded within your HTML web page. Open up your text editor with the page you want.

```
<html>
  <head>
    <link rel="stylesheet" type="text/css"
    <style>
      body {
        font-family: 'Tangerine', serif;
        font-size: 48px;
      }
    </style>
  </head>
  <body>
    <div>Making the Web Beautiful!</div>
  </body>
```

19 Paste the code

Paste the code in the <head> part. If you want effects such as bold, add the word bold to the code after the font name: family=Gorditas:bold.

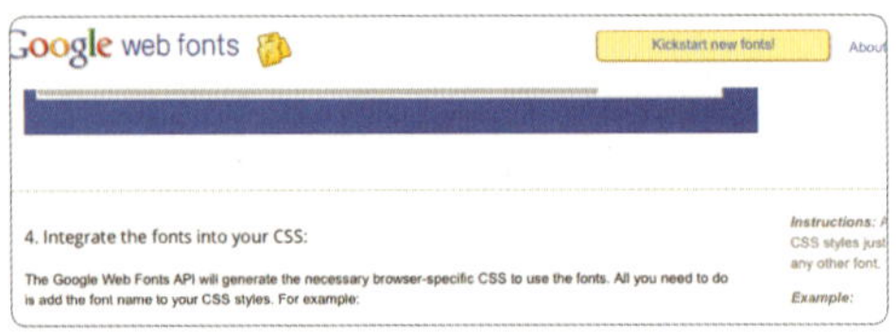

20 CSS code

Copy the code under Integrate the Fonts into then add to your CSS styles by writing in your <head> section:

```
<style>
  body {
    font-family: 'Gorditas', cursive;
    font-size: 48px;
  }
</style>
```

21 And that's it

Now test your website. It will contain the font that you chose. You can also add some styles. Such as text-shadow: 4px 4px 4px #aaa for a shadow.

The interface

Become familiar with the workings of Google Fonts

Search

If you know the name of the font that you want you can go straight to it by inserting its name into the search box on the Web Font main page

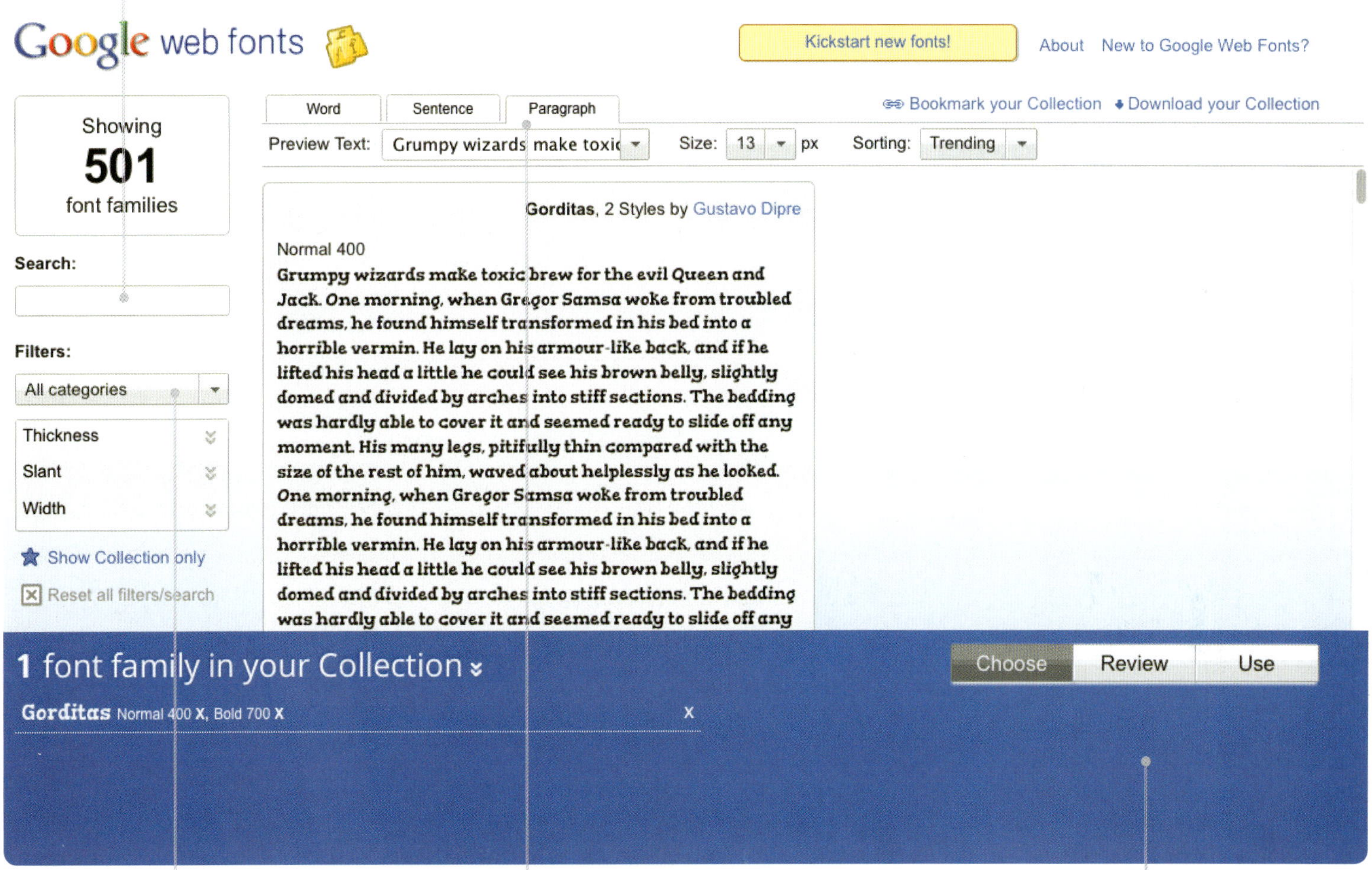

Filters

You can narrow down your search until you get the exact kind of font that you are after from the hundreds that are on display, and you can reset these at any time

The tabs

You can choose from a single word, sentence or paragraph when deciding how you want your search results to display on the webpage

The view

All of your text is displayed in the main section of the website with all fonts that you have chosen placed in the blue box at the bottom

Google Fonts alternatives

Typekit

Adobe's Typekit operates with a subscription model, but does allow free access to its Trial Library. Subscriptions range from $24.99-$99.99 (approx £15-£60) a year.

WebInk

WebInk's stylish web font service also features a subscription model with a free option, and its pricing ranges from $20-$120 (approx £12-75) per year.

FontSquirrel

The strangely named FontSquirrel offers web fonts that are 100% free for commercial use, like Google Fonts. Its layout is fantastic and the site is easy to use.

FontDeck

If you're looking for a more professional option, then try FontDeck. You only pay for the fonts you need, when you need them, with a typical price of $7.50 (approx £5) per font.

Browse

If you can't find any fonts you like in the other sites, just try a quick Google search for 'Free web fonts' and you may be surprised at how many sites turn up!

Produce an image slider

Make a visual impact using a graphical slider

If you want to make a major visual statement on your website, then a slider is an ideal choice for displaying information. It allows you to display some bold imagery and it also means you can flag up some of the content within your website. You could have, for example, a large image of yourself on holiday pointing to more holiday snaps within your site. It is a far better way of drawing attention to features on your site than text could alone.

A typical slider will span the entire width of your website. Images, therefore, have to be chosen for their visual impact. For this tutorial we are using a service called WOW Slider. It is free to use for anyone producing a site for themselves or for charity. Indeed, as long as you don't make a profit, you are fine to use the slider without payment, and you can read its terms on the site **http://wowslider.com**.

All of the slider's content is controlled via an app which can be downloaded for both PC or Apple Mac computers. It's an intuitive program, the only downside being that it doesn't just generate some code that you can simply embed into your site's script. To get this code, you have to create an HTML file using a text editor (just save your document with the .html suffix) and then view the code which you can do via most web browsers.

"A slider is the ideal choice for displaying information and bold imagery"

Working with images

Ensure the images you use for the slider are perfect

Image size
Change the image size using the drop-down box. If you don't want the picture to stretch or become distorted, ensure you tick the box for Preserve Aspect Ratio. You can opt to stretch small images, though

Templates galore
To make life easier and to ensure some great professional effects, choose a template to suit you from the many on offer. Each has a preview so you can check out the ones that are best for your page

Choose the quality
The slider lets you alter the quality of the image. The better the quality, the more bandwidth it would take up and this could have an effect on the fluidity of your slider

Alter the slider
Choose a transition effect to see a preview of it, alter the delay between slides and the effect duration. You can watermark images to prevent them from being stolen and you can choose the text to display within it

TRANSITIONS
A transition is the effect that takes place when an image enters the slider. There are many different types. You could have it so that there is a blur between one image and another or you could have the pictures fly in. There is no right or wrong transition. It's all about preference and what suits your site.

01 Download the app

You can download the WOW Slider app for free by going to **http://wowslider.com**. Install the app by following the steps.

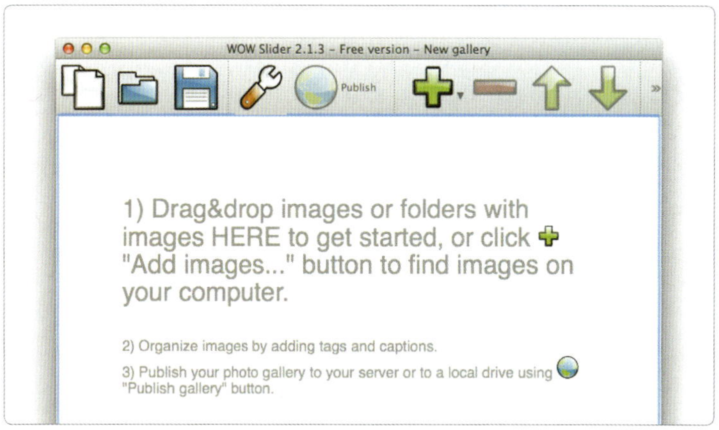

02 Add the fields

Open WOW Slider. There are two ways to add an image. You can click on the + symbol or you can drag and drop pictures into the main window.

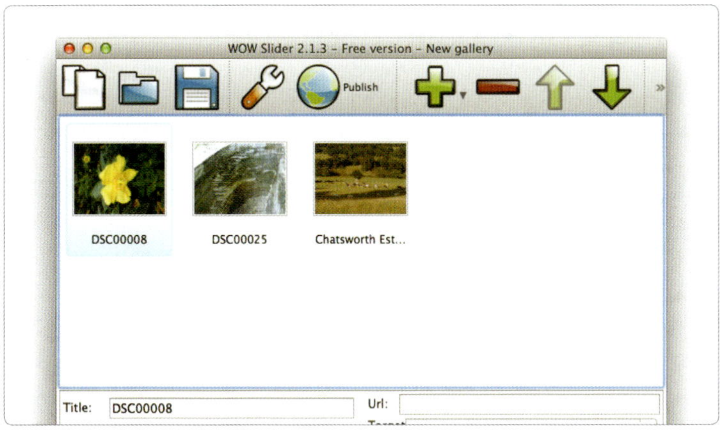

03 Include the URLs

Click on an image and you will see information about it. Fill in the URL – this is the address to send people when they click on your slider image.

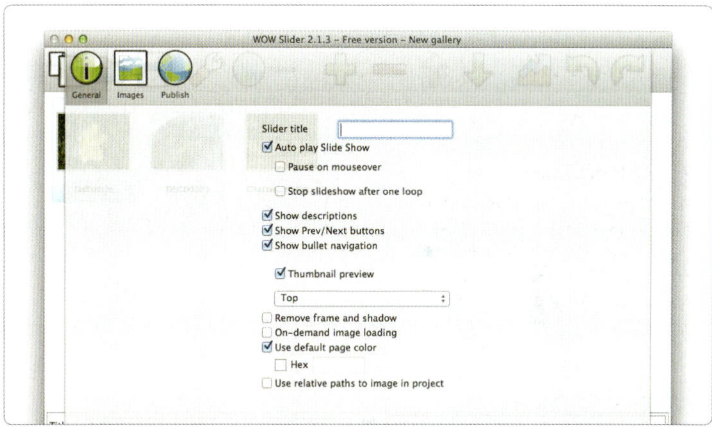

04 Slider options

Click on the Spanner icon and choose if you want the slider to auto-play and whether descriptions, previous and next buttons should show.

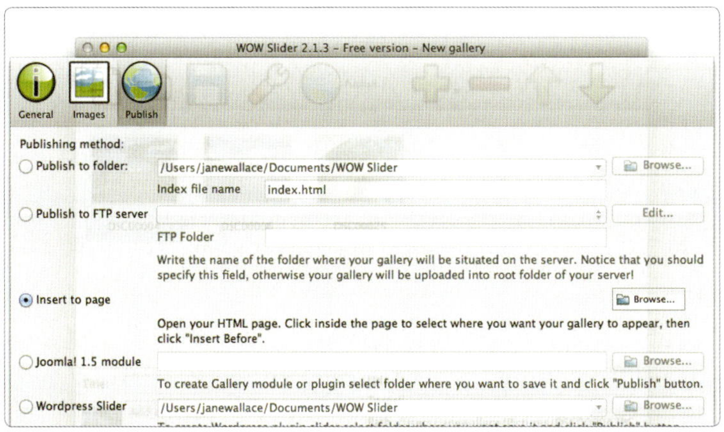

05 Publish the slider

Click on the Publish icon. To embed it, click Insert to Page. Create a blank text document, save it as an HTML file and then open this.

06 Pasting the code

Select Insert Before then copy all the WOW Slider code from the HEAD and BODY tag. Paste them into the <head> and <body> of your website's code.

Create email newsletters and let people subscribe

Creating a newsletter script for your site need not be hard with a little help from MailChimp

In order to promote your website, you may want to consider producing an email newsletter. These are sent out to subscribers, keeping them up to date with the latest additions to your webpages. The idea is that it keeps driving traffic and shows that you are still up and running.

In order to be effective, you will want to add a newsletter script to your webpage. This will produce a form into which people can insert their email address to sign up for your regular updates. Once subscribed, they will automatically receive your newsletter every time you produce it. It can also be a good idea to have an Unsubscribe button somewhere on your website, maybe in the About Us section. They are more likely to try it out if they know they can leave.

The easiest way to set up a newsletter script is via MailChimp. Although the service can charge, if you have fewer than 2,000 subscribers and don't send more than 12,000 emails each month, there is no charge at all. You don't need to input any payment details either to sign up which is a plus. MailChimp is an easy app to use and it is all done online with menus and wizards, ensuring you will be up and running in next to no time.

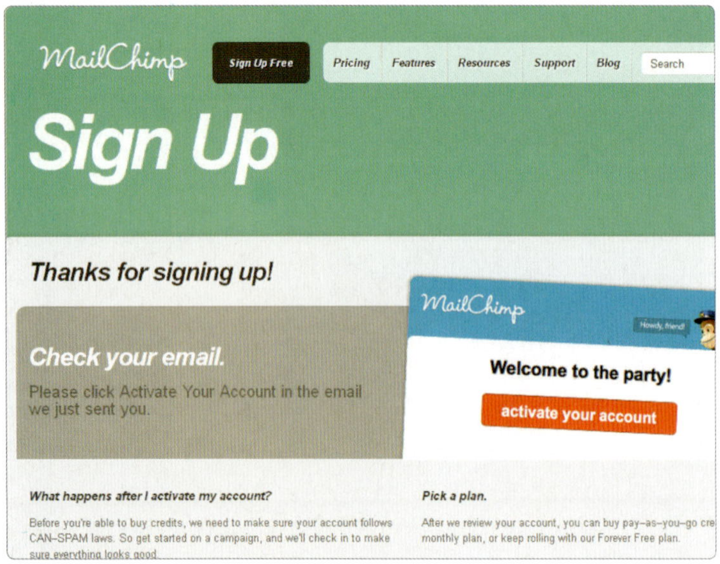

01 Sign up to MailChimp

Go to **http://mailchimp.com** and click the Sign Up Free button. Fill in your email, username and password where prompted and you'll then be sent an email with a link. Click this to activate your account. Complete the signup with your name, address and website details.

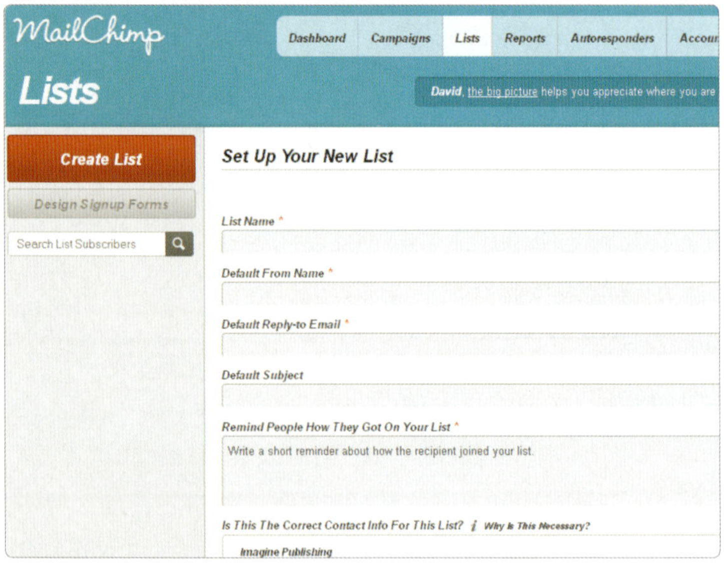

02 Create a list

The first thing you need to do to get your newsletter up and running is to create a list into which the subscriber details will be inserted. Give it a name, say who you want the emails to come from, give a reply address and a default email subject.

The design interface

How to design and build your form

Signup Form

Click the Signup Form drop-down menu and you will see many other different types of forms that you can use for your sign up process. These include Unsubscribe options and confirmation replies

Email address

The only required box – denoted by an *– is the email field. This is because you need to know where the email with your newsletter is going to be sent

CAMPAIGN BUILDER

MailChimp has a Campaign Builder option which enables you to create newsletters that can then be sent out to the list of your choice. As people subscribe to your newsletter, they will be added to the list and become a recipient of it. All you have to do is keep creating your newsletters. These templates can be set up at **https://us5.admin.mailchimp.com/templates.**

Share it

Clicking on here will give you the form that you can then embed into your website. When people fill in the form, it will subscribe them to your email newsletter

Add a Field

The items to the right show the various fields that you can use for your form. You can ask people to give you their address, phone number, URL and birthday, for instance

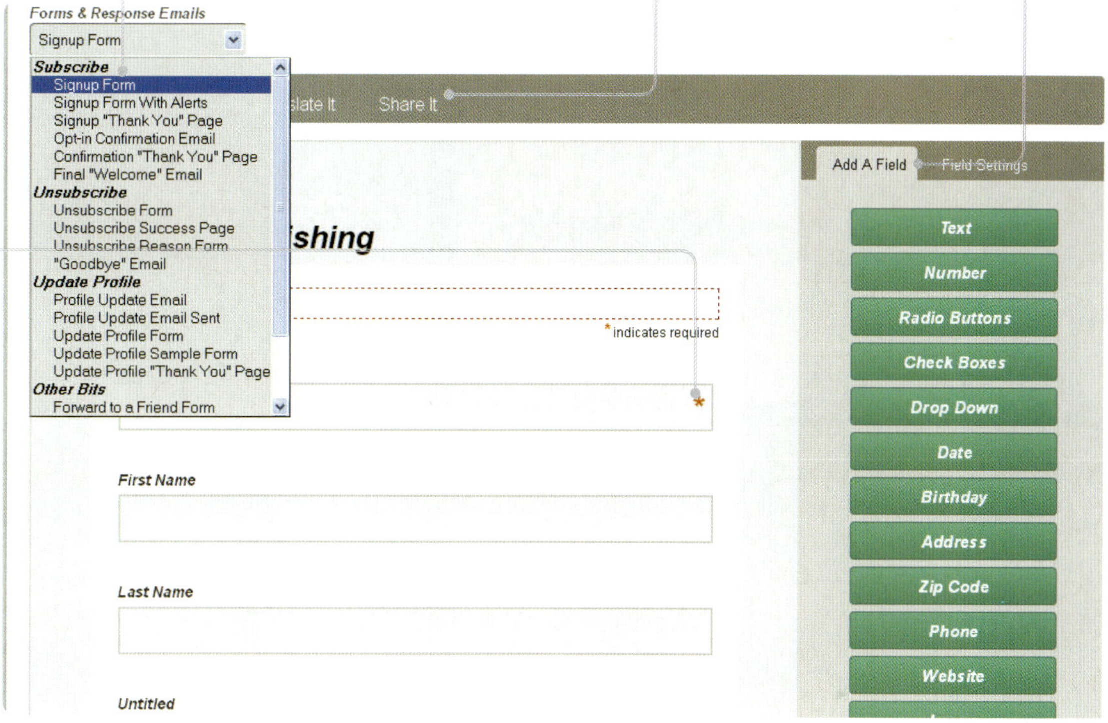

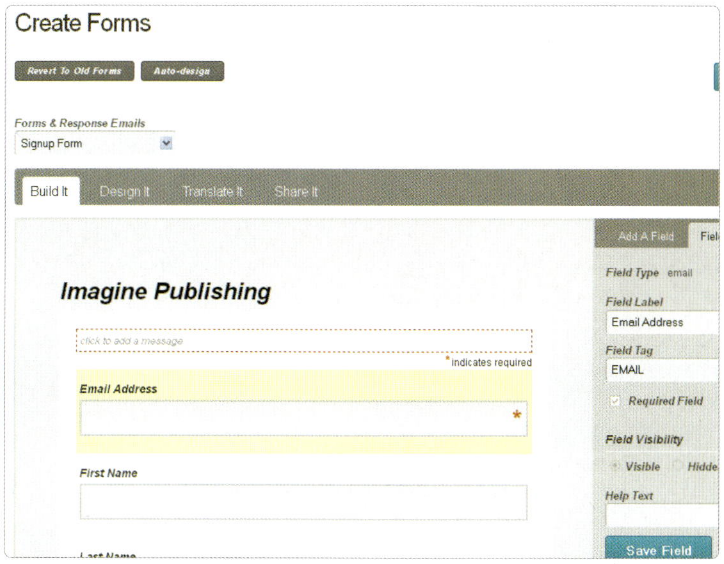

03 Design Signup Forms

The next stage is to click on the Design Signup Forms button. Click on a field in the left-hand box to alter the settings to your liking. Under the Add a Field tab, you can include new fields from date to birthday. Build your form the way you want it.

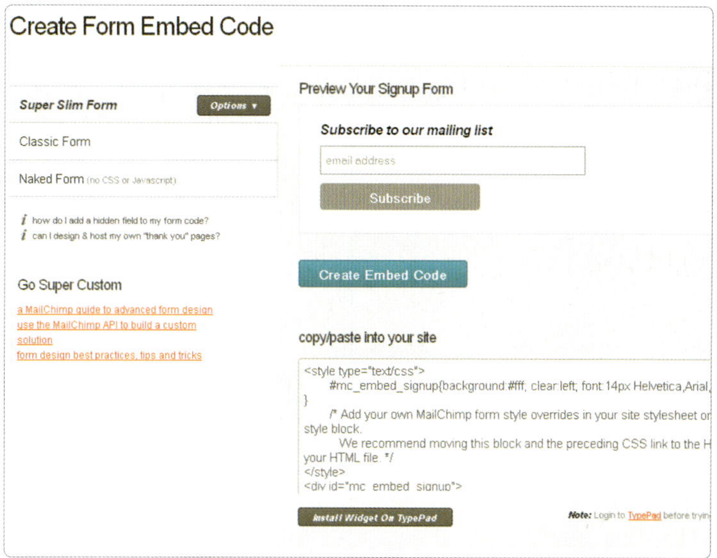

04 Get the code

The Design It tab lets you alter the form's look. When happy, click the Share It tab. Click the Create HTML Code for a Small Subscribe Form button. Choose the perfect form type for you and the embed code appears. Copy and paste it into your site.

Add a favourites icon

Produce an icon that will sit alongside the URL in a browser

Look at the address bar of a website such as the BBC. Now look to the left and you will see a very small BBC logo. This is an example of a favicon. Short for favourites icon, it adds a little extra sheen to your website. Not only does a favicon appear next to the URL on a browser but it also appears in a favourites list of bookmarks so it's a good chance to make a neat impression.

A favicon is small. To be more precise, they're 16 by 16 pixels. You can produce them in any graphics package such as Paint on a PC, for instance. Set the attributes for the area in which you are working to this size and work within it. You will notice that the area is tiny so you can't be massively elaborate. Keep things simple and eye catching.

The favicon needs to be uploaded onto your web server with all of your other webpage files. To do this, you can use an FTP package or go to the website of your web hosting provider and find details of how you can access the files. You will also need to alter the HTML code of your webpage in order for it to pull the file in.

> "A favicon appears next to the URL on a browser, so it's a good chance to make a neat impression"

How the favicon works

Where the fruits of your labour will have an impact

Within the bookmarks
When you bookmark a file, the favicon will be inserted next to the name of the website for easy recognition. Some of these are blank – don't let your website be one

Small size
Notice just how small the icons are. It is important for you to make them as simple as you possibly can. A bold and unique shape is usually best

The URL bar
The favicon will appear next to the URL bar on your internet browser. This is better than having a blank or generic browser favicon, and it gives your site a professional sheen

On the tabs
The favicon will also appear on the tabs. When someone has a lot of tabs open, it is good for them to be able to easily identify where your site is

WHAT'S AN ICO FILE?
An ICO file is an image file format for computer icons. It was introduced as far back as 1985 with the first Windows. Although it is possible to use other image file formats with most browsers, Internet Explorer only supports ICO files, which is why it is prudent to ensure that your favicon is of this type rather than any other.

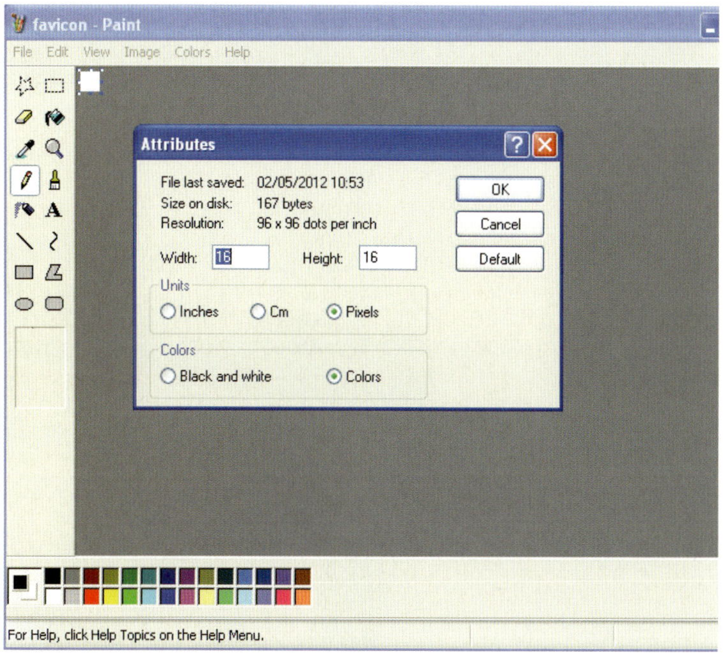

01 Creating a map

Open a paint app on your computer and create an image that is 16 pixels wide and 16 pixels in depth. Start designing your favicon and, when you have completed it and are happy, save it as a PNG or GIF file. We would suggest you name the file 'favicon'.

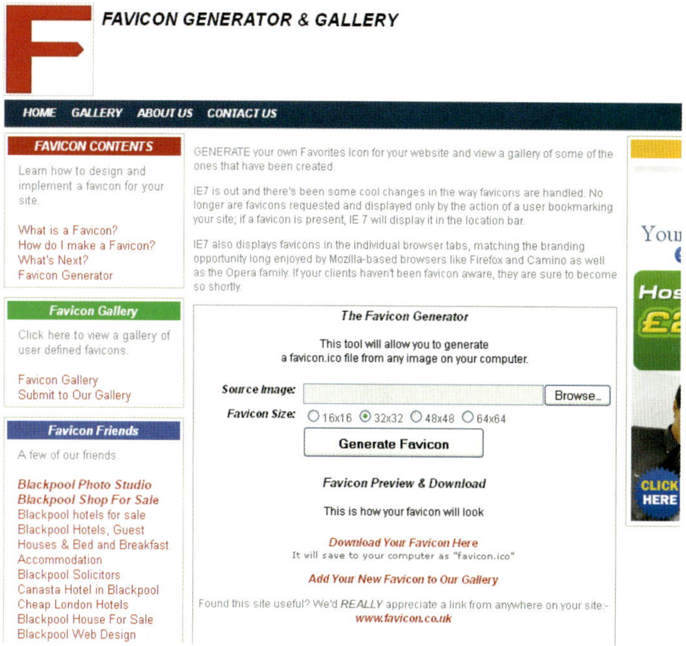

02 Convert to ICO

A favicon needs to be of the ICO file type. Go to a favicon conversion website such as **www.favicon.co.uk**. Click browse and find the image you created in step 1. Select 16x16 and click Generate Favicon. Click Download Your Favicon to save it.

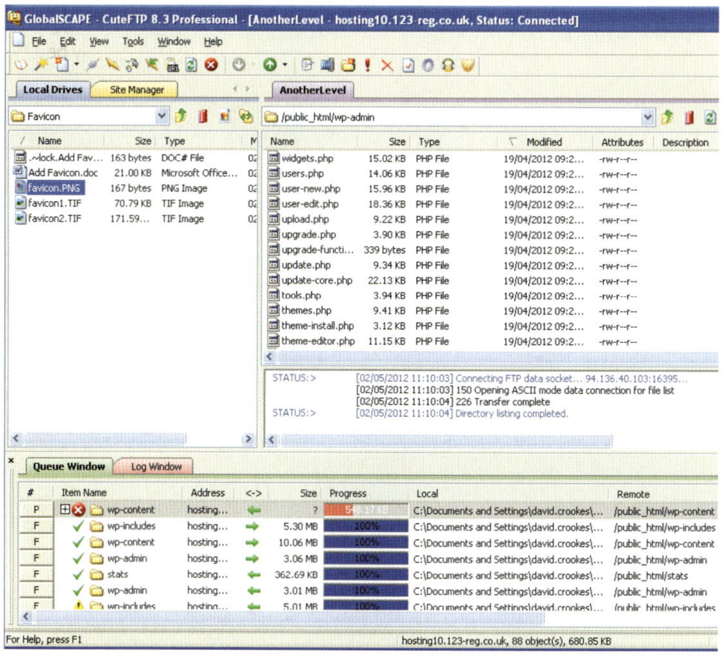

03 Upload the favicon

You will now have an ICO file. This needs to be uploaded to the server on which your website is stored. It also needs to be in the same directory as the webpage that it is for. Use an FTP package or your website host's own upload service.

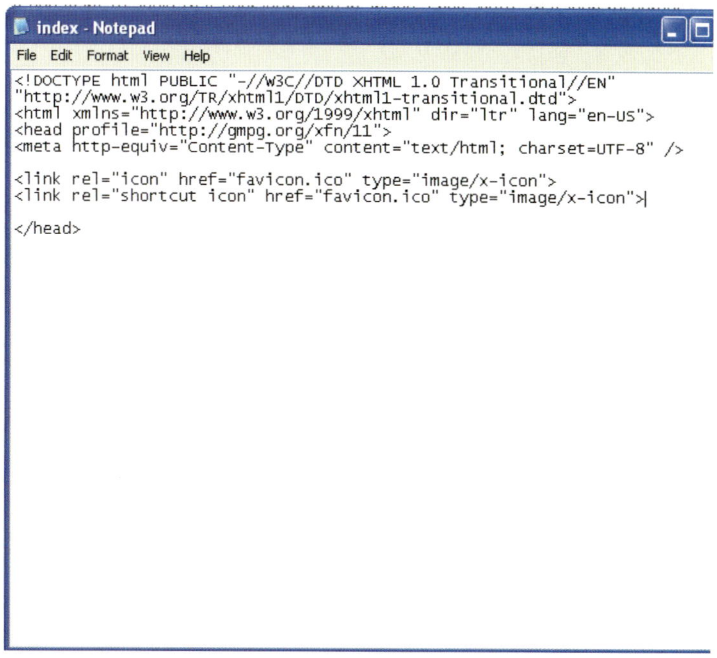

04 Insert code

Select the webpage HTML file that you want to associate with the favicon in your web editor. Within the <head> section, add the lines shown (changing 'favicon.ico' with the file name of your favicon). Finally, upload your HTML file to your web server.

Web design FAQs

Top solutions to common web design and hosting problems

When you're just starting out with web design and are building your first website, there may be a few areas you are unsure about. For example, you might be wondering what happens if someone with an iPad, iPhone or other smartphone tries to access your website. Will it be okay or will they struggle to view the pages, read the text and navigate the sections? Don't worry because we have some excellent advice and tips for making your website mobile-friendly. It's not as difficult as you might imagine.

There are many web languages and platforms that we haven't covered in this book, such as PHP, Java, XML, Flash and more. However, that's not a complete list by any means, so which ones are the best to learn? Which are the ones that could be left until later when you're more experienced? We have some advice for beginners.

It is possible to find web hosting companies that will give you free space for your website, so why bother to pay for it? The pros and cons of free vs paid hosting are analysed here. If you decide that paid hosting is best, you will want to recuperate your costs and perhaps generate an income. For some people it's their sole income, so we have tips for improving your site's popularity and for making money.

After you've built your site you may find that progress is slow, but we provide some simple steps you can take to speed it up. There's also advice on presenting a more professional image with a personalised email address.

Finally, you'll want people to find your site, so we provide help with boosting its popularity and ensuring search engines like Google can find it. Remember: building websites should be fun, so we hope these tips and solutions will help smooth the path to completion.

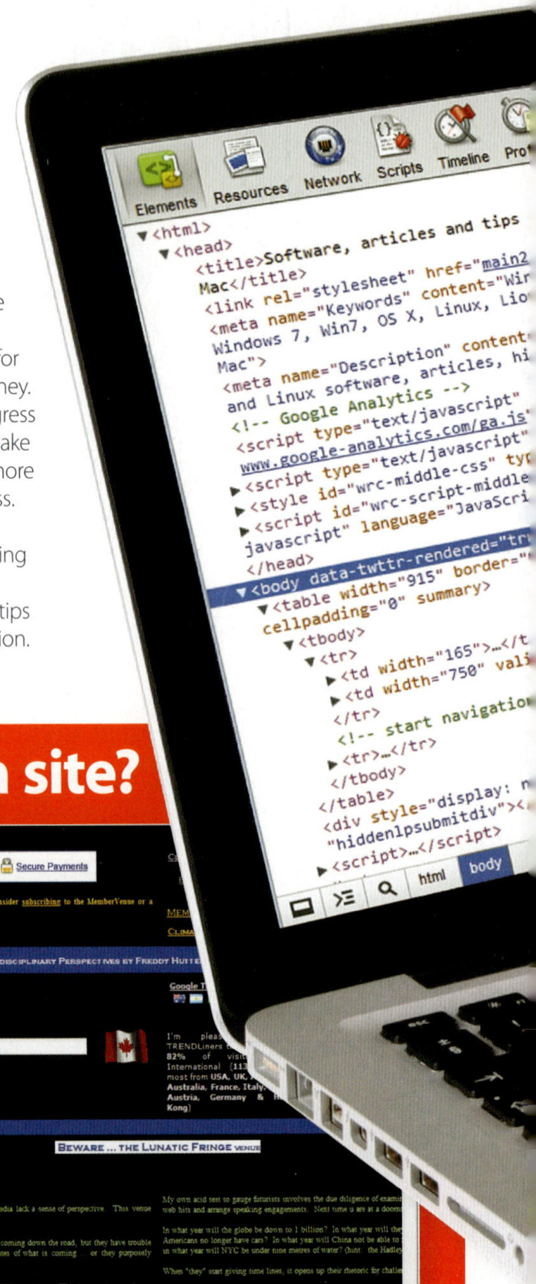

What should I avoid when designing a site?

Whole books have been written about bad website design and there are many pitfalls to watch out for. For example, don't use a splash screen – in other words, a fancy image or Flash animation before you get to the real home page. Flash is yesterday's technology and doesn't work on tablets and smartphones, which are used increasingly these days.

Don't create very long pages that scroll forever and are filled with images or videos. It's common with blogs, but you can limit the number of items shown. Large images saved in the wrong file format, like photos as 24-bit bmp or png files are deadly. Resize them and save them as compressed JPEGs.

Choosing the correct colours is important. Poor contrast, such as light grey text on a white background, is hard to read, but oddly common these days. If you've got something to say, make it easy to read and don't use colour schemes such as red on blue, black on red, green on red and other eye-watering combinations.

Don't fill the page with adverts – visitors come for the content and it should be the main focus. Avoid over-complicated navigation, such as images or icons whose purpose is only revealed when the mouse hovers over them. Flash should not be used for navigation because some visitors won't be able to navigate the site.

What are the main web design languages?

Web developers are spoilt for choice when it comes to creating web pages and there are a number of technologies and languages that can be used. At the heart of all web content though is HTML (HyperText Markup Language) and this is the fundamental language used to build pages. HTML consists of tags or markers that are used to mark sections of the web page's content. There is a tag to mark the start and finish of a page, the beginning and end of the main body, the start and end of a paragraph, where an image is to be placed and so on. It is the first language you should learn.

The second most important language is CSS (Cascading Style Sheets). It has grown in popularity in recent years and like HTML it is used to define how the text, images and other page content looks and where it is positioned. It consists of a series of definitions or rules that tell the web browser how to display the content. The third language is JavaScript, which is a true programming language and it provides much of the interactivity in web pages. Other web languages such as Java, PHP, Perl and Python are similar to JavaScript.

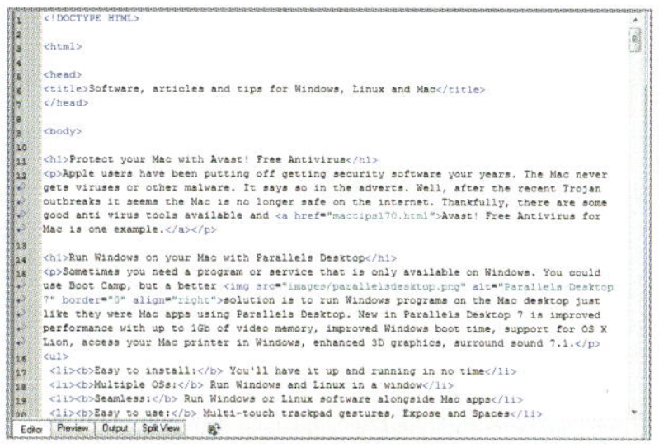

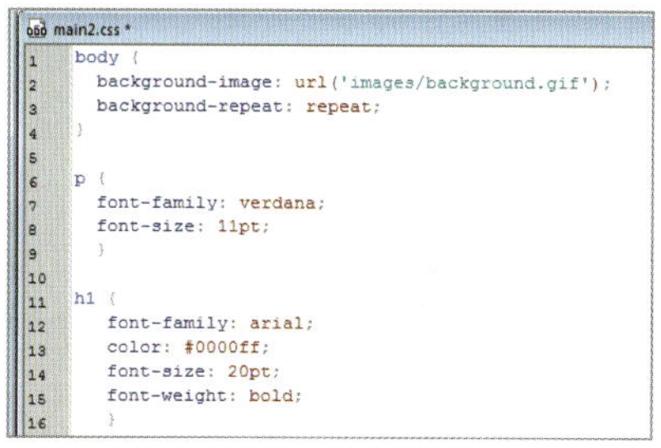

01 Enter the HTML

HTML is used to create basic web pages. It defines the different parts of the file, such as the header and the body, it marks the content and shows where headings are, where paragraphs start and end, and where lists should be placed.

02 Define the CSS

CSS can be included in the HTML file; however, it is usually contained in a separate file and then linked to. In the CSS file you define the fonts, styles and positions of the elements on the page. This overrides the way HTML works.

03 Write the JavaScript

Small amounts of JavaScript are often included in the web page itself, but large amounts of code or code that you want to reuse on many web pages are best placed in their own files. A link can be placed in the HTML to load it.

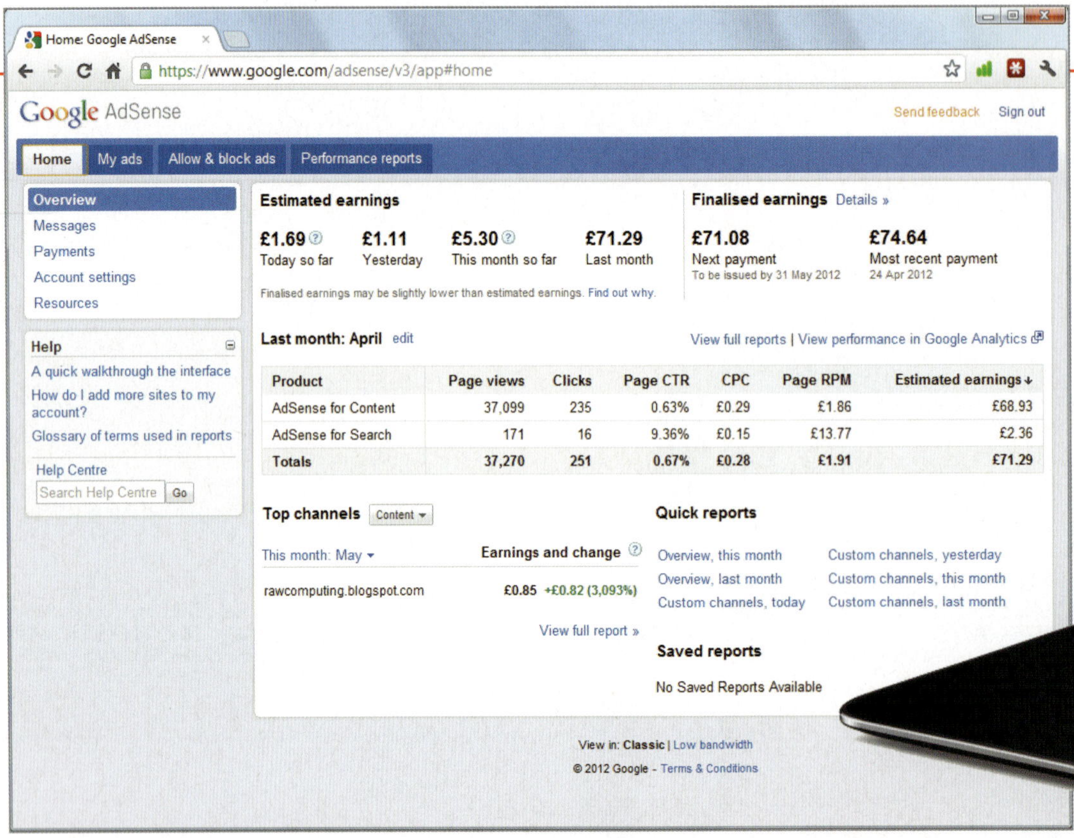

"An easy way to make money is by displaying adverts on your site"

What are the best ways to monetise my site?

If you have built a website or are planning to build one, sooner or later your thoughts will turn to money. How can you earn an income from it? Some people may simply want to cover the cost of web hosting, but others might want to boost their salary or even give up the day job completely and make money from the web.

An easy way to make money is by displaying company adverts on your site. Google is an organisation that immediately springs to mind, but there are others out there. Sign up for Google AdSense (**www.google.com/adsense**) and you'll get some code you can copy and paste into your web pages. When someone views your web page they'll see an advert, and if they click on that advert you will receive a few pence from Google.

You can also sell goods from your website or provide content that can only be viewed by paying subscribers. PayPal (**www.paypal.co.uk**) is the best known online payment service and after signing up you can create 'Buy Now' buttons, 'Subscribe' buttons and more to place on your site. Affiliate schemes like Commission Junction (**uk.cj.com**) are popular. They offer an alternative to selling your own goods and you simply place links or banners on your site. When someone buys something, you receive a commission.

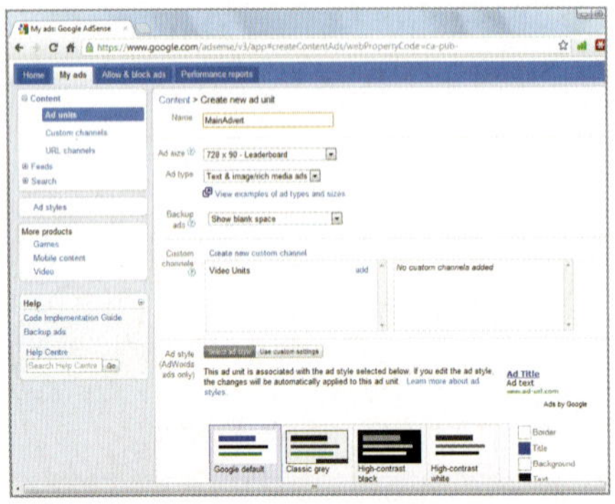

01 Use Google AdSense

Sign up to Google AdSense and then choose the option to create a new advert. Select a type, such as text or image, and the size. Banners, skyscrapers and squares are available. You are then given the code for your web pages.

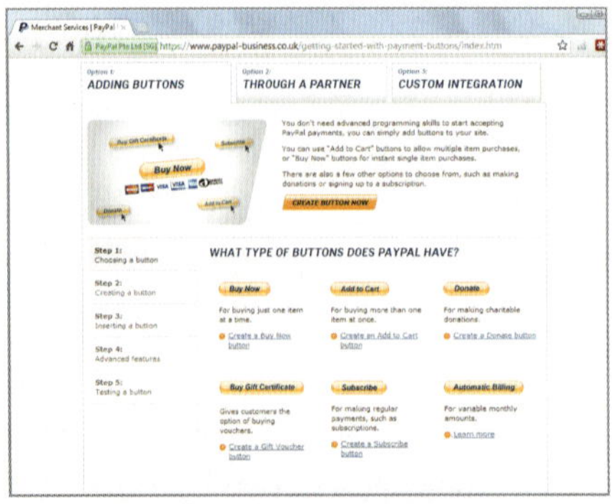

02 Build PayPal buttons

To create a PayPal button, sign in and go to Merchant Services then click the Website Payments Standard link. There are six buttons to choose from and a step-by-step guide to creating it. Just follow the instructions then copy the code.

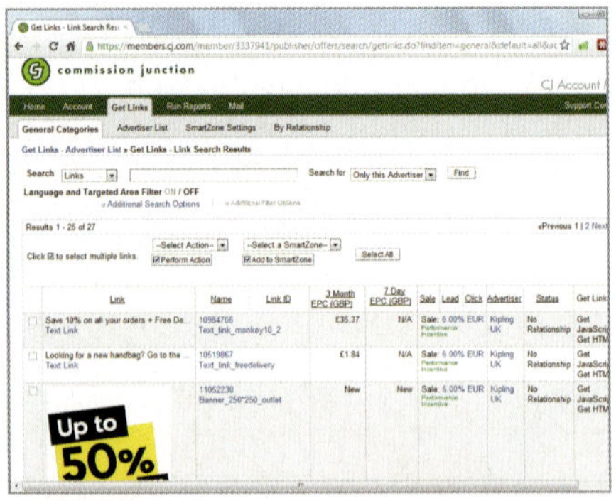

03 Become an affiliate

Commission Junction is one of many affiliate services and you can select from a wide range of advertisers and products to sell on your site. Choose the product and advert, copy the link code that is provided and paste it into your pages.

How can I create a personalised email address for myself?

With email provided by Hotmail, Yahoo!, Gmail or your ISP, you can only choose the first part of your address, such as 'your.name@hotmail.com'. To stand out from the crowd or to present a more professional business image you need a personalised address like 'firstname@lastname.com' or 'name@company.co.uk'. There are several options and if you have created a website then when you sign up with a web hosting company a domain name and email account may be part of the bundle. You choose your domain name when you sign up, such as 'yourname.co.uk', and then email is 'something@yourname.co.uk'. It's common to create several email accounts, such as 'support@company.co.uk' and 'info@company.co.uk'.

The domain name (the bit after the @) must be unique. When you sign up, your proposed address will be checked and you'll need to think of another one if it is already in use.

Web hosting isn't the only way to get a personalised email address and some companies can register a domain name for you just for email purposes. At www.123-reg.co.uk, for example, a personalised email address of your own costs just 99 pence a month. You can also just buy a domain name and then have your email forwarded to your current email account. At www.godaddy.com it's £1.25 for the domain name and then 89 pence a month for email. Shop around for the best deal.

Should I consider free hosting?

Free web hosting is a decent way to get started with web development because it doesn't cost anything and you can use it to learn how to create pages in HTML, experiment with different designs, and hone your skills. It is adequate for a personal or family website; however, there are some limitations. For example, the domain name may reflect the free hosting company and not your name or company like 'mysite.theirsite.co.uk' instead of 'mysite.co.uk'. There may be limited bandwidth, which roughly means the number of visitors a month you can have. If your site really takes off you don't want visitors to be greeted with a "Site exceeded bandwidth" message. There may be other limitations, such as disk space, no ecommerce (selling), limited software and so on.

Paid hosting usually comes with your own domain name and there may be one-click setup of popular software like Wordpress, Joomla, Drupal and others, there are advanced features like PHP programming, access via FTP and more. You can buy as much space or bandwidth as you need and your site can grow with you. The hosting company will back up your site and restore it if there's ever a problem. You can put adverts on it, shopping carts and ecommerce, and make money from it. Having complete control over the site and fewer limitations makes it more fun.

How can I make my website mobile friendly?

Your visitors may be using a mobile phone or tablet and they need special consideration

01 Check your website stats

If you already have a website you need to know whether it is being visited by people using mobile phones and tablets. Google Analytics (**www.google.com/analytics**) and similar services will tell you which OS and devices visitors are using. Go to the Mobile section on the left and then click Devices. This provides you with a list of devices and their popularity.

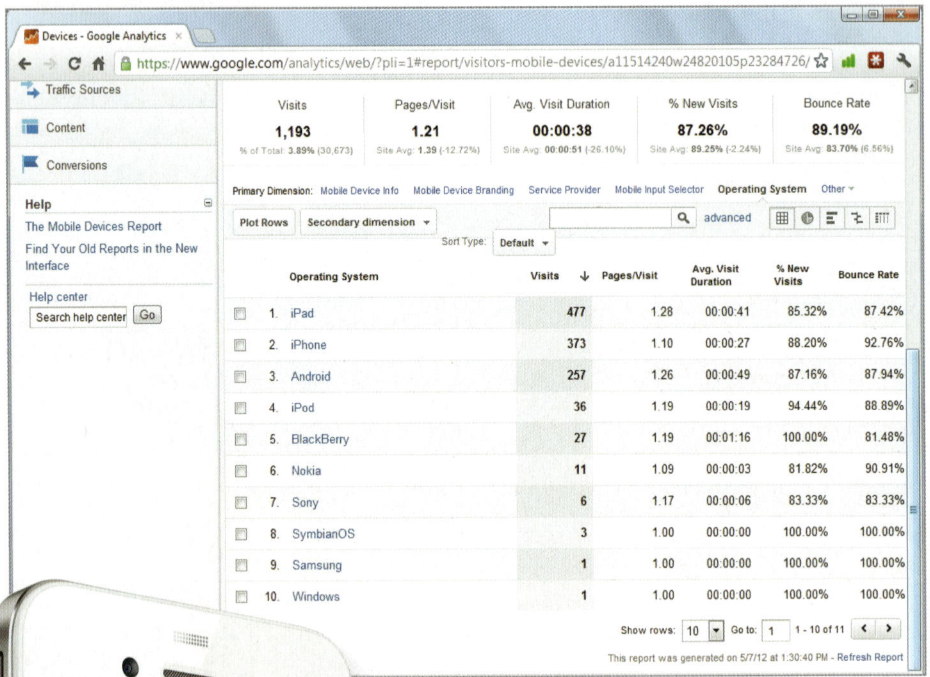

02 Test your site on mobiles

During the design and building of your website you should use a mobile to see what it looks like. It may work already and you might not need to make any changes, which is great, but more than likely you will find that some things don't work well on the mobile device. This screen shot (below) of a bistro's website is blank apart from the logo. It shouldn't be.

03 Avoid using unsupported technologies

Handheld devices aren't as powerful as desktops and their web browsers have limited capabilities. The iPad, iPhone and iPod touch do not support Flash or Java, and anyone trying to access a page that uses them won't see anything, apart from the message shown in the screenshot to the left. Mobile devices that do support Flash and Java do so poorly.

04 Use a WordPress mobile plugin

If you are using WordPress you should visit the plugin directory (**bit.ly/TthqP**) to find WPtouch. Install this plugin and when someone visits your site using a mobile device, it will change the design to accommodate the device. There's a link in the footer to allow visitors to switch to the standard site view.

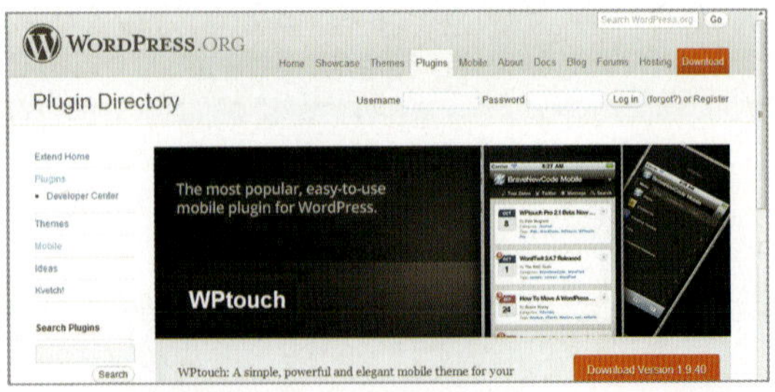

05 Limit the number of images

Your mobile visitors may not always have a good internet connection and they could be using 3G, Edge or even GPRS. Keep the pages small and lightweight with just a few small images. Optimise them by using 256-colour PNGs for illustrations and compressed JPEGs for photos. RIOT (luci.criosweb.ro/riot/) is one of many image optimisation tools you could use.

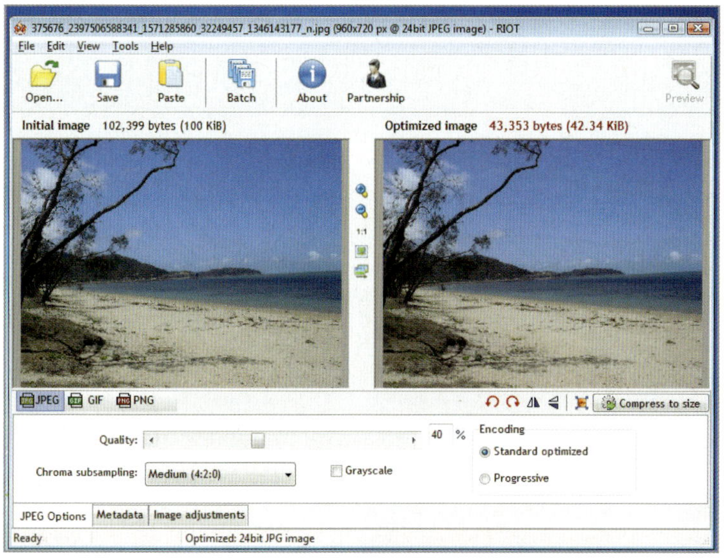

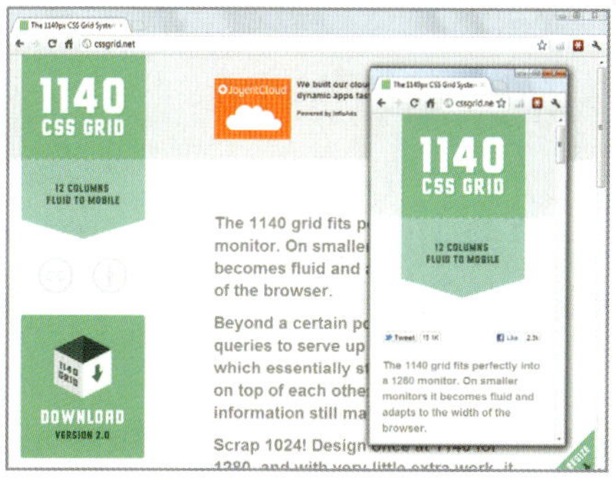

06 Use a mobile-aware template

Responsive website design is popular among web designers right now, and it means creating a page that automatically adapts to the dimensions of the screen or device. It's a trick that CSS can perform and if you Google the term you will find many free and premium templates you can use on your own website. Use them as they are or customise them.

07 Simplify the navigation

A mobile device is not like a desktop computer and rollover buttons and navigation controls that use mouse hover attributes don't work. Make the navigation simple and obvious to use. Use large buttons or links for the navigation. Remember that a mouse can be positioned with pixel accuracy, but fingers on mobiles are big, fat and stubby. Don't make things too small.

08 Blogs and more on mobiles

We've been through setting up a WordPress site, but it is not the only blogging platform. Whatever system you use, look for the mobile options. In Blogger, for example, go to 'Template' and then look at the mobile template options. There are several to choose from. If you use Joomla then go to **www.mobilejoomla.com** to enable it to be displayed on mobile devices.

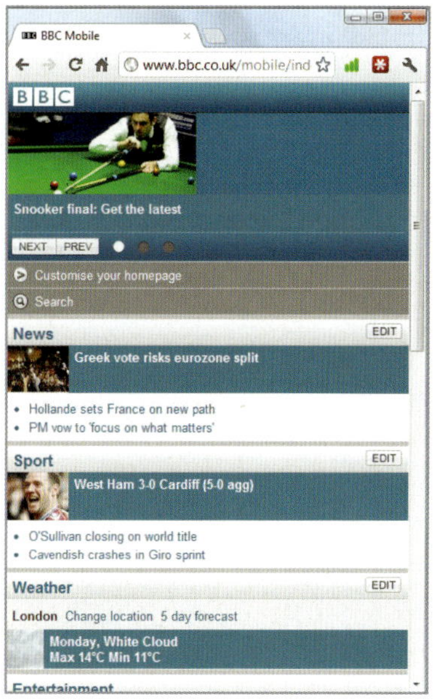

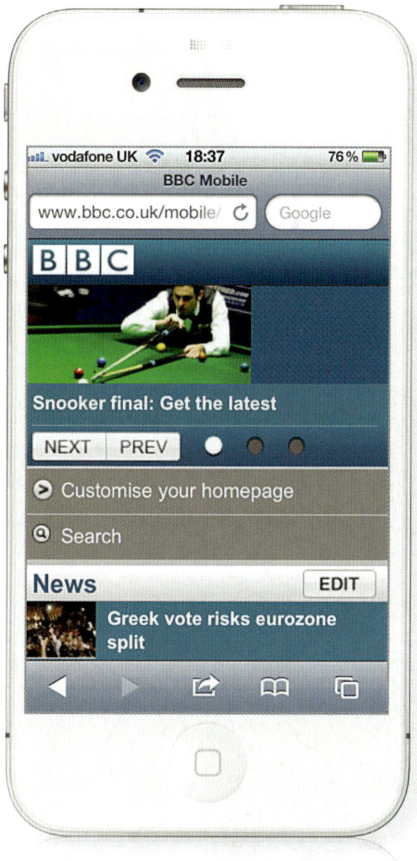

09 Avoid absolute sizes and positions

When you are designing the layout for your pages, you should avoid using absolute sizes and positioning for the elements on the page. The problem is that mobiles and tablets come in many different sizes and the screen may not be wide or tall enough to display the content. Wherever possible you should use percentages like setting the width of an image or text to 50% and so on.

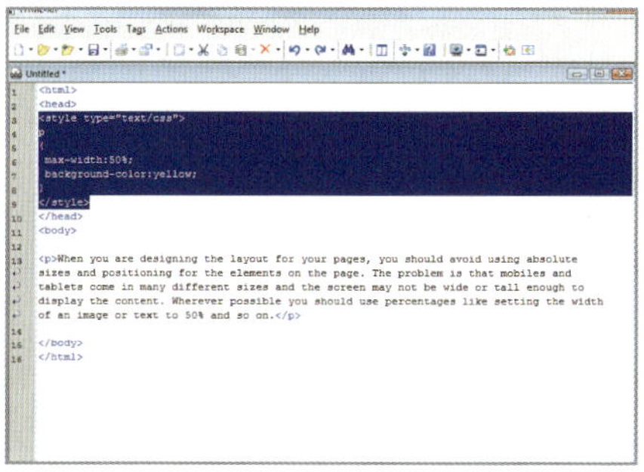

10 Create a site to be accessed by mobiles

In an ideal world it would be brilliant if there was only one site and the content automatically adjusted according to the device's size and capabilities. However, it is quite difficult to do this yourself and you may find that it is easier to create a separate mobile section, such as **mysite.com/mobile**. JavaScript on the home page can detect mobile browsers and then redirect the user to the mobile page.

"Give each page a descriptive title and include keywords"

How can I increase my website's popularity?

You may have a great website, but you won't have any visitors if no one knows it exists, so add it to every search engine. Start with Google and Bing, and find others at **thesearchenginelist.com** and Wikipedia. Go to the search engine and enter 'add a website to' whatever the engine is called. It links to the page you need. Tools like **submitexpress.com/free-submission.html** submit your site to 70+ search engines and are very useful indeed.

Search engines analyse your web pages and try to make sense of the content, so make them easy to understand and more people will find your site. Give each page a descriptive title in the header and include keywords, words that people might search for. Add meta tags in the header that list the keywords and description, but don't go overboard or the search engine might think you are trying to cheat the system. Use headings within the page using h1, h2 and so on to describe the content and include keywords. Use simple and obvious navigation links so the search engine can find all the pages on your site. Make each file name descriptive and include keywords if possible. Use **www.alexa.com/siteinfo** to check your website's popularity.

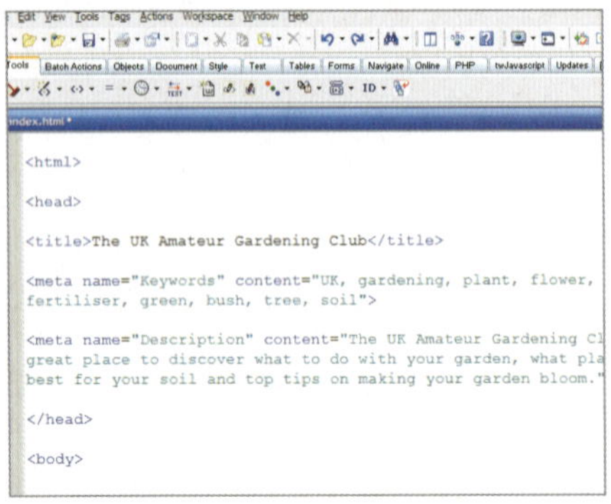

01 Add meta tags

Here we have used a descriptive, easily searchable title for this web page that includes keywords and phrases that many people may put into a search engine. There is a meta tag that contains a list of keywords associated with this site and also a meta tag that includes a description of the content.

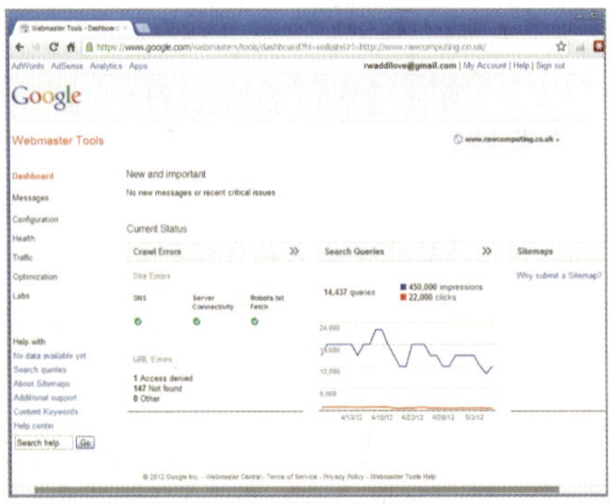

02 Webmaster Tools

Google Webmaster Tools (**www.google.com/webmasters/tools/**) are useful and you can see crawl errors (problems adding pages). You can submit a sitemap (**www.sitemaps.org**), which is a description of all the pages on your website so that Google doesn't miss any.

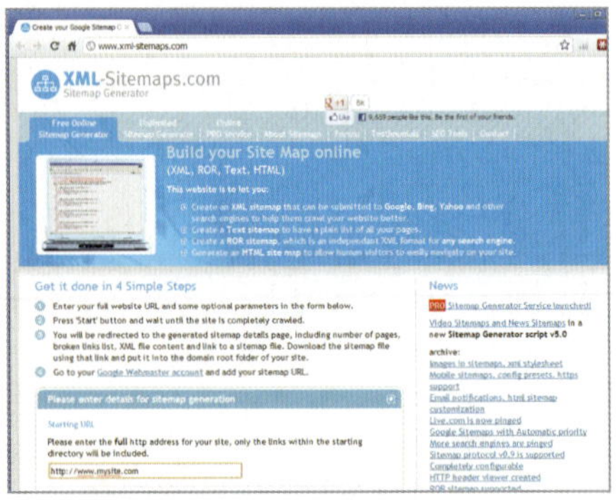

03 Create a sitemap

If you don't have any software available for creating a sitemap there are a number of services online that are able to do it for you. The one above (**www.xml-sitemaps.com**) is typical and there are free services and paid ones that offer a superior range of features.

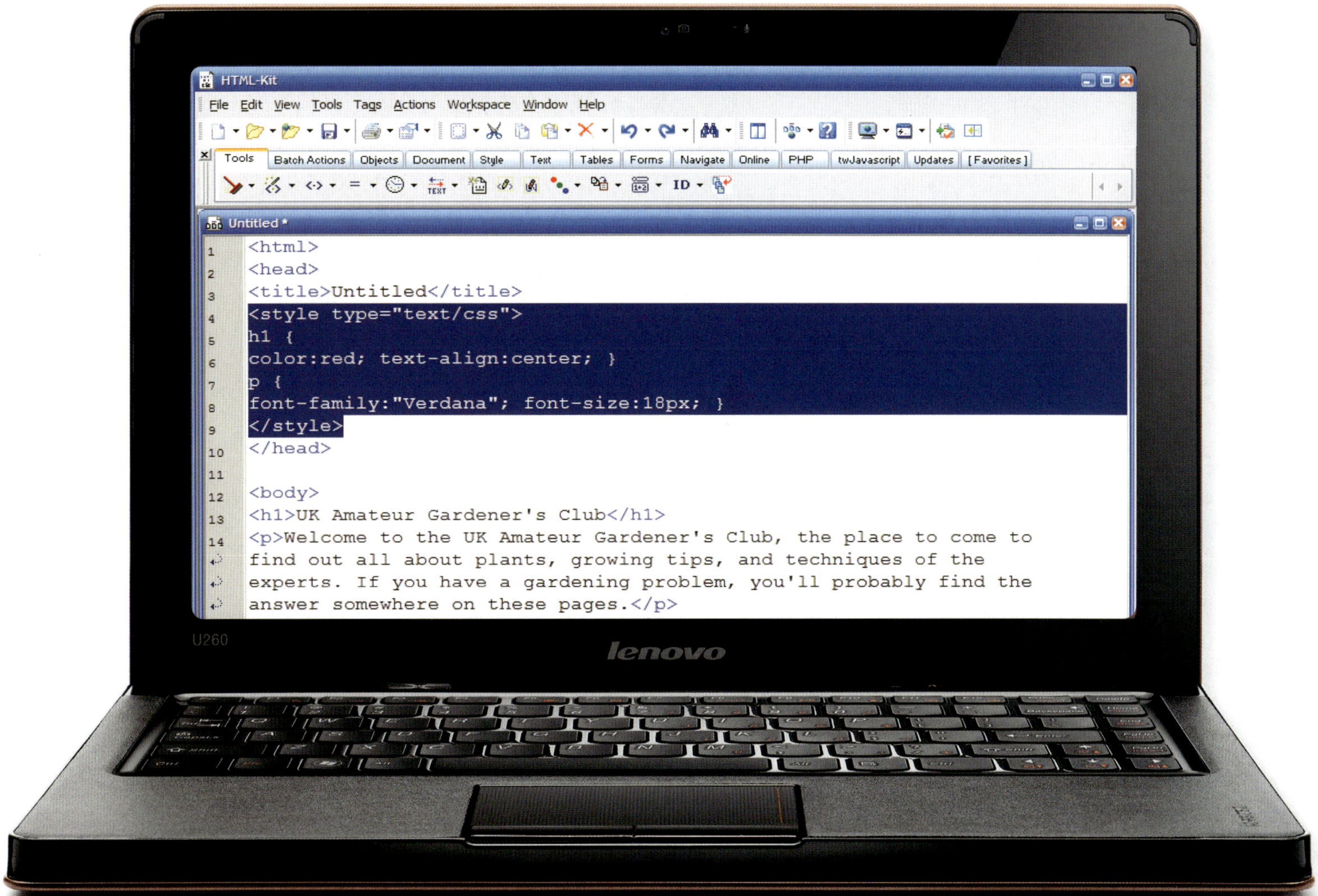

What's the difference between HTML & CSS?

HTML and CSS might at first appear to be similar and do much of the same job; however, they have very different functions when building websites. HTML is the language that is used to define the structure (paragraphs, inserted images and so on) of a web page, separating the header section that contains titles, JavaScript, meta tags and other elements, from the body of the page containing the content. HTML defines the elements on the page, such as text, images, and links. It is used to create forms that allow information to be entered, it marks where videos and images should be placed and so on. HTML is specific to the page it is on.

On the other hand, CSS is used to define how the content should look, such as which font should be used and how it is displayed for the text, its colour and its size. This programming language can create margins or borders around text or images, it can make images appear semi-transparent, align different elements across the page, and turn lists into navigation bars. In some cases the same function can be performed in both languages, but CSS is the preferred choice for display because it has more features, greater flexibility and better control over the attributes. You can mix the two languages, but try to use CSS where possible.

CSS can be specific to a page or can work across a whole site. Change one CSS font definition and all text on all pages in the whole website can also be changed. This makes it a powerful tool that saves time and effort.

> "Use CSS to define how the content should look in terms of font type and size, margins and borders"

How can I prevent my site and its content from being copied?

Unfortunately, you cannot prevent your site's content from being copied by someone that is determined to steal it. However, there are several techniques you can use that can make it harder for thieves to reproduce your work. One simple addition you should make to your web pages is a copyright notice and a request that people email you if they want to use anything from your site. Most people are honest and will respect this.

If you want to prevent people from copying images then this CSS code will help: <span style="background-image:url('photo.jpg')"><img src="clear.gif" width="100" height="100"></span>. It displays a transparent GIF on top of an image on your website, which you'll need to make. This trick is possible in HTML via old-fashioned tables too. To stop people from copying the text, use this body tag: <body ondragstart="return false" onselectstart="return false">. Neither of these methods are fool-proof though and there are ways around them.

There are services you can use that try to discover if your site, pages or content have been copied and used elsewhere, such as Copyscape (**www.copyscape.com**), Plagiarism Checker (**www.plagiarismchecker.com**), Plagium (**www.plagium.com**) and Plagiarisma (**plagiarisma.net**). They work by entering the URL of a page you want to check or by copying and pasting in some text. They perform a Google or Bing search on the page or text and then show the URLs or the page where it appears.

Why is my site loading so slowly?

Any website will become unresponsive if too many people try to access it at the same time, which you may have discovered if you have ever tried to buy tickets online for a popular event. Assuming you don't have thousands of people trying to access your site, the reason is because of the page content.

The number and size of images is the first item to check. Smaller images display faster, so load larger pictures into a photo editor and reduce their width and height. Crop an image as tightly as possible and use CSS padding if you need space around it and instead of using a large background image, create a small one that can be tiled. Photos and detailed artwork should be saved as JPEGs. A compression or quality setting is available when saving them and slightly more compression often isn't noticeable, but loads faster. Simple illustrations and plain images are best saved as PNG files. Photo editors can often reduce the colours to 256 without affecting the quality and this produces smaller, faster files.

Adverts may be necessary to produce an income, but they can slow down the page display. Keep them to a minimum. Other files linked to in the page also affect the speed and Flash movies, such as from YouTube, can take time to display, so don't put too many on one page.

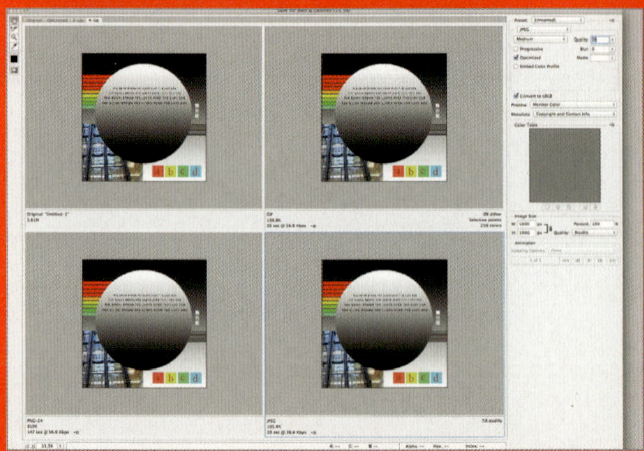

What is jQuery and how does it work?

jQuery is a JavaScript library that was created by John Resig and released in 2006 with the goal of providing web designers and developers with an easy way to write client-side web interactivity. The biggest downside of using JavaScript has been the syntax, which can be long-winded and tricky to understand. jQuery is an open-source library, so there are no licensing fees associated with using it, but the distribution of jQuery is protected by the MIT or GNU licence.

The jQuery project is now managed by a team of core developers and regularly updated with new features. The open-source community provides a large support network, offering the opportunity for web designers and developers to release their own jQuery code snippets and plug-ins and also find help when needed.

jQuery can be thought of as a framework, but it is really a library of methods (functions) that extend native JavaScript functions to provide an API (application programming interface). The API gives you total control over the DOM (document object model) in a much easier-to-understand format, and by including the jQuery library in your webpage, you will immediately have full access to all of the functionality that it provides. The true power behind jQuery is in the simplicity of the syntax (the patterns and words that make up the language). Most programming languages – such as PHP, Java and Visual Basic – have a dauntingly steep learning curve when it comes to understanding how to write code – but jQuery is the opposite. The syntax is shorter and more efficient than traditional JavaScript, leaving you with less code to write, therefore you can rapidly create scripts for your own websites. There are other JavaScript libraries such as YUI, Prototype, Dojo and MooTools that allow for similar functionality, but jQuery has the easiest syntax, which has made it the library of choice among web designers and developers.

> "jQuery is an open-source library, so there are no fees associated with it"

Turning to its format, the library is divided into ten categories that include jQuery core methods, selectors, attributes, traversing, manipulation, CSS (cascading style sheets), events, effects, AJAX and utilities. Within each of these ten categories, there are upwards of 40 different methods that you are able to utilise in your scripts.

jQuery has grown to include not only the core desktop browser library, but also a mobile version. The jQuery team also supports an effects and user interactions plug-in called jQuery UI. In August 2010, jQuery Mobile was announced as an addition to the jQuery family. jQuery Mobile is currently in Beta 3 release and working towards an official version 1 due out in the next few months.

The browser wars are not getting any easier. With four versions of Internet Explorer, three versions of Firefox, two versions of Safari and Chrome and many others popping up all the time, cross-browser compatibility is always at the top of every web designer's agenda. jQuery supports all of the popular and not-so-popular desktop browsers including: Microsoft Internet Explorer 6.0+, Firefox 2.0+, Safari, Chrome and Opera. jQuery Mobile supports Apple iOS, Google Android, BlackBerry, Palm OS and Firefox Mobile to name just the most popular ones. For a full list of all supported browsers, you can visit **http://jquerymobile.com/gbs**, as compatible platforms are ever changing with the library getting closer to its version 1 release.

Sniffing out jQuery Tools for detecting the script

If you are ever on a website and are interested to find out whether it is using jQuery, without having to view page source, you can find out by using a browser extension.

There are a few free tools for web browsers that enable you to 'sniff out' the web frameworks such as Drupal, WordPress and JavaScript libraries that are being employed on a site. Chrome has a free extension called Chrome Sniffer, while Firefox's free add-on is called Wappalyzer.

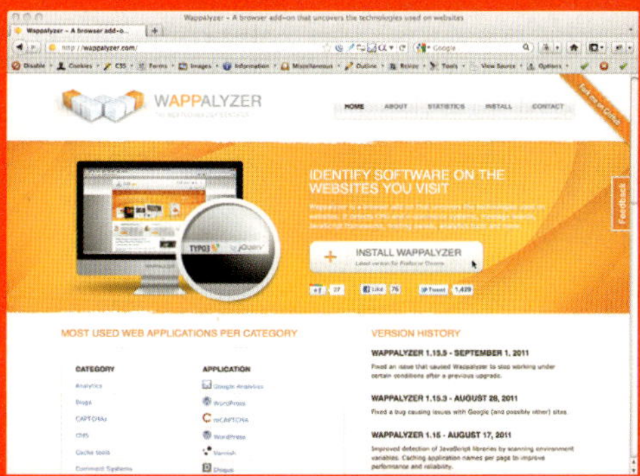

Wappalyzer is a cost-free plug-in for Mozilla Firefox which is used for detecting technologies that are being employed by websites including jQuery and jQuery UI.

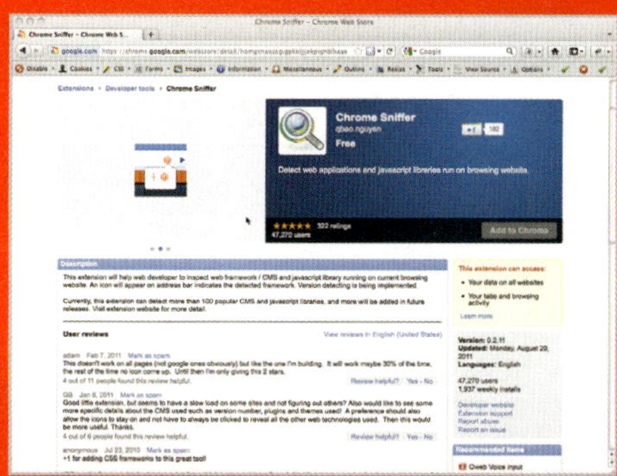

Chrome Sniffer is a Google Chrome browser extension that enables web developers to find out which frameworks or libraries a website is utilising, if any.

Web design glossary

Most specialisms have their own language and there are many specific terms related to web design. We look through some of the key terms to clear up any confusion

Above the fold

Anything which resides in the web browser window when your webpage first loads is referred to as above the fold. Imagine it as a large newspaper – above the fold is the top part with the name of the paper.

Accessibility

This is the extent to which a website is able to be used by people with a disability. Ideally, a website will be accessible for people with visual and hearing problems and those who are colour blind or physically disabled.

Address bar

Also referred to as the URL bar. This is where you type in the web address in a browser.

AJAX

Standing for asynchronous JavaScript and XML, AJAX is a group of technologies which include HTML, CSS and JavaScript. It allows data from a web server to be loaded after a webpage has loaded, without altering its performance.

Backlink

A link which refers from another website to yours. The more the merrier because search engines look for the number of links to your site and this helps raise it up the rankings.

Bandwidth

The amount of data requested from your website. Your host web server will have a set limit and you may be charged extra if you go over. Either that or requests are denied.

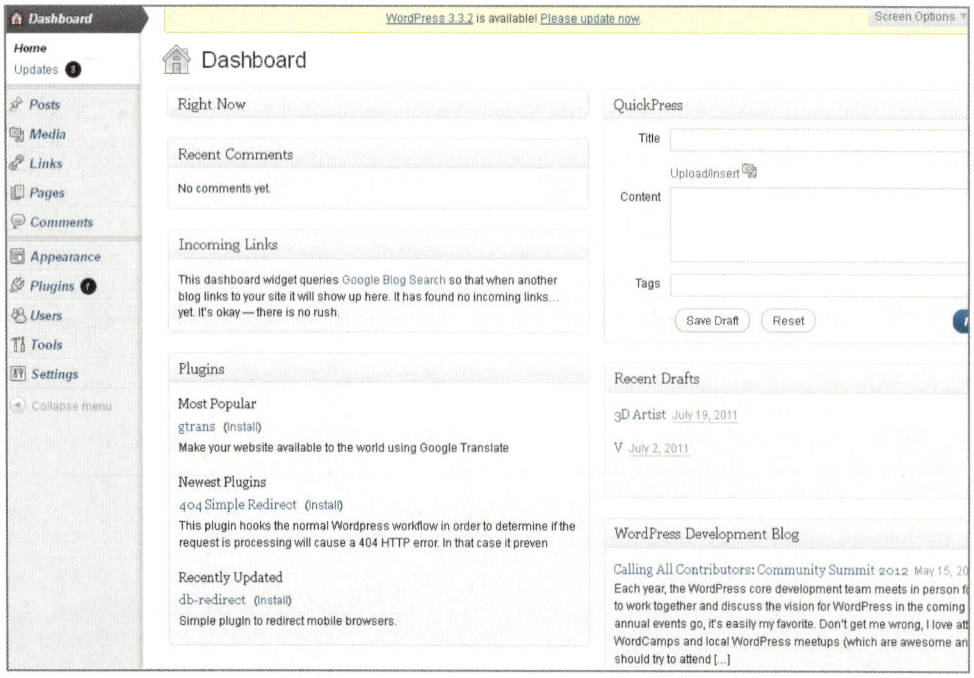

■ *Content management systems such as WordPress remove the hassle of coding and ensure updating a site is easy*

Blog

Short for weblog. It's a common form of website in which small items of news or opinion are frequently posted.

Breadcrumb

Refers to the navigation elements at the top of the webpage. These not only show you the site you are on but where it lies in the site hierarchy so that you can see the process of clicks that got you there. It can enhance navigation because they can quickly get to a higher-level page.

Captcha

Captchas are places within web forms. They are the sometimes undecipherable words which you have to work out and type in when you want to submit a form within a site. The idea behind making you type these correctly is to reduce the levels of spam that would otherwise be generated from automated computer bots.

Content management system

A CMS manages aspects of your site using a backend tool. Popular examples include WordPress. Commonly, you will be able to create posts, add headlines, text and images within a simple form in the admin area for your site that, when published, appear online. The various elements are usually separated so that content is set aside from design.

Cookie

Cookies are useful for remembering what a visitor did when they last landed on a webpage. A cookie can hold all sorts of data including any customised elements, ensuring they do not have to tailor the site for their needs each time.

CSS

Cascading style sheets have superseded HTML tables, telling a web browser how its pages

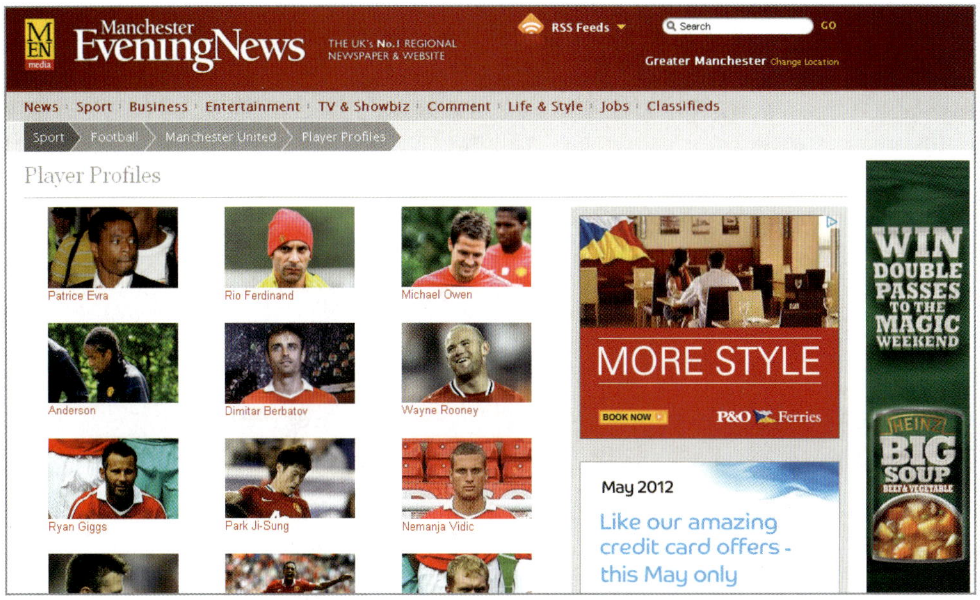

Here you can see how this site shows a breadcrumb trail letting you jump to football or sport very quickly

should look. The language specifies the layout and style of a site, giving information about the fonts, colour, typeface, border, alignment, width, height and much more.

Domain

A website domain refers to the name of the site. For example imagine-publishing is the domain for the publisher of this bookazine. The .co.uk suffix is the domain's extension.

Dots per inch

DPI refers to the resolution of an image. Typically an image for the web will need to be 72dpi. This is low when compared to print. The images in this bookazine, for example, are 300dpi.

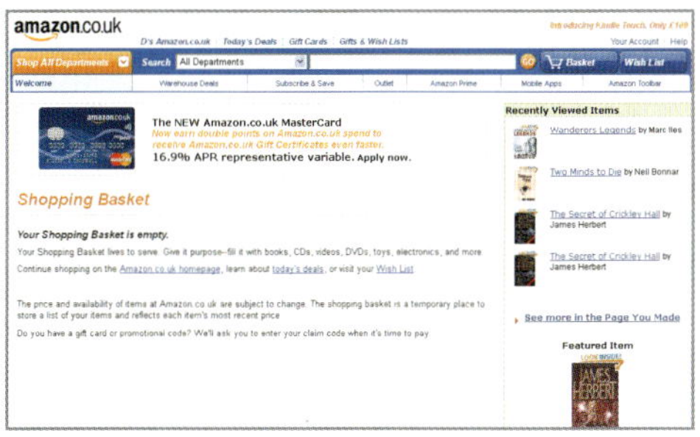

Shopping carts are key features of eCommerce websites and will be identifiable to anyone who has bought items online

eCommerce

Sites which allow the buying and selling of items online are examples of eCommerce.

Embed code

Many sites such as YouTube, Facebook, Twitter and so on allow you to feed their content into your own site. This is done via embed code which can be copied and pasted into the relevant area of your own page code. The site will then pull in content, be it a video, tweets, images and more.

Favicon

The 16x16 pixel icon which appears next to the address bar in the browser to identify the site.

Focal point

The area where the eye is naturally drawn is called the focal point so you need to make sure that if something is catching the attention more than anything else, that it is the part you wish to draw attention to. A focal point can be anything but you want it to be something that stands out.

Font family

Fonts refer to the characters that make up the words on your webpage. A font family is a group of typefaces which look similar, for example Arial and Arial Black, Arial MT Std and so on.

Font weight

The thickness or thinness of a font.

Form

Rather than just have a link to an email address (<a href="mailto:youremail@email.com>email</a>), you can use a form. They are great for interactivity and for allowing people to fill in details directly on the page. You can code them yourself or use third-party software to generate a form which can then be embedded.

GIF

An image file which refers to graphic interchange format. GIFs can also be animated. In that case a series of images (or maybe just two) is created and it gives an illusion of movement.

Hosting

A website has to be stored on a computer. This is referred to as a server. The server has to be connected to the internet. Servers are owned by host companies, hence hosting is the act of providing the service.

HTML

Hypertext markup language enables you to create webpages. It is an adaptable language that is used to provide website content and can incorporate elements of design. HTML5 is the latest iteration and it adds new syntactical features including <video> and <audio>.

HTTP

Hypertext transfer protocol is most often used as part of a URL. It sets out the rules of exchange on the web between the server and browser. HTTP does this over a secure and encrypted connection and it is used when sensitive information is being sent online.

Hyperlink

Where text or an image can be clicked so that the user is sent to another page or website, this is referred to as a hyperlink. When hyperlinks are carried within text, they will be shown in a different colour or underlined. The cursor will also change when a hyperlink is available on a section of your webpage.

Hyperlinks are familiar to web users. Often coloured or underlined, they point you to other areas of the website or internet

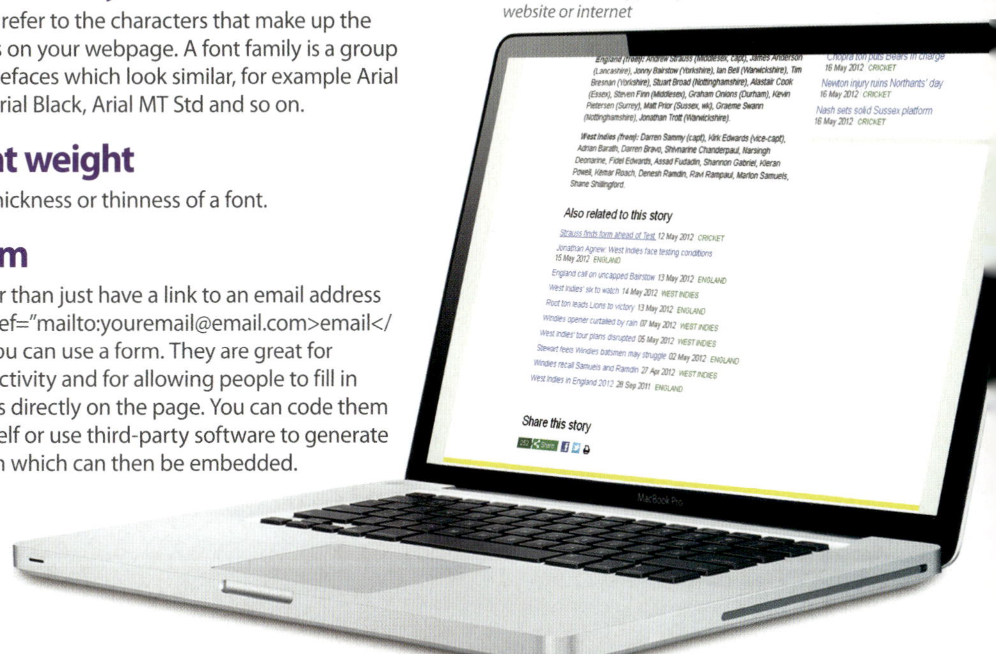

Glossary

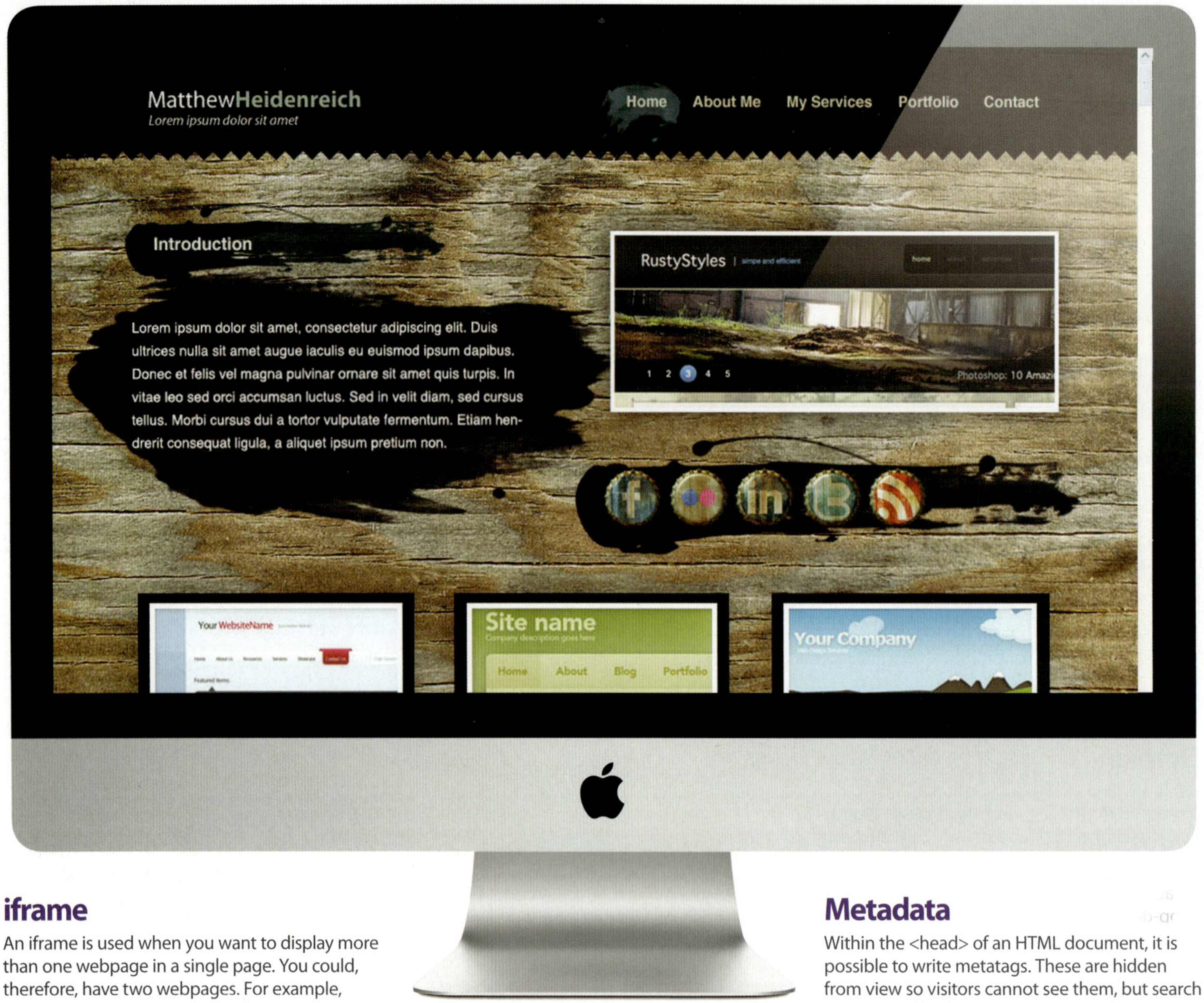

iframe

An iframe is used when you want to display more than one webpage in a single page. You could, therefore, have two webpages. For example, there could be a menu where clicking on a hyperlink will open a new webpage in a frame on the same page while retaining the menu area.

Image map

Coded in XHTML, an image map is a picture that is broken down into different clickable areas, each of which send the user to different URLs.

JPEG

A file format which reduces an image's file size, therefore making pictures quicker to download when they are placed within a webpage.

Keywords

Search engines are important because they point people to your website. Search engine optimisation is therefore crucial and keywords – the terms which people will use to search for your page or content – are one element of that. A keyword used prominently on a page will ensure a better ranking.

Liquid layout

A website with a liquid layout will alter depending on the physical size of the browser window. So if someone minimises their browser, the content will optimise to fit the window, whereas a non-liquid layout will hide some of the content. The containers on the page have their widths defined in percentage terms.

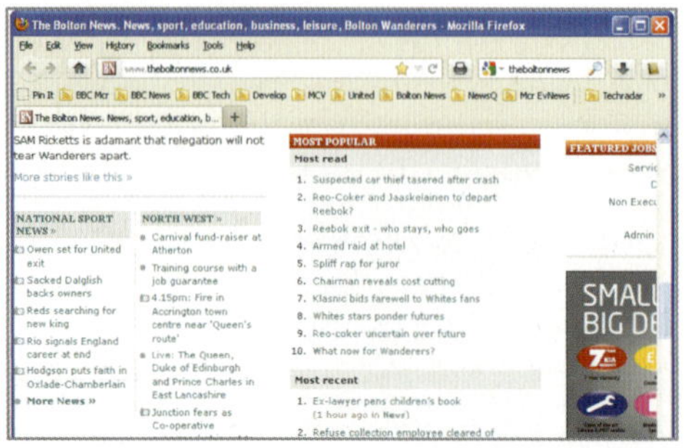

This is an example of a non-liquid layout where resizing the browser cuts into the page. A liquid layout readjusts to fit

Metadata

Within the <head> of an HTML document, it is possible to write metatags. These are hidden from view so visitors cannot see them, but search engines will find and make use of such metadata.

Navigation

Refers to the way people move around your webpages. Your navigation needs to be as simple as possible so that people do not become lost. Navigation is usually in the form of menus but it can also be via links on a page.

Non-breaking space

In HTML, this refers to a white-space character. Use it when a single white-space is needed such as when indenting a line. It is also referred to by the indicator .

Outbound link

A hyperlink which sends people to another website. Also called an external link.

PDF

A portable document format file provides information in a layout that is fixed. PDFs can be used for a variety of purposes such as making a printed leaflet available to download from your site or a timetable of events that is too intricate to be placed on a webpage.

Plug-in

Some web content requires a plug-in – an extra piece of software that expands the possibilities of an existing app. For a browser, for instance, you could have a Flash plug-in to be able to play Flash video. Plug-ins are also available for content management systems. An example of this is an eCommerce plug-in for WordPress to allow users to set up an online store and accept payments.

Podcast

Web design is not just about the visual. You should be aiming for all sorts of content including audio. A podcast – which can also be video – is a recording to which visitors can subscribe or download.

RSS

Really simple syndication not only allows websites to pull in content feeds from other sites, but it also allows web managers to give visitors the option of subscribing to their feeds. A feed will typically show you a website's headlines and sometimes the first paragraph of text.

Script

JavaScript is an example of a script, a code that is placed within an HTML page that produces interactive and dynamic elements. This could be a drop-down menu or pop-ups.

SEO

Search engine optimisation is the act of enhancing your website so that it is picked up by the likes of Google and Bing. It's a complicated area but metadata, inbound and outbound links and allowing RSS feeds to encourage your content to be used within other sites helps.

Shopping cart

Online shops do not usually require you to buy items individually. Most often you place them in a basket or cart and then check out, paying for them all at the same time.

Sitemap

If you have lots of content, a sitemap can be used to make sense of it. It is a list of all of the items within your site, organised by their hierarchy or importance, depending on the type of site.

Social media

Most people are dab hands with social media nowadays. From Facebook to Blogger, Twitter to YouTube, there is a rich tapestry of content

■ *Many websites make it simple to add dynamic content via embed code such as this on the YouTube site*

provided by users. These elements can be inserted into a webpage. They help to drive people to your site too. The developer areas of such sites often carry embed code and individual elements are also embeddable.

Template

Commonly associated with content management systems, templates (and themes) give websites a standardised and consistent look and feel, which helps to ensure they appear more professional.

Text editor

A fancy web design package is not needed if you know HTML. All you need is a simple text editor program such as Notepad on the PC, saving the file with the extension .html.

Traffic

When people come to your site for whatever reason, they will download data. The amount they transfer is called traffic, although this term is also used to describe the number of people visiting a site.

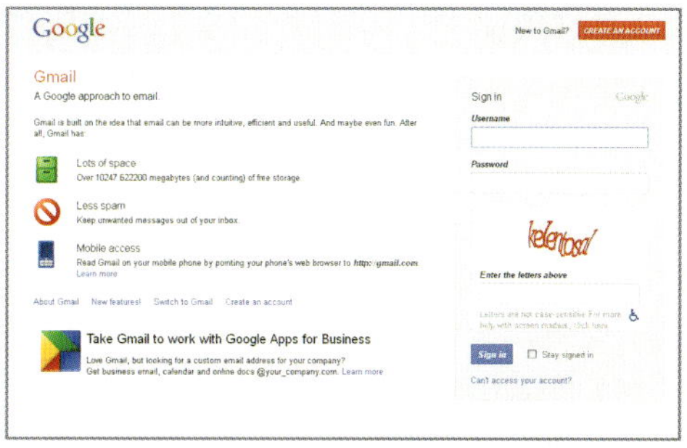

■ *Having a captcha on a web form bars it from being overrun by automated bots that scour the web and randomly fill them in*

Visitor

The unique individual who visits your website as opposed to the same person coming back time after time (which counts as one visitor).

WYSIWYG

What you see is what you get refers to a program that will publish a webpage on the internet that appears exactly as it did within the app. One good example of this is Apple's intuitive and easy-to-use iWeb.

XHTML

Standing for extensible hypertext markup language, it refers to HTML which complies with XML rules.

XML

Extensible markup language is a markup language that is used to write other markup languages.

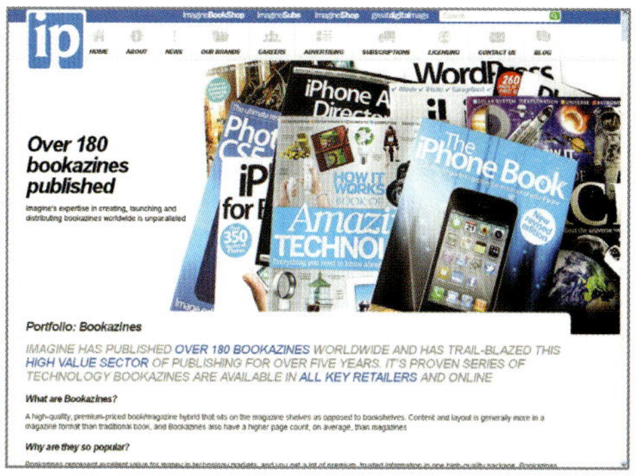

■ *The top of a webpage – the part that shows – is referred to as above the fold. You can scroll to see the rest*

On your free disc

Resources and code to help you get to grips with web design

Attached on the opposite page is your free **Web Design for Beginners** disc. Here you'll find files you need to help you with the tutorials in this book, as well as some other top resources that will help you to improve your web design projects. On offer are seven exceptional video tutorials on DreamWeaver, a free WordPress theme and a free image slider. Everything is easy to access and downloads straight from the disc, meaning you can be experimenting with these fantastic tools in no time at all. So if you're raring to let your creative side run wild, pop the disc into your Mac/PC and away you go!

Navigate
Upon start-up, this is the screen you'll be taken to. From here you can navigate your way around the disc

Video tutorials
KillerSites University has kindly provided us with seven video tutorials on Adobe Dreamweaver

Image slider

For those who are wishing to build a website to house their photography or modelling portfolio, then an image slider is ideal. This free continuous slider from Flabell (worth $8) can randomise your image and link to different areas of your site.

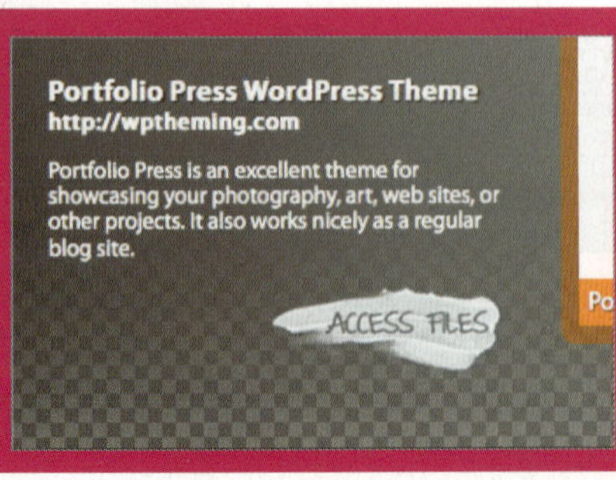

WordPress theme

The five-star-rated Portfolio Press WordPress template is ideal for bloggers who enjoy photography. You can click the link on the CD to see video tutorials on how it works, and how to make the most of it.